Nonverbal Communication: The State of the Art *by Robert G. Harper, Arthur N. Weins, and Joseph D. Matarazzo*

A Biodevelopmental Approach to Clinical Child Psychology: Cognitive Controls and Cognitive Control Theory *by Sebastiano Santostefano*

Handbook of Infant Development *edited by Joy D. Osofsky*

Understanding the Rape Victim: A Synthesis of Research Findings *by Sedelle Katz and Mary Ann Mazur*

Childhood Pathology and Later Adjustment: The Question of Prediction *by Loretta K. Cass and Carolyn B. Thomas*

Intelligent Testing with the WISC-R *by Alan S. Kaufman*

Adaptation in Schizophrenia: The Theory of Segmental Set *by David Shakow*

Psychotherapy: An Eclectic Approach *by Sol L. Garfield*

Handbook of Minimal Brain Dysfunctions *edited by Herbert E. Rie and Ellen D. Rie*

Handbook of Behavioral Interventions: A Clinical Guide *edited by Alan Goldstein and Edna B. Foa*

Art Psychotherapy *by Harriet Wadeson*

Handbook of Adolescent Psychology *edited by Joseph Adelson*

Psychotherapy Supervision: Theory, Research and Practice *edited by Allen K. Hess*

Psychology and Psychiatry in Courts and Corrections: Controversy and Change *by Ellsworth A. Fersch, Jr.*

Personal Construct Psychology: Psychotherapy and Personality *edited by Alvin W. Landfield and Larry M. Leitner*

Mothers, Grandmothers, and Daughters: Personality and Child Care in Three-Generation Families *by Bertram J. Cohler and Henry U. Grunebaum*

Further Explorations in Personality *edited by A.I. Rabin, Joel Aronoff, Andrew M. Barclay, and Robert A. Zucker*

Hypnosis and Relaxation: Modern Verification of an Old Equation *by William E. Edmonston, Jr.*

Handbook of Clinical Behavior Therapy *edited by Samuel M. Turner, Karen S. Calhoun, and Henry E. Adams*

Handbook of Clinical Neuropsychology *edited by Susan B. Filskov and Thomas J. Boll*

Handbook of Innovative Psychotherapies *edited by Raymond J. Corsini*

The Role of the Father in Child Development (Second Edition) *edited by Michael E. Lamb*

Handbook for the Practice of Pediatric Psychology *edited by June M. Tuma*

Change Through Interaction: Social Psychological Processes of Counseling and Psychotherapy *by Stanley R. Strong and Charles D. Claiborn*

Drugs and Behavior (Second Edition) *by Fred Leavitt*

Handbook of Research Methods in Clinical Psychology *edited by Philip C. Kendall and James N. Butcher*

A Social Psychology of Developing Adults *by Thomas O. Blank*

Loneliness: A Sourcebook of Current Theory, Research and Therapy *edited by Letitia Anne Peplau and Daniel Perlman*

Hyperactivity: Current Issues, Research, and Theory (Second Edition) *by Dorothea M. Ross and Sheila A. Ross*

Review of Human Development *edited by Tiffany M. Field, Aletha Huston, Herbert C. Quay, Lillian Troll, and Gordon E. Finley*

Agoraphobia: Multiple Perspectives on Theory and Treatment *edited by Dianne L. Chambless and Alan J. Goldstein*

The Rorschach: A Comprehensive System. Volume III: Assessment of Children and Adolescents *by John E. Exner, Jr. and Irving B. Weiner*

Handbook of Play Therapy *edited by Charles E. Schaefer and Kevin J. O'Connor*

Adolescent Sexuality in a Changing American Society: Social and Psychological Perspectives for the Human Service Professions (Second Edition) *by Catherine S. Chilman*

(continued on back)

THE RORSCHACH: A COMPREHENSIVE SYSTEM

Volume
2

Interpretation

Second Edition

THE RORSCHACH
A COMPREHENSIVE SYSTEM
VOLUME 2: INTERPRETATION
SECOND EDITION

JOHN E. EXNER, JR.

A **WILEY-INTERSCIENCE** PUBLICATION

JOHN WILEY & SONS, INC.

New York • Chichester • Brisbane • Toronto • Singapore

Library of Congress Cataloging-in-Publication Data

Exner, John E.
    The Rorschach : a comprehensive system.   Volume 2, Interpretation
/ John E. Exner, Jr. — 2nd ed.
        p.   cm. — (Wiley series on personality processes)
    Includes bibliographical references and indexes.
    ISBN 0-471-85080-2
    1. Rorschach Test. I. Title. II. Series.
    [DNLM: 1. Rorschach Test.   WM 145 E96ra]
    RC473.R6E96   1991
    155.2′842—dc20
    DNLM/DLC
    for Library of Congress   90-13160
                                                              CIP

Printed in the United States of America

91 92 10 9 8 7 6 5 4 3 2

To Doris

When we were young and very new
I pledged my deepest love to you,
And as we've grown along the way
That love grows deeper every day

J.E.E. (1978)

Now as leaves begin to turn
And autumn knocks upon our door,
I'll say it once again to you,
I pledge my deepest love once more

J.E.E. (1991)

Series Preface

This series of books is addressed to behavioral scientists interested in the nature of human personality. Its scope should prove pertinent to personality theorists and researchers, as well as to clinicians concerned with applying an understanding of personality processes to the amelioration of emotional difficulties in living. To this end, the series provides a scholarly integration of theoretical formulations, empirical data, and practical recommendations.

Six major aspects of studying and learning about human personality can be designated: personality theory, personality structure and dynamics, personality development, personality assessment, personality change, and personality adjustment. In exploring these aspects of personality, the books in the series discuss a number of distinct but related subject areas: the nature and implications of various theories of personality; personality characteristics that account for consistencies and variations in human behavior; the emergence of personality processes in children and adolescents; the use of interviewing and testing procedures to evaluate individual differences in personality; efforts to modify personality styles through psychotherapy, counseling, behavior therapy, and other methods of influence; and patterns of abnormal personality functioning that impair individual competence.

IRVING B. WEINER

University of South Florida
Tampa, Florida

Preface

A preface is supposed to introduce a work by offering some hints about what it contains. I see no useful purpose in attempting to do that here as the subtitle *Interpretation* should suffice, but it may be worthwhile to offer some explanation about why this volume exists. Although it is called *Volume 2*, it is really the fifth volume to be written in the series concerning the *Comprehensive System*. Twenty years have passed since the decision was made to integrate the empirically defensible components of five major Rorschach Systems into a single, standardized approach to Rorschach's Test. It was decided to call the new approach *A Comprehensive System* because the effort involved the integration of elements from each of the five *Systems*. The first edition of *Volume 2*, released in 1978, was simply an extension of the first edition of *Volume 1*. It was necessary because *Volume 1* was so incomplete, although I did not realize how incomplete when the manuscript was finished in late 1973.

The original decision to create the *Comprehensive System* was not reached quickly or easily. Although the actual decision to do it occurred 20 years ago, the seed for the idea existed well before then. Thirty-eight years ago I first laid hands on a set of Rorschach blots. I remember it vividly for I was awestruck at the prospect of being permitted into the inner sanctum of clinical psychology. During the next two years I became even more excited about the test as I served briefly as a summer intern, first with Samual Beck and then with Bruno Klopfer. There were no limits to my admiration for the seemingly magical ways that they culled information about people from no more than a handful of Rorschach answers. They became two of my professional models, not just because of the wonders they could perform with the Rorschach but because they were also extraordinarily sensitive about people. At that time I had no idea about my own future with the test, but I did sense that something was wrong because of the considerable animosity that Beck and Klopfer conveyed about each other. I was truly baffled when I learned that they had no communication with each other after 1939 and as I studied their disagreements during the middle to late 1950s my awareness of the need for a standard approach to the Rorschach probably began to develop.

It clearly existed in 1960 when I approached Beck and Klopfer with the grandiose notion of permitting me to serve in the role of a monitor while they would discuss and hopefully resolve their many differences. They were both kind but firm in their refusals and the idea might have died then had not Beck added the suggestion that I should write a paper describing the differences between he and Klopfer. When Klopfer cautiously endorsed the notion of a comparison of his and Beck's work the seed took on new dimensions.

When I began the comparative analysis in 1961 I envisaged a reasonably long paper that would contrast the two approaches, but I found it difficult to write about Klopfer without also mentioning the contributions that Piotrowski had made to Klopfer's approach. Consequently I began corresponding and meeting with Piotrowski to try to understand why he had broken away from the Klopfer group and ultimately created his own approach to the test. I was also very aware of the contributions of Rapaport and Schafer and had passing familiarity with some of the work of Hertz. Thus by late 1962, an obvious logical conclusion surfaced. The project should be expanded to compare the work of all five approaches rather than focus exclusively on Beck and Klopfer.

During the next six years I devoted as much of my free time as possible to the project, which I found very knotty because each of the *Systematizers* often used the same concepts or scoring symbols but with different definitions and/or interpretations. Although it was a laborious task, there were two rewards that more than offset the effort. First, I found myself with a vast bank of knowledge concerning the development and use of the test. Second, and more important, were the delightful personal relationships that I formed with these Rorschach legends. Rapaport died early into the project so that much of his personal input was not to be, but Beck, Hertz, Klopfer, and Piotrowski gave generously to the effort and there is no way to acknowledge the warmth and support that each devoted to the project. Not only were they eager to clarify their own positions, but they also shared many personal and private bits of history to aid in helping me to gain a more complete understanding of their work with the test.

As more and more information accumulated it became easy to understand how many criticisms of the test had originated and how some were clearly justified. When the manuscript, published as *The Rorschach Systems* (Grune & Stratton, 1969), was finished I arranged for it to be sent to Beck, Hertz, Klopfer, Piotrowski, and Schafer mainly to insure that there was no historically incorrect material and to receive some assurance that I had presented their positions fairly and objectively. Klopfer was the first to respond. He was complimentary, suggesting one or two minor changes but also expressing some disappointment about the fact that I had drawn no conclusions about the respective merits of the *Systems*. Two days later I met with Beck and heard almost the same commentary, including his sense of disappointment that I had drawn no conclusions.

A few weeks later the seed of the original idea began to emerge again. I visited Klopfer, and with his usual marvelous sensitivity he brought up the issue of our mutual disappointment about the lack of conclusions in the book. He said, "but maybe you should look further." On returning to my office a few days later I found a letter from Beck. In it he asked if I had any plans to investigate the various *Systems* further in an effort to arrive at the "missing conclusions." Not long thereafter Piotrowski offered access to his files if I decided to pursue the issue of the missing conclusions further, and Hertz, in her customarily charming manner added to the challenge with the contention that any thorough research concerning the different *Systems* would show that they all reach the same conclusions.

The friendly and sincere encouragement from these Rorschach Godfathers (and Godmother) could not be ignored, and in 1968 the *Rorschach Research Foundation,* which quickly became known as *Rorschach Workshops,* was created. Its purpose was not to integrate, but to find the missing conclusions. Which *Sys-*

tem had the greatest empiricial sturdiness? Which *System* had the greatest clinical efficacy? Those were the questions that nourished the seed and caused it to finally emerge. Nearly three years of considerable research ensued and by late 1970 the results of those early investigations highlighted three inescapable conclusions. First, there were really five Rorschach tests that were extremely diverse. Second, although each included some highly valuable components, each was also scored by serious liabilities. None was uniformly superior to the others. One might be superior in one area, yet inferior in several other areas. Third, the professional Rorschach community seemed prone to ignore the vast intersystem differences and lay praise or criticism to the Rorschach as if only one test did exist. Thus the seed finally blossomed into a decision. Integration of the best of each approach was not only wise, but necessary if the integrity of Rorschach's test was to be established.

Before the final decision was made I took a two week period during which I met with Klopfer, Piotrowski, Beck, and Hertz, in that order. I prefaced my visits with a written communication concerning our findings and included a description of my intentions. Bruno Klopfer was in poor health and we spoke only briefly during a luncheon lovingly prepared by his wife Erna. His words were, "work as you will to find the truth." He died less than a year later and I have always regreted that I could not share my conclusions with him. Zygmunt Piotrowski was quite enthusiastic and optimistic about the notion of a *Comprehensive System*. He continued to offer suggestions and hypotheses for testing during the first 10 years of our work at *Rorschach Workshops*. Sam Beck was also quite favorable about the project, seemingly delighted that it would provoke a new wave of Rorschach research. Marguerite Hertz, even though skeptical at first, probably offered the greatest emotional support for an integrated approach. After reviewing the findings of our research concerning the *Systems,* she acknowledged that personalities probably played a much more important role in the test development than should have been the case and in her warm but straightforward manner said, "if you can make it better, do the best you can."

Hertz' advice has been a guideline for the development of the *Comprehensive System*. At the onset, I naively assumed that all of the pieces to the puzzle were already in place and the task would be to select those pieces that fit neatly together to make the complete test. It was the product of that selection that constituted most of the original *Volume 1*. But even as the manuscript was completed many gaps in information remained obvious. Data for nonpatients were sparse, the new approach contained no special scores, something was not quite right with the form quality definitions, and components of the developmental quality distributions overlapped. And so the research effort continued, provoking additions and changes and the first edition of *Volume 2* was a natural byproduct of the work.

But *Volume 2* also became outdated as new findings accumulated, and new findings continued to accumulate rapidly due to the efforts of a small army of dedicated and enthusiastic project directors, workshop assistants, and field examiners. Their numbers varied from year to year, ranging from as few as a dozen when the first pieces of the *System* were put into place to nearly 100 during the span of years from 1977 to 1981. Although most all worked on a part-time, underpaid basis, their productivity exceeded anything that might have been expected.

By 1982 the raw data input had far out distanced data analyses. After the completion of many studies concerning children, including the collection of nearly 2000 records from nonpatient youngsters, *Volume 3* in the series about the *System* was released. Shortly thereafter, the number of data collection projects was scaled back and the focus of attention shifted to a more careful and systematic culling through the thousands of records from dozens of groups that had accumulated since 1971.

The number of changes and additions in the *System* had become so numerous by 1984 that the original *Volume 1* had little utility. A major revision of it was released in 1986, but as the research and data analyses have continued more changes and additions have occurred. I have addressed these in the first chapter of this work, but that should not be construed to mean that this work replaces *Volume 1*. On the contrary, as with the first edition, this is an extension that focuses on the interpretive process.

I have tried to spell out, as best I can, how to use this remarkable test. Writing has always been a slow and painful process for me and this volume has been more difficult to write than any preceding undertaking. Possibly that is because it has required so much attention to detail, which breeds boredom and frustration, but more likely it is because of the constant struggle to translate interpretive concepts and procedures into words that are meaningful and sentences that are not concrete or mechanistic. If this work reads easily it is because of the many people who have read pieces of the manuscript and offered many constructive suggestions. If it does not read easily, it is probably because I foolishly ignored some of those suggestions.

Far too many people to list here have been involved in the research effort at *Rorschach Workshops* during the past decade. I hope that they know of my appreciation and affection. There are are 10 who worked tirelessly. They undertook the terrible task of rescoring thousands of records as each new change would occur, and they deserve special recognition: Doris Alinski, Earl Bakeman, Eileen Carter, Ruth Cosgrove, Lisa Hillman, Nancy Latimore, Theresa Sabo, John Talkey, Eugene Thomas, and Edward Walker. I would also be remiss if I did not thank Alicia Stewart, Cina Lundy, my daughter Andrea, and my wife Doris for keeping our main office in some semblence of order during the several years since our transition to North Carolina. Their tolerance of my tendency to hide away from the day-to-day routines has made it possible for this work to be completed.

Finally, I noted in the *Preface* to the 1978 *Volume 2,* "the test itself continues to pose many mysteries, and there is no end in sight to the continuing research needs." We seem to have solved some of those mysteries and have continued to move forward in the research endeavor, but the quote remains true and I look forward to seeing the younger researchers of the present and future continuing to address these issues as faithfully as possible. I offer to them a paraphrase of the Klopfer and Hertz advice that has meant much to me—go and seek out the truth as best you can, and never settle for the pedestrian way.

J.E.E.

Asheville, North Carolina
February 1991

Contents

Tables

PART I

Introduction

CHAPTER 1

Developments in the Comprehensive System 1985–1990

RECENT DEVELOPMENTS

The *Comprehensive System* began to take shape in late 1971 after the cumulative findings from a series of studies that had been initiated between 1967 and 1970 revealed that, although each of the five markedly different approaches to the Rorschach (Beck, Hertz, Klopfer, Piotrowski, & Rapaport-Schafer) had considerable merit, each was also flawed by features that could not be supported empirically. In light of those findings, a plan was formulated to integrate the empirically defensible features of each of those approaches to create a standard format for the test that could stand the test of scientific scrutiny and provide a basis from which investigations regarding various issues of reliability and validity could proceed.

The first *Comprehensive System* manuscript was completed late in 1973 and published in 1974. Soon after the first volume was released, however, it became clear that the task was far from complete. What had seemed like a fairly straightforward series of decisions in 1973, began to appear more like a never-ending task by 1977. Research completed from 1973 to 1977 made it obvious that some of the 1973 decisions were more questionable than had been anticipated and, although the data from many newly completed studies served to offer more clarification about the test and flesh out the *System*, they also continued to highlight some of its complex mysteries. The first edition of *Volume 2* seemed to be a logical extension of the earlier work and the manuscript was completed late in 1977 and published in 1978.

During the next several years the *System* continued to evolve and a major revision of *Volume 1* was released in 1986 but even then the work remained incomplete. Fortunately, major advances in computer technology have occurred in almost every year that the *System* has been under development, and they have made it progressively easier to process and analyze large chunks of data. That technology has provided an important impetus in bringing about further refinements to the *System* and enhancing its interpretive validity. Therefore, a new edition of *Volume 2* is appropriate.

This new work represents the culmination of research concerning the test that has evolved during the past decade, and brings a sense of closure to a lengthy effort. The *Comprehensive System* appears to be about as complete as possible if the data that are available in the pool of records at the Rorschach Research Foundation are used as a basis from which to form that opinion. This is not to suggest that it cannot be fine-tuned further. Many questions about the test, or

3

the variables of the test, remain unanswered or their answers are only partially satisfying to the Rorschach scholar. The structural variables appear to be in place however, and much has been learned about how best to approach the data when the focus is on interpretation.

Findings derived during the most recent phase of investigation concerning the test have generated several changes and additions to the *System*. These changes and additions have occurred since completing the revision of *Volume 1* in late 1985 and, therefore, it seems best to review them before going more deeply into the contemporary status of the *System*.

CHANGES AND ADDITIONS IN SCORING

Nature, Botany, and Landscape

Many responses contain more than one content, and all should be included in the coding, *with two exceptions* that concern the categories Nature (*Na*), Botany (*Bt*), and Landscape (*Ls*).

First, *Na* always takes priority over *Bt* or *Ls*. In other words, if a response includes *Na* and *Bt* and/or *Ls, only Na* is scored. For example, a subject might answer, "This is an animal stepping on some stones that are in the water. He's trying to get to this bush." This answer contains four contents, animal (*A*), stones (*Ls*), water (*Na*), and bush (*Bt*), but the correct content coding is *A,Na*. Second, if a response does not include *Na* but contains both *Bt* and *Ls, only* one of the two is scored. Thus, if the response were, "An animal stepping over some stones next to this bush," the correct content coding would be *A,Bt* or *A,Ls*. The reason for the rule concerning Nature, Botany, and Landscape is that all are included in the new calculation of the *Isolation Index,* and the rule is designed to ensure that no single answer will contribute excessively to that calculation.

[handwritten margin note: Na priority]

[handwritten margin note: Bt or Ls]

Alphabet *(Al)* Content Category Dropped

The original content categories were selected from the results of a study in which the frequencies for each of 35 categories used by Beck (1944) were tallied for nearly 7500 responses. It was decided that any with a frequency of 10 or more were included in the *System*. At that time the Alphabet (*Al*) category met criterion but the Science category did not. By 1984, the frequency for science contents was increasing substantially, apparently as a result of an increasing awareness of computer and space technology plus the advent of the video game. Consequently, the content category Science (*Sc*) was added to the list in the revision of *Volume 1*. Recently, all content categories again were studied for frequency using a pool of approximately 15,000 responses. Because Alphabet responses occurred only twice, it seems reasonable to drop *Al* from the formal listing.

Vocational *(Vo)* Content Category Dropped

The 1973 decision to include the Vocational *(Vo)* category in the *System* as a secondary content was based on the historical premise that some occupational groups were prone to give atypically elevated frequencies of some contents because of their occupations or occupational interests. For instance, those in the medical professions were expected to give more anatomy and/or X-ray answers, artists to give more art responses, and so on. Thus, *Vo* was thought to provide a useful datum that could be used as a guideline in interpreting the presence of an elevated frequency for some content categories. A review of 1000 protocols of nonpatient adults, sorted by occupation, reveals that the premise underlying *Vo* was somewhat faulty. Although subjects from the medical professions do have slightly higher frequencies of anatomy responses (but not X-ray responses) and professional artists do give slightly higher frequencies of art answers, these are very modest, nonsignificant differences. In other words, when a significant frequency occurs for a content that may be occupationally related, the finding is still important and the interpretation should not be tempered because of an apparent occupational linkage. In that context, the *Vo* category serves no apparent usefulness and its use has been discontinued.

Human Experience *(Hx)* Content Category Added

Abstract (*Ab*) has been included as a content category since the beginning of the *System* but recent research suggests that it should probably be a special score (*AB*). Therefore, the new content category Human Experience (*Hx*) has been   *Hx* created to code some types of answers that previously would have been coded *Ab*. The most common of these are formless Movement (*M*) responses that involve a human emotion or sensory experience (e.g., love, hate, anger, depression, happiness, sound, smell, fear), but some *M* answers that contain form also include the *Hx* coding. For example, the response, "Two people who are deeply in love, gazing longingly at each other," that involves the *D9* areas of Card III would be scored, $D+ M^po$ 2 H,Hx P 4.0. Many answers for which the *Hx* coding is used also include the use of *AB* as a special score.

Z Scores and Use of White Space

If white space use involves *Z*, other areas of the blot *also must* be used. For   *not* instance, the white areas of Card I are commonly reported as eyes and/or mouth   *why* in face responses to all, or nearly all, of the blot. Similarly, the *DS5* area of Card   *alone* II is often reported as a spaceship, with the red *D3* area used as an exhaust. Both meet the criteria for *Z*. On the other hand, if *DS5* is reported as a rocket, but no other blot area is included in the response, the criterion for *Z* is not met.

Recent research concerning the relationships between figure and ground in the various blots suggests that some assumptions about the integration of white space with other blot areas have not been correct. For instance, when defining the location of an object, a subject may outline an area of the blot that includes   *Must* white space but *fail to specify* that the white space is actually being used as part   *specify* of the object. When this happens, *ZS* should *not* be scored.   *W*

The erroneous scoring of *ZS* has occurred most often on Cards III and X, in which the blot areas are more broken than solid. Sometimes, the various parts of a blot are collectively identified as a face and specified as eyes, nose, mouth, ears, beard, and so on. When the subject specifies the area being used, arbitrary lines are drawn that encompass the various parts and also encompass much of the white ground, leading to the logical conclusion that the white is also being integrated. *But this is not true.* In most of these answers the subject is simply manifesting the gestalt principle of closure and *ignoring* the white background. Thus, *ZS* is *not* scored. In some face responses to Cards III and X, the white space is integrated. These answers contain specific use of the white area, as in, "It's the face of a clown. These are the eyes and the nose, and he has *white* paint on." *ZS is* scored for this type of answer.

Active and Passive Superscripts for the Same Answer

For some answers, the active (a) and passive (p) superscripts are both assigned to the same movement determinant. These are responses in which *two or more objects* are described in movement but at least one is active while the other(s) are passive. For example, the statement, "Two people dancing [active] around a person standing [passive] in the middle," is scored $M^{a\text{-}p}$. The determinant is entered and counted only once in the frequency tally for *M,* but both superscripts are counted when tallying the number of active and passive movement answers. Both superscripts are assigned to a single movement determinant only when more than one object is involved in the movement. Some answers will be given in which the same object is involved in both active and passive movement, such as, "A dog sitting there [passive] howling at the moon [active]." When this occurs, *only* the active movement is coded, FM^{a}.

NEW AND REVISED CALCULATIONS

EB Pervasive *(EBPer)*

The *EB* Pervasive (*EBPer*) ratio concerns the dominance of an *EB* (*Erlebnistypus*) style in decision making activity. It is calculated by dividing the larger number in the *EB* by the smaller number. For example, if the *EB* is $7 : .0$, the larger *EB* value (7) is divided by the smaller (4.0), with a result of 1.8. *EBPer* is calculated *only* when a marked style is indicated in the *EB;* that is, if the value of *EA* (experience actual) is 10.0 or less, one side of the *EB* must be *at least 2 points* greater than the other side, or if the value of *EA* is more than 10.0, one side of the *EB* must be *at least 2.5 points* greater than the other.

EBPer has interpretive relevance when its value is 2.5 or greater. Beginning with Rorschach's own work, a great deal of information has evolved that highlights the significant differences between introversive and extratensive subjects. Whereas the former prefers a more ideational style of coping in which affect plays only a peripheral role, the latter tends to merge affect more freely into ideation in problem solving situations. Introversives and extratensives tend to manifest substantial physiological differences when in coping demand (Blatt & Feirstein, 1977; Exner, Thomas, & Martin, 1980) and differ markedly for the actual number of overt operations they complete before reaching the solution to a problem (Exner, 1978; Rosenthal, 1954).

Although the two styles are discrete for many features, the issue of homogeneity within each style has received little empirical scrutiny. As a result most interpretations of the *EB* tend to assume that the overall approach to problem solving is similar and relatively consistent within each style and that variations within a style are produced by other psychological features. For instance, it has been demonstrated that marked differences may exist within either style for tasks requiring greater persistence (Exner, 1974; Piotrowski, 1957; Wiener-Levy & Exner, 1981). Generally, those differences appear to be related to D Scores and to the magnitude of *EA*. In other words, as one's capacity for control and resource accessibility increases, problems in being persistent in a meaningful but frustrating task are reduced.

The type and quality of *M* responses and chromatic color answers also correlate with variations within a style concerning the effectiveness and characteristics of the style. Subjects who give an above average number of "cooperative *M*'s" are generally more oriented toward socially effective behaviors (Exner, 1987, 1988; Piotrowski, 1957), and a positive relationship exists between assertive *M*'s and the tendency to be field independent (Witkin, Dyk, Faterson, Goodenough, & Karp, 1962). Although all introversives tend to be ideational in their coping activities, the manifestations of the style will be notably different for the introversive with a higher *es* and predominantly aggressive *M*'s and for the introversive with a higher *EA* and predominantly cooperative *M*'s.

The behavioral variability within any group of extratensives is probably greater than that for introversives. This is because the introversive is defined by a single form of answer, the *M*, whereas the extratensive is defined by any combination of three types of chromatic color answers, *FC, CF,* and *C*. Thus, the extratensive whose record consists mainly of *CF* and *C* responses probably differs considerably in coping activity from the extratensive whose record is marked predominantly by *FC* responses. Again, the presence of a higher *EA* or higher *es* contributes significantly to the manifestations of the coping activity, as do many other personality features.

The accumulated findings regarding differences within styles tend to reinforce the theoretical formulation of Singer and Brown (1977). They speculated on the possibility that the two basic dimensions of the *EB*, introversive and extratensive, may be constitutionally predetermined, but they also pointed to many findings in the developmental psychology literature to emphasize how these styles may be reinforced or inhibited in their "natural" development. They suggested that a revised *EB*, derived from more precisely defined criteria than the crude and simple ratio devised by Rorschach, could yield much information concerning the patterns of fantasy, affectivity, motility, and the spontaneity potential in the ideation and affect of the individual.

Logically, any attempt to create a revised *EB* should be prefaced by more information than has been published regarding the consistency or homogeneity of the introversive and extratensive styles. In other words, if other seemingly important variables are held constant, such as *FC* : *CF* + *C,* D Scores, *X* + %, type of *M*, etc., are the problem solving activities within each style consistent even though the absolute values in the *EB* differ considerably? For example, would an introversive with an *EB* of 6 : 1.0 manifest problem solving behaviors highly similar to those of the introversives who have *EB*'s of 7 : 4.0, or 6 : 3.0, or 6 : 3.5?

A hint that this might not be true evolved from a reexamination of the data from a problem solving study (Exner, Bryant, & Leura, 1975) reported in the first edition of *Volume 2* (Exner, 1978) and is of sufficient importance to review again. It involved three groups of 15 subjects each, selected from a college population on the basis of the *EB,* the Adjusted D Score, and SAT Verbal Scores, which were between 575 and 600. One group was clearly extratensive, defined by *Sum C* exceeding *M* by 3.0 or more; a second group was clearly introversive, defined by *M* exceeding *Sum C* by at least 3.0; and the third group consisted of ambitents, defined as *Sum C* being within 0.5 point of *M*. All subjects had Adjusted D Scores of 0 or +1, and the frequencies for each did not differ among the groups.

The problem solving apparatus used was the Logical Analysis Device (LAD) (Langmuir, 1958). The subject is provided with a display panel containing nine indicating lights arranged in a circle. Each of the lights is controlled manually through the use of an adjacent pushbutton. A 10th light is located in the center of the circle and is known as the "target" light. It has no switch. Information about the relationships of the various lights is provided by an arrow diagram placed within the circle of nine indicator lights. Each arrow indicates one relationship, either between the indicator lights on the circle, or between any of these lights and the target light. The only information that the subject does not have is the nature of the relationship between two lights. Figure 1 shows the display panel at which the subject works.

Any of three kinds of relationships may exist between two lights: (1) an effector relation (the activation of one light activates another light), (2) a preventor relation (if one light is on, a second is prohibited from lighting), and (3) a combinor relation (the combination of two lights simultaneously activated acts either as an effector or preventor for a third light). The object of the task is to light the center light, using only operations created by the switches for the three lower peripheral lights.

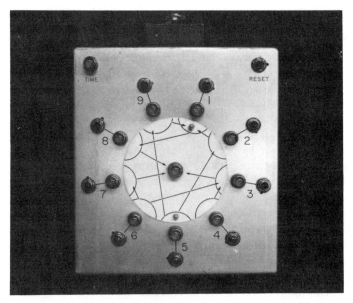

Figure 1.   Subject Display Panel for the Logical Analysis Device.

Before the first problem, the subject is taught the rules of solution by demonstration, explanation, and practice. The subject may ask questions, take notes, and repeat practice operations. The task of finding the correct combination of operations, using only the three lower switches, is one of logical analysis, developed by trial and error, with each trial representing an experimental question posed by the subject concerning various relationships. Ultimately, the subject must synthesize the information developed from each operation to cause the target light to be turned on.

The problems vary in complexity. Some may contain as few as 15 or 20 information yielding operations, whereas others may have as many as 50 operations that can yield relevant information. Each operation is such that many other possible operations can be eliminated by logical deduction. This procedure is demonstrated and explained during the instruction period, but each subject must ultimately decide how many operations to explore, and in what sequence, before attempting a final solution. Each operation is electronically recorded, so that the total recording provides data regarding total number of (1) operations to solution, (2) extraneous or irrelevant operations, and (3) repeated operations. The latter can be subdivided into repeated relevant and repeated extraneous operations. The time between operations and the total time spent solving the problem are also recorded.

Subjects vary enormously in their approach to these problems. Some work in an overly systematic manner, exploring the functions for each of the nine peripheral lights, even though some are often obviously irrelevant to the task. Others tend to repeat, or "verify" information over and over. Still others move almost immediately to the switches controlling the three lower lights that must ultimately be used in the final solution. This latter group, which Langmuir labeled as "organ grinders," typically has the most difficulty because they seldom pause to contemplate the results of their actions, and they rarely alter their approach in favor of the more elementary analytic procedure provided in the initial instructions. Data accumulated for a reasonably large number of subjects suggest that problem solving approaches can be defined along a broad continuum of efficiency that ranges from the hyperactively haphazard, crude, and redundant to the deliberately systematic, flexible, and sophisticated.

The 45 subjects were asked to solve four problems of gradually increasing difficulty, with time limits of 10, 15, 20, and 30 minutes, respectively. Two examiners were assigned randomly across subjects. Neither was aware of the basis on which the subjects had been selected. Subjects were not aware of time limits and were encouraged to continue working on the problem for as long as they desired, but the data analyses were restricted to operations performed within the time limits for the respective problems. All 45 subjects completed Problems 1 and 2 within the time limits. Problem 3 was completed within the time limit by 13 extratensives, 12 introversives, and 12 ambitents. Problem 4 was completed within the time limit by 12 extratensives, 12 introversives, and 11 ambitents.

In the original analyses, the data for each problem were addressed separately, using a 3×3 analysis of variance (ANOVA), with total operations, total errors, and average time between operations as the dependent measures. Separate analyses were performed for repeated operations, repeated errors, and total average time to completion for those finishing within the time limits. Means and standard deviations for each of these variables are shown in Table 1.

Table 1. Means and Standard Deviations for Six Variables in Four Logical Analysis Device Problems for Three Groups

Variables	Introversive N = 15		Extratensive N = 15		Ambitent N = 15	
	M	SD	M	SD	M	SD
PROBLEM 1 (10 MIN)						
Total operations	11.4[b]	3.7	16.3	4.2	19.9	4.9
Total errors	3.1[b]	1.6	6.1	2.8	5.4	2.3
Time betw operations (sec)	19.3[a]	3.6	13.1	3.3	15.6	3.6
Repeated operations	1.8[b]	1.1	4.6	1.4	3.9	1.6
Repeated errors	0.7[d]	0.4	2.3	1.2	2.8	1.5
Time to solution (sec)	220.2	43.1	213.6	41.7	310.2[d]	54.1
PROBLEM 2 (15 MIN)						
Total operations	19.8[a]	4.3	28.4	7.1	23.7	6.7
Total errors	5.7[b]	2.3	11.7	4.8	8.8	3.6
Time betw operations (sec)	21.4	3.7	14.7[c]	4.2	20.9	4.1
Repeated operations	3.6[c]	1.2	7.2	2.6	6.7	2.8
Repeated errors	2.1[c]	0.8	4.1	2.0	5.9	2.4
Time to solution (sec)	423.6	44.2	417.6	49.7	495.6[c]	57.4
PROBLEM 3 (20 MIN)						
Total operations	41.2[b]	9.8	61.8	17.1	56.3	15.2
Total errors	11.7[d]	3.9	26.4	6.7	18.9	5.1
Time betw operations (sec)	24.6	6.8	15.9[c]	4.8	20.4	5.1
Repeated operations	7.3	3.1	9.7	4.7	15.3[d]	3.8
Repeated errors	3.5[d]	1.2	6.9	3.3	11.4[d]	2.7
Time to solution (sec) (passed only)	1013.5	67.1	982.6	69.7	1148.6[c]	61.2
PROBLEM 4 (30 MIN)						
Total operations	51.2[a]	12.1	70.6	11.3	64.9	13.7
Total errors	13.6[c]	4.2	29.8	8.7	21.7	7.5
Time betw operations (sec)	18.2	5.1	13.7	4.4	16.3	4.9
Repeated operations	12.7	3.8	16.2	4.1	24.1[d]	6.8
Repeated errors	4.3	1.6	6.9	2.7	12.8[d]	3.3
Time to solutions (sec) (passed only)	931.8	57.6	967.2	61.8	1057.9[c]	63.1

[a]Significantly different from one other group, $p < .05$.
[b]Significantly different from one other group, $p < .01$.
[c]Significantly different from both other groups, $p < .05$.
[d]Significantly different from both other groups, $p < .01$.

The results indicate that introversives and extratensives work through problem solving tasks at nearly the same rate. Introversives used substantially fewer operations to achieve their goal, whereas extratensives explored many more possibilities, often needlessly and with much greater replication of operations and errors, even though they took slightly less time to achieve the target. The introversives appear to be a bit slower but more systematic in their decisions, and the accuracy of their decisions compensates for the slowness of operation. The extratensives appear to be more "doer" oriented in problem solving. They are more willing to make mistakes, but they apparently profit from those mistakes so that their solution times are generally a bit shorter than the more reflective introversives.

These results parallel the findings of Rosenthal (1954), who used the Katona Matchstick problems with groups of high M and high *Sum C* subjects. Rosenthal found that the high M group was more thoughtful and took longer to finish the task. Although the approaches to problem solving differed for the two groups, they were equally proficient in terms of achieving solutions.

The results also indicate that the ambitents are clearly less efficient when compared with either of the other groups. They use more time to solution, but, more importantly, they repeat more operations and more errors than the other groups. In the last two LAD problems, ambitents repeated almost twice as many errors as the extratensives, and nearly three times as many as the introversives.

It appears that the ambitent needs to verify each maneuver or operation, and that he or she does not profit as much from mistakes as do the other kinds of subjects. The ambitent is probably more prone to vacillate during problem solving, tending to fluctuate between alternatives rather than manifesting a consistent coping approach. This lack of consistency can breed more vulnerability to disruption under stress conditions. This does not mean that ambitents are less well adjusted or effective, but a lack of consistency can become a significant liability under various circumstances.

As noted earlier, a reexamination of these findings hinted that less homogeneity exists within the introversive and extratensive styles than might appear at first glance. Although the data suggest that introversive and extratensive groups are difficult to discriminate in terms of efficiency if time to solution is used as the criterion, that implication is subject to challenge if the results for Problems 3 and 4 are studied separately.

In the original analysis, time to solution was calculated for those two problems *only* for subjects completing the task within the allowed time limits. In fact, when the two groups are subdivided, using completion within the time limit as the basis for the subdivision, some of the results appear rather striking.

Twelve introversives and 13 extratensives completed Problem 3 within the time limit. Twelve subjects from each of those groups completed Problem 4 within the time limit. The five subjects who failed to complete Problem 3 within the time limit also failed to complete Problem 4 within the time limit. All subjects continued working until a correct solution was reached on each problem.

Table 2 shows the means for Problems 3 and 4 for all of the variables studied, after the introversive and extratensive groups were subdivided on the basis of completion of the problems within the time limit. The size of the noncompleting samples is far too small to attempt any statistical comparisons. Nonetheless, the data do appear to highlight some characteristics.

In general, the data for the noncompleters in each group appear substantially different from those for the completers. For instance, the noncompleter introversives had substantially fewer total operations and much longer times between operations than the completer introversives for each problem. The noncompleter extratensives had substantially more total operations and less time between operations than the completer extratensives.

In effect, the noncompleters in each group are *outliers* whose scores for Problems 3 and 4 tended to make the differences between the two groups appear more notable than may have been the case. In other words, although the differences between the two completer groups still seem obvious, they are less substantial than

Table 2.   Means for Six Variables in Two Logical Analysis Device Problems for Introversives and Extratensives Subdivided Based on Completion of the Problems Within the Time Limit

	Introversives		Extratensives	
	Completers	Noncompleters	Completers	Noncompleters
PROBLEM 3 (20 MIN)				
	N = 12	N = 3	N = 13	N = 2
Variables	M	M	M	M
Total operations	46.1	31.2	56.9	70.3
Total errors	13.9	10.1	21.4	30.3
Seconds betw op's	20.5	32.6	17.4	11.3
Repeated op's	7.8	6.4	9.1	10.6
Repeated errors	4.1	3.1	5.8	7.7
Seconds to solution	1013.5	1381.3	982.6	1282.1
PROBLEM 4 (30 MIN)				
	N = 12	N = 3	N = 12	N = 3
Variables	M	M	M	M
Total operations	58.4	41.6	63.8	79.1
Total errors	15.4	11.2	23.9	34.6
Seconds betw op's	16.4	22.1	15.1	12.0
Repeated op's	14.9	10.6	15.2	19.3
Repeated errors	4.9	3.7	5.7	8.4
Seconds to solution	931.8	1979.5	967.2	1876.3

first thought and, in several instances (e.g., seconds between operations or repeated operations) the differences are not statistically significant.

These findings stimulated a review of other characteristics of the six Problem 4 noncompleters. All had SAT Verbal Scores within a 15-point range; all had D Scores and Adjusted D Scores of 0; all had $X + \%$'s between 72 and 86%; all had $FC : CF + C$ ratios that contained more FC responses, and no Pure C responses; and none had Zd scores of less than 0.5. The one common Rorschach feature was that all six had EB's in which the higher number was at least three times the lower number, and in three cases the higher number was four or more times greater than the lower number. A review of the protocols for 24 Problem 4 completers revealed that only two subjects had EB's in which the higher value was at least three times greater than the lower value.

The finding regarding the extensive difference between the values for M and $Sum\ C$ among the noncompleters led to the postulate that, as the magnitude of the difference between the values in the EB increases, the basic characteristics of the style become more dominating or consistent. Stated differently, the hypothesis suggests that, as the difference between values in the EB becomes substantial, the dominance of the style tends to inhibit flexibility in its applications.

A post hoc test of the hypothesis was organized by culling through more than 325 Rorschach protocols of subjects who had completed within the time limits the same sequence of the four LAD problems, or a parallel series that has the same difficulty level and the same number of information yielding operations. Those subjects completed LAD problems while participating in various projects at the

Rorschach Research Foundation from 1974 to 1982. The objective was to create four groups, two introversive and two extratensive, differentiated by the *EB,* and among which differences in demography and other major Rorschach variables would be minimal.

The sorting process yielded four groups of 13 subjects each. The classification criterion for assignment to the target groups (pervasive introversive or pervasive extratensive) was that the higher value in the *EB* be at least 2.5 times that of the lower value. The criterion for the control group assignment (typical introversive or typical extratensive) was that the higher *EB* value be less than 2.5 times that of the lower value, but at least 2 points higher if the *EA* was 10 or less or at least 2.5 points higher if the *EA* was greater than 10. The label "typical" was selected after reviewing adult nonpatient normative data and determining that only about 25 to 28% of introversives and extratensives have a larger *EB* value that is at least 2.5 times that of the lower value.

The subjects ranged in age from 19 to 34, with an average for each group of between 22 and 24 years. Four from each group had been outpatients when they were tested. The other 36 were nonpatients who participated in the standardization sample or served as controls in psychiatric studies. All had completed at least 13 years of education, with the average for each group of between 13.6 and 14.7 years. All had Rorschachs in which the D Score and Adjusted D Score were 0 or +1; had *X* + %'s between 73 and 86%; had at least six Popular answers; had *FC* : *CF* + *C* ratios containing as much or more *FC* and there were no Pure *C*'s; contained at least 10 *Zf;* and had *Zd* values no lower than −1.5 (four subjects in each of three groups and three subjects in the fourth group had *Zd* scores greater than +3.0). Table 3 shows the performance data for each group through the four problems.

The results appear to afford some support for the hypothesis that basic features of the introversive and extratensive coping styles are more dominant and less flexible when the greater *EB* value is at least 2.5 times larger than the lesser value. In Problems 1 and 2, which are relatively easy problems that most subjects solve within the time limits, the data for the introversive groups are very similar, as are the data for the extratensive groups. As might be expected, both extratensive groups used significantly more operations, made more errors, tended to repeat more operations, and had significantly shorter intervals between operations than the introversives. The pattern of differences shifts considerably for the last two problems.

Problem 3 is much more difficult than Problem 2 because it involves more complex combinor relationships. In Problem 3, both extratensive groups used significantly more operations than the pervasive introversive group but not than the typical introversive group. In fact, there are *no* significant differences between the typical introversive and extratensive groups. Conversely, the pervasive extratensive group differed from the pervasive introversive group for all six variables and had more errors and shorter intervals between operations than the typical extratensive group. The pervasive introversive group averaged significantly more time to solve the problem than any of the other groups. Problem 4 is even more complex than Problem 3. As with Problem 3, there are no significant differences between the typical introversive and typical extratensive groups, but

Table 3.   Means for Six Variables in Four Logical Analysis Device Problems for Introversives and Extratensives Subdivided on the Basis of *M:SUM C* Difference

	Introversives		Extratensives	
	Extreme N = 13	Typical N = 13	Extreme N = 13	Typical N = 13
	M	M	M	M
PROBLEM 1 (10 MIN)				
Total Operations	10.1	11.3	17.7**	16.8**
Total Errors	2.8	3.6	6.4**	5.6*
Seconds Betw Op's	20.9	20.2	13.2**	13.3**
Repeated Op's	2.6	2.8	5.7**	5.4*
Repeated Errors	1.5	1.9	2.1	3.0
Seconds to Solution	231.6	222.4	213.9	217.5
PROBLEM 2 (15 MIN)				
Total Operations	19.4	20.7	31.8**	29.9**
Total Errors	4.6	5.4	12.7**	12.2**
Seconds Betw Op's	23.3	21.7	12.2**	14.1**
Repeated Op's	3.9	4.4	9.1**	7.0
Repeated Errors	1.9	1.8	5.8**	4.1
Seconds to Solution	441.6	419.9	414.5	421.2
PROBLEM 3 (20 MIN)				
Total operations	36.8	45.1	64.6*	55.9*
Total errors	10.3	13.8	27.9**	19.7***
Seconds betw op's	29.7	23.6	12.3**	18.4***
Repeated op's	5.8	7.1	11.4*	7.7
Repeated errors	3.6	4.7	8.1*	6.1
Seconds to solution	1126.6	1001.9*	981.2*	963.3*
PROBLEM 4 (30 MIN)				
Total operations	42.1	54.3*	77.7**	61.0***
Total errors	9.3	16.2*	31.2**	21.1***
Seconds betw op's	24.8	17.6	12.3*	15.6
Repeated op's	10.8	14.3	19.5*	15.1
Repeated errors	4.6	4.3	7.1	5.4
Seconds to solution	1254.6	952.7***	1049.8*	927.4***

*   = significantly different from extreme introversive group, $p < .01$
**   = significantly different from both introversive groups, $p < .02$
*** = significantly different from both extreme groups, $p < .02$

both differ substantially from the two pervasive groups. Actually, the performance of the typical extratensive group is more like that of the typical introversive group than the pervasive extratensive group.

An examination of the trends within groups across all four problems seems to indicate that the two typical groups profited more from the problem solving experience or at least tended to modify their problem solving approaches more. For the last two problems, the typical introversives began using more operations, made more errors, had shorter intervals between operations, and achieved solution in nearly the same amount of time as the typical extratensives. Likewise, the typical extratensives began using fewer operations, made fewer errors, lengthened the time intervals between operations, and had the lowest average time to solution. In other words those in the typical groups appeared to show greater flexibility by adopting some of the problem solving features of the opposite style and, in doing so, enhanced their performance. Those in the pervasive groups did not appear to do this. Their approach to each problem was consistent with their approach to the preceding problem. In this instance, that lack of flexibility probably reduced efficiency.

These findings raised intriguing questions concerning the pervasive style and prompted a review of other data for subjects in the protocol pool. Although only 25% of introversive and extratensive nonpatient adults do have a pervasive style, the percentages are considerably higher for some psychiatric groups. For instance, about 60% of schizophrenics are introversive and nearly two-thirds of those do have pervasive styles. Nearly half of inpatient depressives are either introversive or extratensive, and about half of those subjects have pervasive styles. About 60% of patients with character disorders are either introversive or extratensive, and about two-thirds have pervasive styles.

The difference between patients and nonpatients for pervasiveness of style prompted a review of some treatment data available for some of the subjects whose records are included in the protocol pool at the Rorschach Research Foundation. Overall, this group comprised nearly 1000 subjects who were tested more than once in the course of treatment effects research. Many data included some information about length of hospitalization and/or number of outpatient treatment visits, premature termination from treatment, rehospitalization, treatment progress, or posttreatment progress. Two target groups were selected from this pool, using as the criterion for selection the fact that the baseline Rorschach included an *EB* that was either introversive or extratensive.

The first target group consisted of 261 first-admission nonschizophrenics. About 70% had been hospitalized for some form of affective disturbance. None of the subjects terminated their hospitalization against medical advice, and none were transferred to other hospitals. The group was subdivided into (1) typical style or (2) pervasive style, disregarding whether the style was introversive or extratensive, and data were analyzed according to (1) length of hospitalization, (2) confirmation of entry into posthospitalization outpatient treatment, and (3) rehospitalization within a year. The results are shown in Table 4.

Table 4. **Some Treatment Data Concerning First Admission Inpatients Subdivided on the Basis of *EBPer***

	Typical *EB* N = 139		Pervasive *EB* N = 122	
Variable	N	%	N	%
Length of Hospitalization				
Less than 16 days	33	24%	24	20%
Between 16 and 30 days	67	48%	35	29%*
More than 30 days	39	28%	63	52%*
Entered Outpatient Care	131	94%	117	96%
Rehospitalized	36	26%	27	22%

* = significantly different from typical group ($p < .01$)

The second target group consisted of 239 outpatients, who were beginning treatment for the first time and who remained in treatment for at least 4 months. Presenting complaints varied considerably for this group, but the majority manifested some depressive features. Like the inpatient target group, they were subdivided on the basis of typical versus pervasive style. Four dependent measures were selected for analysis: (1) terminations against advice, (2) terminations with a favorable outcome within a year, (3) therapist progress evaluations for the first two months, (4) therapist progress evaluations for the second two months. The results are shown in Table 5.

The credibility of the results shown in Tables 4 and 5 are clearly subject to question because so many variables, such as type of treatment, presenting symptoms, subject demography, and other personality variables, have not been considered. Nonetheless, they are compelling because of their consistency. Among the inpatient group, more pervasive style subjects were hospitalized for a longer period, even though there is no difference for the proportions entering outpatient care or being rehospitalized. Among the outpatients, significantly fewer pervasive style subjects terminated care within one year and proportionally more were evaluated negatively for progress by their therapists after both two and four months.

The collective data concerning those with pervasive styles seems to have sufficient substance to warrant the inclusion of *EBPer* into the *System*. It is probably best to regard it as somewhat of an experimental index and, although it is premature to speculate on any relationship between the pervasive style and the onset or maintenence of pathology, these do appear to be issues worth further exploration. It is also important to emphasize that there are probably many situations in which a dominant or pervasive style might be a distinct asset.

Intellectualization Index $\{2AB + (Art + Ay)\}$

The original Intellectualization Index was calculated as $Ab + Art$, but, as noted earlier, new research concerning Abstract suggests that it is more appropriately

Table 5.   Some Treatment Data Concerning First Time Outpatients Subdivided on the Basis of *EBPer*

	Typical *EB* N = 137		Pervasive *EB* N = 102	
Variable	N	%	N	%
Terminated against advice	26	19%	17	17%
Favorable termination within one year	80	58%	39	38%*
Evaluations—1st two months				
Negative	22	16%	30	29%*
Neutral	51	37%	28	27%
Favorable	64	47%	44	43%
Evaluations—2nd two months				
Negative	29	21%	36	35%*
Neutral	26	19%	15	15%
Favorable	82	60%	51	50%

* = significantly different from typical group (p < .01)

applied as a special score (*AB*). Some of that research also indicates that it accounts for much more variance in identifying the intellectualization process and that the content category for anthropology (*AY*) also contributes. Thus, the revised index includes all three variables, with the special score *AB* weighted double. The index is calculated as two times the number of *AB* answers plus the number of *Art* and *Ay* contents. Both primary and secondary contents are included.

In the original Intellectualization Index, values of 5 or more were considered significant. Reexamination of the same validation criteria from which the index was developed indicates that, when the revised index is applied, values of 4 and 5 have some limited interpretive significance. Subjects with values of 4 and 5 do tend to intellectualize more often than most others but it is erroneous to assume that this defensive strategy is a major, or frequently used, feature in the psychological operations of the individual. On the other hand, when the value is 6 or greater, it is much more likely that the subject employs intellectualization as a major tactic to neutralize some of the impact of emotion.

Isolation Index {(2*Cl* + 2*Na* + *Bt* + *Ge* + *Ls*)/*R*}

The original Isolation Index involved the straightforward addition of the primary and secondary contents in five content categories—Botany (*Bt*), Clouds (*Cl*), Geography (*Ge*), Landscape (*Ls*), and Nature (*Na*)—and then dividing that sum by *R*. Additional research, using a regression model to correlate the index with other measures of social isolation revealed that both *Na* and *Cl* account for considerably more variance than do *Bt, Ge,* or *Ls.* Consequently, it was decided that both should be weighted more heavily in the calculation for the index, provided that the new rule regarding the scoring of *Na, Bt,* and *Ls* be invoked when any combination of the three appear in a single answer. In doing so, the predictive correlation for the index is increased from the mid .60s to the upper .70s when the resulting value exceeds .25, and into the .80s when the value exceeds .33. Thus, in calculating the index, the raw sum for the two categories, *Cl* and *Na,* should be doubled, that sum added to the raw sum of *Bt* + *Ge* + *Ls,* and the total divided by *R.*

S – %

The variable *S* – % evolved during the research on the Schizophrenia Index (SCZI). It is one of 10 variables that loads significantly in discriminant function analyses that differentiate false positives from true positives. The data revealed that many false positive cases, on both the original SCZI and many of the experimental SCZI's, were created because of three variables: a low *X* + %, a high *X* – %, and at least one *M*– answer. Although the proportion of false positive cases was within reasonably acceptable limits for most groups (less than 6%), it was unacceptably high among three groups: inpatient affective disorders, inpatient adolescents, and children having academic difficulties.

A sort of minus responses, card by card by location, for those three groups plus a target group of schizophrenics, yielded a highly significant difference. Namely, the nonschizophrenics, especially younger clients, tended to give many more *S*– answers than did the schizophrenics. Further investigation revealed that, although the absolute raw score for $S-$ answers did provide some useful discrimination, a proportional score or percentage substantially improved the discrimination. Thus an $S-\%$ has been added to the *System,* calculated as the number of $S-$ answers divided by the total number of *minus* answers.

The $S-\%$ also provides information about the extent to which mediational distortions may relate to some affective interference or influence. Minus responses are quite intriguing because they defy or distort the contours of the stimulus field. During the response process the subject has the opportunity to rescan the stimulus field often, and alter or discard potential answers that had been created during the first scan of the field. This opportunity to make internal corrections before giving an answer is an important part of the test, yet most people give some minus answers. For instance, 605 of the 700 adult nonpatients who constitute the new normative sample gave at least one minus response. Earlier research suggested that many minus answers have projected features, promoted by sets and/or preoccupations. Thus, when the $S-\%$ exceeds 33%, particularly in records that have more than three minus answers, it is reasonable to postulate that strong sets, created by negativism or anger, are contributing to mediational distortions. Obviously, such findings have considerable importance in planning intervention.

SPECIAL SCORES

Research and data analyses, completed since the publication of the second edition of *Volume 1*, have led to the identification of two new special scores and a tactic for differentiating four of the six critical special scores that relate to cognitive slippage.

A Special Score for Abstractions (*AB*)

The *AB* coding is used for two classes of answers. The first are those for which the content code Human Experience (*Hx*) has been used to note human emotion or sensory experience. The second are responses in which the subject articulates a clear and specific symbolic representation. Abstract paintings *are not* scored *AB* unless a specific representation is included. Some examples of *AB* answers are, "A statue representing communist tyranny"; "It just reminds me of depression"; "A modern dance representing the beauty of women"; "It's just a horrible smell, please take it back"; "A mask that represents evil"; "Two dancers from the musical *A Chorus Line*"; and "A Blake painting of man's struggle for purity."

A Special Score for Cooperative Movement (COP)

The COP coding is assigned to any movement response (*M, FM,* or *m*) involving two or more objects in which the interaction is *clearly* positive or cooperative. The positive or cooperative characteristic of the interaction must be *unequivocal.* Thus, looking or talking are *not* scored COP. Some examples of COP responses are, "Two men lifting something up"; "Two insects trying to knock down this post"; "Two people leaning toward each other, sharing a secret";

"Three people doing a dance together"; "A bird feeding her young"; "Two children playing on a see-saw"; and "Two wolves attacking some other animal."

COP answers appear at least once in almost 80% of the 700 adult nonpatient records that constitute the normative sample ($M = 2.07$, mode = 2, range = 0 to 6). On the other hand, COP answers appear at least once in only about 65% of outpatient protocols, about half of the records from inpatient schizophrenics and depressives, and less than 40% of the protocols from patients with character disorders.

COP is not easily reported on some cards. A review of the COP answers indicates that it occurs in less than 20% of the M and less than 15% of the FM answers on Cards I, VIII, IX, and X. It is almost nonexistent among answers to Cards IV and VI and has a very low frequency in answers to Card V. COP answers occur most often to Card III, and next most frequently to Cards II and VII. The validational data seem to offer a strong argument that, with the possible exception of Card III, COP answers represent a form of projection related to an interpersonal style or interest.

In two sociometric studies, one consisting of peer nominations from 25 third-year high school students and the second consisting of the same type of peer nominations collected from 35 female college freshmen living in the same dormitory, a subject who had more than two COP answers was identified by peers at a rate five times greater than other subjects as being the one who "Is the most fun to be with," "Is the easiest to be around," "Is a class leader," and "Is the most trustworthy." Four subjects from the group of high school students and five of the college students whose records contained no COP responses were never nominated by their peers for any of those four items. Conversely, those nine subjects did receive the most nominations for relatively negative items, such as "Is the person I know least about," "Is a person who does not seem to have many friends," and "Is a person I would probably not vote for a class office."

COP also correlates with the group therapy process. A review of the audio recordings of 17 subjects in two groups, taken during three group therapy sessions, reveals that four subjects with more than two COP answers talked more frequently and for longer intervals, and directed remarks to more group members than did others in the groups. Six subjects with no COP responses talked less frequently and directed remarks to the therapist more often than did others in the groups.

Treatment effects data suggest that COP is probably an important variable regarding successful termination and/or discharge from hospitalization. For instance, a stratified random sample of 70 outpatients was drawn from the pool of subjects at the Rorschach Research Foundation who had participated in a multiple retest, treatment effects study. The criteria for selection was fourfold: (1) that each had entered treatment because of interpersonal problems, (2) that each had participated in the study for at least two years, (3) that each had terminated treatment before the 18th month, and (4) that the pretreatment protocol contained either no COP or one COP response. The selection yielded 31 cases with no COP responses in the pretreatment record and 39 cases with one COP response.

Information concerning the subjects indicated that all had entered one of four treatment models (cognitive therapy, $N = 23$; rational emotive therapy,

$N = 14$; behavioral modeling therapy, $N = 13$; dynamic psychotherapy, $N = 20$). All 70 subjects terminated treatment between the 8th and 15th month. All were retested during the 9th or 10th month after the onset of treatment, and again between the 18th and 20th month. In the first retest, 37 gave at least two COP responses, 15 gave one, and the remaining 18 gave none (none of these 18 had COP responses in the first test).

In the second retest, the COP response distribution showed very little change. All 37 subjects who had two or more COP answers in the first retest had at least two COP responses in the second retest and 34 of the 37 (92%) reported a favorable interpersonal adjustment. Two of the 15 subjects who had one COP answer in the 10-month retest had two COP responses in the second retest and the remaining 13 continued to have one COP response. Twelve of these subjects (80%) also reported a favorable interpersonal adjustment, but three reported recurring problems and one had entered treatment again. None of the 18 subjects who had no COP answers in the first retest gave COP responses in the second retest. Ten of the 18 (56%) reported a favorable interpersonal adjustment, but eight (44%) reported recurring interpersonal problems and five of the eight had entered treatment again.

A second study focused on a review of follow-up data for 100 first-admission inpatient affective disorders. Among the admission protocols, 31 contained two or more COP answers, 36 contained one COP response, and 33 had no COP answer. All were retested at discharge, which occurred between 21 and 45 days after admission. At that time, 37 records contained two or more COP answers, 29 had one COP response, and 34 had no COP answers. All subjects entered or reentered outpatient care, and 78 were continuing as outpatients at the time of a follow-up given at 9 to 10 months postdischarge. Favorable progress was reported by 30 of the 37 (81%) who had two or more COP answers at discharge. Three had been rehospitalized within eight months of being discharged. Favorable progress was reported by 19 of the 29 subjects (66%) who had given one COP answer at discharge; however, six of the remaining 10 had been rehospitalized during the first eight months following discharge. Favorable progress was reported by only 18 of the 34 subjects (53%) whose discharge protocols contained no COP responses, and nine of the remaining 16 subjects had been rehospitalized during the eight months following discharge.

Obviously, it is dangerous to interpret the presence or absence of COP answers in isolation. Findings generated from many other sources are necessary to put the COP data in proper perspective. For instance, preliminary findings suggest that interpersonal relationships are likely to be less stable for those whose protocols contain more than two aggressive movement (AG) answers even though multiple COP answers also appear in the record. Nonetheless, COP does seem to be a linchpin variable in the cluster of variables related to interpersonal perception.

The relationship between no texture (T) responses and no COP responses differs considerably for patients and nonpatients. For instance, a review of 700 adult nonpatient records in the normative sample found that 145 contained no COP but only 33 (23%) of those gave no T, although 80 subjects in the total sample gave no T. Conversely, a reference group of 320 schizophrenic records (Exner, 1990) contains 162 with no COP responses. No T responses were given in 148 (91%) of those cases. Likewise, a reference group of 315 inpatient depressives (Exner,

1990) includes 156 who gave no COP answers, of whom 82 (53%) gave no *T* responses. No COP answers appear in 123 of 300 protocols collected from outpatients beginning treatment for the first time and *T* is also absent in 94 of the 123 records (76%).

Level 1–Level 2 Differentiation for Four Special Scores

Shortly after the original Schizophrenia Index (SCZI) was developed in 1981, it became obvious that the experimental weighted values assigned to the six critical special scores (DV, INCOM, DR, FABCOM, ALOG, and CONTAM) did not always reflect the degree of cognitive slippage manifest in the answers. Consequently, several variations in assigning weights were explored but to no avail because none of those tactics could contend with the fact that, within each category of special score, variations in slippage are considerable.

For example, many people, especially children, inadvertently identify the presence of hands or arms when explaining either of the Popular Bat responses to Cards I or V. Technically, these are INCOM responses that represent the mild forms of slippage that sometimes occur when people do not pay close attention to how they are expressing themselves. On the other hand, a subject might say, "This is a bat that has four nostrils on its wings." This response is also an IN-COM, and under the original scoring criteria would be assigned the same quantitative values as the answer describing hands or arms on a bat even though it is much more bizarre.

Several experimental criteria were devised in an attempt to provide more accurate differentiation for degrees of slippage reflected in the special scores, but most were discarded because of problems with interscorer reliability. The criteria that have been adopted are the most simplistic in some ways, but that simplicity has been required to establish satisfactory interscorer reliability. It involves the assignment of a value of 1 or 2 to each of the four special scores, DV, INCOM, DR, and FABCOM, depending on whether the answer is clearly bizarre.

A value of 1 is assigned to answers in which a mild or modest instance of illogical, fluid, or peculiar thinking is evident. Although each Level 1 answer meets the criteria for the special score, usually they are not markedly different from the cognitive slips that often occur when people do not attend closely to their expressions or to the judgments that they are making. These answers often sound like the products of immaturity, limited education, or judgments that are not well thought out. Some examples of Level 1 scores are shown below:

Two dogs with their hands together	FABCOM1
It looks like crabs but I don't like them very much	DR1
It's a circus elephant, he's wearing a pointy cap	DV1
It looks like two red wolves	INCOM1
It looks like worms, my father used to tease me about them	DR1
It's a fly with those thing-a-jigs on it	DV1
A tiny little rabbit	DV1
Like two sheep or something playing basketball	FABCOM1
It's a cat's face but it's got white eyes	INCOM1

A value of 2 is assigned to answers in which a moderate or severe instance of dissociated, illogical, fluid, or circumstantial thinking is present. They deviate markedly in the flawed judgment that is conveyed and/or the very unusual mode of expression that is used. Level 2 answers stand out because of their bizarreness and seldom leave doubt concerning their scoring. In instances when a scorer has legitimate doubts about whether a response meets the Level 2 criteria, the Level 1 score should be assigned. Some examples of Level 2 responses are shown below:

Ah ha, its a quartet of four ants	DV2
It's the destituteness of the world, evil and hollow	DR2
It's the universal hole of a female vagina	DV2
It looks like two men have raped some stones	FABCOM2
It's a face with Cousteaus's bra across the mouth	FABCOM2
It looks like the double twin two peaks of Mt. Rushmore	DV2
A person with a heart so big it's pushing on his chin	INCOM2
A man tormented by the black bile in his lungs	INCOM2

The decision about whether to assign a value of 1 or 2 should be based *exclusively* on the substance and verbiage of the answer. Extraneous elements, such as age, educational level, or cultural background, should never be considered in this differentiation.

It had been expected that the Level 1–Level 2 differentiation of these four special scores would contribute significantly to the revision of the SCZI, but the actual input to the new index was far less than expected. This is because Level 2 special scores do appear among other groups. In the adult nonpatient normative sample, 23 of the 700 subjects gave at least one Level 2 response. The frequency is much more substantial among nonpatient children. For instance, at least one Level 2 special score appears in 27 of the 120 nonpatient eight-year-olds that comprise the normative sample for that age. More striking is the fact that Level 2 scores appear in 24 of the 100 records that comprise the normative sample for 13-year-olds. The frequency is more marked among psychiatric groups. Level 2 scores appear at least once in the protocols of 225 of 315 first-admission inpatient depressives; 62 of 180 outpatients with character disorders; and 96 of a mixed group of 250 outpatients, none of whom are diagnosed with schizophrenia or character disorders.

These data indicate that the presence of a Level 2 special score in a protocol has no precise meaning, other than to reflect the fact that some of the ideational activities of the subject are marked by much more slippage and/or strangeness than might be expected. In other words, a single Level 2 score does not necessarily signal pathological thinking.

NEW INDICES

The Schizophrenia Index (SCZI)

Investigations designed to improve the Schizophrenia Index (SCZI) began in 1986 and several were developed that improved both true positive and false positive rates. However, only after the research concerning Level 1 and Level 2 Special Scores was completed and the $S - \%$ was formulated, did the improvements became more substantial. Following from a large number of correlational and discriminant function analyses, it became apparent that at least 10 variables loaded positively in attempting to correctly identify the presence of schizophrenia.

Subsequently, more than 50 discriminant function analyses were conducted, each involving a variety of subject samples that included nonpatients, schizophrenics, and nonschizophrenic patients. The objective of each analysis was to determine the best weightings and/or cutoff scores for the 10 variables that would produce the largest percentage of true positive cases and the smallest percentage of false positives among the various control samples. The control samples included both inpatients and outpatients, as well as adults and children. The best combination of the variables, weightings, and cutoffs resulted in the new SCZI, which involves six tests. The 10 variables used in the six tests are as follows:

1. $X + \% < .61$ **and** $S - \% < .41$ **or** $X + \% < .50$
2. $X - \% > .29$
3. *Sum FQ-> Sum FQu* **or** *Sum FQ-> Sum (FQo + FQ +)*
4. *Sum* Level 2 Special Scores > 1 **and** FABCOM2 > 0
5. *Sum* 6 Special Scores > 6 **or** *Weighted Sum* 6 Special Scores > 17 (Cutoffs should be adjusted for children as > 1 *SD* above mean)
6. $M- > 1$ **or** $X - \% > .40$.

The critical value in the SCZI is 4; that is, a value of 4 indicates a significant probability that schizophrenia is present but also a possibility of a false positive. Values of 5 or 6 are more definitive, indicating a strong likelihood of schizophrenia and a very low probability of a false positive. This is probably best illustrated by the results of a "Monte Carlo" procedure.

The procedure involved five random drawings. In each draw, 100 subjects were randomly selected from each of five groups consisting of (1) DSM-III diagnosed first-admission schizophrenics ($N = 1238$), (2) DSM-III-SADS diagnosed first-admission major affective disorders ($N = 1421$), and (3) outpatients beginning treatment for the first time ($N = 926$), (4) adolescent behavior disorders ($N = 764$), and (5) adult nonpatients ($N = 1364$). (The outpatients represented a variety of diagnoses, but more than half had depression as one of the presenting symptoms.) The program for the procedure was written so that, after a record was included in one draw, it would be excluded from the pool and not available for subsequent draws.

The results are shown in Table 6.

The false positive rates vary from 0 to 11% depending on the group studied. However, 76 of the 105 false positive records (72%), have SCZI values of 4. For this reason, SCZI values of 4 must be approached with caution. False negative rates are also relatively modest, ranging from 12 to 22% across all five draws. Sixty-seven of 83 (81%) of the false negative protocols have fewer than 17 responses.

The Depression Index (DEPI)

Anyone working with the *System* for very long can attest to the problems with the original Depression Index (DEPI). The false negative rate was unacceptably high,

Table 6.   Frequency of SCZI Values of 4 or More for Five Random Selections of 100 Subjects From Each of Five Groups

	Schizophrenic Disorder	Affective Disorder	Outpatient Mixed Group	Adolescent Behav Prob	Adult Nonpt
	N	N	N	N	N
DRAW 1					
SCZI = 6	32	0	0	0	0
SCZI = 5	29	1	1	3	0
SCZI = 4	23	6	4	3	0
TOTAL	84	7	5	6	0
DRAW 2					
SCZI = 6	31	0	0	0	0
SCZI = 5	33	0	0	4	0
SCZI = 4	22	10	4	5	1
TOTAL	86	10	4	9	1
DRAW 3					
SCZI = 6	26	1	0	1	0
SCZI = 5	34	3	2	1	0
SCZI = 4	21	5	3	6	0
TOTAL	81	9	5	8	0
DRAW 4					
SCZI = 6	34	1	0	0	0
SCZI = 5	33	1	0	2	0
SCZI = 4	21	6	2	4	0
TOTAL	88	8	2	6	0
DRAW 5					
SCZI = 6	32	1	0	1	0
SCZI = 5	24	3	1	1	0
SCZI = 4	22	7	5	7	1
TOTAL	78	11	6	9	1

often exceeding 60% for some groups of clearly depressed subjects. Part of the problem stemmed from the fact that the index was overly conservative, but the problem was exacerbated by the changing definitions of depression and the affective disorders that have appeared during the past decade. During the same period, the literature concerning affective disturbances often has been marked by contradictory positions and many of the research findings, based on non-Rorschach sources, have been equivocal. Obviously, depression, as a complaint, continues to rank among the most commonly presented symptoms, but even the most stringent advocate of the DSM position will openly admit that findings of homogeneity among depressed patients are, at best, scarce.

A review of the positions and findings regarding depression easily lends itself to the conclusion that at least three different kinds of people tend to be diagnosed as being depressed or as having an affective disorder: (1) those who are emotionally distraught; (2) those who are cognitively pessimistic, lethargic, and self-defeating in their behaviors; and (3) those who are helpless in the face of contending with a complex society. Obviously, these are not discrete states and considerable overlap can be expected, but some of the positions and findings do tend to support the hypothesis that they reflect *primary* features in the psychological organization of the person. In 1986, that postulate formed the basis for a series of studies regarding the DEPI, with the tentative objective of creating three DEPI's to replace the original.

The first step involved an effort to subdivide the more than 1400 cases in the protocol pool, collected from subjects diagnosed as affectively disturbed, into three broad groups using non-test data as the basis for the sort. The groups were arbitrarily defined as (1) emotionally depressed, (2) cognitively depressed, and (3) helpless. The sort was impossible for more than 650 cases because of insufficient data, but three groups ultimately were formed, each containing more than 200 subjects. Factor analyses yielded interesting but unclear findings. A five-factor solution generated two common factors for all three groups, two factors common to two groups but not the third, and one factor that made no sense. At best, the results suggested that the groups were probably different in some ways. The next steps involved a series of multivariate analyses of variance (MANOVA's), intergroup correlational analyses, and discriminant function analyses. This time, the yield was more distinct.

The data for the first two groups (emotional and cognitive) overlapped considerably, but the data for the third group were much more discrete. No matter what tactic was employed, it was impossible to empirically disentangle the first two groups, so they were collapsed into a single group ($N = 471$) that was used as a target sample from which to search out a new DEPI. This was done using a series of discriminant analyses and contingency tables. The third group (helpless; $N = 213$) was held out to be used as a sample against which results might be tested. The findings revealed that at least 15 variables must be considered if the presence of depression or an affective disturbance was to be identified. Those 15 variables form the basis for seven tests that constitute the new DEPI:

1. $(FV + VF + V) > 0$ **or** $FD > 2$
2. Color-Shading Blends > 0 **or** $S > 2$
3. $3r + (2)/R > .44$ **and** $Fr + rF = 0$ **or** $3r + (2)/R < .33$
4. $Afr < .46$ **or** Blends < 4
5. *Sum of Shading* $> FM + m$ **or** *Sum C'* > 2
6. MOR > 2 **or** $(2AB + Art + Ay) > 3$
7. COP < 2 **or** Isolation Index $> .24$.

A value of 5 is critical but not necessarily definitive in the new DEPI. In other words, a value of 5 indicates that the subject has many of the features that are common among those diagnosed as being depressed or having an affective disorder, but other diagnoses may be assigned depending on presenting symptoms and history. In effect, the value of 5 probably reflects the presence of a psychological organization that can easily give rise to experiences of depression or fluctuations in mood.

Values of 6 and 7 are more definitive. Subjects having these values in the DEPI are almost always diagnosed as having some significant affective problem (the exceptions to this occur most often among schizophrenics who are depressed but who have schizophrenia as the primary diagnosis).

The first test of the new DEPI focused on the sample of subjects that had been categorized as helpless, and the results were disappointing. Only 36 of the 213 subjects (17%) showed values of 5, 6, or 7 on the new DEPI. This seemed very striking because the final contingency table for the DEPI indicated that values of 5, 6, or 7 correctly identified 402 of the 471 subjects (85%) in the target sample that had been used to formulate the index.

A second test of the DEPI was accomplished using the 663 subjects who could not be subdivided into the exploratory groups (emotional, cognitive, helpless) because of lack of data. About 81% (539) had values of 5, 6, or 7, and 469 (71%) had values of 6 or 7.

Similar testing of the DEPI was completed using groups of schizophrenics, outpatients, character disorder patients, and nonpatients. Children and adolescents were included in each test. The false positive results have been very favorable. About 3% of nonpatient adults are positive on the DEPI, as are less than 2% of nonpatient children. On the other hand, about 19% of schizophrenics are positive (most obtaining values of 5), as are about 13% of patients with character disorders (almost all obtaining values of 5). The outpatient sample has about 18% who are positive on the DEPI, with about 78% of those having values of 5.

A review of the validation data concerning each of the variables included in the DEPI indicates that they reflect a substantial mixture, with each related either to a cognitive or affective feature. For instance, MOR responses, the egocentricity index, *FD* answers, and the intellectualization index involve a greater emphasis on cognitive activities, whereas color-shading blends, C' answers, or the *Afr* are much more directly related to affect. The fact that a composite was required to achieve the desired efficacy level seems to indicate that most people who are diagnosed with dysthymia or an affective disorder have difficulties in both areas, even though they might be differentiated as being either cognitively or affectively distressed or disturbed if some other criteria are applied.

The Coping Deficit Index (CDI)

A very important by-product of the research leading to the new DEPI is the development of the Coping Deficit Index (CDI). As noted above, the DEPI was not effective in identifying very many subjects from the depression–affective disorders pool who had been categorized as "helpless." Consequently, the records from the helpless group that were not positive on the DEPI—that is, those having a DEPI value of less than 5 ($N = 177$)—were combined with the 69 false negatives from the original target group to create a new sample to study ($N = 246$). It was anticipated that a second depression index might be formulated by using a series of intercorrelational and discriminant function analyses.

The group proved to be reasonably homogeneous for a grouping of 11 variables. Several mixtures of those 11 variables were tested and it was determined that they yielded the greatest efficacy when used in a composite to test five issues and 1 point was assigned for each issue proving to be positive. Thus, by using critical values of 4 or 5, 194 of the 246 subjects in the new target group (79%) were correctly identified, including 143 of the 177 subjects in the helpless group (81%).

The 11 variables and five tests used are as follows:

1. *EA* < 6 **or** Adj D < 0
2. COP < 2 **and** AG < 2
3. Weighted *Sum C* < 2.5 **or** *Afr* < .46
4. *Passive* movement > *active* movement + 1 **or** Pure H < 2
5. *Sum T* > 1 **or** Isolation Index > .24 **or** Food > 0.

When this new index was calculated for the group of 663 subjects from the depression–affective disorders pool who had not been subcategorized in the original analyses leading to the DEPI, 219 (33%) were positive, including 93 of the 124 subjects who were negative on the DEPI.

A review of scores on this new index for several other groups were then calculated as a logical next step in evaluating its usefulness. The results indicate that about 3% of nonpatient adults have values of 4 or 5, although the percentages are higher among nonpatient children (6 to 24%). Between 20 and 25% of schizophrenics have values of 4 or 5, as do nearly 50% of nonadjudicated character disorders. The highest percentages of positive indices were found among three groups: inadequate personalities (88%), alcohol and substance abusers (74%), and adjudicated character disorders (69%).

The substantial percentages of positive indices among the various psychiatric groups made it reasonably clear that this new index is not a second depression index. Nonetheless, 79% of subjects diagnosed with affective disorders *who were not positive on the DEPI* also obtained values of 4 or 5 on this index, which poses some compelling data. At first glance the variables in the index appear to be a strange mix. On closer study, however, it is apparent that most have some relationship to social/interpersonal activity. In other words, people who have scores of 4 or more on this index are likely to have impoverished or unrewarding social relationships. Hypothetically, they are probably people who have difficulty contending with the natural demands of a social world. Conceptually, the index appears to afford a measure that identifies those who have coping limitations or deficiencies, and thus the label Coping Deficit Index.

It seems reasonable to postulate that potential coping difficulties can give rise to the kinds of features and experiences that might easily be translated or defined in ways that are commensurate with the diagnostic criteria for some types of depression. This seems to be especially true for those people who tend to be helpless or inept in social situations. Thus, it seems reasonable to assume that those who are positive on the CDI will have histories marked by social chaos and/or ineptness.

Some support for that postulate is found in the data for 440 outpatients beginning treatment for the first time. Initial interviews for those patients were coded for a variety of variables, including major presenting complaints. The presenting complaints were coded as (1) depression, (2) anxiety, (3) ideational control, (4) emotional control, (5) somatic difficulties, and (6) interpersonal difficulties, and as many as three were entered for each subject. A sorting program was used to create two groups. The target group included all subjects for whom Item 6 (interpersonal difficulties) had been coded, and a control group consisted of the remaining subjects for whom Item 6 had not been coded as being among the

Table 7. The Frequency of CDI Values of 4 or 5 Among Two Groups of Outpatients Sorted on the Basis of Interpersonal Complaints

	INTERPERSONAL COMPLAINT N = 204		NO INTERPERSONAL COMPLAINT N = 236	
	N	%	N	%
CDI = 4	36	18%	18	8%
CDI = 5	61	30%*	10	4%
TOTAL POSITIVE CDI	97	48%*	28	12%

* = significantly different from other group (p < .001)

presenting complaints. The CDI was calculated from the 440 records and 125 had values of 4 or 5. The distribution of those positive CDI records is shown for both groups in Table 7.

These data do not mean that the subjects in the target group actually did have more interpersonal problems than the subjects in the other group, for that is unlikely. The data do indicate, however, that the subjects who complained about interpersonal difficulties were apparently more acutely aware of those problems.

Although the CDI is not a depression index, the presence of a positive CDI among subjects diagnosed as being depressed seems to have considerable relevance for treatment planning. The reference group of first admission inpatient depressives (published in the third edition of *A Rorschach Workbook for the Comprehensive System,* Exner, 1990, and reproduced in Chapter 2 of this work) is a random sample of 315 subjects representing approximately 25% of protocols available for that group. The selection was stratified to include approximately half who were admitted to private psychiatric hospitals and half who were admitted to public hospitals.

The DEPI results for this sample indicate that 237 (75%) have values of 5 or more, and 80 of the 237 also have CDI values of 4 or 5. The CDI results indicate that 138 of the 315 subjects (44%) have values of 4 or more. This means that 58 of the 78 subjects (74%) who had DEPI values of less than 5 (false negatives) had CDI values of 4 or more. Stated differently, 25% of the group is positive on both the DEPI and CDI, 50% are positive on the DEPI but not on the CDI, and 18% are positive on the CDI but not on the DEPI. Taken together, the two indices identify slightly more than 93% of the total group.

None of the 315 subjects remained hospitalized for longer than 42 days. Six-month posthospitalization data were available for 271 of the 315 subjects in the sample. Those data reveal that 72 of the 271 were rehospitalized during that period. A review of the baseline records for those 72 subjects shows that 33 were positive on both the DEPI and CDI, 24 were positive on the CDI but not the DEPI, 13 were positive only on the DEPI, and the remaining two subjects had not been positive on either the DEPI or CDI. In other words, 79% of the relapsers had been positive on the CDI at the time of their first admission. This is a significantly greater proportion than the 43% of the subjects in the original sample who were positive on the CDI.

Obviously, many variables, both internal and external, contribute to relapse and it would be an error to assume that the 10 variables that make up the CDI form a nucleus of "best" predictors. Nevertheless, the disproportionately high percentage of relapsers who were positive on the CDI suggests that issues of interpersonal skills and adjustment may not have been adequately addressed during hospitalization or in posthospitalization outpatient care.

The accumulated data regarding the CDI, although limited, seem sufficiently compelling to warrant the inclusion of the index in the *System*. Nonetheless, the fact that it is very new argues that it should be regarded as experimental, and subject to much additional investigation.

The Hypervigilance Index (HVI)

The Hypervigilance Index (HVI) evolved from attempts to validate a cluster of five variables that, at first glance, appeared to be related to paranoid characteristics. They included $T = 0$, $Zf > 13$, $Zd > +3.0$, $S > 3$, and $H + A : Hd + Ad < 4 : 1$ when reduced (Exner, 1986, p. 470). In studying the cluster in more detail, it became obvious that the term *paranoid* was not really appropriate.

The cluster had first been discovered during a study of 150 paranoid schizophrenics. In that sample more than 70% were positive for all five variables and more than 85% were positive for at least four of the five. In contrast, only 13% of a comparison group of 150 schizophrenics who manifest no paranoid features were positive for all five variables and only 17% were positive for four of the five. The findings seemed conceptually logical because of validational data related to each of the five variables: the absence of T tends to indicate more guarded and distant relations with others; an emphasis on Hd and Ad responses usually involves head, profiles, and so forth; elevations in S correlate with negativism and anger; and elevations in Zf and Zd indicate cautious processing. The next step in the investigation was to review the protocols of 20 outpatients diagnosed with paranoid personality disorder. All five variables were positive in 12 of the 20 cases, and at least four of the five variables were positive in 16 of the cases. This seemed to confirm the initial hypothesis that the cluster did, indeed, relate to paranoid features.

Unfortunately, additional findings concerning false positive cases required that the conceptual model for the cluster be reconsidered. The five variables were sometimes positive for patients who do not manifest any obvious paranoid characteristics, and four of the five variables were positive for a substantial percentage of several groups. For instance, all five variables were positive in about 10% of a randomly drawn group of 200 depressives, and four of the five were positive for nearly 20% of that group. Similarly, all five variables were positive among 10% of a randomly drawn group of 100 patients with character disorders, and four of the five were positive in more than 30% of that group. In fact, at least four of the five variables were positive among 48 (8%) of the original normative sample of 600 adult nonpatients.

These findings prompted a new series of discriminant function analyses for the original samples of 150 paranoid schizophrenics and 20 patients with paranoid personality disorder, plus a group of 200 randomly drawn adult nonpatients and a second group of 200 outpatients for whom considerable information regarding behaviors, relationships, and progress in treatment had been provided from three sources: (1) the patient, (2) the therapist, and (3) a significant other. This latter group provided an excellent source of cross-validational data.

The results of the discriminant function analyses for the combined group of paranoid schizophrenics and paranoid personality disorder patients broadened the cluster to include seven variables, but also revealed that one of the variables ($T = 0$) accounted for nearly half of the variance. Consequently, a new experimental index was created in which the absence of T is prerequisite. If that condition is positive, the remaining tests in the index proceed, but if T is present in the record, the entire index is considered to have a negative result. Ultimately, an eighth variable was added. In light of various studies, the decision evolved to identify the index as a method of detecting the presence of a hypervigilant state.

Calculation of HVI involves one primary variable ($T = 0$) and seven secondary variables. When the primary variable is positive and any four of the seven secondary variables are also positive, the HVI is positive. If the primary variable is not positive or less than four secondary variables are positive, the HVI is negative. The seven secondary variables are:

1. $Zf > 12$ (for a child more than 1 SD above the age group mean)
2. $Zd > +3.5$
3. $S > 3$
4. The sum of all human content $[H + (H) + Hd + (Hd)] > 6$
5. The sum of parenthesized contents (human and animal) > 3
6. The ratio $H + A : Hd + Ad$ is less than $4:1$ when reduced
7. $Cg > 3$.

The HVI is positive for 132 of the 150 (88%) paranoid schizophrenics sampled and 18 of the 20 paranoid personality disorder patients. It also is positive among small segments of other groups. For example, it is positive for about 10% of the first-admission inpatient depressives reference group ($N = 315$), 7% of the character disorders reference group ($N = 180$), and about 9% of the outpatient reference sample ($N = 440$). It is also positive for about 3% of the adult nonpatient reference sample and, although it is not positive for any nonpatient children in the normative samples for ages five through 10, it does appear in 1 to 3% of the protocols of nonpatient children for ages 11 to 16. It seems likely that these are *not* false positive cases.

Probably the best understanding of the HVI is derived from the non-test data available for the sample of 200 outpatients mentioned earlier, which was used as one of the groups to develop the index. Only 23 of those subjects were positive on the HVI, but they form a rather discrete sample. Interestingly, only three of the 23 subjects were described by their therapists as having paranoid-like features, or by their significant others as being irrationally suspicious of others. Instead, they were uniformly identified as people who tended to be hyperalert during most of their daily routines. This hyperalertness was described by most of the therapists as like a subtle state of apprehensiveness or pessimistic anticipation in which the subject assumes a psychological preparedness even though there may be no clues or stimuli in the environment to warrant it. They tend to view the world more cynically than most people, and tend to avoid creating close relationships with others. In fact, most are described as being more mistrusting of others, and overly concerned with issues of personal space. They are very slow to respond to treatment, and eight of the 23 subjects terminated prematurely.

Although the general description of those positive on the HVI is quite small, the striking homogeneity among the reports of therapists and significant others argues for their validity. Apparently, these are people who consider themselves to be possible victims of the environment and believe that they must be alert to avoid such victimization. Obviously, if this set or style becomes magnified or intensified as a result of pathology, more direct paranoid-like features are likely to manifest, as in the instance of the group diagnosed with paranoid personality disorder and the group diagnosed as paranoid schizophrenic.

The Obsessive Style Index (OBS)

The final addition to the *System,* which occurred in 1990, is also a by-product of other searches. During the course of testing and cross-validating the SCZI and the DEPI, it was important to test those indices against other psychiatric groups that included subjects who were neither schizophrenic nor seriously depressed. Among those were two groups, one consisting of 32 outpatients who had been diagnosed with obsessive–compulsive disorders and another consisting of 114 outpatients who had been diagnosed with compulsive personality disorders. Most cases included anxiety as the presenting symptom, but 33 also were marked by impairing phobic features.

A discriminant function analysis for these 146 protocols produced considerable homogeneity among seven conditions for six variables. In fact, when those conditions were applied in various combinations, 101 of the 146 subjects (69%) were correctly identified. Two of the conditions weigh much more heavily than the other five; thus, in calculating the Obsessive Style Index (OBS), any of four combinations yields a positive finding. The calculation begins by determining if any of the following conditions are positive: (1) $Dd > 3$, (2) $Zf > 12$, (3) $Zd > +3.0$, (4) Popular > 7, and (5) $FQ+ > 1$. The OBS is positive if:

1. Conditions 1 through 5 are all positive
2. $FQ+ > 3$ **and** two or more of Conditions 1 through 4 are positive
3. $X+\% > .89$ **and** three or more of Conditions 1 through 5 are positive
4. $FQ+ > 3$ **and** $X+\% > .89$.

If OBS is positive, it is highly probable that the subject is prone to be perfectionistic, overly preoccupied with details, and often indecisive, and is likely to have some difficulty in expressing emotion. The frequency of positive OBS findings in other groups is extremely low. It does not appear among any cases in the schizophrenic, depressive, or character disorder reference groups, although it is positive for 56 of the 440 (13%) subjects in the outpatient reference sample. In the normative samples, the OBS is positive for two of the 1390 nonpatient children protocols and in 13 of the 700 (2%) nonpatient adult records.

SUMMARY

The *System* has grown considerably during more than two decades. The basics, first published in 1974, remain in place but they have been supplemented by many additions designed to tighten the empirical integrity of the test and increase its clinical efficacy. The additions and modifications that have occurred since 1985 appear to have served those purposes, as well as to provide grist for new research efforts that will continue the fine-tuning of the test.

REFERENCES

Beck, S. J. (1944). *Rorschach's Test I. Basic processes.* New York: Grune & Stratton.

Blatt, S. J., and Feirstein, A. (1977). Cardiac response and personality organization. *Journal of Consulting and Clinical Psychology, 45,* 111–123.

Exner, J. E. (1974). *The Rorschach: A Comprehensive System. Volume 1.* New York: Wiley.

Exner, J. E. (1978). *The Rorschach: A Comprehensive System. Volume 2: Current research and advanced interpretation.* New York: Wiley.

Exner, J. E. (1986). *The Rorschach: A Comprehensive System. Volume 1: Basic foundations* (2nd ed.). New York: Wiley.

Exner, J. E. (1987). *1987 Alumni Newsletter.* Asheville, NC: Rorschach Workshops.

Exner, J. E. (1988). *1988 Alumni Newsletter.* Asheville, NC: Rorschach Workshops.

Exner, J. E. (1990). *A Rorschach workbook for the Comprehensive System* (3rd ed.). Asheville, NC: Rorschach Workshops.

Exner, J. E., Bryant, E. L., and Leura, A. V. (1975). *Variations in problem solving by three EB types* [Workshops Study No. 217, unpublished]. Rorschach Workshops, Bayville, NY.

Exner, J. E., Thomas, E. A., and Martin, L. S. (1980). *Alterations in GSR and cardiac and respiratory rates in Introversives and Extratensives during problem solving* [Workshops Study No. 272, unpublished]. Rorschach Workshops, Bayville NY.

Langmuir, C. R. (1958). *Varieties of decision making behavior: A report of experiences with the Logical Analysis Device.* Washington, DC: American Psychological Association.

Piotrowski, Z. (1957). *Perceptanalysis.* New York: Macmillan.

Rosenthal, M. (1954). *Some behavioral correlates of the Rorschach Experience Balance.* Unpublished doctoral dissertation, Boston University.

Singer, J. L., and Brown, S. L. (1977). The experience type: Some behavioral correlates and theoretical implications. In M. A. Rickers-Ovsiankina (Ed.), *Rorschach psychology.* Huntington, NY: Robert E. Krieger, pp. 325–372.

Wiener-Levy, D., and Exner, J. E. (1981). The Rorschach EA-ep variable as related to persistence in a task frustration situation under feedback conditions. *Journal of Personality Assessment, 45,* 118–124.

Witkin, H. A., Dyk, R. B., Faterson, H. F., Goodenough, D. R., and Karp, S. A. (1962). *Psychological differentiation: Studies of development.* New York: Wiley.

CHAPTER 2

Normative Data and Reference Samples

A small table of mean values for only 27 variables was included in the first edition of *Volume 1* (Exner, 1974). Two years later, the first normative data for nonpatient adults and children appeared, together with reference samples for schizophrenics, depressives, outpatients, and character problems (Exner, Weiner, & Schuyler, 1976). The adult samples were expanded and refined in the first edition of *Volume 2* (Exner, 1978). The completed normative data for nonpatient children were published in *Volume 3* (Exner & Weiner, 1982) and for nonpatient adults in the second edition of *Volume 1* (Exner, 1986).

Unfortunately, almost all of the normative and reference samples that were published through 1986 included protocols of questionable validity because they contained too few answers. The problem of the validity of brief records was not discovered until early 1987 (Exner, 1988). Once the problem concerning brief records was discovered, all records containing fewer than 14 answers were culled from the data pool at the Rorschach Research Foundation and various samples that had been published earlier for normative or reference purposes were reanalyzed.

This chapter contains the tables of the revised normative data for adults and children, plus tables of reference data for several psychiatric groups. They are important to the understanding and utilization of the test. For the most part, the revised data are not extraordinarily different from previously published normative and reference data (Exner, 1978, 1985, 1986; Exner & Weiner, 1982) but there are some notable changes. Many brief records that were excluded from the pool contained very high Lambda values, which tended to elevate means and create false impressions concerning the range for that variable. Similarly, many of the brief records with high Lambda values contained very low values for *EA* and/or *es,* thereby creating some distortions in the descriptive statistics for those variables and the variables that contribute to them.

THE ADULT NORMATIVE SAMPLE

The adult nonpatient normative sample probably was affected least by the exclusion of brief records. Fewer than 50 were discarded from the original sample of 600 and that sample subsequently was increased to 700 subjects and equalized for sex.

This sample was randomly selected from an available group of 1332 adult nonpatient records. The final selection was stratified to include 350 males and

350 females, 140 subjects from each of five geographic areas: Northeast, South, Midwest, Southwest, and West. Attempts were made to equalize the numbers of males and females from each region but that was not always possible because the samples for some regions are markedly uneven for sex. Thus, the number of males and females are nearly equal for four regions but the Southwest group includes 83 females and 57 males and the Midwest group contains 81 males and 59 females.

The mean age for the group is 32.36 ($SD = 11.93$, median = 30, mode = 22), with a range of 19 to 70 years. The subjects average 13.25 years of education, with a range of 8 to 18. A breakdown for demographic variables is shown in Table 8.

The data for socioeconomic status (SES) have been collapsed in Table 8. The coding for SES was done using a 9-point variation of the Hollingshead and Redlich Scale. It includes three subgroups for each of the categories, upper, middle, and lower. Thus, SES 2 equals middle-upper class, SES 5 equals middle-middle class, and so on, with SES 9 being restricted to subjects exclusively on public assistance. The sample contains no subjects from SES 1 and the group shown in Table 8 as "Lower" includes 52 subjects from SES 9.

A multivariate model was used to search out significant differences among the three broad categories and among the subgroups. The only significant findings occur between the SES 9 subgroup and other subgroups. The SES 9 group has a significantly higher average Lambda and significantly lower mean values for *EA* and *es*. Consequently, the group has lower mean values for most of the determinants that contribute to *EA* and *es*. The data for all 700 subjects were compared with a modified sample of 648 subjects that excluded all of the SES 9 subjects. In general, it was found that the inclusion of that group in the sample does not alter means or standard deviations significantly. Apparently, this is because the number of subjects in that group is modest, representing only 7% of the total group.

Several descriptive statistics for 111 Rorschach variables for the adult nonpatient sample are shown in Table 9. Standard deviations are shown in brackets for many of the variables, signifying that the variable *is not* parametric (i.e., the distribution of scores for the variable deviates significantly from a normal distribution). Thus, in most instances the standard deviation should not be used to

Table 8.   Demography Variables for 700 Nonpatient Adults

MARITAL STATUS			AGE			RACE		
Single	193	28%	18–25	236	34%	White	567	81%
Lives w/s.o	57	8%	26–35	267	38%	Black	81	12%
Married	332	47%	36–45	100	14%	Hispanic	43	6%
Separated	28	4%	46–55	44	6%	Asian	9	1%
Divorced	71	10%	56–65	34	5%			
Widowed	19	3%	OVER 65	19	3%			

EDUCATION			RESIDENCE			SOCIO-ECONOMIC LEVEL		
Under 12 Yrs	53	8%	Urban	259	37%	Upper	65	9%
12 Yrs	214	31%	Suburban	280	40%	Middle	411	59%
13–15 Yrs	346	49%	Rural	162	23%	Lower	224	32%
16+ Yrs	87	12%						

Table 9. Descriptive Statistics for 700 Adult Nonpatients

VARIABLE	MEAN	SD	MIN	MAX	FREQ	MEDIAN	MODE	SK	KU
R	22.67	4.23	14.00	38.00	700	23.00	23.00	0.54	1.37
W	8.55	1.94	3.00	20.00	700	9.00	9.00	1.28	8.87
D	12.89	3.54	0.00	22.00	698	13.00	14.00	−0.38	1.02
Dd	1.23	[1.70]	0.00	15.00	452	1.00	0.00	3.89	22.18
S	1.47	[1.21]	0.00	10.00	600	1.00	1.00	2.44	11.43
DQ+	7.31	2.16	2.00	13.00	700	7.00	6.00	0.27	−0.39
DQo	13.64	3.46	5.00	34.00	700	14.00	15.00	0.95	4.67
DQv	1.30	[1.26]	0.00	6.00	477	1.00	0.00	0.93	0.38
DQv/+	0.41	[0.66]	0.00	2.00	219	0.00	0.00	1.35	0.53
FQx+	0.90	0.92	0.00	5.00	427	1.00	0.00	1.21	2.26
FQxo	16.99	3.34	7.00	29.00	700	17.00	17.00	0.04	0.52
FQxu	3.25	1.77	0.00	13.00	667	3.00	3.00	0.94	3.37
FQx−	1.44	1.04	0.00	6.00	605	1.00	1.00	0.95	0.93
FQxNone	0.09	[0.33]	0.00	3.00	58	0.00	0.00	4.00	18.52
MQ+	0.55	0.73	0.00	3.00	297	0.00	0.00	1.23	1.02
MQo	3.52	1.89	0.00	8.00	693	3.00	3.00	0.46	−0.60
MQu	0.20	0.45	0.00	2.00	123	0.00	0.00	2.23	4.31
MQ−	0.03	[0.19]	0.00	2.00	22	0.00	0.00	5.90	36.99
MQNone	0.01	[0.11]	0.00	1.00	8	0.00	0.00	9.21	83.11
SQual−	0.18	[0.49]	0.00	3.00	102	0.00	0.00	3.16	11.29
M	4.31	1.92	1.00	9.00	700	4.00	3.00	0.51	−0.74
FM	3.70	1.19	1.00	9.00	700	4.00	4.00	−0.05	0.46
m	1.12	0.85	0.00	4.00	530	1.00	1.00	0.51	0.32
FC	4.09	1.88	0.00	9.00	690	4.00	5.00	0.31	−0.13
CF	2.36	1.27	0.00	6.00	670	2.00	3.00	0.40	−0.12
C	0.08	[0.28]	0.00	2.00	51	0.00	0.00	3.73	14.14
Cn	0.01	[0.08]	0.00	1.00	5	0.00	0.00	11.73	135.98
Sum Color	6.54	2.52	1.00	12.00	700	7.00	5.00	−0.04	−0.79
WSumC	4.52	1.79	0.50	9.00	700	4.50	3.50	0.02	−0.69
Sum C'	1.53	[1.25]	0.00	10.00	551	1.00	1.00	1.32	5.24
Sum T	1.03	[0.58]	0.00	4.00	620	1.00	1.00	1.35	5.39
Sum V	0.26	[0.58]	0.00	3.00	137	0.00	0.00	2.39	5.54
Sum Y	0.57	[1.00]	0.00	10.00	274	0.00	0.00	4.08	28.70
Sum Shading	3.39	2.15	0.00	23.00	689	3.00	3.00	3.03	20.65
Fr+rF	0.08	[0.35]	0.00	4.00	47	0.00	0.00	6.06	49.54
FD	1.16	[0.87]	0.00	5.00	553	1.00	1.00	1.00	2.57
F	7.99	2.67	2.00	19.00	700	8.00	8.00	0.65	1.21
(2)	8.68	2.15	1.00	14.00	700	8.00	8.00	0.06	0.63
Lambda	0.58	0.26	0.14	2.25	700	0.56	0.50	2.23	9.91
FM+m	4.82	1.51	1.00	10.00	700	5.00	5.00	0.27	0.30
EA	8.83	2.18	2.00	14.50	700	9.00	9.50	−0.30	0.15
es	8.20	2.98	3.00	31.00	700	8.00	7.00	1.90	10.18
D Score	0.04	1.08	−10.00	2.00	244	0.00	0.00	−3.29	24.95
AdjD	0.20	0.87	−5.00	2.00	272	0.00	0.00	−1.11	6.04
a (active)	6.48	2.14	2.00	13.00	700	6.00	6.00	0.57	−0.09
p (passive)	2.69	1.52	0.00	9.00	659	2.00	2.00	0.54	0.26
Ma	3.04	1.59	0.00	7.00	679	3.00	2.00	0.45	−0.38
Mp	1.31	0.94	0.00	5.00	568	1.00	1.00	0.59	0.34
Intellect	1.56	1.29	0.00	6.00	546	1.00	1.00	0.78	0.25
Zf	11.81	2.59	5.00	23.00	700	12.00	12.00	0.27	1.47
Zd	0.72	3.06	−6.50	9.50	644	0.50	−1.00	0.48	0.09
Blends	5.16	1.93	1.00	12.00	700	5.00	5.00	0.04	−0.37
Blends/R	0.23	0.09	0.04	0.67	700	0.23	0.26	0.76	1.55
Col-Shd Bld	0.46	[0.69]	0.00	3.00	252	0.00	0.00	1.45	1.66
Afr	0.69	0.16	0.27	1.29	700	0.67	0.91	0.40	0.30
Populars	6.89	1.39	3.00	10.00	700	7.00	8.00	−0.47	−0.13

(continued)

Table 9.   (Continued)

VARIABLE	MEAN	SD	MIN	MAX	FREQ	MEDIAN	MODE	SK	KU
X+%	0.79	0.08	0.50	1.00	700	0.80	0.80	−0.23	1.17
F+%	0.71	0.17	0.25	1.00	700	0.71	1.00	−0.24	−0.24
X−%	0.07	0.05	0.00	0.43	605	0.05	0.04	1.86	8.97
Xu%	0.14	0.07	0.00	0.37	667	0.14	0.15	0.17	0.41
S−%	0.08	[0.23]	0.00	1.00	102	0.00	0.00	2.93	7.99
Isolate/R	0.20	0.09	0.00	0.47	689	0.19	0.16	0.39	−0.23
H	3.40	1.80	0.00	9.00	694	3.00	3.00	0.90	0.30
(H)	1.20	0.98	0.00	4.00	499	1.00	1.00	0.41	−0.35
HD	0.69	0.89	0.00	7.00	348	0.00	0.00	2.06	8.03
(Hd)	0.14	0.35	0.00	2.00	99	0.00	0.00	2.14	2.95
Hx	0.01	[0.11]	0.00	1.00	8	0.00	0.00	9.21	83.11
All H Cont	5.42	1.63	1.00	11.00	700	5.00	6.00	0.23	−0.10
A	8.18	2.04	3.00	15.00	700	8.00	7.00	0.43	0.17
(A)	0.17	[0.47]	0.00	3.00	95	0.00	0.00	3.27	12.22
Ad	2.21	[1.18]	0.00	9.00	665	2.00	2.00	1.14	4.65
(Ad)	0.05	[0.26]	0.00	2.00	33	0.00	0.00	5.14	28.41
An	0.42	[0.65]	0.00	4.00	244	0.00	0.00	1.54	2.46
Art	0.91	0.83	0.00	4.00	448	1.00	1.00	0.50	−0.41
Ay	0.34	[0.48]	0.00	2.00	236	0.00	0.00	0.78	−1.09
Bl	0.15	[0.40]	0.00	2.00	96	0.00	0.00	2.64	6.55
Bt	2.48	1.29	0.00	6.00	652	3.00	3.00	−0.02	−0.47
Cg	1.29	0.93	0.00	4.00	572	1.00	1.00	0.62	0.12
Cl	0.15	[0.38]	0.00	2.00	102	0.00	0.00	2.32	4.54
Ex	0.13	[0.34]	0.00	1.00	93	0.00	0.00	2.17	2.71
Fi	0.42	[0.67]	0.00	2.00	221	0.00	0.00	1.33	0.44
Food	0.23	[0.50]	0.00	2.00	136	0.00	0.00	2.11	3.65
Ge	0.04	[0.21]	0.00	2.00	25	0.00	0.00	5.74	35.68
Hh	0.93	0.85	0.00	4.00	458	1.00	1.00	0.76	0.32
Ls	0.89	0.78	0.00	3.00	460	1.00	1.00	0.45	−0.50
Na	0.38	[0.60]	0.00	2.00	222	0.00	0.00	1.34	0.72
Sc	0.91	[0.97]	0.00	6.00	411	1.00	0.00	1.25	2.99
Sx	0.07	[0.39]	0.00	5.00	30	0.00	0.00	8.41	85.78
Xy	0.03	[0.18]	0.00	2.00	17	0.00	0.00	7.25	57.98
Idio	1.85	1.29	0.00	7.00	599	2.00	2.00	0.75	1.08
DV	0.70	[0.79]	0.00	4.00	373	1.00	0.00	1.12	1.20
INCOM	0.52	[0.65]	0.00	4.00	323	0.00	0.00	1.39	3.56
DR	0.15	[0.38]	0.00	2.00	103	0.00	0.00	2.30	4.44
FABCOM	0.17	[0.41]	0.00	2.00	111	0.00	0.00	2.27	4.43
DV2	0.01	[0.10]	0.00	1.00	7	0.00	0.00	9.87	95.70
INC2	0.00	[0.07]	0.00	1.00	3	0.00	0.00	15.21	229.99
DR2	0.00	[0.04]	0.00	1.00	1	0.00	0.00	26.46	700.00
FAB2	0.02	[0.13]	0.00	1.00	12	0.00	0.00	7.46	53.74
ALOG	0.04	[0.22]	0.00	2.00	29	0.00	0.00	5.23	29.28
CONTAM	0.00	0.00	0.00	0.00	0	0.00	0.00	—	—
Sum6 Sp Sc	1.62	1.26	0.00	7.00	564	1.00	1.00	0.73	0.35
Sum6 Sp Sc2	0.03	[0.18]	0.00	1.00	23	0.00	0.00	5.25	25.66
WSum6	3.28	2.89	0.00	15.00	564	3.00	0.00	1.07	1.15
AB	0.15	[0.40]	0.00	2.00	98	0.00	0.00	2.57	6.17
AG	1.18	1.18	0.00	5.00	466	1.00	1.00	1.04	0.62
CFB	0.00	0.00	0.00	0.00	0	0.00	0.00	—	—
COP	2.07	1.52	0.00	6.00	555	2.00	2.00	0.25	−0.84
CP	0.02	[0.14]	0.00	1.00	13	0.00	0.00	7.15	49.23
MOR	0.70	[0.82]	0.00	4.00	356	1.00	0.00	1.03	0.60
PER	1.05	1.00	0.00	5.00	478	1.00	1.00	1.38	3.27
PSV	0.05	[0.22]	0.00	1.00	34	0.00	0.00	4.21	15.76

NOTE: Standard deviations shown in brackets indicate that the value is probably unreliable and/or misleading because the variable is nonparametric.

estimate the expected or average range for the variable. Obviously, variables that have standard deviations in brackets should not be included in most types of parametric analyses.

Although the sorts of descriptive statistics provided in Table 9 often are of valuable use in understanding the test and test results, some can be quite misleading unless clarified by other information concerning the distributions of scores. The distribution for the *Erlebnistypus* (*EB*) probably offers the best illustration of this. As it involves the relation between *M* and *Sum C*, those naive to the Rorschach might be prone to estimate the "average" *EB* by reviewing the normative data for those variables. The data in Table 8 indicate that mean for *M* is 4.31 (*SD* = 1.92, median = 4, mode = 3) and the mean for *Sum C* is 6.54 (*SD* = 2.52, median 7.0, mode = 5.0).

Table 10.   Frequencies and Percentages for 33 Structural Variables for 700 Adult Nonpatients

EB STYLE			FORM QUALITY DEVIATIONS		
Introversive	251	36%	X+% > .89	49	7%
Pervasive	68	10%	X+% < .70	71	10%
Ambitent	143	20%	X+% < .61	12	2%
Extratensive	306	44%	X+% < .50	0	0%
Pervasive	86	12%	F+% < .70	313	45%
			Xu% > .20	109	16%
D SCORE			X−% > .15	24	3%
D Score > 0	156	22%	X−% > .20	9	1%
D Score = 0	455	65%	X−% > .30	2	0%
D Score < 0	89	13%			
D Score < −1	30	4%			
ADJUSTED D SCORE			**FC:CF+C RATIO**		
Adj D Score > 0	206	29%	FC > (CF+C)+2	220	31%
Adj D Score = 0	428	61%	FC > (CF+C)+1	345	49%
Adj D Score < 0	66	9%	(CF+C) > FC+1	30	4%
Adj D Score < −1	30	4%	(CF+C) > FC+2	9	1%
Zd > +3.0 (Overincorp)	127	18%	S−Con Positive	0	0%
Zd < −3.0 (Underincorp)	37	5%	HVI Positive	13	2%
			OBS Positive	14	2%

SCZI = 6	0	0%	DEPI = 7	1	0%	CDI = 5	3	0%
SCZI = 5	0	0%	DEPI = 6	3	0%	CDI = 4	18	3%
SCZI = 4	2	0%	DEPI = 5	21	3%			

MISCELLANEOUS VARIABLES					
Lambda > .99	38	5%	(2AB+Art+Ay) > 5	52	7%
Dd > 3	33	5%	Populars < 4	9	1%
DQv + DQv/+ > 2	200	29%	Populars > 7	293	42%
S > 2	72	10%	COP = 0	145	21%
Sum T = 0	80	11%	COP > 2	271	39%
Sum T > 1	75	11%	AG = 0	234	33%
3r+(2)/R < .33	112	16%	AG > 2	95	14%
3r+(2)/R > .44	169	24%	MOR > 2	22	3%
Fr + rF > 0	47	7%	Lvl 2 Sp.Sc. > 0	23	3%
PureC > 0	51	7%	Sum 6 Sp.Sc. > 6	1	0%
PureC > 1	3	0%	Pure H < 2	69	10%
Afr < .40	11	2%	Pure H = 0	6	1%
Afr < .50	50	7%	p > a+1	6	1%
(FM+m) < Sum Shad	106	15%	Mp > Ma	72	10%

Either of two erroneous conclusions could be drawn from those data. One is that the majority of subjects in the sample are extratensive because the mean for *Sum C* exceeds the mean for *M* by more than 2 points. The second is that most subjects in the sample are ambitents because there is considerable overlap among the variances for the two variables. Unfortunately, neither conclusion is correct. Actually, about 36% of the subjects are introversives, about 44% are extratensives, and only 20% are ambitents. The means and standard deviations are misleading because the distribution of the data is bimodal; that is, introversives tend to give more *M*'s than represented by the mean, whereas extratensives tend to have more *Sum C*'s than indicated by the mean.

Table 10 includes some important information concerning the distribution of scores, with a particular focus on scores that are often critical in evaluating ratios and percentages.

The equal distribution of the number of males and females in the adult normative sample makes it relatively easy to study the group for sex differences. During the past decade the question of sex differences often has been raised but very little data has been published concerning the issue. Tables 11 through 14 contain the adult nonpatient data by sex, for the same variables listed in Tables 9 and 10.

ADULT NORMATIVE DATA BY COPING STYLE

It is apparent from examination of Tables 11 through 14 that the differences between males and females for almost all variables are inconsequential. Therefore, the data for the total sample usually afford a useful guideline for the interpreter or researcher. However, data for the total sample are not necessarily the best data source from which to judge marked deviations. On the contrary, some of the data can be very misleading because the total sample contains three subgroups that are substantially different from each other for numerous variables.

These three subgroups are created by the different coping or decision making styles that are represented in the total group. As already mentioned, the data for *M* and *Sum C* tend to be misleading because the distribution of the scores is bimodal, mainly because of the differences between the introversive and extratensive subjects. They tend to be rather discrete for several variables and both groups also tend to differ from ambitents for several other variables.

Subjects from all three groups, introversive, extratensive, and ambitent, could be subdivided further using other features as the basis for classification. For instance, distinctive stylistic features of personality are represented by values for Lambda that are greater than 0.99, the presence of one or more reflection responses plus a high Egocentricity Index, passive movement exceeding active movement by more than 1 point, a positive Hypervigilance Index, or a positive Obsessive Style Index. Any or all could be used to subclassify the groups further. Unfortunately, the total sample is not large enough to do this and maintain the integrity of the data, but the sample is large enough to present data for the three basic coping styles. These findings are presented in Tables 15 through 20 in the same format used for the preceding tables. Data for introversives are presented in Tables 15 and 16, extratensives in Tables 17 and 18, and ambitents in Tables 19 and 20.

Table 11.   Descriptive Statistics for 350 Adult Nonpatient Females

VARIABLE	MEAN	SD	MIN	MAX	FREQ	MEDIAN	MODE	SK	KU
R	22.14	3.94	14.00	35.00	350	22.00	23.00	0.29	1.12
W	8.39	1.94	3.00	20.00	350	9.00	9.00	1.13	7.92
D	12.59	3.52	0.00	21.00	348	13.00	14.00	−0.74	1.40
Dd	1.17	[1.67]	0.00	12.00	209	1.00	0.00	3.36	15.89
S	1.34	[1.22]	0.00	10.00	284	1.00	1.00	2.81	14.77
DQ+	7.19	2.20	2.00	12.00	350	7.00	6.00	0.32	−0.54
DQo	13.17	3.29	5.00	29.00	350	13.00	15.00	0.77	3.95
DQv	1.37	[1.20]	0.00	5.00	249	1.00	1.00	0.65	−0.31
DQv/+	0.41	[0.70]	0.00	2.00	101	0.00	0.00	1.41	0.52
FQx+	0.84	0.89	0.00	4.00	203	1.00	0.00	0.98	0.76
FQxo	16.68	3.43	7.00	29.00	350	17.00	17.00	−0.02	0.50
FQxu	3.23	1.67	0.00	11.00	327	3.00	4.00	0.25	0.85
FQx−	1.29	0.95	0.00	6.00	302	1.00	1.00	1.42	3.45
FQxNone	0.09	[0.32]	0.00	2.00	29	0.00	0.00	3.63	13.58
MQ+	0.51	0.72	0.00	3.00	134	0.00	0.00	1.20	0.50
MQo	3.31	1.73	0.00	8.00	346	3.00	3.00	0.48	−0.29
MQu	0.20	0.43	0.00	2.00	67	0.00	0.00	1.91	2.73
MQ−	0.04	[0.19]	0.00	1.00	13	0.00	0.00	4.92	22.30
MQNone	0.01	[0.11]	0.00	1.00	4	0.00	0.00	9.23	83.72
SQual−	0.14	[0.42]	0.00	2.00	38	0.00	0.00	3.19	9.78
M	4.07	1.81	1.00	9.00	350	3.00	3.00	0.66	−0.61
FM	3.67	1.27	1.00	9.00	350	4.00	4.00	0.08	0.44
m	1.14	0.90	0.00	4.00	256	1.00	1.00	0.49	0.15
FC	4.02	1.99	0.00	9.00	343	4.00	3.00	0.44	0.03
CF	2.16	1.21	0.00	5.00	330	2.00	1.00	0.31	−0.53
C	0.07	[0.26]	0.00	1.00	26	0.00	0.00	3.26	8.68
Cn	0.01	[0.09]	0.00	1.00	3	0.00	0.00	10.71	113.31
Sum Color	6.27	2.54	1.00	12.00	350	6.00	5.00	0.12	−0.80
WSumC	4.29	1.78	0.50	9.00	350	4.00	3.50	0.16	−0.73
Sum C'	1.47	[1.40]	0.00	10.00	262	1.00	1.00	1.77	6.67
Sum T	1.09	[0.64]	0.00	4.00	313	1.00	1.00	1.41	4.11
Sum V	0.27	[0.55]	0.00	2.00	78	0.00	0.00	1.90	2.63
Sum Y	0.56	[1.10]	0.00	10.00	127	0.00	0.00	4.70	33.23
Sum Shading	3.39	2.45	0.00	23.00	344	3.00	2.00	3.47	22.92
Fr+rF	0.09	[0.39]	0.00	4.00	25	0.00	0.00	6.81	59.91
FD	1.18	[0.86]	0.00	5.00	279	1.00	1.00	0.84	1.89
F	7.89	2.60	2.00	17.00	350	8.00	8.00	0.27	0.39
(2)	8.59	2.19	1.00	14.00	350	8.00	8.00	0.04	0.58
Lambda	0.59	0.27	0.14	2.14	350	0.56	0.50	1.72	5.99
FM+m	4.81	1.64	1.00	10.00	350	5.00	5.00	0.35	0.12
EA	8.35	2.10	2.00	13.50	350	8.50	10.50	−0.42	−0.08
es	8.20	3.34	3.00	31.00	350	8.00	7.00	2.24	11.75
D Score	−0.01	1.28	−10.00	2.00	142	0.00	0.00	−3.31	21.81
AdjD	0.17	1.02	−5.00	2.00	153	0.00	0.00	−1.34	5.46
a (active)	6.30	2.19	3.00	13.00	350	6.00	5.00	0.71	0.13
p (passive)	2.61	1.57	0.00	9.00	325	2.00	2.00	0.62	0.75
Ma	2.85	1.57	0.00	7.00	339	2.00	2.00	0.64	−0.14
Mp	1.25	1.01	0.00	5.00	266	1.00	1.00	0.78	0.87
Intellect	1.51	1.35	0.00	6.00	259	1.00	1.00	0.89	0.37
Zf	11.63	2.61	5.00	23.00	350	12.00	14.00	0.06	0.46
Zd	0.76	3.24	−6.50	9.50	324	0.50	2.00	0.57	0.11
Blends	5.10	1.96	1.00	12.00	350	5.00	6.00	0.22	−0.10
Blends/R	0.24	0.10	0.06	0.67	350	0.23	0.12	1.02	1.97
Col−Shd Bld	0.42	[0.72]	0.00	3.00	107	0.00	0.00	1.86	3.12
Afr	0.68	0.16	0.27	1.29	350	0.67	0.56	0.44	0.21
Populars	6.89	1.46	3.00	10.00	350	7.00	8.00	−0.59	−0.19

(continued)

Table 11.   (Continued)

VARIABLE	MEAN	SD	MIN	MAX	FREQ	MEDIAN	MODE	SK	KU
X+%	0.79	0.08	0.50	1.00	350	0.80	0.80	−0.07	1.05
F+%	0.70	0.18	0.29	1.00	350	0.71	1.00	−0.19	−0.35
X−%	0.06	0.05	0.00	0.43	302	0.05	0.04	2.87	16.77
Xu%	0.14	0.07	0.00	0.37	327	0.15	0.14	−0.01	0.54
S−%	0.07	[0.23]	0.00	1.00	38	0.00	0.00	3.29	9.84
Isolate/R	0.21	0.10	0.00	0.47	344	0.21	0.24	0.26	−0.43
H	3.17	1.68	0.00	8.00	348	3.00	3.00	0.88	0.21
(H)	1.11	0.94	0.00	4.00	236	1.00	0.00	0.26	−0.93
HD	0.70	0.85	0.00	4.00	178	1.00	0.00	1.36	1.88
(Hd)	0.15	0.35	0.00	1.00	51	0.00	0.00	2.02	2.08
Hx	0.01	[0.11]	0.00	1.00	4	0.00	0.00	9.23	83.72
All H Cont	5.13	1.61	1.00	9.00	350	5.00	4.00	0.17	−0.47
A	8.21	2.14	3.00	15.00	350	8.00	8.00	0.33	0.11
(A)	0.17	[0.41]	0.00	3.00	54	0.00	0.00	2.67	8.65
Ad	2.21	[1.24]	0.00	9.00	332	2.00	2.00	1.32	5.34
(Ad)	0.03	[0.17]	0.00	1.00	10	0.00	0.00	5.68	30.48
An	0.42	[0.62]	0.00	3.00	124	0.00	0.00	1.35	1.35
Art	0.85	0.81	0.00	4.00	217	1.00	1.00	0.70	0.29
Ay	0.31	[0.47]	0.00	2.00	108	0.00	0.00	0.90	−0.97
Bl	0.13	[0.36]	0.00	2.00	41	0.00	0.00	2.82	7.62
Bt	2.61	1.32	0.00	6.00	331	3.00	3.00	−0.01	−0.54
Cg	1.24	0.89	0.00	4.00	282	1.00	1.00	0.51	−0.03
Cl	0.15	[0.39]	0.00	2.00	49	0.00	0.00	2.52	5.86
Ex	0.15	[0.36]	0.00	1.00	52	0.00	0.00	1.98	1.95
Fi	0.33	[0.63]	0.00	2.00	85	0.00	0.00	1.72	1.66
Food	0.28	[0.55]	0.00	2.00	82	0.00	0.00	1.82	2.34
Ge	0.03	[0.18]	0.00	2.00	8	0.00	0.00	7.53	62.80
Hh	0.99	0.94	0.00	4.00	227	1.00	1.00	0.79	0.15
Ls	0.82	0.73	0.00	3.00	225	1.00	1.00	0.52	−0.24
Na	0.47	[0.65]	0.00	2.00	137	0.00	0.00	1.03	−0.06
Sc	0.77	[0.79]	0.00	3.00	194	1.00	0.00	0.50	−1.01
Sx	0.06	[0.31]	0.00	3.00	17	0.00	0.00	5.83	39.26
Xy	0.02	[0.14]	0.00	1.00	7	0.00	0.00	6.89	45.69
Idio	1.71	1.26	0.00	7.00	293	2.00	1.00	0.91	1.56
DV	0.73	[0.76]	0.00	3.00	198	1.00	0.00	0.89	0.47
INCOM	0.44	[0.61]	0.00	4.00	137	0.00	0.00	1.43	3.23
DR	0.16	[0.37]	0.00	2.00	54	0.00	0.00	2.06	2.81
FABCOM	0.17	[0.41]	0.00	2.00	56	0.00	0.00	2.25	4.38
DV2	0.01	[0.12]	0.00	1.00	5	0.00	0.00	8.22	65.97
INC2	0.01	[0.09]	0.00	1.00	3	0.00	0.00	10.71	113.31
DR2	0.00	[0.05]	0.00	1.00	1	0.00	0.00	18.71	350.00
FAB2	0.02	[0.13]	0.00	1.00	6	0.00	0.00	7.47	54.14
ALOG	0.05	[0.24]	0.00	2.00	15	0.00	0.00	5.39	31.57
CONTAM	0.00	0.00	0.00	0.00	0	0.00	0.00	—	—
Sum6 Sp Sc	1.59	1.13	0.00	5.00	286	2.00	2.00	0.47	−0.09
Sum6 Sp Sc2	0.04	[0.20]	0.00	1.00	15	0.00	0.00	4.53	18.66
WSum6	3.21	2.73	0.00	15.00	286	3.00	0.00	1.11	1.72
AB	0.17	[0.43]	0.00	2.00	54	0.00	0.00	2.46	5.53
AG	1.19	1.25	0.00	5.00	225	1.00	0.00	1.05	0.35
CFB	0.00	0.00	0.00	0.00	0	0.00	0.00	—	—
COP	2.14	1.52	0.00	6.00	284	2.00	2.00	0.20	−0.80
CP	0.03	[0.18]	0.00	1.00	11	0.00	0.00	5.39	27.26
MOR	0.65	[0.79]	0.00	3.00	167	0.00	0.00	0.95	0.06
PER	1.18	1.10	0.00	5.00	248	1.00	1.00	1.35	2.80
PSV	0.05	[0.23]	0.00	1.00	19	0.00	0.00	3.95	13.69

NOTE: Standard deviations shown in brackets indicate that the value is probably unreliable and/or misleading because the variable is nonparametric.

Table 12.   Frequencies and Percentages for 33 Structural Variables for 350 Adult Female Nonpatients

EB STYLE			FORM QUALITY DEVIATIONS		
Introversive	116	33%	X+% > .89	30	9%
Pervasive	29	8%	X+% < .70	36	10%
Ambitent	79	23%	X+% < .61	6	2%
Extratensive	155	44%	X+% < .50	0	0%
Pervasive	42	12%	F+% < .70	157	45%
			Xu% > .20	56	16%
D SCORE			X−% > .15	10	3%
D Score > 0	84	24%	X−% > .20	4	1%
D Score = 0	208	59%	X−% > .30	2	1%
D Score < 0	58	17%			
D Score < −1	19	5%			
ADJUSTED D SCORE			**FC:CF+C RATIO**		
Adj D Score > 0	108	31%	FC > (CF+C)+2	119	34%
Adj D Score = 0	197	56%	FC > (CF+C)+1	176	50%
Adj D Score < 0	45	13%	(CF+C) > FC+1	14	4%
Adj D Score < 1	17	5%	(CF+C) > FC+2	5	1%
Zd > +3.0 (Overincorp)	62	18%	S−Con Positive	0	0%
Zd < −3.0 (Underincorp)	21	6%	HVI Positive	2	1%
			OBS Positive	4	1%

SCZI = 6	0	0%	DEPI = 7	0	0%	CDI = 5	3	1%
SCZI = 5	0	0%	DEPI = 6	2	1%	CDI = 4	8	2%
SCZI = 4	2	1%	DEPI = 5	9	3%			

MISCELLANEOUS VARIABLES

Lambda > .99	22	6%	(2AB+Art+Ay) > 5	30	9%
Dd > 3	15	4%	Populars < 4	8	2%
DQv + DQv/+ > 2	104	30%	Populars > 7	151	43%
S > 2	28	8%	COP = 0	66	19%
Sum T = 0	37	11%	COP > 2	143	41%
Sum T > 1	49	14%	AG = 0	125	36%
3r+(2)/R < .33	66	19%	AG > 2	56	16%
3r+(2)/R > .44	104	30%	MOR > 2	7	2%
Fr + rF > 0	25	7%	Lvl 2 Sp.Sc. > 0	15	4%
PureC > 0	26	7%	Sum 6 Sp.Sc. > 6	0	0%
PureC > 1	0	0%	Pure H < 2	44	13%
Afr < .40	7	2%	Pure H = 0	2	1%
Afr < .50	27	8%	p > a+1	5	1%
(FM+m) < Sum Shad	59	17%	Mp > Ma	46	13%

Table 13. Descriptive Statistics for 350 Nonpatient Adult Males

VARIABLE	MEAN	SD	MIN	MAX	FREQ	MEDIAN	MODE	SK	KU
R	23.20	4.44	14.00	38.00	350	23.00	23.00	0.66	1.31
W	8.72	1.93	3.00	20.00	350	9.00	9.00	1.47	10.13
D	13.19	3.54	3.00	22.00	350	13.00	13.00	−0.04	0.48
Dd	1.29	[1.73]	0.00	15.00	243	1.00	1.00	4.38	27.82
S	1.61	[1.19]	0.00	9.00	316	1.00	1.00	2.15	8.83
DQ+	7.44	2.13	2.00	13.00	350	7.00	6.00	0.23	−0.19
DQo	14.11	3.56	7.00	34.00	350	14.00	16.00	1.09	5.25
DQv	1.24	[1.31]	0.00	6.00	228	1.00	0.00	1.18	0.98
DQv/+	0.41	[0.62]	0.00	2.00	118	0.00	0.00	1.25	0.47
FQx+	0.95	0.96	0.00	5.00	224	1.00	1.00	1.39	3.27
FQxo	17.29	3.23	9.00	27.00	350	17.00	17.00	0.16	0.51
FQxu	3.27	1.87	0.00	13.00	340	3.00	3.00	1.42	4.84
FQx−	1.59	1.11	0.00	5.00	303	1.00	1.00	0.59	−0.31
FQxNone	0.10	[0.35]	0.00	3.00	29	0.00	0.00	4.26	21.70
MQ+	0.59	0.74	0.00	3.00	163	0.00	0.00	1.26	1.49
MQo	3.73	2.02	0.00	8.00	347	3.00	3.00	0.36	−0.89
MQu	0.19	0.48	0.00	2.00	56	0.00	0.00	2.46	5.36
MQ−	0.03	[0.18]	0.00	2.00	9	0.00	0.00	7.02	54.49
MQNone	0.01	[0.11]	0.00	1.00	4	0.00	0.00	9.23	83.72
SQual−	0.23	[0.54]	0.00	3.00	64	0.00	0.00	3.00	10.51
M	4.55	2.00	1.00	9.00	350	4.00	3.00	0.36	−0.83
FM	3.73	1.09	1.00	7.00	350	4.00	4.00	−0.22	0.36
m	1.09	0.78	0.00	4.00	274	1.00	1.00	0.52	0.44
FC	4.16	1.76	0.00	9.00	347	4.00	5.00	0.15	−0.41
CF	2.55	1.30	0.00	6.00	340	3.00	3.00	0.44	0.04
C	0.08	[0.30]	0.00	2.00	25	0.00	0.00	4.01	16.88
Cn	0.01	[0.08]	0.00	1.00	2	0.00	0.00	13.17	172.48
Sum Color	6.80	2.47	1.00	12.00	350	7.00	8.00	−0.19	−0.68
WSumC	4.76	1.77	0.50	9.00	350	5.00	5.00	−0.12	−0.54
Sum C'	1.58	[1.07]	0.00	5.00	289	2.00	2.00	0.35	−0.02
Sum T	0.97	[0.50]	0.00	4.00	307	1.00	1.00	0.92	6.61
Sum V	0.24	[0.61]	0.00	3.00	59	0.00	0.00	2.77	7.62
Sum Y	0.59	[0.89]	0.00	8.00	147	0.00	0.00	2.79	15.14
Sum Shading	3.38	1.82	0.00	14.00	345	3.00	3.00	1.66	5.89
Fr+rF	0.08	[0.32]	0.00	2.00	22	0.00	0.00	4.44	20.47
FD	1.14	[0.88]	0.00	5.00	274	1.00	1.00	1.17	3.27
F	8.10	2.75	3.00	19.00	350	8.00	8.00	0.97	1.77
(2)	8.77	2.11	1.00	14.00	350	8.00	8.00	0.10	0.70
Lambda	0.56	0.25	0.18	2.25	350	0.54	0.50	2.90	15.88
FM+m	4.83	1.37	1.00	9.00	350	5.00	5.00	0.14	0.41
EA	9.31	2.16	2.00	14.50	350	9.50	9.50	−0.26	0.30
es	8.21	2.58	3.00	22.00	350	8.00	7.00	1.04	3.00
D Score	0.09	0.82	−6.00	2.00	102	0.00	0.00	−2.08	14.01
AdjD	0.24	0.69	−2.00	2.00	119	0.00	0.00	0.00	2.07
a (active)	6.66	2.09	2.00	13.00	350	6.00	6.00	0.45	−0.23
p (passive)	2.76	1.47	0.00	6.00	334	2.00	2.00	0.47	−0.35
Ma	3.22	1.60	0.00	7.00	340	3.00	2.00	0.28	−0.46
Mp	1.37	0.87	0.00	3.00	302	1.00	1.00	0.37	−0.51
Intellect	1.61	1.22	0.00	6.00	287	1.00	1.00	0.67	0.12
Zf	11.98	2.56	5.00	23.00	350	12.00	12.00	0.50	2.50
Zd	0.69	2.87	−6.50	9.50	320	0.50	−1.00	0.34	−0.06
Blends	5.22	1.89	1.00	10.00	350	5.00	5.00	−0.16	−0.62
Blends/R	0.23	0.09	0.04	0.50	350	0.24	0.26	0.21	−0.07
Col−Shd Bld	0.50	[0.65]	0.00	2.00	145	0.00	0.00	0.94	−0.22
Afr	0.70	0.15	0.30	1.14	350	0.69	0.63	0.38	0.46
Populars	6.90	1.31	3.00	10.00	350	7.00	8.00	−0.30	−0.18
X+%	0.79	0.07	0.50	1.00	350	0.79	0.78	−0.49	1.17

Table 13.   (Continued)

VARIABLE	MEAN	SD	MIN	MAX	FREQ	MEDIAN	MODE	SK	KU
F+%	0.72	0.16	0.25	1.00	350	0.72	0.67	−0.27	−0.12
X−%	0.07	0.05	0.00	0.27	303	0.05	0.04	0.81	1.24
Xu%	0.14	0.06	0.00	0.34	340	0.13	0.13	0.37	0.31
S−%	0.09	[0.22]	0.00	1.00	64	0.00	0.00	2.59	6.32
Isolate/R	0.19	0.09	0.00	0.47	345	0.17	0.16	0.48	0.03
H	3.62	1.89	0.00	9.00	346	3.00	3.00	0.87	0.21
(H)	1.28	1.01	0.00	4.00	263	1.00	1.00	0.51	−0.04
HD	0.67	0.92	0.00	7.00	170	0.00	0.00	2.61	12.53
(Hd)	0.14	0.36	0.00	2.00	48	0.00	0.00	2.28	3.86
Hx	0.01	[0.11]	0.00	1.00	4	0.00	0.00	9.23	83.72
All H Cont	5.72	1.61	2.00	11.00	350	6.00	6.00	0.30	0.17
A	8.15	1.94	4.00	14.00	350	8.00	7.00	0.56	0.21
(A)	0.17	[0.52]	0.00	3.00	41	0.00	0.00	3.48	12.67
Ad	2.20	[1.13]	0.00	8.00	333	2.00	2.00	0.89	3.54
(Ad)	0.08	[0.32]	0.00	2.00	23	0.00	0.00	4.33	19.42
An	0.43	[0.67]	0.00	4.00	120	0.00	0.00	1.68	3.25
Art	0.97	0.84	0.00	3.00	231	1.00	1.00	0.31	−0.92
Ay	0.37	[0.50]	0.00	2.00	128	0.00	0.00	0.68	−1.19
Bl	0.18	[0.44]	0.00	2.00	55	0.00	0.00	2.45	5.45
Bt	2.35	1.25	0.00	6.00	321	3.00	3.00	−0.07	−0.44
Cg	1.35	0.98	0.00	4.00	290	1.00	1.00	0.68	0.12
Cl	0.15	[0.37]	0.00	2.00	53	0.00	0.00	2.09	2.97
Ex	0.12	[0.32]	0.00	1.00	41	0.00	0.00	2.39	3.74
Fi	0.51	[0.70]	0.00	2.00	136	0.00	0.00	1.03	−0.26
Food	0.18	[0.44]	0.00	2.00	54	0.00	0.00	2.48	5.65
Ge	0.05	[0.23]	0.00	2.00	17	0.00	0.00	4.74	23.69
Hh	0.86	0.75	0.00	3.00	231	1.00	1.00	0.53	−0.17
Ls	0.96	0.82	0.00	3.00	235	1.00	1.00	0.37	−0.72
Na	0.29	[0.55]	0.00	2.00	85	0.00	0.00	1.75	2.13
Sc	1.05	[1.11]	0.00	6.00	217	1.00	0.00	1.32	2.87
Sx	0.07	[0.46]	0.00	5.00	13	0.00	0.00	8.55	80.69
Xy	0.03	[0.21]	0.00	2.00	10	0.00	0.00	6.83	50.77
Idio	2.00	1.31	0.00	7.00	306	2.00	2.00	0.61	0.84
DV	0.67	[0.81]	0.00	4.00	175	0.50	0.00	1.33	1.87
INCOM	0.61	[0.67]	0.00	4.00	186	1.00	1.00	1.35	3.84
DR	0.15	[0.39]	0.00	2.00	49	0.00	0.00	2.52	5.86
FABCOM	0.17	[0.40]	0.00	2.00	55	0.00	0.00	2.29	4.57
DV2	0.01	[0.08]	0.00	1.00	2	0.00	0.00	13.17	172.48
INC2	0.00	[0.00]	0.00	0.00	0	0.00	0.00	—	—
DR2	0.00	[0.00]	0.00	0.00	0	0.00	0.00	—	—
FAB2	0.02	[0.13]	0.00	1.00	6	0.00	0.00	7.47	54.14
ALOG	0.04	[0.20]	0.00	1.00	14	0.00	0.00	4.71	20.35
CONTAM	0.00	0.00	0.00	0.00	0	0.00	0.00	—	—
Sum 6 Sp Sc	1.65	1.37	0.00	7.00	278	1.00	1.00	0.83	0.35
Lvl 2 Sp Sc	0.02	[0.15]	0.00	1.00	8	0.00	0.00	6.41	39.35
WSum6	3.34	3.04	0.00	15.00	278	2.00	2.00	1.03	0.71
AB	0.13	[0.37]	0.00	2.00	44	0.00	0.00	2.67	6.66
AG	1.17	1.10	0.00	5.00	241	1.00	1.00	1.00	0.93
CFB	0.00	0.00	0.00	0.00	0	0.00	0.00	—	—
COP	1.99	1.52	0.00	5.00	271	2.00	2.00	0.30	−0.87
CP	0.01	[0.08]	0.00	1.00	2	0.00	0.00	13.17	172.48
MOR	0.75	[0.85]	0.00	4.00	189	1.00	0.00	1.08	0.91
PER	0.93	0.88	0.00	5.00	230	1.00	1.00	1.20	3.00
PSV	0.04	[0.20]	0.00	1.00	15	0.00	0.00	4.53	18.66

NOTE: Standard Deviations shown in brackets indicate that the value is probably unreliable and/or misleading because the variable is nonparametric.

Table 14.   Frequencies and Percentages for 33 Structural Variables for 350 Adult Nonpatient Males

EB STYLE			FORM QUALITY DEVIATIONS		
Introversive	135	39%	X+% > .89	19	5%
Pervasive	39	11%	X+% < .70	35	10%
Ambitent	64	18%	X+% < .61	6	2%
Extratensive	151	44%	X+% < .50	0	0%
Pervasive	44	13%	F+% < .70	156	45%
			Xu% > .20	53	15%
D SCORE			X−% > .15	14	4%
D Score > 0	72	21%	X−% > .20	5	1%
D Score = 0	247	71%	X−% > .30	0	0%
D Score < 0	31	9%			
D Score < −1	11	3%			
ADJUSTED D SCORE			**FC:CF+C RATIO**		
Adj D Score > 0	98	28%	FC > (CF+C)+2	101	29%
Adj D Score = 0	231	66%	FC > (CF+C)+1	169	48%
Adj D Score < 0	30	9%	(CF+C) > FC+1	16	5%
Adj D Score < −1	11	3%	(CF+C) > FC+2	4	1%
Zd > +3.0 (Overincorp)	65	19%	S−Con Positive	0	0%
Zd < −3.0 (Underincorp)	16	5%	HVI Positive	9	3%
			OBS Positive	10	3%

SCZI = 6	0	0%	DEPI = 7	1	0%	CDI = 5	0	0%
SCZI = 5	0	0%	DEPI = 6	1	0%	CDI = 4	10	3%
SCZI = 4	0	0%	DEPI = 5	12	3%			

MISCELLANEOUS VARIABLES					
Lambda > .99	16	5%	(2AB+Art+Ay) > 5	22	6%
Dd > 3	18	5%	Populars < 4	1	0%
DQv + DQv/+ > 2	196	27%	Populars > 7	142	41%
S > 2	44	13%	COP = 0	79	23%
Sum T = 0	43	12%	COP > 2	128	37%
Sum T > 1	26	7%	AG = 0	109	31%
3r+(2)/R < .33	46	13%	AG > 2	39	11%
3r+(2)/R > .44	65	19%	MOR > 2	15	4%
Fr + rF > 0	22	6%	Lvl 2 Sp.Sc. > 0	8	2%
PureC > 0	25	7%	Sum 6 Sp.Sc. > 6	1	0%
PureC > 1	3	1%	Pure H < 2	25	7%
Afr < .40	4	1%	Pure H = 0	4	1%
Afr < .50	23	7%	p > a+1	1	0%
(FM+m) < Sum Shad	47	13%	Mp > Ma	26	7%

Table 15. Descriptive Statistics for 251 Adult Nonpatient Introversives

VARIABLE	MEAN	SD	MIN	MAX	FREQ	MEDIAN	MODE	SK	KU
R	23.50	4.76	14.00	38.00	251	24.00	20.00	0.50	0.46
W	8.71	2.26	3.00	20.00	251	9.00	8.00	1.53	8.71
D	13.25	3.63	2.00	22.00	251	14.00	14.00	0.20	0.81
Dd	1.54	[1.62]	0.00	10.00	191	1.00	1.00	2.48	9.39
S	1.43	[1.39]	0.00	10.00	204	1.00	1.00	2.61	11.21
DQ+	8.48	2.29	4.00	13.00	251	9.00	8.00	−0.22	−0.72
DQo	13.15	3.88	5.00	26.00	251	12.00	12.00	0.75	0.65
DQv	1.53	[1.36]	0.00	5.00	187	1.00	1.00	0.67	−0.64
DQv/+	0.34	[0.61]	0.00	2.00	68	0.00	0.00	1.59	1.38
FQx+	0.99	1.02	0.00	5.00	161	1.00	1.00	1.39	2.78
FQxo	17.46	3.42	9.00	27.00	251	18.00	18.00	0.32	0.29
FQxu	3.63	1.73	0.00	12.00	246	4.00	4.00	0.79	3.26
FQx−	1.39	0.99	0.00	4.00	217	1.00	1.00	0.87	0.33
FQxNone	0.02	[0.15]	0.00	1.00	6	0.00	0.00	6.27	37.63
MQ+	0.59	0.81	0.00	3.00	107	0.00	0.00	1.34	1.22
MQo	5.38	1.42	1.00	8.00	251	5.00	5.00	−0.27	0.08
MQu	0.38	0.59	0.00	2.00	82	0.00	0.00	1.29	0.64
MQ−	0.04	[0.21]	0.00	2.00	8	0.00	0.00	6.32	43.98
MQNone	0.01	[0.11]	0.00	1.00	3	0.00	0.00	9.04	80.29
SQual−	0.17	[0.40]	0.00	2.00	40	0.00	0.00	2.18	3.88
M	6.40	1.23	4.00	9.00	251	7.00	7.00	−0.13	−0.48
FM	3.65	1.26	1.00	7.00	251	4.00	4.00	0.07	−0.13
m	1.38	0.84	0.00	3.00	211	1.00	2.00	−0.05	−0.65
FC	3.20	1.39	0.00	7.00	246	3.00	3.00	0.28	0.27
CF	1.54	0.71	0.00	3.00	235	2.00	2.00	−0.15	−0.20
C	0.01	[0.11]	0.00	1.00	3	0.00	0.00	9.04	80.29
Cn	0.00	[0.00]	0.00	0.00	0	0.00	0.00	—	—
Sum Color	4.75	1.62	1.00	9.00	251	5.00	5.00	0.07	0.27
WSumC	3.16	1.04	0.50	5.50	251	3.50	3.50	−0.19	0.28
Sum C'	1.21	[1.08]	0.00	4.00	168	1.00	0.00	0.49	−0.59
Sum T	0.99	[0.47]	0.00	3.00	226	1.00	1.00	0.90	5.78
Sum V	0.29	[0.56]	0.00	2.00	59	0.00	0.00	1.82	2.32
Sum Y	0.33	[0.81]	0.00	6.00	53	0.00	0.00	3.81	19.45
Sum Shading	2.82	1.75	0.00	9.00	244	3.00	2.00	1.05	1.47
Fr+rF	0.08	[0.42]	0.00	4.00	12	0.00	0.00	7.48	63.71
FD	1.17	[0.87]	0.00	4.00	194	1.00	1.00	0.48	0.20
F	8.04	2.91	2.00	19.00	251	7.00	6.00	0.65	0.16
(2)	9.11	2.01	3.00	14.00	251	9.00	8.00	0.45	0.71
Lambda	0.54	0.21	0.17	1.12	251	0.50	0.50	0.60	−0.23
FM+m	5.02	1.47	1.00	9.00	251	5.00	5.00	0.38	−0.12
EA	9.56	2.11	4.50	14.50	251	9.50	9.50	−0.16	−0.22
es	7.84	2.61	3.00	16.00	251	7.00	7.00	0.52	0.21
D Score	0.24	0.80	−3.00	2.00	90	0.00	0.00	−0.46	3.29
AdjD	0.48	0.74	−2.00	2.00	122	0.00	0.00	−0.06	0.97
a (active)	7.90	2.12	4.00	13.00	251	8.00	6.00	0.27	−0.78
p (passive)	3.55	1.60	0.00	9.00	241	3.00	3.00	−0.02	0.14
Ma	4.62	1.20	1.00	7.00	251	5.00	4.00	−0.16	0.06
Mp	1.80	1.06	0.00	5.00	224	2.00	1.00	0.18	−0.20
Intellect	1.27	1.20	0.00	5.00	176	1.00	1.00	0.90	0.26
Zf	12.65	2.92	6.00	23.00	251	13.00	12.00	0.25	1.81
Zd	−0.43	3.04	−6.50	8.50	235	−1.00	−3.00	0.53	−0.15
Blends	4.39	1.90	1.00	10.00	251	4.00	3.00	0.29	−0.80
Blends/R	0.19	0.09	0.07	0.57	251	0.17	0.12	1.18	1.70
Col–Shd Bld	0.25	[0.48]	0.00	2.00	56	0.00	0.00	1.80	2.43
Afr	0.67	0.14	0.30	1.14	251	0.67	0.67	0.58	1.54
Populars	6.78	1.28	3.00	10.00	251	6.00	6.00	−0.00	−0.16

(continued)

Table 15.   (Continued)

VARIABLE	MEAN	SD	MIN	MAX	FREQ	MEDIAN	MODE	SK	KU
X+%	0.79	0.07	0.56	1.00	251	0.80	0.80	−0.32	1.50
F+%	0.71	0.17	0.29	1.00	251	0.71	0.80	−0.57	−0.04
X−%	0.06	0.04	0.00	0.13	217	0.05	0.04	0.22	−0.48
Xu%	0.15	0.06	0.00	0.37	246	0.15	0.15	0.30	1.26
S−%	0.09	[0.22]	0.00	1.00	40	0.00	0.00	2.83	7.74
Isolate/R	0.19	0.10	0.00	0.47	243	0.17	0.12	0.48	−0.19
H	5.09	1.70	1.00	9.00	251	5.00	5.00	0.05	−0.47
(H)	1.04	1.06	0.00	4.00	155	1.00	0.00	0.89	0.21
HD	0.34	0.66	0.00	4.00	68	0.00	0.00	2.54	8.51
(Hd)	0.08	0.28	0.00	2.00	18	0.00	0.00	3.77	14.45
Hx	0.01	[0.11]	0.00	1.00	3	0.00	0.00	9.04	80.29
All H Cont	6.55	1.34	2.00	11.00	251	7.00	7.00	0.02	0.43
A	8.10	1.94	3.00	15.00	251	8.00	8.00	0.32	1.10
(A)	0.29	[0.58]	0.00	3.00	58	0.00	0.00	2.14	4.62
Ad	2.39	[1.12]	0.00	7.00	235	3.00	3.00	0.06	1.54
(Ad)	0.04	[0.22]	0.00	2.00	10	0.00	0.00	5.52	33.19
An	0.47	[0.70]	0.00	2.00	89	0.00	0.00	1.15	−0.05
Art	0.73	0.76	0.00	3.00	137	1.00	0.00	0.55	−0.90
Ay	0.40	[0.50]	0.00	2.00	100	0.00	0.00	0.50	−1.51
Bl	0.01	[0.11]	0.00	1.00	3	0.00	0.00	9.04	80.29
Bt	2.00	1.20	0.00	5.00	225	2.00	3.00	0.01	−0.98
Cg	1.54	1.13	0.00	4.00	206	1.00	1.00	0.36	−0.88
Cl	0.16	[0.40]	0.00	2.00	37	0.00	0.00	2.43	5.37
Ex	0.26	[0.44]	0.00	1.00	65	0.00	0.00	1.11	−0.78
Fi	0.26	[0.49]	0.00	2.00	58	0.00	0.00	1.74	2.17
Food	0.12	[0.32]	0.00	1.00	29	0.00	0.00	2.42	3.89
Ge	0.01	[0.09]	0.00	1.00	2	0.00	0.00	11.14	122.97
Hh	1.16	0.92	0.00	4.00	184	1.00	1.00	0.45	−0.01
Ls	1.22	0.82	0.00	3.00	197	1.00	1.00	−0.06	−0.87
Na	0.39	[0.65]	0.00	2.00	75	0.00	0.00	1.42	0.76
Sc	1.02	[1.09]	0.00	6.00	158	1.00	0.00	1.68	4.98
Sx	0.08	[0.50]	0.00	5.00	11	0.00	0.00	8.14	73.81
Xy	0.02	[0.14]	0.00	1.00	5	0.00	0.00	6.91	46.16
Idio	1.92	1.25	0.00	7.00	219	2.00	2.00	0.70	1.61
DV	0.79	0.90	0.00	4.00	136	1.00	0.00	1.02	0.45
INCOM	0.50	[0.71]	0.00	4.00	102	0.00	0.00	1.82	4.76
DR	0.10	[0.35]	0.00	2.00	22	0.00	0.00	3.64	13.52
FABCOM	0.19	[0.42]	0.00	2.00	45	0.00	0.00	2.05	3.38
DV2	0.01	[0.09]	0.00	1.00	2	0.00	0.00	11.14	122.97
INC2	0.01	[0.11]	0.00	1.00	3	0.00	0.00	9.04	80.29
DR2	0.00	[0.00]	0.00	0.00	0	0.00	0.00	—	—
FAB2	0.03	[0.18]	0.00	1.00	8	0.00	0.00	5.36	26.97
ALOG	0.04	[0.23]	0.00	2.00	8	0.00	0.00	6.47	44.89
CONTAM	0.00	0.00	0.00	0.00	0	0.00	0.00	—	—
Sum 6 Sp Sc	1.68	1.42	0.00	7.00	190	1.00	1.00	0.66	−0.11
Lvl 2 Sp Sc	0.05	[0.22]	0.00	1.00	13	0.00	0.00	4.07	14.68
WSum6	3.35	3.17	0.00	15.00	190	3.00	0.00	1.08	1.18
AB	0.07	[0.32]	0.00	2.00	12	0.00	0.00	5.05	25.71
AG	1.16	1.11	0.00	5.00	175	1.00	1.00	1.10	1.06
CFB	0.00	0.00	0.00	0.00	0	0.00	0.00	—	—
COP	2.63	1.70	0.00	6.00	210	3.00	3.00	−0.07	−1.05
CP	0.00	[0.00]	0.00	0.00	0	0.00	0.00	—	—
MOR	0.81	[0.90]	0.00	4.00	138	1.00	0.00	0.98	0.50
PER	1.02	0.90	0.00	5.00	170	1.00	1.00	0.82	1.76
PSV	0.03	[0.17]	0.00	1.00	7	0.00	0.00	5.77	31.53

NOTE: Standard Deviations shown in brackets indicate that the value is probably unreliable and/or misleading because the variable is nonparametric.

Table 16. Frequencies and Percentages for 33 Structural Variables for 251 Adult Nonpatient Introversives

EB STYLE			FORM QUALITY DEVIATIONS		
Introversive	251	100%	X+% > .89	12	5%
Pervasive	68	27%	X+% < .70	23	9%
Ambitent	0	0%	X+% < .61	4	2%
Extratensive	0	0%	X+% < .50	0	0%
Pervasive	0	0%	F+% < .70	106	42%
			Xu% > .20	40	16%
D SCORE			X–% > .15	0	0%
D Score > 0	72	29%	X–% > .20	0	0%
D Score = 0	161	64%	X–% > .30	0	0%
D Score < 0	18	7%			
D Score < –1	7	3%			
ADJUSTED D SCORE			**FC:CF+C RATIO**		
Adj D Score > 0	113	45%	FC > (CF+C)+2	68	27%
Adj D Score = 0	129	51%	FC > (CF+C)+1	115	46%
Adj D Score < 0	9	4%	(CF+C) > FC+1	6	2%
Adj D Score < –1	4	2%	(CF+C) > FC+2	4	2%
Zd > +3.0 (overincorp)	34	14%	S–Con Positive	0	0%
Zd < –3.0 (Underincorp)	26	10%	HVI Positive	2	1%
			OBS Positive	6	2%

SCZI = 6	0	0%	DEPI = 7	0	0%	CDI = 5	0	0%
SCZI = 5	0	0%	DEPI = 6	1	0%	CDI = 4	0	0%
SCZI = 4	0	0%	DEPI = 5	9	4%			

MISCELLANEOUS VARIABLES

Lambda > .99	11	4%	(2AB+Art+Ay) > 5	7	3%
Dd > 3	16	6%	Populars < 4	2	1%
DQv + DQv/+ > 2	78	31%	Populars > 7	95	38%
S > 2	27	11%	COP = 0	41	16%
Sum T = 0	25	10%	COP > 2	135	54%
Sum T > 1	18	7%	AG = 0	76	30%
3r+(2)/R < .33	36	14%	AG > 2	27	11%
3r+(2)/R > .44	61	24%	MOR > 2	12	5%
Fr + rF > 0	12	5%	Lvl 2 Sp.Sc. > 0	13	5%
PureC > 0	3	1%	Sum 6 Sp.Sc. > 6	1	0%
PureC > 1	0	0%	Pure H < 2	2	1%
Afr < .40	7	3%	Pure H = 0	0	0%
Afr < .50	14	6%	p > a+1	2	1%
(FM+m) < Sum Shad	15	6%	Mp > Ma	9	4%

Table 17.   Descriptive Statistics for 306 Nonpatient Adult Extratensives

VARIABLE	MEAN	SD	MIN	MAX	FREQ	MEDIAN	MODE	SK	KU
R	22.76	2.93	15.00	36.00	306	23.00	23.00	0.44	2.61
W	8.73	1.63	4.00	19.00	306	9.00	9.00	1.76	11.70
D	13.21	3.00	1.00	21.00	306	13.00	13.00	−0.75	1.69
Dd	0.83	[1.17]	0.00	11.00	163	1.00	0.00	4.48	35.43
S	1.35	[0.82]	0.00	5.00	275	1.00	1.00	0.93	2.26
DQ+	6.88	1.70	3.00	11.00	306	6.00	6.00	0.63	−0.03
DQo	14.32	2.09	8.00	23.00	306	15.00	15.00	−0.30	2.22
DQv	1.13	[1.14]	0.00	6.00	197	1.00	0.00	1.18	1.92
DQv/+	0.44	[0.64]	0.00	2.00	111	0.00	0.00	1.15	0.19
FQx+	0.93	0.86	0.00	4.00	199	1.00	1.00	0.86	1.05
FQxo	17.32	2.66	11.00	24.00	306	17.00	17.00	−0.06	0.11
FQxu	3.04	1.65	0.00	9.00	286	3.00	3.00	0.42	0.22
FQx−	1.37	1.02	0.00	4.00	258	1.00	1.00	0.89	0.40
FQxNone	0.11	[0.33]	0.00	2.00	30	0.00	0.00	3.15	9.76
MQ+	0.62	0.68	0.00	3.00	156	1.00	0.00	0.71	−0.34
MQo	2.23	0.96	0.00	4.00	303	2.00	2.00	0.07	−0.86
MQu	0.04	0.20	0.00	1.00	13	0.00	0.00	4.56	18.91
MQ−	0.00	[0.00]	0.00	0.00	0	0.00	0.00	—	—
MQNone	0.00	[0.00]	0.00	0.00	0	0.00	0.00	—	—
SQual−	0.12	[0.35]	0.00	2.00	36	0.00	0.00	2.74	7.00
M	2.89	0.78	1.00	5.00	306	3.00	3.00	−0.22	0.61
FM	3.78	0.99	1.00	6.00	306	4.00	4.00	−0.29	0.02
m	0.81	0.66	0.00	4.00	212	1.00	1.00	0.78	2.55
FC	5.16	1.70	1.00	9.00	306	5.00	5.00	0.21	−0.08
CF	3.34	1.02	1.00	6.00	306	3.00	3.00	0.29	0.65
C	0.10	[0.30]	0.00	1.00	30	0.00	0.00	2.72	5.42
Cn	0.01	[0.08]	0.00	1.00	2	0.00	0.00	12.31	150.47
Sum Color	8.61	1.59	5.00	12.00	306	8.00	8.00	−0.21	−0.38
WSumC	6.07	1.07	4.00	9.00	306	6.00	6.00	0.20	−0.25
Sum C'	1.58	[1.11]	0.00	5.00	258	1.00	1.00	0.58	0.03
Sum T	1.09	[0.58]	0.00	4.00	284	1.00	1.00	1.77	5.58
Sum V	0.19	[0.47]	0.00	2.00	47	0.00	0.00	2.53	5.78
Sum Y	0.66	[0.73]	0.00	3.00	161	1.00	0.00	0.88	0.33
Sum Shading	3.52	1.53	1.00	9.00	306	3.00	3.00	0.88	0.58
Fr+rF	0.07	[0.30]	0.00	2.00	17	0.00	0.00	4.77	23.78
FD	1.06	[0.70]	0.00	5.00	254	1.00	1.00	1.18	5.58
F	8.12	2.30	4.00	19.00	306	8.00	8.00	0.73	2.66
(2)	8.54	1.76	5.00	12.00	306	8.00	8.00	0.32	−0.82
Lambda	0.58	0.23	0.24	1.88	306	0.56	0.56	1.99	9.41
FM+m	4.58	1.34	1.00	9.00	306	5.00	5.00	0.13	0.41
EA	8.96	1.65	5.50	13.00	306	9.00	8.50	0.03	−0.21
es	8.11	2.34	4.00	18.00	306	8.00	7.00	0.70	1.14
D Score	0.16	0.74	−3.00	2.00	95	0.00	0.00	−0.21	3.67
AdjD	0.20	0.70	−2.00	2.00	96	0.00	0.00	0.28	2.04
a (active)	5.44	1.57	3.00	10.00	306	5.00	5.00	0.38	−0.41
p (passive)	2.08	1.05	0.00	7.00	293	2.00	2.00	0.84	2.50
Ma	1.95	0.91	0.00	4.00	285	2.00	2.00	−0.28	−0.19
Mp	0.98	0.69	0.00	3.00	236	1.00	1.00	0.33	0.07
Intellect	1.94	1.24	0.00	6.00	282	2.00	1.00	0.84	0.67
Zf	11.59	2.02	7.00	19.00	306	11.00	11.00	0.23	0.08
Zd	1.75	2.81	−3.00	9.50	276	1.00	2.00	0.76	0.21
Blends	5.72	1.59	2.00	12.00	306	6.00	6.00	0.29	0.46
Blends/R	0.25	0.07	0.08	0.57	306	0.26	0.26	0.46	1.59
Col−Shd Bld	0.69	[0.80]	0.00	3.00	155	1.00	0.00	1.01	0.42
Afr	0.73	0.16	0.44	1.09	306	0.74	0.91	0.22	−0.47
Populars	7.07	1.31	4.00	9.00	306	7.00	8.00	−0.70	−0.12
X+%	0.80	0.08	0.60	1.00	306	0.81	0.86	0.09	0.38

Table 17. (Continued)

VARIABLE	MEAN	SD	MIN	MAX	FREQ	MEDIAN	MODE	SK	KU
F+%	0.74	0.16	0.29	1.00	306	0.75	1.00	−0.16	−0.24
X−%	0.06	0.04	0.00	0.19	258	0.05	0.04	0.76	0.08
Xu%	0.13	0.06	0.00	0.28	286	0.13	0.14	−0.03	−0.24
S−%	0.07	[0.21]	0.00	1.00	36	0.00	0.00	3.56	12.12
Isolate/R	0.22	0.09	0.05	0.45	306	0.21	0.29	0.43	−0.64
H	2.43	0.82	0.00	5.00	304	2.00	3.00	0.14	0.73
(H)	1.19	0.86	0.00	3.00	229	1.00	2.00	0.02	−0.98
HD	0.88	0.85	0.00	4.00	197	1.00	1.00	0.97	0.93
(Hd)	0.21	0.41	0.00	1.00	65	0.00	0.00	1.41	−0.00
Hx	0.00	[0.00]	0.00	0.00	0	0.00	0.00	—	—
All H Cont	4.71	1.30	2.00	9.00	306	4.00	4.00	0.33	−0.24
A	8.27	2.03	4.00	14.00	306	8.00	7.00	0.71	−0.20
(A)	0.10	[0.37]	0.00	3.00	25	0.00	0.00	4.79	28.25
Ad	2.13	[0.91]	0.00	5.00	299	2.00	2.00	0.29	0.21
(Ad)	0.07	[0.31]	0.00	2.00	18	0.00	0.00	4.61	22.27
An	0.37	[0.55]	0.00	4.00	108	0.00	0.00	1.72	6.17
Art	1.19	0.74	0.00	4.00	258	1.00	1.00	0.40	0.60
Ay	0.30	[0.48]	0.00	2.00	91	0.00	0.00	1.04	−0.44
Bl	0.25	[0.47]	0.00	2.00	72	0.00	0.00	1.61	1.64
Bt	3.16	1.12	0.00	6.00	301	3.00	3.00	−0.02	−0.04
Cg	1.13	0.72	0.00	4.00	254	1.00	1.00	0.43	0.84
Cl	0.10	[0.30]	0.00	1.00	30	0.00	0.00	2.72	5.42
Ex	0.02	[0.14]	0.00	1.00	6	0.00	0.00	6.96	46.80
Fi	0.61	[0.77]	0.00	2.00	131	0.00	0.00	0.81	−0.87
Food	0.36	[0.60]	0.00	2.00	90	0.00	0.00	1.46	1.07
Ge	0.07	[0.28]	0.00	2.00	19	0.00	0.00	4.31	19.74
Hh	0.86	0.73	0.00	3.00	211	1.00	1.00	0.77	0.82
Ls	0.73	0.67	0.00	3.00	188	1.00	1.00	0.50	−0.17
Na	0.40	[0.56]	0.00	2.00	112	0.00	0.00	1.01	0.03
Sc	0.91	[0.92]	0.00	3.00	184	1.00	0.00	0.72	−0.39
Sx	0.03	[0.16]	0.00	1.00	8	0.00	0.00	5.97	33.85
Xy	0.00	[0.00]	0.00	0.00	0	0.00	0.00	—	—
Idio	1.99	1.32	0.00	7.00	274	2.00	1.00	0.71	0.61
DV	0.59	[0.63]	0.00	3.00	158	1.00	0.00	0.66	−0.12
INCOM	0.54	[0.56]	0.00	2.00	156	1.00	0.00	0.39	−0.85
DR	0.17	[0.39]	0.00	2.00	52	0.00	0.00	1.90	2.19
FABCOM	0.10	[0.30]	0.00	2.00	28	0.00	0.00	3.13	9.18
DV2	0.01	[0.10]	0.00	1.00	3	0.00	0.00	10.00	98.63
INC2	0.00	[0.00]	0.00	0.00	0	0.00	0.00	—	—
DR2	0.00	[0.06]	0.00	1.00	1	0.00	0.00	17.49	306.00
FAB2	0.00	[0.00]	0.00	0.00	0	0.00	0.00	—	—
ALOG	0.05	[0.22]	0.00	1.00	15	0.00	0.00	4.20	15.73
CONTAM	0.00	0.00	0.00	0.00	0	0.00	0.00	—	—
Sum 6 Sp Sc	1.46	1.05	0.00	5.00	254	1.00	1.00	0.58	−0.03
Lvl 2 Sp Sc	0.01	[0.11]	0.00	1.00	4	0.00	0.00	8.62	72.72
WSum6	2.86	2.46	0.00	13.00	254	2.00	2.00	1.19	1.65
AB	0.22	[0.45]	0.00	2.00	63	0.00	0.00	1.86	2.61
AG	1.14	1.26	0.00	5.00	186	1.00	0.00	1.11	0.57
CFB	0.00	0.00	0.00	0.00	0	0.00	0.00	—	—
COP	1.83	1.33	0.00	4.00	241	2.00	2.00	0.14	−1.10
CP	0.04	[0.20]	0.00	1.00	13	0.00	0.00	4.56	18.91
MOR	0.62	[0.72]	0.00	3.00	152	0.00	0.00	0.98	0.54
PER	1.13	1.13	0.00	5.00	217	1.00	1.00	1.61	3.27
PSV	0.05	[0.22]	0.00	1.00	16	0.00	0.00	4.04	14.43

NOTE: Standard deviations shown in brackets indicate that the value is probably unreliable and/or misleading because the variable is nonparametric.

Table 18.   Frequencies and Percentages for 33 Structural Variables for 306 Adult Nonpatient Extratensives

EB STYLE			FORM QUALITY DEVIATIONS		
Introversive	0	0%	X+% > .89	28	9%
Pervasive	0	0%	X+% < .70	24	8%
Ambitent	0	0%	X+% < .61	2	1%
Extratensive	306	100%	X+% < .50	0	0%
Pervasive	86	28%	F+% < .70	115	38%
			Xu% > .20	49	16%
D SCORE			X–% > .15	13	4%
D Score > 0	68	22%	X–% > .20	0	0%
D Score = 0	211	69%	X–% > .30	0	0%
D Score < 0	27	9%			
D Score < –1	6	2%			
ADJUSTED D SCORE			**FC:CF+C RATIO**		
Adj D Score > 0	73	24%	FC > (CF+C)+2	113	37%
Adj D Score = 0	210	69%	FC > (CF+C)+1	166	54%
Adj D Score < 0	23	8%	(CF+C) > FC+1	19	6%
Adj D Score < –1	6	2%	(CF+C) > FC+2	3	1%
Zd > +3.0 (overincorp)	68	22%	S–Con Positive	0	0%
Zd < –3.0 (Underincorp)	0	0%	HVI Positive	1	0%
			OBS Positive	5	2%

SCZI = 6	0	0%	DEPI = 7	0	0%	CDI = 5	0	0%
SCZI = 5	0	0%	DEPI = 6	0	0%	CDI = 4	8	3%
SCZI = 4	0	0%	DEPI = 5	4	1%			

MISCELLANEOUS VARIABLES

Lambda > .99	11	4%	(2AB+Art+Ay) > 5	33	11%
Dd > 3	2	1%	Populars < 4	0	0%
DQv + DQv/+ > 2	81	26%	Populars > 7	139	45%
S > 2	22	7%	COP = 0	65	21%
Sum T = 0	22	7%	COP > 2	98	32%
Sum T > 1	35	11%	AG = 0	120	39%
3r+(2)/R < .33	58	19%	AG > 2	50	16%
3r+(2)/R > .44	52	17%	MOR > 2	5	2%
Fr + rF > 0	17	6%	Lvl 2 Sp.Sc. > 0	4	1%
PureC > 0	30	10%	Sum 6 Sp.Sc. > 6	0	0%
PureC > 1	0	0%	Pure H < 2	35	11%
Afr < .40	0	0%	Pure H = 0	2	1%
Afr < .50	15	5%	p > a+1	2	1%
(FM+m) < Sum Shad	57	19%	Mp > Ma	55	18%

Table 19. Descriptive Statistics for 143 Adult Nonpatient Ambitents

VARIABLE	MEAN	SD	MIN	MAX	FREQ	MEDIAN	MODE	SK	KU
R	21.00	5.06	14.00	38.00	143	21.00	23.00	0.87	1.21
W	7.89	1.84	3.00	13.00	143	8.00	8.00	−0.20	0.49
D	11.57	4.12	0.00	20.00	141	12.00	14.00	−0.43	−0.14
Dd	1.54	[2.46]	0.00	15.00	98	1.00	1.00	3.66	15.59
S	1.80	[1.50]	0.00	9.00	121	2.00	2.00	2.00	6.79
DQ+	6.20	1.87	2.00	9.00	143	7.00	5.00	−0.36	−0.78
DQo	13.07	4.61	5.00	34.00	143	13.00	14.00	1.86	6.62
DQv	1.28	[1.26]	0.00	5.00	93	1.00	0.00	0.90	0.40
DQv/+	0.46	[0.78]	0.00	2.00	40	0.00	0.00	1.30	−0.06
FQx+	0.66	0.84	0.00	4.00	67	0.00	0.00	1.28	1.88
FQxo	15.43	4.02	7.00	29.00	143	15.00	19.00	0.35	0.38
FQxu	3.01	1.97	0.00	13.00	135	3.00	4.00	1.94	7.78
FQx−	1.70	1.14	0.00	6.00	130	1.00	1.00	1.08	1.89
FQxNone	0.20	[0.51]	0.00	3.00	22	0.00	0.00	2.93	9.32
MQ+	0.32	0.63	0.00	3.00	34	0.00	0.00	2.17	4.59
MQo	3.02	1.42	0.00	7.00	139	3.00	3.00	0.17	−0.15
MQu	0.21	0.44	0.00	2.00	28	0.00	0.00	1.93	2.90
MQ−	0.10	[0.30]	0.00	1.00	14	0.00	0.00	2.74	5.56
MQNone	0.04	[0.18]	0.00	1.00	5	0.00	0.00	5.12	24.53
SQual−	0.33	[0.78]	0.00	3.00	26	0.00	0.00	2.38	4.61
M	3.68	1.29	1.00	7.00	143	4.00	3.00	0.26	0.11
FM	3.63	1.42	1.00	9.00	143	4.00	4.00	0.11	0.80
m	1.32	1.00	0.00	4.00	107	1.00	2.00	0.42	0.17
FC	3.37	1.81	0.00	8.00	138	3.00	5.00	0.30	−0.41
CF	1.68	1.04	0.00	4.00	129	2.00	1.00	0.40	−0.50
C	0.15	[0.41]	0.00	2.00	18	0.00	0.00	2.89	8.17
Cn	0.02	[0.14]	0.00	1.00	3	0.00	0.00	6.76	44.26
Sum Color	5.22	2.13	1.00	9.00	143	5.00	5.00	0.01	−0.80
WSumC	3.59	1.45	0.50	6.50	143	3.50	3.50	−0.06	−0.81
Sum C'	1.97	[1.61]	0.00	10.00	125	2.00	1.00	1.92	7.01
Sum T	0.95	[0.71]	0.00	4.00	110	1.00	1.00	1.05	3.58
Sum V	0.36	[0.78]	0.00	3.00	31	0.00	0.00	2.20	3.95
Sum Y	0.81	[1.56]	0.00	10.00	60	0.00	0.00	3.86	18.60
Sum Shading	4.10	3.36	0.00	23.00	139	3.00	3.00	3.07	13.36
Fr+rF	0.13	[0.33]	0.00	1.00	18	0.00	0.00	2.28	3.24
FD	1.34	[1.14]	0.00	5.00	105	1.00	2.00	0.94	1.31
F	7.65	2.97	2.00	18.00	143	7.00	7.00	0.68	1.36
(2)	8.22	2.89	1.00	13.00	143	8.00	8.00	−0.09	−0.13
Lambda	0.63	0.38	0.14	2.25	143	0.56	0.44	2.20	6.23
FM+m	4.95	1.84	1.00	10.00	143	5.00	6.00	0.12	0.01
EA	7.27	2.48	2.00	12.00	143	7.50	7.50	−0.01	−0.58
es	9.05	4.37	3.00	31.00	143	9.00	9.00	2.18	8.07
D Score	−0.54	1.72	−10.00	2.00	59	0.00	0.00	−3.04	12.73
AdjD	−0.27	1.16	−5.00	2.00	54	0.00	0.00	−1.67	4.77
a (active)	6.20	1.87	2.00	11.00	143	6.00	6.00	0.42	0.26
p (passive)	2.47	1.53	0.00	6.00	125	2.00	2.00	0.25	−0.36
Ma	2.58	0.99	1.00	6.00	143	2.00	2.00	0.75	1.11
Mp	1.13	0.82	0.00	3.00	108	1.00	1.00	0.13	−0.78
Intellect	1.27	1.35	0.00	5.00	88	1.00	0.00	0.90	−0.04
Zf	10.78	2.61	5.00	17.00	143	11.00	14.00	−0.20	−0.58
Zd	0.55	2.84	−6.50	8.00	133	0.00	−1.00	0.59	0.25
Blends	5.29	2.18	1.00	10.00	143	5.00	5.00	−0.07	−0.66
Blends/R	0.26	0.11	0.04	0.67	143	0.25	0.26	0.88	1.55
Col−Shd Bld	0.34	[0.58]	0.00	2.00	41	0.00	0.00	1.50	1.26
Afr	0.65	0.16	0.27	1.29	143	0.63	0.63	0.62	1.13
Populars	6.69	1.67	3.00	10.00	143	7.00	8.00	−0.49	−0.39

(continued)

Table 19.   (Continued)

VARIABLE	MEAN	SD	MIN	MAX	FREQ	MEDIAN	MODE	SK	KU
X+%	0.77	0.09	0.50	1.00	143	0.78	0.81	−0.43	1.09
F+%	0.64	0.18	0.25	1.00	143	0.63	0.50	0.35	−0.02
X−%	0.09	0.07	0.00	0.43	130	0.07	0.04	2.11	7.43
Xu%	0.14	0.07	0.00	0.34	135	0.13	0.13	0.43	0.30
S−%	0.11	[0.25]	0.00	1.00	26	0.00	0.00	2.21	3.77
Isolate/R	0.18	0.09	0.00	0.47	140	0.17	0.21	0.57	0.64
H	2.50	1.20	0.00	7.00	139	3.00	3.00	0.73	2.16
(H)	1.48	0.98	0.00	4.00	115	2.00	2.00	0.12	−0.25
HD	0.87	1.11	0.00	7.00	83	1.00	0.00	2.78	12.16
(Hd)	0.11	0.32	0.00	1.00	16	0.00	0.00	2.49	4.25
Hx	0.04	[0.18]	0.00	1.00	5	0.00	0.00	5.12	24.53
All H Cont	4.96	1.67	1.00	10.00	143	5.00	5.00	0.54	1.18
A	8.13	2.25	4.00	14.00	143	9.00	9.00	0.12	−0.40
(A)	0.11	[0.39]	0.00	3.00	12	0.00	0.00	4.64	25.84
Ad	2.05	[1.68]	0.00	9.00	131	2.00	2.00	1.97	4.99
(Ad)	0.04	[0.18]	0.00	1.00	5	0.00	0.00	5.12	24.53
An	0.45	[0.74]	0.00	3.00	47	0.00	0.00	1.73	2.61
Art	0.64	0.92	0.00	3.00	53	0.00	0.00	1.11	−0.11
Ay	0.32	[0.47]	0.00	1.00	45	0.00	0.00	0.81	−1.37
Bl	0.19	[0.49]	0.00	2.00	21	0.00	0.00	2.62	6.11
Bt	1.87	1.11	0.00	4.00	126	2.00	2.00	−0.02	−0.84
Cg	1.21	0.88	0.00	4.00	112	1.00	1.00	0.46	0.21
Cl	0.26	[0.47]	0.00	2.00	35	0.00	0.00	1.52	1.26
Ex	0.15	[0.36]	0.00	1.00	22	0.00	0.00	1.94	1.78
Fi	0.29	[0.59]	0.00	2.00	32	0.00	0.00	1.89	2.41
Food	0.16	[0.47]	0.00	2.00	17	0.00	0.00	2.99	8.15
Ge	0.03	[0.17]	0.00	1.00	4	0.00	0.00	5.79	31.93
Hh	0.64	0.88	0.00	3.00	63	0.00	0.00	1.34	1.05
Ls	0.65	0.73	0.00	3.00	75	1.00	0.00	1.09	1.19
Na	0.32	[0.61]	0.00	2.00	35	0.00	0.00	1.74	1.83
Sc	0.71	[0.82]	0.00	2.00	69	0.00	0.00	0.58	−1.27
Sx	0.13	[0.50]	0.00	3.00	11	0.00	0.00	4.65	22.59
Xy	0.10	[0.34]	0.00	2.00	12	0.00	0.00	3.74	14.51
Idio	1.43	1.24	0.00	7.00	106	1.00	1.00	1.05	2.23
DV	0.76	[0.86]	0.00	4.00	79	1.00	0.00	1.21	1.40
INCOM	0.53	[0.69]	0.00	4.00	65	0.00	0.00	1.71	4.93
DR	0.20	[0.40]	0.00	1.00	29	0.00	0.00	1.49	0.24
FABCOM	0.29	[0.52]	0.00	2.00	38	0.00	0.00	1.53	1.44
DV2	0.01	[0.12]	0.00	1.00	2	0.00	0.00	8.37	68.94
INC2	0.00	[0.00]	0.00	0.00	0	0.00	0.00	—	—
DR2	0.00	[0.00]	0.00	0.00	0	0.00	0.00	—	—
FAB2	0.03	[0.17]	0.00	1.00	4	0.00	0.00	5.79	31.93
ALOG	0.04	[0.20]	0.00	1.00	6	0.00	0.00	4.62	19.60
CONTAM	0.00	0.00	0.00	0.00	0	0.00	0.00	—	—
Sum 6 Sp Sc	1.87	1.34	0.00	6.00	120	2.00	2.00	0.68	0.47
Lvl 2 Sp Sc	0.04	[0.20]	0.00	1.00	6	0.00	0.00	4.62	19.60
WSum6	4.04	3.07	0.00	13.00	120	3.00	3.00	0.67	0.01
AB	0.16	[0.37]	0.00	1.00	23	0.00	0.00	1.87	1.50
AG	1.29	1.12	0.00	4.00	105	1.00	1.00	0.78	0.10
CFB	0.00	0.00	0.00	0.00	0	0.00	0.00	—	—
COP	1.58	1.26	0.00	4.00	104	2.00	0.00	0.19	−1.09
CP	0.00	[0.00]	0.00	0.00	0	0.00	0.00	—	—
MOR	0.69	[0.86]	0.00	3.00	66	0.00	0.00	1.00	−0.01
PER	0.93	0.87	0.00	5.00	91	1.00	1.00	0.85	1.81
PSV	0.08	[0.27]	0.00	1.00	11	0.00	0.00	3.21	8.42

NOTE: Standard deviations shown in brackets indicate that the value is probably unreliable and/or misleading because the variable is nonparametric.

Table 20. Frequencies and Percentages for 33 Structural Variables for 143 Adult Nonpatient Ambitents

EB STYLE			FORM QUALITY DEVIATIONS		
Introversive	0	0%	X+% > .89	9	6%
Pervasive	0	0%	X+% < .70	24	17%
Ambitent	143	100%	X+% < .61	6	4%
Extratensive	0	0%	X+% < .50	0	0%
Pervasive	0	0%	F+% < .70	92	64%
			Xu% > .20	20	14%
D SCORE			X−% > .15	11	8%
D Score > 0	16	11%	X−% > .20	9	6%
D Score = 0	84	59%	X−% > .30	2	1%
D Score < 0	43	30%			
D Score < −1	17	12%			
ADJUSTED D SCORE			**FC:CF+C RATIO**		
Adj D Score > 0	20	14%	FC > (CF+C)+2	39	27%
Adj D Score = 0	89	62%	FC > (CF+C)+1	64	45%
Adj D Score < 0	34	24%	(CF+C) > FC+1	5	3%
Adj D Score < −1	15	10%	(CF+C) > FC+2	2	1%
Zd > +3.0 (Overincorp)	25	17%	S−Con Positive	0	0%
Zd < −3.0 (Underincorp)	11	8%	HVI Positive	6	4%
			OBS Positive	2	1%

SCZI = 6	0	0%	DEPI = 7	1	1%	CDI = 5	3	2%
SCZI = 5	0	0%	DEPI = 6	2	1%	CDI = 4	9	6%
SCZI = 4	2	1%	DEPI = 5	8	6%			

MISCELLANEOUS VARIABLES					
Lambda > .99	16	11%	2AB+Art+Ay) > 5	12	8%
Dd > 3	15	10%	Populars < 4	7	5%
DQv + DQv/+ > 2	41	29%	Populars > 7	59	41%
S > 2	23	16%	COP = 0	39	27%
Sum T = 0	33	23%	COP > 2	38	27%
Sum T > 1	22	15%	AG = 0	38	27%
3r+(2)/R < .33	18	13%	AG > 2	18	13%
3r+(2)/R > .44	56	39%	MOR > 2	5	3%
Fr + rF > 0	18	13%	Lvl 2 Sp.Sc. > 0	6	4%
PureC > 0	18	13%	Sum 6 Sp.Sc. > 6	0	0%
PureC > 1	3	2%	Pure H < 2	29	20%
Afr < .40	4	3%	Pure H = 0	4	3%
Afr < .50	21	15%	p > a+1	2	1%
(FM+m) < Sum Shad	34	24%	Mp > Ma	8	6%

THE NORMATIVE SAMPLES FOR CHILDREN AND ADOLESCENTS

The normative samples for younger subjects have changed much more than the adult sample. The 1982 normative samples for ages 5 to 16 included 1580 protocols, with the number for each year ranging between 105 (age six) to 150 (ages 9, 11, and 16). A total of 239 of the 1580 protocols (15%) were discarded from the sample because of a low *R*.

Nearly half of the discarded records were from ages five through eight. Thus, the data for those ages most likely changed most, but every age group was affected. Some records of nonpatient children that were not selected for use in the 1982 norms have been added to replace about 20% of those that were discarded

Table 21.   Distribution of Demographic Variables, by Age, for 1390 Nonpatient Children and Adolescents

						AGE GROUPS						
	5	6	7	8	9	10	11	12	13	14	15	16
TOTAL	90	80	120	120	140	120	135	120	110	105	110	140
Male	50	46	68	54	72	64	70	63	45	43	·53	68
Female	40	34	52	66	68	56	65	57	65	62	57	72
RACE												
White	71	60	106	88	106	97	110	87	80	76	81	107
Black	11	15	9	16	14	11	13	19	20	18	16	21
Hispanic	8	5	5	14	13	12	9	10	8	9	8	11
Asian	0	0	0	2	7	0	3	4	2	3	5	1
SES & GEOGRAPHIC												
Upper	22	17	21	15	21	25	27	19	14	15	20	17
Middle	47	38	63	64	80	63	77	67	68	61	57	84
Lower	21	25	36	41	39	32	31	34	28	29	33	39
Urban	31	21	34	34	45	27	41	34	37	24	43	46
Suburban	26	27	39	42	51	41	51	43	39	44	35	49
Rural	33	32	46	44	44	52	43	43	34	37	32	44

but samples for all years remain smaller than the originals, and the discarding and replacement procedure has altered the stratification pattern, based on geographic distribution and socioeconomic level that was applied in the original sample. The total sample now consists of 1390 protocols.

The 1390 records were collected by 87 examiners, for an average of 16 protocols each. Actually, 12 examiners collected between 21 and 26 protocols, but no examiner collected fewer than seven records. Eighty-four school districts, from 33 states plus the District of Columbia, are represented. No school district contributed more than 33 subjects or more than 10 records for any age group. Most minority subjects were recruited from the Northeast, Southwest, and Western United States.

Table 21 provides some demographic data concerning sex, race, SES and residential geography for each age group.

Tables 22 and 23, include the revised normative data for nonpatient children.

THE PSYCHIATRIC REFERENCE GROUPS

Tables 24 through 31 include data for the same variables listed in the normative tables for four groups of adult psychiatric subjects. These tables are considerably different from those previously published in that none contain records of fewer than 14 answers. Each group represents a random selection of between 25 and 50% of the records available for each group.

Although the records for the groups have been randomly selected from larger samples, no stratification effort has been made, except to choose relatively equal samples of public and private hospital subjects for the two inpatient groups. Therefore, the data for these four groups *should not be considered normative* in any sense.

Table 22.   Descriptive Statistics for 1390 Nonpatient Children and Adolescents by Age

5 YEAR OLDS (N = 90)

VARIABLE	MEAN	SD	MIN	MAX	FREQ	MEDIAN	MODE	SK	KU
R	17.64	1.44	14.00	20.00	90	18.00	18.00	−0.83	−0.25
W	9.97	1.65	7.00	12.00	90	9.00	11.00	0.24	−1.35
D	7.10	2.61	3.00	12.00	90	8.00	6.00	−0.83	−0.24
Dd	0.58	[0.65]	0.00	2.00	44	0.00	0.00	0.70	−0.53
S	1.40	[1.14]	0.00	3.00	64	1.00	0.00	0.14	−1.39
DQ+	5.47	1.43	2.00	8.00	90	5.50	4.00	0.35	−1.29
DQo	10.72	2.07	7.00	13.00	90	12.00	13.00	−1.25	0.05
DQv	1.37	[0.62]	0.00	4.00	83	1.00	1.00	0.36	−0.63
DQv/+	0.09	[0.29]	0.00	1.00	8	0.00	0.00	2.94	6.78
FQX+	0.00	0.00	0.00	0.00	0	0.00	0.00	—	—
FQXo	11.54	2.50	6.00	15.00	90	13.00	13.00	−0.70	−0.52
FQXu	3.59	1.96	1.00	7.00	90	4.00	1.00	0.13	−1.19
FQX−	1.46	0.64	0.00	3.00	86	1.00	1.00	0.04	−0.19
FQXNone	0.87	[0.62]	0.00	2.00	63	1.00	1.00	0.36	−0.63
MQ+	0.00	0.00	0.00	0.00	0	0.00	0.00	—	—
MQo	1.13	0.34	1.00	2.00	90	1.00	1.00	2.19	2.88
MQu	0.38	0.66	0.00	2.00	25	0.00	0.00	1.53	1.00
MQ−	0.19	[0.39]	0.00	1.00	17	0.00	0.00	1.62	0.63
MQNone	0.00	[0.00]	0.00	0.00	0	0.00	0.00	—	—
S−	0.91	[0.69]	0.00	3.00	62	1.00	1.00	0.45	−0.83
M	1.70	1.00	1.00	4.00	90	1.00	1.00	1.26	0.36
FM	5.00	0.95	4.00	7.00	90	5.00	4.00	0.32	−1.20
m	0.78	0.80	0.00	3.00	49	1.00	0.00	0.43	−1.32
FM+m	5.78	1.19	4.00	9.00	90	6.00	5.00	0.65	0.50
FC	0.71	0.46	0.00	1.00	64	1.00	1.00	−0.95	−1.13
CF	3.02	1.41	1.00	6.00	90	3.00	3.00	0.53	−0.20
C	0.67	[0.62]	0.00	2.00	63	1.00	1.00	0.36	−0.63
Cn	0.00	[0.00]	0.00	0.00	0	0.00	0.00	—	—
FC+CF+C+Cn	4.40	1.10	2.00	6.00	90	4.00	4.00	−0.39	−0.11
WGSum C	4.38	1.09	2.50	6.50	90	4.00	4.00	0.27	−0.73
Sum C'	0.63	[0.48]	0.00	1.00	57	1.00	1.00	−0.56	−1.72
Sum T	0.83	[0.48]	0.00	2.00	57	1.00	1.00	0.42	2.42
Sum V	0.00	[0.00]	0.00	0.00	0	0.00	0.00	—	—
Sum Y	0.36	[0.33]	0.00	2.00	20	0.00	0.00	−0.65	2.71
SumShd	1.77	0.97	0.00	2.00	57	2.00	2.00	−0.56	−1.72
Fr+rF	0.38	[0.45]	0.00	2.00	29	0.00	0.00	1.01	−1.00
FD	0.28	[0.63]	0.00	1.00	16	0.00	0.00	1.77	0.58
F	6.98	1.26	4.00	9.00	90	6.00	6.00	0.19	−0.35
PAIR	9.08	1.96	5.00	11.00	90	9.00	11.00	−0.91	−0.29
3r(2)/R	0.69	0.14	0.33	1.00	90	0.60	0.64	0.28	0.57
LAMBDA	0.86	0.15	0.36	1.25	90	0.75	0.60	0.76	−0.52
EA	5.08	1.34	2.50	8.50	90	5.50	5.00	−0.24	−0.75
es	7.04	1.14	5.00	9.00	90	7.00	7.00	0.10	−0.60
D	−0.24	0.43	−1.00	0.00	90	0.00	0.00	−1.21	−0.55
AdjD	−0.20	0.40	−1.00	0.00	90	0.00	0.00	−1.53	0.33
a (active)	6.28	0.95	5.00	8.00	90	6.00	6.00	0.38	−0.70
p (passive)	1.20	1.37	0.00	4.00	49	1.00	0.00	0.82	−0.60
Ma	1.42	0.67	1.00	3.00	90	1.00	1.00	1.32	0.47
Mp	0.28	0.45	0.00	1.00	25	0.00	0.00	1.01	−1.00
Intellect	0.17	0.38	0.00	1.00	90	0.00	0.00	1.82	1.34
Zf	10.08	2.18	8.00	14.00	90	10.00	14.00	0.15	−1.52
Zd	−1.13	2.60	−5.00	4.50	90	−1.75	−2.50	0.70	0.09
Blends	2.86	1.92	0.00	5.00	77	3.00	5.00	−0.21	−1.56
Col Shd Bl	0.18	[0.56]	0.00	1.00	5	0.00	0.00	1.81	−2.37
Afr	0.88	0.13	0.50	1.00	90	0.90	0.80	−0.65	−0.08
Popular	4.66	1.69	3.00	10.00	90	4.00	4.00	0.55	−0.94

NOTE: Standard Deviations shown in brackets indicate that the value is probably unreliable and/or misleading and should not be used to estimate expected ranges. Ordinarily these variables should not be included in most parametric analyses.

(continued)

Table 22.   (Continued)

5 YEAR OLDS (N = 90)

VARIABLE	MEAN	SD	MIN	MAX	FREQ	MEDIAN	MODE	SK	KU
X+%	0.78	0.10	0.47	0.83	90	0.75	0.70	–0.28	–0.68
F+%	0.84	0.13	0.50	1.00	90	0.83	0.83	–0.62	0.28
X–%	0.08	0.04	0.00	0.17	86	0.07	0.11	–0.02	–0.16
Xu%	0.14	0.11	0.06	0.40	90	0.12	0.06	0.09	–1.44
S–%	0.49	[0.46]	0.00	1.00	52	0.50	0.00	0.02	–1.83
Isolate	0.17	0.06	0.11	0.27	90	0.17	0.11	0.58	–0.88
H	2.19	0.50	1.00	3.00	90	2.00	2.00	0.38	0.34
(H)	1.46	0.50	1.00	2.00	90	1.00	1.00	0.18	–2.01
Hd	0.36	0.48	0.00	1.00	32	0.00	0.00	0.61	–1.66
(Hd)	0.46	0.57	0.00	2.00	13	0.00	0.00	1.42	1.54
Hx	0.00	[0.00]	0.00	0.00	0	0.00	0.00	—	—
All H Cont	4.00	1.15	2.00	6.00	90	4.00	3.00	0.41	–0.90
A	10.69	2.32	6.00	14.00	90	11.00	12.00	–0.88	–0.28
(A)	0.37	[0.48]	0.00	1.00	33	0.00	0.00	0.56	–1.72
Ad	0.71	[0.60]	0.00	2.00	57	1.00	1.00	0.23	–0.57
(Ad)	0.00	[0.00]	0.00	0.00	0	0.00	0.00	—	—
An	0.37	[0.49]	0.00	3.00	18	0.00	0.00	0.46	2.01
Art	0.17	0.38	0.00	1.00	15	0.00	0.00	1.82	1.34
Ay	0.00	[0.00]	0.00	0.00	0	0.00	0.00	—	—
Bl	1.13	[0.46]	0.00	2.00	86	1.00	1.00	0.54	1.30
Bt	0.28	0.45	0.00	1.00	25	0.00	0.00	1.01	–1.00
Cg	3.73	1.35	2.00	6.00	90	3.00	3.00	0.62	–0.92
Cl	0.58	[0.74]	0.00	2.00	42	0.00	0.00	1.21	0.83
Ex	0.22	[0.51]	0.00	2.00	16	0.00	0.00	2.31	4.54
Fi	0.22	[0.51]	0.00	2.00	16	0.00	0.00	2.31	4.54
Fd	0.41	[0.53]	0.00	2.00	21	0.00	0.00	2.16	2.38
Ge	0.00	[0.00]	0.00	0.00	0	0.00	0.00	—	—
Hh	0.71	0.65	0.00	3.00	61	1.00	1.00	–0.48	1.96
Ls	2.68	0.63	2.00	4.00	90	3.00	3.00	0.38	–0.65
Na	0.36	[0.51]	0.00	2.00	19	0.00	0.00	1.42	–0.39
Sc	0.52	[0.43]	0.00	2.00	37	0.00	0.00	1.35	3.58
Sx	0.00	[0.00]	0.00	0.00	0	0.00	0.00	—	—
Xy	0.00	[0.00]	0.00	0.00	0	0.00	0.00	—	—
Idio	0.14	0.35	0.00	1.00	13	0.00	0.00	2.06	2.28
DV	1.16	[1.05]	0.00	4.00	83	1.00	1.00	1.00	0.57
INCOM	1.96	[0.70]	0.00	4.00	76	1.00	1.00	0.06	–0.93
DR	0.11	[0.21]	0.00	1.00	9	0.00	0.00	4.50	18.63
FABCOM	0.89	[0.57]	0.00	3.00	72	1.00	1.00	–0.02	0.06
DV2	0.00	[0.00]	0.00	0.00	0	0.00	0.00	—	—
INC2	0.09	[0.29]	0.00	1.00	8	0.00	0.00	2.94	6.78
DR2	0.09	[0.29]	0.00	1.00	8	0.00	0.00	2.94	6.78
FAB2	0.22	[0.42]	0.00	1.00	20	0.00	0.00	1.36	–0.16
ALOG	0.61	[0.50]	0.00	1.00	57	0.00	0.00	0.37	–1.91
CONTAM	0.00	0.00	0.00	0.00	0	0.00	0.00	—	—
Sum6 Sp Sc	6.88	2.01	3.00	9.00	90	6.00	5.00	0.45	–0.65
Sum6 Sp Sc2	0.40	[0.58]	0.00	2.00	32	0.00	0.00	1.12	0.30
WSum6	14.88	4.68	4.00	22.00	90	14.00	7.00	–0.10	–1.05
AB	0.00	[0.00]	0.00	0.00	0	0.00	0.00	—	—
AG	1.23	0.67	0.00	3.00	82	1.00	1.00	0.60	0.74
CFB	0.00	0.00	0.00	0.00	0	0.00	0.00	—	—
COP	1.08	0.52	0.00	3.00	81	1.00	1.00	0.10	0.67
CP	0.23	[0.81]	0.00	1.00	2	0.00	0.00	3.38	11.55
MOR	0.78	[0.75]	0.00	2.00	53	1.00	0.00	0.39	–1.10
PER	0.18	0.41	0.00	2.00	21	0.00	0.00	0.69	4.73
PSV	0.63	[0.48]	0.00	1.00	57	1.00	1.00	–0.56	–1.72

Table 22. (Continued)

6 YEAR OLDS (N = 80)

VARIABLE	MEAN	SD	MIN	MAX	FREQ	MEDIAN	MODE	SK	KU
R	18.91	0.98	14.00	20.00	80	19.00	20.00	–0.23	–1.25
W	10.79	1.17	7.00	10.00	80	11.00	9.00	–0.56	–1.16
D	7.94	1.01	7.00	11.00	80	7.00	8.00	–1.38	2.27
Dd	0.30	[0.46]	0.00	1.00	24	0.00	0.00	0.89	–1.24
S	0.79	[0.76]	0.00	3.00	51	1.00	1.00	1.09	1.67
DQ+	4.42	0.59	3.00	5.00	80	4.00	4.00	–0.46	–0.66
DQo	11.31	1.35	9.00	13.00	80	11.00	13.00	0.11	–1.45
DQv	2.54	[1.19]	1.00	5.00	80	3.00	3.00	0.14	–0.89
DQv/+	0.45	[0.64]	0.00	1.00	38	1.00	1.00	–1.18	–0.63
FQX+	0.00	0.00	0.00	0.00	0	0.00	0.00	——	——
FQXo	13.39	1.22	12.00	16.00	80	14.00	14.00	0.25	–0.92
FQXu	4.01	1.29	3.00	7.00	80	4.00	4.00	0.75	–0.32
FQX–	0.94	0.50	0.00	6.00	66	0.00	0.00	0.21	–2.01
FQXNone	0.74	[0.48]	0.00	2.00	68	1.00	1.00	–0.58	–1.70
MQ+	0.00	0.00	0.00	0.00	0	0.00	0.00	——	——
MQo	1.96	0.75	1.00	3.00	80	2.00	2.00	0.06	–1.22
MQu	0.00	0.00	0.00	0.00	0	0.00	0.00	——	——
MQ–	0.23	[0.67]	0.00	1.00	6	0.00	0.00	1.24	4.12
MQNone	0.00	[0.00]	0.00	0.00	0	0.00	0.00	——	——
S–	0.42	[0.78]	0.00	0.50	11	0.00	0.00	0.98	3.15
M	1.96	0.75	1.00	3.00	80	2.00	2.00	0.06	–1.22
FM	4.52	0.81	4.00	8.00	80	5.00	4.00	–1.25	2.76
m	1.40	1.48	0.00	4.00	51	1.00	0.00	0.81	–0.72
FM+m	5.92	0.99	7.00	10.00	80	8.00	8.00	1.11	0.35
FC	1.11	1.09	0.00	3.00	42	2.00	0.00	0.07	–1.72
CF	3.51	0.94	1.00	5.00	80	3.00	3.00	–0.36	0.83
C	0.94	[0.48]	0.00	2.00	68	1.00	1.00	–0.58	–1.70
Cn	0.06	[0.09]	0.00	1.00	1	0.00	0.00	4.15	35.81
FC+CF+C+Cn	5.56	1.63	1.00	7.00	80	6.00	6.00	–0.94	0.29
WGSum C	5.02	1.42	1.00	6.50	80	5.50	5.50	–1.23	1.26
Sum C'	0.58	[0.50]	0.00	1.00	46	1.00	1.00	–0.31	–1.95
Sum T	0.83	[0.22]	0.00	1.00	69	1.00	1.00	–1.21	6.12
Sum V	0.00	[0.00]	0.00	0.00	0	0.00	0.00	——	——
Sum Y	0.54	[0.48]	0.00	1.00	37	0.00	0.00	0.70	–1.55
SumShd	1.95	0.88	0.00	3.00	76	2.00	2.00	–0.18	–0.89
Fr+rF	0.28	[0.40]	0.00	2.00	17	0.00	0.00	1.83	0.35
FD	0.48	[0.68]	0.00	1.00	29	0.00	0.00	1.49	2.34
F	5.77	1.47	3.00	10.00	80	4.00	4.00	3.10	10.34
PAIR	9.61	1.79	5.00	12.00	80	10.00	11.00	–0.88	0.30
3r(2)/R	0.67	0.15	0.25	0.90	80	0.66	0.60	0.38	0.61
LAMBDA	0.79	0.17	0.18	1.50	80	0.78	0.65	–1.56	0.64
EA	6.98	1.42	2.00	8.50	80	6.00	5.00	0.85	1.77
es	7.87	1.00	8.00	11.00	80	7.00	6.00	0.13	–1.52
D	–0.41	0.59	–2.00	0.00	80	0.00	0.00	–1.11	0.28
AdjD	–0.21	0.41	–2.00	0.00	80	0.00	0.00	–1.43	0.05
a (active)	6.03	1.27	5.00	9.00	80	6.00	5.00	0.43	–1.17
p (passive)	1.85	1.90	1.00	6.00	80	2.00	1.00	0.51	–1.49
Ma	0.98	0.84	0.00	2.00	51	1.00	0.00	0.05	–1.59
Mp	0.99	1.35	0.00	3.00	29	0.00	0.00	0.70	–1.44
Intellect	0.96	0.51	0.00	2.00	80	1.00	1.00	–0.06	0.93
Zf	10.15	1.44	6.00	12.00	80	11.00	9.00	–0.45	–1.21
Zd	–1.38	2.20	–5.00	1.00	80	0.00	0.00	–0.91	–0.93
Blends	2.16	0.49	1.00	3.00	80	2.00	2.00	0.38	0.64
Col Shd Bl	0.44	[0.64]	0.00	1.00	18	0.00	0.00	2.13	4.67
Afr	0.87	0.26	0.25	1.11	80	0.82	0.78	–0.76	–0.36
Popular	5.02	1.43	4.00	9.00	80	5.00	5.00	0.14	–0.70

NOTE: Standard Deviations shown in brackets indicate that the value is probably unreliable and/or misleading and should not be used to estimate expected ranges. Ordinarily these variables should not be included in most parametric analyses.

(continued)

Table 22.   (Continued)

6 YEAR OLDS (N = 80)

VARIABLE	MEAN	SD	MIN	MAX	FREQ	MEDIAN	MODE	SK	KU
X+%	0.76	0.07	0.55	0.84	80	0.70	0.60	−0.31	−0.93
F+%	0.74	0.25	0.50	1.00	80	0.75	0.75	0.63	1.02
X−%	0.09	0.08	0.00	0.25	80	0.10	0.10	0.25	−1.92
Xu%	0.17	0.06	0.16	0.35	80	0.22	0.15	0.52	−0.56
S−%	0.25	[0.67]	0.00	0.00	28	0.33	0.20	0.88	2.13
Isolate	0.24	0.08	0.12	0.39	80	0.22	0.15	0.31	−1.21
H	2.63	1.14	1.00	4.00	80	3.00	3.00	−0.47	−1.24
(H)	0.78	0.50	0.00	1.00	66	1.00	1.00	−0.31	−1.95
Hd	0.64	0.62	0.00	2.00	45	1.00	1.00	0.43	−0.63
(Hd)	0.23	0.63	0.00	1.00	16	0.00	0.00	1.28	3.16
Hx	0.00	[0.00]	0.00	0.00	0	0.00	0.00	—	—
All H Cont	4.28	0.68	2.00	6.00	80	4.00	4.00	0.22	−0.83
A	8.24	0.96	6.00	10.00	80	8.00	8.00	−0.06	0.32
(A)	0.30	[0.46]	0.00	1.00	24	0.00	0.00	0.89	−1.24
Ad	0.95	[0.22]	0.00	1.00	76	1.00	1.00	−4.21	16.12
(Ad)	0.00	[0.00]	0.00	0.00	0	0.00	0.00	—	—
An	0.33	[0.50]	0.00	1.00	11	0.00	0.00	0.99	2.02
Art	0.96	0.51	0.00	2.00	68	1.00	1.00	−0.06	0.93
Ay	0.00	[0.00]	0.00	0.00	0	0.00	0.00	—	—
Bl	0.25	[0.44]	0.00	1.00	20	0.00	0.00	1.18	−0.63
Bt	1.52	0.60	0.00	2.00	76	2.00	2.00	−0.84	−0.25
Cg	1.02	0.70	0.00	3.00	49	1.00	1.00	0.47	−0.68
Cl	0.11	[0.32]	0.00	1.00	9	0.00	0.00	2.50	4.36
Ex	0.20	[0.40]	0.00	1.00	16	0.00	0.00	1.53	0.35
Fi	0.64	[0.48]	0.00	1.00	51	1.00	1.00	−0.58	−1.70
Fd	0.58	[0.50]	0.00	1.00	46	1.00	1.00	−0.31	−1.95
Ge	0.05	[0.22]	0.00	1.00	4	0.00	0.00	4.21	16.12
Hh	1.26	0.55	1.00	3.00	80	1.00	1.00	2.01	3.16
Ls	1.27	0.78	0.00	3.00	80	1.00	1.00	2.21	3.84
Na	0.81	[0.75]	0.00	2.00	49	1.00	1.00	0.32	−1.14
Sc	0.69	[0.57]	0.00	2.00	51	1.00	1.00	0.08	−0.59
Sx	0.00	[0.00]	0.00	0.00	0	0.00	0.00	—	—
Xy	0.00	[0.00]	0.00	0.00	0	0.00	0.00	—	—
Idio	0.15	0.36	0.00	1.00	12	0.00	0.00	2.00	2.04
DV	0.26	[0.24]	0.00	2.00	35	0.00	0.00	0.68	1.87
INCOM	2.35	[0.48]	2.00	3.00	80	2.00	2.00	0.64	−1.63
DR	0.78	[0.56]	0.00	2.00	36	0.00	0.00	0.57	2.76
FABCOM	0.58	[0.50]	0.00	1.00	46	1.00	1.00	−0.31	−1.95
DV2	0.00	[0.00]	0.00	0.00	0	0.00	0.00	—	—
INC2	0.15	[0.36]	0.00	2.00	13	0.00	0.00	1.94	2.56
DR2	0.00	[0.00]	0.00	0.00	0	0.00	0.00	—	—
FAB2	0.20	[0.45]	0.00	1.00	10	0.00	0.00	1.74	0.96
ALOG	0.64	[0.48]	0.00	1.00	51	1.00	1.00	−0.58	−1.70
CONTAM	0.00	0.00	0.00	0.00	0	0.00	0.00	—	—
Sum6 Sp Sc	6.63	1.38	2.00	8.00	80	6.00	5.00	−0.03	−1.54
Sum6 Sp Sc2	0.72	[0.98]	0.00	2.00	20	0.00	0.00	1.94	2.05
WSum6	13.30	5.03	4.00	20.00	80	13.00	10.00	−0.33	−1.71
AB	0.00	[0.00]	0.00	0.00	0	0.00	0.00	—	—
AG	0.30	0.56	0.00	3.00	20	0.00	0.00	1.74	2.11
CFB	0.00	0.00	0.00	0.00	0	0.00	0.00	—	—
COP	2.40	0.54	0.00	3.00	76	2.00	2.00	−4.21	16.12
CP	0.18	[0.30]	0.00	1.00	2	0.00	0.00	2.73	11.95
MOR	0.60	[0.57]	0.00	3.00	37	0.00	0.00	0.55	2.15
PER	0.23	1.06	0.00	3.00	14	0.00	0.00	0.78	3.24
PSV	0.64	[0.77]	0.00	2.00	28	0.00	0.00	1.21	3.85

Table 22. (Continued)

7 YEAR OLDS (N = 120)

VARIABLE	MEAN	SD	MIN	MAX	FREQ	MEDIAN	MODE	SK	KU
R	19.93	1.25	14.00	24.00	120	19.00	19.00	-0.10	-0.50
W	10.33	2.01	5.00	12.00	120	9.00	9.00	0.02	-1.34
D	9.09	2.86	7.00	15.00	120	9.00	7.00	0.07	-1.77
Dd	0.82	[0.32]	0.00	3.00	74	0.00	0.00	0.42	2.91
S	1.44	[1.06]	0.00	4.00	102	2.00	2.00	-0.49	-0.38
DQ+	6.48	0.80	6.00	9.00	120	6.00	6.00	0.11	-0.41
DQo	11.15	0.98	10.00	13.00	120	11.00	11.00	0.36	-0.92
DQv	1.63	[0.58]	0.00	3.00	89	2.00	1.00	0.28	-0.71
DQv/+	0.28	[0.45]	0.00	1.00	33	0.00	0.00	1.02	-0.98
FQX+	0.00	0.00	0.00	0.00	0	0.00	0.00	—	—
FQXo	14.37	1.46	12.00	18.00	120	15.00	14.00	0.24	-1.28
FQXu	2.08	0.69	1.00	3.00	120	2.00	2.00	-0.10	-0.86
FQX-	1.99	1.27	0.00	4.00	117	2.00	1.00	0.36	-1.18
FQXNone	1.10	[0.30]	0.00	3.00	72	1.00	1.00	2.70	5.38
MQ+	0.00	0.00	0.00	0.00	0	0.00	0.00	—	—
MQo	2.51	1.16	2.00	6.00	120	3.00	2.00	1.25	0.67
MQu	0.56	0.34	0.00	1.00	13	0.00	0.00	2.20	4.96
MQ-	0.45	[0.22]	0.00	2.00	28	0.00	0.00	2.18	11.75
MQNone	0.00	[0.00]	0.00	0.00	0	0.00	0.00	—	—
S-	0.12	[0.32]	0.00	1.00	14	0.00	0.00	2.42	3.91
M	3.02	1.22	2.00	6.00	120	3.00	2.00	1.15	0.12
FM	5.92	1.20	3.00	7.00	120	6.00	6.00	-1.11	0.14
m	1.06	0.40	0.00	2.00	114	1.00	1.00	0.52	3.35
FM+m	6.08	1.14	5.00	8.00	120	7.00	8.00	-0.80	-0.79
FC	2.17	0.93	1.00	4.00	120	2.00	2.00	0.27	-1.82
CF	3.19	0.98	1.00	6.00	120	3.00	3.00	-0.71	0.47
C	0.99	[0.30]	0.00	3.00	72	0.00	0.00	2.70	5.38
Cn	0.00	[0.00]	0.00	0.00	0	0.00	0.00	—	—
FC+CF+C+Cn	6.15	1.39	4.00	10.00	120	5.00	5.00	0.70	-1.11
WGSum C	4.97	1.14	3.00	7.00	120	4.00	4.00	0.16	-1.17
Sum C'	1.25	[0.86]	0.00	2.00	87	2.00	2.00	-0.51	-1.47
Sum T	0.93	[0.78]	0.00	2.00	110	1.00	1.00	0.42	4.14
Sum V	0.00	[0.00]	0.00	0.00	0	0.00	0.00	—	—
Sum Y	0.23	[0.42]	0.00	1.00	37	0.00	0.00	1.33	-0.23
SumShd	2.48	1.12	1.00	4.00	120	3.00	3.00	-0.05	-1.37
Fr+rF	0.30	[0.39]	0.00	2.00	22	0.00	0.00	2.70	5.38
FD	0.13	[0.70]	0.00	1.00	14	0.00	0.00	1.31	-2.94
F	7.62	1.60	3.00	10.00	120	7.00	8.00	-0.68	-0.31
PAIR	9.73	1.94	7.00	12.00	120	9.00	8.00	0.03	-1.75
3r(2)/R	0.65	0.12	0.33	0.90	120	0.62	0.60	0.14	0.28
LAMBDA	0.79	0.16	0.20	1.25	120	0.70	0.62	-0.17	-0.32
EA	7.48	1.04	4.00	9.00	120	8.00	7.00	-0.41	-1.07
es	8.56	1.67	4.00	12.00	120	8.00	7.00	0.01	-0.98
D	-0.53	0.67	-2.00	0.00	120	0.00	0.00	-0.92	-0.32
AdjD	-0.47	0.58	-2.00	0.00	120	0.00	0.00	-0.79	-0.35
a (active)	6.97	1.24	4.00	8.00	120	7.00	8.00	-1.00	-0.19
p (passive)	3.03	1.28	2.00	6.00	120	2.00	2.00	0.91	-0.50
Ma	2.82	0.87	2.00	5.00	120	3.00	2.00	0.84	-0.07
Mp	0.20	0.40	0.00	1.00	24	0.00	0.00	1.52	0.31
Intellect	0.27	0.44	0.00	1.00	120	0.00	0.00	1.07	-0.87
Zf	11.51	1.46	10.00	15.00	120	11.00	14.00	-0.08	-1.14
Zd	-1.04	2.41	-3.50	3.00	120	-1.00	-3.50	0.39	-1.46
Blends	5.11	0.65	3.00	7.00	120	4.00	5.00	-0.72	0.74
Col Shd Bl	0.36	[0.64]	0.00	1.00	20	0.00	0.00	2.12	8.35
Afr	0.79	0.09	0.45	0.83	120	0.67	0.75	0.02	-1.21
Popular	4.75	0.79	2.00	8.00	120	6.00	4.00	-0.35	-0.16

NOTE: Standard Deviations shown in brackets indicate that the value is probably unreliable and/or misleading and should not be used to estimate expected ranges. Ordinarily these variables should not be included in most parametric analyses.

(continued)

Table 22. (Continued)

			7 YEAR OLDS (N = 120)						
VARIABLE	MEAN	SD	MIN	MAX	FREQ	MEDIAN	MODE	SK	KU
X+%	0.81	0.05	0.45	0.89	120	0.82	0.76	−0.62	−0.33
F+%	0.66	0.17	0.33	0.88	120	0.63	0.88	−0.08	−0.98
X−%	0.08	0.07	0.10	0.30	107	0.09	0.12	0.33	−1.09
Xu%	0.11	0.03	0.05	0.15	120	0.11	0.11	−0.68	−0.56
S−%	0.15	[0.14]	0.00	0.50	24	0.00	0.00	2.60	5.18
Isolate	0.25	0.05	0.17	0.35	120	0.25	0.25	0.41	−1.08
H	1.87	0.79	1.00	3.00	120	1.00	1.00	0.65	−1.10
(H)	1.64	0.88	0.00	3.00	93	2.00	2.00	−0.29	−1.00
Hd	0.38	0.49	0.00	1.00	45	0.00	0.00	0.52	−1.76
(Hd)	0.74	0.87	0.00	3.00	63	1.00	0.00	1.15	0.71
Hx	0.00	[0.00]	0.00	0.00	0	0.00	0.00	—	—
All H Cont	4.63	0.89	2.00	7.00	120	5.00	4.00	0.17	−0.94
A	9.26	0.77	8.00	10.00	120	9.00	10.00	−0.48	−1.16
(A)	1.18	[0.81]	0.00	2.00	90	1.00	2.00	−0.35	−1.39
Ad	0.68	[0.79]	0.00	2.00	57	0.00	0.00	0.65	−1.10
(Ad)	0.05	[0.22]	0.00	1.00	6	0.00	0.00	4.18	15.75
An	0.37	[0.48]	0.00	1.00	44	0.00	0.00	0.56	−1.72
Art	0.10	0.30	0.00	1.00	12	0.00	0.00	2.70	5.38
Ay	0.17	[0.37]	0.00	1.00	20	0.00	0.00	1.81	1.30
Bl	0.48	[0.45]	0.00	2.00	43	0.00	0.00	1.02	−0.98
Bt	2.11	0.56	1.00	3.00	120	2.00	2.00	0.03	0.12
Cg	1.15	0.36	1.00	2.00	120	1.00	1.00	1.98	1.97
Cl	0.38	[0.57]	0.00	1.00	21	0.00	0.00	2.78	6.10
Ex	0.41	[0.64]	0.00	2.00	19	0.00	0.00	2.46	4.84
Fi	0.48	[0.50]	0.00	1.00	57	0.00	0.00	0.10	−2.02
Fd	0.20	[0.40]	0.00	1.00	24	0.00	0.00	1.52	0.31
Ge	0.00	[0.00]	0.00	0.00	0	0.00	0.00	—	—
Hh	1.45	0.88	0.00	3.00	58	1.00	1.00	0.73	1.40
Ls	1.21	0.93	0.00	3.00	92	1.00	1.00	0.93	1.59
Na	0.96	[0.77]	0.00	2.00	82	1.00	1.00	0.07	−1.31
Sc	1.54	[1.14]	0.00	4.00	96	1.00	1.00	0.39	−0.62
Sx	0.00	[0.00]	0.00	0.00	0	0.00	0.00	—	—
Xy	0.00	[0.00]	0.00	0.00	0	0.00	0.00	—	—
Idio	0.53	0.59	0.00	2.00	57	0.00	0.00	0.64	−0.53
DV	1.39	[0.49]	1.00	2.00	120	1.00	1.00	0.45	−1.83
INCOM	1.39	[0.58]	0.00	2.00	114	1.00	1.00	−0.34	−0.71
DR	0.46	[0.63]	0.00	2.00	56	0.00	0.00	1.06	0.06
FABCOM	0.49	[0.46]	0.00	3.00	55	0.00	0.00	0.93	−1.16
DV2	0.00	[0.00]	0.00	0.00	0	0.00	0.00	—	—
INC2	0.29	[0.57]	0.00	1.00	13	0.00	0.00	2.58	5.05
DR2	0.10	[0.34]	0.00	1.00	7	0.00	0.00	2.98	7.45
FAB2	0.08	[0.26]	0.00	1.00	9	0.00	0.00	3.27	8.83
ALOG	0.48	[0.49]	0.00	2.00	55	0.00	0.00	0.52	−1.76
CONTAM	0.01	0.09	0.00	1.00	1	0.00	0.00	10.95	120.00
Sum6 Sp Sc	5.92	1.25	1.00	7.00	120	5.00	5.00	−0.31	−0.12
Sum6 Sp Sc2	0.18	[0.26]	0.00	1.00	19	0.00	0.00	3.27	8.83
WSum6	12.18	4.66	1.00	29.00	120	10.00	4.00	0.86	0.69
AB	0.00	[0.00]	0.00	0.00	0	0.00	0.00	—	—
AG	1.20	0.40	1.00	2.00	120	1.00	1.00	1.52	0.31
CFB	0.00	0.00	0.00	0.00	0	0.00	0.00	—	—
COP	1.57	0.59	0.00	4.00	108	2.00	2.00	−0.06	−0.28
CP	0.00	[0.00]	0.00	0.00	0	0.00	0.00	—	—
MOR	1.64	[0.58]	1.00	3.00	120	2.00	2.00	0.23	−0.70
PER	2.22	0.57	1.00	4.00	120	1.00	2.00	2.51	4.94
PSV	0.54	[0.50]	0.00	1.00	65	1.00	1.00	−0.17	−2.01

Table 22. (Continued)

8 YEAR OLDS (N = 120)

VARIABLE	MEAN	SD	MIN	MAX	FREQ	MEDIAN	MODE	SK	KU
R	18.73	2.46	14.00	23.00	120	18.00	16.00	0.21	-1.57
W	10.03	1.01	6.00	11.00	120	11.00	8.00	0.55	-1.05
D	7.00	1.28	7.00	11.00	120	7.00	7.00	0.41	-1.12
Dd	1.70	[0.84]	0.00	3.00	104	1.00	0.00	0.40	-1.47
S	1.73	[0.58]	1.00	3.00	119	2.00	2.00	0.08	-0.43
DQ+	6.80	1.74	4.00	10.00	120	6.00	6.00	0.64	-0.57
DQo	11.27	1.40	9.00	14.00	120	12.00	12.00	-0.04	-0.68
DQv	0.90	[0.62]	0.00	3.00	99	1.00	1.00	0.50	-0.59
DQv/+	0.17	[0.25]	0.00	1.00	19	0.00	0.00	3.56	11.07
FQX+	0.00	0.00	0.00	0.00	0	0.00	0.00	—	—
FQXo	13.22	1.83	10.00	17.00	120	13.00	12.00	0.44	-0.37
FQXu	3.47	1.37	2.00	6.00	120	4.00	2.00	0.24	-1.34
FQX–	1.72	0.76	1.00	4.00	120	2.00	1.00	0.53	-1.07
FQXNone	0.43	[0.48]	0.00	1.00	43	0.00	0.00	0.73	-1.53
MQ+	0.00	0.00	0.00	0.00	0	0.00	0.00	—	—
MQo	3.12	1.62	1.00	6.00	120	2.00	2.00	0.68	-0.97
MQu	0.20	0.40	0.00	1.00	24	0.00	0.00	1.54	0.38
MQ–	0.07	[0.25]	0.00	1.00	10	0.00	0.00	3.56	11.07
MQNone	0.00	[0.00]	0.00	0.00	0	0.00	0.00	—	—
S–	0.13	[0.34]	0.00	1.00	29	0.00	0.00	2.21	3.00
M	3.38	1.85	1.00	7.00	120	3.00	2.00	0.79	-0.49
FM	4.72	1.37	3.00	8.00	120	4.00	4.00	0.71	-0.30
m	0.57	0.50	0.00	3.00	57	0.00	0.00	0.14	-2.05
FM+m	5.28	1.56	3.00	8.00	120	5.00	4.00	0.20	-1.29
FC	1.80	0.84	1.00	3.00	120	2.00	1.00	0.40	-1.47
CF	2.73	0.78	1.00	4.00	120	3.00	3.00	-0.38	-0.01
C	0.43	[0.48]	0.00	1.00	43	0.00	0.00	0.73	-1.53
Cn	0.00	[0.00]	0.00	0.00	0	0.00	0.00	—	—
FC+CF+C+Cn	4.87	0.72	3.00	6.00	120	5.00	5.00	-0.90	1.37
WGSum C	4.13	0.77	3.00	6.00	120	4.00	3.50	0.80	0.22
Sum C'	1.30	[0.89]	0.00	3.00	102	1.00	1.00	0.92	-0.26
Sum T	1.08	[0.60]	0.00	2.00	107	1.00	1.00	0.76	2.58
Sum V	0.00	[0.00]	0.00	0.00	0	0.00	0.00	—	—
Sum Y	0.92	[0.85]	0.00	2.00	68	1.00	0.00	0.37	-1.54
SumShd	2.90	1.47	1.00	5.00	120	2.00	2.00	0.18	-1.46
Fr+rF	0.33	[0.48]	0.00	1.00	33	0.00	0.00	0.73	-1.53
FD	0.53	[0.34]	0.00	2.00	39	0.00	0.00	2.21	3.00
F	6.98	1.64	5.00	10.00	120	7.00	7.00	0.67	-0.58
PAIR	7.97	1.19	6.00	10.00	120	8.00	8.00	0.07	-0.60
3r(2)/R	0.62	0.12	0.30	0.90	120	0.67	0.60	0.28	0.39
LAMBDA	0.77	0.27	0.29	1.35	120	0.65	0.70	0.91	-0.21
EA	7.51	1.45	4.00	11.50	120	7.00	6.50	0.48	-0.31
es	8.18	2.51	4.00	12.00	120	7.00	6.00	0.07	-1.31
D	-0.22	0.64	-2.00	1.00	120	0.00	0.00	-1.38	2.44
AdjD	-0.15	0.61	-2.00	1.00	120	0.00	0.00	-1.82	4.40
a (active)	6.73	1.63	4.00	10.00	120	6.00	6.00	0.15	-0.34
p (passive)	1.93	1.30	0.00	5.00	112	2.00	1.00	0.89	0.20
Ma	3.12	1.66	1.00	6.00	120	3.00	2.00	0.52	-1.01
Mp	0.37	0.45	0.00	2.00	46	0.00	0.00	1.08	-0.86
Intellect	0.46	0.98	0.00	1.50	120	0.00	0.00	2.46	3.15
Zf	11.27	1.49	10.00	15.00	120	12.00	11.00	0.28	-1.27
Zd	-0.70	1.93	-4.50	5.00	120	-1.00	0.00	1.23	3.73
Blends	4.88	1.03	3.00	6.00	120	5.00	5.00	-0.54	-0.82
Col Shd Bl	0.30	[0.40]	0.00	1.00	34	0.00	0.00	1.54	0.38
Afr	0.69	0.09	0.36	0.90	120	0.68	0.63	0.64	0.00
Popular	5.68	0.80	3.00	7.00	120	6.00	6.00	-0.57	-1.22

NOTE: Standard Deviations shown in brackets indicate that the value is probably unreliable and/or misleading and should not be used to estimate expected ranges. Ordinarily these variables should not be included in most parametric analyses.

(continued)

Table 22.   (Continued)

8 YEAR OLDS (N = 120)

VARIABLE	MEAN	SD	MIN	MAX	FREQ	MEDIAN	MODE	SK	KU
X+%	0.77	0.07	0.45	0.85	120	0.75	0.70	0.02	−1.34
F+%	0.59	0.07	0.43	0.71	120	0.60	0.60	−0.47	0.10
X−%	0.10	0.04	0.05	0.25	120	0.09	0.06	0.82	−0.25
Xu%	0.13	0.06	0.12	0.32	120	0.16	0.13	0.91	−0.12
S−%	0.06	[0.15]	0.00	0.50	24	0.00	0.00	2.38	4.02
Isolate	0.23	0.04	0.14	0.27	120	0.24	0.19	−0.66	−0.44
H	1.87	1.03	1.00	4.00	120	1.00	1.00	0.66	−1.06
(H)	1.47	0.62	1.00	3.00	120	1.00	1.00	1.00	0.00
Hd	0.27	0.45	0.00	1.00	32	0.00	0.00	1.08	−0.86
(Hd)	1.20	0.55	1.00	3.00	120	1.00	1.00	2.69	6.06
Hx	0.00	[0.00]	0.00	0.00	0	0.00	0.00	—	—
All H Cont	4.80	1.92	3.00	9.00	120	4.00	3.00	0.89	−0.41
A	9.27	1.45	7.00	12.00	120	9.00	8.00	0.35	−1.06
(A)	1.73	[0.58]	1.00	3.00	120	2.00	2.00	0.08	−0.43
Ad	0.33	[0.48]	0.00	1.00	40	0.00	0.00	0.73	−1.53
(Ad)	0.13	[0.34]	0.00	1.00	16	0.00	0.00	2.21	3.00
An	0.20	[0.40]	0.00	1.00	24	0.00	0.00	1.54	0.38
Art	0.59	0.64	0.00	1.00	13	0.00	0.00	2.41	4.58
Ay	0.10	[0.35]	0.00	1.00	4	0.00	0.00	4.87	11.65
Bl	0.33	[0.48]	0.00	1.00	40	0.00	0.00	0.73	−1.53
Bt	1.45	0.65	0.00	3.00	118	1.00	1.00	0.77	0.10
Cg	1.80	1.18	1.00	4.00	120	1.00	1.00	0.92	−0.92
Cl	0.13	[0.34]	0.00	1.00	16	0.00	0.00	2.21	3.00
Ex	0.43	[0.34]	0.00	2.00	35	0.00	0.00	2.20	3.13
Fi	0.33	[0.48]	0.00	1.00	40	0.00	0.00	0.73	−1.53
Fd	0.20	[0.40]	0.00	1.00	41	0.00	0.00	1.54	0.38
Ge	0.00	[0.00]	0.00	0.00	0	0.00	0.00	—	—
Hh	0.45	0.36	0.00	3.00	48	0.00	0.00	1.01	2.11
Ls	0.93	0.25	0.00	1.00	112	1.00	1.00	−3.56	11.07
Na	0.80	[0.40]	0.00	1.00	96	1.00	1.00	−1.54	0.38
Sc	2.45	[0.62]	1.00	3.00	120	3.00	3.00	−0.68	−0.46
Sx	0.00	[0.00]	0.00	0.00	0	0.00	0.00	—	—
Xy	0.00	[0.00]	0.00	0.00	0	0.00	0.00	—	—
Idio	0.53	0.62	0.00	2.00	56	0.00	0.00	0.74	−0.40
DV	1.33	[0.71]	0.00	2.00	104	1.00	2.00	−0.58	−0.80
INCOM	2.07	[0.45]	1.00	3.00	120	2.00	2.00	0.32	2.18
DR	0.47	[0.62]	0.00	2.00	48	0.00	0.00	1.00	0.00
FABCOM	0.55	[0.89]	0.00	3.00	84	1.00	1.00	1.63	1.78
DV2	0.07	[0.25]	0.00	1.00	7	0.00	0.00	3.56	11.07
INC2	0.13	[0.34]	0.00	1.00	15	0.00	0.00	2.21	3.00
DR2	0.00	[0.00]	0.00	0.00	0	0.00	0.00	—	—
FAB2	0.13	[0.34]	0.00	1.00	16	0.00	0.00	2.21	3.00
ALOG	0.73	[0.45]	0.00	1.00	88	1.00	1.00	−1.08	−0.86
CONTAM	0.00	0.00	0.00	0.00	0	0.00	0.00	—	—
Sum6 Sp Sc	6.15	1.96	2.00	10.00	120	6.00	5.00	0.74	0.52
Sum6 Sp Sc2	0.33	[0.48]	0.00	1.00	27	0.00	0.00	0.73	−1.53
WSum6	14.33	5.12	5.00	28.00	120	14.00	13.00	0.72	1.86
AB	0.00	[0.00]	0.00	0.00	0	0.00	0.00	—	—
AG	0.93	0.58	0.00	4.00	96	1.00	1.00	−0.00	0.11
CFB	0.00	0.00	0.00	0.00	0	0.00	0.00	—	—
COP	1.93	1.01	1.00	4.00	120	2.00	1.00	0.55	−1.05
CP	0.08	[0.40]	0.00	1.00	2	0.00	0.00	3.17	16.45
MOR	1.13	[0.34]	1.00	3.00	120	1.00	1.00	2.21	3.00
PER	0.33	0.48	0.00	2.00	40	0.00	0.00	0.73	−1.53
PSV	0.46	[0.78]	0.00	2.00	18	0.00	0.00	2.74	9.86

Table 22.   (Continued)

9 YEAR OLDS (N = 140)

VARIABLE	MEAN	SD	MIN	MAX	FREQ	MEDIAN	MODE	SK	KU
R	20.53	2.46	14.00	26.00	140	21.00	19.00	0.41	0.57
W	10.33	1.57	6.00	12.00	140	11.00	9.00	0.55	0.05
D	9.00	1.28	7.00	13.00	140	9.00	8.00	0.41	0.84
Dd	1.20	[0.84]	0.00	4.00	102	1.00	0.00	0.40	3.47
S	1.73	[0.58]	0.00	4.00	108	2.00	1.00	1.78	3.43
DQ+	6.40	1.94	3.00	12.00	138	7.00	6.00	0.64	2.57
DQo	11.67	1.80	7.00	14.00	140	11.00	10.00	-0.04	-0.68
DQv	1.61	[0.65]	0.00	4.00	72	1.00	0.00	0.50	-0.59
DQv/+	0.45	[0.65]	0.00	1.00	23	0.00	0.00	3.56	11.07
FQX+	0.26	0.31	0.00	1.00	5	0.00	0.00	4.18	13.67
FQXo	14.22	1.83	10.00	18.00	140	14.00	12.00	0.44	-0.37
FQXu	3.49	1.37	2.00	6.00	140	4.00	2.00	0.24	-1.34
FQX-	2.04	0.76	1.00	3.00	140	2.00	1.00	0.53	-1.07
FQXNone	0.38	[0.48]	0.00	2.00	31	0.00	0.00	0.73	-1.53
MQ+	0.00	0.00	0.00	0.00	0	0.00	0.00	—	—
MQo	3.12	1.62	1.00	6.00	140	2.00	2.00	0.68	-0.97
MQu	0.20	0.40	0.00	1.00	22	0.00	0.00	1.54	0.38
MQ-	0.37	[0.25]	0.00	2.00	7	0.00	0.00	3.27	10.61
MQNone	0.00	[0.00]	0.00	0.00	0	0.00	0.00	—	—
S-	0.13	[0.34]	0.00	1.00	29	0.00	0.00	2.21	3.00
M	3.12	1.85	1.00	7.00	140	3.00	2.00	0.79	-0.49
FM	4.22	1.47	3.00	9.00	140	4.00	4.00	0.71	0.64
m	0.67	0.58	0.00	3.00	66	0.00	0.00	0.14	3.65
FM+m	5.64	1.86	2.00	9.00	140	6.00	4.00	0.20	0.59
FC	1.89	0.86	0.00	3.00	131	2.00	1.00	0.40	2.47
CF	2.79	0.78	1.00	4.00	140	3.00	2.00	-0.38	2.01
C	0.43	[0.48]	0.00	2.00	22	0.00	0.00	0.73	2.53
Cn	0.00	[0.00]	0.00	0.00	0	0.00	0.00	—	—
FC+CF+C+Cn	4.15	0.72	3.00	9.00	140	6.00	5.00	-0.90	1.37
WGSum C	5.13	1.07	2.50	7.50	140	4.00	3.50	0.80	0.22
Sum C'	1.16	[0.79]	0.00	4.00	104	1.00	1.00	0.92	1.66
Sum T	0.97	[0.63]	0.00	2.00	123	1.00	1.00	0.24	3.58
Sum V	0.00	[0.00]	0.00	0.00	0	0.00	0.00	—	—
Sum Y	0.83	[0.85]	0.00	3.00	102	1.00	1.00	0.37	-1.76
SumShd	2.96	1.27	1.00	6.00	140	2.00	2.00	0.18	-1.46
Fr+rF	0.42	[0.43]	0.00	1.00	26	0.00	0.00	0.73	2.53
FD	0.63	[0.34]	0.00	1.00	64	0.00	0.00	2.45	3.13
F	9.14	1.84	5.00	11.00	140	8.00	8.00	0.67	-0.58
PAIR	8.97	1.69	5.00	12.00	140	9.00	8.00	0.07	-0.60
3r(2)/R	0.57	0.12	0.30	0.88	140	0.60	0.55	0.18	0.54
LAMBDA	0.81	0.37	0.29	1.45	140	0.85	0.70	0.91	0.21
EA	8.25	1.95	4.00	11.50	140	8.00	6.50	0.38	0.56
es	8.60	2.59	4.00	13.00	140	7.00	6.00	0.07	1.31
D	-0.18	0.54	-3.00	1.00	140	0.00	0.00	1.18	1.44
AdjD	-0.10	0.41	-2.00	1.00	140	0.00	0.00	-1.32	3.44
a (active)	6.26	1.23	3.00	11.00	140	7.00	6.00	0.12	0.30
p (passive)	2.51	1.40	0.00	5.00	76	2.00	1.00	0.89	0.70
Ma	2.72	1.36	1.00	6.00	134	3.00	2.00	0.52	-1.01
Mp	0.27	0.45	0.00	1.00	61	0.00	0.00	1.28	1.86
Intellect	1.03	0.98	0.00	1.00	140	0.00	0.00	2.68	10.89
Zf	11.16	1.54	7.00	15.00	140	11.00	11.00	0.28	0.47
Zd	0.40	2.03	-4.50	6.00	140	0.00	0.00	0.23	0.73
Blends	4.38	1.23	2.00	7.00	140	5.00	5.00	-0.44	-0.92
Col Shd Bl	0.90	[0.56]	0.00	3.00	59	0.00	0.00	1.04	0.34
Afr	0.79	0.13	0.38	1.05	140	0.76	0.68	-0.44	0.03
Popular	5.78	0.63	4.00	7.00	140	6.00	5.00	-0.52	-1.02

NOTE: Standard Deviations shown in brackets indicate that the value is probably unreliable and/or misleading and should not be used to estimate expected ranges. Ordinarily these variables should not be included in most parametric analyses.

(continued)

Table 22. (Continued)

9 YEAR OLDS (N = 140)

VARIABLE	MEAN	SD	MIN	MAX	FREQ	MEDIAN	MODE	SK	KU
X+%	0.77	0.09	0.53	0.90	140	0.76	0.71	–0.02	0.64
F+%	0.70	0.08	0.43	1.00	140	0.75	0.67	–0.37	0.15
X–%	0.08	0.06	0.05	0.25	140	0.07	0.09	–0.32	0.25
Xu%	0.15	0.07	0.10	0.33	140	0.18	0.15	0.81	–0.15
S–%	0.06	[0.15]	0.00	1.00	29	0.00	0.00	1.34	4.22
Isolate	0.16	0.05	0.06	0.32	140	0.14	0.17	–0.67	–0.34
H	2.87	1.03	0.00	6.00	138	2.00	2.00	0.66	–1.06
(H)	1.32	0.61	1.00	3.00	140	1.00	1.00	0.84	1.25
Hd	0.57	0.40	0.00	2.00	46	0.00	0.00	1.58	0.36
(Hd)	0.74	0.58	0.00	2.00	62	0.00	0.00	1.60	4.06
Hx	0.00	[0.00]	0.00	0.00	0	0.00	0.00	——	——
All H Cont	5.50	1.62	2.00	8.00	140	5.00	4.00	0.59	–0.41
A	8.28	1.59	5.00	13.00	140	9.00	8.00	0.35	0.06
(A)	0.73	[0.68]	0.00	3.00	101	1.00	1.00	0.28	1.63
Ad	0.53	[0.98]	0.00	2.00	80	1.00	1.00	–0.63	2.73
(Ad)	0.23	[0.39]	0.00	1.00	13	0.00	0.00	3.27	4.00
An	0.36	[0.60]	0.00	3.00	34	0.00	0.00	2.54	2.38
Art	0.32	0.71	0.00	2.00	31	0.00	0.00	1.38	3.09
Ay	0.13	[0.28]	0.00	1.00	11	0.00	0.00	3.94	8.28
Bl	0.33	[0.48]	0.00	1.00	28	0.00	0.00	1.03	1.33
Bt	1.45	0.65	0.00	3.00	129	1.00	1.00	0.97	1.10
Cg	1.84	1.08	1.00	4.00	133	1.00	1.00	0.92	1.92
Cl	0.16	[0.39]	0.00	1.00	40	0.00	0.00	2.01	3.34
Ex	0.26	[0.54]	0.00	1.00	21	0.00	0.00	1.93	4.06
Fi	0.69	[0.68]	0.00	1.00	68	0.00	0.00	0.33	2.73
Fd	0.18	[0.46]	0.00	1.00	15	0.00	0.00	2.54	4.38
Ge	0.00	[0.00]	0.00	0.00	0	0.00	0.00	——	——
Hh	0.59	0.36	0.00	1.00	49	0.00	0.00	2.11	2.07
Ls	0.93	0.59	0.00	3.00	107	1.00	1.00	–0.28	0.83
Na	0.70	[0.48]	0.00	2.00	96	1.00	1.00	–0.54	1.38
Sc	1.55	[0.72]	0.00	3.00	102	2.00	1.00	0.68	2.46
Sx	0.00	[0.00]	0.00	0.00	0	0.00	0.00	——	——
Xy	0.00	[0.00]	0.00	0.00	0	0.00	0.00	——	——
Idio	0.63	0.42	0.00	1.00	48	0.00	0.00	0.84	1.40
DV	1.01	[0.61]	0.00	2.00	97	1.00	1.00	–0.08	2.80
INCOM	1.37	[0.75]	0.00	3.00	81	1.00	1.00	0.32	2.18
DR	0.67	[0.72]	0.00	2.00	91	1.00	1.00	–0.73	2.00
FABCOM	1.05	[0.89]	0.00	3.00	102	1.00	1.00	0.63	1.68
DV2	0.07	[0.21]	0.00	1.00	6	0.00	0.00	1.56	12.07
INC2	0.11	[0.59]	0.00	1.00	7	0.00	0.00	1.27	11.40
DR2	0.00	[0.00]	0.00	0.00	0	0.00	0.00	——	——
FAB2	0.05	[0.39]	0.00	1.00	3	0.00	0.00	0.68	13.00
ALOG	0.61	[0.49]	0.00	1.00	56	0.00	0.00	1.08	3.86
CONTAM	0.00	0.00	0.00	0.00	0	0.00	0.00	——	——
Sum6 Sp Sc	5.95	2.16	1.00	9.00	140	6.00	6.00	0.74	0.52
Sum6 Sp Sc2	0.27	[0.51]	0.00	2.00	14	0.00	0.00	0.63	6.53
WSum6	13.06	4.72	3.00	26.00	140	12.00	11.00	0.92	0.86
AB	0.00	[0.00]	0.00	0.00	0	0.00	0.00	——	——
AG	1.37	0.78	0.00	4.00	128	2.00	1.00	0.67	1.11
CFB	0.00	0.00	0.00	0.00	0	0.00	0.00	——	——
COP	2.03	1.14	0.00	5.00	136	2.00	2.00	0.18	1.05
CP	0.00	[0.00]	0.00	0.00	0	0.00	0.00	——	——
MOR	0.87	[0.64]	0.00	4.00	116	1.00	1.00	–0.41	1.87
PER	1.16	0.78	0.00	6.00	99	1.00	1.00	0.73	–1.53
PSV	0.26	[0.61]	0.00	2.00	29	0.00	0.00	1.04	4.14

Table 22. (Continued)

10 YEAR OLDS (N = 120)

VARIABLE	MEAN	SD	MIN	MAX	FREQ	MEDIAN	MODE	SK	KU
R	20.97	1.92	18.00	25.00	120	19.00	19.00	0.85	−0.39
W	9.52	0.87	9.00	12.00	120	9.00	9.00	1.59	1.46
D	10.10	1.48	8.00	13.00	120	10.00	9.00	0.31	−1.32
Dd	1.35	[0.44]	0.00	3.00	119	0.00	0.00	1.17	−0.64
S	1.48	[0.70]	1.00	3.00	107	1.00	1.00	1.12	−0.08
DQ+	7.68	0.96	3.00	9.00	120	8.00	7.00	−0.48	−0.18
DQo	12.07	1.78	9.00	17.00	120	12.00	11.00	0.08	0.01
DQv	0.53	[0.50]	0.00	2.00	64	1.00	1.00	−0.14	−2.02
DQv/+	0.38	[0.28]	0.00	1.00	36	0.00	0.00	3.05	7.45
FQX+	0.30	0.50	0.00	1.00	11	0.00	0.00	4.04	9.15
FQXo	15.80	1.98	13.00	21.00	120	15.00	15.00	0.81	0.33
FQXu	2.95	0.79	1.00	4.00	120	3.00	3.00	−0.54	0.12
FQX−	1.58	1.03	0.00	6.00	104	2.00	2.00	1.74	6.56
FQXNone	0.13	[0.34]	0.00	1.00	29	0.00	0.00	2.19	2.82
MQ+	0.08	0.21	0.00	1.00	2	0.00	0.00	4.80	13.25
MQo	3.23	1.48	1.00	6.00	120	3.00	3.00	0.22	−0.78
MQu	0.25	0.44	0.00	1.00	30	0.00	0.00	1.17	−0.64
MQ−	0.17	[0.37]	0.00	2.00	21	0.00	0.00	1.81	1.30
MQNone	0.00	[0.00]	0.00	0.00	0	0.00	0.00	—	—
S−	0.12	[0.32]	0.00	1.00	14	0.00	0.00	2.42	3.91
M	3.65	1.63	1.00	7.00	120	4.00	3.00	−0.04	−0.69
FM	5.53	1.46	3.00	7.00	120	6.00	7.00	−0.43	−1.38
m	1.08	0.28	1.00	2.00	120	1.00	1.00	3.05	7.45
FM+m	6.62	1.40	4.00	8.00	120	7.00	8.00	−0.56	−1.06
FC	2.55	0.96	1.00	4.00	120	2.00	2.00	0.44	−1.03
CF	3.68	1.29	2.00	6.00	120	3.50	5.00	0.14	−1.27
C	0.13	[0.34]	0.00	2.00	29	0.00	0.00	2.19	2.82
Cn	0.00	[0.00]	0.00	0.00	0	0.00	0.00	—	—
FC+CF+C+Cn	6.37	1.50	4.00	8.00	120	7.00	8.00	−0.41	−1.30
WGSum C	5.16	1.25	3.00	7.00	120	5.00	4.00	−0.23	−1.26
Sum C'	0.79	[0.85]	0.00	4.00	73	1.00	1.00	0.41	0.44
Sum T	0.98	[0.39]	0.00	2.00	106	1.00	1.00	−0.16	3.86
Sum V	0.02	[0.13]	0.00	1.00	2	0.00	0.00	7.65	57.43
Sum Y	0.43	[0.65]	0.00	2.00	34	0.00	0.00	0.82	−0.37
SumShd	1.83	1.32	1.00	6.00	120	3.00	4.00	0.06	−1.16
Fr+rF	0.35	[0.36]	0.00	1.00	36	0.00	0.00	1.98	1.97
FD	0.67	[0.58]	0.00	2.00	78	1.00	1.00	1.33	0.81
F	6.38	2.04	3.00	12.00	120	5.50	5.00	0.57	−0.73
PAIR	9.62	1.36	6.00	12.00	120	9.00	9.00	−0.29	0.09
3r(2)/R	0.54	0.07	0.29	0.68	120	0.52	0.47	−0.71	6.30
LAMBDA	0.49	0.23	0.19	1.11	120	0.36	0.36	0.90	−0.23
EA	8.81	1.36	4.00	11.00	120	9.00	7.00	−0.37	1.09
es	8.45	1.90	5.00	12.00	120	8.00	7.00	−0.33	−0.89
D	−0.15	0.44	−2.00	1.00	120	0.00	0.00	−1.89	5.07
AdjD	−0.12	0.49	−2.00	1.00	120	0.00	0.00	−1.17	3.81
a (active)	7.15	1.37	6.00	11.00	120	8.00	7.00	0.32	−0.74
p (passive)	3.27	0.66	1.00	4.00	120	2.00	2.00	1.46	1.91
Ma	2.82	1.09	1.00	5.00	120	3.00	3.00	−0.10	−0.63
Mp	0.98	0.83	0.00	3.00	88	1.00	1.00	0.93	0.76
Intellect	0.53	0.56	0.00	2.00	120	0.50	0.00	0.44	−0.81
Zf	13.52	1.19	11.00	16.00	120	13.50	13.00	−0.19	−0.27
Zd	−0.13	2.32	−5.00	5.00	120	0.00	−3.00	0.22	−0.35
Blends	5.80	1.05	3.00	7.00	120	6.00	7.00	−0.39	−0.70
Col Shd Blend	0.42	[0.13]	0.00	1.00	22	0.00	0.00	7.65	57.43
Afr	0.63	0.09	0.50	0.85	120	0.58	0.58	0.94	−0.05
Popular	6.07	0.84	3.00	7.00	120	6.00	6.00	−1.01	1.55s

NOTE: Standard Deviations shown in brackets indicate that the value is probably unreliable and/or misleading and should not be used to estimate expected ranges. Ordinarily these variables should not be included in most parametric analyses.

(continued)

Table 22.   (Continued)

							10 YEAR OLDS	(N = 120)
VARIABLE	MEAN	SD	MIN	MAX	FREQ	MEDIAN	MODE	SK	KU
---	---	---	---	---	---	---	---	---	---
X+%	0.76	0.08	0.45	0.88	120	0.79	0.75	−0.86	1.39
F+%	0.55	0.14	0.33	0.82	120	0.50	0.50	0.39	−1.03
X−%	0.08	0.06	0.00	0.25	104	0.07	0.05	1.46	5.42
Xu%	0.15	0.05	0.05	0.21	120	0.16	0.16	−0.44	−0.53
S−%	0.12	[0.14]	0.00	1.00	34	0.00	0.00	2.82	6.34
Isolate	0.19	0.03	0.14	0.26	120	0.19	0.16	0.67	−0.53
H	2.47	1.12	1.00	5.00	120	3.00	3.00	0.01	−0.83
(H)	1.48	0.74	0.00	2.00	102	2.00	2.00	−1.06	−0.37
Hd	0.25	0.47	0.00	2.00	28	0.00	0.00	1.65	1.80
(Hd)	0.85	0.36	0.00	1.00	102	1.00	1.00	−1.98	1.97
Hx	0.00	[0.00]	0.00	0.00	0	0.00	0.00	—	—
All H Cont	5.05	1.64	2.00	8.00	120	6.00	6.00	−0.59	−0.59
A	8.92	1.18	7.00	11.00	120	9.00	9.00	0.54	−0.43
(A)	1.20	[0.77]	0.00	3.00	96	1.00	1.00	−0.14	−0.88
Ad	1.35	[1.08]	0.00	3.00	76	2.00	2.00	−0.25	−1.49
(Ad)	0.07	[0.25]	0.00	1.00	8	0.00	0.00	3.52	10.56
An	0.67	[0.57]	0.00	2.00	74	1.00	1.00	0.14	−0.66
Art	0.53	0.56	0.00	2.00	60	0.50	0.00	0.44	−0.81
Ay	0.23	[0.41]	0.00	1.00	12	0.00	0.00	2.95	11.25
Bl	0.60	[0.59]	0.00	2.00	66	1.00	1.00	0.37	−0.70
Bt	2.17	0.74	1.00	4.00	120	2.00	2.00	0.49	0.33
Cg	1.48	1.03	0.00	3.00	102	1.00	1.00	0.33	−1.10
Cl	0.08	[0.28]	0.00	1.00	10	0.00	0.00	3.05	7.45
Ex	0.08	[0.28]	0.00	1.00	10	0.00	0.00	3.05	7.45
Fi	0.75	[0.44]	0.00	1.00	90	1.00	1.00	−1.17	−0.64
Fd	0.53	[0.50]	0.00	1.00	64	1.00	1.00	−0.14	−2.02
Ge	0.00	[0.00]	0.00	0.00	0	0.00	0.00	—	—
Hh	0.60	0.49	0.00	1.00	72	1.00	1.00	−0.41	−1.86
Ls	1.00	0.45	0.00	2.00	108	1.00	1.00	0.00	2.14
Na	0.30	[0.46]	0.00	1.00	36	0.00	0.00	0.88	−1.24
Sc	2.85	[0.40]	2.00	4.00	120	3.00	3.00	−1.17	1.62
Sx	0.00	[0.00]	0.00	0.00	0	0.00	0.00	—	—
Xy	0.00	[0.00]	0.00	0.00	0	0.00	0.00	—	—
Idio	0.08	0.28	0.00	1.00	10	0.00	0.00	3.05	7.45
DV	1.03	[0.61]	1.00	3.00	112	1.00	1.00	1.72	4.91
INCOM	1.35	[0.51]	1.00	3.00	103	1.00	1.00	1.01	−0.16
DR	0.18	[0.28]	0.00	1.00	30	0.00	0.00	3.05	7.45
FABCOM	0.65	[0.48]	0.00	1.00	82	0.00	0.00	0.64	−1.62
DV2	0.00	[0.00]	0.00	0.00	0	0.00	0.00	—	—
INC2	0.23	[0.43]	0.00	1.00	5	0.00	0.00	1.28	−0.38
DR2	0.02	[0.13]	0.00	1.00	2	0.00	0.00	7.65	57.43
FAB2	0.02	[0.09]	0.00	1.00	1	0.00	0.00	8.31	69.82
ALOG	0.47	[0.48]	0.00	1.00	49	0.00	0.00	0.56	−1.72
CONTAM	0.00	0.00	0.00	0.00	0	0.00	0.00	—	—
Sum6 Sp Sc	5.15	1.20	2.00	8.00	120	4.00	4.00	1.37	0.95
Sum6 Sp Sc2	0.09	[0.44]	0.00	1.00	10	0.00	0.00	1.17	−0.64
WSum6	10.22	3.79	3.00	17.00	120	7.00	7.00	1.08	0.65
AB	0.08	[0.28]	0.00	1.00	2	0.00	0.00	4.15	10.34
AG	1.57	0.62	1.00	3.00	120	1.50	1.00	0.61	−0.55
CFB	0.00	0.00	0.00	0.00	0	0.00	0.00	—	—
COP	1.73	0.84	1.00	4.00	120	2.00	2.00	1.41	1.94
CP	0.00	[0.00]	0.00	0.00	0	0.00	0.00	—	—
MOR	0.75	[0.62]	0.00	3.00	78	1.00	1.00	0.67	−0.50
PER	0.75	0.44	0.00	1.00	90	1.00	1.00	−1.17	−0.64
PSV	0.05	[0.22]	0.00	1.00	6	0.00	0.00	4.18	15.75

Table 22. (Continued)

11 YEAR OLDS (N = 135)

VARIABLE	MEAN	SD	MIN	MAX	FREQ	MEDIAN	MODE	SK	KU
R	21.29	2.43	15.00	27.00	135	22.00	19.00	0.93	0.29
W	9.61	0.95	9.00	12.00	135	9.00	9.00	1.49	1.06
D	10.01	1.31	9.00	13.00	135	11.00	11.00	0.05	−1.09
Dd	1.67	[1.13]	0.00	4.00	128	0.00	0.00	2.12	3.75
S	1.75	[0.68]	1.00	3.00	135	2.00	2.00	0.36	−0.81
DQ+	8.07	1.22	6.00	10.00	135	8.00	7.00	0.10	−1.08
DQo	12.08	2.14	9.00	17.00	135	12.00	11.00	0.73	0.25
DQv	0.64	[0.88]	0.00	3.00	63	0.00	0.00	1.57	1.99
DQv/+	0.50	[0.69]	0.00	2.00	41	0.00	0.00	1.98	2.39
FQX+	0.21	0.38	0.00	1.00	9	0.00	0.00	3.08	11.42
FQXo	15.83	1.40	13.00	18.00	135	16.00	17.00	−0.29	−1.09
FQXu	3.18	1.26	1.00	6.00	135	3.00	3.00	0.52	0.49
FQX−	2.20	1.87	0.00	7.00	125	2.00	2.00	1.73	2.02
FQXNone	0.18	[0.27]	0.00	1.00	18	0.00	0.00	3.09	7.69
MQ+	0.11	0.45	0.00	1.00	3	0.00	0.00	4.24	13.85
MQo	3.59	1.38	1.00	6.00	135	4.00	3.00	−0.15	−0.69
MQu	0.33	0.47	0.00	1.00	44	0.00	0.00	0.75	−1.46
MQ−	0.20	[0.40]	0.00	1.00	27	0.00	0.00	1.52	0.30
MQNone	0.00	[0.00]	0.00	0.00	0	0.00	0.00	–––	–––
S−	0.31	[0.46]	0.00	1.00	52	0.00	0.00	0.82	−1.34
M	4.12	1.67	1.00	7.00	135	4.00	3.00	0.08	−0.56
FM	4.48	1.21	2.00	7.00	135	6.00	4.00	−0.51	−0.65
m	1.00	0.89	0.00	2.00	122	1.00	1.00	0.84	1.69
FM+m	5.48	1.21	4.00	8.00	135	7.00	7.00	−0.51	−0.65
FC	2.93	0.95	1.00	4.00	135	3.00	4.00	−0.19	−1.29
CF	3.43	1.13	2.00	6.00	135	4.00	4.00	0.10	−1.14
C	0.28	[0.27]	0.00	1.00	17	0.00	0.00	3.09	7.69
Cn	0.00	[0.00]	0.00	0.00	0	0.00	0.00	–––	–––
FC+CF+C+Cn	6.44	1.39	4.00	8.00	135	7.00	7.00	−0.57	−0.93
WGSum C	4.02	1.15	2.50	8.00	135	5.00	4.00	−0.36	−1.06
Sum C'	1.06	[0.71]	0.00	2.00	105	1.00	1.00	−0.09	−0.99
Sum T	0.94	[0.47]	0.00	2.00	116	1.00	1.00	−0.20	1.55
Sum V	0.00	[0.00]	0.00	0.00	0	0.00	0.00	–––	–––
Sum Y	0.85	[0.70]	0.00	2.00	91	1.00	1.00	0.21	−0.92
SumShd	2.85	1.10	1.00	4.00	135	3.00	4.00	−0.32	−1.31
Fr+rF	0.21	[0.41]	0.00	1.00	29	0.00	0.00	1.40	−0.03
FD	0.91	[0.84]	0.00	2.00	92	0.00	0.00	0.59	−1.34
F	6.70	2.37	4.00	12.00	135	6.00	5.00	1.12	0.09
PAIR	9.90	1.08	7.00	12.00	135	10.00	10.00	−0.31	0.86
3r(2)/R	0.53	0.04	0.35	0.75	135	0.58	0.50	0.44	0.38
LAMBDA	0.68	0.22	0.27	1.50	135	0.69	0.60	0.89	−0.62
EA	8.14	1.37	7.00	12.00	135	8.00	7.00	0.57	−0.53
es	8.33	1.72	4.00	12.00	135	9.00	7.00	−0.22	−1.08
D	−0.09	0.29	−1.00	0.00	135	0.00	0.00	−2.92	6.63
AdjD	−0.06	0.34	−1.00	1.00	135	0.00	0.00	−1.00	5.32
a (active)	7.89	1.42	6.00	11.00	135	8.00	7.00	0.67	−0.27
p (passive)	2.79	1.60	2.00	8.00	135	2.00	2.00	2.08	3.12
Ma	2.81	1.01	1.00	5.00	135	3.00	3.00	0.29	−0.01
Mp	1.38	1.33	0.00	5.00	104	1.00	1.00	1.26	0.76
Intellect	0.77	0.65	0.00	2.00	135	1.00	1.00	0.26	−0.67
Zf	13.70	1.22	11.00	16.00	135	14.00	15.00	−0.30	−0.72
Zd	0.60	2.74	−4.50	4.50	135	1.00	4.50	−0.07	−1.15
Blends	6.04	1.41	3.00	8.00	135	6.00	7.00	−0.28	−1.05
Col Shd Bl	0.00	[0.00]	0.00	0.00	0	0.00	0.00	–––	–––
Afr	0.62	0.09	0.47	0.80	135	0.58	0.58	0.33	−0.90
Popular	6.06	0.86	4.00	9.00	135	7.00	5.00	−0.76	−0.78

NOTE: Standard Deviations shown in brackets indicate that the value is probably unreliable and/or misleading and should not be used to estimate expected ranges. Ordinarily these variables should not be included in most parametric analyses.

(continued)

Table 22.   (Continued)

				11 YEAR OLDS (N = 135)					
VARIABLE	MEAN	SD	MIN	MAX	FREQ	MEDIAN	MODE	SK	KU
X+%	0.75	0.08	0.52	0.90	135	0.77	0.79	−1.65	2.46
F+%	0.54	0.16	0.27	1.00	135	0.50	0.60	0.75	0.92
X−%	0.10	0.07	0.00	0.26	125	0.09	0.09	1.42	1.41
Xu%	0.15	0.05	0.05	0.24	135	0.16	0.14	−0.35	−0.35
S−%	0.11	[0.19]	0.00	0.50	42	0.00	0.00	1.47	0.42
Isolate	0.20	0.05	0.14	0.37	135	0.18	0.17	2.07	4.31
H	2.80	1.27	1.00	5.00	131	3.00	3.00	0.23	−0.71
(H)	1.51	0.66	0.00	2.00	123	2.00	2.00	−1.01	−0.12
Hd	0.52	0.66	0.00	2.00	58	0.00	0.00	0.90	−0.30
(Hd)	0.87	0.33	0.00	1.00	118	1.00	1.00	−2.28	3.25
Hx	0.00	[0.00]	0.00	0.00	0	0.00	0.00	—	—
All H Cont	5.70	1.80	2.00	9.00	135	6.00	6.00	−0.22	0.04
A	8.58	1.25	7.00	11.00	135	8.00	8.00	0.83	−0.19
(A)	1.00	[0.83]	0.00	2.00	89	1.00	0.00	0.00	−1.54
Ad	1.54	[0.95]	0.00	3.00	101	2.00	2.00	−0.75	−0.78
(Ad)	0.16	[0.36]	0.00	1.00	21	0.00	0.00	1.92	1.72
An	0.73	[0.64]	0.00	2.00	85	1.00	1.00	0.30	−0.66
Art	0.56	0.50	0.00	1.00	76	1.00	1.00	−0.26	−1.96
Ay	0.21	[0.59]	0.00	2.00	17	0.00	0.00	2.62	5.19
Bl	0.44	[0.57]	0.00	2.00	54	0.00	0.00	0.87	−0.24
Bt	2.10	0.67	1.00	4.00	135	2.00	2.00	0.65	1.16
Cg	1.60	0.99	0.00	3.00	122	1.00	1.00	0.26	−1.15
Cl	0.16	[0.24]	0.00	1.00	18	0.00	0.00	3.77	12.44
Ex	0.23	[0.17]	0.00	2.00	14	0.00	0.00	3.61	9.92
Fi	0.85	[0.36]	0.00	1.00	72	1.00	1.00	−2.00	2.04
Fd	0.64	[0.48]	0.00	1.00	67	1.00	1.00	−0.61	−1.65
Ge	0.10	[0.27]	0.00	1.00	6	0.00	0.00	3.97	13.57
Hh	0.81	0.46	0.00	2.00	106	1.00	1.00	−0.65	0.55
Ls	1.28	0.61	0.00	2.00	124	1.00	1.00	−0.23	−0.58
Na	0.35	[0.48]	0.00	1.00	47	0.00	0.00	0.64	−1.61
Sc	2.96	[0.36]	2.00	4.00	135	3.00	3.00	−0.57	4.57
Sx	0.00	[0.00]	0.00	0.00	0	0.00	0.00	—	—
Xy	0.09	[0.29]	0.00	1.00	9	0.00	0.00	2.92	6.63
Idio	0.06	0.34	0.00	2.00	4	0.00	0.00	5.61	29.92
DV	1.21	[0.41]	1.00	2.00	135	1.00	1.00	1.46	0.13
INCOM	1.44	[0.63]	0.00	3.00	131	1.00	1.00	0.42	−0.06
DR	0.22	[0.32]	0.00	1.00	26	0.00	0.00	2.39	3.75
FABCOM	0.46	[0.48]	0.00	2.00	48	0.00	0.00	0.61	−1.65
DV2	0.00	[0.00]	0.00	0.00	0	0.00	0.00	—	—
INC2	0.12	[0.32]	0.00	1.00	16	0.00	0.00	2.39	3.75
DR2	0.03	[0.17]	0.00	1.00	4	0.00	0.00	5.61	29.92
FAB2	0.00	[0.00]	0.00	0.00	0	0.00	0.00	—	—
ALOG	0.28	[0.43]	0.00	1.00	39	0.00	0.00	1.20	−0.56
CONTAM	0.00	0.00	0.00	0.00	0	0.00	0.00	—	—
Sum6 Sp Sc	4.36	1.16	2.00	6.00	135	3.00	3.00	0.69	−0.54
Sum6 Sp Sc2	0.15	[0.36]	0.00	1.00	20	0.00	0.00	2.00	2.04
WSum6	8.93	3.04	3.00	16.00	135	8.00	7.00	0.78	1.10
AB	0.21	[0.39]	0.00	1.00	8	0.00	0.00	3.38	11.45
AG	1.42	0.57	1.00	4.00	135	1.00	1.00	0.94	−0.11
CFB	0.00	0.00	0.00	0.00	0	0.00	0.00	—	—
COP	1.56	0.50	1.00	4.00	135	2.00	2.00	−0.23	−1.98
CP	0.00	[0.00]	0.00	0.00	0	0.00	0.00	—	—
MOR	0.72	[0.57]	0.00	3.00	82	0.00	0.00	0.94	−0.11
PER	0.88	0.53	0.00	2.00	107	1.00	1.00	−0.11	0.38
PSV	0.09	[0.25]	0.00	1.00	8	0.00	0.00	4.47	18.26

Table 22.   (Continued)

			12 YEAR OLDS (N = 120)						
VARIABLE	MEAN	SD	MIN	MAX	FREQ	MEDIAN	MODE	SK	KU
R	21.40	2.05	14.00	23.00	120	20.00	22.00	–1.03	0.96
W	8.79	1.85	1.00	14.00	120	9.00	9.00	–1.94	7.05
D	10.85	1.96	1.00	13.00	120	11.00	12.00	–3.26	12.20
Dd	1.76	[1.11]	0.00	5.00	117	1.00	1.00	3.51	16.47
S	1.92	[0.76]	0.00	5.00	118	2.00	2.00	1.30	4.92
DQ+	8.16	1.90	2.00	10.00	120	8.00	10.00	–1.42	2.39
DQo	12.12	1.07	9.00	15.00	120	12.00	12.00	–0.13	1.90
DQv	1.03	[0.26]	0.00	2.00	72	1.00	1.00	0.65	2.43
DQv/+	0.38	[0.38]	0.00	2.00	16	0.00	0.00	3.62	13.45
FQX+	0.30	0.54	0.00	2.00	10	0.00	0.00	4.16	16.95
FQXo	15.34	2.32	5.00	17.00	120	16.00	17.00	–2.40	6.80
FQXu	3.77	0.89	1.00	5.00	120	4.00	3.00	–0.95	1.08
FQX–	1.95	1.04	1.00	7.00	120	2.00	2.00	3.71	16.47
FQXNone	0.43	[0.26]	0.00	2.00	42	0.00	0.00	2.65	7.43
MQ+	0.10	0.30	0.00	1.00	5	0.00	0.00	7.45	45.23
MQo	3.21	1.52	1.00	5.00	120	3.00	5.00	–0.33	–1.26
MQu	0.67	0.51	0.00	2.00	78	1.00	1.00	–0.32	–1.01
MQ–	0.22	[0.41]	0.00	1.00	26	0.00	0.00	1.39	–0.06
MQNone	0.02	[0.13]	0.00	1.00	2	0.00	0.00	7.65	57.43
S–	0.57	[0.62]	0.00	3.00	63	1.00	1.00	1.02	2.14
M	4.21	2.06	1.00	7.00	120	4.00	4.00	–0.22	–1.07
FM	5.02	1.66	0.00	9.00	118	6.00	4.00	–1.34	1.64
m	1.00	0.45	0.00	3.00	112	1.00	1.00	2.26	12.57
FM+m	6.02	1.70	1.00	9.00	120	7.00	7.00	–1.44	1.83
FC	2.87	1.17	0.00	4.00	106	3.00	3.00	–1.61	1.77
CF	3.14	1.40	0.00	5.00	112	3.00	3.00	–0.55	–0.30
C	0.39	[0.13]	0.00	1.00	38	0.00	0.00	1.65	7.43
Cn	0.00	[0.00]	0.00	0.00	0	0.00	0.00	—	—
FC+CF+C+Cn	6.03	2.29	0.00	8.00	119	7.00	7.00	–1.49	1.26
WGSum C	4.05	1.78	0.00	6.50	120	5.00	6.50	–1.17	0.69
Sum C'	1.08	[0.88]	0.00	3.00	99	1.00	1.00	0.38	–0.47
Sum T	0.88	[0.32]	0.00	1.00	106	1.00	1.00	–2.42	3.91
Sum V	0.07	[0.36]	0.00	2.00	4	0.00	0.00	5.27	26.16
Sum Y	1.01	[0.67]	0.00	2.00	108	2.00	2.00	–1.04	–0.13
SumShd	3.74	1.37	0.00	6.00	114	4.00	4.00	–0.98	1.25
Fr+rF	0.20	[0.13]	0.00	1.00	15	0.00	0.00	3.65	17.43
FD	1.48	[0.83]	0.00	2.00	94	2.00	2.00	–1.11	–0.61
F	5.84	1.65	5.00	13.00	120	5.00	5.00	2.75	7.47
PAIR	9.09	1.89	1.00	10.00	120	10.00	10.00	–2.89	9.00
3r(2)/R	0.54	0.08	0.10	0.50	120	0.55	0.50	–3.53	16.28
LAMBDA	0.66	0.58	0.29	4.25	120	0.70	0.50	5.18	30.28
EA	8.26	2.38	1.00	12.00	120	8.50	7.00	–1.38	1.99
es	8.97	2.59	1.00	13.00	120	8.00	6.00	–2.08	3.95
D	–0.21	0.53	–2.00	1.00	120	0.00	0.00	–1.17	2.25
AdjD	–0.11	0.67	–2.00	2.00	120	0.00	0.00	–0.04	1.74
a (active)	6.53	1.45	2.00	8.00	120	7.00	6.00	–1.34	2.04
p (passive)	4.00	2.01	0.00	8.00	118	3.00	2.00	0.50	–0.57
Ma	2.47	0.80	0.00	4.00	118	2.00	2.00	0.32	0.24
Mp	1.73	1.60	0.00	5.00	92	2.00	2.00	–0.06	–1.04
Intellect	1.05	0.59	0.00	4.00	120	1.00	1.00	2.96	12.69
Zf	13.14	1.96	5.00	16.00	120	14.00	14.00	–2.25	6.48
Zd	1.67	2.11	–4.50	5.00	120	1.50	1.50	–0.24	–0.26
Blends	6.67	2.29	0.00	9.00	118	7.00	8.00	–1.79	2.12
Col Shd Bl	0.05	[0.22]	0.00	1.00	6	0.00	0.00	4.18	15.75
Afr	0.65	0.11	0.21	0.67	120	0.69	0.67	–0.80	0.75
Popular	6.22	1.10	2.00	7.00	120	7.00	6.00	–1.53	2.56

NOTE: Standard Deviations shown in brackets indicate that the value is probably unreliable and/or misleading and should not be used to estimate expected ranges. Ordinarily these variables should not be included in most parametric analyses.

(continued)

Table 22. (Continued)

12 YEAR OLDS (N = 120)

VARIABLE	MEAN	SD	MIN	MAX	FREQ	MEDIAN	MODE	SK	KU
X+%	0.75	0.09	0.29	0.88	120	0.77	0.77	–3.33	14.09
F+%	0.54	0.11	0.18	0.88	120	0.60	0.60	–0.10	1.95
X–%	0.10	0.05	0.05	0.41	120	0.09	0.09	4.05	19.33
Xu%	0.15	0.04	0.05	0.29	120	0.15	0.14	–0.27	2.29
S–%	0.27	[0.28]	0.00	1.00	63	0.33	0.00	0.42	–0.71
Isolate	0.15	0.04	0.00	0.33	120	0.16	0.18	0.19	5.42
H	3.38	1.64	1.00	5.00	120	3.00	5.00	–0.37	–1.42
(H)	1.24	0.84	0.00	4.00	97	1.00	1.00	0.38	0.53
Hd	0.59	0.69	0.00	3.00	61	1.00	0.00	1.37	2.75
(Hd)	0.78	0.41	0.00	1.00	94	1.00	1.00	–1.39	–0.06
Hx	0.13	[0.34]	0.00	1.00	2	0.00	0.00	7.57	46.38
All H Cont	6.00	2.56	2.00	11.00	120	5.00	5.00	–0.24	–1.18
A	7.70	1.29	4.00	13.00	120	8.00	7.00	0.65	4.48
(A)	0.47	[0.50]	0.00	1.00	57	0.00	0.00	0.10	–2.02
Ad	1.97	[0.45]	0.00	3.00	116	2.00	2.00	–2.44	11.96
(Ad)	0.36	[0.54]	0.00	2.00	20	0.00	0.00	3.10	5.86
An	1.14	[0.60]	0.00	2.00	106	1.00	1.00	–0.06	–0.27
Art	0.92	0.28	0.00	1.00	110	1.00	1.00	–3.05	7.45
Ay	0.03	[0.18]	0.00	1.00	4	0.00	0.00	5.27	26.16
Bl	0.26	[0.44]	0.00	1.00	31	0.00	0.00	1.12	–0.76
Bt	1.52	0.65	0.00	2.00	110	2.00	2.00	–1.04	–0.03
Cg	1.90	1.06	0.00	4.00	116	1.00	1.00	0.12	–1.63
Cl	0.22	[0.13]	0.00	1.00	12	0.00	0.00	7.65	57.43
Ex	0.47	[0.38]	0.00	2.00	40	0.00	0.00	3.16	4.84
Fi	0.57	[0.26]	0.00	2.00	81	1.00	1.00	–1.61	12.13
Fd	0.37	[0.34]	0.00	1.00	29	0.00	0.00	2.19	4.82
Ge	0.02	[0.13]	0.00	1.00	2	0.00	0.00	7.65	57.43
Hh	0.88	0.32	0.00	1.00	106	1.00	1.00	–2.42	3.91
Ls	1.36	0.60	0.00	2.00	112	1.00	1.00	–0.36	–0.65
Na	0.10	[0.35]	0.00	2.00	10	0.00	0.00	3.79	14.82
Sc	2.47	[0.87]	0.00	3.00	112	3.00	3.00	–1.72	2.12
Sx	0.02	[0.13]	0.00	1.00	2	0.00	0.00	7.65	57.43
Xy	0.06	[0.12]	0.00	1.00	7	0.00	0.00	4.95	21.11
Idio	0.15	0.51	0.00	3.00	12	0.00	0.00	4.02	17.31
DV	1.21	[0.55]	0.00	2.00	112	1.00	1.00	0.08	–0.13
INCOM	1.35	[0.57]	0.00	3.00	116	1.00	1.00	0.34	–0.10
DR	0.44	[0.43]	0.00	1.00	39	0.00	0.00	1.22	–0.51
FABCOM	0.46	[0.53]	0.00	2.00	36	0.00	0.00	1.95	2.99
DV2	0.02	[0.16]	0.00	1.00	3	0.00	0.00	6.16	36.58
INC2	0.17	[0.56]	0.00	3.00	13	0.00	0.00	3.54	12.65
DR2	0.02	[0.16]	0.00	1.00	3	0.00	0.00	6.16	36.58
FAB2	0.04	[0.20]	0.00	1.00	5	0.00	0.00	4.65	19.91
ALOG	0.41	[0.68]	0.00	2.00	27	0.00	0.00	1.94	3.61
CONTAM	0.00	0.00	0.00	0.00	0	0.00	0.00	—	—
Sum6 Sp Sc	4.06	0.95	1.00	6.00	120	3.00	4.00	–0.47	–1.06
Sum6 Sp Sc2	0.27	[0.68]	0.00	4.00	22	0.00	0.00	3.47	14.40
WSum6	8.86	3.85	2.00	19.00	120	8.00	4.00	2.33	9.04
AB	0.05	[0.22]	0.00	1.00	6	0.00	0.00	4.18	15.75
AG	1.08	0.66	0.00	2.00	99	1.00	1.00	–0.09	–0.65
CFB	0.00	0.00	0.00	0.00	0	0.00	0.00	—	—
COP	1.93	0.53	0.00	4.00	114	3.00	2.00	0.18	–0.19
CP	0.00	[0.00]	0.00	0.00	0	0.00	0.00	—	—
MOR	0.67	[0.37]	0.00	3.00	58	0.00	0.00	1.81	1.30
PER	0.93	0.36	0.00	2.00	108	1.00	1.00	–0.89	4.40
PSV	0.03	[0.18]	0.00	1.00	4	0.00	0.00	5.27	26.16

Table 22. (Continued)

13 YEAR OLDS (N = 110)

VARIABLE	MEAN	SD	MIN	MAX	FREQ	MEDIAN	MODE	SK	KU
R	21.20	3.30	14.00	33.00	110	20.00	20.00	1.07	3.51
W	8.57	2.15	1.00	14.00	110	9.00	9.00	-1.07	3.04
D	11.15	3.09	1.00	21.00	110	11.00	12.00	-0.25	3.08
Dd	1.46	[1.66]	0.00	6.00	93	1.00	1.00	2.74	7.81
S	1.33	[1.16]	0.00	7.00	106	2.00	1.00	1.93	5.93
DQ+	7.70	2.54	2.00	15.00	110	8.00	8.00	0.24	1.27
DQo	12.40	2.02	8.00	20.00	110	12.00	12.00	0.73	2.74
DQv	0.45	[0.99]	0.00	4.00	24	0.00	0.00	2.31	4.70
DQv/+	0.24	[0.57]	0.00	2.00	18	0.00	0.00	2.33	4.18
FQX+	0.20	0.59	0.00	3.00	14	0.00	0.00	3.25	10.63
FQXo	15.24	3.04	5.00	23.00	110	15.00	17.00	-0.70	2.09
FQXu	3.27	1.53	0.00	8.00	106	3.00	3.00	0.42	1.24
FQX-	2.00	1.42	0.00	7.00	108	2.00	2.00	2.15	4.81
FQXNone	0.07	[0.32]	0.00	2.00	6	0.00	0.00	4.81	23.90
MQ+	0.13	0.43	0.00	2.00	10	0.00	0.00	3.52	11.76
MQo	3.23	1.66	1.00	8.00	110	3.00	5.00	0.34	-0.38
MQu	0.54	0.66	0.00	3.00	51	0.00	0.00	1.23	2.00
MQ-	0.14	[0.51]	0.00	2.00	12	0.00	0.00	2.08	3.61
MQNone	0.02	[0.13]	0.00	1.00	2	0.00	0.00	7.31	52.42
S-	0.52	[0.81]	0.00	4.00	43	0.00	0.00	2.16	5.84
M	4.14	2.24	1.00	11.00	110	4.00	4.00	0.50	-0.01
FM	4.42	1.94	0.00	8.00	108	4.00	6.00	-0.25	-0.89
m	1.25	0.94	0.00	5.00	98	1.00	1.00	1.88	4.46
FM+m	5.67	2.10	1.00	11.00	110	6.00	7.00	-0.28	-0.34
FC	2.95	1.72	0.00	9.00	96	3.00	3.00	0.42	1.72
CF	2.70	1.50	0.00	5.00	102	3.00	3.00	-0.07	-0.98
C	0.07	[0.26]	0.00	1.00	8	0.00	0.00	3.34	9.30
Cn	0.00	[0.00]	0.00	0.00	0	0.00	0.00	----	----
FC+CF+C+Cn	5.73	2.61	0.00	10.00	110	6.50	8.00	-0.71	-0.33
WGSum C	4.29	1.94	0.00	7.50	110	4.75	6.50	-0.61	-0.49
Sum C'	1.20	[0.89]	0.00	3.00	87	1.00	1.00	0.48	-0.37
Sum T	0.97	[0.51]	0.00	3.00	90	1.00	1.00	0.64	4.99
Sum V	0.14	[0.48]	0.00	2.00	10	0.00	0.00	3.31	9.70
Sum Y	1.02	[0.81]	0.00	2.00	80	1.00	2.00	-0.22	-1.44
SumShd	3.34	1.44	0.00	6.00	104	4.00	4.00	-0.55	-0.07
Fr+rF	0.45	[0.23]	0.00	1.00	32	0.00	0.00	2.98	4.08
FD	1.27	[0.87]	0.00	3.00	82	2.00	2.00	-0.39	-1.25
F	6.90	2.52	3.00	13.00	110	6.00	5.00	0.93	-0.20
PAIR	8.64	2.30	1.00	14.00	110	9.50	10.00	-1.18	2.59
3r(2)/R	0.49	0.10	0.20	0.66	110	0.48	0.50	-1.84	4.97
LAMBDA	0.67	0.61	0.20	4.33	110	0.38	0.33	4.44	24.00
EA	8.43	2.69	1.00	15.00	110	9.00	7.50	-0.60	0.64
es	9.01	3.01	1.00	14.00	110	10.00	8.00	-0.83	-0.02
D	-0.09	0.82	-2.00	3.00	110	0.00	0.00	0.78	3.45
AdjD	0.10	0.84	-2.00	3.00	110	0.00	0.00	0.74	2.06
a (active)	6.23	1.89	2.00	11.00	110	6.00	6.00	-0.34	0.13
p (passive)	3.61	2.11	0.00	8.00	104	3.00	3.00	0.45	-0.49
Ma	2.49	1.30	0.00	8.00	106	2.00	2.00	1.80	6.06
Mp	1.67	1.44	0.00	5.00	84	2.00	2.00	0.12	-0.80
Intellect	1.22	0.95	0.00	4.00	110	1.00	1.00	1.24	1.45
Zf	12.64	3.02	5.00	23.00	110	13.00	11.00	0.05	2.17
Zd	1.37	2.27	-4.50	5.00	110	1.50	-0.50	-0.35	-0.40
Blends	5.81	2.43	0.00	9.00	108	7.00	7.00	-0.90	-0.34
Col Shd Blend	0.16	[0.37]	0.00	1.00	18	0.00	0.00	1.84	1.42s
Afr	0.69	0.15	0.28	1.00	110	0.58	0.67	0.10	0.52
Popular	6.19	1.34	2.00	9.00	110	7.00	6.00	-0.59	0.79

NOTE: Standard Deviations shown in brackets indicate that the value is probably unreliable and/or misleading and should not be used to estimate expected ranges. Ordinarily these variables should not be included in most parametric analyses.

(continued)

Table 22. (Continued)

13 YEAR OLDS (N = 110)

VARIABLE	MEAN	SD	MIN	MAX	FREQ	MEDIAN	MODE	SK	KU
X+%	0.76	0.11	0.30	1.00	110	0.77	0.77	-1.86	5.39
F+%	0.61	0.18	0.18	1.00	110	0.60	0.60	0.39	0.14
X-%	0.10	0.07	0.00	0.38	108	0.09	0.09	2.67	8.99
Xu%	0.16	0.07	0.00	0.33	106	0.15	0.14	-0.03	0.76
S-%	0.20	[0.28]	0.00	1.00	43	0.00	0.00	1.11	0.35
Isolate	0.16	0.06	0.00	0.33	110	0.16	0.18	0.59	1.30
H	3.09	1.72	1.00	8.00	110	3.00	5.00	0.42	-0.57
(H)	1.25	1.02	0.00	5.00	84	1.00	1.00	1.06	2.35
Hd	0.68	0.83	0.00	3.00	55	0.50	0.00	1.24	1.11
(Hd)	0.56	0.53	0.00	2.00	60	1.00	1.00	0.11	-1.21
Hx	0.00	[0.00]	0.00	0.00	0	0.00	0.00	----	----
All H Cont	5.59	2.46	2.00	11.00	110	5.00	5.00	0.13	-1.03
A	7.96	1.81	4.00	13.00	110	8.00	7.00	0.63	0.65
(A)	0.37	[0.49]	0.00	1.00	41	0.00	0.00	0.53	-1.75
Ad	2.00	[0.81]	0.00	4.00	106	2.00	2.00	0.42	1.71
(Ad)	0.00	[0.00]	0.00	0.00	0	0.00	0.00	----	----
An	0.84	[0.69]	0.00	2.00	74	1.00	1.00	0.22	-0.89
Art	0.85	0.48	0.00	2.00	88	1.00	1.00	-0.36	0.78
Ay	0.11	[0.31]	0.00	1.00	12	0.00	0.00	2.54	4.55
Bl	0.19	[0.39]	0.00	1.00	21	0.00	0.00	1.59	0.55
Bt	1.74	0.98	0.00	5.00	98	2.00	2.00	0.44	1.35
Cg	1.62	1.10	0.00	4.00	98	1.00	1.00	0.47	-0.93
Cl	0.05	[0.23]	0.00	1.00	6	0.00	0.00	3.98	14.08
Ex	0.09	[0.29]	0.00	1.00	10	0.00	0.00	2.89	6.44
Fi	0.76	[0.54]	0.00	2.00	78	1.00	1.00	-0.12	-0.23
Fd	0.42	[0.52]	0.00	2.00	46	1.00	0.00	-0.10	-1.15
Ge	0.04	[0.19]	0.00	1.00	4	0.00	0.00	5.02	23.65
Hh	1.07	0.81	0.00	4.00	90	1.00	1.00	1.35	2.87
Ls	1.10	0.97	0.00	6.00	84	1.00	1.00	2.28	10.32
Na	0.22	[0.50]	0.00	2.00	20	0.00	0.00	2.25	4.39
Sc	1.97	[1.14]	0.00	5.00	96	2.00	3.00	-0.18	-0.48
Sx	0.07	[0.42]	0.00	3.00	4	0.00	0.00	6.43	42.22
Xy	0.00	[0.00]	0.00	0.00	0	0.00	0.00	----	----
Idio	0.78	1.14	0.00	4.00	44	0.00	0.00	1.26	0.28
DV	1.01	[0.70]	0.00	3.00	86	1.00	1.00	0.32	0.05
INCOM	1.07	[0.79]	0.00	3.00	84	1.00	1.00	0.33	-0.33
DR	0.30	[0.66]	0.00	4.00	27	0.00	0.00	3.54	16.72
FABCOM	0.42	[0.71]	0.00	3.00	34	0.00	0.00	1.71	2.45
DV2	0.02	[0.13]	0.00	1.00	2	0.00	0.00	7.31	52.42
INC2	0.22	[0.60]	0.00	3.00	16	0.00	0.00	3.06	9.49
DR2	0.04	[0.19]	0.00	1.00	4	0.00	0.00	5.02	23.65
FAB2	0.07	[0.32]	0.00	2.00	3	0.00	0.00	4.81	23.90
ALOG	0.34	[0.19]	0.00	1.00	18	0.00	0.00	5.02	23.65
CONTAM	0.00	0.00	0.00	0.00	0	0.00	0.00	----	----
Sum6 Sp Sc	2.94	1.46	0.00	9.00	110	3.00	2.00	1.55	5.03
Sum6 Sp Sc2	0.34	[0.77]	0.00	4.00	24	0.00	0.00	2.73	8.42
WSum6	7.54	6.99	0.00	40.00	108	6.00	3.00	2.89	9.56
AB	0.13	[0.33]	0.00	1.00	14	0.00	0.00	2.27	3.20
AG	1.18	0.91	0.00	4.00	85	1.00	1.00	0.67	0.48
CFB	0.00	0.00	0.00	0.00	0	0.00	0.00	----	----
COP	1.84	1.22	0.00	6.00	101	2.00	1.00	1.59	3.11
CP	0.02	[0.13]	0.00	1.00	1	0.00	0.00	7.31	52.42
MOR	0.49	[0.74]	0.00	3.00	40	0.00	0.00	1.42	1.38
PER	1.05	0.89	0.00	5.00	90	1.00	1.00	2.31	7.82
PSV	0.04	[0.21]	0.00	1.00	5	0.00	0.00	3.68	14.48

Table 22.   (Continued)

14 YEAR OLDS (N = 105)

VARIABLE	MEAN	SD	MIN	MAX	FREQ	MEDIAN	MODE	SK	KU
R	21.72	3.36	14.00	33.00	105	20.00	20.00	1.11	3.43
W	8.92	2.19	4.00	14.00	105	9.00	9.00	-1.01	2.83
D	11.13	3.16	1.00	21.00	105	11.00	10.00	-0.23	2.82
Dd	1.67	[1.70]	0.00	6.00	98	2.00	1.00	2.67	7.31
S	1.32	[1.09]	0.00	7.00	101	2.00	2.00	1.89	5.56
DQ+	7.81	2.55	2.00	15.00	105	8.00	8.00	0.33	1.36
DQo	12.69	2.06	8.00	20.00	105	12.00	12.00	0.73	2.58
DQv	0.58	[1.01]	0.00	4.00	27	0.00	0.00	2.23	4.30
DQv/+	0.65	[0.58]	0.00	2.00	48	0.00	0.00	2.25	3.79
FQX+	0.14	0.50	0.00	2.00	11	0.00	0.00	3.16	9.97
FQXo	15.17	3.09	5.00	23.00	105	15.00	15.00	-0.64	1.93
FQXu	3.27	1.56	0.00	8.00	101	3.00	3.00	0.42	1.10
FQX-	1.84	1.25	0.00	5.00	103	2.00	2.00	2.10	4.46
FQXNone	0.02	[0.53]	0.00	1.00	4	0.00	0.00	4.69	22.65
MQ+	0.11	0.44	0.00	2.00	6	0.00	0.00	3.42	11.04
MQo	3.21	1.66	1.00	8.00	105	3.00	1.00	0.43	-0.26
MQu	0.51	0.67	0.00	3.00	46	0.00	0.00	1.34	2.18
MQ-	0.13	[0.50]	0.00	2.00	11	0.00	0.00	2.18	4.01
MQNone	0.00	[0.00]	0.00	0.00	0	0.00	0.00	----	----
S-	0.39	[0.82]	0.00	3.00	31	0.00	0.00	2.24	6.00
M	4.06	2.24	1.00	11.00	105	4.00	4.00	0.59	0.16
FM	4.35	1.96	0.00	8.00	103	4.00	6.00	-0.17	-0.92
m	1.27	0.96	0.00	5.00	93	1.00	1.00	1.81	4.08
FM+m	5.62	2.14	1.00	11.00	105	6.00	7.00	-0.21	-0.42
FC	2.93	1.76	0.00	9.00	91	3.00	3.00	0.45	1.59
CF	2.70	1.53	0.00	5.00	97	3.00	3.00	-0.08	-1.05
C	0.10	[0.27]	0.00	1.00	9	0.00	0.00	3.14	7.67
Cn	0.00	[0.00]	0.00	0.00	0	0.00	0.00	----	----
FC+CF+C+Cn	5.71	2.67	1.00	10.00	105	7.00	8.00	-0.69	-0.44
WGSum C	4.29	1.98	0.50	7.50	105	5.00	6.50	-0.60	-0.58
Sum C'	1.11	[0.91]	0.00	3.00	82	1.00	1.00	0.44	-0.50
Sum T	0.99	[0.52]	0.00	3.00	85	1.00	1.00	0.66	4.71
Sum V	0.13	[0.50]	0.00	2.00	8	0.00	0.00	3.21	9.06
Sum Y	0.88	[0.84]	0.00	2.00	75	1.00	2.00	-0.14	-1.44
SumShd	3.10	1.47	0.00	6.00	99	4.00	4.00	-0.49	-0.19
Fr+rF	0.38	[0.43]	0.00	1.00	15	0.00	0.00	3.97	10.25
FD	1.24	[0.87]	0.00	3.00	71	1.00	2.00	-0.31	-1.30
F	6.96	2.56	3.00	13.00	105	6.00	5.00	0.87	-0.35
PAIR	8.59	2.34	1.00	14.00	105	9.00	10.00	-1.12	2.38
3r(2)/R	0.47	0.10	0.05	0.56	105	0.45	0.50	-1.79	4.60
LAMBDA	0.67	0.62	0.20	4.33	105	0.38	0.33	4.34	22.96
EA	8.34	2.70	1.00	15.00	105	9.00	7.50	-0.55	0.60
es	8.92	3.06	1.00	13.00	105	9.00	9.00	-0.76	-0.15
D	-0.09	0.84	-2.00	3.00	105	0.00	0.00	0.78	3.19
AdjD	0.09	0.86	-2.00	3.00	105	0.00	0.00	0.74	1.95
a (active)	6.20	1.92	2.00	11.00	105	6.00	7.00	-0.32	0.06
p (passive)	3.49	2.07	0.00	8.00	99	3.00	3.00	0.52	-0.35
Ma	2.59	1.32	0.00	8.00	101	2.00	2.00	1.81	5.93
Mp	1.49	1.36	0.00	5.00	89	2.00	2.00	0.17	-0.74
Intellect	1.23	0.97	0.00	4.00	105	1.00	1.00	1.18	1.22
Zf	12.56	3.06	5.00	23.00	105	13.00	14.00	0.12	2.11
Zd	1.27	2.26	-4.50	5.00	105	1.50	-0.50	-0.30	-0.38
Blends	5.74	2.46	0.00	9.00	103	7.00	7.00	-0.84	-0.47
Col Shd Blend	0.17	[0.38]	0.00	1.00	18	0.00	0.00	1.77	1.15
Afr	0.69	0.16	0.31	0.89	105	0.68	0.67	0.03	0.47
Popular	6.02	1.17	3.00	9.00	105	7.00	6.00	-0.53	0.67

NOTE: Standard Deviations shown in brackets indicate that the value is probably unreliable and/or misleading and should not be used to estimate expected ranges. Ordinarily these variables should not be included in most parametric analyses.

(continued)

Table 22.   (Continued)

14 YEAR OLDS   (N = 105)

VARIABLE	MEAN	SD	MIN	MAX	FREQ	MEDIAN	MODE	SK	KU
X+%	0.76	0.12	0.49	0.95	105	0.79	0.75	-1.81	5.01
F+%	0.69	0.18	0.38	1.00	105	0.60	0.60	0.34	0.03
X-%	0.09	0.07	0.00	0.27	105	0.09	0.05	2.60	8.43
Xu%	0.16	0.07	0.00	0.33	105	0.15	0.14	-0.03	0.61
S-%	0.19	[0.28]	0.00	1.00	38	0.00	0.00	1.27	0.76
Isolate	0.16	0.06	0.00	0.33	105	0.16	0.16	0.60	1.15
H	3.00	1.71	1.00	8.00	105	3.00	1.00	0.54	-0.35
(H)	1.23	1.03	0.00	5.00	79	1.00	1.00	1.14	2.44
Hd	0.67	0.85	0.00	3.00	52	0.00	0.00	1.28	1.07
(Hd)	0.56	0.54	0.00	2.00	57	1.00	1.00	0.13	-1.19
Hx	0.00	[0.00]	0.00	0.00	0	0.00	0.00	----	----
All H Cont	5.46	2.44	2.00	11.00	105	5.00	5.00	0.22	-0.91
A	7.97	1.85	4.00	13.00	105	8.00	7.00	0.60	0.49
(A)	0.39	[0.49]	0.00	1.00	41	0.00	0.00	0.46	-1.83
Ad	2.00	[0.83]	0.00	4.00	101	2.00	2.00	0.41	1.50
(Ad)	0.23	[0.41]	0.00	1.00	13	0.00	0.00	4.16	29.15
An	0.84	[0.71]	0.00	2.00	49	1.00	0.00	0.24	-0.97
Art	0.85	0.50	0.00	2.00	83	1.00	1.00	-0.32	0.62
Ay	0.15	[0.32]	0.00	1.00	14	0.00	0.00	2.46	4.13
Bl	0.20	[0.40]	0.00	1.00	20	0.00	0.00	1.52	0.32
Bt	1.73	1.00	0.00	5.00	91	2.00	2.00	0.44	1.22
Cg	1.55	1.08	0.00	4.00	94	1.00	1.00	0.60	-0.69
Cl	0.06	[0.23]	0.00	1.00	8	0.00	0.00	3.87	13.24
Ex	0.09	[0.29]	0.00	1.00	19	0.00	0.00	2.80	5.94
Fi	0.75	[0.55]	0.00	2.00	63	1.00	1.00	-0.06	-0.32
Fd	0.30	[0.53]	0.00	2.00	31	1.00	1.00	-0.02	-1.16
Ge	0.04	[0.19]	0.00	1.00	3	0.00	0.00	4.90	22.40
Hh	1.08	0.83	0.00	4.00	82	1.00	1.00	1.30	2.58
Ls	1.06	0.97	0.00	6.00	79	1.00	1.00	2.47	11.28
Na	0.23	[0.50]	0.00	2.00	24	0.00	0.00	2.18	4.01
Sc	1.93	[1.15]	0.00	5.00	96	2.00	3.00	-0.10	-0.48
Sx	0.08	[0.43]	0.00	1.00	3	0.00	0.00	6.27	40.17
Xy	0.04	[0.20]	0.00	1.00	5	0.00	0.00	5.18	31.60
Idio	0.82	1.16	0.00	4.00	44	0.00	0.00	1.19	0.10
DV	0.98	[0.69]	0.00	3.00	81	1.00	1.00	0.38	0.22
INCOM	1.05	[0.79]	0.00	3.00	79	1.00	1.00	0.39	-0.24
DR	0.29	[0.66]	0.00	4.00	25	0.00	0.00	3.61	16.99
FABCOM	0.44	[0.72]	0.00	3.00	34	0.00	0.00	1.64	2.18
DV2	0.02	[0.14]	0.00	1.00	2	0.00	0.00	7.14	49.92
INC2	0.12	[0.60]	0.00	3.00	6	0.00	0.00	3.06	9.40
DR2	0.03	[0.17]	0.00	1.00	2	0.00	0.00	5.74	31.57
FAB2	0.08	[0.33]	0.00	1.00	3	0.00	0.00	4.69	22.65
ALOG	0.11	[0.19]	0.00	1.00	10	0.00	0.00	4.90	22.40
CONTAM	0.00	0.00	0.00	0.00	0	0.00	0.00	----	----
Sum6 Sp Sc	2.89	1.38	0.00	8.00	103	3.00	2.00	1.61	5.11
Sum6 Sp Sc2	0.14	[0.38]	0.00	1.00	9	0.00	0.00	2.75	8.37
WSum6	7.42	7.14	0.00	20.00	105	6.00	3.00	2.85	9.12
AB	0.13	[0.34]	0.00	1.00	12	0.00	0.00	2.19	2.84
AG	1.30	0.92	0.00	4.00	89	1.00	1.00	0.63	0.36
CFB	0.00	0.00	0.00	0.00	0	0.00	0.00	----	----
COP	1.75	1.14	0.00	5.00	95	1.00	1.00	1.57	2.91
CP	0.00	[0.00]	0.00	0.00	0	0.00	0.00	----	----
MOR	0.61	[0.75]	0.00	3.00	48	0.00	0.00	1.35	1.17
PER	1.01	0.81	0.00	4.00	80	1.00	1.00	2.25	7.32
PSV	0.03	[0.12]	0.00	1.00	3	0.00	0.00	5.87	23.24

Table 22. (Continued)

15 YEAR OLDS (N = 110)

VARIABLE	MEAN	SD	MIN	MAX	FREQ	MEDIAN	MODE	SK	KU
R	21.94	4.21	14.00	32.00	110	21.00	20.00	0.94	1.14
W	8.87	2.20	3.00	20.00	110	9.00	9.00	1.57	9.58
D	11.42	3.66	0.00	20.00	109	12.00	12.00	-0.31	1.91
Dd	1.65	[1.31]	0.00	7.00	91	1.00	1.00	1.31	3.76
S	1.44	[1.31]	0.00	5.00	104	2.00	1.00	2.66	12.86
DQ+	7.88	2.02	2.00	13.00	110	8.00	8.00	-0.33	0.15
DQo	12.67	3.62	5.00	29.00	110	12.00	12.00	1.49	5.43
DQv	0.75	[1.29]	0.00	4.00	40	0.00	0.00	1.84	2.46
DQv/+	0.14	[0.42]	0.00	2.00	12	0.00	0.00	3.22	10.13
FQX+	0.36	0.70	0.00	3.00	27	0.00	0.00	1.81	2.20
FQXo	16.35	3.34	7.00	29.00	110	16.00	15.00	0.60	2.79
FQXu	3.08	1.57	0.00	11.00	108	3.00	3.00	1.37	5.75
FQX-	1.60	0.91	0.00	6.00	99	2.00	2.00	0.81	3.89
FQXNone	0.04	[0.25]	0.00	2.00	4	0.00	0.00	6.07	39.81
MQ+	0.25	0.57	0.00	3.00	22	0.00	0.00	2.46	6.34
MQo	3.54	2.01	0.00	8.00	108	3.00	1.00	0.20	-0.91
MQu	0.44	0.52	0.00	2.00	48	0.00	0.00	0.43	-1.36
MQ-	0.12	[0.32]	0.00	1.00	13	0.00	0.00	2.40	3.82
MQNone	0.00	[0.00]	0.00	0.00	0	0.00	0.00	----	----
S-	0.38	[0.57]	0.00	2.00	37	0.00	0.00	1.22	0.52
M	4.35	2.17	1.00	9.00	110	4.00	4.00	0.06	-0.97
FM	4.82	1.73	1.00	9.00	110	5.00	6.00	-0.20	-0.80
m	1.17	0.78	0.00	4.00	97	1.00	1.00	1.49	3.79
FM+m	5.99	1.78	2.00	10.00	110	6.00	7.00	-0.14	-0.67
FC	3.14	1.14	0.00	6.00	107	3.00	3.00	-0.56	0.76
CF	2.85	1.53	0.00	6.00	101	3.00	2.00	-0.11	-0.73
C	0.03	[0.16]	0.00	1.00	3	0.00	0.00	5.88	33.24
Cn	0.02	[0.13]	0.00	1.00	2	0.00	0.00	7.31	52.42
FC+CF+C+Cn	6.04	2.01	1.00	10.00	110	7.00	8.00	-0.62	-0.37
WGSum C	4.47	1.68	0.50	8.00	110	4.50	3.50	-0.33	-0.64
Sum C'	1.63	[1.35]	0.00	10.00	94	1.00	1.00	2.49	12.61
Sum T	1.06	[0.51]	0.00	3.00	101	1.00	1.00	2.62	13.12
Sum V	0.18	[0.49]	0.00	2.00	12	0.00	0.00	2.75	6.73
Sum Y	1.30	[1.27]	0.00	10.00	83	1.00	2.00	3.35	20.69
SumShd	4.17	2.55	0.00	23.00	109	4.00	4.00	4.04	27.31
Fr+rF	0.50	[0.45]	0.00	2.00	26	0.00	0.00	6.67	53.57
FD	1.33	[0.97]	0.00	5.00	83	1.50	2.00	0.35	0.78
F	6.48	2.71	2.00	17.00	110	5.00	5.00	1.31	2.02
PAIR	9.10	2.00	1.00	14.00	110	10.00	10.00	-1.37	4.47
3r(2)/R	0.44	0.10	0.05	0.79	110	0.45	0.50	-0.58	4.63
LAMBDA	0.65	0.22	0.14	1.71	110	0.36	0.33	2.27	8.94
EA	8.82	2.34	2.00	13.50	110	9.50	9.50	-0.69	0.39
es	9.16	3.40	4.00	17.00	110	10.00	9.00	2.13	12.31
D	-0.45	1.39	-10.00	2.00	39	0.00	0.00	-3.73	20.85
AdjD	-0.25	1.07	-5.00	2.00	43	0.00	0.00	-1.71	5.14
a (active)	6.99	1.73	3.00	12.00	110	7.00	8.00	0.18	0.32
p (passive)	3.36	1.93	0.00	9.00	106	3.00	3.00	0.75	0.31
Ma	2.58	1.44	1.00	7.00	110	2.00	2.00	0.96	0.38
Mp	1.77	1.46	0.00	5.00	81	2.00	2.00	0.48	-0.51
Intellect	1.04	0.83	0.00	4.00	110	1.00	1.00	1.59	3.76
Zf	12.68	2.59	5.00	23.00	110	13.00	13.00	0.01	2.61
Zd	1.03	2.96	-6.50	9.00	110	0.50	-0.50	0.17	0.11
Blends	6.34	2.16	1.00	12.00	110	7.00	7.00	-0.63	0.03
Col Shd Blend	0.22	[0.51]	0.00	2.00	19	0.00	0.00	2.35	4.69
Afr	0.65	0.18	0.27	1.29	110	0.67	0.67	0.97	1.69
Popular	6.33	1.23	3.00	9.00	110	7.00	7.00	-0.59	0.22

NOTE: Standard Deviations shown in brackets indicate that the value is probably unreliable and/or misleading and should not be used to estimate expected ranges. Ordinarily these variables should not be included in most parametric analyses.

(continued)

Table 22.   (Continued)

15 YEAR OLDS (N = 110)

VARIABLE	MEAN	SD	MIN	MAX	FREQ	MEDIAN	MODE	SK	KU
X+%	0.78	0.07	0.50	0.90	110	0.77	0.75	-0.46	2.72
F+%	0.62	0.18	0.29	1.00	110	0.60	0.60	0.54	-0.44
X-%	0.07	0.05	0.00	0.43	99	0.09	0.05	3.29	23.26
Xu%	0.14	0.06	0.00	0.37	108	0.15	0.14	0.45	1.97
S-%	0.18	[0.27]	0.00	1.00	37	0.00	0.00	1.28	0.76
Isolate	0.15	0.07	0.00	0.47	110	0.15	0.16	1.76	8.18
H	3.42	1.96	0.00	8.00	109	3.00	5.00	0.49	-0.51
(H)	1.04	0.90	0.00	4.00	75	1.00	1.00	0.52	-0.15
Hd	0.57	0.82	0.00	4.00	48	0.00	0.00	1.97	5.02
(Hd)	0.54	0.50	0.00	1.00	59	1.00	1.00	-0.15	-2.01
Hx	0.00	[0.00]	0.00	0.00	0	0.00	0.00	----	----
All H Cont	5.57	2.28	1.00	9.00	110	5.00	5.00	-0.15	-0.95
A	7.98	1.96	3.00	15.00	110	8.00	7.00	0.55	1.91
(A)	0.36	[0.55]	0.00	3.00	37	0.00	0.00	1.55	3.35
Ad	2.08	[1.20]	0.00	9.00	102	2.00	2.00	2.26	11.70
(Ad)	0.05	[0.30]	0.00	2.00	4	0.00	0.00	5.80	34.15
An	0.43	[0.79]	0.00	3.00	43	1.00	0.00	0.24	-1.02
Art	0.85	0.63	0.00	4.00	82	1.00	1.00	1.01	4.67
Ay	0.14	[0.34]	0.00	1.00	15	0.00	0.00	2.15	2.66
Bl	0.22	[0.41]	0.00	1.00	24	0.00	0.00	1.38	-0.09
Bt	1.68	0.82	0.00	4.00	102	2.00	2.00	-0.05	-0.06
Cg	1.47	1.11	0.00	4.00	93	1.00	1.00	0.59	-0.80
Cl	0.09	[0.35]	0.00	2.00	8	0.00	0.00	4.12	17.53
Ex	0.12	[0.32]	0.00	1.00	13	0.00	0.00	2.40	3.82
Fi	0.69	[0.52]	0.00	2.00	73	1.00	1.00	-0.23	-0.72
Fd	0.30	[0.51]	0.00	2.00	25	1.00	1.00	-0.20	-1.47
Ge	0.01	[0.09]	0.00	1.00	1	0.00	0.00	10.49	110.00
Hh	0.89	0.60	0.00	4.00	88	1.00	1.00	1.36	7.28
Ls	1.12	0.71	0.00	2.00	88	1.00	1.00	-0.18	-1.00
Na	0.12	[0.35]	0.00	2.00	12	0.00	0.00	3.02	9.12
Sc	1.70	[1.34]	0.00	6.00	77	2.00	3.00	0.03	-0.83
Sx	0.11	[0.44]	0.00	3.00	8	0.00	0.00	4.64	23.43
Xy	0.04	[0.19]	0.00	1.00	4	0.00	0.00	5.02	23.65
Idio	1.09	1.47	0.00	7.00	52	0.00	0.00	1.49	2.28
DV	0.98	[0.70]	0.00	3.00	84	1.00	1.00	0.35	0.03
INCOM	0.88	[0.74]	0.00	4.00	76	1.00	1.00	0.75	1.58
DR	0.13	[0.33]	0.00	1.00	14	0.00	0.00	2.27	3.20
FABCOM	0.23	[0.46]	0.00	2.00	23	0.00	0.00	1.87	2.73
DV2	0.03	[0.16]	0.00	1.00	3	0.00	0.00	5.89	33.24
INC2	0.01	[0.09]	0.00	1.00	1	0.00	0.00	10.49	110.00
DR2	0.01	[0.09]	0.00	1.00	1	0.00	0.00	10.49	110.00
FAB2	0.04	[0.19]	0.00	1.00	4	0.00	0.00	5.02	23.65
ALOG	0.05	[0.26]	0.00	2.00	5	0.00	0.00	5.37	31.19
CONTAM	0.00	0.00	0.00	0.00	0	0.00	0.00	----	----
Sum6 Sp Sc	2.27	1.36	0.00	5.00	110	2.00	2.00	-0.11	-0.96
Sum6 Sp Sc2	0.08	[0.27]	0.00	1.00	9	0.00	0.00	3.09	7.71
WSum6	4.71	3.33	0.00	15.00	110	4.00	3.00	0.60	0.27
AB	0.03	[0.16]	0.00	1.00	3	0.00	0.00	5.89	33.24
AG	1.14	0.91	0.00	4.00	82	1.00	1.00	0.53	-0.05
CFB	0.00	0.00	0.00	0.00	0	0.00	0.00	----	----
COP	1.54	0.97	0.00	5.00	98	1.00	1.00	0.75	0.98
CP	0.00	[0.00]	0.00	0.00	0	0.00	0.00	----	----
MOR	0.54	[0.83]	0.00	4.00	41	0.00	0.00	1.74	3.06
PER	0.92	0.65	0.00	5.00	89	1.00	1.00	2.31	14.11
PSV	0.04	[0.19]	0.00	1.00	4	0.00	0.00	5.02	23.65

Table 22. (Continued)

16 YEAR OLDS (N = 140)

VARIABLE	MEAN	SD	MIN	MAX	FREQ	MEDIAN	MODE	SK	KU
R	22.89	5.16	14.00	31.00	140	21.00	20.00	0.94	1.70
W	8.96	2.37	3.00	20.00	140	9.00	9.00	1.70	8.32
D	11.91	3.74	0.00	21.00	139	12.00	12.00	-0.23	1.41
Dd	2.02	[1.82]	0.00	7.00	121	2.00	1.00	3.49	15.11
S	1.24	[1.23]	0.00	5.00	132	2.00	2.00	2.70	14.04
DQ+	7.94	2.04	2.00	13.00	140	8.00	8.00	-0.28	-0.13
DQo	13.12	3.47	5.00	27.00	140	12.00	12.00	1.23	4.58
DQv	0.89	[1.35]	0.00	5.00	59	0.00	0.00	1.59	1.62
DQv/+	0.84	[0.53]	0.00	2.00	46	0.00	0.00	2.21	3.98
FQX+	0.54	0.83	0.00	3.00	48	0.00	0.00	1.26	0.31
FQXo	16.43	3.36	7.00	29.00	140	16.00	15.00	0.59	2.16
FQXu	3.19	1.56	0.00	11.00	138	3.00	3.00	1.18	4.32
FQX-	1.58	0.91	0.00	5.00	126	2.00	2.00	0.70	2.97
FQXNone	0.06	[0.26]	0.00	2.00	7	0.00	0.00	5.01	27.20
MQ+	0.35	0.64	0.00	3.00	38	0.00	0.00	1.96	3.75
MQo	3.50	2.01	0.00	8.00	138	3.00	1.00	0.29	-0.86
MQu	0.37	0.50	0.00	2.00	51	0.00	0.00	0.71	-1.07
MQ-	0.09	[0.29]	0.00	1.00	13	0.00	0.00	2.84	6.13
MQNone	0.00	[0.00]	0.00	0.00	0	0.00	0.00	----	----
S-	0.34	[0.55]	0.00	2.00	43	0.00	0.00	1.32	0.81
M	4.31	2.13	1.00	9.00	140	4.00	4.00	0.20	-0.88
FM	4.58	1.66	1.00	9.00	140	4.00	4.00	0.04	-0.73
m	1.14	0.80	0.00	4.00	117	1.00	1.00	1.10	2.43
FM+m	5.72	1.78	2.00	10.00	140	6.00	7.00	0.03	-0.73
FC	3.43	1.34	0.00	8.00	137	3.00	3.00	0.14	1.16
CF	2.78	1.45	0.00	6.00	130	3.00	3.00	-0.05	-0.59
C	0.04	[0.20]	0.00	1.00	6	0.00	0.00	4.56	19.10
Cn	0.01	[0.12]	0.00	1.00	2	0.00	0.00	8.27	67.44
FC+CF+C+Cn	6.26	2.08	1.00	11.00	140	7.00	8.00	-0.56	-0.16
WGSum C	4.56	1.66	0.50	8.00	140	5.00	3.50	-0.42	-0.49
Sum C'	1.15	[1.27]	0.00	6.00	118	1.00	1.00	2.48	13.59
Sum T	1.02	[0.48]	0.00	3.00	128	1.00	1.00	2.44	13.39
Sum V	0.19	[0.51]	0.00	2.00	20	0.00	0.00	2.64	6.03
Sum Y	1.04	[1.21]	0.00	5.00	95	2.00	1.00	3.25	20.79
SumShd	3.44	2.35	0.00	23.00	139	4.00	4.00	4.25	31.18
Fr+rF	0.48	[0.41]	0.00	3.00	32	0.00	0.00	6.27	48.14
FD	1.31	[0.93]	0.00	5.00	108	1.00	2.00	0.33	0.77
F	6.85	2.69	2.00	17.00	140	6.00	5.00	0.96	0.93
PAIR	9.04	2.00	1.00	14.00	140	9.00	10.00	-0.90	3.36
3r(2)/R	0.43	0.09	0.05	0.79	140	0.45	0.50	-0.32	3.89
LAMBDA	0.65	0.21	0.24	1.71	140	0.68	0.63	1.85	7.03
EA	8.87	2.23	2.00	13.50	140	9.00	8.50	-0.59	0.63
es	9.21	3.29	4.00	17.00	140	10.00	8.00	2.09	12.09
D	-0.31	1.31	-10.00	2.00	140	0.00	0.00	-3.70	22.64
AdjD	-0.11	1.04	-5.00	2.00	140	0.00	0.00	-1.56	5.47
a (active)	6.82	1.71	3.00	12.00	140	7.00	6.00	0.25	0.13
p (passive)	3.22	1.89	0.00	9.00	133	3.00	2.00	0.70	0.33
Ma	2.62	1.42	1.00	7.00	140	2.00	2.00	0.88	0.20
Mp	1.69	1.38	0.00	5.00	106	2.00	2.00	0.55	-0.32
Intellect	1.14	0.93	0.00	5.00	140	1.00	1.00	1.38	2.72
Zf	12.61	2.64	5.00	23.00	140	13.00	13.00	0.37	3.18
Zd	1.12	2.96	-6.50	9.00	140	0.75	-0.50	0.09	0.15
Blends	6.11	2.13	1.00	12.00	140	7.00	7.00	-0.44	-0.26
Col Shd Blends	0.24	[0.50]	0.00	2.00	28	0.00	0.00	2.08	3.56
Afr	0.65	0.17	0.27	1.29	140	0.67	0.67	0.80	1.61
Popular	6.46	1.27	3.00	10.00	140	7.00	7.00	-0.35	0.39

NOTE: Standard Deviations shown in brackets indicate that the value is probably unreliable and/or misleading and should not be used to estimate expected ranges. Ordinarily these variables should not be included in most parametric analyses.

(continued)

Table 22.   (Continued)

TABLE 22.   16 YEAR OLDS   (N = 140)

VARIABLE	MEAN	SD	MIN	MAX	FREQ	MEDIAN	MODE	SK	KU
X+%	0.78	0.07	0.50	0.90	140	0.79	0.75	-0.42	2.27
F+%	0.74	0.18	0.29	1.00	140	0.70	0.67	0.36	-0.58
X-%	0.07	0.05	0.00	0.25	126	0.07	0.05	3.08	22.84
Xu%	0.14	0.06	0.00	0.37	138	0.15	0.15	0.45	1.42
S-%	0.16	[0.27]	0.00	1.00	43	0.00	0.00	1.48	1.38
Isolate	0.16	0.07	0.00	0.47	140	0.16	0.16	1.31	4.09
H	3.39	1.94	0.00	8.00	139	3.00	3.00	0.62	-0.28
(H)	1.07	0.89	0.00	4.00	97	1.00	1.00	0.36	-0.43
Hd	0.59	0.81	0.00	4.00	62	0.00	0.00	1.79	4.08
(Hd)	0.46	0.50	0.00	1.00	64	0.00	0.00	0.17	-2.00
Hx	0.00	[0.00]	0.00	0.00	0	0.00	0.00	----	----
All H Cont	5.51	2.12	1.00	9.00	140	5.00	5.00	-0.06	-0.76
A	8.04	1.97	3.00	15.00	140	8.00	7.00	0.46	1.18
(A)	0.32	[0.54]	0.00	3.00	41	0.00	0.00	1.73	3.69
Ad	2.11	[1.15]	0.00	9.00	131	2.00	2.00	1.98	10.34
(Ad)	0.07	[0.33]	0.00	2.00	7	0.00	0.00	4.94	24.56
An	0.41	[0.79]	0.00	4.00	32	1.00	0.00	0.45	-0.96
Art	0.83	0.68	0.00	4.00	97	1.00	1.00	0.79	2.33
Ay	0.19	[0.41]	0.00	2.00	25	0.00	0.00	1.95	2.75
Bl	0.21	[0.43]	0.00	2.00	29	0.00	0.00	1.68	1.61
Bt	1.87	1.03	0.00	6.00	130	2.00	2.00	0.62	1.27
Cg	1.39	1.06	0.00	4.00	116	1.00	1.00	0.65	-0.57
Cl	0.11	[0.36]	0.00	2.00	14	0.00	0.00	3.33	11.30
Ex	0.31	[0.32]	0.00	1.00	26	0.00	0.00	2.45	4.06
Fi	0.39	[0.57]	0.00	2.00	42	1.00	0.00	0.20	-0.76
Fd	0.31	[0.52]	0.00	2.00	31	0.50	0.00	0.13	-1.62
Ge	0.01	[0.12]	0.00	1.00	2	0.00	0.00	8.28	67.44
Hh	0.91	0.67	0.00	4.00	108	1.00	1.00	1.14	3.97
Ls	1.07	0.74	0.00	3.00	108	1.00	1.00	-0.00	-0.87
Na	0.17	[0.41]	0.00	2.00	22	0.00	0.00	2.36	5.05
Sc	1.51	[1.31]	0.00	6.00	93	2.00	0.00	0.23	-0.82
Sx	0.11	[0.41]	0.00	3.00	11	0.00	0.00	4.58	23.67
Xy	0.04	[0.19]	0.00	1.00	5	0.00	0.00	5.06	23.93
Idio	1.31	1.45	0.00	7.00	81	1.00	0.00	1.07	1.04
DV	0.99	[0.71]	0.00	3.00	107	1.00	1.00	0.39	0.11
INCOM	0.83	[0.75]	0.00	4.00	91	1.00	1.00	0.81	1.34
DR	0.14	[0.37]	0.00	2.00	19	0.00	0.00	2.48	5.51
FABCOM	0.21	[0.44]	0.00	2.00	28	0.00	0.00	1.89	2.75
DV2	0.02	[0.14]	0.00	1.00	3	0.00	0.00	6.68	43.26
INC2	0.01	[0.12]	0.00	1.00	2	0.00	0.00	8.28	67.44
DR2	0.01	[0.08]	0.00	1.00	1	0.00	0.00	11.83	140.00
FAB2	0.04	[0.19]	0.00	1.00	5	0.00	0.00	5.06	23.93
ALOG	0.05	[0.25]	0.00	2.00	6	0.00	0.00	5.49	32.88
CONTAM	0.00	0.00	0.00	0.00	0	0.00	0.00	----	----
Sum6 Sp Sc	2.22	1.34	0.00	8.00	124	3.00	2.00	0.03	-0.90
Sum6 Sp Sc2	0.08	[0.27]	0.00	1.00	11	0.00	0.00	3.17	8.14
WSum6	4.57	3.23	0.00	15.00	140	4.00	3.00	0.67	0.32
AB	0.06	[0.25]	0.00	1.00	9	0.00	0.00	3.59	11.06
AG	1.20	0.99	0.00	5.00	106	1.00	1.00	1.03	1.98
CFB	0.00	0.00	0.00	0.00	0	0.00	0.00	----	----
COP	1.60	1.10	0.00	5.00	120	1.00	1.00	0.69	0.45
CP	0.00	[0.00]	0.00	0.00	0	0.00	0.00	----	----
MOR	0.58	[0.81]	0.00	4.00	59	0.00	0.00	1.57	2.57
PER	0.96	0.72	0.00	5.00	110	1.00	1.00	1.60	7.12
PSV	0.04	[0.20]	0.00	1.00	4	0.00	0.00	4.56	29.10

Table 23. Frequencies for 33 Variables for 1390 Nonpatient Children and Adolescents by Age

	AGE 5 (N = 90) Freq	%	AGE 6 (N = 80) Freq	%	AGE 7 (N = 120) Freq	%	AGE 8 (N = 120) Freq	%	AGE 9 (N = 140) Freq	%	AGE 10 (N = 120) Freq	%
EB STYLE												
Introversive	2	2%	1	1%	9	8%	16	13%	33	24%	26	22%
Pervasive	0	0%	0	0%	0	0%	0	0%	3	2%	0	0%
Ambitent	24	27%	20	25%	44	37%	48	40%	51	36%	38	32%
Extratensive	64	71%	59	74%	67	56%	56	47%	56	40%	56	47%
Pervasive	62	69%	46	58%	40	33%	32	27%	15	11%	26	22%
D SCORE & ADJUSTED D SCORE												
D Score > 0	0	0%	0	0%	0	0%	6	5%	7	5%	2	2%
D Score = 0	68	76%	51	64%	69	58%	90	75%	117	84%	100	83%
D Score < 0	22	24%	29	36%	51	43%	24	20%	16	11%	18	15%
D Score < -1	4	4%	4	5%	12	10%	8	7%	9	6%	2	2%
Adj D Score > 0	0	0%	0	0%	0	0%	6	5%	9	6%	6	5%
Adj D Score = 0	72	80%	63	79%	69	58%	98	82%	121	86%	96	80%
Adj D Score < 0	18	20%	17	21%	51	43%	16	13%	10	7%	18	15%
Adj D Score < -1	3	3%	4	5%	5	4%	8	7%	7	5%	2	2%
Zd > +3.0 (Overincorp)	3	3%	0	0%	0	0%	8	7%	28	20%	30	25%
Zd < -3.0 (Underincorp)	23	26%	27	34%	32	27%	19	16%	22	16%	19	16%
FORM QUALITY DEVIATIONS												
X+% > .89	0	0%	0	0%	0	0%	0	0%	1	1%	0	0%
X+% < .70	51	57%	28	35%	22	18%	56	47%	48	34%	12	10%
X+% < .61	25	28%	13	16%	12	10%	16	13%	11	8%	13	11%
X+% < .50	4	4%	0	0%	0	0%	3	3%	3	2%	3	3%
F+% < .70	15	17%	27	34%	81	68%	68	57%	67	48%	92	77%
Xu% > .20	49	54%	59	74%	0	0%	32	27%	36	26%	22	18%
X-% > .15	9	10%	12	15%	12	10%	14	12%	21	15%	17	14%
X-% > .20	1	1%	1	1%	6	5%	2	2%	2	1%	8	7%
X-% > .30	0	0%	0	0%	0	0%	0	0%	0	0%	0	0%
FC:CF+C RATIO												
FC > (CF+C) + 2	0	0%	0	0%	9	8%	1	1%	0	0%	1	1%
FC > (CF+C) + 1	0	0%	0	0%	12	10%	9	8%	10	7%	14	12%
(CF+C) > FC+1	87	97%	71	89%	17	14%	48	40%	30	21%	60	50%
(CF+C) > FC+2	43	48%	49	61%	11	9%	32	27%	19	14%	21	18%

(continued)

Table 23. (Continued)

	AGE 5 (N = 90) Freq	%	AGE 6 (N = 80) Freq	%	AGE 7 (N = 120) Freq	%	AGE 8 (N = 120) Freq	%	AGE 9 (N = 140) Freq	%	AGE 10 (N = 120) Freq	%
CONSTELLATIONS & INDICES												
HVI Positive	0	0%	0	0%	0	0%	0	0%	0	0%	0	0%
OBS Positive	0	0%	0	0%	0	0%	0	0%	0	0%	0	0%
SCZI = 6	0	0%	0	0%	0	0%	0	0%	0	0%	0	0%
SCZI = 5	0	0%	0	0%	0	0%	0	0%	0	0%	0	0%
SCZI = 4	0	0%	0	0%	0	0%	0	0%	0	0%	0	0%
DEPI = 7	0	0%	0	0%	0	0%	0	0%	0	0%	0	0%
DEPI = 6	0	0%	0	0%	0	0%	0	0%	0	0%	0	0%
DEPI = 5	0	0%	0	0%	0	0%	0	0%	0	0%	0	0%
CDI = 5	1	1%	2	2%	3	3%	3	3%	0	0%	0	0%
CDI = 4	11	12%	10	13%	13	11%	8	7%	9	6%	18	15%
MISCELLANEOUS VARIABLES												
Lambda > .99	12	12%	9	11%	14	12%	20	17%	20	14%	13	11%
S > 2	21	23%	4	5%	37	31%	9	8%	12	9%	14	12%
Sum T = 0	33	37%	11	14%	10	8%	8	7%	17	12%	14	12%
Sum T > 1	0	0%	0	0%	2	2%	8	7%	6	4%	8	7%
3r+(2)/R < .33	0	0%	4	5%	0	0%	1	1%	7	5%	4	3%
3r+(2)/R > .44	86	96%	68	85%	86	72%	82	68%	56	40%	110	92%
PureC > 1	14	16%	31	39%	9	8%	3	3%	9	6%	2	2%
Afr < .40	0	0%	12	15%	0	0%	1	1%	8	6%	2	2%
Afr < .50	13	14%	19	24%	9	8%	12	10%	16	11%	16	13%
(FM+m) < Sum Shading	0	0%	0	0%	2	2%	10	8%	14	10%	8	7%
Populars < 4	6	7%	8	10%	3	3%	4	3%	0	0%	4	3%
COP = 0	13	14%	13	16%	12	10%	6	5%	4	3%	6	5%
COP > 2	6	6%	5	6%	16	13%	30	25%	37	26%	21	18%
AG = 0	8	9%	40	50%	0	0%	24	20%	12	9%	3	3%
AG > 2	4	4%	4	5%	3	3%	13	11%	19	14%	18	15%
MOR > 2	3	3%	5	6%	6	5%	3	3%	11	8%	13	11%
Level 2 Sp.Sc. > 0	32	36%	16	20%	19	16%	13	11%	14	10%	10	8%
Sum 6 Sp. Sc. > 6	19	21%	22	27%	22	18%	32	27%	23	16%	21	18%
Pure H < 2	4	4%	24	30%	63	52%	32	27%	31	22%	36	30%
Pure H = 0	1	1%	8	10%	2	2%	4	3%	2	1%	4	3%
p > a+1	7	8%	5	6%	16	13%	10	8%	19	14%	12	10%
Mp > Ma	9	10%	9	11%	11	9%	14	12%	17	12%	14	12%

	AGE 11 (N = 135)		AGE 12 (N = 120)		AGE 13 (N = 110)		AGE 14 (N = 105)		AGE 15 (N = 110)		AGE 16 (N = 140)	
	Freq	%	Freq	%	Freq	%	Freq	%	Freq	%	Freq	%
EB STYLE												
Introversive	41	30%	38	32%	34	31%	36	34%	41	37%	52	37%
Super-Introversive	0	0%	8	7%	10	9%	10	10%	8	7%	12	9%
Ambient	34	25%	39	33%	39	35%	26	25%	23	21%	27	19%
Extratensive	60	44%	43	36%	37	34%	43	41%	46	42%	61	44%
Super-Extratensive	14	10%	22	18%	18	16%	18	17%	18	16%	23	16%
EA - es DIFFERENCES: D-SCORES												
D Score > 0	0	0%	4	3%	14	13%	10	10%	9	8%	14	10%
D Score = 0	123	91$	90	75%	70	64%	69	66%	71	65%	110	79%
D Score < 0	12	9%	26	22%	26	24%	26	25%	30	27%	16	11%
D Score < -1	5	4%	3	3%	4	4%	3	3%	10	9%	9	6%
Adj D Score > 0	4	3%	14	12%	25	23%	21	20%	16	15%	17	12%
Adj D Score = 0	119	88%	80	67%	65	59%	70	67%	67	61%	86	61%
Adj D Score < 0	11	8%	26	22%	20	18%	14	13%	27	25%	12	9%
Adj D Score < -1	4	3%	2	2%	2	2%	2	2%	6	5%	7	5%
Zd > +3.0 (Overincorp)	36	27%	34	28%	30	27%	21	20%	25	23%	30	21%
Zd < -3.0 (Underincorp)	14	10%	20	17%	15	14%	16	15%	16	15%	14	10%
FORM QUALITY DEVIATIONS												
X+% > .89	2	1%	0	0%	2	2%	1	1%	7	6%	8	6%
X+% < .70	21	16%	18	15%	16	15%	16	15%	7	6%	12	9%
X+% < .61	14	10%	6	5%	8	7%	8	8%	3	3%	3	2%
X+% < .50	0	0%	4	3%	6	5%	4	4%	0	0%	0	0%
F+% < .70	117	87%	91	76%	82	75%	57	54%	77	70%	72	51%
Xu% > .20	26	19%	16	13%	16	15%	14	13%	9	8%	16	11%
X-% > .15	20	15%	6	5%	12	11%	10	10%	2	2%	2	1%
X-% > .20	18	13%	4	3%	6	5%	4	4%	2	2%	2	1%
X-% > .30	0	0%	2	2%	2	2%	0	0%	1	1%	0	0%
FC:CF+C RATIO												
FC > (CF+C) + 2	3	2%	8	7%	6	5%	4	4%	10	9%	18	13%
FC > (CF+C) + 1	17	13%	12	10%	12	11%	8	8%	20	18%	38	27%
(CF+C) > FC+1	45	33%	24	20%	19	17%	16	15%	23	21%	23	16%
(CF+C) > FC+2	14	10%	0	0%	3	3%	3	3%	2	2%	2	1%

(continued)

Table 23. (Continued)

	AGE 11 (N = 135)		AGE 12 (N = 120)		AGE 13 (N = 110)		AGE 14 (N = 105)		AGE 15 (N = 110)		AGE 16 (N = 140)	
	Freq	%	Freq	%	Freq	%	Freq	%	Freq	%	Freq	%
CONSTELLATIONS & INDICES												
HVI Positive	3	2%	4	3%	3	3%	1	1%	0	0%	1	1%
OBS Positive	0	0%	0	0%	0	0%	0	0%	1	1%	1	1%
SCZI = 6	0	0%	0	0%	0	0%	0	0%	0	0%	0	0%
SCZI = 5	0	0%	0	0%	0	0%	0	0%	0	0%	0	0%
SCZI = 4	0	0%	0	0%	0	0%	0	0%	0	0%	0	0%
DEPI = 7	0	0%	0	0%	0	0%	0	0%	0	0%	0	0%
DEPI = 6	0	0%	0	0%	0	0%	0	0%	0	0%	0	0%
DEPI = 5	0	0%	1	1%	1	1%	0	0%	0	0%	0	0%
CDI = 5	0	0%	0	0%	0	0%	0	0%	1	1%	1	1%
CDI = 4	12	9%	29	24%	14	13%	13	12%	11	10%	12	9%
MISCELLANEOUS VARIABLES												
Lambda > .99	16	12%	10	8%	10	9%	7	7%	8	7%	9	6%
S > 2	18	13%	10	8%	16	15%	13	12%	17	15%	18	13%
Sum T = 0	19	14%	14	12%	20	18%	17	16%	6	5%	12	9%
Sum T > 1	11	8%	0	0%	4	4%	2	2%	9	8%	11	8%
3r+(2)/R < .33	0	0%	6	5%	18	16%	18	17%	7	6%	10	7%
3r+(2)/R > .44	123	91%	85	71%	62	56%	59	56%	49	45%	74	53%
PureC > 1	0	0%	0	0%	0	0%	0	0%	0	0%	0	0%
Afr < .40	0	0%	6	5%	8	7%	6	6%	5	5%	6	4%
Afr < .50	13	10%	45	38%	33	30%	24	23%	19	17%	21	15%
(FM+m) < Sum Shading	10	7%	12	10%	11	10%	9	9%	17	15%	20	14%
Populars < 4	0	0%	4	3%	4	4%	1	1%	3	3%	4	3%
COP = 0	6	4%	6	5%	10	9%	13	12%	12	11%	20	14%
COP > 2	13	10%	19	16%	16	15%	18	17%	15	14%	24	17%
AG = 0	5	4%	21	18%	25	23%	19	18%	28	25%	34	24%
AG > 2	10	7%	15	13%	8	7%	10	10%	8	7%	11	8%
MOR > 2	6	4%	6	5%	2	2%	5	5%	4	4%	5	4%
Level 2 Sp.Sc. > 0	20	15%	22	18%	13	12%	9	9%	9	8%	7	5%
Sum 6 Sp. Sc. > 6	22	16%	17	14%	16	15%	12	11%	9	8%	9	6%
Pure H < 2	27	20%	30	25%	28	25%	18	17%	23	21%	14	10%
Pure H = 0	4	3%	0	0%	0	0%	0	0%	1	1%	1	1%
p > a+1	12	9%	10	8%	7	6%	13	12%	13	12%	15	11%
Mp > Ma	20	15%	18	15%	9	8%	8	8%	16	15%	17	12%

Table 24. Descriptive Statistics for 320 Inpatient Schizophrenics

VARIABLE	MEAN	SD	MIN	MAX	FREQ	MEDIAN	MODE	SK	KU
R	23.44	8.66	14.00	45.00	320	21.00	19.00	1.21	0.88
W	8.79	5.11	0.00	22.00	317	9.00	10.00	0.68	0.11
D	9.79	6.47	0.00	32.00	313	10.00	10.00	0.82	0.47
Dd	4.86	[5.04]	0.00	21.00	300	3.00	2.00	1.98	3.47
S	2.77	[2.49]	0.00	10.00	257	2.00	2.00	0.96	0.33
DQ+	6.93	4.32	0.00	20.00	288	7.00	6.00	0.23	-0.56
DQo	14.87	7.80	3.00	42.00	320	12.00	9.00	1.46	1.45
DQv	1.43	[1.74]	0.00	8.00	216	1.00	1.00	2.20	5.55
DQv/+	0.21	[0.45]	0.00	2.00	63	0.00	0.00	1.93	2.92
FQX+	0.07	0.31	0.00	2.00	15	0.00	0.00	5.12	26.51
FQXo	8.92	3.39	2.00	18.00	320	9.00	8.00	0.39	0.01
FQXu	4.89	3.17	0.00	14.00	316	4.00	3.00	0.83	-0.12
FQX-	8.95	5.32	0.00	27.00	317	7.00	7.00	1.24	1.30
FQXNone	0.61	[0.95]	0.00	4.00	129	0.00	0.00	1.95	3.85
MQ+	0.05	0.29	0.00	2.00	10	0.00	0.00	6.07	36.52
MQo	2.40	1.96	0.00	7.00	263	2.00	1.00	0.62	-0.63
MQu	1.06	1.17	0.00	5.00	195	1.00	0.00	1.37	2.02
MQ-	2.42	[2.46]	0.00	10.00	256	2.00	1.00	1.32	0.81
MQNone	0.07	[0.25]	0.00	1.00	21	0.00	0.00	3.53	10.49
S-	1.61	[1.77]	0.00	6.00	191	1.00	0.00	0.91	-0.21
M	6.00	4.33	0.00	16.00	289	6.00	6.00	0.57	-0.42
FM	2.41	2.43	0.00	13.00	246	2.00	1.00	1.23	1.24
m	1.18	1.17	0.00	5.00	207	1.00	0.00	1.00	0.87
FM+m	3.59	2.92	0.00	15.00	277	3.00	3.00	0.89	0.35
FC	1.54	1.60	0.00	7.00	227	1.00	1.00	1.12	0.44
CF	1.24	1.38	0.00	5.00	198	1.00	0.00	1.15	0.55
C	0.42	[0.72]	0.00	3.00	101	0.00	0.00	1.97	3.88
Cn	0.06	[0.29]	0.00	2.00	13	0.00	0.00	5.56	31.66
FC+CF+C+Cn	3.25	2.61	0.00	11.00	320	3.00	1.00	1.02	0.82
WGSum C	2.63	2.23	0.00	10.50	320	2.00	1.50	1.13	1.21
Sum C'	1.50	[1.57]	0.00	6.00	224	1.00	1.00	1.27	1.04
Sum T	0.46	[0.99]	0.00	7.00	97	0.00	0.00	3.88	19.29
Sum V	0.60	[1.20]	0.00	7.00	112	0.00	0.00	3.46	14.31
Sum Y	2.12	[2.62]	0.00	9.00	189	1.00	0.00	1.11	-0.07
SumShd	4.68	4.51	0.00	23.00	268	3.50	0.00	1.51	2.90
Fr+rF	0.17	[0.48]	0.00	2.00	41	0.00	0.00	2.83	7.15
FD	0.60	[1.08]	0.00	6.00	108	0.00	0.00	2.56	8.29
F	10.46	6.42	1.00	32.00	320	9.00	6.00	1.15	1.01
PAIR	8.53	4.90	0.00	29.00	320	8.00	7.00	0.53	0.33
3r(2)/R	0.38	0.18	0.10	0.75	320	0.37	0.33	-0.08	-0.49
LAMBDA	1.57	3.47	0.05	29.00	320	0.85	0.33	6.08	41.06
EA	8.63	5.39	2.00	24.00	320	8.00	8.00	0.77	0.43
es	8.27	5.99	3.00	28.00	320	6.50	2.00	0.83	0.07
D	0.14	1.58	-7.00	4.00	320	0.00	0.00	-1.10	5.39
AdjD	0.69	1.45	-4.00	4.00	320	0.00	0.00	0.37	0.74
a (active)	5.51	3.94	0.00	16.00	290	5.00	4.00	0.76	0.19
p (passive)	4.25	3.28	0.00	14.00	291	4.00	2.00	0.81	-0.17
Ma	3.38	2.76	0.00	10.00	267	3.00	2.00	0.68	-0.44
Mp	2.75	2.54	0.00	9.00	260	2.00	1.00	0.89	-0.22
Intellect	1.32	1.88	0.00	8.00	320	1.00	0.00	1.84	3.08
Zf	12.67	5.21	2.00	26.00	320	12.00	11.00	0.66	0.44
Zd	1.33	4.93	-11.50	13.50	320	1.50	-5.00	0.08	-0.21
Blends	4.28	3.97	0.00	19.00	273	3.00	0.00	1.43	2.27
Col Shd Blends	0.67	[1.26]	0.00	7.00	109	0.00	0.00	2.73	8.99
Afr	0.52	0.20	0.18	1.25	320	0.50	0.33	0.77	0.95
Popular	4.67	2.08	1.00	10.00	320	5.00	4.00	0.29	-0.30

NOTE: Standard Deviations shown in brackets indicate that the value is probably unreliable and/or misleading and should not be used to estimate expected ranges. Ordinarily these variables should not be included in most parametric analyses.

(continued)

Table 24.   (Continued)

VARIABLE	MEAN	SD	MIN	MAX	FREQ	MEDIAN	MODE	SK	KU
X+%	0.40	0.14	0.13	0.77	320	0.40	0.35	0.22	-0.18
F+%	0.42	0.20	0.00	1.00	301	0.40	0.50	0.39	0.75
X-%	0.37	0.14	0.05	0.72	320	0.37	0.32	-0.11	0.14
Xu%	0.20	0.09	0.00	0.43	316	0.19	0.27	0.35	-0.29
S-%	0.20	[0.22]	0.00	0.83	191	0.14	0.00	0.92	-0.04
Isolate	0.15	0.13	0.00	0.54	320	0.13	0.00	1.15	1.17
H	3.17	2.44	0.00	9.00	273	3.00	2.00	0.62	-0.36
(H)	1.60	1.45	0.00	8.00	267	1.00	1.00	1.80	4.27
Hd	1.88	2.18	0.00	9.00	212	1.00	0.00	1.61	2.35
(Hd)	0.77	0.98	0.00	6.00	168	1.00	0.00	2.12	7.38
Hx	0.14	[0.49]	0.00	3.00	27	0.00	0.00	3.89	15.22
All H Cont	7.41	4.19	0.00	21.00	315	7.00	8.00	0.69	0.47
A	8.21	3.53	3.00	27.00	320	7.00	7.00	1.08	2.00
(A)	0.53	[0.85]	0.00	3.00	109	0.00	0.00	1.50	1.24
Ad	2.03	[1.88]	0.00	10.00	235	2.00	0.00	1.06	1.76
(Ad)	0.27	[0.62]	0.00	3.00	57	0.00	0.00	2.38	4.90
An	0.98	[1.49]	0.00	8.00	148	0.00	0.00	2.11	5.12
Art	0.73	1.41	0.00	7.00	102	0.00	0.00	2.67	7.84
Ay	0.21	[0.48]	0.00	5.00	62	0.00	0.00	3.96	29.41
Bl	0.32	[0.79]	0.00	5.00	73	0.00	0.00	4.09	20.40
Bt	0.82	1.04	0.00	5.00	162	1.00	0.00	1.54	2.85
Cg	1.83	1.88	0.00	9.00	232	1.00	0.00	1.38	1.93
Cl	0.26	[0.66]	0.00	4.00	60	0.00	0.00	3.55	15.34
Ex	0.11	[0.33]	0.00	2.00	33	0.00	0.00	3.02	8.82
Fi	0.38	[0.59]	0.00	2.00	103	0.00	0.00	1.31	0.69
Fd	0.32	[0.67]	0.00	4.00	74	0.00	0.00	2.61	7.45
Ge	0.18	[0.53]	0.00	2.00	39	0.00	0.00	2.79	6.43
Hh	0.38	0.93	0.00	6.00	72	0.00	0.00	3.38	12.92
Ls	0.44	0.85	0.00	4.00	88	0.00	0.00	2.20	4.59
Na	0.72	[1.00]	0.00	4.00	138	0.00	0.00	1.35	1.04
Sc	0.49	[0.69]	0.00	3.00	124	0.00	0.00	1.25	0.92
Sx	1.36	[2.16]	0.00	8.00	146	0.00	0.00	1.85	2.63
Xy	0.16	[0.45]	0.00	2.00	42	0.00	0.00	2.83	7.43
Idio	2.56	2.33	0.00	10.00	266	2.00	1.00	1.38	2.04
DV	0.78	[1.18]	0.00	7.00	141	0.00	0.00	2.11	5.25
INCOM	1.53	[1.44]	0.00	6.00	226	1.00	0.00	0.90	0.44
DR	0.97	[1.49]	0.00	7.00	148	0.00	0.00	2.31	6.04
FABCOM	0.72	[1.07]	0.00	5.00	140	0.00	0.00	1.99	4.37
DV2	0.28	[0.57]	0.00	5.00	75	0.00	0.00	2.96	15.03
INC2	1.17	[1.68]	0.00	7.00	157	0.00	0.00	1.76	2.78
DR2	1.90	[2.80]	0.00	14.00	182	1.00	0.00	1.97	4.04
FAB2	1.83	[2.04]	0.00	9.00	202	1.00	0.00	1.12	0.39
ALOG	0.93	[1.40]	0.00	6.00	141	0.00	0.00	1.83	3.32
CONTAM	0.13	0.41	0.00	2.00	35	0.00	0.00	3.18	9.84
Sum6 Sp Sc	5.07	3.23	0.00	15.00	320	5.00	4.00	1.09	1.29
Sum6 Sp Sc2	5.18	[4.92]	0.00	25.00	277	3.00	1.00	1.09	0.57
WSum6	44.69	35.40	0.00	173.00	320	32.00	32.00	1.07	0.74
AB	0.19	[0.45]	0.00	2.00	52	0.00	0.00	2.40	5.18
AG	1.26	1.85	0.00	9.00	161	1.00	0.00	2.05	4.49
CFB	0.05	0.26	0.00	2.00	8	0.00	0.00	6.12	38.81
COP	0.81	1.03	0.00	5.00	158	0.00	0.00	1.36	1.73
CP	0.04	[0.19]	0.00	1.00	12	0.00	0.00	4.89	22.07
MOR	1.47	[1.71]	0.00	7.00	192	1.00	0.00	1.31	1.31
PER	1.22	1.97	0.00	15.00	166	1.00	0.00	2.95	11.91
PSV	0.13	[0.37]	0.00	2.00	37	0.00	0.00	2.95	8.56

Table 25. Frequency Data for 320 Inpatient Schizophrenics

DEMOGRAPHY VARIABLES

MARITAL STATUS			AGE			RACE		
Single	232	73%	18-25	154	48%	White	271	85%
Lives w/S.O.	0	0%	26-35	83	26%	Black	26	8%
Married	70	22%	36-45	45	14%	Hispanic	23	7%
Separated	8	2%	46-55	14	4%	Asian	0	0%
Divorced	10	3%						
Widowed	0	0%				EDUCATION		
						Under 12	47	15%
SEX						12 Years	133	42%
Male	153	48%				13-15 Yrs	94	29%
Female	167	52%				16+ Yrs	46	14%

RATIOS, PERCENTAGES AND SPECIAL INDICES

EB STYLE			FORM QUALITY DEVIATIONS		
Introversive	191	60%	X+% > .89	0	0%
Pervasive	128	40%	X+% < .70	309	97%
Ambitent	95	30%	X+% < .61	300	94%
Extratensive	34	11%	X+% < .50	234	73%
Pervasive	19	6%	F+% < .70	286	89%
			Xu% > .20	142	44%
D SCORE & ADJUSTED D SCORE			X-% > .15	290	91%
D Score > 0	99	31%	X-% > .20	288	90%
D Score = 0	152	48%	X-% > .30	221	69%
D Score < 0	69	22%			
D Score < -1	19	6%	FC:CF+C RATIO		
			FC > (CF+C) + 2	38	12%
Adj D Score > 0	132	41%	FC > (CF+C) + 1	51	16%
Adj D Score = 0	153	48%	(CF+C) > FC+1	81	25%
Adj D Score < 0	35	11%	(CF+C) > FC+2	44	14%
Adj D Score < -1	12	4%			
			S-Constellation Positive	18	6%
Zd > +3.0 (Overincorp)	121	38%	HVI Positive	56	18%
Zd < -3.0 (Underincorp)	82	26%	OBS Positive	0	0%

SCZI = 6	106	33%	DEPI = 7	3	1%	CDI = 5	22	7%
SCZI = 5	83	26%	DEPI = 6	15	5%	CDI = 4	57	18%
SCZI = 4	72	23%	DEPI = 5	42	13%			

MISCELLANEOUS VARIABLES

Lambda > .99	124	39%	(2AB+Art+Ay) > 5	38	12%
Dd > 3	151	47%	Populars < 4	101	32%
DQv + DQv/+ > 2	63	20%	Populars > 7	20	6%
S > 2	136	43%	COP = 0	162	51%
Sum T = 0	223	70%	COP > 2	23	7%
Sum T > 1	22	7%	AG = 0	159	50%
3r+(2)/R < .33	112	35%	AG > 2	53	17%
3r+(2)/R > .44	115	36%	MOR > 2	71	22%
Fr + rF > 0	41	13%	Level 2 Sp.Sc. > 0	277	87%
PureC > 0	101	32%	Sum 6 Sp. Sc. > 6	217	68%
PureC > 1	21	7%	Pure H < 2	92	29%
Afr < .40	99	31%	Pure H = 0	47	15%
Afr < .50	151	47%	p > a+1	60	19%
(FM+m) < Sum Shading	131	41%	Mp > Ma	111	35%

Table 26.   Descriptive Statistics for 315 Inpatient Depressives

VARIABLE	MEAN	SD	MIN	MAX	FREQ	MEDIAN	MODE	SK	KU
R	22.70	8.52	14.00	41.00	315	19.00	19.00	1.56	2.59
W	8.48	4.13	0.00	18.00	306	9.00	9.00	-0.07	-0.79
D	9.94	6.01	1.00	30.00	315	8.00	7.00	1.06	0.95
Dd	4.28	[5.25]	0.00	21.00	275	3.00	2.00	2.55	7.97
S	2.51	[2.30]	0.00	10.00	261	2.00	1.00	1.35	1.97
DQ+	5.96	3.33	0.00	18.00	308	5.00	4.00	0.77	0.82
DQo	13.99	7.86	4.00	46.00	315	12.00	11.00	1.73	3.57
DQv	2.46	[1.97]	0.00	8.00	262	2.00	1.00	0.72	-0.08
DQv/+	0.29	[0.63]	0.00	3.00	64	0.00	0.00	2.12	3.58
FQX+	0.04	0.24	0.00	3.00	11	0.00	0.00	7.80	76.85
FQXo	11.76	4.28	4.00	28.00	315	11.00	11.00	0.82	1.06
FQXu	5.20	3.24	1.00	14.00	315	5.00	2.00	0.79	0.10
FQX-	4.70	3.35	0.00	18.00	302	4.00	2.00	1.37	2.71
FQXNone	1.00	[1.29]	0.00	6.00	166	1.00	0.00	1.46	1.73
MQ+	0.02	0.18	0.00	2.00	7	0.00	0.00	7.71	65.72
MQo	2.25	1.46	0.00	6.00	288	2.00	2.00	0.69	0.12
MQu	0.64	0.95	0.00	5.00	127	0.00	0.00	1.93	5.19
MQ-	0.58	[0.81]	0.00	4.00	127	0.00	0.00	1.33	1.57
MQNone	0.08	[0.27]	0.00	1.00	25	0.00	0.00	3.13	7.83
S-	1.04	[1.21]	0.00	5.00	179	1.00	0.00	1.27	1.16
M	3.57	2.17	0.00	9.00	300	3.00	4.00	0.50	-0.31
FM	3.12	2.76	0.00	14.00	278	3.00	2.00	1.86	4.81
m	1.69	1.89	0.00	11.00	217	1.00	0.00	2.15	7.45
FM+m	4.81	3.62	0.00	15.00	294	4.00	3.00	1.06	0.89
FC	1.58	1.95	0.00	11.00	194	1.00	0.00	1.97	5.60
CF	1.58	1.38	0.00	8.00	236	1.00	1.00	1.09	2.16
C	0.72	[0.99]	0.00	4.00	142	0.00	0.00	1.51	2.00
Cn	0.03	[0.18]	0.00	1.00	10	0.00	0.00	5.37	26.98
FC+CF+C+Cn	3.91	2.52	0.00	12.00	291	4.00	2.00	0.53	0.11
WGSum C	3.45	2.15	0.00	9.00	291	3.50	4.00	0.27	-0.66
Sum C'	2.16	[1.79]	0.00	8.00	245	2.00	0.00	0.68	0.10
Sum T	0.86	[1.35]	0.00	7.00	136	0.00	0.00	2.29	6.25
Sum V	1.09	[1.23]	0.00	5.00	175	1.00	0.00	0.94	0.06
Sum Y	1.81	[1.40]	0.00	8.00	247	2.00	3.00	0.78	1.92
SumShd	5.92	3.72	0.00	18.00	309	5.00	4.00	0.90	0.48
Fr+rF	0.12	[0.36]	0.00	2.00	33	0.00	0.00	3.18	10.12
FD	0.82	[1.03]	0.00	4.00	159	1.00	0.00	1.26	1.00
F	9.20	5.68	1.00	33.00	315	8.00	9.00	1.62	3.76
PAIR	7.01	3.94	1.00	21.00	315	6.00	5.00	1.18	1.51
3r(2)/R	0.33	0.15	0.06	0.67	315	0.31	0.33	0.48	-0.47
LAMBDA	0.94	1.68	0.08	15.00	315	0.67	0.36	7.50	60.29
EA	7.03	3.56	2.00	18.00	315	6.00	5.00	0.81	0.60
es	10.73	5.48	1.00	27.00	315	11.00	13.00	0.34	-0.06
D	-1.22	1.72	-6.00	3.00	315	-1.00	0.00	-0.67	0.27
AdjD	-0.57	1.52	-6.00	3.00	315	0.00	0.00	-1.14	3.09
a (active)	4.79	3.19	0.00	14.00	292	5.00	6.00	0.56	-0.16
p (passive)	3.66	2.53	0.00	11.00	293	3.00	3.00	0.82	0.32
Ma	1.94	1.68	0.00	7.00	245	2.00	2.00	0.95	0.56
Mp	1.67	1.41	0.00	6.00	242	2.00	2.00	0.96	1.05
Intellect	2.39	2.10	0.00	10.00	315	2.00	0.00	0.86	0.66
Zf	11.38	4.31	1.00	25.00	315	12.00	13.00	0.15	0.11
Zd	-0.33	4.90	-12.50	13.00	315	0.50	4.50	-0.40	0.01
Blends	4.50	3.17	0.00	15.00	292	4.00	6.00	0.67	0.15
Col Shd Blends	0.95	[1.13]	0.00	5.00	179	1.00	0.00	1.44	2.03
Afr	0.47	0.16	0.16	1.00	315	0.43	0.36	0.85	0.85
Popular	5.22	1.90	2.00	10.00	315	5.00	4.00	0.19	-0.91

Table 26. (Continued)

VARIABLE	MEAN	SD	MIN	MAX	FREQ	MEDIAN	MODE	SK	KU
X+%	0.53	0.11	0.27	0.81	315	0.51	0.47	-0.05	-0.50
F+%	0.52	0.21	0.00	1.00	302	0.54	0.50	-0.55	0.34
X-%	0.20	0.10	0.00	0.44	302	0.18	0.13	0.15	-0.70
Xu%	0.22	0.10	0.04	0.47	315	0.24	0.24	0.03	-0.59
S-%	0.21	[0.25]	0.00	1.00	179	0.13	0.00	1.16	0.98
Isolate	0.17	0.12	0.00	0.53	315	0.16	0.00	0.50	-0.05
H	2.05	1.45	0.00	7.00	291	2.00	1.00	0.96	0.53
(H)	1.12	1.02	0.00	6.00	226	1.00	1.00	1.35	3.70
Hd	1.26	1.44	0.00	6.00	192	1.00	0.00	1.38	1.68
(Hd)	0.78	1.11	0.00	5.00	151	0.00	0.00	1.99	4.52
Hx	0.04	[0.19]	0.00	1.00	12	0.00	0.00	4.85	21.65
All H Cont	5.21	2.92	1.00	15.00	315	5.00	4.00	1.04	1.22
A	7.57	3.28	3.00	17.00	315	7.00	5.00	0.82	0.05
(A)	0.48	[0.97]	0.00	5.00	96	0.00	0.00	3.08	11.07
Ad	2.37	[2.69]	0.00	19.00	258	2.00	1.00	3.80	20.97
(Ad)	0.20	[0.43]	0.00	2.00	60	0.00	0.00	1.94	2.92
An	1.05	[1.57]	0.00	7.00	150	0.00	0.00	1.94	3.66
Art	1.62	1.67	0.00	9.00	215	1.00	0.00	1.24	2.10
Ay	0.27	[0.50]	0.00	2.00	76	0.00	0.00	1.69	2.01
Bl	0.48	[1.06]	0.00	6.00	73	0.00	0.00	2.95	10.48
Bt	0.94	1.22	0.00	5.00	158	1.00	0.00	1.35	1.19
Cg	1.80	1.47	0.00	8.00	267	1.00	1.00	1.36	2.90
Cl	0.29	[0.54]	0.00	2.00	78	0.00	0.00	1.71	2.02
Ex	0.17	[0.44]	0.00	2.00	46	0.00	0.00	2.61	6.30
Fi	0.57	[0.74]	0.00	3.00	140	0.00	0.00	1.26	1.25
Fd	0.37	[0.64]	0.00	3.00	93	0.00	0.00	1.71	2.49
Ge	0.16	[0.47]	0.00	4.00	42	0.00	0.00	4.48	28.11
Hh	0.53	0.87	0.00	4.00	115	0.00	0.00	2.11	5.08
Ls	1.04	1.18	0.00	5.00	175	1.00	0.00	0.99	0.27
Na	0.49	[0.71]	0.00	3.00	119	0.00	0.00	1.19	0.42
Sc	0.75	[1.10]	0.00	5.00	130	0.00	0.00	1.69	2.97
Sx	0.73	[1.22]	0.00	5.00	110	0.00	0.00	1.76	2.30
Xy	0.16	[0.46]	0.00	2.00	41	0.00	0.00	2.84	7.40
Idio	1.73	1.55	0.00	7.00	244	1.00	1.00	1.14	1.47
DV	0.69	[0.98]	0.00	6.00	136	0.00	0.00	1.96	6.54
INCOM	1.18	[1.20]	0.00	6.00	206	1.00	0.00	1.11	1.41
DR	0.88	[1.41]	0.00	5.00	116	0.00	0.00	1.49	0.91
FABCOM	0.52	[1.01]	0.00	5.00	100	0.00	0.00	2.85	9.31
DV2	0.22	[0.58]	0.00	4.00	54	0.00	0.00	3.59	16.67
INC2	0.64	[0.95]	0.00	5.00	134	0.00	0.00	1.92	4.12
DR2	0.55	[1.27]	0.00	6.00	95	0.00	0.00	2.77	7.31
FAB2	0.50	[0.85]	0.00	5.00	79	0.00	0.00	2.31	6.60
ALOG	0.13	[0.34]	0.00	2.00	39	0.00	0.00	2.49	5.06
CONTAM	0.00	0.00	0.00	0.00	0	0.00	0.00	----	----
Sum6 Sp Sc	3.40	2.20	1.00	9.00	315	3.00	3.00	0.78	0.31
Sum6 Sp Sc2	1.41	[2.18]	0.00	7.00	225	1.00	0.00	1.76	3.63
WSum6	18.20	13.68	2.00	55.00	315	16.00	4.00	0.91	0.41
AB	0.25	[0.61]	0.00	3.00	54	0.00	0.00	2.39	4.83
AG	0.56	0.93	0.00	4.00	109	0.00	0.00	1.77	2.63
CFB	0.00	0.00	0.00	0.00	0	0.00	0.00	----	----
COP	0.72	0.83	0.00	3.00	159	1.00	0.00	0.85	-0.22
CP	0.04	[0.20]	0.00	1.00	13	0.00	0.00	4.63	19.60
MOR	1.56	[1.87]	0.00	8.00	219	1.00	1.00	1.79	2.82
PER	1.85	2.40	0.00	9.00	180	1.00	0.00	1.38	1.05
PSV	0.33	[0.67]	0.00	2.00	69	0.00	0.00	1.76	1.53

NOTE: Standard Deviations shown in brackets indicate that the value is probably unreliable and/or misleading and should not be used to estimate expected ranges. Ordinarily these variables should not be included in most parametric analyses.

Table 27.   Frequency Data for 315 Inpatient Depressives

DEMOGRAPHY VARIABLES

MARITAL STATUS			AGE			RACE		
Single	110	35%	18-25	58	18%	White	254	81%
Lives w/S.O.	0	0%	26-35	56	18%	Black	36	11%
Married	161	51%	36-45	70	22%	Hispanic	25	8%
Separated	17	5%	46-55	75	24%	Asian	0	0%
Divorced	19	6%	56-65	24	8%			
Widowed	8	3%	OVER 65	6	2%	EDUCATION		
						Under 12	43	14%
SEX						12 Years	104	33%
Male	129	41%				13-15 Yrs	69	22%
Female	186	59%				16+ Yrs	99	31%

RATIOS, PERCENTAGES AND SPECIAL INDICES

EB STYLE			FORM QUALITY DEVIATIONS		
Introversive	80	25%	X+% > .89	0	0%
Pervasive	39	12%	X+% < .70	294	93%
Ambitent	177	56%	X+% < .61	229	73%
Extratensive	58	18%	X+% < .50	129	41%
Pervasive	33	10%	F+% < .70	248	79%
			Xu% > .20	193	61%
D SCORE & ADJUSTED D SCORE			X-% > .15	188	60%
D Score > 0	37	12%	X-% > .20	143	45%
D Score = 0	105	33%	X-% > .30	51	16%
D Score < 0	173	55%			
D Score < -1	140	44%	**FC:CF+C RATIO**		
			FC > (CF+C) + 2	30	10%
Adj D Score > 0	56	18%	FC > (CF+C) + 1	53	17%
Adj D Score = 0	125	40%	(CF+C) > FC+1	116	37%
Adj D Score < 0	134	43%	(CF+C) > FC+2	60	19%
Adj D Score < -1	68	22%			
			S-Constellation Positive	16	5%
Zd > +3.0 (Overincorp)	81	26%	HVI Positive	32	10%
Zd < -3.0 (Underincorp)	79	25%	OBS Positive	0	0%

SCZI = 6	2	1%	DEPI = 7	28	9%	CDI = 5	50	16%
SCZI = 5	6	2%	DEPI = 6	95	30%	CDI = 4	88	28%
SCZI = 4	24	8%	DEPI = 5	114	36%			

MISCELLANEOUS VARIABLES

Lambda > .99	93	30%	(2AB+Art+Ay) > 5	94	30%
Dd > 3	110	35%	Populars < 4	59	19%
DQv + DQv/+ > 2	158	50%	Populars > 7	57	18%
S > 2	130	41%	COP = 0	156	50%
Sum T = 0	179	57%	COP > 2	9	3%
Sum T > 1	71	23%	AG = 0	206	65%
3r+(2)/R < .33	163	52%	AG > 2	19	6%
3r+(2)/R > .44	75	24%	MOR > 2	58	18%
Fr + rF > 0	33	10%	Level 2 Sp.Sc. > 0	225	71%
PureC > 0	142	45%	Sum 6 Sp. Sc. > 6	118	37%
PureC > 1	58	18%	Pure H < 2	142	45%
Afr < .40	107	34%	Pure H = 0	24	8%
Afr < .50	180	57%	p > a+1	72	23%
(FM+m) < Sum Shading	191	61%	Mp > Ma	107	34%

Table 28. Descriptive Statistics for 440 Outpatients

VARIABLE	MEAN	SD	MIN	MAX	FREQ	MEDIAN	MODE	SK	KU
R	19.41	5.68	14.00	55.00	440	18.00	19.00	2.77	12.65
W	7.72	3.02	1.00	16.00	440	7.00	7.00	0.19	−0.74
D	8.59	5.18	0.00	26.00	424	8.00	5.00	1.02	1.04
Dd	3.09	[3.30]	0.00	26.00	378	3.00	1.00	3.42	19.81
S	1.87	[1.69]	0.00	7.00	324	1.50	0.00	0.80	0.17
DQ+	5.85	3.23	0.00	15.00	438	5.00	3.00	0.85	0.97
DQo	11.92	5.26	5.00	47.00	440	11.00	9.00	3.03	16.55
DQv	1.42	[1.63]	0.00	6.00	267	1.00	0.00	1.15	0.45
DQv/+	0.22	[0.57]	0.00	5.00	80	0.00	0.00	4.25	26.28
FQx+	0.61	1.38	0.00	5.00	101	0.00	0.00	2.29	3.87
FQxo	11.63	3.15	6.00	26.00	440	11.00	12.00	0.46	0.39
FQxu	3.41	2.69	0.00	17.00	412	3.00	3.00	1.86	5.30
FQx−	3.14	2.59	0.00	19.00	407	3.00	1.00	2.42	11.46
FQxNone	0.62	[0.99]	0.00	3.00	154	0.00	0.00	1.43	0.72
MQ+	0.48	1.10	0.00	4.00	89	0.00	0.00	2.23	3.60
MQo	2.31	1.65	0.00	8.00	403	2.00	1.00	0.92	0.60
MQu	0.51	0.77	0.00	3.00	161	0.00	0.00	1.51	1.69
MQ−	0.39	[0.71]	0.00	4.00	126	0.00	0.00	2.14	5.57
MQNone	0.00	[0.00]	0.00	0.00	0	0.00	0.00	—	—
SQual−	0.69	[0.98]	0.00	5.00	200	0.00	0.00	1.83	3.84
M	3.68	2.49	0.00	11.00	408	4.00	4.00	0.86	0.81
FM	2.30	1.70	0.00	8.00	372	2.00	2.00	0.79	0.55
m	1.19	1.24	0.00	5.00	267	1.00	0.00	0.88	0.17
FC	1.23	1.27	0.00	6.00	312	1.00	1.00	1.58	2.67
CF	1.32	1.42	0.00	6.00	281	1.00	0.00	1.20	1.27
C	0.64	[1.01]	0.00	4.00	163	0.00	0.00	1.57	1.62
Cn	0.02	[0.15]	0.00	1.00	10	0.00	0.00	6.43	39.48
Sum Color	3.22	1.95	0.00	9.00	424	3.00	3.00	1.03	1.26
WSumC	2.90	1.96	0.00	9.50	424	3.00	1.50	1.14	1.88
Sum C'	0.86	[1.12]	0.00	5.00	231	1.00	0.00	1.64	2.37
Sum T	0.46	[0.78]	0.00	3.00	140	0.00	0.00	1.87	2.97
Sum V	0.42	[0.78]	0.00	3.00	116	0.00	0.00	1.82	2.32
Sum Y	0.88	[0.93]	0.00	6.00	264	1.00	0.00	1.22	2.32
Sum Shading	2.61	2.32	0.00	11.00	391	2.00	1.00	1.27	0.97
Fr+rF	0.18	[0.63]	0.00	6.00	42	0.00	0.00	4.37	23.74
FD	0.87	[0.91]	0.00	5.00	269	1.00	1.00	1.36	2.96
F	8.93	5.11	2.00	39.00	440	8.00	7.00	2.47	10.43
(2)	7.53	3.79	2.00	24.00	440	7.00	5.00	1.77	4.46
Lambda	1.16	1.26	0.11	7.67	440	0.77	1.00	3.00	9.96
FM+m	3.48	2.31	0.00	11.00	388	4.00	4.00	0.39	0.10
EA	6.58	3.42	0.00	16.50	439	6.50	5.50	1.03	1.34
es	6.09	3.78	1.00	17.00	440	5.00	5.00	0.60	−0.37
D Score	0.11	1.23	−4.00	5.00	199	0.00	0.00	−0.01	3.45
AdjD	0.38	1.12	−3.00	5.00	211	0.00	0.00	0.77	2.66
a (active)	3.92	2.44	0.00	11.00	414	3.00	3.00	0.55	−0.25
p (passive)	3.24	2.52	0.00	11.00	378	2.00	2.00	0.52	−0.61
Ma	1.90	1.65	0.00	8.00	349	2.00	2.00	1.08	1.10
Mp	1.78	1.53	0.00	8.00	320	2.00	2.00	0.84	1.19
Intellect	1.98	1.96	0.00	7.00	311	2.00	0.00	0.86	−0.36
Zf	10.62	3.55	2.00	23.00	440	10.00	10.00	0.34	1.04
Zd	0.10	4.09	−9.00	10.00	431	−0.50	5.00	0.46	−0.50
Blends	2.91	2.23	0.00	8.00	384	3.00	1.00	0.58	−0.65
Blends/R	0.16	0.12	0.00	0.50	384	0.14	0.00	0.63	−0.17
Col−Shd Bld	0.63	[0.78]	0.00	3.00	207	0.00	0.00	1.09	0.58
Afr	0.53	0.18	0.13	1.25	440	0.50	0.50	1.80	4.14

(continued)

Table 28.   (Continued)

VARIABLE	MEAN	SD	MIN	MAX	FREQ	MEDIAN	MODE	SK	KU
Populars	5.56	2.22	0.00	10.00	428	5.50	5.00	−0.27	−0.35
X+%	0.64	0.14	0.27	0.89	440	0.64	0.63	−0.25	−0.50
F+%	0.66	0.19	0.13	1.00	440	0.67	0.71	−0.45	0.22
X−%	0.16	0.10	0.00	0.44	407	0.14	0.07	0.61	−0.14
Xu%	0.17	0.10	0.00	0.42	412	0.15	0.11	0.35	−0.47
S−%	0.21	[0.29]	0.00	1.00	200	0.00	0.00	1.36	1.03
Isolate/R	0.14	0.16	0.00	0.81	347	0.11	0.00	2.75	9.01
H	2.10	1.29	0.00	7.00	422	2.00	1.00	1.00	1.32
(H)	1.07	1.18	0.00	5.00	250	1.00	0.00	0.91	0.08
HD	1.45	2.19	0.00	18.00	311	1.00	1.00	4.58	28.90
(Hd)	0.54	0.82	0.00	3.00	156	0.00	0.00	1.33	0.70
Hx	0.06	[0.30]	0.00	2.00	16	0.00	0.00	5.74	32.95
All H Cont	5.16	3.24	0.00	27.00	424	5.00	4.00	2.98	17.20
A	7.50	2.65	3.00	15.00	440	7.00	5.00	0.61	−0.30
(A)	0.33	[0.67]	0.00	3.00	107	0.00	0.00	2.37	5.67
Ad	1.69	[1.70]	0.00	11.00	343	1.00	1.00	1.92	4.85
(Ad)	0.08	[0.29]	0.00	2.00	35	0.00	0.00	3.54	12.54
An	0.56	[0.86]	0.00	5.00	171	0.00	0.00	2.01	5.67
Art	1.22	1.22	0.00	5.00	273	1.00	0.00	0.68	−0.48
Ay	0.16	[0.37]	0.00	1.00	71	0.00	0.00	1.85	1.42
Bl	0.26	[0.61]	0.00	3.00	85	0.00	0.00	2.92	9.21
Bt	1.18	1.23	0.00	4.00	279	1.00	0.00	0.98	0.07
Cg	1.71	1.58	0.00	6.00	305	2.00	0.00	0.72	−0.21
Cl	0.14	[0.43]	0.00	2.00	47	0.00	0.00	3.21	9.76
Ex	0.19	[0.46]	0.00	2.00	70	0.00	0.00	2.45	5.40
Fi	0.25	[0.46]	0.00	2.00	102	0.00	0.00	1.60	1.52
Food	0.25	[0.53]	0.00	2.00	88	0.00	0.00	2.08	3.40
Ge	0.02	[0.13]	0.00	1.00	8	0.00	0.00	7.24	50.60
Hh	0.60	0.99	0.00	4.00	141	0.00	0.00	1.62	2.04
Ls	0.68	1.07	0.00	6.00	171	0.00	0.00	2.05	5.46
Na	0.23	[0.79]	0.00	4.00	49	0.00	0.00	4.13	16.56
Sc	0.51	[0.81]	0.00	5.00	157	0.00	0.00	2.15	7.06
Sx	0.51	[0.95]	0.00	5.00	131	0.00	0.00	2.27	5.49
Xy	0.11	[0.31]	0.00	1.00	48	0.00	0.00	2.52	4.35
Idio	0.92	1.16	0.00	5.00	222	1.00	0.00	1.26	0.93
DV	0.95	[1.18]	0.00	5.00	247	1.00	0.00	1.81	3.86
INCOM	1.01	[1.09]	0.00	4.00	264	1.00	0.00	1.04	0.45
DR	0.25	[0.72]	0.00	4.00	57	0.00	0.00	3.22	10.50
FABCOM	0.51	[0.80]	0.00	4.00	155	0.00	0.00	1.67	2.82
DV2	0.10	[0.30]	0.00	1.00	45	0.00	0.00	2.63	4.96
INC2	0.19	[0.58]	0.00	4.00	53	0.00	0.00	3.92	18.00
DR2	0.10	[0.71]	0.00	10.00	25	0.00	0.00	12.74	175.89
FAB2	0.21	[0.62]	0.00	3.00	58	0.00	0.00	3.40	11.46
ALOG	0.17	[0.49]	0.00	3.00	55	0.00	0.00	3.13	9.81
CONTAM	0.00	0.00	0.00	0.00	0	0.00	0.00	—	—
Sum 6 Sp Sc	3.48	2.99	0.00	21.00	407	3.00	1.00	1.67	4.97
Lvl 2 Sp Sc	0.60	[1.28]	0.00	11.00	156	0.00	0.00	4.63	28.43
WSum6	9.59	10.96	0.00	97.00	407	8.00	1.00	3.35	19.27
AB	0.30	[0.52]	0.00	3.00	120	0.00	0.00	1.72	3.18
AG	0.87	1.24	0.00	8.00	199	0.00	0.00	2.37	9.40
CFB	0.00	0.00	0.00	0.00	0	0.00	0.00	—	—
COP	1.09	1.20	0.00	6.00	267	1.00	0.00	1.35	2.31
CP	0.02	[0.13]	0.00	1.00	8	0.00	0.00	7.24	50.60
MOR	1.03	[1.21]	0.00	6.00	285	1.00	1.00	1.84	3.49
PER	1.06	1.60	0.00	10.00	201	0.00	0.00	2.23	7.45
PSV	0.15	[0.48]	0.00	3.00	49	0.00	0.00	3.98	17.92

Table 29. Frequency Data for 440 Outpatients

DEMOGRAPHY VARIABLES

MARITAL STATUS			AGE				RACE		
Single	132	30%	18–25		84	19%	White	341	78%
Lives w/S.O.	46	10%	26–35		170	39%	Black	47	11%
Married	175	40%	36–45		104	24%	Hispanic	41	9%
Separated	49	11%	46–55		18	4%	Asian	11	3%
Divorced	34	8%	56–65		34	8%			
Widowed	4	1%	OVER	65	7	2%	EDUCATION		
							Under 12	58	13%
SEX							12 Yrs	96	22%
Male	186	42%					13–15 Yrs	211	48%
Female	254	58%					16+ Yrs	75	17%

RATIOS, PERCENTAGES AND SPECIAL INDICES

EB STYLE			FORM QUALITY DEVIATIONS		
Introversive	154	35%	X+% > .89	0	0%
Pervasive	118	27%	X+% < .70	277	63%
Ambient	173	39%	X+% < .61	173	39%
Extratensive	113	26%	X+% < .50	54	12%
Pervasive	81	18%	F+% < .70	237	54%
			Xu% > .20	151	34%
D SCORE			X–% > .15	202	46%
D Score > 0	112	25%	X–% > .20	138	31%
D Score = 0	241	55%	X–% > .30	34	8%
D Score < 0	87	20%			
D Score < –1	25	6%			
ADJUSTED D SCORE			**FC:CF+C RATIO**		
Adj D Score > 0	153	35%	FC > (CF+C)+2	26	6%
Adj D Score = 0	229	52%	FC > (CF+C)+1	60	14%
Adj D Score < 0	58	13%	(CF+C) > FC+1	153	35%
Adj D Score < –1	13	3%	(CF+C) > FC+2	88	20%
Zd > +3.0 (Overincorp)	106	24%	S-Con Positive	35	8%
Zd < –3.0 (Underincorp)	123	28%	HVI Positive	39	9%
			OBS Positive	56	13%

SCZI = 6	4	1%	DEPI = 7	6	1%	CDI = 5	41	9%
SCZI = 5	2	0%	DEPI = 6	12	3%	CDI = 4	84	19%
SCZI = 4	5	1%	DEPI = 5	71	16%			

MISCELLANEOUS VARIABLES

Lambda > .99	167	38%	(2AB+Art+Ay) > 5	94	21%
Dd > 3	177	40%	Populars < 4	69	16%
DQv + DQv/+ > 2	108	25%	Populars > 7	98	22%
S > 2	148	34%	COP = 0	173	39%
Sum T = 0	300	68%	COP > 2	43	10%
Sum T > 1	41	9%	AG = 0	241	55%
3r+(2)/R < .33	121	28%	AG > 2	14	3%
3r+(2)/R > .44	136	31%	MOR > 2	42	10%
Fr + rF > 0	42	10%	Lvl 2 Sp.Sc. > 0	156	35%
PureC > 0	163	37%	Sum 6 Sp.Sc. > 6	51	12%
PureC > 1	76	17%	Pure H < 2	173	39%
Afr < .40	66	15%	Pure H = 0	18	4%
Afr < .50	209	48%	p > a+1	124	28%
(FM+m) < Sum Shad	129	29%	Mp > Ma	146	33%

Table 30.   Descriptive Statistics for 180 Character Disorders

VARIABLE	MEAN	SD	MIN	MAX	FREQ	MEDIAN	MODE	SK	KU
R	18.44	4.29	14.00	34.00	180	18.00	18.00	1.74	3.23
W	6.94	3.86	1.00	23.00	180	7.00	5.00	0.89	1.96
D	8.64	4.56	0.00	21.00	178	8.00	12.00	0.44	-0.05
Dd	2.84	[2.21]	0.00	10.00	161	2.50	1.00	1.00	0.94
S	1.92	[1.86]	0.00	7.00	123	2.00	0.00	0.87	0.22
DQ+	4.13	2.55	0.00	10.00	176	4.00	2.00	0.69	-0.29
DQo	12.74	5.09	4.00	27.00	180	12.00	9.00	0.67	0.33
DQv	1.12	[1.12]	0.00	4.00	108	1.00	0.00	0.64	-0.44
DQv/+	0.43	[0.72]	0.00	3.00	57	0.00	0.00	1.73	2.56
FQX+	0.03	0.16	0.00	1.00	5	0.00	0.00	5.79	31.94
FQXo	10.56	3.03	4.00	18.00	180	10.00	11.00	0.56	0.24
FQXu	3.71	2.13	0.00	9.00	169	3.00	3.00	0.34	-0.45
FQX-	3.72	2.01	0.00	10.00	174	4.00	4.00	0.97	1.89
FQXNone	0.41	[0.73]	0.00	3.00	51	0.00	0.00	1.81	2.63
MQ+	0.03	0.16	0.00	1.00	5	0.00	0.00	5.80	31.94
MQo	1.55	1.47	0.00	6.00	135	1.00	1.00	1.00	0.28
MQu	0.61	0.89	0.00	3.00	75	0.00	0.00	1.53	1.60
MQ-	0.47	[0.78]	0.00	3.00	57	0.00	0.00	1.52	1.34
MQNone	0.00	[0.00]	0.00	0.00	0	0.00	0.00	----	----
S-	0.97	[1.23]	0.00	4.00	89	0.00	0.00	1.12	0.09
M	2.66	2.54	0.00	10.00	149	2.00	1.00	1.34	1.48
FM	1.57	1.17	0.00	5.00	153	1.00	1.00	1.02	1.24
m	1.02	1.06	0.00	4.00	107	1.00	0.00	0.79	-0.26
FM+m	2.59	1.74	0.00	7.00	160	2.00	2.00	0.55	-0.07
FC	0.98	1.29	0.00	5.00	85	0.00	0.00	1.21	0.64
CF	0.86	1.08	0.00	5.00	89	0.00	0.00	1.28	1.29
C	0.47	[0.86]	0.00	3.00	49	0.00	0.00	1.68	1.60
Cn	0.01	[0.10]	0.00	1.00	2	0.00	0.00	9.41	87.45
FC+CF+C+Cn	2.32	2.00	0.00	7.00	180	2.00	0.00	0.45	-0.88
WGSum C	2.06	1.91	0.00	6.00	180	1.50	0.00	0.63	-0.76
Sum C'	0.83	[1.05]	0.00	4.00	88	0.00	0.00	1.26	1.14
Sum T	0.31	[0.52]	0.00	2.00	50	0.00	0.00	1.44	1.16
Sum V	0.24	[0.55]	0.00	2.00	32	0.00	0.00	2.25	3.95
Sum Y	0.65	[0.95]	0.00	4.00	77	0.00	0.00	1.71	2.71
SumShd	2.03	1.82	0.00	9.00	141	2.00	2.00	1.25	2.13
Fr+rF	0.47	[0.43]	0.00	4.00	36	0.00	0.00	2.62	6.45
FD	0.33	[0.65]	0.00	2.00	42	0.00	0.00	1.74	1.61
F	10.86	4.90	2.00	25.00	180	11.00	11.00	0.66	0.77
PAIR	6.87	3.55	0.00	20.00	180	6.00	4.00	1.30	2.70
3r(2)/R	0.46	0.17	0.20	0.93	180	0.48	0.30	0.68	0.81
LAMBDA	2.12	2.39	0.15	16.00	180	1.62	3.00	4.96	33.89
EA	4.72	3.40	0.50	14.00	180	4.00	2.50	1.16	1.50
es	4.62	3.03	2.00	13.00	180	6.00	4.00	0.81	0.25
D	0.03	1.06	-3.00	3.00	180	0.00	0.00	-0.21	2.18
AdjD	0.19	1.05	-3.00	3.00	180	0.00	0.00	-0.01	1.47
a (active)	2.82	2.31	0.00	10.00	150	2.00	2.00	0.91	0.50
p (passive)	2.43	1.89	0.00	10.00	157	2.00	2.00	1.63	4.30
Ma	1.39	1.67	0.00	8.00	115	1.00	0.00	1.83	3.81
Mp	1.27	1.30	0.00	6.00	125	1.00	1.00	1.39	2.28
Intellect	1.44	2.13	0.00	11.00	104	1.00	0.00	2.59	7.92
Zf	9.40	4.20	2.00	24.00	180	10.00	8.00	0.28	0.10
Zd	0.20	4.83	-18.50	9.00	180	0.50	-1.00	-1.14	2.26
Blends	2.14	1.90	0.00	7.00	133	2.00	0.00	0.62	-0.46
Col Shd Blends	0.32	[0.57]	0.00	3.00	51	0.00	0.00	1.95	4.71
Afr	0.49	0.19	0.20	1.08	180	0.46	0.50	0.75	0.38
Popular	4.93	1.67	1.00	8.00	180	5.00	6.00	0.03	-0.50

Table 30. (Continued)

VARIABLE	MEAN	SD	MIN	MAX	FREQ	MEDIAN	MODE	SK	KU
X+%	0.58	0.12	0.29	0.82	180	0.57	0.61	0.01	-0.25
F+%	0.59	0.16	0.25	1.00	180	0.58	0.50	-0.11	-0.31
X-%	0.20	0.10	0.00	0.43	174	0.20	0.20	0.15	-0.36
Xu%	0.20	0.10	0.00	0.50	169	0.20	0.20	0.10	0.10
S-%	0.24	[0.30]	0.00	1.00	89	0.00	0.00	1.08	0.13
Isolate	0.14	0.12	0.00	0.50	180	0.11	0.00	1.10	0.79
H	1.94	1.65	0.00	7.00	156	1.00	1.00	1.41	1.97
(H)	0.83	1.01	0.00	4.00	97	1.00	0.00	1.35	1.31
Hd	1.39	1.47	0.00	6.00	118	1.00	0.00	1.14	0.84
(Hd)	0.40	0.67	0.00	3.00	55	0.00	0.00	1.65	2.14
Hx	0.09	[0.35]	0.00	2.00	12	0.00	0.00	4.27	18.33
All H Cont	4.56	2.97	0.00	12.00	168	4.00	5.00	0.72	0.05
A	7.67	3.30	2.00	21.00	180	7.00	7.00	1.19	2.25
(A)	0.27	[0.49]	0.00	2.00	45	0.00	0.00	1.58	1.60
Ad	1.90	[1.57]	0.00	7.00	146	2.00	1.00	1.02	1.07
(Ad)	0.14	[0.41]	0.00	2.00	21	0.00	0.00	3.05	9.13
An	0.87	[1.33]	0.00	5.00	75	0.00	0.00	1.70	2.27
Art	0.80	0.96	0.00	4.00	93	1.00	0.00	1.14	0.70
Ay	0.11	[0.31]	0.00	1.00	20	0.00	0.00	2.50	4.28
Bl	0.26	[0.59]	0.00	3.00	34	0.00	0.00	2.51	6.29
Bt	0.86	1.02	0.00	5.00	101	1.00	0.00	1.73	4.28
Cg	0.99	1.11	0.00	4.00	101	1.00	0.00	1.03	0.39
Cl	0.14	[0.38]	0.00	2.00	23	0.00	0.00	2.72	7.06
Ex	0.08	[0.31]	0.00	2.00	12	0.00	0.00	4.27	19.31
Fi	0.22	[0.51]	0.00	2.00	32	0.00	0.00	2.29	4.38
Fd	0.17	[0.38]	0.00	1.00	31	0.00	0.00	1.75	1.08
Ge	0.15	[0.57]	0.00	4.00	18	0.00	0.00	5.38	32.48
Hh	0.29	0.50	0.00	2.00	48	0.00	0.00	1.47	1.20
Ls	0.58	0.92	0.00	4.00	65	0.00	0.00	1.62	2.03
Na	0.32	[0.55]	0.00	2.00	49	0.00	0.00	1.56	1.52
Sc	0.29	[0.61]	0.00	3.00	43	0.00	0.00	2.66	8.29
Sx	0.43	[0.83]	0.00	4.00	53	0.00	0.00	2.58	7.29
Xy	0.11	[0.31]	0.00	1.00	19	0.00	0.00	2.59	4.76
Idio	0.84	1.01	0.00	5.00	101	1.00	0.00	1.52	2.55
DV	0.76	[0.85]	0.00	3.00	98	1.00	0.00	1.04	0.54
INCOM	1.06	[1.36]	0.00	6.00	91	1.00	0.00	1.39	1.94
DR	0.35	[0.61]	0.00	3.00	52	0.00	0.00	1.85	3.56
FABCOM	0.63	[0.57]	0.00	2.00	70	0.00	0.00	1.54	1.42
DV2	0.14	[0.41]	0.00	2.00	21	0.00	0.00	3.05	9.13
INC2	0.36	[0.68]	0.00	2.00	30	0.00	0.00	2.27	5.48
DR2	0.20	[0.57]	0.00	3.00	23	0.00	0.00	3.04	8.86
FAB2	0.36	[0.79]	0.00	3.00	21	0.00	0.00	2.80	8.81
ALOG	0.30	[0.65]	0.00	2.00	25	0.00	0.00	3.77	14.60
CONTAM	0.00	0.00	0.00	0.00	0	0.00	0.00	----	----
Sum6 Sp Sc	2.62	2.10	0.00	9.00	180	2.00	2.00	0.83	0.44
Sum6 Sp Sc2	0.76	[1.29]	0.00	4.00	62	1.00	0.00	1.07	0.18
WSum6	11.31	10.77	0.00	48.00	180	8.00	7.00	1.42	1.62
AB	0.27	[0.89]	0.00	5.00	22	0.00	0.00	4.09	17.29
AG	0.41	0.67	0.00	2.00	56	0.00	0.00	1.36	0.54
CFB	0.00	0.00	0.00	0.00	0	0.00	0.00	----	----
COP	0.57	0.85	0.00	3.00	69	0.00	0.00	1.40	1.08
CP	0.00	[0.00]	0.00	0.00	0	0.00	0.00	----	----
MOR	1.07	[1.62]	0.00	7.00	76	0.00	0.00	1.73	2.77
PER	0.93	1.51	0.00	9.00	77	0.00	0.00	2.47	8.37
PSV	0.19	[0.63]	0.00	5.00	25	0.00	0.00	5.37	35.91

NOTE: Standard Deviations shown in brackets indicate that the value is probably unreliable and/or misleading and should not be used to estimate expected ranges. Ordinarily these variables should not be included in most parametric analyses.

Table 31.   Frequency Data for 180 Character Disorders

DEMOGRAPHY VARIABLES

MARITAL STATUS			AGE			RACE		
Single	118	66%	18-25	57	32%	White	147	82%
Lives w/S.O.	7	4%	26-35	39	22%	Black	16	9%
Married	39	22%	36-45	12	7%	Hispanic	17	9%
Separated	2	1%	46-55	18	10%	Asian	0	0%
Divorced	14	8%	56-65	4	2%			
Widowed	0	0%	OVER 65	0	0%	EDUCATION		
						Under 12	55	31%
SEX						12 Years	62	34%
Male	112	62%				13-15 Yrs	49	27%
Female	68	38%				16+ Yrs	14	8%

RATIOS, PERCENTAGES AND SPECIAL INDICES

EB STYLE			FORM QUALITY DEVIATIONS		
Introversive	63	35%	X+% > .89	0	0%
Super-Introversive	33	18%	X+% < .70	147	82%
Ambitent	74	41%	X+% < .61	113	63%
Extratensive	43	24%	X+% < .50	37	21%
Super-Extratensive	34	19%	F+% < .70	123	68%
			Xu% > .20	83	46%
EA - es DIFFERENCES: D-SCORES			X-% > .15	121	67%
D Score > 0	38	21%	X-% > .20	76	42%
D Score = 0	111	62%	X-% > .30	26	14%
D Score < 0	31	17%			
D Score < -1	13	7%	FC:CF+C RATIO		
			FC > (CF+C) + 2	8	4%
Adj D Score > 0	51	28%	FC > (CF+C) + 1	21	12%
Adj D Score = 0	102	57%	(CF+C) > FC+1	45	25%
Adj D Score < 0	27	15%	(CF+C) > FC+2	29	16%
Adj D Score < -1	10	6%			
Zd > +3.0 (Overincorp)	50	28%	S-Constellation Positive	3	2%
Zd < -3.0 (Underincorp)	31	17%	HVI Positive	13	7%
			OBS Positive	0	0%

SCZI = 6	0	0%	DEPI = 7	0	0%	CDI = 5	18	10%
SCZI = 5	0	0%	DEPI = 6	1	0%	CDI = 4	69	38%
SCZI = 4	4	2%	DEPI = 5	23	13%			

MISCELLANEOUS VARIABLES

Lambda > .99	122	68%	(2AB+Art+Ay) > 5	17	9%
Dd > 3	55	31%	Populars < 4	40	22%
DQv + DQv/+ > 2	48	27%	Populars > 7	16	9%
S > 2	61	34%	COP = 0	111	62%
Sum T = 0	130	72%	COP > 2	8	4%
Sum T > 1	5	3%	AG = 0	124	69%
3r+(2)/R < .33	62	34%	AG > 2	0	0%
3r+(2)/R > .44	60	33%	MOR > 2	31	17%
Fr + rF > 0	36	20%	Level 2 Sp.Sc. > 0	62	34%
PureC > 0	49	27%	Sum 6 Sp. Sc. > 6	29	16%
PureC > 1	28	16%	Pure H < 2	91	51%
Afr < .40	54	30%	Pure H = 0	24	13%
Afr < .50	94	52%	p > a+1	42	23%
(FM+m) < Sum Shading	54	30%	Mp > Ma	64	36%

Rather, they afford a comparative review of these samples with findings from adult nonpatients, which may be useful in establishing a conceptual framework concerning each of the groups, but is by no means diagnostically practical.

Tables 24 and 25 present data for 320 schizophrenics, 147 from private hospitals and 173 from public hospitals, randomly selected from approximately 1100 available records. Tables 26 and 27 include data for 315 inpatient depressives, 184 from private hospitals and 131 from public hospitals, randomly selected from approximately 1300 available records. Tables 28 and 29 show data for a group of 440 outpatients, beginning treatment for the first time. They reflect a considerable variety of diagnoses, although more than half presented features or complaints of depression during their initial screening. They were randomly selected from a group of nearly 900 available protocols. Tables 30 and 31 contain data for 180 outpatient character problems. Although some have forensic related problems, none have been adjudicated. They were selected from approximately 370 available records.

Demographic data for each group concerning sex, age, race, marital status, and completed education are included for each group in the tables of frequency data.

REFERENCES

Exner, J. E. (1974). *The Rorschach: A Comprehensive System. Volume 1*. New York: Wiley.

Exner, J. E. (1978). *The Rorschach: A Comprehensive System. Volume 2: Recent research and advanced interpretation*. New York: Wiley.

Exner, J. E. (1985). *A Rorschach Workbook for the Comprehensive System* (2nd ed.). Bayville, NY: Rorschach Workshops.

Exner, J. E. (1986). *The Rorschach: A Comprehensive System. Volume 1: Basic foundations* (2nd ed.). New York: Wiley.

Exner, J. E. (1988). Problems with brief Rorschach protocols. *Journal of Personality Assessment, 4*, 640–647.

Exner, J. E., and Weiner, I. B. (1982). *The Rorschach: A Comprehensive System. Volume 3: Assessment of children and adolescents*. New York: Wiley.

Exner, J. E., Weiner, I. B., and Schuyler, W. (1976). *A Rorschach workbook for the Comprehensive System*. Bayville, NY: Rorschach Workshops.

PART II

Prerequisites to Interpretation

CHAPTER 3

The Rorschach Procedure

OVERVIEW

Rorschach interpretation is much more complex and demanding than collecting the basic data of the test, but is not independent of that procedure. The objective—to develop a reasonably accurate description of the personality organization and psychological functioning of the subject—is achieved only if the entire Rorschach procedure is completed skillfully.

The Rorschach procedure involves three discrete, but interrelated operations: (1) collecting the responses, (2) coding or scoring the responses and calculating the Structural Summary, and (3) interpreting the data. All three require considerable expertise and, although interpretation is somewhat more complex and requires higher level skills, the importance of the first two operations should never be underestimated.

Accurate interpretation is contingent upon data that have been accurately collected and tallied. Collection of the test data requires adherence to fairly straightforward, standardized procedures that can be accomplished by any reasonably intelligent person who has appropriate training. It involves some subject preparation, and then the responses are collected. The challenges to the examiner are threefold: (1) recording all of the verbalizations verbatim, (2) thinking through the inquiry phase carefully and intelligently so that the accumulated information is easily scorable, and (3) scoring or coding each answer correctly.

Usually, the response phase of the test is not very lengthy. Most subjects deliver all of their answers in 20 minutes or less. A well-thought-out Inquiry usually requires an additional 25 to 40 minutes, depending on how cooperative and articulate a subject is. *No* answers are random or accidental. Instead, each is the product of a very complicated set of psychological operations that culminates in the decision to deliver a response in lieu of others that are available. Thus, each answer is some indirect representation of the psychological operations of the subject but, unfortunately, most answers reveal little about the subject if studied separately. Nonetheless, each contributes in some way to the final conclusions about the subject. Obviously, correct scoring is crucial to ensure the accuracy of that contribution.

The importance of correct scoring cannot be overemphasized. Because much of the interpretation is generated from the structural data, if they are inaccurate, the interpretation will miss the mark no matter how skillful the interpreter. The coding or scoring of each answer contributes to the numerous frequency tallies and ultimately relates to the many ratios and derivations that become the nucleus for interpretation. Each also contributes some information about the sequencing of decisions as they have occurred. Single responses that contain highly unusual characteristics or direct projected representations can play an important role in the interpretive process, but most have limited interpretive importance when studied separately. Nevertheless, any answer might have some special interpretive importance when considered in light of those immediately preceding and/or following it.

Likewise, the absence of some types of answers can be of particular value to the interpretive effort. Failure to deliver some classes of predictable answers often signals the presence of psychological elements or operations that take precedence over some decision activities of the subject and affect the subject's cognitive and affective behaviors in adverse ways.

In most instances, the collection of responses, their scoring, and the calculations required to complete the Structural Summary require no more than 1.5 to 2 hours. Interpretation of the data usually takes no longer, and in some instances may require less time. However, the data in some protocols can be very knotty, making the interpretive process painfully slow. Competent Rorschach interpretation is contingent upon a sophisticated knowledge of personality, psychopathology, behavior, and the tactics regularly employed in various intervention routines. These essentials are critical in sorting through the variety of postulates and questions that arise during the interpretive process. They are also crucial to the integration of test findings with other data concerning the subject and the ultimate formulation of conclusions and/or recommendations.

Any Rorschach examiner or interpreter must have a thorough understanding of the test and be able to use that knowledge in ways that give direction to the tactics and pace of the interpretive process. At times, the data are crystal clear and interpretation can proceed rapidly with minimal regard for the order in which data sets are approached. In other instances, the complexity and/or special features of certain responses or data sets may favor a particular sequencing of the interpretive approach. An understanding of the *response process* (i.e., how the data evolve) is often very important during each of the three segments of the Rorschach procedure. It often affords direction to the tactics and pace of administration, provides clarification when difficult scoring issues arise, and provides the conceptual understanding of how and why certain data sets are interpreted in specific ways. It can provide some direction to the tactics of interpretation, is important in weighing the merits of the myriad of interpretive hypotheses, and contributes to final conclusions derived from the test data.

THE RESPONSE PROCESS

Although the research concerning the response process has yielded mainly inferential data, the considerable data that have accumulated from various studies regarding patterns of visual scanning of the blots, stimulus characteristics of the blots, response frequencies, set influences, and impact of personality and/or cognitive style differences on responses suggest that the process should probably be conceptualized as consisting of at least three phases. It is unrealistic to envision each phase as totally discrete from the others, but it does seem very likely that each phase involves decision operations that are often somewhat independent of decision operations in each of the other phases. The three phases are illustrated in Table 32.

Table 32.   Response Process Phases and Operations

PHASE I	PHASE II	PHASE III
1. ENCODING THE STIMULUS FIELD	3. RESCANNING THE FIELD TO REFINE POTENTIAL ANSWERS	5. FINAL SELECTION FROM REMAINING POTENTIAL ANSWERS
2. CLASSIFYING THE ENCODED IMAGE & ITS PARTS INTO POTENTIAL ANSWERS	4. DISCARDING UNUSABLE OR UNWANTED ANSWERS BY PAIRED-COMPARISON RANKING OR CENSORSHIP	6. ARTICULATION OF THE SELECTED ANSWER

The response process is initiated by the question to the subject, "What might this be?" The implication is that the subject should report what the blot or blot's areas look like. The task is seemingly simple at the onset, but quickly becomes intricate as the subject is confronted with the first figure.

Phase I: Encoding and Classification

There is little doubt that most subjects form multiple potential answers very shortly after a blot has been presented (Colligan & Exner, 1985; Exner, 1980, 1986; Exner, Armbruster, & Mittman, 1978). During this first phase or segment of the test process, the subject scans the blot quite rapidly and encodes the product of that scan. Once the initial encoding has occurred, information is retrieved from long term storage and the subject begins to make comparisons with the image that has been encoded. These comparisons lead to classifications of the blot, or portions of it, into *potential* answers. The number of potential answers increases as the scan continues and as the initial encoding is modified. Although many questions remain unanswered concerning this phase of the test, it seems certain that the vast majority of subjects formulate many more potential answers during the first *two or three seconds* of blot exposure than ultimately are given as responses. The actual number of potential responses that are formed probably varies to some extent from subject to subject, and clearly varies from blot to blot. For example, Colligan and Exner (1985) found that subjects averaged only slightly more than one answer per card when the blots were tachistoscopically exposed for 600 milliseconds or less. Conversely, Exner, Armbruster, and Mittman (1978) found that, when each blot was exposed for a full minute with instructions to find as many answers as possible, responses by nonpatient subjects ranged from an average of slightly more than five answers to Card IV to an average of more than 15 answers to Card X. Apparently, the more solid the stimulus field, such as in Cards IV, V, and VI, the fewer potential answers are formed easily as contrasted with blots having a partially broken field (I, II, VII, IX) or blots in which the pattern is well dispersed (III, VIII, X). Even when the blots are relatively solid, however, most people can develop three or four potential answers even if the blot is exposed for a brief interval.

Exner and Persell (1985) used a tachistoscopic presentation of Cards IV, V, and VI for two seconds each to 17 volunteer high school students. The subjects were asked to give as many answers as they could, beginning the first answer after a tone sounded at the end of the exposure. All 17 gave at least four answers to Cards IV and VI (range = 4 to 7), and 13 of the 17 gave at least two common detail (*D*) responses to each of those blots. None gave fewer than two answers to Card V (range = 2 to 5), although only four of the 17 gave a *D* answer. A brief location inquiry was conducted after all three cards had been exposed so that form quality could be calculated. The $X + \%$ range for Card IV was 66 to 90% (median = 75%); for Card V, 50 to 100% (median = 100%); and for Card VI, 50 to 86% (median = 72%).

The Role of Critical Stimulus Bits in Classification Phase I classifications seem to occur rapidly, in accord with the intent to create available answers. It is likely that most are unrefined and the majority are probably form dominated. For instance, Colligan and Exner (1985) found that, when the blots were exposed to subjects for only 600 milliseconds or less, the majority of answers given were Pure *F* and about 20% were minus answers. Most minus responses were given to Cards II, III, VIII, IX, and X, and many were "face" responses, suggesting that the subjects did not have enough time to complete the scan of the entire blot and simply used a gestalt-like procedure of closure in encoding the stimulus field. Colligan and Exner (1986) completed a pilot replication of the basic design with 15 subjects, but increased the exposure time to one second per blot. The data from this pilot reveal an average of nearly 15 total responses, with fewer than half being Pure *F* and less than 10% minus answers. Almost 80% of the minus responses were given to Cards III and X, suggesting that the one-second exposure time is insufficient for most subjects to complete an adequate encoding of these very broken fields. On the other hand, the $X + \%$ for the answers given to the remaining eight blots was 76% ($SD = 9\%$), suggesting that, if sufficient time is available to complete the encoding of the field, most subjects translate it in a relatively conventional way. This is because the blots are not nearly as ambiguous as has often been purported.

Although the Rorschach blots do not have the precisely defined stimulus parameters of a specific object, such as a glass, a spoon, or an automobile, the blots also *are not* totally ambiguous. Quite the contrary, *all* have discrete stimulus features that limit the parameters of translation or classification or, stated differently, that encourage certain translations or classifications to occur. The importance of the *Dd*34 projections to the classification of Card I as a winged object is a good example. Exner and Martin (1981) used a photographically modified version of Card I, in which the *Dd*34 projections had been eliminated, and administered the entire test to 30 adult nonpatients. None of those 30 subjects gave the bat response to Card I and only two gave winged object answers (one butterfly, one bird). These findings suggest that the *Dd*34 projections have some important role in promoting the winged object class of answer while discouraging other classifications of the blot.

That premise seems supported by findings from another study (Exner, Persell, & Thomas, 1985) in which 48 high school seniors were randomized into two groups of 24 each. The control group was shown the standard Card I projected on a screen for 45 seconds and asked to write at least four answers for the blot. The experimental group was shown the modified version of Card I that excluded the

Dd34 areas for the same interval and with the same instructions. All 24 of the control subjects listed at least one winged object in their list, and seven included two. Conversely, only one experimental subject included a winged object (bird) in the list. Nine of the control subjects included a face or mask answer in their lists, whereas 21 of the experimental subjects included such a response. After the lists were completed, the subjects were asked to review their answers and identify which one they would prefer to have scored for accuracy. All 24 control subjects selected a winged object (bat = 13, butterfly = 9, bird = 2) as their preferred answer. Fourteen of the experimental subjects selected the face or mask as their preferred response and the one subject who had listed a bird selected a human figure.

A similar design was used with 46 first-year college students who were randomized into groups of 23 each (Exner & Simon, 1985). One group was shown the standard version of Card VIII projected on a screen for 45 seconds with instructions to write four responses to the blot. The second group viewed a modified version of Card VIII, in which the D1 areas (popular animal) had been eliminated, for the same exposure time and with the same instructions. All 23 control subjects included an animal to the D1 area in their list, and 17 of the 23 integrated the animal with the rest of the blot, thus creating a whole (W) response, such as an animal climbing a tree or a mountain, or an animal on a bush. On the other hand, only one of the 23 experimental subjects listed a W response (a ship). Sixteen of the 23 included "flags" to the D5 area and 14 included the answer "mountain" to the D4 area. When asked to review their lists and select the answer to be scored for accuracy, all 23 control subjects chose the answer that included the use of the D1 area as an animal, whereas 14 of the 16 experimental subjects who had listed flags to the D5 area identified that as their preferred answer.

Data such as these provide considerable support for the premise that the blots are not totally ambiguous. Instead, each blot has critical stimulus elements or bits that, when viewed separately or in the gestalt pattern of the figure, tend to promote specific kinds of classifications while limiting or inhibiting other classifications. These potent or high valence stimulus features play a significant role in the test process. They create the parameters within which the blot, or areas of the blot, may be classified appropriately without resorting to distortion or some process that disregards their presence.

These findings are not surprising when considered in light of the relatively low number of responses or classes of response that meet the frequency criterion used to define *ordinary* (o) form quality. The Form Quality Table for the Comprehensive System (Exner, 1985) was developed from 7500 protocols containing 162,427 responses. The frequency criterion used to define an ordinary response to W and D areas is that an answer must have appeared in at least 150 (2%) of the 7500 records. *Only 831 responses or classes of response met that criterion.* Even if the response classes are subdivided, such as counting all of the animals that are consistent with the contours of D1 on Card VIII, the number meeting criterion is still only slightly more than 1000 responses. Although this may seem like a large number, it is not if considered in relation to the fact that 89 W and D areas are available. In other words, the stimulus features in those areas create limitations on the range of answers that can be generated without violating the properties or realities of the field. In effect, those features contribute to the formation of at least four of every five answers given by nonpatient subjects and are probably responsible in no small way for the high retest correlations for most variables that have been found in numerous temporal consistency studies (Exner, 1978, 1980, 1983, 1986; Exner, Armbruster, & Viglione, 1978; Exner & Weiner, 1982; Haller & Exner, 1985). Obviously, the blots and blot areas can be classified in less conventional ways without violating the stimulus properties. The more than 140 ordinary (*o*) *Dd* answers and 1700 *unusual* (*u*) responses listed in the Form Quality Table attest to this. It seems likely, however, that those types of responses are formed less rapidly than the more conventional answers, probably as the blot is rescanned during the second phase of the response process. Less than 2% of the answers listed by the subjects in the group tachistoscopic studies were scorable as *Dd* or *u*. This issue remains fertile ground for investigation.

Although it appears that most critical or potent stimulus elements in the blots involve contour, it is also clear that some do not. For instance, Exner (1959) demonstrated that the formulation of the bat response to Card I is closely related to the coloring of the blot. Similarly, Exner and Wylie (1977) demonstrated that the blue coloring in the *D*1 areas of Card X clearly facilitates the frequency with which the spider and crab answers are given to that area.

Unfortunately, information about the stimulus characteristics of the blots remains far too limited. This is especially true about the specific stimulus features of each *D* area and the relationships between each of the *D* areas within a blot. For instance, pilot work indicates that if the blue *D*1 area of Card X is presented separately, none of 21 adult nonpatients viewing it give either a spider or crab response. Eighteen of the 21 subjects reported that it is a "drop of water." Similarly, if the *D*4 area of Card I is presented alone, only three of 20 adult nonpatients identify it as a human female figure. The remaining 17 subjects identified it as an insect.

Some *D* areas have a negative potency or valence as related to some blot classifications. For example, if the *D*1 area is deleted from Card IV, the frequency of a human-like figure answer is nearly doubled. If only the *D*1 area of Card VII is shown, the frequency of human head or profile answers is increased by one-third as contrasted to when the *D*2 area is shown. When the latter is presented, about 35% of the respondents identify the area as being a small animal, usually a rabbit. The presence of these negative or limiting relationships probably contributes significantly to the reduction in the number of very high frequency answers (Populars) and to an increase in the number of ordinary responses or response classes.

Phase II: Rank Ordering and Discarding

The second segment or phase of the test process is the most intriguing and probably the most complex. Although the subject is able to generate a substantial number of answers shortly after the onset of blot exposure, there is no need to give all of them. The examiner gives no instructions about the number of responses (*R*) except to encourage the subject who gives only one answer to Card I, implying that one answer is not enough. Otherwise, the decision concerning the number of responses is left to the subject. Most subjects apparently find it uneconomical, redundant, disconcerting, or even embarrassing to report all of what they have "seen." Because the subjects review and discard some of the potential answers that were developed in the Phase I classification of the blot, this portion of the test process is the most time-consuming.

Refinement of Potential Answers and Paired Comparison   Early in Phase II, a judgmental process begins in which the merits of each potential answer are weighed in relation to each other and in relation to the task at hand *as the subject perceives it.* The subject's perception of the task includes not only the instructions that have been given but also any of a variety of sets that the subject may have concerning the test and test situation. The judgments that ensue probably entail a more precise rescanning of the blot or blot area than may have occurred initially, with the intent of validating the first impression, and possibly challenging its efficacy. Much of the resulting discarding of potential answers undoubtedly is based on a simple paired comparison tactic in which the subject judges one response to be more favorable or less favorable than another in light of the stimulus features of the blot. Most experienced examiners have heard subjects verbalize this process at times by saying, "I could say it looks like a . . . , or I could say it looks like a . . . . I guess I'll say a . . ." In the majority of these decisions, the subject probably relies mainly on the stimulus features of the blot as the primary source for the judgment, but the weights assigned to those features apparently differ across subjects. The bat response to Card I can be used to illustrate.

The importance of the $Dd34$ projections to the classification of Card I as a winged object has already been mentioned. That class of answer can be subdivided into five more specific responses that meet the frequency criterion to be scored or coded as ordinary (o), but the proportional frequencies for each vary considerably from the others. They include (1) bat = 48%, (2) butterfly = 40%, (3) bird = 8%, (4) winged insect = 3%, and (5) moth = 2%. It seems reasonable to assume that most subjects develop at least one and possibly more of these as potential answers during the Phase I classification process. In Exner, Persell, and Thomas's (1985) study, seven of the 24 control subjects included two in their list of five answers. A review of the 700 nonpatient adult protocols that constitute the normative sample for the *Comprehensive System* reveals that 39 subjects (6%) actually gave two of these answers in responding to Card I, and a review of the reference sample of 180 outpatient character problems (Exner, 1990) shows that 37 subjects (21%) gave two of these answers. Nonetheless, in every sample studied except children under age 10, the bat answer occurs with the highest frequency. Although the potency of the contours promotes the "winged object" class of answer, the *coloring* of Card I seems very important to the subclassification of bat rather than butterfly. If all other stimulus features are held constant but the color is changed to any of several chromatic varieties, the frequency of the bat answer is reduced dramatically, and in some instances is eliminated completely (Exner, 1959).

The most parsimonious explanation to account for the preferential differences in rank ordering, such as bat versus bird, butterfly versus bat, and so on, is that responses are generated from a variety of cognitive or stylistic features that promote mediational and decisional habits. For instance, the subject who rejects the potential butterfly response in favor of the bat response may simply be more conventional, or more precise, or conservative in decision operations, and for that type of subject the coloring of the blot may take on greater importance. The subject who retains the butterfly answer and discards the bat response may be more committed to rely on contour and/or more willing to disregard the incongruity of the coloring. There is support for this notion in the data concerning the coloring in Card V.

The proportional frequencies of the bat and butterfly answers to Card I are essentially reversed for the standard version of Card V. For Card V, the butterfly answer occurs in approximately 46% and the bat answer in only 36% of nonpatient records, and the bird response occurs substantially more often than to Card I (13%). If the color of the blot is altered to any of a variety of chromatic hues and all other stimulus features are held constant, the butterfly answer increases very substantially, whereas the bat answer is almost completely eliminated and the frequency for the bird response remains unchanged. In other words, the contours of the blot are more congruent to those that people tend to identify as a butterfly, whereas the standard achromatic version of the blot seems to become more potent for the bat answer because of the coloring. Thus, subjects who give the butterfly answer are seemingly attracted to the contours, whereas subjects oriented to giving the bat answer seem to place greater emphasis on the coloring.

Sets and Censorship   Although much discarding is based on paired comparison tactics, some potential answers clearly are discarded because of sets and/or censorship. Exner and Leura (1976) and Thomas, Exner, and Leura (1977) demonstrated that subjects more readily report responses involving sexuality, injury, or violence as much easier to find when set to believe that such answers commonly are give by businessmen rather than by schizophrenics. Potential sex responses can be generated to the blots much more easily than is suggested by the low frequency with which they occur under standard test conditions. Exner and Bromley (1984) set 44 graduating high school seniors to believe that locating objects commonly associated with sexuality, such as penis, vagina, breasts, and buttocks, is easier for younger people who identify with contemporary cultural values than for older people whose values are conservative. Slides were used to display each blot for one minute and subjects were provided with location sheets on which to record their findings. They were asked to search each blot for such objects and outline the corresponding area of each one discovered on the location sheet, also entering an M or F next to that area to indicate a male or female organ. Male subjects averaged 17.3 sexual objects, whereas female subjects averaged 22.6, and less than 10% involved form distortion.

Although the effect of such sets concerning acceptable answers plays an important role in judgments related to discarding, the relationship between subject and examiner can also contribute. Exner, Armbruster, and Mittman (1978) demonstrated that less discarding occurs when a close relationship exists between subject and examiner.

Patients tested by their own therapists gave an average of 10 more answers than did patients tested by unknown examiners. Nine of the 10 patients tested by their own therapists gave at least three sex responses, whereas most of the patients tested by unknown examiners gave none. In a similar study, eighth-grade students tested by their own teachers averaged 16 more answers than did eighth-grade students tested by unknown teachers (Exner & Weiner, 1982).

Phase III: Final Selection and Articulation

In some respects, Phase III operations are merely an extension of some Phase II activity but there is probably less cognitive shifting than during Phase II. Censorship operations have been completed by this time and most paired comparison judgments involving the same location area have led to discarding. Additional discarding has resulted from rank ordering. For some subjects, Phase III involves little more than the articulation of the remnants of the Phase II activities; however, for most subjects, the array of potential answers available continues to exceed the demands of the task. Therefore, some final selection is required.

Sets concerning the test and/or the test situation most likely continue as influences during this final phase, but data from numerous temporal consistency (test–retest) studies indicate that two elements, (1) the subject's psychological organization and (2) the subject's psychological state, have a primacy influence in the selection decisions. Retest correlations from both short term (3-day to 30-day retest) and long term (6-month to 3-year retest) studies indicate that subjects are highly consistent for the characteristics of responses that they select (Exner, 1978, 1980, 1983, 1986; Exner, Armbruster, & Viglione, 1978; Exner & Weiner, 1982). Some of the temporal consistency is provoked by the stimulus potency features of the blot, but even when subjects are asked to remember their original answers and provide different responses during the retest, the distribution of scores from both tests are remarkably similar (Exner, 1980; Haller & Exner, 1985). These findings suggest that enduring features of the individual, whether called response styles, traits, or habits, direct many or most of the selection decisions, but that situational elements, such as transient needs, stresses, and so on, including sets about the test and/or test situation, can also contribute to some selections. As noted earlier these elements have already been influential during much of the Phase II censoring and discarding and simply continue to have an impact as the decision operations shift toward the necessity of final selection.

THE ROLE OF PROJECTION IN THE
RESPONSE PROCESS

The operations that have been described as occurring during the three phases of the response process—scanning, encoding, classifying, refining, evaluating, discarding, and selecting—are fundamental cognitive operations, similar to those evoked in processing visual stimuli related to problem solving or decision making tasks. Projection is not included among the operations because, in many of those situations, projection is *not required or forced,* and in some may even be discouraged. The Rorschach situation does not discourage projection but, unlike tests that are designed to force projection, such as the Thematic Apperception Test (TAT) in which the subject is asked to create a story that goes well beyond the stimulus field (What is happening? What are the characters feeling or thinking? What led up to the event? What will be the outcome?), the subject taking the Rorschach is simply asked, "What might this be?" This instruction creates a somewhat narrow set of parameters for the subject, which are made even more so by the fact that the blots are not completely ambiguous.

Although the limited ambiguity of the stimulus fields of the blots plus the nature of the task do not encourage projection, they do not prohibit or discourage the unique translations or embellishments that almost certainly have some projected properties. As a result, projected features do seem to occur in some but not necessarily all answers, and some subjects give a reliable, valid protocol *without* including any projected material in the responses. Unfortunately, the Rorschach has been erroneously mislabeled as a "projective test" for far too long, and that label has created many faulty implications about the test process and tactics of interpreting the test data.

The term *projection* was introduced by Freud in 1894 and explained as a tactic of attribution. He elaborated further in 1896, describing it as a process of defensively attributing one's own feelings or drives to others or the world to avoid awareness of those feelings or drives. In 1913, he expanded or clarified the concept in "Totem and Taboo" by stating:

> But projection was not created for the purpose of defense; it also occurs where there is no conflict. The projection outward of internal perceptions is a primitive mechanism, to which . . . our sense perceptions are subject, and which . . . plays a very large part in determining the form taken by our external world. Under conditions whose nature has not yet been sufficiently established, internal perceptions of emotional and thought processes can be projected outwards [and] . . . are employed for building up the external world, though they should by rights remain part of the internal world. (p. 64)

In effect, Freud was describing projection as it is probably most applicable when speaking of projective tests or responses that include projection when given to test stimuli. A paraphrase of his statement—that is, given ambiguity, internal percepts may be projected into the translation of the stimulus field to afford it specificity—coincides reasonably well with Murray's 1938 explanation of the TAT: "When a person interprets an ambiguous social situation, he is apt to expose his own personality as much of the phenomena to which he is attending" (p. 531). Thus, as Lindzey (1961) and Shneidman (1965) pointed out, Murray created a link between the concept of projection and a method for the measurement of personality. Frank (1939) is usually credited with making the link more precise in his formulation of the "projective hypothesis" and his conception of projective tests as emphasizing the idiographic nature of human perception. In doing so, he became the theoretical leader of projective psychology, although the terms projection and projective techniques were subject to various definitions and spirited disagreements during the next two decades. Some, such as Abt (1950), Bellak (1950), Rapaport, Gill, and Schafer (1946), and Schafer (1948, 1954), developed definitions or concepts of projection focused mainly on its defensive or homeostatic role. Others, such as White (1944), MacCorquodale and Meehl (1948), Murray (1951, 1955), and Cattell (1957), chose to conceptualize projection as a process that yields information concerning personality structures.

Naturally, the Rorschach inkblots afforded an attractive centerpiece for those involved in the projective psychology movement and responses were variously described as perceptive projections (Murray, 1938), constitutive projections (Frank,

1939, 1948), imaginative projections (Murray, 1951; White, 1944) interpretive projections (Symonds, 1946), apperception distortions (Bellak, 1950), misperceptions (Cattell, 1957), voluntary indirect free responses (Campbell, 1957), and associations (Lindzey, 1961).

By the early 1950s, the proliferation in the definitions of projection and projective techniques caused much concern about the way in which projective psychology was developing. For instance, Murray (1951) wrote:

> Up to now most of us have been more ambitious to exhibit the gold extracted from the deep earth of personality . . . than we have to discover, explain, and if possible, remedy the failures and limitations of the method . . . As a result, in the realm of projective techniques today we must deal with anarchy. (p. xi)

Murray was especially critical of definitions that expanded the concept of projection well beyond that intended by Freud. He noted that, "If the term [projection] is used to denote all forms of expression . . . then we must find a new word to stand for the process of projection. . . . If 'projection' means everything it means nothing" (p. xiii). Murray also called attention to the fact that, when the projective process is stimulated, not all of the resulting response can be called projection.

Unfortunately, those seeking to interpret projected material in Rorschach responses have often been misled by faulty assumptions concerning the stimulus characteristics of the blots. As a result, a flawed logic system has often been endorsed, namely (A) the more ambiguous a stimulus field, the more a response to it will reflect the personality of the perceiver; (B) the Rorschach blots are very ambiguous; and, therefore, (C) all Rorschach responses will include some projections by the respondent. Numerous empirical findings question Assumption A concerning the relation between degrees of ambiguity and projection (Murstein, 1965). Other findings refute Assumption B concerning the ambiguity of the inkblots (Exner, 1978, 1986). Yet, this flawed logic chain has persisted among many who use the Rorschach. As a result, interpreters often make the error of trying to glean some meaning for each Rorschach answer even though some, many, or all of the responses may not contain projected material. Thus, an unwanted and sometimes disastrously misleading "noise effect" is often injected into the interpretation.

Projection is only a possibility in the Rorschach. Freud and Murray both endorsed the notion that a relationship exists between ambiguity and projection, and Murray argued that the less ambiguity in a stimulus field, or in the instructions and/or demands related to the classification of a field, the less likely it is that projection will occur. Because the inkblots are far less ambiguous than has been assumed, some answers simply result from classifying a blot or blot area in ways that are compatible with the stimulus field. They *are not* projections. But projections can and do occur despite the more limited ambiguity of the stimuli. In fact, there are probably two types of projected responses, one formed during the Phase I operations and the second formed during the Phase II or Phase III operations.

Projection and Phase I

The first type of projection that may occur in Rorschach answers is similar in some ways to Bellak's (1950) notion of apperceptive distortion and Cattell's (1957) concept of misperception. For instance, most people shown a glass and asked what it is respond that it is a glass. The distinct stimulus features of the object (glass) reduce the parameters of its definition rather sharply. It also can be identified functionally, such as, "Something you drink from," or even syncretistically, such as, "It's a thing that is made by man," but the range of adequate responses is quite limited. If a subject who is not perceptually impaired misidentifies the glass by calling it a boiler, or a devil, or a kidney, or a stomach, it is not unreasonable to assume that some element of projection has occurred because the stimulus field has been markedly distorted and/or ignored.

While the potent stimulus elements within each blot tend to facilitate the formation of certain responses or classes of response, the demands or restrictions created by their characteristics also tend to reduce the likelihood that projection will be involved in most Phase I operations. Nonetheless, classifications of blots or blot areas in ways that violate or ignore these prevalent features do occur. Technically, they are minus answers, and if they are not the product of some neurophysiologically related dysfunction in perceptual operations, it seems logical to postulate that they are the result of some form of cognitive mediation in which internal psychological sets or operations have superseded a reality oriented translation of the field. In other words, some form of projection may be involved.

Some limited support for the hypothesis that projection may be influential in the formation of some minus answers can be gleaned from a study of the minus responses in the protocols of three groups of subjects (Exner, 1989). One group consisted of 76 first-admission male paranoid schizophrenics. The second was a mixed group of 68 adult males with physical problems, including 27 who were tested within six days after a cardiac infarction and 41 beginning outpatient treatment for chronic gastrointestinal problems that had a psychogenic relationship. The third group, used as a control comparison, consisted of 70 protocols randomly drawn from the adult nonpatient male sample used in creating normative data for the *Comprehensive System*. The tactic used in this investigation involved a simple computer sort of the minus answers by content classes.

Although the three groups did not differ in the proportional frequencies of minus answers given for any single content class, a notable differentiation among the groups did occur for three composite classes of contents. These include the composite of *Hd + Ad* answers, which does not include the parenthesized (*Hd*) or (*Ad*) content categories; the composite of parenthesized content classes *(H) + (Hd) + (A) + (Ad)*; and the composite of *An + Xy*. The frequencies and proportions of minus answers for each of the composite classes of contents are shown for each group in Table 33.

It is intriguing to note that more than one-third of the minus answers given by the schizophrenic group involve human or animal details, or parenthesized contents, whereas more than one-third of the minus answers given by the group with physical problems consist of anatomy and X-ray contents. These data suggest that a set or preoccupation exists within each group that contributes to the distortion or misperception that occurs when the minus answer is formed. In such a circumstance the preoccupation apparently is not only of sufficient strength to promote the distortion but also to sustain the distortion through the remainder of the response process. Although these findings are compelling they fall far short of supporting the notion that all minus answers are related to projections. It is more

Table 33.   Frequencies and Proportions of Minus Responses in Each of Three Composite Content Classes for Three Groups

GROUP	TOTAL R	TOTAL MINUS	%	Hd+Ad Freq	%	Parens Freq	%	An + Xy Freq	%
PAR SCZ (N = 76)	1611	419	26	94	22*	62	15*	39	9
PHY PROB (N = 68)	1537	138	9	16	12	10	7	48	35*
CONTROL (N = 70)	1523	106	7	11	10	6	6	13	12

* = significantly greater proportion than all other groups ($p < .02$)

parsimonious to assume that many minus answers are the product of faulty scanning and/or encoding of the stimulus field. Moreover, the homogeneity that exists among the minus answers for these two groups does not occur among other groups. Computer sorts of minus responses, by content classes and composite content classes for several other groups, including a mixed group of schizophrenics, patients with sex problems, adolescents recently placed in foster programs, chronic headache patients, depressives, and so on, do not yield significant findings. Thus, although it is possible for projection to play some role during the Phase I classifications, no simple tactic permits the easy differentiation of projected versus nonprojected minus answers in most protocols. The exceptions are those records in which a substantial number of minus answers cluster in a single content category or among categories that are clearly related.

Projection and Phases II and III

Although projection may play a role during the Phase I classifications of the blot, it seems much more likely that the impact of the process, if it occurs, is greater during Phases II and III. During these later operations, a type of process such as that described by Symonds (1946) as interpretive projection and by White (1944) and Murray (1951) as imaginative projection may become involved if the subject overelaborates or departs from the stimulus field. As each potential answer is reviewed, judged, and refined, the circumstance exists during which a subject may embellish the answer. For instance, as noted earlier, most people who are shown a glass and asked what it is answer that it is a glass. Even within the parameters of that narrow stimulus field, however, a subject might expand the answer, such as, "It is a glass that was made by a very conscientious person." Likewise, most people who are asked, "How much are two times two?" answer "four," but they might embellish the answer in a projected manner, such as, "The answer is four, which is my favorite number because it represents the four seasons of the year that are so important to the cycle of life." Such an elaboration clearly seems to reflect something about the person because nothing in the stimulus field *or* in the question provokes it.

   In each of these examples the nature of the tasks (i.e., multiplying numbers or identifying an object) reduces the probability that projection will occur. It can occur but usually does not because the parameters of the task and the field are very narrow. In the Rorschach, however, the parameters of both the task and the field are broader. Although the limited ambiguity of the stimulus field plus the nature of the task do not encourage projection, they do not prohibit or discourage the unique translations or embellishments that almost certainly have some projected properties. As a result projected characteristics do occur in the formation of some answers and they continue to be weighed positively during the Phase III operations and ultimately appear in the protocol.

As suggested by Piotrowski (1957, 1969), the majority of answers that include this kind of projection do not require much interpretive translation because the embellishment is usually obvious by its departure from, or overelaboration of the stimulus field, such as occurs in many movement responses or answers in which an object is described with excessive specificity. It is quite rare, however, for any single seemingly projected answer to provide a wealth of interpretive information concerning the subject. Instead, it is the classes of projected material that generate the greatest interpretive yield. Some responses that appear to have projected features may be nothing more than straightforward translations of the blot stimuli.

For instance, most people give at least one passive movement answer, which has little interpretive significance, but research concerning high frequencies of passive movement answers has contributed much to the understanding of both passive-dependent and passive-aggressive coping styles, and, when passive features are predominant among human movement answers, it signals an abusive use of fantasy as a defensive tactic (Exner, 1978, 1986). Similarly, most people deliver at least one embellished response containing morbid (MOR) content, which alone means little, but data reveal that subjects who give high frequencies of MOR answers feel more damaged, unwanted, or unqualified, and harbor much more pessimism about themselves and their world than do those who give few MOR responses (Exner, 1986; Exner & Weiner, 1982). Data concerning aggressive movement (AG) answers indicates that subjects who give higher than average frequencies of AG answers manifest significantly more aggressive verbal and nonverbal behaviors than those who do not give AG answers (Exner, 1986). When they occur with an elevated frequency, AG answers are not indirect representations of the psychological features of people. Instead, as Piotrowski argued, they are probably very direct reflections concerning the feelings and/or behaviors of people.

The importance of using higher than average frequencies as a guideline in attempting to interpret these kinds of seemingly projected answers is possibly best illustrated by some of the data related to the development of the scoring for cooperative movement (COP) responses. The criterion for COP evolved from the failure to detect correlates for active movement, plus the positive findings concerning aggressive movement. One of the preliminary tests for COP involved the Rorschach's of 150 outpatients selected by using data from the Katz Adjustment Scale, Form R (KAS-R), a behavioral inventory completed by a patient's significant other (Katz & Lyerly, 1963). Fifty were selected because they scored high on subscales related to interpersonal cooperativeness and low on subscales related to aggression. Fifty were selected who had scored high on subscales related to aggressiveness, and 50 were selected who had scored high for depressive features. While all 50 subjects who scored high for interpersonal cooperativeness on the KAS-R gave at least two COP answers and 39 gave more than three, more than 20% gave at least one AG and a third gave at least more than one MOR. Similarly, although 41 of the 50 subjects scoring high for aggressiveness on the KAS-R gave at least two AG answers and 32 gave three or more, 19 of those subjects also gave at least one COP answer. Thirty-six subjects scoring high for depression on the KAS-R gave more than two MOR responses, although 18 of these subjects gave two or more AG answers and 16 gave at least two COP responses.

Although the data for each of the three scores do discriminate the groups, the sometimes strange mixture of seemingly projected responses led to the formulation of two interrelated experiments (Exner, 1989). The first was designed to establish some baseline data about whether each of the three kinds of answers, COP, AG, and MOR, could be identified easily in the same blot areas. This information is important in distinguishing the projected answer from the simple stimulus classification response. In other words, if all three options are easily available to the subject, just as the bat and butterfly options are probably available to most people for Cards I and V, the selection of any of the three can be considered as a projection as each type of answer departs from, or embellishes on, the stimulus field.

Forty-five nonpatient adults, naive to the test, were randomized and tested in groups of 15 subjects each. Each group was shown 7 of the 10 blots (I, II, III, V, VII, IX, and X) using a slide projector set for an exposure interval of 15 seconds per blot with a 10-second interval between exposures. Prior to the exposures, subjects were provided with a looseleaf booklet containing the seven location figures of the blots, each mounted one blot per page. Each page also had one response for the blot printed above the location figure. Subjects were not permitted to open the booklets or to turn subsequent pages until the corresponding blot was exposed on the screen. They were instructed to view the exposed blot, find the target answer, and then outline on the location figure the area of the blot involved.

Twenty-one reasonably specific target responses, three for each of the seven blots, were used. Seven were COP responses, seven were AG responses, and the remaining seven consisted of MOR answers. Responses were selected in accord with the criteria that each set of three responses would be to the same blot area and each of the three were also listed as *ordinary* responses for that area in the Form Quality Table. They were randomized so that, as each group of 15 subjects was tested, five were asked to find COP content in the seven blots, five were to find AG content, and the remaining five were to locate MOR content. The frequencies by which subjects correctly located the target answers that they were requested to find are shown in Table 34.

The results indicate that, given the set for the response, each response type in the set of three can be located with about the same ease as each of the others in the set. The only possible, but not statistically significant, exceptions to this are the MOR answers to Card III (broken bone structure), to which four subjects selected only the $D7$ area, and Card X (missile blowing up), to which two subjects selected the entire blot and one failed to respond.

These findings may indicate that, when a subject is refining and weighing the merits of potential answers during Phase II and III operations, any or all of the three kinds of responses may be included among the possibilities. On the other

Table 34. Frequencies by Which 45 Subjects Correctly Located Target Responses Provided During 15 Seconds of Blot Esposure

CARD, RESPONSE & LOCATION		TARGET RESPONSES		
		COP N = 15	AG N = 15	MOR N = 15
I	People dancing (W)	15	—	—
I	People beating another person (W)	—	13	—
I	A dead butterfly (W)	—	—	15
II	Dogs playing (D1)	15	—	—
II	Dogs fighting (D1)	—	15	—
II	Hurt animals (D1)	—	—	15
III	People lifting something (D1)	15	—	—
III	People fighting (D1)	—	15	—
III	A broken bone structure (D1)	—	—	11
V	People resting back to back (W)	14	—	—
V	Animals butting heads (W)	—	13	—
V	Dead bird (W)	—	—	15
VII	Children playing (W)	15	—	—
VII	Women arguing (W)	—	15	—
VII	Cloud formation breaking up (W)	—	—	15
IX	Clowns laughing (D3)	13	—	—
IX	Spacemen shooting at each other (D3)	—	14	—
IX	Flames consuming something (D3)	—	—	15
X	Insects lifting somthing (D11)	14	—	—
X	Insects fighting over something (D11)	—	15	—
X	A missile blowing up (D11)	—	—	12

hand, it could be argued that the subject is most likely to translate and/or elaborate the given blot area more in keeping with internal sets, which will have some impact in determining the specific features of the translation. If the latter is true, the resulting answer reflects those sets in some way or, in other words, includes some projection. This does not necessarily mean that the answer will be delivered, because it is still subject to discarding through censorship or through being judged less satisfactory than other potential answers.

In the second experiment, 45 nonpatient adults, naive to the Rorschach, were recruited to participate in a study about social sensitivity. They were randomized into three groups of 15 each and administered the test by one of three examiners who had no knowledge about the nature of the study. Each examiner tested five subjects from each group. Before meeting an examiner, the subject was interviewed briefly for demographic information and completed a 30-item questionnaire concerning vocational, avocational, and social activities. After the questionnaire was completed the subject was given a brief explanation of the Rorschach and the sets were introduced. Each subject heard the following explanation with the appropriate ending: "People find all kinds of things in the blots, and what they find often provides information about them. For instance, people who are more alert to the feelings of others usually find it easier to see _____." The end of the sentence for subjects set to report (COP) answers was, "humans or animals in some kind of cooperative behavior such as dancing, playing, talking, etc."; for subjects set to report AG responses, "aggression and violence between humans or animals such as fighting, arguing, etc."; and for subjects set to report MOR answers, "the products of violence such as things broken, damaged or destroyed." Data for each of the three types of answers by group are shown in Table 35.

The data in Table 35 suggest that the sets, even though presumably transient, did have some influence on the decisions of the subjects concerning what kind of answers to give during the test. Whereas all three groups gave essentially the same average number of M and FM answers, significantly fewer of the protocols given by subjects in the group set for AG responses contained COP answers when compared with the other two groups and all 15 subjects in that group gave at least one aggressive M and one aggressive FM. On the other hand, only four subjects in the group set to give COP answers gave AG responses, whereas all 15 gave at least one COP M and one COP FM. Interestingly, although all 15 subjects in the group set to give MOR answers did so, 14 of the 15 also gave at least one COP answer and nine gave at least one AG answer.

Projection is usually conceptualized as a process about which the subject has little or no conscious awareness and, because it is impossible to ascertain the extent to which these subjects retained a conscious awareness of the sets inserted during the pretest preparation, the data must be approached cautiously. Nonetheless, the findings are relevant to issues concerning projection in two respects. First, extrapolation from these data lends support to the postulate that if internal transient sets are influential in the Rorschach decision process, so too will be more enduring sets that are created by the potent features of personality organization such as needs, interests, attitudes, conflicts, and so forth. Second, and possibly more important, is the fact that in each group the sets did manifest with substantial frequencies, but other answers that ordinarily are considered to contain projected material also occurred within each group with frequencies

Table 35.   Descriptive Statistics for R, M, and FM, Plus Each of Three Special Scores, COP, AG, and MOR, Given by Three Groups of Nonpatient Adults Under Set Conditions

VARIABLE	GROUP 1 SET COP N = 15			GROUP 2 SET AG N = 15			GROUP 3 SET MOR N = 15		
	M	SD	FREQ	M	SD	FREQ	M	SD	FREQ
R	22.6	4.9	—	20.8	3.8	—	21.2	4.4	—
TOTAL M	4.7	2.6	15	4.3	1.9	15	3.7	2.1	15
TOTAL FM	4.9	2.3	15	5.2	2.4	15	4.2	2.6	15
M COP	3.6	1.8	15	0.8	1.1	5*	2.1	1.3	13
FM COP	2.9	1.6	15	0.4	1.2	3*	1.9	1.8	14
TOTAL COP	6.5	1.9	15	1.3	1.4	6*	4.1	1.9	14
M AG	0.7	1.3	3	3.1	1.4	15**	1.2	0.9	8
FM AG	0.3	0.7	4	3.8	1.7	15*	0.9	0.8	6
TOTAL AG	1.1	0.9	4	6.9	1.9	15**	2.1	1.0	9
MOR	0.8	0.9	6*	2.7	1.8	12	3.6	1.8	15

* = significantly different from both groups (p < .01)
** = significantly different from Group 1 (p < .01)

that cannot be disregarded. More than one-fourth of the subjects set for COP answers also gave AG answers and more than one-third gave MOR answers. More than one-third of the subjects set for AG answers also gave COP answers and three-fourths also gave MOR responses. Among subjects set for MOR content, all but one also gave COP responses and 60% gave AG answers.

It could be argued that all of these answers, regardless of the sets, represent some form of projection. Although that premise may have merit, it stretches the data beyond reasonable limits. It is more reasonable to assume that many of the "nonset" answers are simply products of blot classification. In other words, the potency of the stimulus features as translated by the subject were of sufficient strength not only to generate the answer, but also to cause it to be articulated. Such a conclusion coincides with other data. For instance, the majority of children's records and nearly half of adult protocols contain one MOR response, the overwhelming majority of which occur to Card VI (dead animal). The most common answer to Card III by both adults and children involves two people in some form of cooperative or aggressive movement. Aggressive movement answers occur in substantial frequencies to both Cards VII and VIII. Passive movement is commonplace to Cards I and IV. This is not to suggest that such answers are unimportant, but rather to reemphasize that, if responses that appear to contain projected features are to be considered in the interpretation, they should be approached with caution and with the knowledge that more valid interpretations will be generated when such responses occur with greater than usual frequencies. Such an approach, albeit conservative, provides some assurance that the test data will not be abused and that the concept of projection will be applied within realistic boundaries.

SUMMARY

Obviously, the test process involves a very complicated set of operations that occur in a relatively brief time span. Each answer that is articulated reflects something about the subject. Some answers are rather straightforward manifestations of processing and mediational activity that occur directly in accordance with the instructions of the test. Others are the products of much more complex activity, in which traits, styles, sets, and preoccupations contribute significantly to the selection and articulation of the answer. If additional data were available concerning the nature of the blot stimuli, it would be easier to glean more precise information concerning which characteristics have contributed to the formulation and selection of specific answers. Even so, the current state of knowledge regarding blot characteristics often provides sufficient information from which clusters of information can be addressed logically and translated in a manner to enhance information concerning the psychological functioning of the subject.

REFERENCES

Abt, L. E. (1950). A theory of projective psychology. In L. E. Abt and L. Bellak (Eds.), *Projective psychology*. New York: Knopf.

Bellak, L. (1950). On the problems of the concept projection. In L. E. Abt and L. Bellak (Eds.), *Projective psychology*. New York: Knopf.

Campbell, D. T. (1957). A typology of testing, projective and otherwise. *Journal of Consulting Psychology,* **21,** 207–210.

Cattell, R. B. (1957). *Personality and motivation structure and measurement.* New York: World Book.

Colligan, S. C., and Exner, J. E. (1985). Responses of schizophrenics and nonpatients to a tachistoscopic presentation of the Rorschach. *Journal of Personality Assessment,* **49,** 129–136.

Colligan, S. C., and Exner, J. E. (1986). *Responses of nonpatients to a one second tachistoscopic exposure of the Rorschach blots* [Workshops Study No. 299, unpublished]. Rorschach Workshops, Asheville, NC.

Exner, J. E. (1959). The influence of chromatic and achromatic color in the Rorschach. *Journal of Projective Techniques,* **38,** 418–425.

Exner, J. E. (1978). *The Rorschach: A Comprehensive System. Volume 2: Recent research and advanced interpretation.* New York: Wiley.

Exner, J. E. (1980). But it's only an inkblot. *Journal of Personality Assessment,* **44,** 562–577.

Exner, J. E. (1983). Rorschach assessment. In I. B. Weiner (Ed.), *Clinical methods in psychology* (2nd ed.). New York: Wiley.

Exner, J. E. (1985). *A Rorschach workbook for the Comprehensive System.* Rorschach Workshops, Bayville, NY.

Exner, J. E. (1986). *The Rorschach: A Comprehensive System. Volume 1: Basic foundations* (2nd ed.). New York: Wiley.

Exner, J. E. (1989). Searching for projection in the Rorschach. *Journal of Personality Assessment,* **53,** 520–536.

Exner, J. E. (1990). *A Rorschach workbook for the Comprehensive System.* Rorschach Workshops, Asheville, NC.

Exner, J. E., Armbruster, G. L., and Mittman, B. (1978). The Rorschach response process. *Journal of Personality Assessment,* **42,** 27–38.

Exner, J. E., Armbruster, G. L., and Viglione, D. (1978). The temporal stability of some Rorschach features. *Journal of Personality Assessment,* **42,** 474–482.

Exner, J. E., and Bromley, R. L. (1984). *Identification of objects associated with sexuality as a function of set concerning values* [Workshops Study No. 289, unpublished]. Rorschach Workshops, Bayville, NY.

Exner, J. E., and Leura, A. V. (1976). *Variations in the ranking of Rorschach responses as a function of a situational set* [Workshops Study No. 221, unpublished]. Rorschach Workshops, Bayville, NY.

Exner, J. E., and Martin, L. S. (1981). *Variations in Rorschach responses to Card I as related to the presence of Dd34* [Workshops Study No. 233, unpublished]. Rorschach Workshops, Bayville, NY.

Exner, J. E., and Persell, R. A. (1985). *Forced responses to Cards IV, V, and VI* [Workshops Study No. 316, unpublished]. Rorschach Workshops, Asheville, NC.

Exner, J. E., Persell, R. A., and Thomas, E. A. (1985). *Response preferences for Card I with and without Dd34* [Workshops Study No. 306, unpublished]. Rorschach Workshops, Asheville, NC.

Exner, J. E., and Simon, B. G. (1985). *Response preferences for Card VIII with and without D1* [Workshops Study No. 307, unpublished.] Rorschach Workshops, Asheville, NC.

Exner, J. E., and Weiner, I. B. (1982). *The Rorschach: A Comprehensive System. Volume 3: Assessment of Children & Adolescents.* New York: Wiley.

Exner, J. E., and Wylie, J. L. (1977). *Differences in the frequency of responses to the D1 area of Card X using an achromatic version* [Workshops Study No. 237, unpublished]. Rorschach Workshops, Bayville, NY.

Exner, J. E., and Wylie, J. L. (1977). Some Rorschach data concerning suicide. *Journal of Personality Assessment,* **41,** 339–348.

Frank, L. K. (1939). Projective methods for the study of personality. *Journal of Psychology,* **8,** 389–413.

Frank, L. (1948). *Projective methods.* Springfield, IL: Thomas.

Freud, S. (1894). The Neuro-psychoses of defense. In J. Strachey (Ed.), (1962) *The standard edition of the complete psychological works of Sigmund Freud* (Vol. 3, pp. 43–69). London: The Hogarth Press.

Freud, S. (1896). Further remarks on the Neuro-psychoses of defense. In J. Strachey (Ed.), (1962) *The standard edition of the complete psychological works of Sigmund Freud* (Vol. 3, pp. 159–188). London: The Hogarth Press.

Freud, S. (1913). Totem and taboo. In J. Strachey (Ed.), (1955) *The standard edition of the complete psychological works of Sigmund Freud* (Vol. 3, pp. 1–161). London: The Hogarth Press.

Haller, N., and Exner, J. E. (1985). The reliability of Rorschach variables for inpatients presenting symptoms of depression and/or helplessness. *Journal of Personality Assessment,* **49,** 516–521.

Katz, M., and Lyerly, S. (1963). Methods for measuring adjustment and behavior in the community. *Psychological Reports,* **13,** 503–535.

Lindzey, G. (1961). *Projective techniques and cross-cultural research.* New York: Appleton-Century-Crofts.

MacCorquodale, K., and Meehl, P. E. (1948). On a distinction between hypothetical constructs and intervening variables. *Psychological Review,* **55,** 95–107.

Murray, H. A. (1938). *Explorations in personality.* New York: Oxford University Press.

Murray, H. A. (1951). Foreword. In H. H. Anderson and G. L. Anderson (Eds.), *An introduction to projective techniques.* Englewood Cliffs, NJ: Prentice-Hall.

Murray, H. A. (1955). American Icarus. In A. Burton and R. E. Harris (Eds.), *Clinical studies of personality.* New York: Harper & Row.

Murstein, B. (1965). Assumptions, adaptation level, and projective techniques. In B. Murstein (Ed.), *Handbook of projective techniques.* New York: Basic Books.

Piotrowski, Z. A. (1957). *Perceptanalysis.* New York: MacMillan.

Piotrowski, Z. A. (1969). A Piotrowski interpretation. In J. E. Exner (Ed.), *The Rorschach Systems.* New York: Grune & Stratton.

Rapaport, D., Gill, M., and Schafer, R. (1946). *Diagnostic psychological testing* (Vol. 2). Chicago: Yearbook.

Schafer, R. (1948). *The Clinical application of psychological tests.* New York: International Universities Press.

Schafer, R. (1954). *Psychoanalytic interpretation in Rorschach testing.* New York: Grune & Stratton.

Shneidman, E. (1965). Projective techniques. In B. Wolman (Ed.), *Handbook of clinical psychology.* New York: McGraw-Hill.

Symonds, P. M. (1946). *The dynamics of human adjustment.* New York: Appleton-Century-Crofts.

Thomas, E. A., Exner, J. E., and Leura, A. V. (1977). *Differences in ranking responses by two groups of nonpatient adults as a function of set concerning the origins of the responses* [Workshops Study No. 251, unpublished]. Rorschach Workshops, Bayville, NY.

White, R. W. (1944). Interpretation of imaginative productions. In J. McV. Hunt (Ed.), *Personality and the behavior disorders.* New York: Ronald.

CHAPTER 4

Validity and Objectives

Although the Rorschach can be a very useful method for addressing matters concerning personality organization and functioning, every interpreter should be aware of two issues to ensure that the test will not be used haphazardly: (1) Are the data of the test interpretively valid? (2) Is the test being used for a purpose that is commensurate with its validity? These issues can be interrelated, but also can be independent. For instance, there are many assessment questions that the data of the Rorschach cannot be used to address. There are other instances in which Rorschach data usually can be used to address an issue, but the test itself may not be interpretively useful.

INTERPRETIVE VALIDITY

For several decades, Rorschachers assumed that, if a subject is presented with the 10 inkblots and gives some responses to them, the results yield information that is both reliable and valid. That Rorschach mythology has intrigued many who have been deeply involved with the test and has led to a substantial abuse of the test. Obviously, any conclusions and/or recommendations about the psychological organization and functioning of a subject that are derived from a protocol that is not reliable and/or valid can be dangerously misleading and, in some instances, can contribute to disastrous recommendations. Similarly, data from invalid protocols that are included among research findings can generate very spurious information.

Two classes of protocols are of questionable reliability and/or validity. Each may have some usefulness under certain conditions in which the assessment issues to be addressed are both narrow and specific, but neither affords the full breadth of information concerning personality organization and functioning that typically is available from the Rorschach. One class includes records that are potentially misleading because the test was administered during a time in which the psychological organization and/or operations of the subject were thrown into severe disarray by transient or situational elements. Those circumstances often create a picture that, although valid for the moment, fails to accurately detect the more salient features of the subject's personality and can produce a distorted psychological portrait. The second includes those records in which the number of responses is too few to produce reliable data. If interpreted, those protocols are likely to produce misleading personality pictures.

Potentially Misleading Records

Unfortunately, some examiners do not or cannot exercise good judgment about when to administer the Rorschach. When referrals are made, schedules and routines become fixed and do not allow for much flexibility in decision making concerning the assessment routine. This lack of flexibility appears to be most common among inpatient settings in which the need to formulate intervention planning often requires that data be collected shortly after an admission. Although the goal is admirable, there are instances in which patients are tested during an actively psychotic or toxic state; either condition will have a significant impact on test performance.

When the Rorschach is administered to a subject who is in a toxic or actively psychotic state, the results will, no doubt, portray the presence of that state. Usually, this will manifest by a lower than average $X + \%$, a higher than average $X - \%$, an elevated number of Critical Special Scores, and, in general, a protocol marked by considerable evidence of bizarreness and/or disorientation. A competent interpreter who reviews the record, knowing nothing about the subject, may conclude that a very serious disturbance exists; however, the data do not reveal the extent to which the presence of the disturbance conceals and/or distorts information regarding the basic personality of the subject. The issue is to what extent the data regarding basic personality styles are valid when the record has been taken while the subject is in a psychotic or toxic state.

The relevance of this issue is highlighted by the protocols of 100 involuntary first admissions that were contributed to the protocol pool of the Rorschach Research Foundation from 14 county and state facilities. All patients were admitted in states of considerable disarray and admission notes include references to psychotic-like features and/or behaviors. Most were suspected of drug induced toxicity, but about 30% were tentatively diagnosed as schizophrenic. The group includes 42 females and 58 males, ranging in age from 19 to 33 years. Fifty of the 100 subjects were tested on the second, third, or fourth day after admission (Group 1), whereas the remaining 50 were tested 7 to 10 days following admission (Group 2). Almost all had been prescribed some medication after admission, including 21 who were taking antipsychotic medication at the time of the testing (eight from Group 1 and 13 from Group 2). Table 36 contains data for each group regarding the interpretive range or directionality for eight variables that are often critical in defining the presence of personality or response styles.

If the assumption is accepted that both groups are drawn from the same population, these findings issue a significant caution regarding the interpretation of records administered shortly after admission when the presenting picture includes a psychotic-like or toxic-like state. This seems especially true when the admission has been involuntary. The data suggest that conclusions regarding response styles, capacity for control, modulation of affective displays, and extent of mediational distortion can be quite misleading.

These findings should not be interpreted to mean that the data are not valid for the moment. In all likelihood, they do illustrate the disarray of the subjects. But they tend to be misleading if taken to represent the basic personality structure of many of the subjects. In this instance, it appears that the intensity of the disarray, which probably includes the products of the stressful experience

Table 36. Range or Directionality Data for Two Groups of Involuntary First Admissions Tested at Different Times

VARIABLE	GROUP 1 N = 50 TESTED 2-4 DAYS AFTER ADMISSION		GROUP 2 N = 50 TESTED 7-10 DAYS AFTER ADMISSION	
	N	%	N	%
EB = AMBITENT	37*	74%	19	38%
D SCORE < 0	44*	88%	16	32%
ADJ D SCORE < 0	34*	68%	11	22%
X–% > .30	39*	78%	17	34%
LAMBDA > 0.99	8	16%	2	4%
EA < 6.0	14	28%	5	10%
CF+C > FC+3	31*	62%	18	36%
p > a+1	5	10%	13	26%

* = significantly different from Group 2 ($p < .01$)

of being admitted involuntarily, created a transient form of dysfunctioning for many of the subjects tested prematurely. Thus, the test results for some subjects probably offered a more dismal picture of the basic personality than may have been the case if the testing had been deferred until the subject had made some adjustments to the situation and the psychotic or toxic episode had subsided.

If the purpose for using the Rorschach for the cases who were tested within two to four days after admission had been to confirm the state of disarray, that objective appears to have been readily achieved. But if the purpose was to generate a valid description of the more enduring personality features, that objective was probably not achieved for many of the cases and, in some instances, intervention decisions could have been made on the basis of data that easily might have been misinterpreted.

Some Rorschach lore suggests that it is preferable to administer the test before medication, especially high potency antipsychotic medication, is prescribed or that it is best to administer the Rorschach as soon as a subject is available to ensure that the test performance is not affected by the onset of intervention. Neither of these presumptions is true. The Rorschach data have the clearest yield when the subject is cooperative and coherent. Pharmacological intervention, especially when the subject has been stabilized reasonably well on the medication, has relatively little impact on most Rorschach variables, and certainly no significant impact on those variables that relate to the core features of the personality structure. Thus, it behooves those using the test to make intelligent decisions about when it should be administered.

Naturally, the decision about when to test should be made in light of the assessment targets that have been selected, but if those targets include the development of a valid picture of the core personality structure, the administration should be deferred until psychotic or toxic episodes have subsided. Otherwise, the interpreter is faced with the incredibly difficult, if not impossible, challenge of deciding which data are temporally reliable.

Brief Records

Unfortunately, brief records, that is, those containing 13 answers or less, occur much more frequently than might be suspected. A review of response frequency data for several groups in the protocol pool at the Rorschach Research Foundation reveals that the proportion of records containing 13 or fewer answers ranges from 6% for nonpatient adults to 14% of inpatient depressives and 17% of children with conduct disorders. The impact of brief records on research findings has been suspect for quite some time. For instance, the original Schizophrenia Index (SCZI) accurately identified between 75 and 85% of randomly selected schizophrenic patients (Exner, 1986). A review of the false negative cases indicates that about 70% consist of records in which 13 or fewer answers were given. Similarly, the original Suicide Constellation (S-Con) correctly identified nearly 80% of subjects who effected their own death within 60 days after taking the Rorschach (Exner & Wylie, 1977). The revised S-Con (Exner, 1986) improved the accuracy to nearly 85%, while continuing to misidentify very few as false positives. A review of the false negative cases shows that 60% are records in which fewer than 13 answers occurred.

These findings prompted review of 10 studies that were completed at the Rorschach Research Foundation between 1974 and 1984 concerning validation issues of test variables (Exner, 1988). These studies were selected because each contained at least 70 records and the data had been subjected to some form of discriminant or correlation analysis. The data for each study were reanalyzed twice using the same statistical procedures employed originally. In the first reanalysis, any protocols containing fewer than 13 responses were deleted from the sample; in the second reanalysis, all records containing fewer than 14 answers were deleted from the sample. The results were striking. When the studies were reanalyzed with records of 12 or fewer answers omitted, the levels of significance that had been detected for positive findings in the original analyses improved substantially. When protocols of 13 or fewer answers were omitted in the second reanalysis, the findings improved even more significantly. None of the new findings changed the basic interpretation of the data, but, *in each study,* conclusions drawn from the original findings were strengthened considerably. For example, in a study concerning the directional stability of ratios, five subjects had shown change of direction for at least one of three ratios in a three-year retest. Four of those five subjects were eliminated from the reanalyses because their first protocols contained fewer than 14 responses. Similarly, in a study concerning aggression, the discrimination between high and low aggression groups changed from $p < .02$ to $p < .001$ when only eight records containing fewer than 13 answers were deleted from the original 70-record pool.

The results of this elementary exercise in data manipulation raised a question about when a Rorschach can be considered as truly representative of the subject. If differences between the original analyses and the two reanalyses are used as guidelines, it would appear clear that the majority of brief records, those with 13 responses or less, are of questionable usefulness and their interpretation could be quite misleading. The findings raised a new issue. Should all brief records be discarded as interpretively suspect, or might there be some way to differentiate the useful from the invalid record? This question was addressed by studying records collected in a variety of temporal consistency studies.

Thirty-six target pairs of protocols were culled from 295 pairs of records from nine short term retest studies. Four involved nonpatient children and five included nonpatient adults, all retested between four and 30 days after the first test (Exner, 1978, 1983, 1986; Exner & Weiner, 1982). In each of the 36 target pairs, one protocol contained 13 or fewer answers and the second contained at least 15 responses (Group LO). A control group of 36 pairs of records was drawn randomly from the remaining pool of 259 subjects who had given at least 15 answers in each of their two records (Group AV).

The first step was a correlational analysis to establish the retest reliabilities for each group, which are shown in Table 37. The correlations in Table 37 seem to offer considerable evidence to support the postulate that the structural data derived from a brief record are likely to be quite different from the structural data for the same subject generated from a record that contains at least 15 answers. The retest correlations for only two variables, m and $X + \%$, are reasonably similar

Table 37. Correlation Coefficients for Two Groups of 36 Subjects Each Tested Between 4 and 30 Days

VARIABLE	DESCRIPTION	GROUP LO R < 14 IN ONE PROTOCOL	GROUP AV R > 14 IN BOTH PROTOCOLS
		r	r
R	No. of Responses	.36	.87
P	Popular Responses	.62	.89
Zf	Z Frequency	.53	.82
F	Pure Form	.48	.79
M	Human Movement	.44	.87
FM	Animal Movement	.28	.74
m	Inanimate Movement	.36	.28
a	Active Movement	.41	.88
p	Passive Movement	.22	.83
FC	Form Color Response	.34	.89
CF	Color Form Responses	.49	.71
C	Pure C Responses	.33	.59
CF+C	Color Dominant Responses	.38	.84
Sum C	Sum Weighted Color	.27	.86
T	Texture Responses	.54	.91
C'	Achromatic Color Responses	.28	.78
Y	Diffuse Shading Responses	.09	.40
V	Vista Responses	.62	.89
RATIOS & PERCENTAGES			
L	Lambda	.46	.83
X+%	Extended Good Form	.81	.92
Afr	Affective Ratio	.49	.89
3r+(2)/R	Egocentricity Index	.51	.87
EA	Experience Actual	.44	.86
es	Experienced Stimulation	.23	.71
D	Stress Tolerance Index	.76	.92
Adj D	Adjusted D Score	.61	.93

for both groups, and the correlations for the group in which one record contained 13 or fewer responses shows only two variables with values above .75 ($X + \%$, D). It seems clear that the probability is considerable for a second record to have substantially different values for most structural variables. Nonetheless, most retest correlations for the group containing one brief record are statistically significant, raising the possibility that some of the retest records might be interpretively similar to the first protocol.

The second analysis involved frequency calculations concerning the interpretive consistency of 17 ratios, indices, and percentages in the test versus the retest. This was done to address the issue of whether the interpretive range would change even though the absolute values might differ substantially from one test to the other. An inspection of the 36 target pairs of records revealed that, for eight subjects, the values for Lambda were .85 or less in both records. None of the values for L in the brief records of the remaining 28 target pairs fell lower than 1.0, and many were greater than 1.5 ($M = 1.48$, $SD = .46$). However, a Lambda value of less than .90 occurred in 22 of the 28 longer protocols for those pairs. Thus, the group was subdivided based on the value for L. Frequency data concerning the number of pairs of records in which the values in 17 ratios, percentages, and indices have the same interpretive directionality or range in both tests were tallied for all 72 pairs of protocols. The results are shown in Table 38, with the eight target pairs in which the value for L was .85 or less shown as a separate group.

As indicated in Table 38, the interpretive directionality or range remained the same for seven variables (*EB*, D, Adj D, $FC : CF + C$, $a : p$, $M^a : M^p$, and

Table 38. Frequencies and Percentages for Three Groups Showing the Number of Pairs of Protocols in Which the Values for 17 Variables Fall in the Same Interpretive Range in Both Tests

| | TARGET GROUPS R < 14 IN ONE PROTOCOL | | | | CONTROL GROUP R > 14 IN BOTH PROTOCOLS N = 36 | |
| | $L < .85$ IN BOTH PROTOCOLS N = 8 | | $L > .99$ IN BRIEF PROTOCOL N = 28 | | | |
VARIABLE	FREQ	%	FREQ	%	FREQ	%
EB	8	100	11*	39	33	92
eb	7	88	13*	46	35	97
D	8	100	21	75	35	97
ADJ D	8	100	16*	57	36	100
a:p	8	100	15*	53	34	94
Ma:Mp	8	100	13*	46	33	92
FC:CF+C	8	100	9*	32	36	100
Afr	5	63	7	25	35*	97
3r+(2)/R	6	75	11*	39	35	97
L	7	88	6*	21	34	94
X+%	8	100	24	86	36	100
X−%	5	63	18	64	32	89
Zd	7	88	13*	46	32	89
W°	3	38	7	25	30*	83
W:M	2	25	6	21	31*	86
ALL H CONT	4	50	11	39	33*	92
ISOLATE:R	6	75	20	71	35	97

* = Proportional Chi Square yields $p < .05$

$X + \%$) in all eight pairs of the target records in which L was less than .85 in both protocols and in seven of the eight pairs for three other variables (*eb, Zd,* and *L*). These findings seem important because a difference of as many as eight answers occurred between the test and the retest records in this group. However, it is equally important to note that, in from three to six of the eight protocols, the interpretive directionality or range shifted for eight other variables. In other words, even when Lambda is less than .85, the data for many of the variables that are important to interpretation are probably not valid.

The findings are much more negative when the value for Lambda exceeds .99. The same interpretive directionality or range existed for only two variables (D, $X + \%$) in three-fourths or more of the remaining 28 target records. In fact, the proportion of pairs among those 28 protocols in which the same interpretive direction or range is found in both records is significantly lower than in both of the other groups for nine variables, and significantly lower than the control group for three additional variables.

These findings, although derived from relatively small samples, highlight the potential hazards of working with brief protocols, whether in a clinical or a research setting. It seems clear that the majority of brief records will not have the level of reliability prerequisite to the assumption of interpretive validity. These results suggest that the interpretation of the structural data of a brief test should be avoided. The data do seem to support the hypothesis that Lambda can be used as a source from which to estimate the probable reliability for a few, *but not all,* variables in brief records.

Data concerning Lambda suggest that it is a crude index of the extent to which a subject is psychologically willing to become involved in a new stimulus field (Exner, 1978, 1986). When Lambda is low it indicates that the subject may become more involved than is customary, sometimes because of an overincorporative style, but more often because of an unusual frequency of psychological demands experienced by the subject. Conversely, when Lambda is substantially above average, it indicates that the subject is prone to minimize the importance of, and/or ignore, some elements of the stimulus field. This may reflect a basic coping style and if so it is of considerable interpretive importance in understanding the psychological organization and functioning of the subject. People with such coping orientations routinely formulate behaviors that are more in accord with their tendency to oversimplify complex stimulus demand situations. In doing so, their behaviors may be less effective in terms of the requirements of the situation and, at times, can even run contrary to social expectations.

The composite of a low number of responses plus a High L can also represent the performance of a highly resistive subject who is simply attempting to avoid the many demands of the test situation. In effect, these performances depict *subtle refusals* to take the test. Unfortunately, there is no easy way to distinguish the low R, high L record that illustrates resistance from the low R, high L record that reflects a valid indicator of a coping style. Thus, when records such as these occur, the interpreter is, at best, very hard pressed to differentiate characteristics that are trait-like from those that might be situationally provoked.

It seems clear that all short records pose potential problems for the interpreter. The retest data for the 36 target pairs of records suggest that four of every five protocols containing 13 or fewer responses are not reliable for most, and possibly all, variables. Even if Lambda has a value of .85 or less, the data for many structural variables are likely to be misleading. Viewed from one perspective, all brief records might be regarded as attempts to conceal. That is probably an accurate conclusion but not very useful in most assessment situations. The data for the eight pairs of records in which the value for Lambda is consistently less than .85 seem to indicate considerable reliability for some of the basic variables concerning capacity for control, coping style, perceptual conventionality, and some information about characteristics of ideation and modulation of affective discharge. If such information is important in the assessment situation, the record probably can be interpreted, but with extreme caution. On the other hand, the remaining sample of target records shows dismal retest reliabilities and percentages for which the values for critical variables fall in the same interpretive range.

Thus, as a rule, protocols in which the number of responses is less than 14 should probably be discarded on the premise that they are unreliable and, as such, are not interpretively valid. There are some obvious exceptions, but these are the protocols of severely disturbed patients in which the $X + \%$ is extremely low, the $X - \%$ is quite high, and two or three bizarre responses occur, *and for which other data exist confirming the magnitude of the disability*.

As noted earlier, brief records occur much more often than might be expected. Some reflect a form of subtle resistance to the test, but some simply may be the result of a subject following instructions very concretely and failing to generalize from encouragement given during Card I. Some subjects, especially young children, want to go through the test as quickly as possible and their haste produces a short record. Whatever the cause, a record of less than 14 answers should not be accepted. In fact, it should not even be inquired.

When a brief record is taken, the examiner/interpreter should consider either of two options. The first is simply to discard the test and rely on other assessment data that are available to formulate an evaluation of the subject. A second option exists if Rorschach data seem to be of importance to the assessment issue(s) that have been posed. It involves an immediate retest following the response phase of the test. To do so, the examiner should interrupt the standard procedure, which ordinarily means proceeding to describe the purpose of the Inquiry, and explain to the subject:

> Now you know how it's done. But there's a problem. You didn't give enough answers for us to get anything out of the test. So we will go through them again and this time I want you to make sure to give me more answers. You can include the same one's you've already given if you like but make sure to give me more answers this time.

Some subjects seek direction under this new circumstance and ask, "How many should I give?" The response should depend mainly on whether the examiner feels that the subject has tried to be cooperative. For example, if the subject has seemed cooperative, it is appropriate to say, "Well, it's really up to you, but you only gave _____ answers and I really need more than that to get anything out of the test." If a subject who has been obviously resistive or guarded asks how many answers are required, the examiner should be more directive, saying, "Well, it's up to you but I really need several more answers than you gave."

Some interpreters may want to consider a third option, namely to deal subjectively with the verbal material in the brief record. This tactic is fraught with potential problems and probably should not be pursued with most brief records. Interpretation of a brief record is often little more than an esoteric exercise in speculation and it easily becomes a pitfall for those who are caught in the Rorschach myth that, once responses have been collected, the data are ripe for interpretation regardless of how many answers have been given. Certainly, in some cases, a wealth of valid history data may be readily available to provide a source from which some cross-validation of interpretive postulates might be gleaned, especially regarding interpersonal behavior. If so, the history in itself probably offers a much more reliable picture of the subject than do propositions generated from the qualitative speculations drawn from a few Rorschach answers.

OBJECTIVES FOR INTERPRETATION

The well-developed Rorschach interpretation yields a useful, valid picture of psychological organization and operations. The picture is drawn together by merging nomothetic and idiographic information in a manner that highlights the uniqueness of the subject. Ideally, the resulting portrait includes reference to both assets and liabilities. Unfortunately, because most test subjects are in distress or disarray, a pervasive tendency exists among interpreters to emphasize liabilities. The result tends to neglect the importance of couching those findings in a broader portrait that captures the core underpinnings of personality in a manner that also recognizes assets.

This oversight in interpretation is not difficult to understand. Many referral questions focus on issues of diagnosis but, even if the assessment issues are of a broader nature, such as a request for a personality description or evaluation, the interpreter is likely to emphasize liabilities. Most who are involved in personality assessment are influenced by an awareness of human frailty and consequently tend to be more oriented toward the detection of flaws in people rather than to search out assets.

This influence is generated by both the theories and concepts of psychology. For instance, most theories of personality tend to focus much more on *problems* of adjustment than on *products* of adjustment, emphasizing the struggles of the individual to develop, identify, cope, adapt, achieve, gratify, accommodate, and assimilate. Similarly, the notions of *normal* and *abnormal* frequently are referred to in ways that imply the presence of vast banks of knowledge concerning each. In reality, the scientific literature is abundant with studies concerning oddness, deviation, maladjustment, and abnormality, but is rather pathetically impoverished for works about adjustment or "normality." Part of the problem is that maladjustment or abnormality seem easily identified or defined, whereas universally acceptable definitions for the concepts of normal or adjusted remain elusive. They have been variously defined using tenets drawn from anthropology, biology, learning theory, philosophy, sociology, theology, statistics, and the numerous theories of personality. Although none of those definitions has proved satisfactory, it has become obvious that the concepts of normality or adjustment cannot be restricted either to internal harmony or external compatibility.

A person may experience considerable satisfaction with his or her own internal state but not be able to interact effectively with the expectations and demands of the environment. It seems probable that many schizophrenics are like this. Their internal tranquility is maintained by ignoring and/or distorting external demands, and they sustain that state until the intensity of external demands breaks through the barriers that have been created. The result is psychological chaos.

Similarly, some people are excessively diligent in striving to interact effectively with the demands and expectations of the environment. Unfortunately, that diligence often requires that they sacrifice much of their own psychological integrity. Although the result is a seemingly admirable pattern of interaction with the external world, the internal condition is far less than satisfactory and is often marked by experiences of frustration, anxiety, pain, and confusion. As those experiences increase in frequency and/or intensity, a breaking point is approached. If that point is breached, the subject is psychologically hurled into a chaotic existence in which neither a sense of internal security nor patterns of effective environmental interaction are possible.

Thus, a major challenge for those interpreting the Rorschach is to create a picture of the individual that is broadly encompassing. It should identify liabilities, but also consider them in the context of assets. It should focus on the integrity and balance of internal operations, but also review them in the context of environmental exchange. It should not be a description that consists of a collection of glib, overgeneralized phrases. Instead, it should capture the psychological substance of the subject, as a person who is similar to others in some ways but, in reality, is different from everyone else. This is not an easy task, but one that can be accomplished. Unfortunately, this objective is often made more difficult because of the nature of some assessment issues that are posed routinely.

DIAGNOSIS, DESCRIPTION, AND PREDICTION

Although the data of the test remain the same, the primary focus of Rorschach assessment often varies. In some cases a referral may request a diagnostic formulation regarding a subject. In other instances, a "personality evaluation" or description is requested. Many referrals are made to obtain inputs concerning treatment planning or treatment evaluation, whereas others may concern disposition. Although the data of the test can be applicable to each of these targets, the efficacy of the yield does vary and the interpreter should be acutely aware of this variability.

Diagnosis

The data of the test converge on internal organization and process. The major yield is *descriptive,* providing an illustration of the subject as he or she is *now.* In most instances, it does not fall neatly into a configuration or profile that equates directly with diagnostic categories, such as those described in the third or third revised editions of the American Psychiatric Association's *Diagnostic and Statistical Manual of Mental Disorders* (DSM-III or DSM-III-R). This should not be surprising as people differ enormously and, as pointed out in the *good pt*

Introduction to DSM-III (APA, 1980), diagnostic labeling is not designed to classify individuals, but rather to classify "disorders that individuals have."

The DSM categories are based on an approach that is mainly atheoretical with regard to etiological elements, except in those few instances for which knowledge about etiology has been well established. The majority of the checklist criteria that have been created to enhance diagnostic decisions are based primarily on self-report and behavioral findings and, for the most part, do not relate directly to the sorts of information derived from Rorschach data. Thus, although diagnostic labeling may be an important task, the Rorschach interpreter usually should not anticipate the discovery of direct diagnostic evidence in the data of the test. There are two important exceptions to this caution. One is the presence of schizophrenia, and the second concerns the probability of frequent and intense experiences of depression. The special indices SCZI and DEPI comprise variable constellations that relate directly to diagnostic labels. The true positive rate for the SCZI ranges between 75 and 85%, whereas the false positive rate is generally less than 10%. The true positive rate for the DEPI ranges from 70 to 85%, whereas the false positive rate is less than 5% when a critical score of *six* or more is applied. Positive findings for either of these indices should be afforded considerable weight in diagnostic decisions.

SCZI + DEPI can be used

Even though Rorschach data do not include configurations or profiles that relate directly to diagnostic classification, the description of the subject that is derived from the data often contributes to the final diagnostic formulation if one is required. But that may not always be the case especially concerning the primary diagnostic classification. Although subjects may be homogeneous for symptoms or problems in adjustment, they may be very heterogeneous for psychological organization or personality structure. Some structural data for two cases, shown in Table 39, may serve to illustrate.

The subjects are both female and are nearly the same age. Case 1 is 30 years old and is recently divorced after eight years of marriage. She and her exhusband share custody of their six-year-old daughter. Case 2 is 31 years old and single. Each has been referred to consulting psychiatrists by their respective physicians. Both have similar complaints concerning symptoms that have existed for more

Table 39.   Some Structural Data for Two Cases

CASE 1—A 30 YEAR OLD FEMALE			CASE 2—A 31 YEAR OLD FEMALE		
R = 23	$L = 0.35$		R = 19	$L = 1.2$	
$EB = 2:7.0$	$EA = 9.0$		$EB = 5:1.0$	$EA = 6.0$	
		$D = -1$			$D = 0$
eb = 6:7	es = 13		eb = 1:3	es = 4	
		AdjD = 0			AdjD = 0
$FM = 4$	$C' = 2$	$T = 3$	$FM = 1$	$C' = 1$	$T = 1$
m = 2	$V = 0$	$Y = 2$	m = 0	$V = 0$	$Y = 1$
$a:p$ = 3:5	$FC:CF+C = 3:5$		$a:p$ = 1:5	$FC:CF+C = 0:1$	
$Ma:Mp = 0:2$	Pure C = 1		$Ma:Mp = 1:4$	Pure C = 0	
Sum6 = 1	Afr = 0.86		Sum6 = 2	Afr = 0.33	

than a month. They report tension, fatigue, headaches, upset stomach, jitteriness, frequent dizziness, anxiety, and difficulties in concentrating. The results of physical examinations are negative and both attending physicians have been unsuccessful in attempting to treat them pharmacologically. The consulting psychiatrists in each case have rendered a preliminary diagnosis of Generalized Anxiety Disorder (DSM-III, 300.02), and both have requested psychological evaluation with a view to treatment planning.

Even though the structural data in Table 39 are only fragmentary, anyone experienced with the Rorschach can see that these two women are extremely different in psychological organization and functioning. The woman in Case 1 is markedly extratensive (EB) and appears to have some difficulties in modulating her affective displays ($FC : CF + C$, Pure C). She is currently in an overload state and prone to impulsiveness (D), and apparently feels quite lonely (T). On the other hand, the woman in Case 2 is markedly introversive (EB) but also seeks to simplify complexity and ambiguity when possible (L). She apparently prefers to avoid affective stimulation (Afr). Although they are quite different in coping preference and emotional responsiveness, they are similar in three other ways: (1) both are experiencing some emotional distress (eb), which is not surprising in light of the presenting complaints; (2) both are very prone to passivity ($a : p$); and (3) both tend to abuse fantasy for purposes of avoiding reality and/or responsibility ($M^a : M^p$).

It could be hypothesized that the similarity in passivity may contribute to the homogeneity in symptoms, but that speculation goes well beyond empirical findings and is not relevant to the diagnostic issue. In view of the presenting symptoms, the tentative diagnosis that has been rendered, Generalized Anxiety Disorder, is clearly appropriate in both cases; however, in view of the findings from the fragments of test data, it is clear that the treatment plans will probably differ considerably for these cases.

Description

A treatment plan is actually a prediction concerning the potential effectiveness of an intervention strategy designed to accomplish specific objectives. The diagnosis can contribute information to this prediction in some cases but, for the most part, the validity of the prediction improves considerably as information concerning the psychological organization and functioning of the subject is included in the array of material to be considered. As noted earlier, the major yield of Rorschach data is descriptive. The variables of the test, when studied in clusters, tend to converge on internal organization and process. Collectively, the findings from the test reveal both general and specific information about some personality features. Most records contain data related to ideation, emotion, coping preferences and response styles, capacity for control, self-perception, information processing, interpersonal perception, cognitive mediation, and routine defensive strategies. Collectively, these data provide much information concerning personality styles, traits, or habits.

Although it is erroneous to expect the findings to fall into neat configurations that differentiate subjects into personality groupings, the cumulative data often make it possible to identify the presence of an overall personality style similar to those proposed by Shapiro (1965). Shapiro focused mainly on a conceptualization of personality structure as it creates a predisposition to maladjustment. He identified as "neurotic styles" the obsessive, the hysteroid, the paranoid, and the impulsive, including two variants of the impulsive style, psychopathic and passive. Although emphasizing the neurotically defensive nature of the characteristics of these personality styles, he was also describing features that are common among people who are not necessarily doomed to a pathological state. In other words, the unique psychological organization of each individual inevitably is marked by features that at times may be assets but at other times may be liabilities.

For instance, a substantial elevation in the Zd score signals the presence of a form of information processing that has been labeled *overincorporation.* Overincorporation is stylistic. Overincorporators tend to invest much more effort than usually is necessary in scanning a field. For whatever reason, they are somewhat more perfectionistic. In many situations this can be an asset but in some situations it can become a significant liability. Its presence, as a type of cognitive style, should not be considered as indicating obsessiveness. Nonetheless, it is a psychological ingredient that is often found in Shapiro's obsessive style.

Similarly, if the $FC : CF + C$ ratio in the record of an adult has a much larger value on the right side, it suggests that the subject does not modulate emotional discharge as much as do most adults. As a consequence, feelings may become overly influential in thinking, in decisions, and in behaviors. These people usually appear more "intense" in their behavioral routines and might be regarded by some as being too emotional. Nonetheless, this feature can be an asset in those situations where openness and intensity is desirable and reinforced. At the same time, it can be a liability in situations that require a more conservative, thoughtful form of behavior. This affective style *cannot* be regarded as indicating the presence of a hysteroid personality, yet it is one of the central components that marks Shapiro's hysterical style.

Any decisions concerning some general categorization of personality can evolve only after a careful study of the many features that comprise the total personality. As noted earlier, Rorschach interpreters often follow the dangerous path of identifying or emphasizing some findings, especially liabilities, without providing a complete description of the psychology of the person, including assets or, at times, without considering apparent liabilities in the broader context of the subject's environment. Table 40 provides an alphabetical listing of seven clusters of variables. In each, the variables relate to each other, and all relate to specific psychological components or functions, which are shown in the column on the left. Some data should be available concerning each of these components in any valid Rorschach protocol. Table 40 also includes one array of variables that relate to situational stress. Those variables do not necessarily relate to each other but all relate to situational stress experience.

Some variables appear in more than one cluster. For example, minus answers relate to both mediation and self-perception. Some movement contents appear in both self-perception and interpersonal perception. A high Lambda is included in both processing and mediation. This repetition across clusters occurs because single variables often have a multiple input. For instance, MOR responses are relevant to both ideation and self-perception. The data regarding MOR indicate that significant elevations in the frequency by which this type of response is given

Table 40.   Variable Clusters Related to Several Psychological Features

COMPONENT OR FUNCTION	VARIABLES
AFFECTIVE FEATURES	EB (extratensive style), EBPer, eb (right side value [C',T,V,Y]), FC:CF+C, PURE C quality, Afr, CP, S, Blends, COL-SH Blends, Shading Blends
CAPACITY FOR CONTROL & STRESS TOLERANCE	D SCORE, ADJD SCORE, EA (Sum M, Sum C), es (FM, T, V, C'), CDI
COGNITIVE MEDIATION	L > .99, P, OBS, X+%, Xu%, X−%, S−% (review minus answers by S, homogeneous clustering, levels of distortion), CONFAB
IDEATION	EB (introversive style), EPPer, eb (left side value [FM,m], a:p, Ma:Mp, 2Ab+(Art+Ay), MOR, 6Sp Sc (Lv1 vs Lv2), MQ, Quality of M responses
INFORMATION PROCESSING	L > .99, OBS, HVI, Zf, W:D:Dd, (W:M), DQ, Zd, PSV, Location Sequencing
INTERPERSONAL PERCEPTION & RELATIONS	p > a+1, CDI, Fd, T, HVI, PER, COP, AG, Isol:R, Content of Movement Responses That Contain a Pair, All Human Content
SELF PERCEPTION	3r+(2)/R (Fr+rF), FD, V, Pure H:Nonpure H, An+Xy, MOR, Content of Minus responses, Content of all movement responses
SITUATION RELATED STRESS	D, ADJ D, EA, EB (zero values), m, Y, T, Blend Complexity, COL-SHD Bl (m & Y), Pure C, Formless M, M−

NOTE: EB IS STYLISTIC *ONLY* IF ONE SIDE EXCEEDS THE OTHER BY 2 OR MORE *IF* EA IS 10 OR LESS, OR MORE THAN 2 IF EA IS GREATER THAN 10

signals the likelihood of two psychological characteristics: (1) the presence of more negative features in self-image, which relates to self-perception, and (2) a tendency for attitudes about the self and the world to be marked by pessimism, which in turn has influence on ideation. Thus, as the interpretive routine proceeds, information about more than one component or function often develops even though the focus of interpretive attention is on a single feature.

As all of the data in each cluster or array are studied, a picture gradually unfolds about a unique person. It should be a descriptive picture *generated from the test data.* Most interpreters tend to intermingle history data or behavioral information about the subject when forming interpretive propositions. They should not be faulted for this, as any good clinician will try to maximize the use of all available data into any global assessment process. However, when doing so, it is crucial that the clinician differentiate the data of the test from other data when weighing the merits of any interpretive postulate. In other words, the test based description should be produced first and then embellished by information from other sources.

Prediction

It could be argued that prediction, as such, is less relevant in the assessment process than is a descriptive understanding of the psychology of the subject. That position has been defended quite well by some in regard to the clinical versus actuarial controversy that was fomented mainly by Meehl during the mid 1950s (Holt, 1958, 1970; Weiner, 1972). But to persist in that position avoids one of the major functions assumed in contemporary assessment, that of planning intervention. Most every form of treatment planning involves the use of predictive descriptions, and diagnosticians or therapists frequently use these descriptions in an attempt to rank order intervention objectives. A second form of prediction frequently requested in assessment referrals concerns behaviors. Generally, either type of prediction poses a difficult task for the Rorschach interpreter but the first is probably the easier to address.

Treatment Predictions   In recent decades, psychology and psychiatry have been marked by many gains in achieving greater diversification among the modes of intervention. Some treatment modalities are highly effective for certain objectives but not necessarily for others. The literature on the many intervention methods has grown rapidly and any intelligent treatment plan should be formulated in concert with this growing knowledge.

There is no magic in the Rorschach from which intervention decisions can be made easily. In fact, taken alone—that is, without some knowledge about the presenting complaints and/or recent behavior of the subject—Rorschach data could easily become misleading in the formation of a treatment plan. This is because, as noted earlier, all humans are somewhat fragile and have liabilities. Most anyone can be psychologically dissected and, if judged against optimal standards, be made to appear much more pathological than is the case. Nonetheless, the use of the Rorschach for the selection of treatment targets and treatment modalities does begin with the so-called optimal state, that is, with the speculative question: What features of the test would be altered if a magic wand were available? Some Rorschach data provide valid indices of response styles and, if the composite of these data are reviewed carefully, those styles can be viewed in terms of their effectiveness, their interrelationships, and possibly most important, whether they are assets or liabilities in the overall functioning of the subject.

Characteristics identified as liabilities become the focal points for treatment consideration, beginning with the question of how serious they seem to be in the total context of the personality, extending through speculation on how easily they can be altered, and ending in a framework of the immediate and long range goals of the subject. Thus, an optimal intervention plan can be formulated that deals with the ideal condition, that is, a design to contend with those liabilities that *might* be viable intervention targets. But Rorschach data do not identify the *reality factors* that are involved in the situation. Not everyone needs or wants treatment and, even for those who do, the most ideal treatment plan may not be realistic or appropriate. Some potential treatment targets are not necessarily the most optimal when viewed in the context of the goals, motivation, or life circumstances of the subject, or the intervention resources that are available.

Any treatment recommendations or decisions should evolve in a framework that considers both internal and external relationships. The optimal intervention design has three objectives. First, it should target on the reduction or elimination of existing stresses and/or symptoms. Second, it should permit the subject to maintain whatever harmony he or she has created with the world. Third, it should improve the psychological sophistication of the subject in ways that will enhance the probability for effective adjustment, both internal and external, in the future.

These seem like simple, straightforward objectives, but that is not always the case. For instance, the elimination of symptoms can, at times, be quite disruptive to pretreatment relationships with the world. Similarly, an increase in the psychological sophistication of a subject can become markedly disruptive to preexisting relationships and patterns of behavior. Thus, any treatment formulation requires a *cost–benefit analysis* in which a myriad of factors must be afforded very careful consideration. Obviously, concern for the psychological organization of the subject is included among those factors and can often provide the core from which the cost–benefit evaluation evolves.

For instance, if only the fragments of structural data presented earlier for Cases 1 and 2 are considered, several *potential* intervention targets can be generated for each. Both women are experiencing anxiety-like symptoms and their discomfort seems evident by the higher right-side values in the Rorschach *eb,* but their marked psychological differences suggest that the treatment selected for one would probably be inappropriate for the other. Case 1 is currently in a state of stimulus overload and is vulnerable to impulsiveness ($D = -1$, Adj $D = 0$). Reduction of the overload is a high priority treatment target and suggests the need for some form of crisis intervention. The data indicate, however, that some of the overload is being created by the experience of considerable loneliness ($T = 3$). This finding could argue that a form of supportive intervention is preferable to a more active crisis model. In addition, it appears that her emotional displays are often overly intense and not well modulated ($FC : CF + C = 3 : 5$, Pure $C = 1$). This issue may well play an important role in formulating treatment objectives. The woman in Case 2 appears to prefer to avoid emotionality (only one color response, $Afr = .33$). Apparently, she prefers to deal with things simplistically ($L = 1.2$), which may be an asset in view of her rather modest resource ($EA = 6.0$), but which also may be a liability if her world is very complex. Any intervention model designed for her must take both of these factors into account. Both of these women also have very passive styles ($p > a + 1$) and apparently use fantasy in a defensively abusive way to avoid reality confrontations ($M^p > M^a$). If those features are deemed to be important treatment targets, the intervention must be planned for a much longer time frame than might be the case if the chosen targets focus only on forms of symptom relief.

Although these apparent liabilities are readily defined from the fragmented Rorschach data, it is possible that some will be discarded as viable objectives in the final treatment formulation for any of several reasons. First, the personality picture drawn from the test data is only fragmented. Much more data require consideration before the total portrait is in place. Second, the issue of etiology of the symptom patterns has not yet been addressed. In other words, if information concerning symptoms or complaints is combined with the descriptive yield concerning the personality, some understanding of the etiology of the problem should emerge rather easily. In turn, an awareness about etiology can be a critical ingredient in any prediction concerning potential solutions to presenting problems. But that information, taken alone, does not necessarily define the most appropriate intervention plan, even though it can be useful in a cost–benefit process to define and prioritize *potential* intervention targets. Other reality factors must be considered. One of the most important of these is the cost factor to the client.

As noted earlier, some treatment objectives require much more time to achieve than others and involve very different forms of intervention. In some cases, it may appear optimal to promote some reconstruction of the personality, an objective that involves a long term intervention plan. A reconstructive approach, however, might jeopardize some other personality features that are precariously interdependent, and the treatment of choice in such a circumstance is one that does not attack the personality organization, but rather focuses on a target of reconstitution of the existing psychological organization in ways that promote symptom reduction or elimination. In many cases, a careful cost–benefit analysis leads to a decision to avoid forcing a client into a treatment modality that goes well beyond what he or she is willing to pay in terms of life disruption. For example, the subjects in Cases 1 and 2 are reporting annoying anxiety-like symptoms, and long term reconstructive models of treatment might seem optimal for either. Other factors may deter such a recommendation, however, or either or both may prefer models of intervention that focus specifically on bringing early relief without requiring any major alterations in their personalities. This does not mean that all of the targets identified from the test data are ignored. Instead, it means that the higher priorities will be those that seem most amenable to change in a briefer, reconstitutive model of treatment and that the intervention will be designed in ways that minimize, or even take advantage of, other liabilities.

Behavior Predictions   Unfortunately, in many instances, assessment issues require a different form of prediction. Sometimes, prediction, which focuses on the issue of future adjustment or maladjustment, is the major focal point of assessment, but often it also becomes a relevant element in treatment planning. For instance, a decision to disregard some potential treatment targets would be unwarranted in cases in which the likelihood of recurring adjustment problems is considerable if features are not altered. Information concerning the substance of personality is usually critical in generating these types of prediction, but this information alone is frequently insufficient to yield a valid prediction. In effect, the prediction focuses on behaviors, including patterns of interaction. The interpreter trying to make predictions regarding the present or future behaviors of a subject is confronted with a difficult challenge. As noted earlier, the test data are most useful for descriptive purposes, that is, providing illustration of the subject as he or she is now. Behavioral prediction is made much more difficult for the Rorschach interpreter because the description generated from the test data renders only limited information about the subject's perceptions of his or her world and even less about interactions with it. The missing ingredients— specific information about the environment in which the subject functions and people with whom the subject interacts—can make some inferences or predictions highly speculative.

This is not to suggest that this type of prediction should be avoided. There are features of personality organization, usually detectable from Rorschach data, that do provide a reasonably sound basis from which to form *some* predictions. These are, of course, the psychological styles that make up a major part of personality organization. They tend to manifest redundantly in decisions and behavioral choices. Information concerning a subject's basic psychological styles can contribute to some general predictions concerning probable patterns of behavior. For example, it would not be unreasonable to predict that, if no change occurs for the subject in Case 1, many of her behaviors will be marked by somewhat intense and possibly volatile emotional displays and that her overall pattern of behavior will be characterized by a passive-dependent routine through which she seeks to avoid responsibility in decision making. It is also reasonable to predict that, when she is under stress, some of her decisions and behaviors will be impulsive and that she will often ignore or deny the harshness of reality by replacing it with the products of her fantasy life.

These general predictions concerning this woman are derived from test variables that are highly stable over lengthy time intervals for adults, and for which considerable validating data have accumulated. In effect, these predictions describe a rather passive hystrionic individual whose controls are limited. It is a negative description and a prediction that implies a considerable potential for maladjustment. However, the negative implications in the predictive description can also be misleading. Maladjustment is not necessarily inevitable for this kind of person. In fact, some of her characteristics might be regarded as tolerable, acceptable, or even desirable in some environmental situations, especially if she has other assets or skills that would enhance her appeal to others. Thus, although the general description is probably correct, it has only limited value in predicting whether these behavior patterns will be effective or ineffective in specific situations. The more specific a behavioral prediction must be, the greater the risk of error if only test data are used to form the prediction. The test data can contribute to the prediction, but more precise information concerning the environment and specific situations in the environment are necessary before those data can be merged into an intelligently thought out behavioral prediction.

The issue of time can also pose substantial difficulties in formulating behavioral predictions. Although data for most test variables remain quite stable over time for adults, none of the retest correlations are perfect. Although it is unlikely that the basic personality structure or response styles of an adult will change much simply as a product of time, some *functional* changes may occur over time as the result of new experiences or new situations. Either can add to the collected wisdom of the person and, in turn, promote behavioral changes. Thus, as the prediction requirement involves a longer time frame, the need for more precise information about external circumstances increases. In some cases, long term predictions based on the test data are impractical. Obviously, this is true for subjects who are actively involved in reconstructive forms of treatment, as they are expected to change, and it is especially true for most children.

Exner, Thomas, and Mason (1985) tested 57 nonpatient children when they were age 8 and subsequently at two-year intervals until they were 16. Correlation coefficients for 23 structural variables were calculated for each of the two-year cohorts. More than half of the 23 coefficients fell below .70 until the interval between ages 14 and 16. In fact, if stability for a variable is defined as one for which $r = .75$ or greater, less than two-thirds of the 23 variables met that criterion across any of the three preceding two-year cohorts (8 to 10, 10 to 12, 12 to 14). These findings should not be surprising because children change quite rapidly and often very remarkably as they develop. Thus, it seems clear that long term predictions about youngsters, based on Rorschach data, should be avoided *unless* there is evidence of major psychopathology.

SUMMARY

Although each of the cautions and issues raised in this chapter is extremely important when using the Rorschach, most will become moot when the test is used by the astute interpreter who approaches the data in a systematic and thorough manner. Such an approach ensures that the data in each cluster of variables are reviewed carefully, and that the findings are organized methodically and efficiently into a broad based, yet specific portrayal of the subject.

REFERENCES

American Psychiatric Association. (1980). *Diagnostic and statistical manual of mental disorders* (3rd ed.). Washington, DC.

Exner, J. E. (1978). *The Rorschach: A Comprehensive System. Volume 2: Recent research and advanced interpretation.* New York: Wiley.

Exner, J. E. (1983). Rorschach assessment. In I. B. Weiner (Ed.), *Clinical methods in psychology* (2nd ed.). New York: Wiley.

Exner, J. E. (1986). *The Rorschach: A Comprehensive System. Volume 1: Basic foundations* (2nd ed.). New York: Wiley.

Exner, J. E. (1988). 1988 *Alumni Newsletter.* Rorschach Workshop, Asheville, NC.

Exner, J. E., Thomas, E. A., and Mason, B. (1985). Children's Rorschach's: Description and prediction. *Journal of Personality Assessment, 49,* 13–20.

Holt, R. R. (1958). Clinical and statistical prediction: A reformulation and some new data. *Journal of Abnormal and Social Psychology, 56,* 1–12.

Holt, R. R. (1970). Yet another look at clinical and statistical prediction: Or is clinical psychology worthwhile? *American Psychologist, 25,* 337–349.

Meehl, P. E. (1954). *Clinical versus statistical prediction.* Minneapolis: University of Minnesota Press.

Shapiro, D. (1965). *Neurotic styles.* New York: Basic Books.

Weiner, I. B. (1972). Does psychodiagnosis have a future? *Journal of Personality Assessment, 36,* 534–546.

PART III

Strategies of
Interpretation

CHAPTER 5

Initial Decisions and Procedures

THE TEST DATA

Obviously, any interpretation of a Rorschach protocol must include careful consideration of all of the data, but the steps by which the interpretation proceeds are not always the same. The data of the test fall into three general groupings: *Structural Summary, Sequence of Scores,* and *Verbalizations.* Unfortunately, these groupings vary considerably with regard to the breadth and sturdiness of their empirical foundations as related to interpretation. When each is scrutinized in the context of psychometric reality, the Structural Summary typically is viewed as constituting the "hard data" of the Rorschach.

Although it is reasonable to expect the structural data to offer the greatest utility in forming interpretive hypotheses, some of those hypotheses can be too general, too narrow, or even misleading. Therefore, it is critically important to review the other data groups intelligently in the context of findings from the structural data. The Sequence of Scores often provides information that clarifies or expands postulates developed from the structural data, and sometimes unusual sequencing effects give rise to new hypotheses. Similarly, although new hypotheses developed from the Verbalizations must be regarded with the utmost caution, the astute interpreter should be able to cull considerable information from the verbal material that can relate to other data in the test. Postulates generated from verbal material are likely to have the greatest validity when derived from a composite of responses that are homogeneous for content or verbiage.

The interpretation should proceed cluster by cluster until all of the data have been exhausted. Although the first steps in addressing a cluster focus on the structural data, this does not mean that the Sequence of Scores and/or the Verbalizations should be ignored until all possible hypotheses have been developed from the structure variables. On the contrary, issues usually arise during the review of the structural variables that necessitate turning to the sequence and/or the verbal material before proceeding to other structural variables.

This flexibility in moving from one data set to another is crucial for a sophisticated interpretation of the test, because structural data easily can be misused. For instance, the novice interpreter sometimes draws premature conclusions from the datum for a single variable. Such errors are usually bred by a faulty conception of the test data that disregards the fact that very few variables are independent of all other variables. Even more experienced interpreters often err because of a naive assumption that, once the data for the structural variables in a cluster relating to a feature or function have been reviewed, no additional input is necessary and/or possible. Either of these errors promotes a concrete and simplistic use of the test that flirts with disaster and inevitably ignores a wealth of available information concerning the organization and functioning of the subject.

It is easy to understand how some errors in interpretive logic occur. Relatively large numbers of studies concerning each variable encourage the notion that each has some discrete meaning. These studies tend to promote the idea that variables can be interpreted in a singular context. Unfortunately, if such an approach is used, the result is a concrete and disconnected picture that, at best, fails to capture the organization of the person or, even worse, presents misleading or distorted conclusions.

Even the discriminant function, intercorrelational, and factorial studies that demonstrate that variables fall into clusters tend to convey the notion that each cluster of variables is somehow insular and should be interpreted as such. Unfortunately, such an interpretive routine serves only to create a fragmented portrait of the subject.

Interpretation should evolve conceptually; that is, each finding is integrated with other findings so that hypotheses and/or conclusions ultimately formulated are based on the total available information. In turn, the hypotheses and conclusions are integrated logically with a careful view of the relationships between the numerous psychological features of the subject. As noted earlier, any valid record contains data related to ideation, emotion, coping preferences and response styles, capacity for control, self-perception, information processing, interpersonal perception, cognitive mediation, and possibly some information about routine defensive strategies. Thus, the challenge for the interpreter is twofold: (1) to search methodically through all of the data concerning each component, and (2) to weave together the resulting yield in a manner that reflects the total person.

VARYING STRATEGIES FOR INTERPRETATION

Once a protocol has been judged to be interpretively valid, a decision is required concerning the interpretive routine to be followed. The order by which each data cluster is evaluated varies from record to record, but the order should never be random. The decision concerning the search strategy is not quite as simple as once seemed the case. During an earlier phase of development of the *Comprehensive System* (Exner, 1978), it was logically concluded that all interpretive routines should begin with a review of the data for four variables (*EB, EA, eb,* and *es*) that had been designated as the *Four Square*. The rule of beginning with the Four Square was based on the logic that the four variables constitute the basic source of information regarding the core features of personality that relate to coping styles and capacity for control. As such, that information would form a nucleus from which the interpretive routine would unfold naturally as each finding raised new issues to be addressed.

The practice of beginning the interpretation with the Four Square worked well for many records, but there was a second group of protocols in which hypotheses formed early during the interpretation required modification or, in some instances, abandonment as findings from other test data unfolded. This unexpected need to backtrack and reorganize hypotheses posed problems for the interpreter as it required a change in set and a reintegration of findings, and sometimes created confusion about how best to weigh findings in the total picture. Any of these challenges, if not properly addressed, risks the richness of the interpretive yield.

In studying many protocols in which hypotheses generated from the data of the Four Square required modification, it became apparent that the recommended tactic for beginning interpretation had failed to appreciate two facts that have become much more apparent as research findings have continued to unfold. First, although the *EB* does provide information regarding coping preferences, other stylistic features of the personality can supersede that preference, or have a more dominating impact on decisions and/or behaviors. Second, in some cases the data of the Four Square may present a less accurate picture because other psychological features (usually pathological) have altered the organization and/or functioning of the person substantially.

This problem was addressed by using a pool of 300 nonschizophrenic patient protocols. In 150 of the records, hypotheses developed from the data of the Four Square subsequently were modified or rejected because of other test data. In the remaining 150 records, used as a control group, hypotheses generated from the data of the Four Square remained viable throughout the interpretive search. Frequency data for each of 241 computer generated interpretive statements, extracted from the *Rorschach Interpretation Assistance Program* (Exner, McGuire, & Cohen, 1985, 1986, 1990), were tallied for the 300 records.

The records were then sorted into seven groups—controls or situational stress, affect, ideation, mediation, processing, self-perception, and interpersonal perception—based on which cluster of variables yielded the largest number of statements for the record. One hundred forty three of the one hundred fifty control group records sorted rather neatly into three groups (controls or stress, $N = 69$; ideation, $N = 36$; affect $N = 38$). Interestingly, these three groupings draw extensively on the data of the Four Square. Five of the remaining seven protocols were sorted into the mediation group, one into self-perception, and one into processing. The sort of the 150 target group records was much more diverse (controls or stress, $N = 33$; ideation, $N = 21$; mediation, $N = 27$; processing, $N = 13$; affect, $N = 22$; self-perception, $N = 25$; interpersonal perception, $N = 9$).

A search program was then applied to determine whether homogeneous data sets within each group would differentiate the groups. The results were very striking but not unexpected. For example, records sorted into the ideation group contained either an introversive *EB* or evidence of markedly strange thinking. Records sorted into the controls or stress group contained a D Score lower than the Adjusted D Score, a minus Adjusted D Score, or a very low *EA;* records sorted into the self-perception group all contained reflection responses; those sorted into the processing group all had Lambda values of 1.0 or more; and so on.

The results of this search yielded 10 *Key* variables that, when set in an order of dominance or priority, actually predicted the results of the sort for 282 of the 300 records. In other words, if a record contained only one positive Key variable, it could be used to predict the cluster from which the largest number of statements would be generated. If a record contained two or more positive Key variables, one had clear precedence in determining the sort and also could be used as a predictor.

The 10 Key variables, in their order of dominance, are (1) Depression Index (DEPI) is greater than 5, (2) D Score is less than Adjusted D (Adj D) Score, (3) Coping Deficit Index (CDI) is greater than 3, (4) Adj D Score is in the minus range, (5) Lambda is greater than 0.99, (6) at least one reflection answer is present, (7) *EB* is introversive, (8) *EB* is extratensive, (9) passive movement is greater than active movement by more than 1 point, and (10) the Hypervigilance Index (HVI) is positive.

The consistency for each group provoked two additional sorts, again using the number of statements from each cluster as the basis for differentiation. The results of the second and third sorts proved to be quite uniform and predictable from the first sort. For instance, if a record had been placed in the ideation group in the first sort, the second and third sorts almost always identified mediation and processing as yielding the next largest number of statements. Conversely, if a record initially had been sorted into affect, the clusters concerning self-perception and interpersonal perception invariably yielded the next largest number of statements.

In effect, the presence of a given Key variable predicted which combination of two or three clusters of data would yield the largest number of statements from the pool of 241 statements. Stated differently, the Key variables permitted the identification of the data sources that would contribute the most substantial information about the core psychological features of the subject. Generally, these are features that will be given considerable emphasis in forming any description of the subject. They are dominant elements of personality structure and have a major impact on psychological organization. They exert a significant influence on the way in which other features are organized and usually afford considerable direction to the psychological functioning of the subject.

SELECTING THE INTERPRETIVE STRATEGY

The findings about Key variables reaffirmed the notion that the interpretive search should not follow the same routine for all protocols. The findings suggested that more logical search strategies could be developed in which the interpretive routine would flow systematically and avoid backtracking and reorganization of hypotheses. In such a format, the first bits of data that are evaluated should provide some information concerning the core elements of the personality structure and/or response styles of the subject. Thus, the decision about which cluster of data to use as the starting point is important because the yield should form a centerpiece in the network of descriptive statements ultimately generated. In turn, the first cluster selected usually should provide direction for the order by which the remaining clusters are reviewed.

An examination of the 10 Key variables suggests that they reflect two sorts of data. Although four of the variables (DEPI > 5, D Score < Adj D Score, CDI > 3, Adj D Score < 0) deal with personality structure, they also focus on the presence of psychopathology or the potential for functional disorganization. The remaining six variables involve more basic personality styles, any of which can form the cornerstone of organization and functioning. This review led to the logical conclusion that an 11th Key variable, a positive Schizophrenia Index (SCZI), should be added to the listing, and afforded priority over all others. The

11 Key variables, and the recommended interpretive search strategies that should be employed, are shown in Table 41.

The Key variables shown in Table 41 are listed in an order of priority. In other words, the first Key variable that is positive defines the interpretive routine for the record. Most of the routines are straightforward but in some cases the entire routine cannot be defined by simply using the first positive Key variable and subsequent Key variables, or Tertiary variables must also be used before the complete routine is established. Each strategy or routine follows in a logical sequence so that each new finding merges neatly with those already developed.

The strategies and routines shown in Table 41 are both empirically and logically developed. They are empirical in the sense that the first two or three clusters reviewed are likely to yield the greatest amount of information concerning the core features of the subject. They are logical in the sense that the sequence is designed so that each new finding merges neatly with those already developed. It is important to note that the 11 search strategies are not markedly discrete. Three clusters, ideation, mediation, and processing are always in tandem because they

Table 41. Interpretive Search Strategies Based on Key Variables

POSITIVE VARIABLE	TYPICAL CLUSTER SEARCH ROUTINE
SCZI > 3	IDEATION → MEDIATION → PROCESSING → CONTROLS → AFFECT → SELF PERCEPTION → INTERPERSONAL PERCEPTION
DEPI > 5	AFFECT → CONTROLS → SELF PERCEPTION → INTERPERSONAL PERCEPTION → PROCESSING → MEDIATION → IDEATION
D < ADJ D	CONTROLS → SITUATION STRESS → (The remaining search routine should be that identified for the next positive key variable or list of tertiary variables)
CDI > 3	CONTROLS → AFFECT → SELF PERCEPTION → INTERPERSONAL PERCEPTION → PROCESSING → MEDIATION → IDEATION
ADJ D IS MINUS	CONTROLS → (The remaining search routine should be that identified for the next positive key variable or list of tertiary variables)
LAMBDA > 0.99	PROCESSING → MEDIATION → IDEATION → CONTROLS → AFFECT → SELF PERCEPTION → INTERPERSONAL PERCEPTION
REFLECTION > 0	SELF PERCEPTION → INTERPERSONAL PERCEPTION → CONTROLS (The remaining search routine should be selected from that identified for the next positive key variable or list of tertiary variables)
EB = INTROVERSIVE	IDEATION → PROCESSING → MEDIATION → CONTROLS → AFFECT → SELF PERCEPTION → INTERPERSONAL PERCEPTION
EB = EXTRATENSIVE	AFFECT → SELF PERCEPTION → INTERPERSONAL PERCEPTION → CONTROLS → PROCESSING → MEDIATION → IDEATION
p > a+1	IDEATION → PROCESSING → MEDIATION → CONTROLS → SELF PERCEPTION → INTERPERSONAL PERCEPTION → AFFECT
HVI POSITIVE	IDEATION → PROCESSING → MEDIATION → CONTROLS → SELF PERCEPTION → INTERPERSONAL PERCEPTION → AFFECT

are interrelated. Likewise, the clusters pertaining to self-perception and interpersonal perception are always in tandem because of their interrelationship.

A REVIEW OF THE KEY VARIABLES

The logic of why these are Key or predictor variables and why they are prioritized as in Table 41 may be worth some review here. Three of the four Special Indices, SCZI, DEPI, and CDI, plus the two D Scores constitute a first tier of decision variables. If any is positive the initial interpretive focus is on the variables that have produced the positive index and on assessing the other data in the clusters containing those variables. This is important for three purposes: (1) to review and possibly challenge the validity of the positive finding, (2) to assess the magnitude of impairment or disorganization implied by the positive finding, and (3) to begin developing a description of the psychological organization of the subject.

SCZI Is Positive

A positive SCZI should always be given preference in the search strategy decision because the presence of schizophrenia or a schizophrenic-like organization will have an impact on all other features of the personality structure. It breeds peculiarity in thinking and often promotes unusual patterns of environmental interaction. The SCZI is based on variables related to two psychological operations commonly impaired among schizophrenics: thinking and perceptual accuracy. Although the index is actuarially sound, both false positive and false negative cases occur. As such, the confirmation or rejection of the positive finding takes on special importance. This can usually be accomplished by assessing the data in the clusters related to ideation and cognitive mediation. They encompass the variables that have contributed to the positive SCZI. The routine begins by focusing on ideation to establish whether the ideational problems implied by the positive SCZI are actually commensurate with those common among schizophrenics, while developing a broader spectrum of information concerning the ideational activity of the subject. The routine continues with an evaluation of the data regarding mediation to determine if the sorts of perceptual distortion common to schizophrenics exist and to generate information regarding the way in which the subject tends to translate inputs.

Ordinarily, a decision concerning the validity of the positive SCZI can be made after these two clusters have been reviewed. If the positive SCZI finding is confirmed, it has major importance for treatment recommendations. Even if the positive finding is rejected after closer inspection of the variables involved, the elevated value in the SCZI suggests that the basic personality style of the subject is marked by ideational and/or perceptual eccentricities that have considerable influence on a wide array of psychological functions.

DEPI Is Greater Than 5

As noted in Chapter 1, a DEPI of 6 or 7 correlates very highly with a diagnosis that emphasizes serious affective problems. A proclivity for affective disruption can exist within any of several personality styles. A careful evaluation of the variables in the clusters related to affect and personal perception in the depressed or depression prone subject often provides important information about some of the core elements in the psychological organization of the subject. In some cases, both the SCZI and the DEPI are positive. When that occurs, the SCZI should continue to be given priority in selecting the interpretive routine, even though the issue of affect is not addressed directly until midway through the search.

The routine selected based on a DEPI value of 6 or 7 begins with a review of the cluster regarding affect. This is because several of the DEPI variables relate to irritating affective experience, and it is important to study their relationship to the subject's overall emotional structure. The search then moves on to the cluster regarding controls, primarily to ascertain whether the disruption suggested by the DEPI has reduced stress tolerance and created a vulnerability to impulsiveness. The third cluster reviewed in the routine concerns self-perception, as information concerning self-views and self-values is often very relevant to an understanding of affective disruption, and two of the variables in this cluster also contribute to the DEPI. The overlap of variables in the clusters regarding personal and interpersonal perception requires that one be reviewed following the other. Thus, interpersonal perception is the fourth cluster to be studied in this routine.

Adjusted D Is Greater Than D

If the Adj D Score is greater than the D Score, regardless of the value of Adj D, it signals the presence of situation-related stress. Although it may seem logical to begin the interpretive search with the array of variables directly related to situational stress, the actual routine should begin with a review of the variables concerning controls to develop information concerning the potentials for control and tolerance for stress. That information becomes very important in understanding the psychological circumstances that have contributed to the lower D Score. Once that understanding has been developed, a review of the variables related to situational stress provide some data regarding the impact of the stress and may offer some clues concerning its origins. The complete interpretive routine is not defined simply because this variable is positive. The remaining strategy usually is selected by using the remaining list of Key variables as a guideline.

CDI Is Greater Than 3

A positive CDI is an ominous finding. Seven of the 11 variables that contribute to CDI relate to interpersonal problems or deficits, and two of the remaining four variables seem to signal emotional avoidance or impoverishment. The other two variables indicate either poor control capacity or limited coping resources. Thus, anyone with a value of 4 or more on the CDI is markedly predisposed to functional disorganization, especially in unusual stress situations or those in which there are high expectations for social/interpersonal effectiveness.

The interpretive search begins with a study of data concerning controls. Those data should provide some clarification about the potential for disorganization, that is, whether a vulnerability to everyday stress exists because of limited control capacity or resource, or whether the vulnerability may be more restricted to situations in which unexpected social demands exist. The second step in the routine involves a review of affective features, which is followed by a study of data regarding personal and interpersonal perception.

Adjusted D Score Is Minus

If the Adj D Score falls in the minus range it signifies several potential problems in the psychological organization and/or operations of the subject. It often indicates a developmental problem that has produced a less mature form of personality organization than might be expected or desired, or it can indicate some psychological deterioration caused by a chronic stimulus overload state. In either event it suggests that problems in both ideational and affective control exist, which in turn set the stage for impulsive behaviors.

The interpretation is initiated by an evaluation of controls and stress tolerance. The magnitude of *EA* and *es,* when evaluated in light of the history, usually clarifies whether the problem is one of immaturity or deterioration. Often, the data for the *EB* and *eb* add considerably in developing an understanding about the potential fragility of the subject. This is the only Key variable that does not predict well which next two clusters will offer the most salient information, and, for this reason, the decision concerning the remainder of the interpretive search must be based on a subsequent positive Key variable or Tertiary variable.

Lambda Is Greater Than 0.99

An elevation in Lambda is always important because it signals the presence of a preferred response style that is oriented toward reducing stimulus situations to their most easily managed level. This often requires a narrowing or simplification of the stimulus field. The behaviors of subjects who have a *High Lambda style* often convey the impression that the simplification occurs at the input level; that is, by using a sort of psychological tunnel vision the subject does not process all of the significant elements of a field. But this explanation does not seem viable in light of the fact that, as a group, High Lambda subjects show neither unusual distributions for *Zf* and *DQv* nor any greater frequency of underincorporation. A more logical explanation posits that the simplification is a defensive process through which some significant elements of a field are viewed as having little importance when judged against the needs of the subject plus the perceived demands of the situation. As such, those elements are afforded little or no attention in the formulation of responses.

The antecedents of the style appear to vary. In some instances it is simply the product of immaturity and social ineptness. In other cases it evolves from a sense of social deprivation and an excessive preoccupation with need gratification. It is often the product of negative sets toward the environment and becomes a tactic through which the subject manifests this negativism. This kind of psychological functioning sets the stage for the formation of some behaviors that fail to meet the demands of a situation and/or deviate from socially expected patterns. Although, the High Lambda style can often interfere with the most well-intended efforts toward social adaptation, this is not always the case. Sometimes a response style designed to simplify external stimuli serves an adaptive, albeit defensive purpose. For example, the subject with limited intellect, flexibility, or stress tolerance may find it important to avoid the myriad of complexities posed by the world in everyday life. Narrowing stimulus fields in ways that make them more easily managed can be highly beneficial to such people, *provided* that in doing so they do not violate social rules and expectations in ways that breed conflict between themselves and their world.

When a High Lambda record occurs, the interpretive search begins with the cognitive triad, determining the extent to which processing is effective, mediation is conventional or atypical, and ideation is clear or clouded. This information is often crucial in determining whether the behaviors of the subject can be expected to align with or disregard social expectations.

One or More Reflection Responses Are Present

The presence of one or more reflection answers triggers an interpretive routine that differs from those previously outlined. The reflection answer is a very important finding that relates to a core characteristic of personality. It signifies the presence of an unrealistically inflated sense of self-value. Although not uncommon among younger children, these types of responses are not expected to appear in the records of older adolescents or adults. If they do occur it is very likely that the subject is strongly influenced by the need to support and defend this narcissistic-like feature, and this need has a marked impact on many psychological operations. In addition, the inflated sense of self-value cannot help but have a direct effect on the interpersonal world of the subject.

The search pattern for records in which the reflection answer is the first positive Key variable begins with the cluster concerning self-perception, and proceeds to interpersonal perception. The first major issues addressed concern the strength of the inflated sense of self-worth and how it is defended, both internally and externally.

EB Indicates an Introversive or Extratensive Style

If the scan of Key variables to this point has not defined the logical interpretive routine, a review of the *EB* frequently provides that identification. The presence of either predominant coping style, introversive or extratensive, offers clear direction to the interpretive chain.

The search of an introversive record begins with the cluster of variables concerning ideation and continues through the other clusters in the cognitive triad, processing and mediation. This style signals a preference for delay and thinking through alternatives before deciding on a response. Many introversives are simply economical and prefer to avoid unnecessary behavior. Others are more cautious and have developed the style as a way of avoiding errors, and some of those become overly preoccupied with caution to the point of obsessiveness. The cognitive triad data typically provide important information concerning the efficiency and effectiveness of the style. The routine continues through the clusters regarding controls and styles and ends with a review of data about affect, self-perception, and interpersonal perception.

If the *EB* indicates an extratensive style, the interpretive routine is almost reversed. It begins with the cluster concerning affect because this *EB* style is one in which feelings play an important role in thinking and behavior. Most extratensives function very well by using this intuitive-like approach to problem solving and decision making. However, the appropriate modulation of emotional discharge is often quite important to the integrity of the style.

p Is Greater Than *a*+1 or the Hypervigilance Index Is Positive

If either of the remaining two Key variables provides the basis for selecting the search strategy, the interpretive routine is the same. If *p* exceeds *a* by a value greater than 1, it suggests that passivity is an integral psychological style that marks many of the subject's coping routines. The passive style usually serves any one of or a combination of several objectives important to the subject. It can provide a convenient way to avoid complexity or responsibility, to manifest aggressiveness, or to perpetuate dependency.

A positive HVI also points to a basic personality style. Subjects with a positive HVI tend to be ill at ease in their world. Thus, they maintain a state of hyperalertness, which is costly in two respects. First, a considerable energy commitment is required to sustain the state of anticipation or guardedness. Second, the orientation that gives rise to the anticipatory state involves a more cautious or guarded set concerning others, which in turn can have a marked impact on interpersonal relationships. People who are hypervigilant are usually less trusting of others and preoccupied with matters of personal space and, when these features are carried to an extreme, a paranoid-like personality results.

Information concerning the ideational features of people with either of these styles is usually crucial to any understanding of the origins or manifestations of the styles. Thus, the first segment of the interpretive routine focuses on the cognitive triad, beginning with ideation and then processing and mediation.

TERTIARY VARIABLES AS STARTING POINTS

Some protocols may contain no positive Key variables. When this occurs, the starting point can be selected from positive findings among numerous Tertiary variables. The list of Tertiary variables has also been selected using frequency tallies for computer statements, developed from the sample of 150 nonschizophrenic patient records in which no Key variables were positive. Unlike the Key variables, Tertiary variables do not have much predictive power. They do tend to highlight which cluster will yield the most significant information about a subject but do not predict which subsequent clusters will contain the most supplementing information. Thus, the search routines developed from them are general guidelines for beginning, but they should not be regarded as inviolate. Rather, they are tactics that are designed to avoid reorganizing or reintegrating findings at a later stage in the interpretive routine and that are based on logic and some general rules that should be followed.

First, when one cluster of the cognitive triad is studied, a review of the other two clusters of the triad should follow immediately. This is because the data in one of the three clusters often affords some clarification about findings in the other clusters, plus the fact that any summary of these cognitive activities—input, translation, and conceptualization—should include attention to their interrelationships. Second, when self-perception is reviewed, a study of variables related to interpersonal perception should follow immediately. As noted earlier, this is because there are significant overlaps in the data of the two clusters. Third, if the cluster regarding affect is reviewed first, the data concerning controls should be studied immediately thereafter. In many instances information regarding controls provides an important clarification regarding modulation issues.

Unlike the Key variables, significant Tertiary variables do not necessarily offer definitive information. Instead, when significant, they simply highlight an issue that *may* be important in the final interpretation. For example, a DEPI of 5 or a higher right-side *eb* value signals the likelihood of distress, which would argue for starting with the cluster concerning affect. On the other hand, a substantial number of Critical Special Scores or the presence of an $M-$ response signifies the probability of cognitive slippage and argues for beginning with a

Table 42. Interpretive Search Strategies Based on Positive Tertiary Variables

POSITIVE VARIABLE	TYPICAL CLUSTER SEARCH ROUTINE
OBS POSITIVE	PROCESSING → MEDIATION → IDEATION → CONTROLS → AFFECT → SELF PERCEPTION → INTERPERSONAL PERCEPTION
DEPI = 5	AFFECT → CONTROLS → SELF PERCEPTION INTERPERSONAL PERCEPTION → PROCESSING → MEDIATION IDEATION
EA > 12	CONTROLS → IDEATION → PROCESSING → MEDIATION → AFFECT → SELF PERCEPTION → INTERPERSONAL PERCEPTION
$M->0$, or Mp > Ma, or SUM6 SPEC SC > 5	IDEATION → MEDIATION → PROCESSING → CONTROLS →AFFECT → SELF PERCEPTION → INTERPERSONAL PERCEPTION
SUM SHAD > FM+m, or CF+C > FC+1, or Afr < 0.46	AFFECT → CONTROLS → SELF PERCEPTION → INTERPERSONAL PERCEPTION → PROCESSING → MEDIATION → IDEATION
X–% > 20%, or Zd > +3.0 or < –3.0	PROCESSING → MEDIATION → IDEATION → CONTROLS → AFFECT → SELF PERCEPTION → INTERPERSONAL PERCEPTION
3r+(2)/R < .33	PERSONAL PERCEPTION → INTERPERSONAL PERCEPTION → AFFECT → CONTROLS → PROCESSING → MEDIATION → IDEATION
MOR > 2, or AG > 2	PERSONAL PERCEPTION → INTERPERSONAL PERCEPTION CONTROLS → IDEATION → PROCESSING → MEDIATION → AFFECT
T = 0 or > 1	PERSONAL PERCEPTION → INTERPERSONAL PERCEPTION AFFECT → CONTROLS → PROCESSING → PROCESSING → IDEATION

review of variables related to ideation. Although significant findings concerning ideation or affect usually take precedence in the decision about where to begin the interpretation, a different cluster is selected sometimes as the starting point if the findings for other variables are striking. For instance, a markedly elevated $X - \%$ prompts a decision to start with the cluster regarding mediation, whereas a large number of MOR answers, a very low Egocentricity Index, or the elevation in or absence of T, warrants beginning with the cluster related to self-perception.

Table 42 provides a list of the Tertiary variables used most frequently to determine the initial interpretive search pattern when *no* Key variables are positive. The recommended search pattern can be altered in some cases, but usually should be followed.

THE SUICIDE CONSTELLATION

The Suicide Constellation (S-CON) should always be reviewed *before* beginning the interpretive routine if the subject is age 15 or older. It has no demonstrated usefulness for subjects of age 14 or under, and attempts to develop a similar constellation for younger subjects have not been successful. In fact, neither the original data set from which the S-CON was developed (Exner and Wilie, 1977) nor the cross-validation data set that was used to modify the constellation (Exner, 1986) contains subjects under the age of 18. However, a study of the few available records of 15- and 16-year-old subjects who effected their own death within 60 days after having been administered the Rorschach indicates that about two-thirds were correctly identifed by the S-CON.

The S-CON does not fall into any of the clusters of variables. This is probably because it is an array of variables from several clusters which, as a collective, has an actuarial usefulness in detecting those who have features similar to individuals who have effected their own death. Some groupings of items in the S-CON have a conceptual similarity, but the entire listing does not.

If a subject's value for the S-CON is 8 or more, the subject does have features similar to those found in people who have committed suicide. If the value for the S-CON is less than 8, it should not be assumed that the subject is not suicidal, but simply that no actuarial data support that contention.

THE WITHIN-CLUSTER ANALYSES

As noted earlier, each Rorschach unit, whether structural data, sequencing effects, or verbal material, ultimately contributes to the interpretation and *none* can be neglected. Each Rorschach is unique in its total configuration, differing from all other Rorschachs and illustrating the idiography of the person who gave it. Thus, the process of interpretation evolves in a step-by-step sequence in which each new datum is reviewed in the context of *all* previously examined data. Interpretation requires inductive and deductive reasoning. At almost every step, whether across clusters or within a cluster, hypotheses are developed that must be tested to the extent possible and confirmed, modified, or rejected. Much of this occurs during the within-cluster analyses.

Once the interpretive search through a cluster begins, all data for the cluster should be reviewed *before* turning to another cluster. This is to ensure that the postulates and/or conclusions developed about the feature being studied are as unambiguous and complete as possible and, above all, that misleading sets or premature conclusions about the subject are not created. Clusters vary considerably in the breadth and/or depth of information concerning organization and functioning that they provide. Consequently, the specificity of propositions and conclusions that are derived also varies.

For example, only five variables relate directly to issues of control and stress tolerance: D Score, Adj D Score, *EA, es,* and CDI. Sometimes, the findings from this cluster are highly important, but, in the majority of cases, the yield is little more than a general statement regarding the availability of resources and the capacity for control. On the other hand, seven structural variables—3r + (2)/R, *Fr + rF, FD, V,* MOR, *An + Xy,* and *H : (H) + Hd + (Hd)*—plus a potentially sizable number of responses (any containing movement, containing MOR, or having a minus form quality) offer information about self-perception. Thus, the yield of information concerning this feature is usually more idiographic. This does not mean, however, that the number of variables in a cluster are directly related to interpretive specificity. On the contrary, the accumulated findings from within-cluster variables dictate whether the resulting information is general or specific. The within-cluster analysis *always* begins with a review of the structural variables in the cluster because they are empirically derived. Although the propositions generated from them are often more general, their validity is less subject to challenge, and typically they lead to the formation of hypotheses that give focus to the remainder of the cluster search.

CASE 1: ANXIETY AND SOMATIC SYMPTOMS

The next four chapters illustrate the issues and routines that ordinarily should be pursued during the interpretation of each cluster. Case 1, shown on the next pages, has been selected to demonstrate the procedures of searching through the variables in each cluster. The subject is 29 years old, is recently separated after five years of marriage, and has a three-year-old daughter for whom custody is being contended. She complains of tension, headaches, fatigue, upset stomach, dizziness, anxiousness, and difficulties concentrating, and she has not responded to pharmacological intervention. She has been referred for evaluation by her family physician.

Case 1 Interpretive Strategy

The record appears to be interpretively valid in that there are 25 answers. The S-CON has a value of 6, which is actuarially meaningless, although this does not rule out the possibility of a suicide potential. An inspection of the Key variables reveals that the first two (SCZI > 3 and DEPI > 5) are negative, but the third (D < Adj D) is positive. Following the guidelines from Table 41, the interpretation begins by focusing first on the cluster concerning controls and then on the variables in the array related to situational stress.

Case 1: A 29-Year-Old Female

Card	Response	Inquiry
I	1. My God that's ugly, it sort of ll a bat	E: (Rpts S's resp) S: Its all black, when I first it all I cld thk of was ugh!
	E: Take ur time & look some more S: Oh, let me look more then	E: I'm not sure I c it as u do S: Oh well u cld make these wgs & ths wld b the body prt, just a bat I guess
	v2. If I turn it ths way it ll a funny ghost house, like it is blowing in the wind	E: (Rpts S's resp) S: Oh its lik in cartoons when u c the spooky ghost houses & thy sort of move like the wind was blowing, c the windows aren't square & that & the funny shape creates that impression to me, ths part is the chmney
II	3. Oh wow, that ll a couple of bears stepping in a bucket of paint or s.t., like black bears gettg in trouble	E: (Rpts S's resp) S: Well ths part is the bears, kind of bent over c their feet r in ths red bucket down here & thy r gettg paint all over them & thyr touchg their paws together up here, just lik thy play lik in Yellowstone park, I've seen it on the TV
	<4. If u turn it ths way red part ll a little red bird, lik a humming bird, I thk thyr red	E: (Rpts S's resp) S: Well it just ll that to me, like a red humming bird, c the head is ths part (points) & the wing goes back to here & the little tiny feet r down here
	5. U kno if I cover everything but ths part it ll a forest fire way off on a mountain top	E: (Rpts S's resp) S: Well its lik way off in the distance & the red is the fire & ths darker part is the mountain, its burning on the side & near the top
III	6. Oh thats a funny one, it ll a lady lookg in the mirror at herself (laughs)	E: (Rpts S's resp) S: She's lik bending inward to get a better look at herself, she has a big purse in her hand & her hair is pulled back tight, c her hi heels & some jewelry or s.t. at her neck
	7. Ths thgs ll red devils that r falling, I dk what ths cntr thg is	E: (Rpts S's resp) S: Well u c littl red devils now & then in cartoons & thyr lik ths but thy ll thy r falling here, like upside dwn w thr long tails out behind them
IV	8. Yuck, its like two snakes on the sides	E: (Rpts S's resp) S: C here (points) lik thy r coiled up w their heads looking around, I don't lik snakes at all, c ths is the head & here is the tail

154

v9. There's two lions here too, one on each side
E: (Rpts S's resp)
S: Thyr just standing there, c one on each side w the long tail sticking out, c ths is the head & the body (points), just lik two lions

V

10. There's a rabbit in the cntr
E: (Rpts S's resp)
S: C the big ears & the little legs & the rabbit face on it so it must be a rabbit

11. There's two liitle birds there too I don't lik ths one much either
E: (Rpts S's resp)
S: U can hardly c them, c here (points) one on each side, just really tiny little birds, just the outline of them

VI

12. I dk what the top cb, mayb the bottm cb a bear skin but the top doesn't fit
E: (Rpts S's resp)
S: Well it really cb, it looks lik one w the legs, lik it was flat & it looks kind of like fur too, c all in the middle (rubs fingers)

13. U kno ther r two dolls ther too
E: (Rpts S's resp)
S: Well just this part (points), like in full gowns, I used to have one like this & I bought one like it for my daughter, c the full skirt & the head & top part of the body, there's one on each side

VII

14. Children, 2 children, lookg at e.o., thyr cute I lik ths one
E: (Rpts S's resp)
S: Its just the upper parts of them, like the chest & the heads & they r like twins, girls, c the hair is all fixed up pretty on top like u do with a comb

v15. If u look ths way its like pieces of Col Sanders chicken
E: (Rpts S's resp)
S: It ll 4 legs and 2 breasts, its all fried up, breaded u kno like it comes in those plastic buckets
E: Fried up?
S: Well it ll it is breaded & fried, when u do that it gets dark in some places & lite in some places, like this is

>16. Ths way it ll a toy dog, lik all fuzzy
E: (Rpts S's resp)
S: It has little legs & here's the ear & the tail stickg out, it ll its artifical fur, its not lik the other one, the bear rug, that looked real, ths one ll artifical, fuzzier & probably softer

VIII

17. Oh look at the colors, its lik a Christmas tree, no more an ornament for one
E: (Rpts S's resp)
S: Its just so colorful, it really strikes u after all those other black ones. Well, its like two thgs on the side, designs & all the pretty designs in the middle & its pointed on the top like an ornament

<18. Oh ths way the side designs ll an animal & he's crawlg ovr thgs & there's water & he can c himself in it
E: (Rpts S's resp)
S: Well here's the little animal, c his head & body & little legs & its lik he's steppg carefully ovr these othr things, I dk what but ths w.b. water & he can c himslf in it, c lik reflected dwn here

(continued)

Case 1: (Continued)

Card	Response	Inquiry
	v19. This way ths part ll a pretty bed jacket, I used to have one lik it	E: (Rpts S's resp) S: It has the arms & the full body like a bed jacket & its got a filmy appearance to it the way tht its colored E: A filmy appearance? S: Well its beautiful, I mean the orange & pink but when it was made they made the colors go together lik, I don't kno what u call it but it looks hazy sort of, filmy the way they made the colors blend together
IX	20. Oh, like a pot boiling over	E: (Rpts S's resp) S: Well if u've ever left a pot on the stove too long, mayb lik cooking cabbage, I did that once, it ll ths, a mess, flames & cabbage all over, c the orange is flames & the green is cabbage & the pink is lik the burner
	<21. Ths way u can c the head of an alligator in there	E: (Rpts S's resp) S: C right in here, just the long nose & the eye, its really like one I don't like them
X	22. Oh my, so many thgs, like a painting of s.t., mayb like from Alice in Wonderland	E: (Rpts S's resp) S: It just so much & so pretty, its not anythg definite, just like a painting, an, a, a, abstract of Alice in Wonderland but Alice isn't there E: I'm not sure I c it lik u do S: Oh its just all colors lik an abstract painting of Alice in Wndrld wld b
	23. I suppose these c.b. crabs	E: (Rpts S's resp) S: Ugh, c all the legs here & here (points), just lik crabs or spiders yuck
	24. There's a rabbit's head in ther too, u can c the littl white nose on him, its cute	E: (Rpts S's resp) S: C rite here in the middl part w the long ears, its its just the face, & the little white nose
	25. That pink is gross, I thot it was bld but I thk that ll the cotton candy u get at a fair	E: (Rpts S's resp) S: Its just pink & fuzzy looking like cotton candy E: Fuzzy looking S: U kno, different colors lik make it fuzzy, just lik cotton candy, its all sticky gooey if u get it on u'r fingers

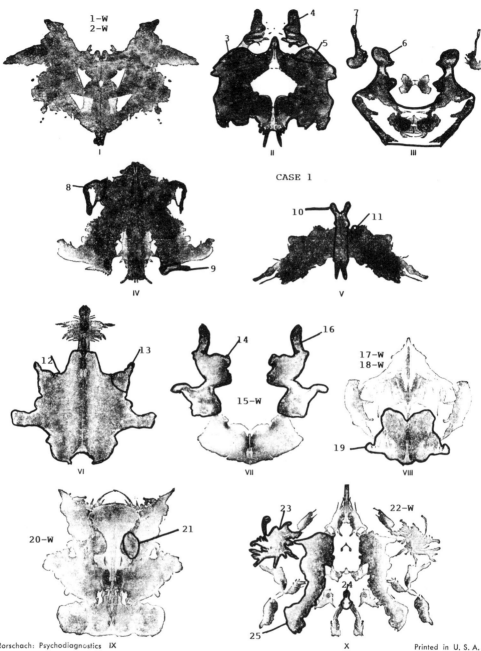

CASE 1

CASE 1. SEQUENCE OF SCORES

CARD	NO	LOC	#	DETERMINANT(S)	(2)	CONTENT(S)	POP	Z	SPECIAL SCORES
I	1	Wo	1	FC'o		A	P	1.0	
	2	WSo	1	mpu		Id		3.5	
II	3	D+	1	FMa.FC.FC'o	2	A,Id,Hh	P	3.0	PER,COP
	4	Do	2	FCu		A			
	5	Dd/	99	ma.CF.FDo		Fi,Ls		3.0	
III	6	D+	1	Mp.Fro		H,Cg	P	3.0	
	7	Do	2	FC.Mpo	2	(H)			
IV	8	Do	4	FMpo	2	A			
	9	Ddo	99	FMp-	2	A			PER
V	10	Do	7	Fo		A			
	11	Ddo	24	Fu	2	A			(DV) PER
VI	12	Do	1	FTo		Ad	P		
	13	Dd+	99	Fu	2	(H),Cg		2.5	PER
VII	14	D+	2	Mpo	2	Hd	P	3.0	
	15	Wo	1	FYo	2	Fd		2.5	
	16	Do	2	FTo		(A)			
VIII	17	Wv	1	CFo	2	Art			
	18	W+	1	FMa.Fro		A,Na	P	4.5	
	19	Do	2	FC.FYu		Cg			PER
IX	20	W/	1	ma.CF-		Hh,Fi,Fd		5.5	PER,MOR
	21	Ddo	99	Fo		Ad			
X	22	Wv	1	C		Art			AB
	23	Do	1	Fo	2	A	P		
	24	DSo	5	FC'o		Ad		6.0	
	25	Dv	9	C.T		Fd			

CASE 1.   STRUCTURAL SUMMARY

===

LOCATION	DETERMINANTS		CONTENTS	S-CONSTELLATION
FEATURES	BLENDS	SINGLE		NO..FV+VF+V+FD>2

```
                                                  H   = 1, 0    YES..Col-Shd Bl>0
Zf    = 11      FM.FC.FC'       M   = 1          (H)  = 2, 0    YES..Ego<.31,>.44
ZSum  = 37.5    m.CF.FD         FM  = 2           Hd  = 1, 0    NO..MOR > 3
ZEst  = 34.5    M.Fr            m   = 1          (Hd) = 0, 0    NO..Zd > +- 3.5
                FC.M            FC  = 1           Hx  = 0, 0    YES..es > EA
W     = 7       FM.Fr           CF  = 1           A   = 9, 0    YES..CF+C > FC
  (Wv  = 2)     FC.FY           C   = 1          (A)  = 1, 0    YES..X+% < .70
D     = 13      m.CF            Cn  = 0           Ad  = 3, 0    NO..S > 3
Dd    = 5       C.T             FC' = 2          (Ad) = 0, 0    NO..P < 3 or > 8
S     = 2                       C'F = 0           An  = 0, 0    YES..Pure H < 2
                                C'  = 0           Art = 2, 0    NO..R < 17
   DQ                           FT  = 2           Ay  = 0, 0     6.....TOTAL
.........(FQ-)                  TF  = 0           Bl  = 0, 0
  +  =  5  ( 0)                 T   = 0           Bt  = 0, 0    SPECIAL SCORINGS
  o  = 15  ( 1)                 FV  = 0           Cg  = 1, 2        Lv1     Lv2
 v/+ =  2  ( 1)                 VF  = 0           Cl  = 0, 0    DV   = 1x1    0x2
  v  =  3  ( 0)                 V   = 0           Ex  = 0, 0    INC  = 0x2    0x4
                                FY  = 1           Fd  = 2, 1    DR   = 0x3    0x6
                                YF  = 0           Fi  = 1, 1    FAB  = 0x4    0x7
                                Y   = 0           Ge  = 0, 0    ALOG = 0x5
    FORM QUALITY                Fr  = 0           Hh  = 1, 1    CON  = 0x7
                                rF  = 0           Ls  = 0, 1       SUM6  = 1
    FQx  FQf  MQual  SQx        FD  = 5           Na  = 0, 1       WSUM6 = 1
  + =  0   0    0    0          F   = 5           Sc  = 0, 0
  o = 16   3    3    1                            Sx  = 0, 0    AB = 1     CP  = 0
  u =  5   2    0    1                            Xy  = 0, 0    AG = 0     MOR = 1
  - =  2   0    0    0                            Id  = 1, 1    CFB = 0    PER = 4
none=  2  --    0    0          (2) = 10                        COP = 1    PSV = 0
```

===

RATIOS, PERCENTAGES, AND DERIVATIONS

```
R = 25          L = 0.25            FC:CF+C = 4: 5     COP = 1     AG = 0
-----------------------------------  Pure C  =    2    Food        = 3
EB = 3: 8.0   EA = 11.0   EBPer= 2.7 Afr     =0.56     Isolate/R =0.12
eb = 7: 8     es = 15       D = -1   S       =    2    H:(H)Hd(Hd) = 1: 3
            Adj es = 12  Adj D =  0   Blends:R= 8:25    (HHd):(AAd) = 2: 1
-----------------------------------  CP      =    0    H+A:Hd+Ad =13: 4
FM = 4  :  C'= 3    T = 3
m  = 3  :  V = 0    Y = 2
                             P   = 7       Zf  =11       3r+(2)/R=0.64
a:p   =  4: 6   Sum6  = 1    X+% =0.64     Zd  = +3.0    Fr+rF   = 2
Ma:Mp =  0: 3   Lv2   = 0    F+% =0.60     W:D:Dd = 7:13: 5  FD  = 1
2AB+Art+Ay= 4   WSum6 = 1    X-% =0.08     W:M  = 7: 3   An+Xy   = 0
M-    =  0      Mnone = 0    S-% =0.00     DQ+  = 5      MOR     = 1
                             Xu% =0.20     DQv  = 3
-------------------------------------------------------------------------
  SCZI = 0    DEPI = 4    CDI = 3    S-CON = 6    HVI = No   OBS = No
```

===

It is important to note that the entire interpretive strategy has not yet been selected. This can be done before beginning the interpretive routine by simply continuing with a review of the list of Key variables. In this case, the next three Key variables are negative (CDI > 3, Adj D < 0, Lambda > 0.99), but the seventh variable (Reflection > 0) is positive. Following from Table 41, this means that the third and fourth data sets to be reviewed concern self-perception and interpersonal perception. Table 41 also indicates that the controls cluster would follow, but in this case that cluster would already have been reviewed. Again, the entire interpretive strategy has not been determined because neither of the positive Key variables that has been identified thus far has that predictive capacity. Therefore, the list of Key variables must be reviewed for a third time to finish planning the routine.

The eighth Key variable (*EB* is introversive) is negative, but the ninth (*EB* is extratensive) is positive. This means that the fifth set of data to be reviewed includes affect, followed by the three clusters in the cognitive triad, processing, mediation, and ideation. Thus, the final interpretive strategy will be:

CONTROLS → SITUATIONAL STRESS → SELF-PERCEPTION → INTERPER-SONAL PERCEPTION → AFFECT → PROCESSING → MEDIATION → IDEATION.

SUMMARY

The importance of careful planning for the interpretive strategy to use in approaching a protocol cannot be overestimated. An enormous number of variables are involved, and they should not be addressed in a random or haphazard manner. To do so risks the possibility of inadvertently neglecting important findings or failing to integrate data appropriately. Each person is a very complex entity, different from all other people. Similarly, each Rorschach is complex and different from all others. If the data of the Rorschach are addressed in a systematic and intelligent manner, each person's uniqueness becomes pervasive as the interpretation evolves.

REFERENCES

Exner, J. E. (1978). *The Rorschach: A Comprehensive System. Volume 2: Recent research and advanced interpretation.* New York: Wiley.

Exner, J. E. (1986). *The Rorschach: A Comprehensive System. Volume 1: Basic foundations* (2nd ed.). New York: Wiley.

Exner, J. E., McGuire, H., and Cohen, J. B. (1985). *Program Proto.* Rorschach Workshops, Bayville, NY.

Exner, J. E., McGuire, H., and Cohen, J. B. (1986). *Rorschach Interpretation Assistance Program* (Version 1). Rorschach Workshops, Bayville, NY.

Exner, J. E., McGuire, H., and Cohen, J. B. (1990). *Rorschach Interpretation Assistance Program* (Version 2). Rorschach Workshops, Asheville, NC.

Exner, J. E., and Wilie, J. R. (1977). Some Rorschach data concerning suicide. *Journal of Personality Assessment,* **41,** 339–348.

CHAPTER 6

Cluster Interpretation: Controls and Stress

The fact that the Case 1 data reveal the presence of some situationally-related stress is not surprising in light of the information that she is separated and apparently involved in a divorce proceeding in which her daughter's custody is being contended. As with any record in which situational stress is indicated, two questions become important: (1) Is this person chronically vulnerable to stimulus overload situations because of limited capacities for control? (2) How does the situational stress impact on the functioning of the subject, and does it create some current vulnerability for which special intervention might be required? The first issue is addressed during the review of the variables related to controls. In turn, those findings provide a basis from which the data in the array of variables concerning situational stress can be used to sort through the second issue.

CAPACITY FOR CONTROL

Some data included in this cluster overlap with the array of variables related to situational stress and, as such, are evaluated twice. The relevant data for Case 1 are shown in Table 43.

Each major element in the cluster, D, Adj D, *EA, es,* and CDI provide important information, but often the values for each of the components of *EA* and/or *es* will provide the keys to fleshing out a broader understanding of the control and stress tolerance features. Stress tolerance is actually a by-product of the capacity for control, which is probably best defined as the ability to draw on available resources to formulate and implement deliberate behaviors designed to contend with demand situations. Thus, as the capacity for control increases, so does the ability to tolerate stress.

Adj D probably is the most direct single Rorschach index of the ability to maintain control under demand or stress situations, and obviously its value is quite important. If studied alone, however, it offers relatively little information about

Table 43. Control-Related Variables for Case 1

EB = 3 : 8.0	*EA* = 11.0	D = −1	CDI = 3
eb = 7 : 8	*es* = 15 Adj*es* = 12	AdjD = 0	
FM = 4 *m* = 3 *C′* = 3 *T* = 3 *V* = 0 *Y* = 2			

161

the capacity for control, and might even render misleading information about stress tolerance. The linchpin in the cluster is *EA,* which is critical to any understanding of capacity for control, especially when considered in the context of various psychological styles that might be present. It is important to emphasize that capacity for control does not necessarily equate with good adjustment, although a limited capacity for control is often a precursor to maladjustment.

Major Issues: The controls cluster is the first to be reviewed in the interpretation when inspection of the Key variables reveals that some control problems appear to exist, and the search through the variables addresses such issues as (1) the source of the problem, (2) the chronicity of the problem, and (3) the extent to which the problem is resulting from a disorganization in previously established patterns of using resources. For instance, in Case 1, the search decision is based on the initial finding that D < Adj D, leading to the proposition that some situationally-related stress condition exists. In this context, the issue of whether the subject is more chronically vulnerable to stress effects becomes a focal point in the search.

When the review of the cluster *does not occur first* in the interpretive routine, the search proceeds with no preconceptions. It is designed to determine if there are any unusual features regarding control and/or stress tolerance. As a matter of routine, the values for all five of the major variables are expected to fall within average limits. In other words, both D scores are expected to have the same value, usually zero, except for younger subjects; the values for *EA* and *es* are expected to be in the average range; and CDI is expected to have a value less than 4. If the observed and expected values coincide, the conclusion is rather simple, namely that the subject appears to have the capacity for control, the tolerance for stress, and a level of resource access that are similar to most other people. Regardless of whether the cluster is addressed first or later in the interpretive routine, the search procedure is the same.

Step 1:   Review the values for Adj D and the CDI to obtain some preliminary information regarding control and stress tolerance.

Potential Finding 1:   Ordinarily, if the value for Adj D is zero and the value for the CDI is less than 4, the subject's capacity for control and tolerance for stress is similar to that of most others. *Proceed to Step 2.*

Potential Finding 2:   If the value of Adj D is zero and the value for the CDI is 4 or 5, the personality organization of the subject may be somewhat less mature than might be expected. This tends to create a vulnerability for problems in coping with the requirements of everyday living. Such difficulties usually are manifest in the interpersonal sphere and can easily contribute to problems in control. *Proceed to Step 2.*

Potential Finding 3:   If the subject's Adj D value is in the *plus* range, the subject has a more sturdy tolerance for stress than do most, and is far less likely to experience problems in control, regardless of the value for the CDI. An Adj D score in the plus range *does not* indicate better adjustment; it simply suggests a greater capacity for control. *Proceed to Step 2.*

Potential Finding 4:   If the Adj D value is −1, it can be postulated that the subject is in a state of chronic stimulus overload. Thus, the subject's control capacity and ability to deal effectively with stress is less than might be expected, regardless of the value for the CDI. Some decisions and behaviors will not be well thought out and/or implemented, and a proclivity for impulsiveness exists. *impulsivity* Although the subject is more vulnerable to control problems or more susceptible to disorganization under stress, those events are less likely to occur in structured, well-defined situations. Unless serious psychological difficulties exist, such people usually function adequately in environments with which they are familiar and in which demands and expectations are routine and predictable. The risk of losing control becomes more substantial as demands and expectations increase beyond levels for which the subject is prepared. *Proceed to Step 2.*

Potential Finding 5:   If the Adj D Score is less than −1, it can be assumed that the subject is highly vulnerable to loss of control and becoming disorganized under stress, regardless of the value for the CDI. People with Adj D Scores of less than −1 usually have histories that include numerous events marked by faulty judgment, emotional disruption, and/or behavioral ineffectiveness. They are chronically vulnerable to ideational and/or affective impulsiveness and typically function adequately for extended periods only in environments that are ✓ highly structured and routine and over which they have some sense of control.

Note that, in some cases the subject's history will contain information about significant achievements in complex endeavors, such as educational or occupational success. High levels of achievement are extremely rare among subjects who have Adj D Scores in the minus range. Therefore, if a minus Adj D Score occurs in the record of a subject with a significant achievement history, it is reasonable to assume that the current minus Adj D Score is the result of some ongoing disorganization. *Proceed to Step 2.*

Case 1 Result: The Adj D Score is zero and the CDI is 3, suggesting that, in most instances, the subject's capacity for control and tolerance for stress is like that of most adults.

Step 2:   Review the *EA* value to evaluate the credibility of the Adj D Score. As noted earlier, *EA* is the centerpiece variable in this cluster. If the Adj D Score is zero, the *EA* is expected to fall at least in the average range. Usually, plus D scores are produced by higher than average values for *EA*. When this is true, it reflects an abundance of available resources but, again, does not necessarily relate to better adjustment or more effective psychological organization. It merely indicates that the subject has identified and/or organized resources more extensively than have most people. But how the resources are used can be an altogether different matter.

$EA = M + WSumC$ available resources

Potential Finding 1:   If the value for *EA* is in the average range, an Adj D Score of zero is expected and probably reflects a reliable and valid index of capacity for control and stress tolerance. *Proceed to Step 3.*

$8.83 SO = 2.8$

Potential Finding 2:   If the value for *EA* is in the average range and the Adj D Score is in the *plus* range, this unusual finding signals a lower than expected value for *es*. Thus, the Adj D Score may be misleading and requires further evaluation during Step 4 of this review. *Proceed to Step 3.*

Potential Finding 3:   If the value for *EA* is in the average range or higher and the Adj D Score is in the *minus* range, this unusual finding signals a higher than average value for *es* after it has been adjusted for stress factors. The unexpected elevation in *es* should be evaluated carefully during Step 4 and conclusions regarding the reliability of Adj D deferred until that time. *Proceed to Step 3.*

Potential Finding 4:   If the value for *EA* exceeds the average range, an Adj D Score in the *plus* range is expected and probably represents a reliable and valid index of capacity for control and tolerance for stress. *Proceed to Step 3.*

Potential Finding 5:   If the value for *EA* exceeds the average range and the Adj D Score is zero, an unexpectedly elevated *es* is present, which may indicate that capacity for control has been greater than currently indicated. This possibility should be carefully evaluated during Step 4. *Proceed to Step 3.*

Potential Finding 6:   An *EA* that is significantly lower than average suggests more limited available resources. In this case, an Adj D Score in the *minus* range is likely. An Adj D Score of zero or greater is possibly misleading because people with a low *EA,* other than young children, are more chronically vulnerable to becoming disorganized by many of the natural everyday stresses of living in a complex society. They function most effectively in environments that are well structured and reasonably free of ambiguity. *Proceed to Step 3.*

Case 1 Result: The subject's *EA* of 11.0 is at the upper end of the average range for nonpatient adults and slightly above average for nonpatient adult females. Therefore, there is no reason to suspect that the current experience of stress is the result of a lack of available resources or that the subject is chronically vulnerable to disorganization.

Step 3:   Review the values on each side of the *EB*. Neither is expected to be zero. A zero on either side of an *EB* in which the other side contains a substantial value casts doubt on the reliability of the *EA* and typically signals the presence of an unusual affective problem that may have served as a predisposition to the current stress state, *or* could be the product of the current stress state.

Potential Finding 1:   If the values on both sides of the *EB* are greater than zero, the resulting *EA* is probably reliable. *Proceed to Step 4.*

Potential Finding 2:   If the value for *M* is zero and the value for *Sum C* is greater than 3, it is reasonable to conclude that the subject is being overwhelmed or flooded by affect. This has a major impact on thinking, especially the ability to invoke the forms of delay in ideational activity that are often necessary to maintain adequate attention and concentration while pursuing decision operations. The possibilities of either ideational or behavioral impulsiveness are increased significantly under this condition. *Proceed to Step 4.*

Potential Finding 3:   If the value for *Sum C* is zero and the value for *M* is greater than 2, the subject is investing considerable energy in a massive containment or shutdown of affect. Usually this requires much more resource than the average person has available, the vulnerability to stimulus overload and the consequent disorganization is considerable. *Proceed to Step 4.*

Case 1 Result: Neither side of the subject's *EB* has a value of zero, the *EA* of 11.0 can be assumed to be reliable.

Step 4:   Review the value for the adjusted *es*. As noted earlier, in some instances, Adj D Scores of zero or *plus* are not the result of an average or higher *EA*, but rather are produced by unexpectedly low values for *es*. Similarly, Adj D Scores in the *minus* range may be produced by an unexpectedly high level of more chronic demands that could indicate much more psychological complexity than is common, or might even signal the presence of a deteriorative state that is creating a picture quite different from what existed previously.

Potential Finding 1:   If the value for Adj *es* is in the average range and no significant findings challenge the reliability of *EA*, it can be concluded that the Adj D Score is reliable. *Proceed to Step 5.*

Potential Finding 2:   If the value for Adj *es* is above average and no significant findings challenge the reliability of *EA*, it is possible that the Adj D Score reflects an underestimate of the subject's capacities for control and stress tolerance. An above average Adj *es* suggests the likelihood of excessive psychological complexity. This possibility should be evaluated carefully during Step 5. *Proceed to Step 5.*

Potential Finding 3:   If Adj *es* is lower than average, the Adj D Score may overestimate the subject's capacities for control and stress tolerance. This possibility should be evaluated carefully during Step 5. *Proceed to Step 5.*

Case 1 Finding: The value of the Adj *es* is 12, which is above average. Although there is no reason to challenge the reliability of *EA*, the Adj D of zero may tend to underestimate the subject's capacities for control under more normal circumstances. This postulate is especially important because she is experiencing situationally-related stress, and the impact could be greater than is reflected by the difference of 1 between the D and Adj D Scores. This postulate should be reviewed again after the review of the next cluster, and in light of the Step 5 findings.

Step 5:   Review the values for *eb* and the values for the variables contributing to *es* that *are not* stress related (*FM, C', T, V*) to assess the kinds of psychological activities that are promoting frequent demands.

Potential Finding 1:   The left-side value in the *eb* is expected to be greater than the right-side value. If the right-side value is greater, regardless of the value for *es* or the Adj *es*, it can be assumed that the subject is experiencing some distress.

Potential Finding 2:   If *FM* is greater than 5, the subject probably is experiencing more seemingly random, disconnected patterns of thinking than is customary. Ideational activity such as this usually is provoked by the presence of more un-gratified needs than typically should be the case. These need-related demands intrude on more deliberate patterns of thought and often interfere with concentration and attention.

Potential Finding 3:   If the value for *FM* is less than 2 it suggests that need states are not being experienced in typical ways, or that they are being acted on more rapidly than is the case for most people.

Potential Finding 4:   The expected value for *C'* is 0 or 1. If the value for *C'* exceeds 2 it indicates an excessive internalization of feelings that the subject would prefer to externalize. This psychological process can lead to any of several experiences of subjective discomfort, including anxiety, sadness, tension, apprehensiveness, and possibly somatic disruption.

Potential Finding 5:   If the value for *V* is greater than zero it suggests that the subject is involved in more self-inspecting behaviors that focus on negative features of the self-image than is common for most people. This type of introspection frequently leads to the experience of discomfort and self-deprecation and is often a precursor to depression and self-destructive thinking.

Potential Finding 6:   If the value for *T* is greater than 1 it signals the presence of experienced emotional deprivation. In *most instances,* this experience may be situationally-related and should be easily identified from a close inspection of the subject's recent history. *If* this is confirmed by the history, a minus value for the Adj D Score may be misleading. In other words, it could reflect a situationally-related problem, such as the recent loss of an emotionally important object. If the recent history does not indicate such a loss, it is more prudent to conclude that the state of emotional deprivation (or loneliness) has a longer standing origin and may even be the product of needs for closeness that exceed the normal parameters experienced in interpersonal relationships.

Potential Finding 7:   If the value for *T* is zero, it is likely that interpersonal relations are marked by superficiality and caution. This can create a vulnerability to stress because supports often derived from closeness with others are not present. In fact, the interpersonal world itself may constitute a source of frequently experienced stress. *Proceed to the next cluster in the interpretive routine.*

Case 1 Findings: The subject's *eb* has a higher right-side value which signals distress. Some of this distress could be the product of the situational condition, but such a conclusion is premature at this time. Significant elevations occur for both *T* and *C'*. The former, indicating a strong sense of emotional deprivation or loneliness, probably has some relation to her situational problems in that she is involved in a marital breakup. It is less likely, but not impossible, that the elevation in *C'* answers has a similar relationship. This finding should be considered again after the review of the next cluster and should be evaluated further when the cluster concerning affect is reviewed.

Case 1 Summary: Controls

The subject has considerable resource organized in ways that make it readily accessible for her use in forming and implementing decisions. Thus, in most instances, her capacities for control and tolerance for stress are at least as robust as those of most adults. However, these features currently have become less effective because of situationally-related stress, which has apparently increased the demands that she is experiencing to levels considerably greater than typically should be the case. Among those demands is a strong irritating sense of affective deprivation that is probably being experienced as loneliness or neglect. This may be situationally-related but it may also have some chronic underpinnings. She also tends to internalize feelings that she would prefer to externalize much more than most people. This also could have some relationship to the current stress situation but it is equally plausible that this is more of a trait-like feature.

SITUATIONALLY-RELATED STRESS

This special array of variables is searched systematically only when the third Key *adj D* variable is positive. In all other interpretive routines, the variables in this array (D, Adj D, *m, Y,* Blend complexity, Color-shading Blends, *T,* Pure *C, M−,* and Formless *M*) are not evaluated as a collective. Instead, they are reviewed during the interpretation of other clusters. As noted earlier, some of the variables in the array are drawn from the cluster related to controls and have already been reviewed once. Nonetheless, when included in this array or collective, they aid in providing some information concerning the overall impact of a situational stress state. The main focus of the interpretive search is to ascertain the effects of the increase in stimulation on the psychological organization and functioning of the subject, and several important issues must be considered.

Major Issues: (1) What is the magnitude of the impact of the current stress? (2) Has the increased stimulation created an overload state? If the stimulus demands that are being experienced by the subject exceed accessible resources, this creates a proclivity for impulsiveness and increases the likelihood for disorganization. (3) Does the increased stimulation have an impact mainly on ideation, or affect, or both? (4) To what extent does the increased stimulation create significantly more psychological complexity and/or affective confusion? The search strategy involves five basic steps, each of which should render useful information. The data for the variables in the array are shown in Table 44.

Proposition: The subject is experiencing a significant increase in stimulus demands as a result of situationally-related stress. Thus, some decisions and/or behaviors may not be as well organized as is usually the case, and the subject is more vulnerable to disorganization as the result of added stresses.

Table 44.   Stress-Related Variables for Case 1

			BLENDS	
D = −1	ADJ D = 0		FM.FC.FC′	m.CF.FD
m = 3,	Y = 2,	T = 3	M.Fr	FC.M
Pure C = 2,		Blends = 8	FM.Fr	FC.FY
M− = 0		MQ none = 0	m.CF	C.T

Step 1:   Calculate the difference between the D Score and the Adj D Score to obtain an estimate of the magnitude of the stress.

Potential Finding: Ordinarily, the resulting value will be 1. If the value exceeds 1, it can be assumed that the subject's experience of the stress is quite severe and that the impact is creating a considerable interference in some of the customary patterns of thinking and/or behavior. *Proceed to Step 2.*

Case 1 Result: The difference between the subject's D and Adj D is 1, thus interference created by the stress can be expected to be more modest than severe.

Step 2:   Review the D Score value to address the issue of stimulus overload.

Potential Finding 1:   If the D Score has a minus value, the potential for impulsiveness in thinking, affect, and/or behavior is considerable. People with D Scores of −1 are vulnerable to disorganization in complex or highly ambiguous situations, and their vulnerability increases as *EA* falls below the average range. If the D Score is less than −1, the potential for disorganization is increased substantially, regardless of the value of *EA*. If this finding is positive, the presence of Pure *C* responses, *M−* answers, or Formless *M* responses is also very important. The presence of one or more Pure *C* answers in this configuration suggests that some of the impulsiveness may manifest in affective displays, whereas the presence of *M−* or Formless *M* responses raises a question about whether ideational controls may be impaired because of the overload state. If this finding is positive, *proceed to Step 3.*

Potential Finding 2:   If the D Score value is zero or greater, no evidence supports the notion that impulsiveness is likely. Nonetheless, the fact that D is less than Adj D does indicate that the subject's stress tolerance is lower than usual and, as noted at Step 2, some interference occurs in the customary patterns of thinking and/or affect. The presence of Pure *C* responses in this configuration *does not* reflect impulsiveness. Instead, it signifies that, in some instances, available resources are not committed to the modulation of affect. The presence of *M−* or Formless *M* answers in this configuration raises a question about more enduring problems in thinking. *Proceed to Step 3.*

Handwritten note at top of page: adj D=visual resources / D = current

Case 1 Result: The subject's D Score is −1, indicating that an overload has created a proclivity for impulsiveness and some potential for disorganization. There are no *M*− or Formless M answers. There are two Pure *C* responses, suggesting that some of the impulsiveness is likely to occur in the form of potentially serious modulation failures during emotional displays. This finding should be afforded some weight in considering intervention routines.

Step 3: Review the values for *T, m,* and *Y* to determine if the impact of the overload has specificity.

Potential Finding 1: If the value for *T* is 2 or more, it can be assumed that some of the stress is related to an experience of emotional loss, which should be confirmed easily by the recent history. If the history does not reveal an obvious recent emotional loss, the possibility of a more chronic state of loneliness or neediness should be considered and investigated more thoroughly.

Potential Finding 2: If the values for *m* and *Y* are not substantially different and the value for *T* is 0 or 1, it can be assumed that the impact of the stress is diffuse. *Proceed to Step 4.*

Potential Finding 3: If the value for *m* is more than three times that of *Y*, it is likely that the overload is having greater impact on thinking. *Proceed to Step 4.*

Potential Finding 4: If the value of *Y* is more than three times that of *m*, it is likely that the greater impact occurs on emotion. *Proceed to Step 4.*

Case 1 Result: Finding 1 is positive, that is, the value for *T* exceeds 1, some of the subject's experience of emotional loss probably translates into feelings of loneliness. The magnitude of the value for *T* (3) suggests that this experience is quite intense. In addition, the values for *m* and *Y* are not markedly disparate, suggesting that the overall impact of the stress is psychologically diffuse. Data from the history reveal that the subject is recently separated and a divorce action is pending. Although these circumstances may account for the elevation in *T,* it is premature to accept that explanation. The entire interpersonal history should be reviewed very carefully.

Step 4: Tally the number of blends that contain the variables *m, Y,* and *T* to assess possible increases in complexity as a result of the increased stimulus demands. If there are blends created *exclusively* by the presence of the *m* and/or *Y* variables, (e.g., *FC.FY, m.CF, m.YF*), subtract the number of these blends from the total number of blends to obtain an estimate of the nonstress level of complexity.

Potential Finding 1: In most records, the composite of these three variables occurs no more than twice among the blends. If the number of blends that include these variables is greater than two, the excess provides a crude, but sometimes useful, index of added psychological complexity being created by the stress condition.

Potential Finding 2:   If the subtraction of blends created by the presence of *m* or *Y* reduces the total from an above average range to an average range or below, it is probable that the current stress is creating substantially more complexity than is common and, as such, is contributing to a vulnerability for disorganization. This factor is especially important if the D Score is in the minus range, because significant increases in complexity also increase the potential for impulsive-like behaviors. *Proceed to Step 5.*

Case 1 Result: Four of the eight blends in the subject's record include *m*, *Y*, or *T*. This pattern suggests that there may be a substantial increase in psychological complexity as a result of the stress condition. In addition, the subtraction of two of the eight blends (*FC.FY, m.CF*) reduces the total from above average to the average range, which suggests that the added complexity may be increasing the potential for impulsiveness.

Step 5:   Review the list of blends for Color-Shading Blends, noting any created exclusively by the combination of chromatic color plus *Y* to assess for situationally-related affective confusion.

Potential Finding: If at least one Color-Shading blend exists based exclusively on the combination of chromatic color plus *Y*, it can be assumed that the stress condition has created and/or increased emotional confusion. *Proceed to the next cluster in the interpretive routine.*

Case 1 Result: There are three Color-Shading blends in the subject's record, *FM.CF.FC'*, *C.T*, and *FC.FY*. The first and possibly the second suggest that this subject often experiences some confusion about her feelings. The third is apparently situation provoked and signifies that the current stress state probably has created some increase in the preexisting potential for ambivalent or mixed feelings.

Case 1 Summary: Situational Stress

The data from the array concerning situational stress has, as expected, provided useful information about the subject that broadens the cornerstone in the total interpretation. Clearly, she is currently experiencing some effects of situationally-related stress. Although the effects are more modest than severe, the added stimulus demands have created an overload state in spite of the fact that she ordinarily has considerable resource available. This overload has created a marked potential for impulsiveness, which is more likely to manifest in emotions than in her thinking. Much of the stress appears to be related to an experience of emotional loss and probably translates psychologically as a strong feeling of loneliness. The stress effects probably are also somewhat diffuse and may account for her complaints of difficulty in concentration as well as the numerous affective symptoms that she presents.

Currently, the subject's psychological state is much more complex than is usually the case and, although she appears to have a long-standing ambivalence or confusion about her feelings, this proclivity has intensified in the current state.

Although the interpretation is far from complete, it seems clear that intervention planning should focus on bringing some relief from the current stress, and the subject's emotional loss and/or loneliness can have considerable importance in determining some of the specific tactics of treatment. This issue will be reviewed again as the remainder of the record is interpreted.

PROCEEDING WITH THE INTERPRETIVE STRATEGY

The findings from the controls cluster and the array of stress-related variables include highlights that will remain quite important for the remainder of the interpretive strategy. First, the *es* value of 15 and the adjusted *es* value of 12 are much higher than expected, and the higher right-side value for *eb* suggests that many of these demands have an affective basis. Second, the composite of the D Score of −1 plus the presence of two Pure *C* answers indicate the likelihood that the subject is vulnerable to serious modulation problems when displaying affect. Third, she appears to have some long-standing ambivalence or confusion about her feelings, which appears to have been increased by the current stress state.

In light of these findings, it seems logical to assume that the data concerning affect will contribute much to the overall interpretation, and some might feel tempted to turn to those data at this point in the routine. As emphasized earlier, however, it is necessary to adhere to the Key variable listing to determine the next steps in the interpretive strategy. In this case, another positive Key variable—the reflection answer—should be given priority. The Case 1 record contains two reflection answers, which is sufficiently important to take precedence in the routine. The selection of this strategy, rather than pursuing the data concerning affect, is important because the reflection finding signals the presence of an unusual core personality feature that tends to influence most psychological functioning, including affect. Thus, by continuing the interpretation with the initial focus on self-perception and interpersonal perception, it is likely that information will be uncovered that can help to understand some of her affective operations more clearly.

CHAPTER 7

Cluster Interpretation: Self-Perception and Interpersonal Perception

Some of the data in the self-perception and interpersonal perception clusters, especially responses containing human content and some of the content of movement responses, overlap. This is one reason why the two clusters are always studied in tandem. The second reason is that findings concerning self-perception frequently contribute substantially to the development of an understanding of interpersonal perceptions and behaviors. Thus, when reviewing the data in the two clusters, the data regarding self-perception are taken first.

SELF-PERCEPTION

The objective in reviewing the self-perception cluster is to develop a picture of self-image and self-esteem. Self-image is the view that one harbors about oneself. It is reflected in an internal lexicon that describes the characteristics of the self, such as bright, dull, beautiful, ugly, talented, vulnerable, kind, selfish, sensitive, and so on. Some of these perceived characteristics may be reality based, whereas others may be more imaginary than real. Regardless of their basis, they form a collective representation of the assets and liabilities of the person *as perceived by the person.* Self-esteem has to do with the value of that collective representation when judged against external sources. It is an estimate of personal worth in relation to others, usually significant others who may be real or imagined. It is involved in both specific and general evaluations and probably has something to do with setting achievement objectives.

Table 45. Self-Perception Variables for Case 1

STRUCTURAL DATA		RESPONSES TO BE READ	
$Fr+rF = 2$	$3r+(2)/R = 0.64$	*MOR* RESPONSE	$= 20$
$FD = 1$	$V = 0$	MINUS RESPONSES	$= 9, 20$
$(H)+Hd+(Hd) = 1:3$		*M* RESPONSES	$= 6, 7, 14$
$An+Xy = 0$		*FM* RESPONSES	$= 3, 8, 9, 18$
$MOR = 1$		*m* RESPONSES	$= 2, 5, 20$

172

Although self-image and self-esteem are interrelated, that relationship is not nearly as direct as might seem to be the case. For example, the Egocentricity Index is more a measure of self-concern and self-value than of self-image. An elevated Egocentricity Index predicts the presence of *FD* responses, which relate to introspective activity, but a low Egocentricity Index does not predict the presence of Vista answers or Morbid content, both of which relate to a negative self-image. Conversely, the presence of at least one Vista answer predicts the presence of more than one MOR response.

The Case 1 structural data for the cluster plus a list of responses to be reviewed for possible projected material are shown in Table 45.

Major Issues: (1) Is the level of self-concern typical or atypical for the age of the subject? That is, when issues of the self versus others arise, what is the result? (2) What are the basic features of the self-image? (3) Is there any evidence of significant distortions in or preoccupations about the self-image?

Step 1:   Review the data for the presence of one or more reflection answers.

Potential Finding 1:   The value for $Fr + rF$ is 0. *Proceed to Step 2.*

Potential Finding 2:   The value for $Fr + rF$ is greater than 0. A nuclear element in the subject's self-image is a narcissistic-like feature that includes a marked tendency to overvalue personal worth. This characteristic is natural among younger children but usually disappears by early adolescence as formal operations begin and social relationships take on a new importance. This inflated sense of personal worth tends to dominate perceptions of the world. It does not automatically predispose pathology, but it can impair the development of a mature balance between a healthy concern for one's own integrity and the integrity of others.

Reflection answers have considerable temporal stability. For instance, 42 subjects included in the outpatient reference group shown in Chapter 2 gave at least one reflection answer when first tested prior to beginning treatment. When retested between 9 and 12 months later, 41 of the 42 gave at least one reflection response. Similarly, a composite of 150 protocols, consisting of 100 nonpatients retested after three years and 50 nonpatients retested after one year, contained 17 in which at least one reflection answer was given in the first test. All 17 subjects gave at least one reflection response in their retest records.

This characteristic forms a basic personality orientation or style that is highly influential in decisions and behaviors because of the need for frequent reaffirmation or reinforcement of the exaggerated sense of personal pride. It often contributes significantly to the development of motives for status and, if that recognition is achieved, it reduces the likelihood that this extreme form of self-centeredness will promote pathology or maladjustment. On the other hand, failures to obtain reaffirmation of the high self-value usually lead to frustration and negativism, and elaborate systems of personal defense are developed to protect the integrity of the belief concerning the extraordinary personal worth. This can create a predisposition to pathology and/or maladjustment. Rationalization, externalization, and denial typically form the core of these defenses. Adolescents and adults with this feature often find it difficult to establish and maintain deep and meaningful interpersonal relationships. In some instances, this provokes self-examining, which may lead to an internal struggle to maintain the inflated self-value versus some awareness that it may not be valid. If the environment has been especially ungiving of reinforcement, asocial and/or antisocial sets can evolve rather easily. *Proceed to Step 2.*

Case 1 Result: The protocol contains two reflection answers indicating that she has an exaggerated sense of personal worth that is important for her to sustain. External attribution of causes for negative events and denial of negative feelings are probably common in her everyday behaviors.

Step 2:   Review the value for the Egocentricity Index to obtain an estimate of self-concern and possibly self-esteem. The index is a crude measure of self-concern or self-attending behavior. If the value falls above the average range it indicates an excessive involvement with the self but *does not necessarily equate with positive self-esteem unless the reflection response is also positive.* On the other hand, if it falls below the average range, it indicates that self-esteem is lower than should be the case; that is, when comparative judgments are made between the self and others, the result tends to be negative.

Potential Finding 1:   An Egocentricity Index greater than .45 for an adult (or greater than 1 *SD* above the mean for the age group of a younger person) suggests that the subject tends to be much more involved with himself or herself than are most people. The presence of a reflection in the record indicates that the narcissistic-like feature is strongly embedded in the psychological organization of the subject and is sustaining favorable judgments concerning the self in relation to others. If no reflection answers appear in the record, a high index signals an unusually strong concern with the self, which easily leads to a neglect of the external world. In many cases, a higher than average index indicates a highly positive estimate of personal worth but, in some instances, this strong concern with the self may signal a sense of dissatisfaction with the self. *Proceed to Step 3.*

Potential Finding 2:   An Egocentricity Index in the range of .33 to .45 for an adult (or in the average range for a younger subject) suggests that the subject is no more or less concerned with the self than are most people. This is an unusual finding if a reflection is present because the narcissistic feature breeds excessive preoccupation with the self. Thus, if this finding is positive in a record containing a reflection, the subject probably has some awareness that the assumption of high personal worth may be faulty and occasional self-doubt and rumination are not uncommon. This finding may be favorable for such a subject as it could indicate the presence of a social maturation process. Conversely, this awareness can lead to an increase in the use of defenses that have been reinforcing in the past, and this can lead to a more chaotic and less effective level of psychological functioning that can include significant mood fluctuations. *Proceed to Step 3.*

Potential Finding 3:   If the value for the Egocentricity Index is .32 or less for an adult (or less than 1 *SD* below the age mean for a younger person), the subject's estimate of personal worth tends to be quite negative. He or she regards themselves less favorably when compared to others. This characteristic is often a precursor to depression. This finding is very uncommon in records containing reflection answers. If it is positive in a protocol containing a reflection response, the subject is likely to be in serious conflict regarding self-image and self-value. The likelihood of mood fluctuations is substantial and behavioral dysfunction is likely. *Proceed to Step 3.*

Case 1 Result: The Egocentricity Index of .64 is consistent with the reflection response finding. It reaffirms the conclusion that the subject has an exaggerated sense of self-value and suggests that she tends to focus excessively on herself. In doing so there is a substantial risk that she will be less sensitive to or less concerned with those around her.

Step 3:   Review the values for *FD* and Vista responses to ascertain the extent to which self-inspecting behavior may be occurring. *FD* answers generally are a positive sign, unless they occur with substantial frequency. Conversely, Vista responses signal the presence of some irritating affective experience that is being produced by self-inspection.

Potential Finding 1:   If no *FD* or Vista answers are in the record, the subject may be less involved with self-awareness than is usually the case. Such people tend to be more naïve about themselves. This finding is common among children and young adolescents. *Proceed to Step 4.*

Potential Finding 2:   If there are no Vista answers and the *FD* value is 1 or 2, it can be assumed that the subject engages in self-inspecting behaviors somewhat routinely. This process can be beneficial as it tends to promote reevaluation of the self-image. *Proceed to Step 4.*

Potential Finding 3:   If the value for *FD* exceeds 2 *or* if the value for Vista exceeds 0, it suggests that some unusual self-inspecting behavior is occurring. This is not necessarily an atypical feature during some stages in the life cycle, such as puberty and aging, or in proximity to critical life events, such as affective loss, failures, and physical or psychological difficulties. Whatever the cause, this finding confirms that considerable self-focusing is occurring. It is a very unusual finding in protocol containing a reflection answer and probably signals the presence of a conflict state concerning self-image. If the Egocentricity Index is in the average range, this finding suggests more rumination concerning the self than is common. If the Egocentricity Index is lower than average, this finding suggests that the unusual frequency of self-inspecting probably relates to the negative self-value held by the subject. If the positive finding includes the presence of one or more vista answers, it signals that some of the self-inspecting behavior is also yielding very negative, irritating feelings. If one or more vista answers appear in a protocol containing a reflection response, it is almost certain that the subject is struggling with the issue of high self-value versus perceived negative features of the self. *Proceed to Step 4.*

Case 1 Result: There is one *FD* answer in the record. This suggests that she does some self inspection. This is probably a favorable finding when considered in light of her current overload state. An issue that should be addressed, if possible, during the interpretation is whether this finding represents a mature attempt by the subject to take distance and review her self-image or whether it might be more directly related to her affective difficulties.

Step 4:   Review the relation between Pure *H* content and other human contents to evaluate the extent to which self-image and/or self-esteem are based on experience.

Potential Finding 1:   If the majority of the human contents include whole figures scored *H,* this suggests that self-image and self-value are probably based more on experience than on imagination. This finding is generally positive but it *should not* be translated to mean that self-image and/or self-value are necessarily accurate or realistic. Rather, it indicates that interactions have contributed significantly to formulations regarding the self.

Potential Finding 2:   If the majority of human contents are scored *Hd* or have parenthesized human contents, this suggests that self-image and/or self-value tend to be based largely on imaginary rather than real experience. Subjects such as this are often less mature and frequently have very distorted notions of themselves. This more limited self-awareness sometimes serves negatively in decision making and problem solving activity and creates a potential for difficulties in relating to others.

Potential Finding 3:   If one or more answers include an *Hx* content, it signals that the subject attempts to deal with issues of self-image and/or self-value in an overly intellectualized manner that tends to ignore reality. People like this often have ideational impulse control problems; as a result, many features of self-image are grossly distorted. *Proceed to Step 5.*

Case 1 Result: The record contains four human contents, none of which have an *Hx* content, but only one of which is Pure *H.* This strongly suggests that the conceptualizations that the subject has about herself are formulated largely on imaginary rather than real experience.

Step 5:   Review the value for *An* + *Xy* to determine if any unusual body preoccupation is present.

Potential Finding 1:   If the value is 0, there is no evidence from which to speculate about body concern. *Proceed to Step 6.*

Potential Finding 2:   If the value is 1 or 2, some body concern may be present but should not necessarily be considered as a major issue in the subject's psychological organization unless the answers have a minus form quality. If they are minus answers, they are included in the Step 8 review of content. *Proceed to Step 6.*

Potential Finding 3:   If the value is 3 or more, some unusual body concern or preoccupation is present. This finding is not uncommon among subjects who have physical problems; however, if no health problem exists, it suggests the likelihood of rumination about body and/or self-image and may indicate an important sense of vulnerability. *Proceed to Step 6.*

Case 1 Result: There are no An or Xy responses in the subject's record.

Step 6:   Review frequency data for MOR to determine if the self-image includes negative or damaged features.

Potential Finding 1:   If the value for MOR does not exceed 1, it is unlikely that the self-image includes markedly negative features. This postulate should be evaluated again during Steps 8 and 9. *Proceed to Step 7* if the value for MOR is 1, or *proceed to Step 8* if the value for MOR is 0.

Potential Finding 2:   If the value for MOR is 2, it is possible that some negative features are included in the self-concept that tend to promote more pessimism in thinking than should be the case. This finding should be evaluated more carefully by a review of the verbal material in the MOR answers. This finding is somewhat unusual in a protocol containing a reflection answer and can signal the presence of conflict concerning self-value. *Proceed to Step 7.*

Potential Finding 3:   If the value for MOR is 3 or more, it is reasonable to assume that the self-image is marked by negative characteristics, and thinking often includes much more pessimism than is ordinary. The verbal material in the MOR answers should provide some additional clarification concerning the negative characteristics. This finding is extremely unusual in a protocol containing one or more reflection responses and suggests the presence of a marked conflict concerning self-image and self-value. *Proceed to Step 7.*

Case 1 Result: The subject's record contains one MOR answer, which is actuarially meaningless but the content of the response may have some importance.

Step 7:   Read the MOR responses to determine if any include a clear projected representation of negative features regarding the self.

Potential Finding 1:   Some MOR answers are common, such as animals in a fight that have been hurt (Card II) or an animal that has been run over (Card VI). They should not be disregarded as being meaningless but any hypotheses generated from them should be considered as *very* tentative and not accepted into the final summary unless cross-validated by other data.

Potential Finding 2:   In some protocols, a key word occurs repeatedly in the MOR answers (e.g., dying, broken, battered, ruined). The cumulative use of such a word can be an important clue regarding the conceptualization of the self. This sort of finding should be used cautiously in the interpretation and not overemphasized unless it is supported from other data sources.

Potential Finding 3:   Some MOR responses are unique and/or dramatic and may provide a rich input to the understanding of self-image. In many instances, these more unique or dramatic answers also have a minus form quality, which tends to increase the likelihood that the answer is a direct projected representation of the self. *Proceed to Step 8.*

Case 1 Result: The subject's one MOR answer, Response 20 to Card IX, is somewhat dramatic and, in fact, is scored minus:

> Oh, like a pot boiling over. (Inquiry) Well, if you've ever left a pot on the stove too long, maybe like cooking cabbage, I did that once, it looks like this, a mess, flames and cabbage all over, see the orange is the flames and the green is the cabbage and the pink is like the burner.

The most obvious translation of this projection focuses on her current state of overload. She is in disarray and having difficulties with controls. A more subtle implication is that something has been ruined by neglect. Although this might relate to her broken marriage, it could also convey something of her current sense of self; that is, neglect has caused her disarray. These postulates are reviewed again as the interpretive search continues.

Step 8:   Read through all minus responses. As noted earlier, there is reason to believe that some minus responses are the product of projection. As such, they often can provide very useful insights into self-image or self-value. However, some minus responses may not be products of projection. They could result from faulty processing or mediation. Thus, it is important to emphasize that the content of the minus answers should be approached very conservatively.

Projected material, especially in minus answers, should be rather obvious. If it is not, the answer should be disregarded because attempts to glean meanings from contents that are not clear become counterproductive to the interpretive process. The minus answers should be read in order and the accumulated postulates summarized after the last one has been reviewed.

Potential Finding 1:   There are no minus responses in the record. *Proceed to Step 9.*

Potential Finding 2:   None of the contents of minus answers include obvious projected material. *Proceed to Step 9.*

Potential Finding 3:   In some cases, a substantial proportion of the minus answers cluster for the content coding, such as *An* or *Sc.* When that occurs, it can be assumed that a preoccupation is being manifest through the projective process.

Potential Finding 4:   Some or all minus answers contain obvious projected material, and these should be used as a source to create postulates or enhance existing postulates. *Proceed to Step 9.*

Case 1 Result: There are two minus responses in the subject's record. The first occurs to Card IV, Response 9:

> There's two lions here too, one on each side. (Inquiry) They are just standing there, see one on each side with the long tail sticking out, see this is the head and the body, just like two lions.

This response has no obvious meaning even though it is given to an unusual location area. Thus, it does not contribute to the formation or enhancement of hypotheses concerning self-image. The second minus answer, Response 20 given to Card IX (pot boiling over), has already been reviewed and postulates formulated from it. Therefore, this step fails to produce any new information for this case.

Step 9: Read through all of the movement responses, developing postulates concerning self-image when they can be appropriately formulated on the basis of obvious projected self-representation. Usually, these answers should be reviewed by studying the human movement (M) responses first because direct self-representation is more likely to be obvious if human content is involved. Once the M answers have been evaluated, the animal movement (FM) answers should be reviewed and then the inanimate movement m responses.

It is important to stress the need for conservatism in generating hypotheses from movement responses. The stimulus features of some blots tend to provoke movement classifications. This is especially true in Cards II ($DS3$, rocket taking off), III ($D1$, people lifting or pulling), V (W, a winged animal in flight), and IX ($D3$, clowns or monsters leaning or fighting). If postulates are formed because of movement answers to these areas, generally they should be based mainly on the presence of more unusual or idiographic features that are included in the answers.

Potential Finding 1: Most protocols contain between four and eight movement answers. Nonetheless, it is possible that the number of movement answers is less than expected and/or that none might be particularly revealing. If this occurs it is inappropriate to attempt the formulation of postulates. *Proceed to Step 10.*

Potential Finding 2: In many instances projected material manifests most directly in the homogeneity of the features of numerous movement answers, such as most being passive, aggressive, markedly emotional, and so on. The probable validity of hypotheses generated from movement content usually can be estimated by using repetition as a basis. In other words, the more often a theme or characteristic occurs among the answers, the more likely it reflects a dimension of self-image or self-esteem. Ordinarily, the more valid postulates are confirmed by significant structural findings.

Potential Finding 3: In some cases the material in one answer may appear inconsistent or even contradictory with the material in other answers. If this occurs, no postulate should be discarded prematurely. Each should be afforded consideration during the summary of findings from the entire cluster, and possibly reconsidered during the summary of the complete interpretation. *Proceed to Step 10.*

Case 1 Result: *The subject's record contains three M's (Responses 6, 7, and 14)* plus four FM and three m answers (Responses 2, 3, 5, 8, 9, 18, and 20). The three human movement answers are:

   6. Oh, that's a funny one, it looks like a lady looking in the mirror at herself. (Inquiry) She's like bending inward to get a better look at herself, she has a big

purse in her hand and her hair is pulled back tight, see her high heels and some jewelry or something at her neck.

7. These things look like red devils that are falling, I don't know what this center thing is. (Inquiry) Well you see little red devils now and then in cartoons and they are like this but they look like they are falling here, like upside down with their long tails out behind them.

14. Children, two children, looking at each other, they are cute I like this one. (Inquiry) It's just the upper parts of them, like the chest and the heads and they are like twins, girls, see the hair is all fixed up pretty on top like you do with a comb.

All three involve passive movement and two of the three focus on inspecting behaviors (looking in the mirror at herself, looking at each other). The two containing real human figures are adorned (big purse, high heels, jewelry; cute, the hair is all fixed up pretty). The passivity suggests that she may not like to make decisions. The inspecting behaviors probably relate to considerable self-focusing behavior, and the adornments could relate to her need to perceive herself quite favorably. The third answer seems to convey feelings of helplessness or loss of control, although it is interesting to note that the characters are not real. They are red devils, which she later clarifies as cartoon characters. This could signal a tendency to deny or neutralize unfavorable experiences.

The four *FM* responses are:

3. Oh wow, a couple of bears stepping in a bucket of paint or something, like black bears getting into trouble. (Inquiry) Well this part is the bears, kind of bent over see their feet are in this red bucket down here and they are getting red paint all over them and they are touching their paws together up here, just like they play like in Yellowstone Park, I've seen it on the TV.

8. Yuck, it's like two snakes on the sides. (Inquiry) See here like they are coiled up with their heads looking around, I don't like snakes at all, see this is the head and here is the tail.

9. There's two lions here too, one on each side. (Inquiry) They are just standing there, see one on each side with the long tail sticking out, see this is the head and the body, just like two lions.

18. Oh this way the side designs look like an animal and he's crawling over things and there's water and he can see himself in it. (Inquiry) Well here's the little animal, see his head and body and little legs and it's like he's stepping carefully over these other things, I don't know what but this would be water and he can see himself in it, see like reflected down here.

Response 3 is the most elaborate. Playing and getting into trouble usually occurs as the result of faulty judgment and could raise a question about maturity. The next two are passive. Neither is especially dramatic but Response 8, "snakes . . . coiled up with their heads looking around," hints about some preparatory defensiveness. Response 18 is the second reflection answer, adding support about the excessive self-focusing, but it may be more important because of other features. It is a "little animal with little legs . . . stepping carefully." Again, there is a hint of preparatory defensiveness or cautiousness.

The three *m* answers include Response 20 (pot boiling over), which has already been reviewed. The remaining two are:

2. If I turn it this way it looks like a funny ghost house, like it is blowing in the wind. (Inquiry) Oh, it's like in cartoons when you see the spooky ghost houses

and they sort of move like the wind was blowing, see the windows aren't square and the funny shape creates that impression to me, this part is the chimney.

5. You know if I cover everything but this part it looks like a forest fire way off on a mountain top. (Inquiry) Well it's way off in the distance and the red is the fire and the darker part is the mountain, it's burning on the side and near the top.

It is not surprising that all three convey a marked sense of vulnerability and loss of control. She seems to attempt to neutralize and/or detach from some of the affective experience. The ghost house is "like in cartoons," and the forest fire is "way off in the distance." This may relate to an attempt to deny the intense affective turmoil that she is experiencing but also suggests that the attempt has only limited success.

Step 10:   Review any responses that have not been read for special embellishments that may reflect some added direct projected self-representation.

Potential Finding 1:   All responses containing embellishments have been read in conjunction with movement answers or special scores. *Proceed to the next cluster in the interpretive routine.*

Potential Finding 2:   Some responses that have not been read may contain dramatic or unusual words or may include some special embellishments that tend to depart from the task at hand. Such findings should be used very cautiously and usually can be merged with other hypotheses or conclusions. However, in some records, especially those that are impoverished for movement answers or special scores, the accumulation of embellishments or unusual wording can sometimes generate hypotheses regarding self-concept that might not be formulated otherwise. *Proceed to the next cluster in the interpretive routine.*

Case 1 Result: In the subject's record, there is no special accumulation of unusual wording or special embellishments that have not already been reviewed.

CASE 1 SUMMARY: SELF-PERCEPTION

The data of this cluster have yielded several important findings. First, and most important, is the presence of the strongly embedded narcissistic-like feature. She greatly overestimates her self-value, and one by-product of this is her tendency to focus much more on herself than on others. This finding also signifies that, generally, she externalizes responsibility, especially for negative events, and tends to avoid and/or deny unpleasantness. One direct consequence is that her interpersonal relationships usually will be more tenuous and less mature. Emotional losses or rejections often have a greater impact on people such as this because they are perceived as insults to the inflated, overglorified sense of personal value.

She does appear to do some self-examining; however, this may represent an attempt to take distance from emotions that are painful or difficult to control. Her self-concept appears to be based much more on imagination than on real experience, a finding that is not surprising in light of her need to defend her exaggerated sense of personal worth. She is acutely aware of her current difficulties with control and is experiencing significant feelings of helplessness, but she also seems to be attempting to deny the intensity of the experience. She is quite cautious and apparently feels that she must be defensively prepared. She is likely the type of person who prefers a more passive role. This issue should be addressed further during the review of the next cluster.

INTERPERSONAL PERCEPTION AND RELATIONS

It is difficult to glean information from the Rorschach about how a subject perceives others and/or relates to them. Most variables that relate to interpersonal perception are also representations of the subject. The variables in this cluster do not relate to self-image or self-value. Instead, they represent some needs, attitudes, sets, and coping styles that often exist in people. As such, they can be quite influential in forming perceptions of the subject's environment and interactions with it. Unfortunately, however, none of the test data reveal information about the subject's real environment or about those with whom the subject interacts. Thus, some postulates generated from this data set tend to be much more inferential and often more general than are those derived from the other clusters. The Case 1 structural data for this cluster and a list of responses to be reviewed are shown in Table 46.

Step 1: Review the value for the Coping Deficit Index (CDI) to determine if there is a predisposition to social/interpersonal problems.

Potential Finding 1: If the value of the CDI is 3 or less, the finding is actuarially meaningless. *Proceed to Step 2.*

Potential Finding 2: If the value of the CDI is 4 or 5, the subject is probably less socially mature than might be expected. This type of person is prone to experience frequent difficulties when interacting with the environment, which often extend into the interpersonal sphere. Thus, interpersonal relationships tend to be more superficial and less easily sustained. Positive CDI people are often regarded by others as being more distant, guarded, inept, or helpless in their dealing with

Table 46.   **Interpersonal Perception Variables for Case 1**

STRUCTURAL VARIABLES	RESPONSES TO BE READ
CDI = 3 HVI = 0+1	MOVEMENT WITH PAIR = 3, 7, 8, 9, 14
$a{:}p$ = 4:6 T = 3 Fd = 3	HUMAN CONTENTS = 6, 7, 13, 14
Isolate/R = 0.12	
Total Human Contents = 4	
PER = 4 COP = 1 AG = 0	

others, and tend to be less sensitive to the needs and interests of others. Positive CDI people often have histories marked by social chaos and interpersonal dissatisfaction. In some instances they tend to back away from social intercourse and settle for a routine of limited, superficial relationships. When that does not happen, their ineptness makes them quite vulnerable to rejections by others. *Proceed to Step 2.*

Case 1 Result: The subject's CDI value is 3.

Step 2:   Review the Hypervigilance Index (HVI) to determine if the tendency to be overly cautious and conservative in relationships with others might be a manifestation of a core personality feature.

Potential Finding 1:   If the HVI is negative, the data are meaningless. *Proceed to Step 3.*

Potential Finding 2:   If the HVI is positive, a hypervigilant style can be assumed to exist as a core element of the subject's psychological structure. The hypervigilant person uses considerable energy to maintain a relatively continuous state of preparedness. This anticipatory or hyperalert state seems to have its origins in a negative or mistrusting attitude toward the environment. People such as this probably feel quite vulnerable and, as a consequence, formulate and implement behaviors very cautiously. They are quite preoccupied with issues of personal space and very guarded in their interpersonal relationships. Typically, they do not have sustained close relationships unless they feel in control of the interactions. They do not expect closeness and often become very suspicious about gestures of closeness by others. Although this feature is not necessarily pathological, exacerbations of it often produce paranoid-like manifestations. *Proceed to Step 3.*

Case 1 Result: The subject's HVI is negative.

Step 3:   Review the active to passive movement ($a : p$) ratio to determine if the subject is stylistically prone to assume a more passive role in interpersonal relationships.

Potential Finding 1:   If the value for passive movement is less than or no more than 1 point greater than the value for active movement, the finding is not significant. *Proceed to Step 4.*

Potential Finding 2:   If the value for passive movement exceeds the value for active movement by more than 1 point, it indicates that the subject generally assumes a more passive, *but not necessarily submissive,* role in interpersonal relationships. Subjects such as this usually prefer to avoid responsibility for decision making and are less prone to search out new solutions to problems or initiate new patterns of behavior. Findings for other variables in this cluster may be important in attempting to discern how the passive style is most commonly manifest in behavior. *Proceed to Step 4.*

Case 1 Result: The value for passive movement exceeds that for active movement by more than 1, signaling the presence of a marked passive style. The subject is the type of person who prefers to let others take the lead and the responsibility for decision making and typically prefers a *status quo* existence.

Step 4:   Review the value for Food (*Fd*) responses to ascertain if there may be some unusual dependency orientation that can affect interpersonal relationships.

Potential Finding 1:   The value for *Fd* is expected to be 0 except in the records of children where the presence of one food answer is not uncommon. If the *Fd* value is 0 (or no more than 1 in the record of a child), there is no evidence from which to speculate the presence of an unusual dependency orientation. *Proceed to Step 5.*

Potential Finding 2:   If the value for *Fd* is greater than 0 in the record of an adolescent or adult, or greater than 1 in the record of a child, the subject can be expected to manifest many more dependency behaviors than usually expected. People such as this tend to rely on others for direction and support and tend to be somewhat more naïve in their expectations concerning interpersonal relationships. In other words, they tend to expect others to be more tolerant of their needs and demands and more willing to act in accord with those needs and demands. If this finding is positive for a subject who also has a passive style, it is reasonable to conclude that a passive-dependent feature is an important core component in the personality structure of the subject. *Proceed to Step 5.*

Case 1 Result: The subject has three *Fd* answers, indicating a very marked dependency orientation in her relationships with others. In light of her passive style, this signifies that many of her interpersonal relationships will be marked by passive-dependent behaviors.

Step 5:   Review the value for Texture (*T*) responses to determine how the experience of needs for closeness may influence interpersonal perceptions and/or behaviors.

Potential Finding 1:   The value for *T* is expected to be 1 for most subjects. The exceptions are children below the age of nine who may fail to articulate tactile impressions. The presence of a single *T* response suggests that the subject experiences needs for closeness in ways similar to most other people. When considered in the context of interpersonal perception and behavior, it suggests that the subject probably is as amenable to close relationships with others as are most people. *Proceed to Step 6.*

Potential Finding 2:   If the value for *T* is 0, it suggests that the subject's experienced needs for closeness are dissimilar to those of most people. *It does not mean that the subject fails to have such needs.* Instead, it indicates that the subject is more conservative in close interpersonal situations than might be expected, especially those involving tactile exchange. People who are *T*-less tend to be overly concerned with personal space and much more cautious about creating or maintaining close emotional ties with others. If this finding is positive in a young child, these postulates should be reviewed in the context of all other available information concerning interpersonal relationships before being accepted or rejected. *Proceed to Step 6.*

Potential Finding 3: A value for *T* that is greater than 1 indicates the presence of very strong needs for closeness. In most cases, the greater than expected intensity of these need experiences has been provoked by a recent emotional loss, but not always. A positive finding could represent a more chronic state that may have been initiated by a loss or disappointment and perpetuated because the loss was never compensated or replaced. People who have these stronger need experiences tend to seek out relationships with others and often become more vulnerable to the manipulations of others. This is especially true for those who are either passive or dependent. *Proceed to Step 6.*

Case 1 Result: As noted in the review of previous clusters, this subject gave three *T* responses. When considered in the context of her interpersonal world, it seems very likely that her strong needs for closeness cause her to strive for relationships that not only reduce those needs, but also permit her to function in a passive-dependent manner while providing some reassurance to her exaggerated estimates concerning personal worth. Obviously, this motivational composite increases her vulnerability to the manipulations of others.

Step 6: Examine the value for the total number of human contents— *H* + *(H)* + *Hd* + *(Hd)*—to obtain some estimate of interest in people. The records of adults and children over the age of eight usually contain between five and seven human contents.

Potential Finding 1: If the total numer of human contents is in the average range it can be assumed that the subject is as interested in others as are most people. *Proceed to Step 7.*

Potential Finding 2: If the total number of human contents is less than average, the subject may not be as interested in others as are most people. This finding is often positive for those who are emotionally withdrawn or socially isolated from their environment. *Proceed to Step 7.*

Potential Finding 3: If the total number of human contents is greater than average, it signifies a strong interest in others. Although this finding often is positive and signifies a healthy interest in people, it can reflect a marked sense of guardedness in some. The latter is especially true for hypervigilant subjects who harbor a strong sense of mistrust for others. *Proceed to Step 7.*

Case 1 Result: The subject gave only four human contents, suggesting that she is not as strongly interested in others as might be expected, particularly in light of her strong needs for closeness. This probably relates to her excessive involvement with herself.

Step 7: Review the number of Personal (PER) responses in the record. They correlate with the use of a form of intellectual authoritarianism to ward off challenges from others. Most people do this from time to time; thus, one PER answer is expected in most protocols, but more than two is unusual.

Potential Finding 1: If the value for PER is 2 or less, the finding should be regarded as nonsignificant. *Proceed to Step 8.*

Potential Finding 2: If the value for PER is 3, the subject tends to be more defensively authoritarian in interpersonal situations than are most people. This does not necessarily impair interpersonal relationships but does signal that the subject is probably less secure in situations involving challenges than might be preferred. *Proceed to Step 8.*

Potential Finding 3: If the value for PER exceeds 3, the subject is most likely quite insecure about his or her personal integrity and tends to be overly authoritarian or argumentative when interpersonal situations appear to pose challenges to the self. People such as this are usually regarded as rigid or narrow by others. Thus, they often have difficulties in maintaining close relationships, especially with those who are not submissive to them. *Proceed to Step 8.*

Case 1 Result: The PER value is 4 in this protocol, indicating that the subject is less secure about herself in interpersonal relationships than are most people and often attempts to conceal this by using a more intellectually authoritarian or argumentative approach to issues.

Step 8: Review the values for cooperative movement (COP) and aggressive movement (AG) responses to obtain some information about sets that the subject may have concerning interactions among people. About 80% of all nonpatient subjects give at least one COP response, and values of 1 or 2 usually have limited interpretive significance. When the COP value is 0 or more than 2, however, some important hypotheses can be drawn concerning the interpersonal perceptions and behaviors of the subject. Similarly, about 70% of all nonpatient subjects have AG values of 0 or 1, and little interpretive significance can be attached to them. AG values of 2 or more are significant and suggest that the subject tends to view interpersonal relationships as being routinely marked by some manifestations of aggression. This does not mean that the aggressiveness is perceived as asocial or antisocial. On the contrary, the subject may perceive the aggression as a regular part of everyday behavior. The data for these two variables often are enriched when they are studied together.

Potential Finding 1: If the value for COP is 0 and the value for AG is 0 or 1, the subject probably does not perceive or anticipate positive interactions among people as a routine event. About 20% of all nonpatients give no COP answers. People such as this tend to feel less secure or less comfortable in interpersonal situations, and they are often regarded by others as being distant or aloof. This does not preclude mature and/or deep relationships with others, but, in general, these people are not perceived by others as being noticeably gregarious and they often remain more in the periphery during group interactions. *Proceed to Step 9.*

Potential Finding 2:   If the value for COP is 0 or 1 and the value for AG is 2, the subject probably tends to perceive aggressiveness as a natural manifestation in interpersonal relationships. Subjects such as this are likely to emit more aggressive behaviors than do those with lower AG values. The specific characteristics of the aggressive pattern (i.e., whether it will be verbal or nonverbal, socially acceptable or asocial, etc.) varies considerably from subject to subject depending on many other personality variables. *Proceed to Step 9.*

Potential Finding 3:   If the value for COP is less than 3 and the value for AG exceeds 2, much of the interpersonal activity of the subject is likely to be marked by forceful and/or aggressive types of behavior that are usually obvious to the frequent observer. These behaviors often represent a defensive tactic designed to contend with a sense of insecurity or discomfort in interpersonal situations. The characteristics of the aggressiveness vary considerably depending on other personality variables, as well as the nature of the environmental situation. *Proceed to Step 9.*

Potential Finding 4:   If the value for COP is 1 or 2 and the value for AG is 0 or 1, it can be assumed that the subject generally perceives positive interactions among people as routine and is willing to participate in them. Specific characteristics of the patterns of interaction usually are defined by other features of the subject, such as coping styles and self-image. *Proceed to Step 9.*

Potential Finding 5:   If the value for COP is 2 or 3 and the value for AG is 2, it suggests that the subject is open and interested in positive interaction, but that many of the interactions are marked by more aggressive forms of exchange. About 17% of the nonpatients give two AG answers, but more than two-thirds of those subjects also give at least one COP answer, and more than half give two COP responses. Thus, many subjects who perceive forms of aggressiveness as a natural mode of exchange between people also anticipate that exchanges generally will be positive. *Proceed to Step 9.*

Potential Finding 6:   If the value for COP is 3 or more and the value for AG is 0 or 1, or if the value for COP is more than 3 and the value for AG is 2 or less, the subject probably is regarded by others as likable and outgoing. Subjects such as this often view interpersonal activity as a very important part of their daily routine and are usually identified by those around them as among the more gregarious in group interactions. Usually, they anticipate and seek out harmonious interactions with others. *Proceed to Step 9.*

Potential Finding 7:   A value for COP of 3 or more and an AG value that exceeds 2 is a very unusual finding and probably signals the presence of some conflict or confusion concerning the appropriate mode of interpersonal behavior. People such as this are likely to be less consistent and/or predictable in their interpersonal routines. *Proceed to Step 9.*

Case 1 Result: The subject's protocol contains one COP response and no AG answers. This suggests that she is probably open to interaction, and there is no evidence to suggest that her interpersonal behaviors are marked by obvious aggressive features. This is not an unexpected finding in light of previously developed hypotheses concerning both self-perception and interpersonal perception.

Step 9:   Review the Isolation Index for evidence of a lack of interest in social relationships, or of social isolation or withdrawal.

Potential Finding 1:   If the Isolation Index value is less than 25% of the number of responses (*R*), the finding is negative and no conclusions should be formulated. *Proceed to Step 10.*

Potential Finding 2:   Nearly 30% of nonpatients have an Isolation Index value that falls between 25 and 30% of *R*. A positive finding in this range usually identifies the person who is less involved in social interaction. It does *not* necessarily reflect social maladjustment or conflict. In most instances, it represents less interest in or possibly more timidity about social intercourse. When the latter is true, the value for COP usually is 3 or more, signifying that interest exists but participation is limited. *Proceed to Step 10.*

Potential Finding 3:   Only about 10% of nonpatients have an Isolation Index value that equals or exceeds one-third of *R*. When this finding is positive, it is very likely that the subject is socially isolated. Almost all subjects for whom this finding is positive have less than two COP responses. People such as this usually find it difficult to create and/or sustain smooth or meaningful interpersonal relationships. Although this finding does not necessarily indicate some pathological kind of withdrawal, that possibility should be carefully explored using other data sources. *Proceed to Step 10.*

Case 1 Result: The subject's Isolation Index value is less than 25% of *R*, and no conclusions are warranted.

Step 10:   Read through all movement responses that contain a coding for a pair (2). These answers have been read previously during the search for information regarding self-perception. Nonetheless, they should be reviewed again for two reasons. First, determine if there is any consistency or patterning in the interactions that are reported. Second, search for unusual words or word usage that might contribute to the formulation of postulates regarding social interaction.

Potential Finding 1:   If the responses lack consistency and fail to be particularly revealing because of word use, no hypotheses can be formulated. *Proceed to Step 11.*

Potential Finding 2:   If a noticeable consistency exists among all or most of the answers, an appropriate postulate should be formulated.

Potential Finding 3:   Sometimes words or word use will stand out in the overall context of the response. If this occurs, a conservative hypothesis may be formulated, *but not incorporated into the cluster summary unless it is clearly supported by other data. Proceed to Step 11.*

Case 1 Result: Five of the subject's movement answers are coded for a pair: Responses 3, 7, 8, 9, and 14. It seems striking that three of the five involve no social interaction (7. red devils falling, 8. snakes coiled up with their heads looking around, 9. lions just standing there). The fourth is passive with very limited social interaction, (14. two children looking at each other). The only one that contains more direct social exchange is somewhat juvenile, and the consequences of the interaction are negative (3. bears getting into trouble). If these answers represent the subject's interpersonal perceptions and/or expectations, it is difficult to avoid the postulate that she is interpersonally cautious and possibly even reluctant. None of the words or wording are especially dramatic, but she does preface two of the five answers with comments that are somewhat unusual for an adult in the test situation: "Oh wow" and "Yuck." Considered in the context of the juvenile movement response (3), they seem to add some support to the proposition that many of her interactions may be less mature than expected of an adult.

Step 11: Review all of the responses that contain human content, focusing on the nouns and adjectives that have been used to describe the human or human-like figures. Some of these data obviously relate to the self and have been reviewed earlier, but sometimes a redundancy may exist among human or human-like figures that has not been reported among movement answers or that, when added to those reported in movement responses, tends to convey some impression about how the subject perceives others.

Potential Finding 1: If most or all of the human or human-like figures have pleasant or positive features, this may suggest a favorable or optimistic attitude toward others. If most have unpleasant or negative features, this could indicate a more negativistic attitude toward others.

Potential Finding 2: In some cases most or all of the human contents are parenthesized. Just as this signifies that the self-conception is based more on imagination than experience, it also suggests that conceptions of others may be more illusory than real. *Proceed to the next cluster in the interpretive routine.*

Case 1 Result: Four answers contain human content, three of which have already been reviewed (6. a lady looking in the mirror, 7. red devils in cartoons, 14. two children . . . they're cute). The fourth is:

> 13. You know there are two dolls there too. (Inquiry) Well just this part, like in full gowns, I used to have one like this and I bought one like it for my daughter, see the full skirt and the head and the top of the body, there's one on each side.

There is no glaring consistency among these answers, but some similarities may exist. Only one is adult and two are unreal play objects. Three of the four are embellished in a positive but somewhat naïve manner. Although the data are sparse, they might be used as the basis for speculation that she prefers less sophisticated and less demanding relationships that are not threatening and are easily controlled.

CASE 1 SUMMARY: INTERPERSONAL PERCEPTION AND RELATIONS

The apparent passivity of the subject plus her very strong dependency orientation serve as focal results for this data set. She probably tends to seek out relationships that coincide with her passive-dependent style but that also afford some reassurance for her overglorified sense of personal worth. In other words, they must be both supportive and nurturing. Such relationships are, at best, difficult to achieve in the adult world and, unfortunately, usually increase one's vulnerability to the manipulations of others. It seems likely that she has some awareness of this, as findings suggest that she is less secure about her interpersonal relationships than are most people. She often attempts to contend with, or conceal these feelings of insecurity or discomfort by using a pseudo-intellectual authoritarian approach to many issues.

Although she is open to social interaction, she is also cautious and possibly even reluctant to initiate exchanges, especially those that may require more tact and sophistication, or those that may create unwanted demands on her or pose hazards regarding control of the situation. Overall, it is doubtful that many of her relationships are marked by maturity and/or depth.

CHAPTER 8

Cluster Interpretation: Affect

People's emotions are complex and often difficult to understand. Feelings permeate all psychological activity. They form a continuing chain of psychological events from birth to death. They intertwine with thinking and impact judgments, decisions, and all manner of behaviors. Sometimes they are subtle and other times intense. Sometimes they are easy to manage and direct, but, at other times, it is difficult to control the influence that they exert in forming or implementing behaviors.

The Rorschach variables that relate to emotion are less numerous and less direct than might be desired in a test designed to study the psychology of a person. The inferential hypotheses drawn from them must be integrated with care. The objective is to determine, to the extent possible, the role of emotion in the psychological organization and functioning of the subject. That role varies considerably from person to person, and numerous issues must be addressed when attempting to gather information concerning this complex psychological unit.

AFFECTIVE FEATURES

Some Rorschach variables that relate to affect also appear in other clusters, but they are addressed somewhat differently here. For instance, the Case 1 data concerning T, Pure C, and the number and types of blends have already been considered in evaluating the array of variables concerning situational stress at which time the data were used to discern some of the effects of the stress. These data are used again in an attempt to uncover a broader picture of the subject's emotional functioning. The relevant data from this cluster for Case 1 are shown in Table 47.

Table 47. Affect-Related Variables for Case 1

			BLENDS	
$EB = 3 : 8.0$	$EBPer = 2.7$	$DEPI = 4$		
$eb = 7 : 8$	$(C' = 3, T = 3, V = 0, Y = 2)$		FM.FC.FC'	m.CF.FD
$FC:CF+C = 4 : 5$	Pure $C = 2$		M.Fr	FC.M
$Afr = 0.56$	$CP = 0$		FM.Fr	FC.FY
$S = 2$	Col-Shd Bl = 3		m.CF	C.T

Beginning the Search: DEPI   The Depression Index (DEPI) actually is not part of the affect cluster. It consists of a variety of affective, cognitive, and interpersonal variables, yet it must always be considered when issues of affect are at hand. Thus, even before addressing the data sets that have been empirically established as being related to affect, the DEPI value should be reviewed.

If the DEPI is positive, either of two propositions should be stated and either one forms a cornerstone against which the data of the cluster are reviewed. The first is when the value for DEPI is 6 or 7. When this occurs it should be assumed that a significant affective problem exists that should be given careful consideration in any diagnostic formulation. Ordinarily, a DEPI value of 6 or 7 is the first positive Key variable and, as such, dictates the interpretive search routine. More often among psychiatric patients, the second proposition is required: When the value for DEPI is 5, this signifies that the personality organization of the subject tends to give rise to frequent and intense experiences of depression and/or affective disruption. This does not mean that the presenting symptoms include depression or affective complaints, or even that a final diagnosis should focus on affective disruption. It does indicate, however, that this feature is present and should not be disregarded or taken lightly in the overall evaluation.

The DEPI is not significant in Case 1; thus, the data regarding affect can be addressed without an initial proposition.

Major Issues: (1) Is the subject's emotion a core element in decision making and the behavioral implementation of those decisions, or are feelings more peripheral when coping or decision making occurs? (2) Is there any evidence of an unusual frequency of negative emotions? (3) To what extent is the subject willing to process emotional stimulation? (4) Are feelings controlled easily and effectively? (5) Do the subject's feelings create unusual sets toward the environment? (6) Is the subject confused about feelings?

Step 1:   Review the *Erlebnistypus* (*EB*) to ascertain whether evidence for an introversive or extratensive style exists. The *EB* reflects a distinct style only if the value on one side exceeds the other by 2 or more points when *EA* is 10 or less, or by more than 2 points when *EA* is greater than 10.

Potential Finding 1:   If the *EB* indicates the presence of an extratensive coping style it can be assumed that, ordinarily, the subject tends to intermingle feelings with thinking during problem solving or decision making activities. People such as this are more prone than others to use and be influenced by emotion and generally prefer to test postulates and assumptions through trial-and-error behaviors. In that trial-and-error behavior is a routine for extratensive subjects, they tend to become more tolerant and less concerned when problem solving errors occur. On the other hand, the emotional impact of chronic failure is often more intense than is usually the case for the nonextratensive subject. People with this style are more inclined to display feelings and often are less concerned about carefully modulating or controlling those displays. *Proceed to Step 2.*

Potential Finding 2:   If the *EB* indicates an introversive style it can be assumed that the subject usually prefers to keep feelings at a more peripheral level during problem solving and decision making. These subjects avoid trial-and-error behaviors when possible and rely more on internal evaluation than on external feedback in formulating judgments. They are prone to be less tolerant of problem solving errors than are nonintroversive people and, because of this, often exercise more caution in decision making than do others. Although they are willing to display feelings openly, they also are inclined to be more concerned about modulating or controlling those displays. *Proceed to Step 2.*

Potential Finding 3: If the *EB* fails to indicate a coping style (*ambitent*), it is likely that the subject's emotions are inconsistent in terms of their impact on thinking, problem solving, and decision making behaviors. In other words, the subject's thinking may be strongly influenced by feelings in one instance, whereas, in a second instance, even though similar to the first, emotions may play only a peripheral role. Because the role of emotions in psychological functioning is not very consistent, the subject is often more vulnerable to their effects. *Proceed to Step 3.*

Case 1 Result: The *EB* of 3:8.0 reveals that the subject is extratensive and, as such, tends to merge feelings with thinking in coping activities. She prefers a trial-and-error approach to problem solving and is disposed toward more open displays of her feelings.

Step 2: Review the value for *EBPer* to determine if the style is markedly pervasive in coping activity. The result affords a rough estimate regarding the dominance of the style in coping activity. The result is not a linear estimate of style pervasiveness, but can be used in a categorical predictive model. The presence of a pervasive style is not necessarily a liability, but does indicate the likelihood of less flexibility in coping and decision making activities.

Potential Finding 1: If the subject is introversive and the value for *EBPer* is less than 2.5, it can be postulated that, although the subject typically uses an ideational style involving delay while keeping feelings in abeyance before reaching a decision, instances do occur in which feelings contribute significantly to decisions. Conversely, if the value for *EBPer* is 2.5 or more, it is reasonable to assume that, in most instances, emotions play a very limited role in decision making activity. *Proceed to Step 3.*

Potential Finding 2: If the subject is extratensive and the value for *EBPer* is less than 2.5, the subject is prone to mix feelings with thinking *much of the time* when coping is required, but instances occur in which feelings are put aside in favor of a more clearly ideational approach. On the other hand, if the value for *EBPer* is equal to or greater than 2.5, it should be assumed that very little decision making occurs that is not markedly influenced by emotion. *Proceed to Step 3.*

Case 1 Result: The value for *EBPer* is 2.7, indicating that her extratensive style is very pervasive in her psychological activity and that, in most instances, emotion plays a significant role in her thinking and implementation of decisions. This lack of flexibility in coping and decision making activity should be weighed carefully in any intervention planning.

eb = Sum Fm + m : Sum all C', all T, all Y, all V

Step 3:   Review the values in the *eb* ratio to ascertain if some unusual distress experiences are occurring. The left-side value is always expected to be the greater number but instances may occur in which the right-side value, although lower than the left-side value, is inordinately high and should receive careful attention.

Potential Finding 1:   If the value of *es* is 11 or less, the left-side value of the *eb* is greater than the right-side value, the value for *T* does not exceed 1, the value for *C'* does not exceed 2, and the value for *V* does not exceed 0, no specific hypothesis is warranted. *Proceed to Step 4.*

Potential Finding 2:   If the value of *es* is 11 or less and the left-side value of the *eb* is greater than the right-side value, but the value for *T* exceeds 1, or the value for *C'* exceeds 2, or the value for *V* exceeds 0, or the value for *Y* exceeds 2, a hypothesis concerning experienced discomfort should be formulated that focuses on the variable(s) related to the discomfort. *Proceed to Step 4.*

Potential Finding 3:   If the total value of the *eb* is greater than 3 and the right-side value is greater than the left-side value, it should be assumed that the subject is in distress. Each variable contributing to the right-side value should be evaluated to discern the source(s) of the distress and an appropriate hypothesis formulated. *Proceed to Step 4.*

Case 1 Result: A higher right-side value exists in the *eb*, which has already been reviewed in the section dealing with situational stress.

Step 4:   Review the $FC:CF + C$ ratio and the value for Pure *C* to obtain information concerning the modulation of emotional discharges or displays. The *FC* response correlates with more well-controlled or modulated emotional experience, whereas the *CF* answers relate to less restrained or modulated forms of affective discharge. Pure *C* answers tend to correlate with the more unrestrained ventilation of feelings; however, it is important to note that the values for *CF* and *C* are considerably less reliable when studied separately than when studied as the unit *CF + C*. Most nonpatient adults give more, or at least as many *FC* as *CF + C* responses. On the other hand, younger subjects typically give more *CF* and *C* answers than *FC* responses.

Potential Finding 1:   If the value for *FC* is at least 1 point more than or as much as twice that of the *CF + C* value *and* the value for Pure *C* is zero, it can be assumed that the subject controls or modulates emotional discharge about as much as do most adults. This is an unexpected finding in the record of a subject younger than age 15 and suggests that more stringent controls are being exerted in contending with emotional display than is common among younger clients. *Proceed to Step 6.*

Potential Finding 2:   If the value for *FC* is more than twice but less than three times that of the *CF + C* value *and* the value for Pure *C* is 0, the subject tends to exert more stringent control of emotional discharges than is typical of most people. This is an extremely unusual finding in the record of a subject younger than age 15. *Proceed to Step 6.*

Potential Finding 3:   If the value for *FC* is three or more times that of the value for *CF + C and* the value for Pure *C* is 0, it should be assumed that the subject is much more overcontrolling of emotional displays than are most people. This finding usually indicates a fearfulness or mistrust of being involved in more intense affective displays. *Proceed to Step 6.*

Potential Finding 4:   If the value for *FC* is at least 1 point more or as much as twice that of the *CF + C* value *and* the value for Pure *C* is 1, it can be assumed that the subject usually modulates emotional discharge about as much as other adults do. In some instances, however, modulation lapses occur during which discharges are less well controlled than is the case for most adults. If this finding is positive in the record of a subject younger than age 15, it suggests that attempts at more stringent control tend to falter and may signal the presence of a conflict state concerning the use and control of emotion. *Proceed to Step 5.*

Potential Finding 5:   If the value for *FC* is more than twice the value for *CF + C and* the value for Pure *C* is 1 or more, this signifies that in most instances emotional displays are tightly modulated, but that the stringent controls are vulnerable to failure. People such as this usually have serious conflicts about emotion and at times these conflicts contribute to a breakdown of the routine efforts at stringent modulation. *Proceed to Step 5.*

Potential Finding 6:   If the record of an adult has an *FC* value that is at least 1 point more than or as much as twice that of the *CF + C* value *and* the value for Pure *C* is greater than 1, this indicates that, although the subject strives to modulate emotional discharge effectively, potentially serious lapses in modulation occur frequently. This is a very unusual finding in the protocol of an adult that should be reviewed in the context of control issues. This finding is not uncommon in the records of children or young adolescents and probably signals the presence of a conflict concerning the appropriate modulation of emotional display. *Proceed to Step 5.*

Potential Finding 7:   If the value for *CF + C* is equal to or as much as 2 points greater than the value for *FC and* the value for Pure *C* is 0 or 1, this signifies that the subject is somewhat less stringent about modulating emotional discharges than are most adults. This is not necessarily a negative finding for an adult, especially if there are no problems with controls. Instead, it reflects a person who tends to be more obvious or intense in expressing feelings than the average adult. Although this is a common finding for most adolescents and many younger children, it is not common for the introversive subject, regardless of age. *Proceed to Step 5 if a Pure* C *response has been given or Step 6 if the value for Pure* C *is 0.*

Potential Finding 8:   If the record of an adult has a value for *CF + C* that is equal to as or much as 2 points greater than the value for *FC and* the value for Pure *C* is greater than 1, this indicates some potentially serious modulation problems. People such as this are often overly intense in their emotional displays and frequently convey impressions of impulsiveness. This problem could be the product of control difficulties; however, it is equally possible that it reflects a less mature psychological organization in which the modulation of affect is not regarded as being very important. Findings such as this are very common among children and tend to represent the affective exuberance and limited modulation that frequently manifests in the behaviors of young subjects. However, this finding is extremely unusual among introversive subjects, regardless of age. If this finding is positive for the introversive subject, it is reasonable to hypothesize that the efficacy or integrity of the ideational style is impaired and often is "short-circuited" by other psychological operations. *Proceed to Step 5.*

Potential Finding 9:   If the value for *CF + C* is 3 or more points greater than the value for *FC and* the value for Pure *C* is 0, the subject modulates emotional discharges much less than others. Adults such as this frequently call attention to themselves because of the intensity with which they express feelings. This is not necessarily a liability as the effectiveness or ineffectiveness of the higher frequency of less restrained emotional displays is determined largely by the acceptability of the displays in the social environment. This finding is very common among younger adolescents and most children. *Proceed to Step 6.*

Potential Finding 10:   If the value for *CF + C* is 3 or more points greater than the value for *FC and* the value for Pure *C* is 1 or more, this reflects a significant laxness in modulating emotion. This finding is most common among younger children. Because it is an unusual finding among adults, such adults frequently are regarded by others as overly emotional and/or less mature. If this finding is positive for an introversive subject it signals a serious problem regarding the functioning and/or effectiveness of the style. *Proceed to Step 5.*

Case 1 Result: The *FC : CF + C* ratio is 4 : 5 and includes two Pure *C* responses, indicating that she has some potentially serious modulation problems. She probably tends to be overly intense when discharging and/or displaying her feelings and often may convey the impression of being impulsive. This is a particularly important finding in light of her extratensive style. People who tend to merge feelings and thinking become more vulnerable to flaws in judgment if the feelings are overly intense or not well modulated. Thus, her well-fixed coping style may be substantially less effective than she would prefer.

Step 5:   Read the Pure *C* responses in the record and evaluate the extent to which they represent a less mature or more primitive type of answer. Although Pure *C* responses reflect a lack of restraint, they vary considerably in their level of sophistication or lack thereof. Some are almost *CF* answers and, although they meet the appropriate coding criteria, are marked by a pseudo-intellectual quality. Responses involving abstract art or decorations often fall into this category. Others stand out because of their more primitive quality. The former suggest that the modulation failures are more subtle and probably more transient, whereas the latter are more likely to indicate forms of modulatory looseness that can easily give rise to behaviors that can be very maladaptive over time.

Potential Finding 1:   If all Pure *C* answers have a defensive and/or psuedo-intellectual quality, they should probably be considered similar to *CF* responses when evaluating whether a serious modulation problem exists. *Proceed to Step 6.*

Potential Finding 2:   If any Pure *C* response has a more childlike or primitive quality the finding should be considered as a significant liability except in the records of young children. This finding probably indicates that, when the modulation lapses occur, the resulting behaviors are likely to be inappropriate and potentially maladaptive. *Proceed to Step 6.*

Case 1 Result: Her two Pure *C* answers both occurred to Card X:

22. Oh my, so many things, like a painting of something, maybe like from *Alice in Wonderland.* (Inquiry) It's just so much and so pretty, just like a painting, an, a, a, abstract of *Alice in Wonderland* but Alice isn't there . . . Oh it's just all colors like an abstract painting of *Alice in Wonderland* would be.
25. That pink is gross, I thought it was blood but I think that it looks like the cotton candy you get at the fair. (Inquiry) It's just pink and fuzzy looking like cotton candy . . . You know, different colors make it look fuzzy, just like cotton candy, it's all sticky gooey if you get it on your fingers.

Response 22 has an intellectualized quality to it, even though somewhat naïve. Response 25 is much more primitive and probably is even more important because it also includes a tactile feature and is her last answer. Last answers often are important because they represent the last decision in the test, implying some sense of satisfaction with the completion of the task. This particular answer reeks of control problems, or at the very least of a level of judgment that is wanting. She notes that the area is "gross," raising a question about why she would bother to respond to it if it seems so negative. She makes matters worse by inserting a "denial" comment, "I thought it was blood. . . ." The nature of these responses, especially the second, appears to add support to the previously developed postulate that her rather pervasive extratensive coping style may be considerably less effective than she would prefer, and gives rise to the speculation that some of her affective displays probably are maladaptive.

Step 6:   Review the value for the *Afr* to obtain some estimate of the subject's interest and/or willingness to process emotional stimulation.

Potential Finding 1:   If the value for the *Afr* is in the average range, the subject appears to be as willing as most people to process emotional stimuli. Generally, this is not a significant finding; however, if the subject tends to have chronic difficulties with the modulation or control of emotion, it may indicate a naïve lack of awareness of either of those problems. Usually, when emotional stimuli are processed, some response or exchange is required. People who have difficulties with control often find it more beneficial to avoid emotional stimuli, thereby reducing demands made on them. *Proceed to Step 7.*

Potential Finding 2:   If the value of the *Afr* exceeds 0.85 for an adult, or is more than one *SD* above the mean for a younger subject, it indicates that the subject is very attracted by emotional stimulation. This finding is more common among extratensives but not exclusive to them. It should not be considered as a liability, but rather simply reflects a stronger interest in emotion. People such as this apparently are more intrigued with or reinforced by emotional stimuli. This can become a liability if they have problems with control and/or modulation, because the tendency to seek out emotional stimuli probably increases the frequency with which emotional exchanges are expected or required. *Proceed to Step 7.*

Potential Finding 3:   If the value for the *Afr* falls in the range from 0.53 to 0.44 for an adult, or is in the first *SD* below the mean for a younger subject, the subject is probably less interested in or less willing to process emotional stimuli. This finding is more common among introversive subjects but not exclusive to them. It should not be considered as a liability, but as a preference to be less involved with emotional stimuli. If other data indicate problems with modulation or control, this finding may signal some awareness of those problems and an inclination to avoid situations in which those difficulties might be exacerbated. *Proceed to Step 7.*

Potential Finding 4:   If the value for the *Afr* falls below 0.44 in the record of an adult, or is more than one *SD* below the mean for a younger subject, it indicates a marked tendency to avoid emotional stimuli. People such as this usually are quite uncomfortable around emotion and, as a result, often become much more socially constrained or even isolated. This finding is particularly important in the protocol of a child or adolescent because it suggests that many of the everyday exchanges that contribute to development are being avoided or approached with excessive caution. *Proceed to Step 7.*

Case 1 Result: The *Afr* of 0.56 falls in the average range, suggesting that she is probably as interested in and willing to process emotional stimuli as most adults.

Step 7:   Review the value for Color Projection (CP) to determine if unusual forms of denial may occur during unpleasant emotional experiences. The value for CP is always expected to be zero. Values greater than zero are extremely unusual and have special importance.

Potential Finding 1:   If the value for CP is 0, the finding is not significant. *Proceed to Step 8.*

Potential Finding 2:   A value for CP greater than 0 signifies that the subject often denies the presence of irritating or unpleasant emotion or emotional stimulation by substituting a false positive emotion or emotional value to the situation. This is a hysteroid-like process that disregards or violates reality. Typically, people who use this process feel very uncomfortable about their ability to deal adequately with negative feelings, and they frequently have problems in modulating their own affective displays. They often bend reality to avoid dealing with perceived or anticipated harshness in the environment, and as a result their interpersonal relationships are prone to suffer. *Proceed to Step 8.*

Case 1 Result: The value for CP is 0.

Step 8:   Review the value for S, and the sequencing of S responses, to determine if the emotional complex includes an unusual negativistic, oppositional, or angry set toward the environment. Most subjects give at least one S response, usually to Cards I or II, and two S answers is not uncommon.

Potential Finding 1:   If the value for S falls between 0 and 2 the finding is not significant. *Proceed to Step 9.*

Potential Finding 2:   If the value for S is 3, and all S responses were given to the first two blots, the subject was probably not well prepared to take the test and responded negativistically to the demands of the situation. Although this may reflect some unusual oppositionality, it is more parsimonious to assume that the negativism is situationally related. *Proceed to Step 9.*

Potential Finding 3:   If the value for S is 4 or 5, and all S answers were given to the first three blots, the subject was quite irritated by the test situation. This probably reflects a tendency to be excessively oppositional when confronted with unwanted challenge but also could reflect a more enduring negative set toward authority. *Proceed to Step 9.*

Potential Finding 4:   If the value for S is 3, and at least one S answer occurred after Card II, the subject probably is disposed to be more negativistic or oppositional toward the environment than are most people. This is not necessarily a liability, but can become detrimental to the formation of harmonious social relationships. *Proceed to Step 9.*

Potential Finding 5:   If the value for S is 4 or more, and at least one S answer was given after Card III, it indicates the presence of a very negative, angry attitude toward the environment. This is a trait-like feature that has some impact on psychological functioning. This does not necessarily mean that the anger will be manifest overtly in the subject's behaviors, but it has some influence on the subject's decision making and coping activities. People such as this often have difficulty sustaining deep and/or meaningful relationships with others as they are prone to be less tolerant of the routine compromises usually required in social intercourse. If problems in control and/or modulation exist, it is likely that the subject's more intense affective displays include some manifestations of the subject's highly negativistic set. *Proceed to Step 9.*

Case 1 Finding: The record contains two S responses, which is not a significant finding.

Step 9:   Review the number of blends in the record to obtain an estimate of the subject's psychological complexity. The expected number of blends differs in relation to *EB*. Introversive subjects tend to give fewer blends than extratensives or ambitents. Typically, about 20% of their responses are blends, and it is somewhat unusual for the proportion to exceed 25% of *R*. The average range for introversive subjects falls between 13 and 26%. Extratensives generally give records in which about 25% of the answers are blends, and it is not unusual for the proportion to be as high as 33% of *R*. The average range for extratensives is from 19 to 33%. Blends given by ambitent subjects also average about 25% of *R* but it is not unusual for the proportion to exceed 35%. The average range for this group is between 16 and 36%.

Potential Finding 1:   If the proportion of blends is in the average range in relation to *EB,* it can be assumed that the level of psychological complexity is not unlike that of others who have a similar style orientation. *Proceed to Step 10.*

Potential Finding 2:   If the proportion of blends in the record falls below the average range in relation to *EB,* it suggests that the subject's psychological functioning is less complex than usual. This is not uncommon for subjects who have Lambda values exceeding 0.99, as their basic style is oriented to avoid complexity. Nonetheless, this finding suggests that some psychological impoverishment may create difficulties in dealing with complex emotional stimuli. If these difficulties occur, they are most likely to manifest in the modulation of emotional displays. *Proceed to Step 10.*

Potential Finding 3:   If the proportion of blends is greater than average in relation to *EB,* the subject's psychological functioning probably is more complex than ordinarily expected. Most blends involve one or more variables related to affect, thus in most instances, the unexpected complexity has an emotional basis. This is not necessarily a liability, provided the subject has considerable resource available to contend with the broad array of emotional experience. If available resources are more limited, however, or if problems in control and/or modulation exist, the complexity of functioning increases the possibility that affect can have detrimental influence on the subject's behavioral consistency and/or stability. *Proceed to Step 10.*

Case 1 Result: The record contains eight blends, constituting 32% of *R*. This proportion falls in the average range for extratensive subjects and suggests that her psychological functioning is probably not more complex than that of most adults with this style.

Step 10:   Tally the number of blends that are created *exclusively* by the presence of *m* and/or *Y* variables, such as *FC.FY, m.CF,* and so on. In most records, one or two such blends are common, but if the number exceeds two, conclusions derived in Step 9 may need to be modified.

Potential Finding 1:   If the number of blends created exclusively by the presence of *m* or *Y* variables is two or less, the finding is not significant and the conclusions derived from Step 9 should be considered valid. *Proceed to Step 11.*

Potential Finding 2:   If the number of blends created exclusively by the presence of *m* and *Y* variables is greater than two, and a subtraction of all but two of those blends yields a proportion of *R* that falls in a different range than established in Step 9, the conclusion derived from Step 9 should be appropriately modified. The modification should include the notation that the current level of complexity has been increased by the presence of situationally-related variables and that less complexity can be expected when those variables are not present. *Proceed to Step 11.*

Case 1 Result: Only two blends (*FC.FY, m.CF*) in the record are created exclusively by the critical variables. Thus, there is no reason to modify the conclusion derived from Step 9.

Step 11:   Review the complexity of the blends in the record to determine if unusual levels of complexity exist that might not be reflected adequately in the Step 9 finding. Approximately three of every four blends involve only two determinants. About one in four have three determinants. It is extremely unusual for a blend to have more than three determinants.

Potential Finding 1:   If no more than one-fourth of the blends contain three determinants, the finding is not significant. *Proceed to Step 12.*

Potential Finding 2:   If more than one-fourth of the blends contain three determinants, or if the record contains one or more blends that include four or more determinants, the conclusion derived from Step 9 should be modified. The modification should include a notation to the effect that, at times, the subject's psychological functioning is inordinately complex. This added complexity is almost always the result of emotional experience. Although this is not necessarily a liability, it can easily contribute to dysfunction, especially if resources are limited or if problems in control and/or modulation exist. *Proceed to Step 12.*

Case 1 Result: Two blends in the subject's record contain three determinants; however, they constitute one-fourth of the blends, so no modification of the Step 9 conclusion is required.

Step 12:   Review the listing of blends to determine if any are Color-Shading blends, which tend to equate with ambivalence or confusion about feelings.

Potential Finding 1:   If there are no Color-Shading blends in the record, *proceed to Step 13.*

Potential Finding 2:   If there is one or more Color-Shading blend, and each is created by the presence of a *Y* variable, it can be assumed that some confusion about feelings exists, but probably as the result of situationally-related events.

Potential Finding 3:   If there is one or more Color-Shading blend in the record, and at least one is created by the presence of a *C', T,* or *V* variable, it should be hypothesized that the subject often is confused by emotion and may frequently experience both positive and negative feelings about the same stimulus situation. People such as this often experience feelings more intensely than others and sometimes have more difficulty bringing closure to emotional situations. This tends to be more common among extratensive subjects, probably because they are more routinely involved with feelings than are others. If this finding is positive for introversive subjects, the impact is probably more disruptive because they are less accustomed to the experience and may have greater difficulty seeking resolution of an issue. *Proceed to Step 13.*

Case 1 Result: The subject's record contains three Color-Shading blends, only one of which can be attributed easily to situational factors. It would appear that she is often plagued by confusion concerning her feelings. This probably has some relationship to the previously noted difficulties with modulation.

Step 13:   Review the listing of blends to determine if any are Shading blends, such as *FT.FC', FV.FY,* and so on. Shading blends are very unusual and never expected.

Potential Finding 1:   If no Shading blends have been given, *proceed to the next cluster in the interpretive routine.*

Potential Finding 2:   If one or more Shading blends have been given, this signals the presence of intensely negative, probably painful emotion. It is impractical to speculate about the source of the negative affect from the coding but it can be concluded that the presence of this kind of intense irritation creates a very disruptive impact on most affective functioning. In other words, it tends to dominate the subject's affective experiences and can become pervasive in influencing thinking. *Proceed to the next cluster in the interpretive routine.*

Case 1 Result: There are no Shading blends in the record.

Case 1 Summary

It seems clear that she is the type of person who uses her emotions a great deal to contend with coping demands and is not very flexible about discarding this style in favor of another approach, even though another approach may be more effective in a given situation. Routinely, she merges her feelings with her thoughts and, thus, much of her decision making is marked by intuitive features. She prefers to test her decisions through trial-and-error activity and is probably not very reluctant to display her feelings.

Unfortunately, the effectiveness of this style is probably impeded by the fact that she is an overly intense person who does not modulate her emotional discharges as much as most adults. As a result, her thinking tends to be vulnerable to judgments that may be excessively influenced by feelings, and it is likely that she often conveys the impression of being impulsive. Some of her emotional structure appears to be more childlike or primitive than is expected for an adult, which creates a marked potential for ineffective or maladaptive emotional behaviors.

On a more positive note, she is no more oriented to involvements with emotional stimuli than are most adults, and she does not appear to have any unusual negative emotional sets toward her environment. Her psychological functioning is marked by considerable emotional complexity, but probably no more so than might be expected in light of her basic coping style. Unfortunately, she is often confused by her feelings. This feature may relate directly to her problems with modulation, but it may have more extensive origins, such as her chronic struggle to maintain her overglorified self-value while creating and sustaining profitable dependency relationships with others.

CHAPTER 9

Cluster Interpretation: The Cognitive Triad

The cognitive triad consists of three clusters that are relatively independent of each other, yet often closely related. They include *information processing* (the procedures involving the input of information), *cognitive mediation* (the procedures of translating or identifying information that has been input), and *ideation* (the procedures of conceptualizing the information that has been translated). Each is related to a relatively distinct element of cognition, but the results of the operations in one element can directly influence the operations in either of the other elements, and collectively they reflect a continuous process that forms the basis for essentially all deliberate and/or meaningful behaviors. The process can be illustrated simply as:

INPUT → TRANSLATION → CONCEPTUALIZATION
(PROCESSING)   (MEDIATION)   (IDEATION)

In reality, a circular illustration might be more appropriate because, in many instances, conceptual sets influence the tactics applied in processing.

The interrelationships among the processes require that the three clusters be studied collectively. Optimally, the triad is approached by beginning with processing, then reviewing mediation, and ending with the data concerning ideation. This search order may not always be practical and, in some cases, it is reversed because findings concerning ideation may be critically important in forming the cornerstone for understanding the subject. Regardless of whether the review of the triad begins with processing or ideation, it is important to remember that the findings from each cluster often provide important clarification for the findings from the other two clusters.

INFORMATION PROCESSING

Although all variables in the information processing cluster are interrelated, they also consist of two subclusters. One affords some information regarding processing effort or motivation (Lambda, OBS, HVI, *Zf*, $W:D:Dd$, $W:M$), whereas the second provides more information about the quality and efficiency of the processing (*DQ, Zd*, PSV, sequencing).

The Case 1 data for the information processing cluster are shown in Table 48.

Major Issues: (1) What sort of effort does the subject put forth in processing information related to problem solving or decision making? (2) Is the quality,

Table 48.   Information Processing Variables for Case 1

$L = 0.25$ OBS = Neg HVI = Neg		LOCATION SEQUENCING		
$Zd = +3.0$	$DQ+$ $= 5$	I W,WS	IV D,Dd	VII D,W,D
$Zf = 11$	$DQv/+ = 2$	II D,D,Dd	V D,Dd	VIII W,W,D
$W{:}D{:}Dd = 7{:}13{:}5$ DQv $= 3$		III D,D	VI D,Dd	IX W,Dd
$W{:}M = 7{:}3$	PSV $= 0$			X W,D,DS,D

efficiency, and consistency of the processing within expected parameters? If a protocol contains a High Lambda, two other issues must also be considered: (3) Is the orientation to economize and/or simplify also reflected in the processing effort? (4) Is the quality and/or efficiency of processing affected by the style?

Step 1:   Review the value for Lambda *(L)* to ascertain if a stylistic tendency to oversimplify stimuli exists.

Potential Finding 1:   If the value for *L* is 1.0 or greater, it can be assumed that the subject's basic response style involves a marked tendency to narrow or simplify stimulus fields perceived as complex or ambiguous. Although this coping style reflects a form of psychological economizing, it also may indicate problems in the processing of information and, as such, can create a potential for a higher frequency of behaviors that do not coincide with social demands and/or expectations. *Proceed to Step 2.*

Potential Finding 2:   If the value for *L* falls between 0.31 and 0.99, the result is not significant. *Proceed to Step 2.*

Potential Finding 3:   If the value for *L* is less than 0.31, it indicates that the subject becomes more involved with stimuli than is common for most people. This may be a consequence of an overincorporative style or may represent a situation in which the subject tends to be influenced by excessive involvement with affect and/or ideation. When the latter is true it does not automatically equate with pathology or maladjustment, although the situation could reflect either state. *Proceed to Step 2.*

Case 1 Result: The value for *L* is 0.25, indicating that the subject is more involved with stimuli than are most people. This could be a product of the previously noted situational stress reaction, but also may represent a more stylistic feature.

Step 2:   Review the findings for the Obsessive Style Index (OBS) and the Hypervigilance Index (HVI) to determine if there is an unusual stylistic orientation toward processing.

Potential Finding 1: If both OBS and HVI are negative, there is no significant meaning. *Proceed to Step 3.*

Potential Finding 2: A positive OBS signals the presence of a marked tendency toward perfectionism and an excessive preoccupation with details. People such as this are very cautious in their processing behaviors because they are strongly influenced by needs to be correct or conventional. This feature often becomes counterproductive because excessive efforts to refine and/or reorganize the details of an input tend to interfere in mediational activities. *Proceed to Step 3.*

Potential Finding 3: A positive HVI signals a state of hyperalertness. People such as this are guarded and mistrusting of the environment. They usually are very concerned about processing information and often invest excessive energy to ensure that all features of a stimulus field are surveyed carefully. In many instances this breeds a superior processing effort; but, if pathology is present the hyperalertness often takes on paranoid-like characteristics in which overly suspicious preoccupations cause an unusual concern for details, which sometimes supersedes concern for the whole stimulus field. When this occurs, the processing activity often becomes chaotic and inefficient and tends to promote faulty mediation. *Proceed to Step 3.*

Case 1 Result: Neither the OBS nor the HVI is positive.

see notes — over/under achievement

Step 3: Review the values for Zf, $W:D:Dd$, and $W:M$ to evaluate the processing effort. All three are expected to fall within average limits.

Zf related to intellectual striving

Potential Finding 1: If the value for L is less than 1.0 and the values for all three variables fall within the average range, it can be surmised that the subject's processing effort is similar to that of most people. *Proceed to Step 4.*

Zf $\bar{x}$ = 11.31 SD = 2.59

Potential Finding 2: If the value for L is 1.0 or higher and the values for all three variables fall within the average range, it can be concluded that the subject's processing effort is similar to that of most people and that the simplification activity associated with the style occurs after processing. *Proceed to Step 4.*

W: $\bar{x}$ = 8.55 SD = 1.94

D $\bar{x}$ = 8.39 SD = 3.54

Potential Finding 3: If the value for Dd is 4 or more, and the value for Zf is less than 13, it usually indicates that the subject prefers to deal with less complex, more easily managed stimulus fields. This finding may represent a tendency to feel uncomfortable about decision making capabilities. If most of the Dd answers include S, the subject probably has a negativistic set toward the test or toward the environment. If this finding is positive, it should be reviewed again during the study of the location sequence. *Review other potential findings for Step 3.*

Dd $\bar{x}$ = 1.23 SD = 1.76

Potential Finding 4: If any two of the following are positive: (1) Zf is higher than average, (2) the value for W exceeds the value for $D + Dd$, and (3) the ratio $W:M$ is equal to or greater than 3:1, it can be concluded that the subject is highly motivated and makes a considerable effort in processing, especially when

Zf $\bar{x}$ = 11.31 SD = 2.59

the information involved relates to problem solving or decision making. This feature can be an asset provided adequate resources are available; however, it can be a liability if resources are limited or if the quality, efficiency, or consistency of the processing is substandard. *Proceed to Step 4.*

Potential Finding 5: If at least two of the following are positive: (1) Zf is less than average, (2) the value for W is less than one-half of the sum for $D + Dd$, and (3) the ratio $W:M$ is less than 1.5:1 when reduced, it is probable that some processing will be affected by very conservative motivation and, as such, may not be very effective. This may reflect a kind of defensive withdrawal from social competitiveness, which can serve a useful purpose if the subject has intellectual limitations or other cognitive handicaps. However, if the subject's intellectual level is at least average, this type of set toward processing typically is the result of a negative self-image. This finding should be reevaluated during the review of the cluster concerning self-perception. *Proceed to Step 4.*

Case 1 Result: Finding 3 is positive, suggesting that she prefers to deal with less complex, more easily managed stimuli. This finding should be reviewed again during the study of the location sequence.

Step 4: Review the values in the DQ distribution to obtain some estimate concerning the quality of the processing activity.

Potential Finding 1: If the value for $DQ+$ is in the average range and the composite value of $DQv/+$ and DQv is no more than 1 point greater than the combined modes for those two variables, it can be assumed that the subject's quality of processing is similar to that of most people. *Proceed to Step 5.*

Potential Finding 2: If the value for $DQ+$ is above average and the composite value of $DQv/+$ and DQv is no more than 1 point greater than the subject's combined modes for those two variables, it can be assumed that the quality of processing usually is complex and sophisticated. This finding is common among more intelligent or more well-educated subjects. However, it is important to emphasize that more complex and/or sophisticated processing does not necessarily equate with more efficient cognition or with more effective patterns of adjustment. It simply means that processing inputs tend to be of a higher quality. *Proceed to Step 5.*

Potential Finding 3: Regardless of the value for $DQ+$, if the composite value of $DQv/+$ and DQv exceeds the combined modes for those two variables by more than 1 point, it can be concluded that, at times, the quality of processing activity falters significantly to an unsophisticated, less mature level. This is common among children but less so among adolescents and adults. Less sophisticated processing often predisposes less effective translations of inputs and can be a precursor to less effective patterns of adjustment. *Proceed to Step 5.*

Case 1 Result: The record contains five $DQ+$ responses, but also contains two $DQv/+$ and three DQv answers, whereas the value for each of those variables is expected to be 0 or 1. This indicates that much of her processing activity is considerably less sophisticated than that of most adults.

Step 5:   Review the values for *Zd* and PSV to obtain some estimate concerning the efficiency of scanning activity involved in processing information. A *Zd* value of between +3.0 and −3.0 is expected, whereas the value for PSV is always expected to be 0.

Potential Finding 1:   If the *Zd* value falls in the average range and the value for PSV is 0, it can be assumed that the scanning efficiency is similar to that of most people. *Proceed to Step 6.*

Potential Finding 2:   Regardless of the *Zd* value, the presence of PSV answers suggests some problems in processing efficiency. Usually, if PSV is present, the value is 1 and it reflects a within-card PSV. If this finding is positive it indicates that, at times, the subject has some difficulty shifting attention, which can produce less efficient processing activities. If the value for PSV is greater than 1, it may signify the presence of very significant difficulties in shifting attention. Usually, this finding is positive only among very young children, subjects who are in considerable psychological disarray, or subjects who have neurologically-related problems. If this finding is positive, a more careful evaluation of cognitive functioning is always warranted.

Potential Finding 3:   If the value for *Zd* is less than −3.0 it usually signifies an *underincorporative* form of scanning activity. In other words, the subject scans hastily and haphazardly and may neglect critical bits or cues that exist in a stimulus field. Underincorporation creates a potential for faulty mediation and can lead to less effective patterns of behavior. *Proceed to Step 6.*

Potential Finding 4:   If the value for *Zd* is greater than +3.0 it usually indicates the presence of an *overincorporative* style. Overincorporation is an enduring trait-like characteristic that prompts the subject to invest more effort and energy into scanning activities. Although somewhat less efficient because of the added effort involved, overincorporation is often an asset because the cautious, thorough approach to scanning usually ensures that all stimulus cues are included in the input. On the other hand, overincorporation is usually present in obsessive styles, and, in those circumstances, it serves only to increase the potential liability of the style. *Proceed to Step 6.*

Case 1 Result: The subject's *Zd* score is +3.0 and there are no PSV answers in the record, thus indicating that her scanning efficiency is unremarkable and similar to that of most others.

Step 6:   Review the Location Sequencing to determine if the subject's approach to processing is consistent. The positioning of *W* answers is especially important; that is, subjects who are consistent typically give most of their *W* answers either as first answers or as last answers but rarely show a mixture of the two. A similar consistency is expected for *Dd* responses when the number of *Dd*'s is elevated in a record.

Potential Finding 1:   If the sequencing of location selections appears reasonably consistent through most of the blots, it can be assumed that the subject's processing habits are regular and predictable.

Potential Finding 2:   If the sequencing patterns vary considerably across cards, it can be concluded that the subject's processing, during problem solving and/or decision making, tends to be irregular. Although this is not uncommon among children, its presence in the record of an older adolescent or adult suggests a failure to have developed economical or efficient processing habits. While this may not be a major liability, an inconsistency in processing habits can increase the potential for faulty inputs or a reduced quality of processing activity. *Proceed to the next cluster in the interpretive routine.*

Case 1 Result: The sequencing is reasonably consistent in the subject's record. She selected *W* responses to five of the blots and gave the *W* response as the first answer in four of the five. Her first answer to each of the remaining six blots was always a *D*. All five *Dd*'s were last responses, and none included *S*. This suggests that she felt the need to reduce the size of the field or to make it more precise in order to sustain her processing effort.

Case 1 Summary

She tends to invest about as much effort in processing as do most adults, but she currently is prone to become overly involved in the complexity of a stimulus field. This excessive involvement is probably more a product of her ongoing situationally-related stress than a chronic style. Generally, the overall quality of her processing is less mature and unsophisticated than is expected for most adults. Although she is usually consistent in her processing habits, she also is much more prone than most people to narrow and/or reorganize a stimulus field in ways that make it easier to manage.

COGNITIVE MEDIATION

Whereas the variables related to information processing focus on the characteristics of input activities, the variables in the cluster concerning mediation provide information about how the input is translated. The basic review of the cluster focuses on eight variables (*L*, OBS, *P*, *X* + %, *Xu*%, *X*–%, *S* – %, CONFAB) plus the frequency data in the Form Quality Distribution (+, *o*, *u*, –). If minus responses have occurred, they are also reviewed for homogeneous clustering and levels of distortion. The Case 1 data for this cluster are shown in Table 49.

Major Issues: (1) What is the likelihood that conventional behaviors will occur in situations in which the expected or accepted behaviors are easily identified? (2) What is the overall orientation toward making conventional translations of inputs? (3) To what extent are translations of inputs more individualistic and less conventional? (4) Does the frequency of perceptual inaccuracy or distortion fall within acceptable limits? (5) Do instances of perceptual inaccuracy or distortion occur in any discernible pattern? (6) Is there evidence

Table 49.   Cognitive Mediation Variables for Case 1

Lambda = 0.25	OBS = Negative	MINUS FEATURES
P = 7	*X* + % = 64	IV 9. *Ddo FMp– 2 A*
FQx+ = 0	*F*+% = 60	IX 20. *Wv/+ ma.CF– Hh,Fi,Fd 5.5 PER,MOR*
*FQx*o = 16	*Xu*% = 20	
*FQx*u = 2	*X*–% = 08	
FQx– = 2	*S*–% = 0	
FQnone = 2	CONFAB = 0	

of severe perceptual inaccuracy or mediational distortion? The search strategy involves 8 basic Steps, which can expand to 11 Steps if minus responses have occurred in the record.

Step 1:   Review the value for Lambda to ascertain if a stylistic tendency to oversimplify stimuli exists. An oversimplifying style often promotes forms of mediation that ignore or distort salient features of the stimulus field. Thus, the data regarding mediation are misleading at times. In other words, low $X + \%$ and high $Xu\%$ or $X - \%$ values may result that do not reflect true difficulties in mediation but rather are simply a product of the psychological orientation of the style.

Potential Finding 1:   If the value for L is 1.0 or greater, it can be assumed that the subject's basic response style involves a marked tendency to narrow or simplify stimulus fields perceived as complex or ambiguous. Although this coping style reflects a form of psychological economizing, it also may promote negligence in the translating of information and, as such, can create a potential for a higher frequency of behaviors that do not coincide with social demands and/or expectations. *Proceed to Step 2.*

Potential Finding 2:   If the value for L is less than 1.0, the result is not significant. *Proceed to Step 2.*

Case 1 Result: The subject's value for L is 0.25.

Step 2:   Review the OBS finding to determine if the subject has an unusual stylistic orientation toward the translation of stimuli.

Potential Finding 1:   If the OBS is positive it signals the presence of a marked tendency toward perfectionism and an excessive preoccupation with details. People such as this are very cautious in translating stimuli, as they are strongly influenced by needs to be correct or conventional. This feature often becomes counterproductive because excessive efforts to refine and/or reorganize the details of an input tend to interfere in mediational activities. *Proceed to Step 3.*

Potential Finding 2:   If OBS is negative, it has no significant meaning. *Proceed to Step 3.*

Case 1 Result: The subject's OBS is negative.

Step 3:   Review the value for Popular (*P*) responses to ascertain the likelihood that the subject will make *obvious* conventional responses to demand situations in which expected or accepted behaviors are easily identified.

Potential Finding 1:   If the value for *P* is at least average, it signifies that, in obvious situations, the subject is likely to make expected or acceptable responses. The probability of less conventional responses occurring in situations that are simple and/or precisely defined is minimal *even* if some processing problems have been noted. Reevaluate this finding at Step 5. *Proceed to Step 4.*

Potential Finding 2:   If the value for *P* is greater than average, it may indicate that a preoccupation with conventionality exists. In other words, the subject may be overly concerned with detecting cues related to socially expected or acceptable behaviors. This is not necessarily a liability, but can reflect a more perfectionistic or obsessive-like style. Reevaluate this finding at Steps 4 and 5. *Proceed to Step 4.*

Potential Finding 3:   If the value for *P* is lower than average, the subject is likely to make less conventional, more individualistic responses, even in situations that are simple and/or precisely defined. This is not necessarily a liability, but can be a problem if difficulties in processing also are noted. Findings at Step 5 are critical in determining whether this tendency contributes to or is a feature of a marked potential for asocial and/or antisocial behavior. *Proceed to Step 4.*

Case 1 Result: The subject's record contains seven Popular answers, a value that is average for adults, suggesting that she is prone to make conventional responses in those situations in which the acceptable or conventional is readily apparent. This reduces the likelihood of inappropriate behaviors in most social situations, even though her processing activities tend to be somewhat unsophisticated.

Step 4:   Observe the value for *FQx*+ to determine if any responses include an overelaborated use of form.

Potential Finding 1:   If the value is 0 or 1, no conclusions can be drawn. *Proceed to Step 5.*

Potential Finding 2:   If the value for *FQx*+ is 2 or 3, it suggests that the subject is oriented to be more precise in mediating stimulus inputs. This is not uncommon among more intelligent or highly educated subjects but can indicate a more perfectionistic or obsessive style. *Proceed to Step 5.*

Potential Finding 3:   If the value for *FQx*+ is greater than 3, it signifies a marked orientation toward perfectionism. Although this is not necessarily a liability, sometimes it does contribute to excessive caution in decision making. *Proceed to Step 5.*

Case 1 Result: There are no *FQx+* answers in the record.

Step 5:   Review $X+\%$ (and $F+\%$ if L is elevated) to establish information concerning the overall disposition of the subject to translate stimuli in conventional ways.

Potential Finding 1:   If the $X+\%$ falls between 70 and 89% (and $F+\%$ is greater than 70% in High L records), it indicates that the subject's frequency rate for making conventional responses is similar to that of most people. *Proceed to Step 6.*

Potential Finding 2:   If the $X+\%$ is greater than 89%, it probably indicates an unusual commitment to conventionality. Although this is not necessarily a liability, it often signals an excessive preoccupation with social acceptability that can lead to a sacrifice of individuality. Elevations in the $X+\%$ may also reflect a marked tendency toward obsessiveness and/or perfectionism. *Proceed to Step 6.*

Potential Finding 3:   If the $X+\%$ (and $F+\%$ in High L records) is less than 70%, it can be concluded that the subject is oriented toward making more unconventional translations of stimuli than do most people. This usually equates with patterns of less conventional behaviors. This tendency is even greater if the number of Popular answers is also less than average. This does not necessarily mean that the less conventional behaviors are unacceptable or antisocial. This feature may reflect a strong emphasis on individualism, may result from social alienation, or could be the product of more serious mediational or affective modulation problems. When this finding is positive in High L records, it is often the result of a strong orientation to maintain distance from and thus cope with an environment that is perceived as threatening, demanding, and ungiving. In other cases, the tendency to produce more unconventional behaviors can result from cognitive difficulties that may include processing and/or perceptual accuracy problems. *Proceed to Step 6.*

Potential Finding 4 (Applicable only to cases in which L *is 1.0 or greater):*   If $X+\%$ is less than 70% but $F+\%$ is 70% or greater, this may signify that when the tactic of simplification is not invoked, or fails, the subject becomes prone to translate stimuli in less conventional ways. This may occur because the subject is irritated or overwhelmed by stimulus complexity and, thus, attempts to deal with the problem by withdrawing from and/or distorting the nature of the stimulus situation. *Proceed to Step 6.*

Potential Finding 5 (Applicable only to cases in which L *is 1.0 or greater):*   If $X+\%$ is 70% or more and $F+\%$ is less than 70%, it is possible that the subject assumes an unconventional or distortional approach during mediation to support the oversimplification process. This is more likely to be true when the $F+\%$ is less than 60%. *Proceed to Step 6.*

Case 1 Result: The subject's $X + \%$ is 0.64, which is slightly below the average range and indicates that she is inclined to produce more unconventional behaviors than most adults. This finding could be a by-product of the problems in affective modulation that were noted earlier. This possibility should be addressed again after reviewing the data in Step 6.

Step 6:   Review the frequency for *FQnone* to determine if a tendency to disregard contour utilization should be considered in evaluating the value for the $X + \%$. Sometimes, especially in the records of younger clients, the presence of "no-form" answers reduces the $X + \%$ considerably. In most instances, the no-form answers are Pure *C* responses.

Potential Finding 1:   Frequencies of 0 or 1 for no-form answers are not significant. *Proceed to Step 7.*

Potential Finding 2:   If the frequency for no-form answers is 2 or more, it can be concluded that failures to modulate either ideation (if no-form movement answers have been given) or affect (if other types of no-form answers have occurred) tend to interfere with the subject's mediational activity. If the value for the $X + \%$ is below average, a second calculation should be completed in which *R* is reduced by the number of no-form responses to determine if the result would place the $X + \%$ in the average range or whether it would remain below average. This finding should be used as a reference in evaluating the results from Step 5 and subsequent Steps. *Proceed to Step 7.*

Case 1 Result: The record contains two no-form answers. When the $X + \%$ is recalculated it is increased to 70%, which is essentially average. This suggests that any unusual frequency of unconventional responses that she may emit are probably the result of modulation failures.

Step 7:   Review *Xu*% in relation to the $X + \%$ to ascertain the extent to which less conventional mediation results from more idiosyncratic or personalized translations. Ordinarily, the value for the *Xu*% falls between 10 and 20%, and is always expected to be greater than the $X - \%$.

Potential Finding 1:   If both the $X + \%$ and the *Xu*% fall within the average range, it can be assumed that the subject expresses idiosyncratic features in mediational activity about as often as most people. *Proceed to Step 8.*

Potential Finding 2:   If the $X + \%$ is less than 70% and the *Xu*% is greater than 20%, it is reasonable to conclude that a higher frequency of behaviors that disregard social demands or expectations may occur because the subject tends to over-personalize in translating stimuli. This may be the product of a unique conflict structure involving the environment and/or of a system of values that varies considerably from those usually endorsed by the environment. *Proceed to Step 8.*

Potential Finding 3:   If the $X + \%$ is less than 70% and the *Xu*% falls between 10 and 20%, it is probable that a higher frequency of less conventional behaviors may occur because of a composite of overpersonalization of translation plus some problems in affective modulation, and/or perceptual accuracy, and/or mediational distortion. Reevaluate this finding at Step 8. *Proceed to Step 8.*

Potential Finding 4:   If the $X + \%$ is less than 70% and the $Xu\%$ is less than 10%, it can be assumed that significant problems in modulation and/or perceptual accuracy are creating a potential for a higher frequency of less conventional behaviors. Reevaluate this finding at Step 8. *Proceed to Step 8.*

Case 1 Result: Finding 3 is positive for the subject. The $X + \%$ is less than 70% and the $Xu\%$ is 20%. The record contains two Pure C responses, and the recalculated $X + \%$ is at 70% if they are disregarded. Nonetheless, the composite of the substantial $Xu\%$, indicating that she does tend to overpersonalize many of her translations, plus the two no-form answers, indicates the likelihood of more unconventional behaviors than is common for adults.

Step 8:   Review the $X - \%$ and the $S - \%$ to determine the extent to which perceptual inaccuracy and/or mediational distortion occur. The value for the $X - \%$ is expected to be less than 15% and the value for the $S - \%$ is always expected to be less than 40% unless the subject gives fewer than four minus answers.

Potential Finding 1:   If the value for the $X - \%$ is 0, end the search and *proceed to the next cluster in the interpretive routine.*

Potential Finding 2:   If the value for the $X - \%$ is less than 15%, it can be concluded that the frequency of perceptual inaccuracy and/or mediational distortion is no greater than for most people. If the value for the $S - \%$ is 40% or more, it is likely that negativism or anger contribute significantly to these events when they occur. *Proceed to Step 9.*

Potential Finding 3:   If the value for the $X - \%$ falls in the range of 15 to 20%, some concern is warranted about the elevated incidence of perceptual inaccuracy and/or mediational distortion. The frequency of minus answers is relevant. Two or three minus responses usually is not cause for major concern; however, four or more minus answers signals that a careful review of the features and distribution of those answers may be critical to a better understanding of mediational activity. If the value for the $S - \%$ is equal to or greater than 40%, this concern should focus on the subject's affective characteristics. This finding should be evaluated further during Steps 9 through 11. *Proceed to Step 9.*

Potential Finding 4:   If the value of the $X - \%$ exceeds 20%, it is likely that the subject has significant problems that promote perceptual inaccuracy and/or mediational distortion. If the value for the $S - \%$ is equal to or greater than 40%, it is probable that negativism and/or anger contributes substantially to the problem. The data concerning affect may shed some light on this issue. If the value for the $S - \%$ is less than 40%, it can be assumed that the inaccuracy or distortion problems are more pervasive. This finding should be evaluated further during Steps 9 through 11.

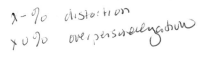
x – % distortion
x o % over persuadelynation

Potential Finding 5:   If the value of the $X - \%$ exceeds 70% and R is greater than 13, regardless of the value for the $S - \%$, it is likely that the subject is attempting to exaggerate or malinger symptoms. Subjects who have an $X - \%$ greater than 70% are usually very difficult or even impossible to test and typically have recent behavioral histories that are consistent with the postulate that an active psychotic-like state exists. If the history does not provide clear and consistent evidence of a psychotic-like state, the probability of malingering is substantial. *Proceed to Step 9.*

Case 1 Result: The subject's $X - \%$ of 8% is not cause for concern. The actual frequency of minus answers is only two, which supports the postulate that serious inaccuracy or distortion is not common. However, the sequencing and characteristics of the minus answers should be reviewed carefully before forming any conclusion.

Step 9:   Review the Sequence of Scores to determine if minus answers occurred within a specific segment. Usually, minus responses are scattered throughout the record in a seemingly haphazard way. If, however, specific patterns are obvious, their presence can be quite meaningful.

Potential Finding 1:   If all minus form quality occurred in answers that cluster within the first three cards, the distortions are most likely a product of the subject's negative resistance toward the test situation. Information regarding the nature of the test situation and the reasons for the evaluation may clarify whether the distortions are situationally related or represent a more habitual pattern of response to unwanted demands. Further clarification of this may also evolve from a review of the cluster concerning controls and stress tolerance. *Proceed to Step 10.*

Potential Finding 2:   If three or more minus answers were given and 40% or more of the minus answers involve S, and those answers are scattered throughout the sequence, some of the distortions probably result from a chronic, trait-like negativistic orientation toward the environment, which is likely to increase the probability of behaviors that may disregard social conventions or expectations. Further information concerning data related to controls, affect, and interpersonal perception should clarify the extent to which this negativism is likely to manifest routinely in responses to demand/coping situations.

Potential Finding 3:   If most minus answers were given to blots containing chromatic color the possibility of affective disruption must be considered. If this problem exists, it usually is confirmed by data concerning affect, which often includes some difficulties in modulating affective displays (higher right-side value for $FC : FC + C$), and in many instances a tendency to avoid emotionally toned stimulus situations (low Afr).

Potential Finding 4:   If more than one minus answer exists and most minus answers are given as first responses to the blots, this may signify a lackadaisical or hasty approach in mediation, especially if subsequent answers within the blot are more conventional.

Potential Finding 5:   If most minus answers are last responses to the blots, two possibilities should be considered. The more common possibility is that those answers are of special significance to the subject and may be quite revealing when their characteristics or content is reviewed. A second possibility is that the subject may be prone, for any of several reasons, to exaggerate features of disturbance. This is particularly likely if the record contains more than three minus answers. *Proceed to Step 10.*

Case 1 Result: The subject gave minus responses as the second answer to Card IV and the first answer to Card IX. No specific clustering is obvious.

Step 10:   Review the Sequence of Scores to assess whether the minus responses include a substantial proportion of the same or very similar characteristics or contents.

Potential Finding 1:   If most minus answers have the same location selections, such as *W* or *Dd,* or the same or similar determinants, the operations associated with those features may contribute to the inaccuracy or distortion. For instance, if most are *W* answers, the subject's disposition to translate the entire field may lead to distortion. Similarly, if most are achromatic or shading answers, the irritating affects associated with those kinds of determinants may contribute to mediational difficulties.

Potential Finding 2:   If minus answers cluster for homogeneous contents, an important preoccupation may be provoking mediational distortion. In some instances, the nature of the preoccupation is reflected by the content category(s); however, in most cases, the preoccupation is clarified only by a careful reading of the responses involved and merging those findings with other findings concerning personal perception. *Proceed to Step 11.*

Case 1 Result: There is no apparent consistency across the two minus answers. One is a *W* response and the second is a *Dd,* and neither the determinants nor the contents are similar.

Step 11:   Read all minus answers to evaluate the degree to which the response violates the properties of the stimulus field. The objective of this review is *not to study content for projected material.* Instead, it should focus on the issue of perceptual or mediational bizarreness. As noted earlier, the vast majority of minus answers given by nonpatients and by nonschizophrenic patients include some features that are clearly congruent with elements of the stimulus field. The location is usually easily identified and, even though the response is scored minus, the examiner or interpreter typically can perceive some components that have contributed to the answer. If minus responses are differentiated into either of two levels of distortion, with Level 1 used for modest distortions and Level 2 used for severe distortions, those in which some significant components are readily apparent are of the Level 1 variety. Illustrations of Level 1 minus answers include face responses to Cards II, III, and X; some anatomy answers to Cards II, III, or VIII; crab responses to Cards IV or V; and a broken cookie or cracker to Card VII. On the other hand, some minus responses reflect an almost complete disregard for the stimulus field. Their location is often difficult to ascertain, and even the most empathic examiner or interpreter may have considerable difficulty in perceiving the object or important components of it. For example, "A group of miners burrowing deeply into the center of the earth" to all of Card I or "Fabulous flights of flaming flamingos" to all of Card X are severe Level 2 distortions. Level 2 minus responses represent an important source of information concerning mediation and often are rich in projected material.

Potential Finding: If Level 2 minus answers appear in the record, they represent a serious breakdown in perceptual-cognitive operations. A positive finding warrants a careful evaluation of data regarding ideation as well as controls. The presence of even one Level 2 minus answer suggests that some of the subject's behaviors may deviate very markedly from those expected and/or acceptable in a demand situation. The presence of multiple Level 2 minus answers suggests that mediational activity often is chaotically disrupted in ways that inevitably breed ineffective and/or inappropriate behaviors. If the record contains multiple Level 2 minus answers, a more extensive review of cognitive functioning than usually is available from Rorschach data is in order. *Proceed to the next cluster in the interpretive routine.*

Case 1 Result: The first minus answer in the record (9) was given to an area not numbered on Card IV, with the card inverted. It is:

> There's two lions here too, one on each side. (Inquiry) They are just standing there, see one on each side with the long tail sticking out, see this is the head and the body, just like two lions.

Although the area involved is quite unusual, most features are readily apparent. Some might even be prone to assign a *u* form quality, but that would be erroneous since nonexistent lines form a significant part of the figure. Nonetheless, it is not a severe distortion.

The second minus response (20) was given using all of Card IX. It is:

> Oh, like a pot boiling over. (Inquiry) Well if you've ever left a pot on the stove too long, maybe like cooking cabbage, I did that once, it looks like this, a mess, flames and cabbage all over, see the orange is flames and the green is cabbage and the pink is like the burner.

Responses such as this are not gross distortions. Most of the items included do not have very specific form requirements, and parts of the response, especially the flames, are congruent with the blot features.

Case 1 Summary

There are no major problems with her mediational operations. She is inclined to translate stimulus fields in ways that are less conventional than most adults, and, at times, this inclination is exacerbated by the problems that she has in modulating affect. Either or both can prompt a slight increase in the frequency of unconventional responses. On the other hand, there are no serious distortions and, in general, she does seem as prone as most adults to make conventional responses when the circumstances of the situation clearly define expected or acceptable answers.

IDEATION

The variables in the ideation cluster address the issue of how the translations of inputs become conceptualized and used. Thinking involves the meaningful organization of a series of symbols or concepts. It constitutes the core of psychological activity from which all decisions and deliberate behaviors evolve. Rorschach data fall far short of uncovering the more subtle nuances of ideational activity. Nonetheless, the data from a composite of variables often provide a useful picture regarding the subject's ideational operations. The Case 1 data for this cluster are shown in Table 50.

Major Issues: (1) Is there evidence to indicate the presence of an ideational coping style? (2) Is there evidence to suggest that ideation is peculiar, disturbed, or marked by poor judgment? (3) Is there evidence to suggest that the subject lacks flexibility when considering decisions? (4) Is there evidence indicating that the subject may not be using this ideation effectively? (5) Is there evidence to suggest that thinking may be marked by unusual or unrealistic sets?

Step 1: Review the *EB* to ascertain if an introversive or extratensive style exists. The *EB* reflects a distinct style only if the value on one side exceeds the other by 2 or more points when *EA* is 10 or less, or by more than 2 points when *EA* is greater than 10.

Potential Finding 1: If the *EB* indicates the presence of an introversive style it can be assumed that the subject ordinarily delays formulating decisions or initiating behaviors until all apparent alternative possibilities have been considered. People such as this usually prefer to keep feelings at a more peripheral level during problem solving and/or decision making and tend to rely heavily on internal

Table 50. Ideation Variables for Case 1

		M QUALITY	CRITICAL SPECIAL SCORES			
EB = 3 : 8.0	*EBPer* = 2.7					
eb = 7 : 8	(*FM* = 4 m = 3)	+ = 0	DV	= 1	DV2	= 0
a:p = 4 : 6	*Ma:Mp* = 0 : 3	o = 3	INC	= 0	INC2	= 0
2*Ab*+(*Art*+*Ay*) = 4		u = 0	DR	= 0	DR2	= 0
MOR = 1		– = 0	FAB	= 0	FAB2	= 0
RESPONSES TO BE READ FOR QUALITY			ALOG	= 0	SUM6	= 1
6, 7, 14			CON	= 0	WSUM6	= 1

evaluation in forming judgments. They generally prefer logic systems that are precise and uncomplicated. They usually avoid engaging in trial-and-error explorations and are less tolerant when problem solving errors occur. *Proceed to Step 2.*

Potential Finding 2: If the *EB* indicates the presence of an extratensive coping style, it can be assumed that the subject usually merges feelings with thinking during problem solving activity. This does not mean that the subject's thinking is less consistent or logical than that of an introversive subject; however, the affective impact on ideation often may give rise to more complex patterns of ideation. Extratensive subjects tend to be more accepting of logic systems that are not precise or are marked by greater ambiguity. Their judgments are often influenced by the external products of trial-and-error activity. *Proceed to Step 2.*

Potential Finding 3: If the *EB* fails to indicate a coping style (*ambitent*), the subject's ideational activity is likely to be less consistent. These people are more prone to reverse previous judgments and often find it more difficult to arrive at a firm decision. Their lack of consistency in thinking, especially during problem solving, makes them more vulnerable to errors in judgment. They tend to profit less from problem solving errors and, as a result, often require more time to reach effective solutions. *Proceed to Step 3.*

Case 1 Result: The subject's *EB* of 3 : 8.0 reveals an extratensive coping style, which suggests that much of her thinking is influenced by feelings and at times may become quite elaborate. She is probably more willing to accept ambiguity in logic and is prone to rely extensively on external feedback in forming judgments.

Step 2: If a style has been detected in the Step 1 evaluation of the *EB,* review the value for *EBPer* to determine if the style is markedly pervasive in coping activity.

Potential Finding 1: If the subject is introversive and the value for *EBPer* is less than 2.5, it can be postulated that, although the subject typically uses an ideational style involving delay, sometimes feelings contribute significantly to decisions. On the other hand, if the value for *EBPer* is 2.5 or more, it should be assumed that emotions usually play only a very limited role in the subject's decision-making activity. *Proceed to Step 3.*

Potential Finding 2: If the subject is extratensive and the value for *EBPer* is less than 2.5, it can be assumed that the subject usually is prone to merge feelings with thinking, but that sometimes feelings are kept more peripheral in favor of a more clear ideational approach. Conversely, if the value for *EBPer* is 2.5 or more, it should be assumed that the style is quite pervasive and that emotions usually have a direct impact on patterns of thinking. *Proceed to Step 3.*

Case 1 Result: The value for *EBPer* is 2.7, indicating that her the style is pervasive and most of her thinking is marked by emotional influences.

Step 3: Review the values for the left side of the *eb, FM,* and *m,* to determine if an unusual level of ideational activity outside of the direct focus of attention might create some interference to deliberate thinking. This peripheral kind of mental activity tends to be produced routinely as a result of need experiences or the subtle awareness of external demand situations. As such, it often serves as a valuable source of alerting stimulation that provokes shifts in attention and foments deliberate decision operations. On the other hand, this kind of ideational activity can create distraction from or interference with more deliberately organized patterns of thought. Typically, the value for *FM* is within the range of 3 to 5, and the value for *m* is from 0 to 2, but always less than the *FM* value. *FM* is the more stable of the two variables and appears to be related to mental activity that is promoted by need states, whereas *m* is a very unstable variable that correlates with mental activity created by situational stress demands.

Potential Finding 1:   In most cases, the left-side value of the *eb* falls between 3 and 6 for an adult, or within one *SD* of the mean for younger subjects, and the value for *FM* is within 1 point of that total, but no greater than 5. If this finding is positive, there is no reason to assume the presence of an unusual level of this somewhat routine form of mental activity. *Proceed to Step 4.*

Potential Finding 2:   If the left-side value for *eb* falls between 3 and 6, or within one *SD* of the mean for younger subjects, and the value for *m* is 2 or more, this indicates that the level of peripheral ideation is being increased by situationally-related stress, even though it falls within expected limits. *Proceed to Step 4.*

Potential Finding 3:   If the left-side value for *eb* exceeds 6, or is more than one *SD* above the mean for a younger subject, it indicates that the subject is experiencing a higher than expected level of ideational activity that is outside the focus of attention. Although this kind of ideational activity can serve as a positive stimulus, it can also become quite distracting once it exceeds natural levels. As a result, concentration tends to be more limited, and the flow of deliberate thinking is likely to be interrupted more often.

Potential Finding 4:   If the left-side *eb* value is 7, and is created exclusively by *FM* responses or includes only one *m* response, or if the left-side *eb* value is greater than 7 and includes more than five *FM* answers, it can be surmised that the subject is experiencing a higher level of peripheral mental activity because of internal need states. It also can be assumed that this situation is more chronic than transient and, as such, increases the likelihood for frequent interference with attention and concentration operations. *Proceed to Step 4.*

Potential Finding 5:   If the left-side *eb* value is 7 or more but includes no more than five *FM* answers, it can be assumed that the subject is experiencing an increase in peripheral mental activity because of situationally-related stress. Ordinarily, this is a transient condition; however, it is important to note that attention and concentration activities can be reduced significantly during its duration. *Proceed to Step 4.*

Potential Finding 6:   Left-side *eb* values of less than 3 are unusual. They appear most often in the protocols of subjects who have high Lambda values.

Low left-side *eb* values suggest that the subject may not be processing more subtle internal and external stimuli, or that the subject tends to react hastily to demands created by such stimuli. The latter is most likely to be true if the *FM* value is 0 or 1, and suggests that the subject is able to minimize or avoid many of the natural stimulus irritations that are common among most people. Although this is positive from a simple homeostatic perspective, it may be a negative finding because hastily formulated responses are often not well thought out and their long term effectiveness can be limited. *Proceed to Step 4.*

Case 1 Result: Finding 5 is positive. The subject's left-side *eb* value is 7, comprised of four *FM* answers and three *m* responses. Thus, an increase in peripheral mental activity appears to be stress related, and may cause some interference problems with attention and concentration activity.

Step 4: Review the values for the $a:p$ ratio to determine if there is evidence to suggest ideational inflexibility. The value on one side of the ratio is usually not more than twice that of the other side. As the values in the ratio become more discrepant, ideational sets and values tend to be more well fixed and difficult to alter.

Potential Finding 1: If the sum of the values in the ratio is 4, and the value for one side is not more than three times that of the other (i.e., no more than $3:1$ or $1:3$), or if the sum of the values in the ratio is 3 or less, the finding is not significant. *Proceed to Step 5.*

Potential Finding 2: If the sum of the values in the ratio is 4 and one value is 0, it can be hypothesized that the subject's thinking and values tend to be less flexible and more well fixed than is ordinary. *Proceed to Step 5.*

Potential Finding 3: If the sum of the values in the ratio exceeds 4, and the value on one side of the ratio is no more than twice that of the other, the finding is not significant. *Proceed to Step 5.*

Potential Finding 4: If the sum of the values in the ratio exceeds 4, and the value on one side is two to three times greater than the value on the other side, it can be presumed that the subject's ideational sets and values are reasonably well fixed and would be somewhat difficult to alter. *Proceed to Step 5.*

Potential Finding 5: If the sum of the values in the ratio exceeds 4, and the value on one side is more than three times greater than the value on the other side, it can be concluded that the subject's ideational sets and values are well fixed and relatively inflexible. People such as this find it very difficult to alter attitudes or opinions, or to view issues from a perspective different from that which they hold. *Proceed to Step 5.*

Case 1 Result: The subject's $a:p$ ratio of $4:6$ is not significant and no conclusions can be drawn.

Step 5: Review the values in the $M^a:M^p$ ratio to determine if any evidence suggests an abusive use of fantasy. The value for M^a is always expected to exceed the value for M^p, and the magnitude of the difference has no interpretive significance. In most instances, however, if the value for M^p is greater than the value for M^a, this very important finding contributes substantially to information concerning the subject's ideational activities.

Potential Finding 1: If the value for M is 1, the data are insufficient for interpretation. *Proceed to Step 6.*

Potential Finding 2: If the value for M is greater than 1 and the value for M^p is 1 point more than the value for M^a, it indicates that the subject has a stylistic tendency to use fantasy excessively. People such as this are prone to defensively substitute fantasy for reality in stress situations much more often than do most people. This form of ideational denial provides some temporary relief from stress by replacing an unpleasant situation with one that is easily managed; however, it also tends to breed a dependency on others because of the implicit assumption that external forces will bring resolution to the situation if it can be avoided long enough. The abuse of this tactic creates risks for any subject, but probably more so for the introversive subject because the basic coping style is being used in ways that are more likely to be ineffective. *Proceed to Step 6.*

Potential Finding 3: If the value for M^p is 2 or more points greater than the value for M^a, it indicates the presence of a marked style in which a flight into fantasy has become a routine tactic for dealing with unpleasant situations. People such as this can be assumed to have a "Snow White syndrome," characterized mainly by the avoidance of responsibility and decision making. They use fantasy with an abusive excess to deny reality, and the results are often counterproductive to many of their own needs. This mode of coping involves the creation of a self-imposed helplessness because it requires a dependency on others. Unfortunately, it also makes them vulnerable to the manipulations of others. The pervasiveness of this coping style is particularly detrimental for the introversive subject because the basic ideational coping orientation becomes subservient to the avoidant-dependent orientation in situations that seem overly complex or potentially stressful. *Proceed to Step 6.*

Case 1 Result: The $M^a:M^p$ ratio of 0:3 indicates that she uses fantasy abusively and probably goes to great lengths to avoid responsibility and decision making. Although she is not introversive, the results of this coping orientation can be especially detrimental because of her strong tendency to overestimate her self-worth.

Step 6: Review the Intellectualization Index $\{2AB + (Art + Ay)\}$ to determine if the defensive tactic of intellectualization is used excessively.

Potential Finding 1: If the Intellectualization Index value is 4, 5, or 6, the subject is prone to deal with feelings on an intellectual level more often than most people. Although this process serves to reduce or neutralize the impact of emotions, it also represents a naïve form of denial that tends to distort the true impact of a situation. *Proceed to Step 7.*

Potential Finding 2: If the Intellectualization Index value exceeds 6, it signifies that the subject uses intellectualization as a major defensive tactic in situations that are perceived as affectively stressful. In effect, it is a pseudo-intellectual process that conceals and/or denies the presence of affect and, as a result, tends to reduce the likelihood that feelings will be dealt with directly and/or realistically. People such as this tend to become more vulnerable to disorganization during intense emotional experiences because the tactic becomes less effective as the magnitude of affective stimuli increases. *Proceed to Step 7.*

Case 1 Result: The value for the Intellectualization Index is 4, suggesting that she tends to intellectualize more often than most people in an effort to reduce or neutralize the effects of emotion that she perceives to be stressful. This somewhat naïve form of denial probably contributes to some of the problems that she has in modulating her emotional displays.

Step 7: Review the number of Morbid (MOR) responses to determine if ideational attitudes or approaches may be marked by unusual pessimism.

Potential Finding 1: If the value for MOR is 2 or less the finding is not significant. *Proceed to Step 8.*

Potential Finding 2: If the value for MOR is 3 or more, it is likely that the subject's thinking is marked frequently by a pessimistic set. People such as this often view their relationships to the world with a sense of doubt and discouragement and tend to anticipate gloomy outcomes for their efforts regardless of the quality of the effort. *Proceed to Step 8.*

Case 1 Result: She gave only one MOR response.

Step 8: Review data for the six Critical Special Scores to assess for the presence of ideational slippage and problems in judgment and/or conceptualization.

Potential Finding 1: If the raw sum for the six Special Scores is 3 or less in an adult record and includes *only* Level 1 DV, INCOM, or DR responses, the finding should be considered unremarkable. If the protocol is from a younger client, the same conclusion is applicable if the value of six Special Scores is within one *SD* of the mean and the value for *each* of the Special Scores DV, INCOM, DR, FABCOM, and ALOG does not exceed the mode for that age by more than 1 point, *and* if these Special Scores include *only* Level 1 responses. *Proceed to Step 9.*

Potential Finding 2: If the raw sum for the six Special Scores is 3 or less in the record of an adult and includes FABCOM and/or ALOG responses, but does not include CONTAM responses or Level 2 answers, it indicates that the subject's ideational activity is marked more by slippage or faulty judgment than is common. This does not necessarily reflect forms of pathological thinking, but does suggest that some of the subject's conceptualizations are less mature or less sophisticated than is typical. *Proceed to Step 9.*

Potential Finding 3:   If the raw sum for the six Special Scores is 4 or 5 in an adult record, and does not include CONTAM or Level 2 responses, and the Weighted Sum6 (WSum6) does not exceed 11, it can be assumed that the subject's ideational activity is marked by more slippage and/or faulty conceptualizations than is usual. This does not necessarily reflect pathological thinking, but does suggest that much of the ideational activity is considerably less sophisticated and/or marked by more faulty judgment than is typical. This postulate is also applicable to the records of younger subjects if the raw sum of the six Special Scores and the WSum6 are greater than one *SD* above the mean but the record does not include CONTAM or Level 2 responses. *Proceed to Step 9.*

Potential Finding 4:   In an adult's record, if the raw sum of the six Special Scores is between 6 and 8, or is less than 6 but has a WSum6 greater than 11, *or* contains at least one CONTAM or Level 2 answer, it indicates serious problems in thinking. Instances of ideational discontinuity and/or faulty conceptualization occur too frequently. They tend to interfere with logic and promote faulty judgment and, as a result, the probability of errors in decision making is increased substantially. This finding is positive for the record of a younger subject if the raw sum of the Special Scores is greater than two *SD* above the mean or includes at least one CONTAM or at least two Level 2 answers. *Proceed to Step 9.*

Potential Finding 5:   If, in the record of an adult, the raw sum of the six Special Scores exceeds 8, or is greater than 6 and contains at least one CONTAM or Level 2 response, it suggests the probability of seriously disturbed thinking. Ideational activity such as this is usually marked by very flawed judgment and conceptualization and disorganized and/or inconsistent patterns of decision making. This finding is positive for the record of a younger subject if the raw sum of the Special Scores and WSum6 are greater than two *SD* above the mean and the record includes at least one CONTAM or more than two Level 2 responses. *Proceed to Step 9.*

Case 1 Result: Only one Level 1 DV response appears in her record. Thus there is no reason to suspect ideational slippage or conceptualization problems.

Step 9:   Read each answer that contains one of the six Critical Special Scores. This subjective evaluation should focus on three issues: (1) the extent to which some or all of the Special Scores reflect subcultural phenomena or educational limitations, (2) the extent to which the answers illustrate problems in judgment, and (3) whether the bizarre features in the CONTAM or Level 2 responses manifest in ways that clearly signal pathological kinds of thinking.

Potential Finding 1:   If the majority of responses containing the six Critical Special Scores appear to reflect common verbiage within the subculture of the subject or for those with similar educational backgrounds, postulates concerning ideational slippage should be tempered but not necessarily rejected. This conclusion should be reevaluated at Step 10. *Proceed to Step 10.*

Potential Finding 2: If none of the answers containing the six Critical Special Scores are bizarre but most reflect forms of flawed logic that are not expected for subjects of this age, it can be postulated that the subject may be socially inept or unable to contain and/or direct ideation adaptively. Data regarding controls may shed some light on this finding. Regardless of findings regarding controls, it is reasonable to conclude that the subject often may manifest ideas and/or behaviors that are the products of faulty judgment. *Proceed to Step 10.*

Potential Finding 3: If the bizarreness of any CONTAM or Level 2 responses seems to clearly evidence markedly disturbed thinking, the behavioral history of the subject probably contains some confirming information about this. If the recent behavioral history fails to provide this confirmation, the possibility of some form of exaggeration or malingering of symptoms should be considered. *Proceed to Step 10.*

Case 1 Result: The single DV occurs in Response 11 and is a minor redundancy, "tiny little," which probably reflects a less mature form of speech rather than cognitive slippage.

Step 10: Review the Form Quality distribution for the *M* responses to assess for disturbed or peculiar thinking.

Potential Finding 1: If all *M* responses have form quality codings of *o* or *u*, no evidence in the data set supports the notion of peculiar or disturbed thinking. *Proceed to Step 12.*

Potential Finding 2: If the value for *M−* is 1, and there are no *formless M* responses, it is reasonable to hypothesize that some characteristics of the subject's thinking are peculiar. A single *M−* often reflects a preoccupation that occasionally interferes with the clarity of thinking, but in some instances even a single *M−* represents a glimpse of a broader form of ideational disarray. When the latter is true, findings concerning the six Critical Special Scores are almost always significant. *Proceed to Step 11.*

Potential Finding 3: If the value for *M−* is 0 but the value for *formless M* is 1, it is reasonable to assume that problems exist that interfere with ideational control. Most *formless M* answers include a clear affective component, such as sadness, rage, pain, ecstasy, and so on, but some have a more esoteric quality, such as illusion, peace, creativeness, intelligence, and so forth. The former seem to represent instances of lability in which feelings overwhelm thinking and lead to a detachment from reality. The latter appear to reflect instances in which ideation becomes fluid and internal preoccupations become superimposed on or replacements for reality. Both signify that the ability to control thinking is impaired; however, the more esoteric *formless M* answers probably include processes that are similar to those that give rise to hallucinatory experiences. *Proceed to Step 11.*

Potential Finding 4:   If the combined value for *M*– and *formless M* is 2 or more, thinking is very likely to be peculiar or disturbed. Although this may be the product of a semi-isolated preoccupation, it more likely represents a broader form of ideational disarray, which probably will be confirmed by other characteristics in the protocol. *Proceed to Step 11.*

Case 1 Result: No *M*– or *formless M* responses appear in the subject's record.

Step 11:   Review the areas used in creating the *M*– responses, focusing on whether the minus represents a Level 1 or Level 2 distortion of the blot's stimulus features.

Potential Finding 1:   If all *M*– answers involve Level 1 distortions and none contain peculiar or bizarre elements, it is likely that some of the subject's thinking patterns are more loose or fluid than might be expected, and this can easily lead to faulty judgments and/or decision making. Nevertheless, this finding, taken alone, is not sufficient to warrant a conclusion that pathologically disturbed thinking exists. *Proceed to Step 12.*

Potential Finding 2:   If one or more *M*– responses involve Level 2 distortions of the stimulus field, it indicates that patterns of thinking are loose and probably dominated frequently by preoccupations and/or disturbance in ways that tend to ignore reality. This finding does not necessarily signify that thinking is pathological; however, these characteristics are often present in pathological thinking. *Proceed to Step 12.*

Case 1 Result: Step 11 is not applicable to Case 1.

Step 12:   Read all *M* responses, focusing on the quality of the responses, that is, whether they are sophisticated, are common, or reflect a more juvenile or primitive form of conceptualization.

Potential Finding: In adult records, the conceptual quality of the movement answers is expected to be common or even sophisticated. If one or more of the *M* answers has a more juvenile or primitive conceptualization, it can be postulated that some of the subject's thinking tends to be less mature or less sophisticated. Conversely, *M* responses given by children or younger adolescents usually include some answers that have more juvenile or primitive characteristics. If the *M* responses of a younger subject contain none of these features, it can be postulated that the subject's thinking tends to be more sophisticated and/or mature than is common for his or her peers. *Summarize findings for this cluster.*

Case 1 Result: The quality of two of her three *M* answers is rather common (a lady looking in the mirror at herself, two children looking at each other). Although both are adorned, neither is very sophisticated. The third *M* is somewhat more juvenile (red devils that are falling), but not markedly so. Thus, it can be speculated that the quality of her thinking is similar to that of most adults but may be marked at times by less maturity than might be expected.

Case 1 Summary

The presence of a pervasive extratensive coping style suggests that most of her thinking is influenced significantly by her feelings and that she is disposed to rely heavily on external feedback in forming judgments. An increase in peripheral mental activity appears to be related to situationally-related stress, which creates some noticeable interference with attention and concentration operations. The subject is the sort of person who is inclined to use her capacities for thinking more to avoid reality than to deal directly with it. She does this by replacing reality with fantasy much more than most people. Her disposition to frequent "flights into fantasy" creates a kind of self-imposed helplessness in which she relies heavily on the actions of others for decision making and problem solving. Apparently, she also attempts to intellectualize somewhat more often than most adults as a way of dealing with emotions that she perceives to be stressful. Although this may be useful at times, the overall quality of her thinking is not very sophisticated, and it is likely that some of these efforts will be more transparent than effective.

SUMMARY

The procedures for searching through the data for each cluster and testing for each potential issue may seem arduous and time-consuming. Rorschach interpretation is an exacting task in which "no stone" can be left unturned. But, the routines tend to be applied much more easily as experience increases, the amount of time required decreases considerably.

If the findings for each cluster have been summarized during the interpretive search, a final summary or report is relatively easy to create. It is accomplished by editing and integrating the summaries, as illustrated in the next chapter.

CHAPTER 10

The Final Description

Usually, the format for the summary or final description should follow the same pattern as the search strategy because many of the more important findings have been generated from the first three or four data sets. As noted in the preceding chapter, the task involves editing and integrating the findings from each cluster in a way that acknowledges both assets and liabilities.

The description rarely constitutes a "final report," mainly because it does not address some of the assessment issues that have been put forth in the referral. However, it usually is included as the bulk of a final report because it serves as a basis from which assessment issues are addressed and recommendations formulated. Case 1 serves as the first illustration of the process, beginning with a review of the most salient findings from the summaries developed from each cluster.

CASE 1

Findings

Controls   She has considerable resource readily accessible. Thus her capacities for control and tolerance for stress are usually at least as robust as those of most adults. These features have become somewhat less effective, however, because of situationally-related stress, which has increased demands substantially. Among these demands is a strong irritating sense of affective deprivation that is probably being experienced as loneliness or neglect. This may be situationally related, but it may also have some chronic underpinnings. She also tends to internalize feelings much more than most people. This also may have some relationship to the current stress situation, but it is equally plausible that this is more of a trait-like feature.

Situational Stress   Although the effects of the situationally-related stress are more modest than severe, the added stimulus demands have produced an overload state that has created a marked potential for emotional impulsiveness. Some of the stress appears related to an experience of emotional loss and probably translates psychologically as a strong feeling of loneliness. The stress effects probably are somewhat diffuse and may account for the subject's complaints of difficulty in concentration, as well as the numerous affective symptoms that she presents. Currently, her psychological state is much more complex than is usually the case and, although she appears to have a long-standing confusion about her feelings, this has intensified.

Self-Perception   Possibly the most important finding is the presence of the subject's strongly embedded narcissistic-like feature. She greatly overestimates her self-value and focuses much more on herself than on others. Generally, she externalizes responsibility, especially for negative events, and tends to avoid and/or deny unpleasantness. One consequence is that her interpersonal relationships usually are more tenuous and less mature. Emotional losses or rejections often have a major impact because they are perceived as insults to the inflated, overglorified sense of personal value. She appears to engage in some introspection, but this may represent an attempt to take distance from emotions that are painful or difficult to control. Her self-concept appears to be based much more on imagination than on real experience. She seems acutely aware of her current difficulties with control and is experiencing significant feelings of helplessness, but she also seems to be attempting to deny the intensity of the experience. She is quite cautious and apparently feels that it is necessary to be defensively prepared.

Interpersonal Perception   She probably tends to seek relationships that both coincide with her passive-dependent style and afford some reassurance for her overglorified sense of personal worth. In other words, they must be with people who are both supportive and nurturing. Such relationships are difficult to achieve in the adult world, and they usually increase one's vulnerability to the manipulations of others. It seems likely that she has some awareness of this, as findings suggest that she is less secure about her interpersonal relationships than are most people. She often attempts to contend with or conceal these feelings of insecurity or discomfort by using a pseudo-intellectual authoritarian approach to many issues. Although she is open to social interaction, she is also cautious and possibly even reluctant to initiate exchanges, especially those that may require more tact and sophistication, or those that may create unwanted demands on her or pose hazards regarding control of the situation. Overall, it is doubtful that many of her relationships are marked by maturity and/or depth.

Affect   She uses her emotions a great deal to contend with coping demands. She usually merges her feelings with her thoughts and because of this, much of her decision making is marked by intuitive features. She likes to test her decisions through trial-and-error activity and is probably not very reluctant to display her feelings. Unfortunately, the effectiveness of this style appears to be impeded by the fact that she is an overly intense person who does not modulate her emotional discharges as much as most adults. Thus, her thinking is often quite vulnerable to judgments that may be excessively influenced by feelings, and it is likely that she often conveys the impression of being impulsive. Some of her emotional structure appears to be more childlike or primitive than is expected for an adult. On a more positive note, she is no more oriented to involvements with emotional stimuli than most adults and she does not appear to have any unusual negative emotional sets toward her environment. She is often confused by her feelings, which may relate directly to her problems with modulation, but may have more extensive origins, such as her chronic struggle to maintain her overglorified self-value while creating and sustaining profitable dependency relations with others.

Processing   She tends to invest about as much effort in processing as do most adults but currently she is prone to become overly involved in the complexity of a stimulus field. This excessive involvement is probably more a product of her ongoing situational stress than a chronic style-like feature. In some instances, the overall quality of her processing is less mature and sophisticated than is expected for adults. Although she is usually consistent in her processing habits, she also is more prone than most people to narrow and/or reorganize a stimulus field in ways that make it easier to manage.

Mediation   There are no major problems with her mediational operations. She is inclined to translate stimuli in less conventional ways, and, at times, this inclination is exacerbated by the problems that she has in modulating affect. Nonetheless, she seems as prone as most adults to make conventional responses when the situational circumstances clearly define expected or acceptable answers.

Ideation   Most of her thinking is influenced considerably by her feelings and she is disposed to rely heavily on external feedback in forming judgments. Currently, she is experiencing an increase in peripheral mental activity that appears to be related to situationally-related stress and this causes noticeable interference with attention and concentration operations. She is inclined to use her thinking more to avoid reality than to deal directly with it. She does this by replacing reality with fantasy much more than do most people. Her disposition to frequent "flights into fantasy" creates a kind of self-imposed helplessness in which she relies heavily on the actions of others for decision making and problem solving. Apparently, she also attempts to intellectualize more often than most adults as a way of dealing with emotions that she perceives to be stressful. Although this may be useful at times, the overall quality of her thinking is not very sophisticated, and it is likely that some of these efforts are more transparent than effective.

Case 1 Final Description

This 29-year-old female has considerable resource organized in ways that make it readily accessible for use in forming and implementing decisions. Thus, her capacities for control and tolerance for stress are usually as robust as those of most adults. However, these features currently are less effective because of some situationally-related stress. The effects of the stress are more modest than severe, but they have created a state of psychological overload. This overload has created a potential for impulsiveness that is more likely to manifest in her emotions than in her thinking.

Much of the subject's stress appears related to an experience of emotional loss and probably translates as strong feelings of loneliness or neglect. The effects of the stress are diffuse and may account for her complaints of difficulty in concentration, as well as the numerous affective symptoms that she presents. Currently, her psychological operations are more complex than usual, and, although she appears to have a long-standing confusion about her feelings, this confusion has become intensified.

Although her feelings of loneliness or neglect are probably stress related, they may also have some chronic features. In other words, she may have stronger needs for emotional attention and closeness than do most people. She tends to internalize feelings more often than she would prefer, which may have some relationship to the current stress situation, but it is equally plausible that this is more of a trait-like feature. The reason that it is difficult to sort out some of the stress effects from more enduring characteristics is because of her basic personality structure.

She is intensely self-centered and greatly overestimates her self-value. One by-product of this is a tendency to focus much more on herself than on others. As a result, her interpersonal relationships usually are more tenuous and less mature. Thus, emotional losses or rejections are likely to have a substantial impact on her because she perceives them as insults to her overglorified sense of personal worth.

Actually, her self-concept is based more on imagination than on real experience. Nonetheless, it is important for her to defend her inflated sense of self and, because of this, she usually externalizes responsibility, especially for negative events, and tends to avoid and/or deny unpleasantness. For instance, she is acutely aware of her current difficulties with control and is experiencing significant feelings of helplessness, but she also seems to be attempting to deny the intensity of the experience. This may account for the fact that her presenting symptoms are more subtle and less precise than might be expected of most people in a stress situation.

A second major personality feature is a strong passive-dependent orientation. She seems prone to seek relationships that are both supportive and nurturing. Unfortunately, this usually increases her vulnerability to the manipulations of others. It seems likely that she has some awareness of this and she seems considerably less secure about her interpersonal relationships than are most people. She attempts to contend with or conceal these feelings of insecurity or discomfort by using a pseudo-intellectual authoritarian approach to many issues. Although she is open to social interaction, she is also cautious and possibly even reluctant to initiate exchanges, especially those that may require more tact and sophistication. She is especially defensive about relationships that may create unwanted demands on her or pose hazards regarding control of the situation. Overall, it is doubtful that many of her relationships are marked by maturity and/or depth.

A third major personality dimension is that she uses her emotions a great deal to contend with coping demands. Typically, she merges her feelings with her thoughts and thus, much of her decision making is markedly influenced by her feelings. She prefers to test her decisions through trial-and-error activity and is probably not very reluctant to display her feelings. Although this is a common approach for many people, the effectiveness of this style is reduced by the fact that she is an overly intense person who does not modulate her emotional discharges as much as most adults. It is likely that she often conveys the impression of being excessively emotional or even impulsive. This may be an even greater liability for her because some of her emotional structure appears to be more childlike or primitive than is expected for an adult, and this creates a marked potential for ineffective or maladaptive emotional behaviors. She is no more oriented to involvements with emotional stimuli than most adults, and she does not appear to have any unusual negative emotional sets toward her environment.

She invests about as much effort in processing information as do most adults, but currently she is prone to become overly involved in the complexity of a stimulus field. This may be a product of the ongoing stress but, even if the stress did not exist, the quality of her processing is often less mature and unsophisticated. Although she is consistent in her processing habits, she is more prone than most people to narrow and/or reorganize a stimulus field in ways that make it easier to manage. She is inclined to translate information in ways that are a bit more personal and less conventional than most adults, and this inclination is exacerbated at times by the problems that she has in modulating affect. Nonetheless, she does not distort, and she seems as prone as most adults to make conventional responses when the circumstances of the situation clearly define expected or acceptable answers.

Although her thinking usually is clear, a current increase in peripheral mental activity appears related to the experience of her feelings of helplessness. This creates some noticeable interference with attention and concentration operations. Unfortunately, she is inclined to use her capacities for thinking more to avoid reality than to deal directly with it. She does this by replacing reality with fantasy much more than do most people. Her disposition to frequent "flights into fantasy" creates a kind of self-imposed helplessness in which she relies heavily on the actions of others for decision making and problem solving. Apparently, she also attempts to intellectualize somewhat more often than most adults as a way of dealing with emotions that she perceives to be stressful. Although this may be useful at times, the overall quality of her thinking is not very sophisticated and some of these efforts are likely to be more transparent than effective.

Recommendations Based on the Final Description

Obviously, the final description can be used in several ways. It can stand alone as a report, or it can be used as a source of questions that might be answerable from other information that is available or that could be collected. For example, additional history information regarding Case 1 might contribute significantly in developing a better understanding of how some of her stylistic features are manifest, such as her self-centeredness, passive-dependency, and problems in modulating affective displays. Similarly, findings from cognitive testing might shed some light on how seriously her attention and concentration are being affected by her stress condition.

In most cases, unless serious pathology is present, the final description does not contain any specific diagnostic formulation, although it can be used as a basis from which one can be generated. For instance, the Case 1 findings include evidence for narcissistic, dependency, and histrionic features. Although these features are not very desirable when considered in light of "optimal" precursors to adjustment, none is so obviously disruptive to the overall psychological organization as to be considered pathological. If a DSM model for diagnosis is applied, any or all of these three features can serve as a basis for an Axis II decision.

Actually, the only findings that might contribute directly to an Axis I diagnostic formulation are those related to the current situational stress. She is in overload and distress, and there is evidence that her attention and concentration are impaired. These findings would support a DSM Axis I diagnosis of Generalized Anxiety Disorder or Adjustment Disorder with Anxious Mood.

but dhisis!
most important!

As is the case with diagnosis, the final description usually does not include specific recommendations for intervention, although it clearly can serve as the basis for various intervention considerations. In Case 1, the findings clearly point to a need for some form of supportive intervention to assist in working through the current stress situation. The findings also highlight the importance of considering her strong passive-dependent orientation, her tendency to externalize cause, and her excessive use of fantasy to replace reality, when selecting the specific form of support to be employed. If a reconstructive model of intervention was to be formulated, several obvious liabilities such as the narcissistic feature, passivity, and affective volatility should be viewed as potential long term treatment targets. If a less lengthy developmental model of treatment were to be considered, such objectives as improving her capacity to modulate emotion and restructuring her interpersonal perception and behavior might be more viable.

these are good
ambi-tious goals,
also - pea?
how?

Regardless of the form of intervention, she has several important assets that can be used to facilitate treatment. First, and most important, she has considerable resource available to her. Second, she has a consistent extratensive coping style. Third, she makes a serious effort to process information. Fourth, ordinarily she does not distort perceptual inputs and, in fact, she usually makes conventional responses when the parameters for expected or accepted responses are obvious. Fifth, her thinking is reasonably clear, and she already engages in some self-inspecting behavior. Finally, she has no obvious negative sets toward the environment. In fact, she is reasonably interested in others, and her current gnawing sense of loneliness should facilitate the development of a working therapeutic relationship.

such as?
translation
needed

Case 1 Epilogue   This subject entered individual treatment with a female therapist whom she visited once weekly. The focus of the treatment was supportive, dealing mainly with the issues of the divorce and the custody arrangements. The divorce was completed six months after the original assessment and joint custody of the daughter was mandated by the court. The therapist reports that most of the presenting symptoms remitted during the first three months of treatment. The therapist also noted that the subject seemed well motivated to deal with issues of social relationships and her dependency on men, however, once the divorce agreement was signed, the subject terminated treatment.

CASE 2: ANXIETY AND SOMATIC SYMPTOMS

The second case regarding the formulation of a final description and its use in generating recommendations involves a subject with presenting symptoms very similar to those of Case 1. Case 2 is a 31-year-old single female who has been employed for the past seven years as a dresser in a theater. She was referred by her physician whom she has visited 13 times in 11 months. She complains of headaches, tension, dizziness, fatigue, upset stomach, anxiety, and difficulties concentrating. After the second visit, a neurological examination was completed and all findings were negative. She has been prescribed various medications but none provide relief consistently. The referral asks if there is any clear evidence of psychological origins for the symptoms and requests recommendations concerning intervention.

She is the third of four children. Her sister, age 39, is married, has a Ph.D. in English, and teaches at a university. Another sister, age 37, has been married for 14 years (and has three children) after completing two years of college. A brother, age 29, is single and has been in the Coast Guard for 10 years. Her father, age 60, owns a small printing firm that he purchased after having worked for a newspaper for 30 years. Her mother, age 65, is a housewife. The father was in psychotherapy during his last two years at the newspaper because of "job-related tension." There is no other psychiatric history in the immediate family. The subject graduated from high school at age 18 and entered a liberal arts college. Although her grades were above average (cumulative grade point average of 3.1), she decided to withdraw after her second year: "Nothing interested me, I wanted to get out in the world." She worked as a pool secretary but quit after one year: "It was boring." Her next position was in the ticket office at the theater for which she now works. Subsequently, she applied for a backstage position and obtained her present position. She says, "It's wonderful work. They are great people to work with."

Her developmental history is unremarkable. She began dating regularly during high school (no one regular), and her first sexual experience was at age 20 while in college: "It was o.k., but I was pretty uptight about it." She says that she has several friends but does not see them often because of her work. She shares an apartment with a 27-year-old female who works in a bank: "We're good friends but we don't talk alot because I work nights." She dates once or twice each week, usually with the 28-year-old ticket manager of the theater in which she works. They have sexual relations "infrequently," and she reports them as being "very satisfying." They have considered marriage but says that she would prefer to wait "for awhile."

The Interpretive Strategy

Because the record contains 18 answers, there is no reason to challenge its interpretive usefulness. The first five Key variables are negative, but the sixth, Lambda > 0.99, is positive as L has a value of 1.0. Thus, unlike Case 1, the complete order by which the clusters should be searched is determined by the single Key variable. The appropriate order is:

PROCESSING → MEDIATION → IDEATION → CONTROLS → AFFECT → SELF PERCEPTION → INTERPERSONAL PERCEPTION.

Initial Proposition   In almost all cases in which the interpretive strategy is decided from a Key variable, an initial proposition should be formulated, based on data concerning the Key variable. In this instance, it is that a basic response style exists that is oriented toward reducing stimulus situations to their most easily managed level. This style often requires a narrowing or simplification of stimulus fields that are perceived as complex or ambiguous. This coping style reflects a form of psychological economizing and can often serve to enhance adjustment, especially for those who may be intellectually limited or neurologically impaired; however, it also may lead to problems in processing information and/or mediation and can create a potential for a higher frequency of behaviors that do not coincide with social demands and/or expectations.

Case 2: A 31-Year-Old Female

Card	Response	Inquiry
I	1. Well it c.b. a bf I suppose but that's all I can c	E: (Rpts S's resp) S: These w.b. the wgs & this is the body part & the antennae r here it has that generl form to it, lik a bf
	E: Most people c more than 1 thg S: Let me look some more	
	2. It c.b. a wm in the cntr I thk, just standg there, thts really all I can c (woman)	E: (Rpts S's resp) S: Well actually its not too good, u can't c a head, these w.b. the arms & ths is the body part & legs, thes bumps up here w.b. a funny hat but u can't c the face E: U said the bumps w.b. a funny hat? S: Yes, sort of a big sun hat I supp.
II	3. Ths c.b. the heads of 2 dogs I really don't c a.t. else	E: (Rpts S's resp) S: Well it ll 2 dogs, c one here & one here, the nose & ear, just this darkr prt
III	4. Ths c.b. 2 wm bending over smthg as if thy were inspecting it	E: (Rpts S's resp) S: One here & here, the legs & the upper body & the heads & these r their arms, thy seem to be lookg into ths cntr thg, mayb a basket of s.s.
	5. Ths c.b. a bf too	E: (Rpts S's resp) S: It has the wgs, larger than the body & the small body part
IV	6. Ths re. me of the hunchback of Notre Dame like he is sitting on a stool there	E: (Rpts S's resp) S: Its a great hulk, stooped over as if in thot, I always liked that book, c the large legs & arms here & ths is the stool E: U said stooped over? S: Rounded like stooped, as if the head were further forward, its his back here E: Its his back here? S: Yes, u'r seeing him from the back w his head bent forward & his shoulders stooped forward as if he was thinking
V	7. Down here u can get the impress of an elf-like figure leaning against a tree	E: (Rpts S's resp) S: Yes, c the little elf hat here & the face & its as if his arms r folded & ths drkr area c.b. a tree, c the ragged edging here mite b leaves or branches
	8. This rem me of a vulture w the big ugly head & beak, its in flight	E: (Rpts S's resp) S: Its wgs r stretched out like it was flyg along looking for prey, w the beak opened & the blackness of it being ugh E: Ugh? S: Its just not very attractive, all black like that

(continued)

235

Case 2: (Continued)

Card	Response	Inquiry
	9. Ths part ll the head of a goose	E: (Rpts S's resp) S: Its just the long neck & the head, u can c the beak here, the liter colored part, whitish, thy r always liter colored than the head I believe
VI	10. I suppose the side part c.b. lik a face w a gigantic nose, s.t. lik Cyrano	E: (Rpts S's resp) S: I didn't mean Cyrano, just like Cyrano, c the big huge nose & this is the forehead & the indentation is where the eye is & the receding chin
	11. I suppose this whole bttm part might b an A skin but the top is nothing that I can think of	E: (Rpts S's resp) S: It is pretty irregular, these cb legs out here & it does hav a furry appearance to it E: Furry appearance? S: The diff shades of coloring there
VII	12. Ths c.b. 2 children, just the heads, looking at e.o.	E: (Rpts S's resp) S: The outlines seem quite clear, 2 littl girls w their hair upswept, the noses & the chins c here (points)
	13. The little forehead part ll it cb a snail too	E: (Rpts S's resp) S: It just re me of that, like a cartoon snail E: Cartoon snail? S: Well not real, but more like u mite c in Fantasia or a cartoon lik tht, it just has that sort of shape
VIII	14. Ths is like an abstract paintg of st, mayb an anatomy representation	E: (Rpts S's resp) S: Its very colorful & laid out in symmetry, the pink cld repr lungs I suppose & there's a rib area & othr features too but I can't identify them, its really an abstact
	15. Oh, the pink cb animals too	E: (Rpts S's resp) S: Thyr small A's, like mice it seems, here r the legs & the head & the body & tail
IX	<16. The only thg I can find here is a man's head, right here	E: (Rpts S's resp) S: Its just a head, roundish, maybe w a mustache, here's the nose & forehead, that's all
X	17. Ths blue cb a spider	E: (Rpts S's resp) S: It has all the legs & the round body in the cntr
	18. Here in the pink is the face of an elf, one on each side,	E: (Rpts S's resp) S: It has that outline, like a child's it ll an imp I think face w the forehead, nose & mouth, its quite clear, just here (points)

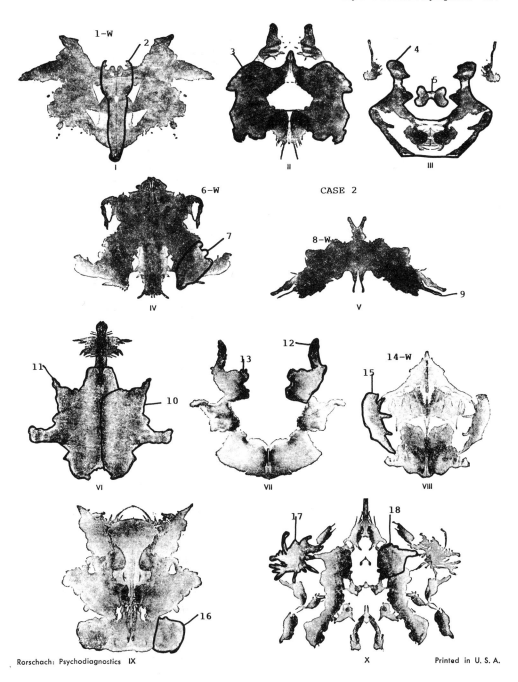

CASE 2

CASE 2. SEQUENCE OF SCORES

CARD	NO	LOC	#	DETERMINANT(S)	(2)	CONTENT(S)	POP	Z	SPECIAL SCORES
I	1	Wo	1	Fo		A	P	1.0	
	2	Dd+	99	Mp-		H,Cg		4.0	
II	3	Do	1	Fo	2	Ad	P		
III	4	D+	1	Mpo	2	H,Hh	P	3.0	
	5	Do	3	Fo		A			
IV	6	W+	1	Mp.FDo		(H),Hh	P	4.0	
	7	Dd+	99	Mp-		(H),Bt,Cg		4.0	
V	8	Wo	1	FMa.FC'o		A		1.0	
	9	Ddo	22	FYu		Ad			
VI	10	Do	4	Fo		Hd			
	11	Do	1	FTo		Ad	P		
VII	12	D+	1	Mpo	2	Hd	P	3.0	
	13	Do	8	Fu		(A)			
VIII	14	Wo	1	CF-		Art,An		4.5	
	15	Do	1	Fo	2	A	P		
IX	16	Do	4	Fo		Hd			
X	17	Do	1	Fo		A	P		
	18	Ddo	99	Fo	2	(Hd)			

```
CASE 2.  STRUCTURAL SUMMARY
=====================================================================================
LOCATION              DETERMINANTS              CONTENTS        S-CONSTELLATION
FEATURES         BLENDS         SINGLE                          NO..FV+VF+V+FD>2
                                            H   = 2, 0          NO..Col-Shd Bl>0
Zf    = 8        M.FD           M  = 4       (H) = 2, 0          YES..Ego<.31,>.44
ZSum  = 24.5     FM.FC'         FM = 0       Hd  = 3, 0          NO..MOR > 3
ZEst  = 24.0                    m  = 0       (Hd)= 1, 0          NO..Zd > +- 3.5
                                FC = 0       Hx  = 0, 0          NO..es > EA
W  = 4                          CF = 1       A   = 5, 0          YES..CF+C > FC
  (Wv = 0)                      C  = 0       (A) = 1, 0          NO..X+% < .70
D  = 10                         Cn = 0       Ad  = 3, 0          NO..S > 3
Dd = 4                          FC'= 0       (Ad)= 0, 0          NO..P < 3 or > 8
S  = 0                          C'F= 0       An  = 0, 1          NO..Pure H < 2
                                C' = 0       Art = 1, 0          NO..R < 17
   DQ                           FT = 1       Ay  = 0, 0          2.....TOTAL
.........(FQ-)                  TF = 0       Bl  = 0, 0
  +  =  5  ( 2)                 T  = 0       Bt  = 0, 1          SPECIAL SCORINGS
  o  = 13  ( 1)                 FV = 0       Cg  = 0, 2             Lv1    Lv2
v/+  =  0  ( 0)                 VF = 0       Cl  = 0, 0          DV  = 0x1    0x2
  v  =  0  ( 0)                 V  = 0       Ex  = 0, 0          INC = 0x2    0x4
                                FY = 1       Fd  = 0, 0          DR  = 0x3    0x6
                                YF = 0       Fi  = 0, 0          FAB = 0x4    0x7
                                Y  = 0       Ge  = 0, 0          ALOG= 0x5
                                Fr = 0       Hh  = 0, 2          CON = 0x7
   FORM QUALITY                 rF = 0       Ls  = 0, 0            SUM6  = 0
                                FD = 0       Na  = 0, 0           WSUM6  = 0
       FQx  FQf  MQual  SQx     F  = 9       Sc  = 0, 0
  +  =  0    0     0     0                   Sx  = 0, 0          AB = 0    CP  = 0
  o  = 13    8     3     0                   Xy  = 0, 0          AG = 0    MOR = 0
  u  =  2    1     0     0                   Id  = 0, 0          CFB= 0    PER = 0
  -  =  3    0     2     0                                       COP= 0    PSV = 0
none=  0    --     0     0      (2) = 5
=====================================================================================
                  RATIOS, PERCENTAGES, AND DERIVATIONS

R = 18         L = 1.00         FC:CF+C = 0: 1     COP = 0     AG = 0
-------------------------------  Pure C  =    0    Food        = 0
EB = 5: 1.0  EA  = 6.0  EBPer= 5.0  Afr  =0.38     Isolate/R  =0.06
eb = 1: 3    es  = 4      D  = 0   S      = 0       H:(H)Hd(Hd)= 2: 6
             Adj es = 4  Adj D = 0  Blends:R= 2:18  (HHd):(AAd)= 3: 1
-------------------------------  CP     = 0        H+A:Hd+Ad  =10: 7
FM = 1 : C'= 1   T = 1
m  = 0 : V = 0   Y = 1
                         P    = 8      Zf  = 8      3r+(2)/R=0.28
a:p    = 1: 5  Sum6  = 0  X+% =0.72    Zd  = +0.5   Fr+rF   = 0
Ma:Mp  = 0: 5  Lv2   = 0  F+% =0.89    W:D:Dd = 4:10: 4  FD   = 1
2AB+Art+Ay= 1  WSum6 = 0  X-% =0.17    W:M  = 4: 5  An+Xy   = 1
M-     = 2     Mnone = 0  S-% =0.00    DQ+  = 5     MOR     = 0
                         Xu% =0.11     DQv  = 0
------------------------------------------------------------------------
   SCZI = 2     DEPI = 4    CDI = 3    S-CON = 2    HVI = No    OBS = No
=====================================================================================
```

Information Processing

The major reason that the information processing cluster is selected first in the search pattern is to determine if the High Lambda style includes processing deficiencies. As noted in Chapter 5, the style is often related to a defensive process in which stimulus elements are ignored or judged unimportant. Usually, this occurs during translation or mediation and processing habits are not affected. Nonetheless, in some instances, deficits in processing activities relate directly to the High Lambda style, and may even have a casual effect. Case 2 data concerning information processing are shown in Table 51.

Case 2 Findings　The six steps involved in searching this cluster, as described in Chapter 9, yield some interesting results. Step 1 (Lambda) has already been noted to be positive because of the Key variable. Step 2 findings (OBS and HVI) are negative, but Step 3 (Zf, $W:D:Dd$, $W:M$), which concerns processing effort, reveals that she is very conservative in her approach to processing new information. Zf is lower than average, W is less than half the value for $D + Dd$, and $W:M$ is less than $1:1$. This finding usually signals some form of withdrawal from or avoidance of social competition. The Step 4 (DQ) evaluation indicates that the record contains five $DQ+$ answers and no v or $v/+$ responses. Thus, although she is conservative in her processing effort, the quality of her processing appears to be similar to that of most people. The Step 5 (Zd, PSV) data appear to support the Step 4 conclusion, as the data for both variables are unremarkable.

The Step 6 review of the Location Sequencing produces two findings. First, she is highly consistent in her approach. Her four W answers are all first responses and her four Dd responses are all last responses. Second, the sequencing also provides additional evidence concerning her conservative approach to processing. Two of the four W's are to blots in which a W is easier to formulate than a D or Dd answer (Cards I and V), and three of the four W's are followed by Dd's, almost as if she sought to escape the challenge of the blot complexity and work only with more easily managed areas. She never gave more than two answers for a blot and, for two of the more difficult blots (II, IX), she gave only one D answer.

Case 2 Summary　She is very cautious and conservative in her motivation to process new information. This is consistent with her orientation to avoid complexity and deal with things on a more simple level as reflected by her High Lambda style. Nevertheless, her tactics of processing appear to be reasonably efficient, and the quality of her processing activity is similar to that of most adults.

Table 51.　Information Processing Variables for Case 2

$L = 1.0$　OBS = Neg　HVI = Neg		LOCATION SEQUENCING		
$Zd = +0.5$	$DQ+$　= 5	I W, Dd	IV W, Dd	VII D, D
$Zf = 8$	$DQv/+ = 0$	II D	V W, Dd	VIII W, D
$W:D:Dd = 4:10:4$	DQv　= 0	III D, D	VI D, D	IX D
$W:M = 4:5$	PSV　= 0			X D, Dd

Thus, there is no reason to believe that her High Lambda style contributes to inputs that are lackadaisical or unsophisticated.

Cognitive Mediation

The data in the cognitive mediation cluster are especially important when a High Lambda style is involved because the style often leads to a disregard for social conventions and/or expectations. Thus, information regarding the way in which stimuli are translated becomes important in evaluating the extent to which the style may predispose behaviors that may be asocial or antisocial. Case 2 data concerning mediation are shown in Table 52.

Case 2 Findings   The High Lambda and negative OBS have already been noted. Thus, the search begins with Step 3 (Populars). The value of *P* is 8, which falls at the upper end of the average range and may even be somewhat higher than expected in light of the modest length of the record. This indicates that the subject definitely is prone to translate stimuli conventionally in situations in which the acceptable or conventional is readily apparent. It also argues against the likelihood of asocial or antisocial behaviors, even though she tends to be overly conservative in processing and prone to simplify stimulus situations. Although the Step 4 (*FOx+*) finding is unremarkable, the Step 5 finding supports the conclusions derived from Step 3. The $X+\%$ of 72% is within the average range, and the $F+\%$ of 89% is slightly above average. The difference between the two values is even more marked when the raw data are studied. Nine of her 18 responses are *Pure F*, and eight of the nine have an *ordinary* form quality. Conversely, four of the remaining nine answers have *unusual* or *minus* form quality. In other words, when she does simplify or ignore stimulus complexity, she is very conventional, more so than most people, but when she becomes involved in translating complexity she is considerably less conventional than would be expected. This seems to support the notion that her High Lambda style plays a very important defensive role for her.

Step 6 (*FOnone*) offers no information, but the yields from Steps 7 (*Xu%*) and 8 (*X−%*) seem important, especially in light of the findings from Step 5. The *Xu%* of 11% is well within the average range, indicting that she is no more likely to translate stimuli in idiosyncratic or overly personalized ways than most people. However, the $X-\%$ of 17% provokes some concern. It is higher than expected, and, even though it represents only three minus answers, the frequency

Table 52. Cognitive Mediation Variables for Case 2

Lambda = 1.0	OBS = Negative		MINUS FEATURES
P = 8	$X+\%$ = .72	I	2. *Dd+ Mp− H,Cg 4.0*
FQx+ = 0	$F+\%$ = .89	IV	7. *Dd+ Mp− (H),Bt,Cg 4.0*
FQxo = 13	$Xu\%$ = .11	VIII	14. *Wo CF− Art,An 4.5*
FQxu = 2	$X-\%$ = .17		
FQx− = 3	$S-\%$ = 0		
FQnon = 0	CONFAB = 0		

seems a bit high for one who is very conservative and conventional otherwise. None are *S* responses. The evaluations for Steps 9 and 10 (sequencing and clustering) do not reveal a clustering effect for all three answers, but two of the three are second answers, both of which have *Dd* locations, and both involve passive human movement. This raises the possibility that, although she is oriented toward making conventional responses, she has some difficulties in thinking that are contributing to mediational distortions more often than is expected. This possibility appears to be reaffirmed by the results of the Step 11 (level of distortion) evaluation.

The first minus answer in the record was given to an area not numbered on Card I. It is in the center, involving a composite of *Dd*21, plus the middle upper section of *Dd*24, plus *D*3:

> It could be a woman in the center I think, just standing there, that's really all I can see. (Inquiry) Well actually it's not too good, you can't see a head, these would be the arms and this is the body part and legs, these bumps up here would be a funny hat but u can't see the face.

Although the area involved is quite unusual, most features are readily apparent. Some examiners might even be prone to assign a *u* form quality, but that would be erroneous since nonexistent lines form a significant part of the figure. Nonetheless, it is not a severe distortion.

The second minus was given to the *Dd*31 area of Card IV:

> Down here you can get the impression of an elf-like figure leaning against a tree. (Inquiry) Yes, see the little elf hat here and the face and it's as if his arms are folded and this darker area could be a tree, see the ragged edging here might be leaves or branches.

This "figure" is very difficult to distinguish in the blot area and apparently is a Level 2 minus answer. The fact that it is an *M* − response reemphasizes the earlier postulate that the subject's thinking may become quite distorted and contribute to mediational problems.

The third minus response was given to the whole Card VIII:

> This is like an abstract painting of something, maybe like an anatomy representation. (Inquiry) It's very colorful and laid out in symmetry, the pink could represent lungs I suppose and there is a rib area and other features too but I can't identify them, it's really an abstract.

As with the first minus answer, this is easy to identify and would not have been scored as minus except for the specificity of lungs.

Case 2 Summary   There are some intriguing issues concerning the subject's mediation. Unlike many High Lambda style subjects, she has no obvious major problems in mediation, but she may have more subtle problems that tend to be concealed or defended against by the use of the style. It is very clear that she is oriented toward making conventional or socially acceptable responses. Thus, the probability that the High Lambda style may lead to asocial or antisocial behaviors is extremely remote. On the other hand, there are significant indications suggesting that, on occasion, her mediation is marked by considerable detachment from reality.

In some respects, the findings seem contradictory, indicating that she strives to be conventional and yet finds it difficult to do so unless she avoids complexity. In fact, in some instances, her thinking seems to become overwhelmed by complexity and results in a disregard for conventionality and serious mediational distortions. This prompts a tentative hypothesis that the High Lambda style and the very conservative approach to processing are intertwined as defensive tactics that are designed to contend with some difficulties that she perceives regarding interactions with her feelings and/or with the environment.

Ideation

Quite often, as is true for Case 2, findings from the two preceding clusters in the cognitive triad raise issues that may be clarified or extended as information concerning thinking becomes available. Data concerning ideation are shown in Table 53.

Case 2 Findings   The results of Steps 1 (*EB*) and 2 (*EBPer*) indicate that she has a markedly pervasive ideational coping style. In most situations, she prefers to delay formulating decisions or initiating behaviors until all apparent possibilities have been considered. She also prefers to keep her feelings at a more peripheral level during decision operations and tends to rely on internal evaluations in making judgments. Unfortunately, the pervasiveness of the style limits her flexibility and its effectiveness depends largely on the clarity of her own logic.

The low value noted in Step 3 (left-side *eb*) is quite intriguing. It suggests that, like many people with a High Lambda style, she does not respond much to more subtle internal and external stimuli or that she reacts quickly to contend with those stimuli. The presence of her pervasive ideational style seems to decrease the likelihood that the latter is true. Thus, if she attempts to avoid or ignore responding to subtle stimuli, a question is raised about whether this may relate to her presenting symptoms. Internal needs do not become dormant simply because of a failure to acknowledge or respond to their presence and, as a result, they often manifest in less direct but clearly disruptive ways.

Table 53.   Variables Related to Ideation for Case 2

		M QUALITY	CRITICAL SPECIAL SCORES		
EB = 5 : 1	*EBPer* = 5.0				
eb = 1 : 3	(*FM* = 1 *m* = 0)	+ = 0	DV = 0	DV2 = 0	
a:p = 1 : 5	*Ma:Mp* = 0 : 5	o = 3	INC = 0	INC2 = 0	
2*Ab*+(*Art*+*Ay*) = 1		u = 0	DR = 0	DR2 = 0	
MOR = 0		– = 2	FAB = 0	FAB2 = 0	
RESPONSES TO BE READ FOR QUALITY			ALOG = 0	SUM6 = 0	
2, 4, 6, 7, 12			CON = 0	WSUM6 = 0	

AND 1:5 see p 221, steps

The Step 4 data ($a:p$) are not significant, but the Step 5 review ($M^a:M^p$) uncovers another very important stylistic feature. She uses fantasy with an abusive excess to avoid and/or deny reality. These somewhat routine flights into fantasy in situations that she regards as being unpleasant serve a temporary defensive purpose but they also create a self-imposed helplessness that requires a dependency on others for decision making. This is especially detrimental for those who have a marked ideational coping style because the effective use of the style is abrogated in favor of an avoidant-dependent orientation in situations that appear to be overly complicated or potentially stressful.

Step 6 (Intellectualization Index) is not significant, and there are no MOR or Special Scores to be considered in Steps 7, 8, and 9. The absence of Special Scores could be a positive finding. It does not rule out the possibility of cognitive slippage, but the probability of significant cognitive slippage is very remote. This may seem somewhat contradictory to the Step 10 (M − frequency) result, which indicates the likelihood of peculiar or disturbed thinking. Slippage usually involves patterns of thought that are loose, fluid, or unsystematically illogical. Peculiar or disturbed thought typically is strange and marked by faulty judgment, but it is not necessarily loose, fluid, or unsystematic. Thus, although her thinking is probably peculiar, there is no reason to suspect that it is loose or unsystematic. This hypothesis is not inconsistent with the results of the Step 11 (M − level of distortion) evaluation. One of the two M − answers does appear to be a Level 2 distortion, suggesting that her thinking is dominated sometimes by an unusually strong preoccupation that causes a disregard for reality.

The Step 12 (quality of M) evaluation shows no evidence of juvenile or primitive thinking. On the contrary, although three of the five movement answers are rather common (2, 4, 12), the remaining two (6. "This reminds me of the hunchback of Notre Dame like he is sitting on a stool there," and 7. "Down here you can get the impression an elf-like figure leaning against a tree") offer a glimpse of reasonably sophisticated thought.

Case 2 Summary Although she prefers to keep her thinking relatively free of emotional influence and delay decisions until all apparent possibilities are considered, the style does not work very well for her, especially in situations that she regards as threatening or stressful. In those instances, she is much more prone to avoid decision making by taking flight into a fantasy world that she controls and that permits her to deny or ignore reality. Unfortunately, this avoidance tactic forces her to become dependent on others for much of her decision making. It also tends to breed and sustain peculiarities in thinking and there is some reason to believe that she may be influenced frequently by some peculiar preoccupation. There is no evidence that her thinking is loose or disturbed. In fact, it is probably rather sophisticated at times. She apparently tries to avoid or ignore some subtle internal experiences that are provoked by her own needs. Although this is consistent with her orientation to simplify or avoid complexity, it may contribute in some way to her presenting symptoms.

Controls

Data for the variables concerning controls are shown in Table 54.

Table 54. Control-Related Variables for Case 2

$EB = 5:1.0$	$EA = 6.0$	$D = 0$	$CDI = 3$
$eb = 1:3$	$es = 4$ Adj$es = 4$	AdjD = 0	
$FM = 1$ $m = 0$ $C' = 1$ $T = 1$ $V = 0$ $Y = 1$			

Case 2 Findings Step 1 (D Scores and CDI) reveals that both D scores are zero and the CDI is not positive. This suggests that her capacity for control and tolerance for stress usually is like those of most adults, but the Step 2 (*EA*) test of the validity of the Adjusted D Score raises questions about the integrity of that conclusion. The *EA* is lower than average, indicating more limited available resource than usually is expected. The Step 3 (*EB*) review affords no information from which to challenge the reliability of *EA*. This leads to the hypothesis that she may be chronically more vulnerable to disruption by many of the natural stresses of everyday living because of more limited access to resources. This hypothesis is fueled by the Step 4 (adjusted *es*) and Step 5 (*eb*) evaluations. The Adjusted *es* is unexpectedly low, mainly because of the absence of *FM* responses, as the values in the right side of the *eb* are all within the expected range.

Case 2 Summary Although her capacity for control currently is adequate, she is more vulnerable to disorganization under perceived stress circumstances because she has fewer resources readily available than do most adults. Apparently, she has some awareness of this and has created an elaborate defense network to minimize demands on her so that her limited resource accessibility will be sufficient to maintain effective controls. That network appears to include a tendency to avoid responding to more subtle internal stimuli, a feature that probably relates directly to her High Lambda style, and is supplemented by her excessive use of fantasy.

Affect

The Case 2 variables related to affective features are shown in Table 55.

Case 2 Findings The DEPI is not positive, thus no initial proposition is warranted. Steps 1 (*EB*) and 2 (*EBPer*) are not applicable in searching this cluster as it

Table 55. Affect-Related Variables for Case 2

$EB = 5:1.0$	$EBPer = 5.0$ DEPI = 4		BLENDS
$eb = 1:3$	$(C = 1, T = 1, V = 0, Y = 1)$	M.FD	FM.FC$'$
$FC:CF + C = 0:1$	Pure $C = 0$		
$Afr = 0.38$	CP = 0		
$S = 0$	Col-Shd Bl = 0		

has previously been established that she has a marked ideational style in which she generally prefers to keep feelings at a peripheral level during decision making and is unlikely to alter that approach very much. Similarly, Step 3 is not applicable as the total values of the *eb* does not exceed 4. The Step 4 finding (*FC : CF + C*) suggests that she may have some trouble modulating her affective discharges, but the data for the ratio are very sparse, making that postulate tenuous. Steps 5 (Pure *C*), 7 (CP), and 8 (*S*) are not applicable but the Step 6 finding (*Afr*) is quite important and probably explains why all of the data for the cluster are sparse. It reflects a marked tendency to avoid emotional stimulation and suggests that she is very uncomfortable around emotion and usually very constrained or isolated in social situations. The very low number of blends, none of which are complex, noted in the review for Steps 9 through 13 is consistent with the High Lambda style and seems to indicate a kind of emotional impoverishment.

Case 2 Summary   This seems to be a person who is very fearful of, and prone to avoid, emotions whenever possible. This could relate to some apprehensiveness that she may have concerning difficulties in control, but it seems much more likely that her avoidance of affect is simply another piece of the defensive network that she has built around her High Lambda style that enables her to ignore or avoid all forms of complexity.

Self-Perception

The Case 2 data for the self-perception cluster are shown in Table 56.

Case 2 Findings   The Step 1 (*Fr + rF*) review yields no information but the Step 2 (Egocentricity Index) result is very important and probably explains some earlier findings. Her estimate of her personal worth tends to be negative, and she regards herself unfavorably in comparison with others. In this case, it probably signals a marked sense of insecurity. If that is true, it seems likely that her High Lambda style and the complex network of defenses that have developed have their origins in this feature. Step 3 (*FD*) indicates that she engages in self-inspecting behavior about as much as most adults, but, considered in light of the Step 2 finding, it seems probable that some of the introspection simply reinforces her negative self-value. The Step 4 *H : (H) + Hd + (Hd)* data are quite

Table 56.   Self-Perception Variables for Case 2

STRUCTURAL DATA		RESPONSES TO BE READ	
Fr+rF = 0	3r+(2)/R = 0.28	*MOR* RESPONSE	=
FD = 1	*V* = 0	MINUS RESPONSES	= 2, 7, 14
H : (H)+ HH)+Hd+(Hd) = 2 : 6		*M* RESPONSES	= 2, 4, 6, 7, 12
An+Xy = 1		*FM* RESPONSES	= 8
MOR = 0		*m* RESPONSES	=

important. They suggest that her self-image tends to be based largely on imagination rather than real experience. People such as this often have a faulty sense of themselves, which can create difficulties in both decision making and interpersonal relationships. The Step 5 ($An + Xy$) finding appears to be unremarkable, but the single An answer is a minus response that may be more revealing during the Step 8 review of contents. Steps 6 and 7 (MOR responses) are not applicable in this case.

The Steps 8 and 9 reviews involve seven answers. The first minus response (2) was given to Card I. It is especially intriguing because she makes the area more precise and in doing so creates imaginary lines, thereby forcing the *minus* form quality. Nonetheless, the answer is not unlike many *ordinary* responses given to all of the *D4* area:

> It could be a woman in the center I think, just standing there, that's really all I can see. (Inquiry) Well actually it's not too good, you can't see a head, these would be the arms and this is the body part and legs, these bumps up here would be a funny hat but u can't see the face.

There are several striking features. First, it is a very cautious, tentative response containing several qualifications (could be, I think, not too good, can't see). Second, it is clearly passive (just standing there). Third, she is critical of it (it's not too good), and finally she tends to overemphasize the fact that the face or head is not apparent (you can't see the head, you can't see the face).

The second minus is also very passive and striking because of the content:

> Down here you can get the impression of an elf-like figure leaning against a tree. (Inquiry) Yes, see the little elf hat here and the face and it's as if his arms are folded and this darker area could be a tree, see the ragged edging here might be leaves or branches.

This answer of a figure that is very difficult to distinguish must have considerable importance for her. It is less tentative than the first minus response but does have some of that quality. Although it is reasonable to assume that there is a direct self-representation in the answer, it is not as clear as might be desired. Historically, the term *elf* was used to describe a figure in the mist, difficult to see. In folklore, elves have magical qualities, are small, and often mischievous. Any or all of these features may relate to her self-concept, but a specific conclusion would be highly speculative.

The third minus answer is:

> This is like an abstract painting of something, maybe like an anatomy representation. (Inquiry) It's very colorful and laid out in symmetry, the pink could represent lungs I suppose and there is a rib area and other features too but I can't identify them, it's really an abstract.

This response is also very cautious and tentative (an abstract of something, maybe; I suppose; I can't identify them). The answer is also striking because it is the only color answer, but the impact is neutralized by her defining the blot as an abstract painting.

The three remaining *M* answers to be evaluated for projected material are 4, 6, and 12. As with the previously examined *M* answers, they are quite similar for their passivity. The first is:

> This could be two women bending over something as if they were inspecting it. (Inquiry) One's here and here, the legs and the upper body and the heads and these are their arms, they seem to be looking into this center thing, maybe a basket of some sort.

This answer is also very tentative (could be, as if, seem to be). The activity is also unusual. They are inspecting something. They are not touching it, pulling on it, picking it up; they are simply inspecting it. This probably illustrates her own tendency to avoid becoming involved.

In the second of the three responses, she provides a glimpse of her own fantasy life, and probably something about her own self-image:

> This reminds me of the Hunchback of Notre Dame like he is sitting on a stool there. (Inquiry) It's a great hulk, stooped over as if in thought, I always liked that book, see the large legs and arms here and this is the stool. . . . Rounded like stooped, as if the head were further forward. (It's his back here?) Yes, you are seeing him from the back with his head bent forward and his shoulders stooped forward as if he was thinking.

The response is considerably less tentative than the others. The figure is deformed, a great hulk seen stooped forward as if he was thinking. This could be a self-representation, especially because she points out, "I always liked that book."

The third answer is very similar to those often given to Card VII.

> This could be two children, just the heads, looking at each other. (Inquiry) The outlines seem quite clear, two little girls with their hair upswept, the noses and the chins see here.

The last answer to be evaluated for content is the only *FM* response in the record:

> This reminds me of a vulture with the big ugly head and beak, it's in flight. (Inquiry) It's wings are stretched out like it was flying along looking for prey, with the beak open and the blackness of it being ugh. (Ugh?) It's just not very attractive, all black like that.

Although the response cannot be scored for either morbidity or aggressiveness, both features clearly exist. It is a vulture and, as she points out, "not very attractive," a phrase that might readily illustrate her own self-conception.

The Step 10 search for unusual wording or embellishments in other responses yield no significant findings.

Case 2 Summary   It seems clear that some very significant problems exist with her self-concept. She tends to regard her own worth negatively, especially when she makes comparisons with others. Although she is introspective, her self-image appears to be based much more on imagination than on experience and is probably very distorted. Thus, the self-examining probably serves only to strengthen misconceptions that she may have about herself. She appears to be very cautious about initiating behavior and tends to perceive herself as having many unattractive or undesirable features. It seems likely that these are long-standing problems that predisposed the development of the High Lambda style and the defensive network related to it that has appeared so prominently in the data reviewed earlier in the interpretation.

Interpersonal Perception

The variables for the interpersonal perception cluster are shown in Table 57.

Case 2 Findings   The yields from Steps 1 (CDI) and 2 (HVI) are negative, but the result for Step 3 ($a:p$) is very significant, although not surprising in light of earlier findings. She is prone to assume a markedly passive role in most of her interpersonal relationships. She relies on the judgments of others in decision making and seeks to avoid responsibility. She is reluctant to search for new solutions to problems or initiate new patterns of behavior. The Step 4 result (*Food*) is not significant, but the presence of a *T* answer noted in Step 5 is a positive finding. Apparently, she does experience needs for emotional contact and is probably amenable to close relationships. This tends to coincide with the Step 6 revelation that she gives an above average number of human contents, signaling a very strong interest in people. Step 7 (PER) is not significant; however, the Step 8 (COP and AG) finding is quite important. It suggests that she does not perceive or anticipate positive interactions among people as a routine event. People such as this often feel less secure or more uncomfortable in interpersonal situations and usually are not perceived by others as being very outgoing. In fact, they are often regarded as distant or aloof because they tend to assume a more peripheral role during group interactions. The Step 9 (Isolation Index) result is not significant, which is somewhat surprising and might be taken as a positive sign in light of other findings. In other words, although she tends to avoid emotional interaction and assumes a markedly passive complaint role, no evidence suggests that she is isolated or withdrawn from the environment.

The Step 10 (movement responses containing a pair) evaluation reaffirms her somewhat timid and passive interpersonal orientation. Only two movement

Table 57.   Interpersonal Perception Variables for Case 2

STRUCTURAL VARIABLES	RESPONSES TO BE READ
CDI = 3 HVI = Neg	MOVEMENT WITH PAIR = 4, 12
$a:p$ = 1:5 T = 1 Fd = 0	HUMAN CONTENTS = 2, 4, 6, 7, 10, 12, 16, 18
Isolate/R = 0.06	
Total Human Contents = 8	
PER = 0 COP = 0 AG = 0	

answers contain a pair (Two women bending over something as if they were inspecting it; Two children, just the heads, looking at each other). The Step 11 (human contents) provides some added information regarding her perception of people. Five of the eight answers have already been reviewed at least once (2. "A woman . . . just standing there . . . it's not too good . . . a funny hat . . . you can't see the face"; 4. Two women bending over something . . . looking into this center thing"; 6. "The Hunchback of Notre Dame . . . a great hulk . . . stooped forward as if he was thinking"; 7. "An elf-like figure leaning against a tree . . . his arms are folded"; 12. "Two children . . . looking at each other . . . with their hair upswept"). Most of these responses are vague or tentative, and all are passive. The remaining three answers containing human content are less tentative, but two contain imaginary figures (10. "a face with a gigantic nose something like Cyrano . . . I didn't mean Cyrano, just like Cyrano"; 16. "a man's head . . . roundish, maybe with a mustache"; 18. "the face of an elf . . . like a child's, it looks like an imp I think"). Overall, three of the eight are nonreal (hunchback, elf, imp) and a fourth (like Cyrano) tends to be in that category. The descriptions of the remaining four (a woman, two women, two children, a man's head) generally are cautious and somewhat concrete. The absence of adjectives (tall, short, fat, ugly, pretty, etc.) makes the descriptions almost sterile, as if she really does not conceptualize people in a dynamic context. Whether this postulate is valid, or whether it simply reflects her conservative, passive, oversimplifying orientation is impossible to discern from the data. Nonetheless, it seems reasonable to conclude that her conceptions of people are not well developed, which in turn suggests that the likelihood of mature interpersonal relationships is somewhat remote.

Case 2 Summary   She seems very interested in people and open to close relationships, but does not seem to perceive or anticipate positive interpersonal relationships as a routine event. She is not very comfortable in most interpersonal situations. In part, this is because she does not have a very good conceptualization of people, probably because she does not have a very good conceptualization of herself. She tends to assume a very passive, almost timid role in which she relies extensively on the judgments of others for decisions and direction. In general, even though she is very interested in others, it seems unlikely that many of her relationships will be very deep or mature.

Case 2 Final Description

This 31-year-old female is a very cautious and conservative person who appears to be quite insecure about herself and her ability to deal effectively with her world. She is especially reluctant to deal with complexity and has developed a basic coping style that orients her toward keeping things on a simple, easily managed level. Although this coping style is not necessarily detrimental, it does serve to reinforce her notions that she is not very capable.

She is a very ideational person who prefers to stop and think things through before reaching a decision or initiating behavior. This decision making style is common among adults and often works quite well, but it does not work very well for her because of her aversion to complexity and preference to keep things simple and easily managed. Actually, she commits much of her ideation to fantasy, which she uses frequently and often abusively to avoid reality. This kind of fantasy substitution for reality permits her to avoid the fact that she regards herself less favorably than others but, to do so, her thinking has to become more strained or distorted than should be the case.

One tactic that she has employed to sustain her avoidance of complexity without causing serious problems for herself is to become very passive in her interpersonal relationships. In doing so, she often sacrifices her own individuality, but this permits her to avoid responsibility and rely on the judgments and directions of others. Her capacity for control is adequate, but she is vulnerable to disorganization under stress because she has fewer resources readily available for use than do most adults. She is very conservative about processing new information but, at the same time, is conscientious and tries to be conventional. She seems to be particularly fearful of feelings and tries to avoid emotional situations whenever possible. This probably even involves suppressing or ignoring some of her own more subtle experiences that are generated by needs.

Overall, the findings suggest that she is a psychologically impoverished and somewhat fragile person. She seems to feel forced to defend herself against an overly complicated world by assuming a passive, submissive interpersonal role. She is very interested in people but her conceptions of them are based more on imagination than on experience. Thus, although she is open to closeness, she seems bewildered about how this might be achieved and concerned about what sacrifices she might be called upon to make in return. The result is a person who tends to live on the periphery of her environment, aware of what goes on but unable to partake in deep or mature relationships and relying mainly on her own fantasy life to sustain her.

Recommendations Based on the Final Description

The referral raises two issues, (1) whether there is any clear evidence of psychological origins for her symptoms (headaches, tension, dizziness, fatigue, upset stomach, anxiety, and difficulties concentrating) and (2) what recommendations can be made concerning intervention. The first is more difficult to address than the second, mainly because no *direct* evidence links her symptoms to her rather inadequate, somewhat schizoid personality structure. It is reasonable to hypothesize that most or all of the symptoms have evolved because she seems to live a very fragile existence, depending on others with whom she is not really close, and not being able to predict how effective or ineffective her avoidant style may be in her day-to-day living. It may be that the realities of her situation gradually are becoming more apparent to her and creating internal alarms for which she is not prepared. Thus, the symptom pattern probably reflects her frequent experiences of confusion and apprehension, and is compounded by many of her own chronically ungratified needs. It also provides her with a socially acceptable reason to seek out additional support through her numerous visits to her physician.

Optimal intervention objectives are easily identified, but an actual intervention strategy is more difficult to define and should be approached cautiously. It seems clear that this woman suffers enormously from many developmental problems. She is not sure who or what she is and seems equally confused about others.

Her limited resources are cause for concern and her abusive use of fantasy serves only to sustain her impoverished plight. A major problem in formulating an intervention plan is that she offers no complaints other than her physical symptoms. In fact, she describes herself as having a "wonderful" job working with a "great bunch" of people. She has a dating relationship and describes her infrequent sexual experiences as "very satisfying." Therefore, the role of the referring physician in recommending intervention will be quite important, as will the initial contact with the prospective therapist.

If confronted with the need for some long term form of developmental treatment, she is likely to bolt as the prospect could be too threatening. Thus, it may be more appropriate to broach the treatment issue in a more specific but open-ended way, possibly by suggesting a focus on broadening social skills and contending with feelings more directly to ease some of the symptoms. Either or both of these targets can be approached through individual or group intervention in which tactics are more directive and supportive. Her experienced need for closeness and her passivity both should be assets to get her started, but the latter will probably become a liability as treatment progresses. It will be very important to caution the therapist about her avoidant, oversimplying style and her abuse of fantasy. Both will pose problems but the former will tend to interfere most, especially when complex issues are addressed. A second evaluation should be recommended after approximately six months to assess progress and review additional treatment objectives.

Case 2 Epilogue   This subject entered individual psychotherapy with a male therapist whom she saw once each week for the first five weeks, after which she requested that the frequency of visits be increased to twice a week. The major impetus of the treatment coincided with a developmental, exploratory model. Her presenting symptoms dissipated after the fourth month, which coincided with her decision to join a women's group. The therapist reports that the relationship between the subject and the ticket manager became more strained during the fifth month of treatment and that the subject was actively involved in the development of more social contacts. The subject was re-evaluated after one year to assess progress and a substantial increase in EA (9.5) was noted, plus the presence of one T response in the retest record. At that time the therapist anticipated that the subject would continue in treatment for at least several additional months.

SUMMARY

The procedures of interpretation, developing the final description, and formulating recommendations from it, which have been illustrated using Cases 1 and 2, are applicable to any Rorschach protocol. Additional illustrations of the procedures follow in the next section.

PART IV

Issues of Diagnosis and Treatment Planning

CHAPTER 11

Issues of Schizophrenia

INTRODUCTION

The issue of identifying schizophrenia accurately has been both complex and controversial for many decades. Although most schemata for the diagnosis of schizophrenia begin with the general agreement that a disturbance in thinking is the most characteristic feature of the condition, there is much less agreement about the way in which that disturbance is manifest, and about which additional features, among the many that characterize schizophrenia, distinguish it from other conditions in which thinking may be impaired. Weiner (1966) traced abundant research support for the thought process dysfunction in the schizophrenic, demonstrating how the condition pervades cognitive focusing, reasoning, and concept formation. Weiner also noted that the schizophrenic has major problems with perceptual accuracy or reality testing; impairment of "reality sense," that is, an inability to differentiate the self accurately; problems in object relations; and a system of coping operations that are limited in terms of their overall effectiveness.

In part, the difficulties posed in differentiating the schizophrenic from the nonschizophrenic stem from the basic theoretical conceptions of schizophrenia. Khouri (1977) pointed to the sharp differences that exist between those who propose a "continuum" concept of schizophrenia and those who identify schizophrenia as a distinct entity, discretely different from all other mental dysfunctions. Moreover, theories of schizophrenia are frequently divided into two camps. One emphasizes the potential genetic element that separates the schizophrenic from the nonschizophrenic, whereas a second focuses on environmental factors as the major cause.

Other past issues that have created problems in differentiating schizophrenia from nonschizophrenia evolved from attempts to refine the diagnosis, for instance, the different categories such as paranoid, hebephrenic, and the like, or the delineation of degrees of schizophrenia, as in the concepts of borderline and incipient schizophrenia. Although some aspects of those difficulties were created by the diversity of perspectives on etiology and symptomatology, they were made more complex by the inclusion of such categories as reactive versus process (Kantor, Wallner, & Winder, 1953; Phillips, 1953), acute versus chronic (Kant, 1941; Meyer, 1907/1948; Wittman, 1941), incipient versus chronic (Kant, 1941; Meyer, 1907/1948; Whittman, 1944), and borderline (Grinker, Werble, & Drye, 1968; Kernberg, 1967; Knight, 1953) or pseudoneurotic (Hoch & Polatin, 1949; Kasanin, 1944; Polatin & Hoch, 1947).

Many of the difficulties noted above have been alleviated in recent years. During the past decade, the once discrete theoretical camps seem to have moved much closer to each other, and the issue of defining schizophrenia appears to have come closer to resolution. For instance, Strauss (1983) posited that schizophrenia is a roughly defined cluster of extreme psychobiological processes that reflect a disorder of function. In elaborating, Strauss pointed out that the presence of schizoaffective conditions suggests that schizophrenia and affective disorders may reflect segments of a continuum rather than discrete diseases. He noted that this view is compatible with findings suggesting separate genetic predispositions to each of these extremes, as discussed by Kendler, Gruenberg, and Strauss (1982).

Andreasen (1989) provided an excellent summary regarding the changing definition of schizophrenia. She noted that the definition has become very narrow and, as such, limits the diagnosis to severe forms. She also pointed out that, at the same time, there has been a greater acceptability of the notion of a schizophrenia spectrum. One segment of this spectrum includes psychotic boundary disorders, including the schizophreniform disorder, delusional disorders, brief reactive psychoses, and the schizoaffective disorder in which there is a persistence of psychotic-like symptoms without affective symptoms. Another segment of the spectrum includes the schizotypal, schizoid, and paranoid personality disorders.

The notion of a schizophrenia spectrum was devised primarily as a research classification based mainly on a series of investigations concerning adoptive children in Denmark (Kety, Rosenthal, Wender, & Schulsinger, 1968; Kety, Rosenthal, Wender, Schulsinger, & Jacobsen, 1975). Although the notion of a spectrum tends to simplify the identification of schizophrenia because of the greater precision of the definition, it also tends to make the diagnostician's challenge much more complex because of the likelihood of an overlap of features among classifications. For example, Rorschach features clearly overlap between the schizophrenic and schizotypal personality disorders (Exner, 1986).

George and Neufeld (1985) provided a thorough review of studies that link cognitive dysfunction to the symptomatology in schizophrenia. Their reviews led them to the speculation that hallucinations occur in conjunction with a disruption in information processing, leading to a spontaneous retrieval of information in long term memory, which, in turn, is represented as mental imagery that is misattributed to external sources. Similarly, they suggested that the cognitive anomalies of the schizophrenic are related to a loosening of associations because of deficits in implementing the network of semantic associations in long term memory. Findings and postulates such as these are important to the Rorschach community because they aid in developing an understanding of how the test works in detecting the presence of schizophrenia.

RORSCHACH IDENTIFICATION OF SCHIZOPHRENIA

Rorschach history is marked by many attempts to identify variables that will provide a valid differentiation of the schizophrenic from the nonschizophrenic (Beck, 1965; Piotrowski & Lewis, 1950; Rapaport, Gill & Schafer, 1946; Theisen, 1952; Watkins & Stauffacher, 1952; Weiner, 1966). All attempts achieved some success but were not uniformly consistent. Early in the development of the *Comprehensive System,* several investigations were mounted that focused on the accurate identification of schizophrenia. By 1978, it was clear that some composite of variables related to ideation (disordered thought) and mediation (perceptual inaccuracy) would have the greatest efficacy in relation to this objective, and a five-variable experimental Schizophrenia Index was designed. As available cases increased, the experimental index was revised in 1981, revised again in 1983, and finally released in 1984 as what is now known as the original SCZI.

THE FALSE POSITIVE PROBLEM

The SCZI was quite effective in identifying the presence of schizophrenia, with accuracy rates of between 75 and 90% for various groups of schizophrenics, and most false negatives could be accounted for because of invalid or highly constricted protocols. Nevertheless, the false positive rates were often disconcertingly high, often between 10 and 20% for some groups, especially adolescent behavior problems, drug induced psychosis, and some of the more severe affective disorders. The false positive problem in the SCZI was highlighted further in a study comparing schizophrenics with schizotypal and borderline personality disorders (Exner, 1986). In that study, 66 of 80 schizophrenics (82%) were correctly identified, but 28 of 76 schizotypals (40%) and 11 of 84 borderlines (13%) were incorrectly identified as being schizophrenic.

The false positive problem stimulated additional investigations designed to modify the SCZI in a way that would maintain the true positive rates but reduce the false positive rates to as close to zero as possible. As noted in Chapter 1, the new SCZI evolved by using a series of discriminant function analyses with a number of relatively large randomly selected groups of both patients and nonpatients. As illustrated in the Monte Carlo procedures (Chapter 1, Table 6), the new SCZI remains at least as effective as the original SCZI in identifying true positive cases, and the false positive rates for affective disorders, outpatients, adolescent behavior problems, and nonpatients have been reduced considerably, but not completely. For instance, in spite of the improvement of SCZI, some diagnostic categories that fall within the schizophrenia spectrum frequently present the most substantial challenge to the differential diagnostic usefulness of the SCZI. This is usually not true for the schizoid (such as Case 2) or paranoid personality disorders because neither tends to manifest a severity of disturbance in both thinking and perceptual accuracy as is found among schizophrenics. But the challenge is substantial among some cases of reactive psychosis, schizoaffective problems, and schizotypal personality disorders. Thus, the SCZI *should never* be interpreted as an absolute. Instead, it should be viewed as an actuarially based index, the results of which are to be tested further by a careful evaluation of all of the test data, including those that contribute to the index.

Usually the issue of a true positive versus a false positive index will be decided as data are addressed during the interpretive search of the first two or three clusters. For instance, as noted above, the original SCZI was positive for 28 of a group of 76 schizotypal patients who were used in a comparative study. When the new

SCZI was applied, the number was reduced to 14 (18%), which is still much higher than preferred. Eight of the 11 false positives have SCZI values of 4, and the remaining six have values of 5. In seven of the eight cases having a SCZI value of 4, the false positive is detected by the time the interpretive search through the first two clusters (ideation and mediation) is complete. In other words, even though the data have produced a positive SCZI, a test of the various issues in each cluster ultimately causes the postulate that schizophrenia exists to be rejected. In most of the remaining false positive cases, the addition of history data causes the postulate concerning the presence of schizophrenia to be rejected or seriously challenged. Similar findings have been noted when examining false positive SCZI's among patients with affective disorders, adolescent behavior problems, and outpatients. This is not to imply that all false positives will be detected easily, and a "wait and see" tactic seems to be the only reasonable solution in some cases, even after the data from all assessment resources have been reviewed.

INITIAL HYPOTHESES BASED ON THE SCZI

At the outset, the approach to interpretating the SCZI should be similar to that used with the Suicide Constellation. If the value is not positive, it does not necessarily rule out schizophrenia, but simply indicates that there is no firm actuarial data on which to develop a postulate that schizophrenia is present. Conversely, if the value for the SCZI is positive, any of three hypotheses may be appropriate depending on the actual value for the SCZI.

If the SCZI value is 4, the initial hypothesis is the most conservative and equivocal, namely that the subject manifests many features that are consistent with those found commonly among schizophrenics and infrequently among other subjects. This suggests a reasonable likelihood that schizophrenia is present and that the interpretive search should include some focus that will attempt to confirm or reject the postulate. The conclusion that schizophrenia is present should not be made unless the data clearly support it.

If the SCZI is 5, the initial hypothesis should be more definitive than if the value were 4; that is, evidence indicates a strong probability of schizophrenia. The interpretive search begins with that assumption, and the routine includes focus on the manifestations of the disorder, as well as awareness of a remote possibility that the hypothesis might be rejected as the specifics of data sets are reviewed. In these cases the hypothesis concerning the likelihood of schizophrenia should not be abandoned in the descriptive summary unless specific findings are very compelling.

If the SCZI value is 6, the initial hypothesis is even more stringent. A value of 6 indicates a very strong likelihood that schizophrenia is present, and the interpretive search begins with that as a given. Whereas cases in which the SCZI value is 4 are approached on the assumption of a possibility, to be accepted or rejected, cases in which the value is 6 are approached on the assumption that schizophrenia is present and only extremely compelling data cause that conclusion to be altered. The application of the SCZI to the interpretive routine and diagnostic conclusions is possibly best illustrated by the following two cases, one a paranoid schizophrenic and the other a patient with a schizotypal disorder.

CASE 3: PARANOID SCHIZOPHRENIA

The subject is a 25-year-old single male. The Rorschach was administered as part of a forensic assessment. He is charged with three homicides, each involving the mutilation and death of young women whose photographs he had apparently taken as part of his work as a free-lance photographer.

The subject is an only child. His parents (father, age 49; mother, age 50) were divorced when he was 10, after which he continued to live with his mother and saw his father infrequently. He graduated from high school at age 18, worked one year in a photography shop, and then completed two years at a technical institute and received an A.A. degree in commercial photography at age 21. After obtaining his degree, he moved out of his mother's home into his own small apartment. During the following two years he was employed full time in the camera-photography section of a large department store, specializing in family and children's portraits and making passport photos. He resigned from that position at age 23. For the next nine months he toured a large section of the United States, taking photographs of landscape and wildlife that he had hoped to sell to nature magazines. Although he sold a few photos, the majority of his pictures were not accepted. Subsequently, he took a part time position with a firm specializing in wedding pictures and used the remainder of his time doing free-lance photography.

Information collected from high school and technical institute records is unremarkable. His grades were slightly above average. He worked as a photographer on the high school newspaper during his junior and senior years. He was described by teachers as quiet and conscientious. He apparently had several friends in high school but no obvious close buddy or girlfriend relationships. He is known to have dated during high school but there is little information concerning his social activities while at the technical institute. He is described by those with whom he has worked recently as a quiet person and a very capable photographer. As part of his free-lance activities he has solicited modeling agencies and has been involved in creating portfolios for both male and female models. Several models who have been interviewed describe him as helpful, very mild mannered, concerned, and very competent.

He was apprehended during a break-in to the apartment of a female model by two of her male neighbors. She was not home at the time. During the resulting police investigation several undergarments and two pieces of jewelry found in his apartment were identified as articles belonging to three women who had been murdered in their homes during the preceding 18 months. In each instance, the victim was apparently strangled and then stabbed numerous times. Forensic experts believe that all three were attacked while sleeping. There was no evidence of sexual assault in any of the cases. When confronted with these findings, the subject confessed to the murders. He maintained that the women were not really models, but had been working as prostitutes. He further maintained that he was able to detect their involvement in prostitution by viewing several of their photographs, which, when placed in a particular relationship to each other, provided the revelation. He stated that he felt selected by some "special force" to take action and that he found he could not sleep until he had completed the acts. His court-appointed attorney stated that the subject looks

Case 3: A 25-Year-Old Male

Card	Response	Inquiry
I	1. A bird taking off, mayb its a queen crow	E: (Rpts S's resp) S: It's a big one, with great big wings, like a special crow, these r the big wgs
	E: Take ur time, I'm sur u find smthg else too	E: A special crow? S: Well crows don't hav big wgs so this must be a special one, lik a queen crow, the size of it lets the other crows know that she is majestic
	2. A face of a frog too	E: (Rpts S's resp) S: Here (outlines), u can c the eyes & the forehead, he's got his mouth open but I can't c his chin E: I c the eyes but I'm not sur about the mouth or why it ll a frog S: It's round lookg lik frog & it's lik he's got big eyes there, frogs always have very big eyes if theyr open E: The mouth open? S: Right here, ths darkr part (points)
II	3. A torn up body, prob an A	E: (Rpts S's resp) S: It's got a hole & it's torn apart & there's a lot of blood E: A lot of blood? S: This red is all blood, up here & dwn here E: I'm not sur why it ll it's torn apart S: There's half on each side, lik smbdy tore som A apart
III	4. Some bones, lik the pelvis & the kidney too	E: (Rpts S's resp) S: These (D1) r all bones of the pelvis & the upper part of the legs & the kidney is in the middl there, in the middl of the pelvis E: Wht maks it ll the kidney? S: Thts where thy r & thyr red & thyr shaped lik ths
	5. Some shoes, lik witch's shoes	E: (Rpts S's resp) S: Thy hav the shape lik shoes tht u c on witches, lik in the movies, thy hav a hi heel & a pointed toe, one on each side. I'v done halloween layouts & I always put boots in lik these
IV	6. A gorilla wearing lumberjack boots, sittg on a stump	E: (Rpts S's resp) S: He's a big hulk lik gorilla's, w a littl head & kinda scrawny arms & he's got these boots on, thy ll the lumberjacks wear, I'v seen lots of them E: U said he's sittg on a stump? S: Here (D1) in the middl, he's just resting

7. There's a face too, lik an evil lookg guy

E: (Rpts S's resp)
S: Up here (D3), u can c him squinting & his mouth looks angry, he's a mean person, lik evil just glaring lik he's really mad at smthg

V

v8. It ll some bone, a chicken bone

E: (Rpts S's resp)
S: It ll a wishbone tht has been pulled, it's still connected but it's partly broken, lik u make a wish and 2 peopl pull, well ths one was pulled but didn't break cuz it wasn't dry enuff so nobody will get a wish

VI

9. A high speed photo of a fist smashing thru smthg, mayb a wall or a board

E: (Rpts S's resp)
S: Ths is the negative, the fist & the arm is up here & it just smashed thru ths thg dwn here, u can get the force of the action by ths stuff spatting out by the arm, it's a real good shot taken w hi speed film, u hav to really plan them rite to catch all the action, I'v done it a few times
E: U said it's a negative?
S: It's all black & grey lik a negative, I'd lik to c the print, I'll bet it's really a good one

v10. It ll sbody was crucified & thy cut off his head & legs *body hanging?*

E: (Rpts S's resp)
S: The pole in the cntr, the arms r out here, lik thyr nailed to the crosspole & the rest is the body but the head & legs aren't there, lik smbody wanted to make a point, to show that if u do wrong thy'll really get u & cut u up & cut off u'r head & leav u hangg there lik this

VII

11. Two littl girls who hav a secret

E: (Rpts S's resp)
S: Thyr just sittg there lookg at e.o., lik thy hav a secret, c ths is the nose & the hair & thyr sittg on ths thg, mayb a big cushion
E: A big cushion? *→ pau ? ngroul receipt?*
S: Mayb, or mayb a rock or a board, I dkno
E: U said thy hav a secret?
S: Thy just ll thyr sharing smthg secret, u kno lik thy hav a secret between them, littl girls do tht

v12. Ths ll a negative of a woman wearing a big hat or scarf

E: (Rpts S's resp)
S: The white is her face, u can't c the features because it's not exposed enuff & the othr part is som weird hat or scarf tht she's got wrapped around her head & it comes dwn around her neck
E: U said a negative?
S: Yeah, it's reversed, lik a negative, the scarf is dark colored & the face is lite colored

VIII

13. A Star Wars mask

E: (Rpts S's resp)
S: It's lik a mask, the white slit is for the eyes & it's pointed at the top & fat at the bottom & it's all diff colors lik some masks, lik in the sc. fict. movies lik Star Wars or smthg, I saw all those movies

(continued)

261

Case 3: (Continued)

Card	Response	Inquiry
v14.	Tht ll smbody mooning	E: (Rpts S's resp)
		S: Smbody w pink drawers, I guess a woman, leaning forward, thes r her arms or elbows (Dd26) & the pink is her drawers & the rest is her ass & her privates, she's doing it on purpose, lik to shock people, mak fun of them
IX	15. Tht's a mask too, but not fr Star Wars, prob from New Orleans or Venice when thy hav those celebrations	E: (Rpts S's resp)
		S: It's lik an A mask, w the big ears & the big and little holes out here (DdS29) for the eyes, it's all diff colors lik the other one. It's lik thy buy for celebrations, it's not a scary one, just smthg to hide behind
X	16. Smbody is taking revenge, lik judgement day	E: (Rpts S's resp)
		S: Everything is being disintegrated, it's all being ripped apart and scattered, lik a quick glimpse of what will happen on judgment day, this is it, it's people & the world all disintegrating in the picture
		E: I'm not sur I'm seeing it lik u r
		S: Everything is coming apart, lik its all disintegrating, people, trees, houses, things, everythg, it's just all coming apart there as if some force is causing everything to be scattered, it's not very nice to look at

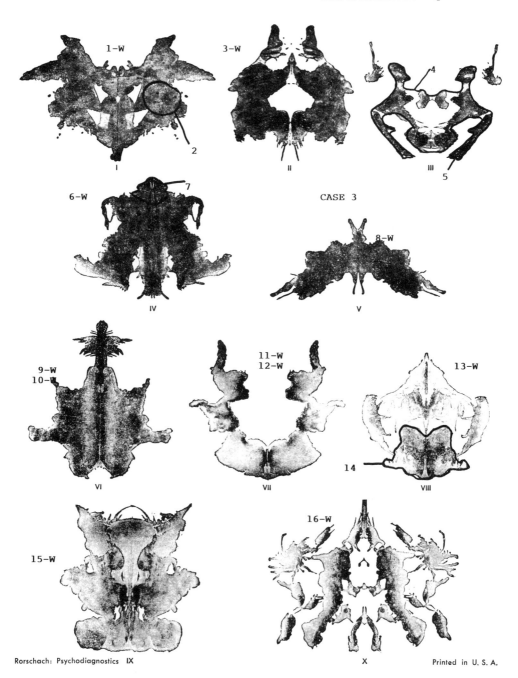

CASE 3

```
CASE 3.   SEQUENCE OF SCORES
===============================================================================
CARD NO  LOC  #      DETERMINANT(S)      (2)  CONTENT(S)   POP Z   SPECIAL SCORES
===============================================================================
I     1  Wo    1 FMau                         A                1.0   ALOG
      2  Ddo  99 FMp-                         Ad

II    3  WSo   1 CF-                      2   Ad,Bl            4.5   MOR

III   4  DS+   1 FCu                          An               4.5   INC2
      5  Ddo  33 Fo                      2    Cg                     PER

IV    6  W+    1 FMpo                         A,Cg,Bt          4.0   FAB,PER
      7  Do    3 Ma-                          Hd                     AG

V     8  Wo    1 F-                           An               1.0   MOR,DR

VI    9  W+    1 Mp.C'F.mpu                    Art,Hd,Id       2.5   AG,MOR,PER
     10  W+    1 mp-                          Hd,Id            2.5   MOR,DR

VII  11  W+    1 Mpo                     2    H,Hh           P 2.5   ALOG
     12  WS+   1 FC'u                         Hd,Cg            4.0

VIII 13  WSo   1 FCu                          (Hd)             4.5   PER
     14  D+    2 Mp.FC.FD-                     Hd,Cg,Sx        3.0   AG

IX   15  WSo   1 FCo                          (Ad)             5.5

X    16  W/    1 Ma.mpu                       (H),Bt,Id        5.5   AG,MOR,DR
===============================================================================
```

```
CASE 3.  STRUCTURAL SUMMARY
================================================================================
   LOCATION              DETERMINANTS              CONTENTS      S-CONSTELLATION
   FEATURES       BLENDS           SINGLE                     NO..FV+VF+V+FD>2
                                              H   = 2, 0       NO..Col-Shd Bl>0
  Zf    = 13    M.C'F.m         M   = 2       (H) = 0, 0      YES..Ego<.31,>.44
  ZSum  = 44.0  M.FC.FD         FM  = 3       Hd  = 4, 1      YES..MOR > 3
  ZEst  = 41.5  M.m             m   = 1       (Hd)= 1, 0       NO..Zd > +- 3.5
                                FC  = 3       Hx  = 0, 0       NO..es > EA
  W   = 11                      CF  = 1       A   = 2, 0       NO..CF+C > FC
   (Wv = 0)                     C   = 0       (A) = 0, 0      YES..X+% < .70
  D   = 3                       Cn  = 0       Ad  = 2, 0      YES..S > 3
  Dd  = 2                       FC'= 1        (Ad)= 1, 0      YES..P < 3 or > 8
  S   = 5                       C'F= 0        An  = 2, 0       NO..Pure H < 2
                                C'  = 0       Art = 1, 0      YES..R < 17
    DQ                          FT  = 0       Ay  = 0, 0        6.....TOTAL
 .........(FQ-)                 TF  = 0       Bl  = 0, 1
  +   = 7   ( 2)                T   = 0       Bt  = 0, 2      SPECIAL SCORINGS
  o   = 8   ( 4)                FV  = 0       Cg  = 1, 3          Lv1    Lv2
 v/+  = 1   ( 0)                VF  = 0       Cl  = 0, 0    DV  =  0x1    0x2
  v   = 0   ( 0)                V   = 0       Ex  = 0, 0    INC =  0x2    1x4
                                FY  = 0       Fd  = 0, 0    DR  =  3x3    0x6
                                YF  = 0       Fi  = 0, 0    FAB =  1x4    0x7
                                Y   = 0       Ge  = 0, 0    ALOG=  2x5
       FORM QUALITY             Fr  = 0       Hh  = 0, 1    CON =  0x7
                                rF  = 0       Ls  = 0, 0    SUM6  = 7
       FQx  FQf  MQual  SQx     FD  = 0       Na  = 0, 0    WSUM6 = 27
  +  =  0    0     0     0      F   = 2       Sc  = 0, 0
  o  =  4    1     1     1                    Sx  = 0, 1    AB  = 0     CP  = 0
  u  =  6    0     2     2                    Xy  = 0, 0    AG  = 4     MOR = 5
  -  =  6    1     2     1                    Id  = 0, 3    CFB = 0     PER = 4
 none=  0   --     0     0       (2) = 3                    COP = 0     PSV = 0
================================================================================
                 RATIOS, PERCENTAGES, AND DERIVATIONS

  R = 16        L =  0.14           FC:CF+C = 4: 1     COP = 0    AG = 4
 ----------------------------------  Pure C   = 0      Food      = 0
  EB = 5: 3.0  EA =  8.0  EBPer= 1.7 Afr     =0.33     Isolate/R =0.13
  eb = 6: 2    es =  8       D  = 0  S       = 4       H:(H)Hd(Hd)= 1: 7
           Adj es =  6   Adj D  = 0  Blends:R= 3:16    (HHd):(AAd)= 2: 1
 ----------------------------------  CP      = 0       H+A:Hd+Ad  = 4: 9
  FM = 3  :  C'= 2   T = 0
  m  = 3  :  V = 0   Y = 0
                            P   = 1        Zf  =13       3r+(2)/R=0.19
  a:p   =  3: 8  Sum6  = 7   X+% =0.25     Zd  = +3.5   Fr+rF    = 0
  Ma:Mp =  2: 3  Lv2   = 1   F+% =0.50  W:D:Dd=11: 3: 2 FD       = 1
  2AB+Art+Ay= 1  WSum6 = 27  X-% =0.38     W:M =11: 5   An+Xy    = 2
  M-    =  2     Mnone = 0   S-% =0.17     DQ+ = 7      MOR      = 4
                            Xu% =0.38     DQv = 0
 -------------------------------------------------------------------------
   SCZI = 5*    DEPI = 5*    CDI = 2    S-CON = 6    HVI =YES   OBS = No
================================================================================
```

forward to the possibility of a trial because it will provide him with an opportunity to explain the special force.

The assessment was conducted in conjunction with routine pretrial procedures with special focus on the issues of whether the subject is competent to stand trial and/or whether a plea of guilty by reason of insanity might be considered as acceptable by the court.

Interpretive Strategy

Although the record contains only 16 responses, there is no reason to challenge its interpretive usefulness. The first Key variable, the SCZI, is positive, having a value of 5. Thus, the complete search order is determined:

IDEATION → MEDIATION → PROCESSING → CONTROLS → AFFECT → SELF-PERCEPTION → INTERPERSONAL PERCEPTION.

Initial Proposition This routine begins with the cognitive triad, but the ideation and processing clusters are addressed in the reverse order from usual because the data regarding ideation are crucial in testing the initial proposition, which is that there is a strong probability that schizophrenia is present. If that postulate is supported, it signals the presence of a psychological organization that is highly vulnerable to chaos because it is marked by warped or distorted thinking and faulty mediational translation. Obviously, if such a core condition exists, its presence affects the interpretation of all other data regarding personality structure and functioning.

Ideation

The most pressing question regarding the subjects ideational features is whether the characteristics of thinking are commensurate with those typical of schizophrenics. As such, this might lead some interpreters to deviate from the recommended order for searching through the data and complete Steps 7 through 11 before turning to Steps 1 through 6. Generally, this is not a good approach because the steps are designed so that the findings at each step provide information from which subsequent findings can be fleshed out more precisely. In this case, an evaluation of ideational quality should be more meaningful when couched in information concerning ideational functioning. For example, poor quality ideation in a pervasive extratensive subject usually has very different roots from those of poor quality ideation in a pervasive introversive subject. Almost 90% of the reference sample of schizophrenics are either introversive (60%) or ambient (30%). Thus, findings concerning the *EB* often become relevant when the validity of a positive SCZI is questioned. Obviously, the summary of findings need not follow a specific order, but the search pattern should be consistent. The basic data for the cluster of variables related to ideation are shown in Table 58.

Case 3 Findings The results of Steps 1 (*EB*) and 2 (*EBPer*) indicate that he is introversive, but that his ideational style is not necessarily pervasive. In other words, in most situations he prefers to keep his feelings at a more peripheral level and think things through before forming a decision or initiating behavior;

Table 58.   Variables Related to Ideation for Case 3

$EB = 5 : 3.0$	$EBPer = 1.7$	M QUALITY		CRITICAL SPECIAL SCORES			
$eb = 6 : 2$	$(FM = 3\ m = 3)$	$+ = 0$	DV	$= 0$	DV2	$= 0$
$a{:}p = 3 : 8$	$Ma{:}Mp = 2 : 3$	$o = 1$	INC	$= 0$	INC2	$= 1$
$2Ab+(Art+Ay) = 1$		$u = 2$	DR	$= 3$	DR2	$= 0$
MOR $= 5$		$- = 2$	FAB	$= 1$	FAB2	$= 0$
RESPONSES TO BE READ FOR QUALITY			ALOG	$= 2$	SUM6	$= 7$
7, 9, 11, 14, 16			CON	$= 0$	WSUM6	$= 27$

but there is some flexibility to this style and his feelings sometimes become more influential in forming decisions and behaviors. Also, there is a possibility of trial-and-error activity in some situations.

The Step 3 finding (left-side eb) indicates no more peripheral ideation than might be expected; however, the current level is apparently increased by the experience of situationally-related stress ($m = 3$). The Step 4 ($a:p$) data show that the right-side value is nearly three times that of the left-side value, which suggests that the ideational sets and values are well fixed and difficult to alter. This is an especially important finding when schizophrenia is present, because disordered thinking often includes obsessional or delusional operations that are well fixed and difficult to challenge. The Step 5 ($M^a:M^p$) finding indicates that he is prone to defensively substitute fantasy for reality. This finding is important when schizophrenia is present because delusional systems usually evolve from elaborate fantasies. Step 6 (Intellectualization Index) data are not significant, but the Step 7 (MOR) datum is important. It indicates that his thinking frequently is marked by a very pessimistic orientation. He is prone to anticipate unfavorable outcomes regardless of the quality of his efforts or behaviors.

The Step 8 (Sum of Critical Special Scores) finding is ominous. The record contains seven Critical Special Scores, of which at least four (INCOM2 = 1, FABCOM = 1, ALOG = 2) reflect more than simply mild cognitive slippage. The seven scores yield a Weighted Sum6 of 27, which, although less than the average of 44 in the reference sample, is much higher than expected, and is even more dramatic in light of the fact that only 16 answers were given. Thus, at the very least, there is clear evidence of serious problems in his thinking that probably include flawed conceptualization and judgment. The Step 9 subjective evaluation of the answers containing Special Scores tends to confirm that his thinking is pathologically bizarre (a kidney in the middle of a pelvis; it wasn't dry enough so nobody will get a wish; if you do wrong they'll cut you up and cut off your head and leave you hanging; somebody is taking revenge) and that his judgment is very flawed and concrete ("the size of it lets other crows know that she is majestic," "they have a secret between them, little girls do that you know").

The Step 10 (frequency of $M-$) data reaffirm the presence of peculiar or disturbed thinking, and the Step 11 evaluation of the two $M-$ answers reveals that either or both could be judged as Level 2 distortions. Both are unique and reflect patterns of thinking that appear to be dominated by preoccupations and/or delusions that tend to disregard reality. Interestingly, the Step 12 evaluation of the quality of the M answers suggests that none are primitive or juvenile. The Card VII Response 11 (two little girls) is somewhat common, but the remaining four (7. "an evil looking guy," 9. "a high speed photo of a fist," 14. "somebody mooning," 16. "somebody is taking revenge") tend to be relatively sophisticated, even though they are all somewhat bizarre.

Case 3 Summary   This subject's thinking is markedly disturbed. It is not well organized and is frequently bizarre. His judgment seems very flawed and concrete at times and it is likely that his thinking is influenced by preoccupations and/or delusions that ignore reality. Unfortunately, he is an ideationally oriented person, preferring to delay decision making until all alternatives have been considered, and keeping emotions at a more detached level during the decision process. Although there is some flexibility to this coping style—that is, instances may occur in which feelings become more influential and may even promote forms of trial-and-error problem solving—his attitudes and values are relatively well fixed, reducing the likelihood that challenges to his way of thinking might be effective. This problem is compounded by two other features. First, his thinking includes a chronically pessimistic set concerning his relationship with the world. He does not anticipate reward or success regardless of the effectiveness of his behaviors. Second, he often takes defensive flight into fantasy when the realities of a situation appear to be threatening. There is no unusual level of peripheral thinking, although the level appears to have been increased by experiences of situational stress, and this could increase his distractibility. Although these findings, taken alone, do not confirm the presence of schizophrenia, the overall pattern of his ideation is consistent with that found among schizophrenics.

Cognitive Mediation

If data from the ideation cluster has not caused the postulate concerning schizophrenia to be rejected, the data in the mediation cluster become the focus from which the issue ordinarily is resolved. As noted earlier, the Rorschach definition of schizophrenia includes clear evidence of serious dysfunction in *both* ideational and mediational operations. The magnitude of dysfunction and/or disorganization for both features typically exceeds that noted in less severe disturbances, and forms a composite of severity that is not usually found in other types of serious disturbance. The basic data regarding variables in this cluster are shown in Table 59.

Case 3 Findings   The Step 1 (Lambda) and 2 (OBS) results are not significant, although the rather low value for Lambda (0.14) suggests that the subject usually does not back away from complexity as much as most people. This finding usually is not important but, when considered in light of the finding regarding his ideational disarray, it suggests that he often processes much more information than he may be able to attend to in a logical, coherent manner. The data reviewed in Step 3 *(P)* seems to support this contention. He gave only one Popular answer, indicating that the likelihood of unconventional translations of inputs is very substantial, even when cues regarding socially acceptable responses are rather obvious.

Table 59.   Cognitive Mediation Variables for Case 3

Lambda = 0.14	OBS = Negative		MINUS FEATURES
P = 1	*X*+% = .25	I	2. *Ddo FMp– Ad*
FQx+ = 0	*F*+% = .50	II	3. *WSo CF– 2 Ad,Bl 4.5 MOR*
FQxo = 4	*Xu*% = .38	IV	7. *Do Ma– Hd AG*
FQxu = 6	*X*–% = .38	V	8. *Wo F– An 1.0 MOR, DR*
FQx– = 6	*S*–% = .17	VI	10. *W+ mp– Hd,Id 2.5 MOR,DR*
FQnone = 0	CONFAB = 0	VIII	14. *D+ Mp.FC.FD– Hd,Cg,Sx 3.0 AG*

The Step 4 (*FQx+*) finding is not significant, but the hypothesis generated in Step 3 seems confirmed by the Step 5 (*X* + %) result. The *X* + % is extraordinarily low, indicating that, regardless of cues that may exist in a situation, the subject simply does not translate inputs conventionally. If behavioral predictions are extrapolated from this finding, it means that the majority of his behaviors are formulated with a disregard for the conventional. The Step 6 *(FQnone)* result is unimportant, but the Step 7 (*Xu*%) finding sheds some light on his disregard for convention. The value for the *Xu*% is nearly three times higher than average for an adult. In other words, he often translates stimuli in a manner that does not distort the input, but rather in a way that is in accord with his own needs and values, even though the translation disregards conventionality. In effect, he tends to "march to his own drummer." Such behavior is often acceptable, and at times even commendable, but a risk of alienating the environment always exists, and the effectiveness of idiosyncratic patterns of behavior invariably is judged against some measure of deviation.

The Step 8 (*X* – %) result suggests that, in this case, the measure of deviation is too extreme for the social palate. The *X* – % is very high, indicating that the subject's mediational translations are abundant with distortion and, as a result, many of his behaviors are inappropriately formulated. It is very important to note that most of these distortions are not rooted in anger. The *S* – % is modest. He simply distorts many inputs. Whether this is the result of faulty conceptualization, as suggested from the data concerning ideation, or whether it may result from faulty retrieval mechanisms cannot be discerned. Whatever the cause, the product is potentially disastrous.

The Step 9 (sequencing) evaluation fails to detect any particular sequencing effect. Two of the minus answers are only responses to cards, whereas the remaining four are second answers. They are spread across six cards with no apparent relationship. The Step 10 review (contents of minus answers) hints at more homogeneity. Five of the six minus responses involve human or animal detail contents, and three of the six have morbid content. This may indicate that some important preoccupation is contributing to the mediational distortion. The Step 11 (levels of distortion) evaluation suggests that at least three of the six answers are simple Level 1 distortions. Two of the remaining three, face responses on Cards I and IV, involve a substantial use of imaginary lines and require considerable effort to discover. The sixth, "sombody mooning" on Card VIII, is also very difficult to perceive. None of the three are clear Level 2 distortions but they are much more severe than most Level 1 answers, and as such tend to emphasize the mediational problem that has unfolded in the review of the data for this cluster.

Case 3 Summary   The findings highlight the presence of a serious mediational problem. He tends to disregard or fails to perceive the conventional. As a result, he tends to translate many stimuli in an overly personalized manner but, in many instances, his mediational efforts are marked by a serious perceptual inaccuracy that promotes a gross distortion of the stimulus. When overpersonalization and distortion occur with a high frequency, as is the case here, it usually indicates patterns of behavior that run contrary to social acceptance or demand. It seems likely that many of his unusual or distorted translations are prompted by some enduring preoccupation. This seems consistent with earlier findings regarding the presence of confused, illogical thinking. The disarray evidenced in his mediational activities is quite severe and commensurate with that found frequently among those suffering from some major psychiatric or neurological disorder. When considered in light of findings regarding a serious thinking problem, it is difficult to avoid the conclusion that a schizophrenic disorder is present.

Information Processing

Information about processing is always important, but more so when a serious disturbance exists. This is because the condition often creates havoc in processing activity. Approaches tend to become more haphazard, motivation is inconsistent, and at times preoccupations direct attention to less relevant details causing important areas to be neglected. The data for this cluster are shown in Table 60.

Case 3 Findings   Step 1 (Lambda) shows a low value for L, indicating more involvement with stimuli than is usual for most adults. In this case, it probably reflects the influence of ideational preoccupations and is not inconsistent with findings generated from the preceding two clusters. The Step 2 (OBS and HVI) result is very important. The HVI is positive, signifying a state of hyperalertness, which, in this case, probably reflects the presence of many paranoid-like features and leads to the hypothesis that he is a paranoid schizophrenic. This revelation also provides some clarification for the very low Lambda. Paranoid

Table 60.   Information Processing Variables for Case 3

$L = 0.14$	OBS = Neg	HVI = Pos		LOCATION SEQUENCING		
$Zd = +3.5$		$DQ+ = 7$	I W,Dd	IV W,D	VIII W,WS	
$Zf = 13$		$DQv/+ = 1$	II WS	V W	VIII WS,D	
$W:D:Dd = 11:3:2$		$DQv = 0$	III D,Dd	VI W,W	IX WS	
$W:M = 11:5$		PSV = 0			X W	

people are often very concerned with complexity, not because they like it, but because they want to make sure that they are not victimized by surprise elements. The data for Step 3 (*Zf, W : D : Dd,* and *W : M*) tend to confirm that he is well motivated to process information. He invests considerable effort in organizing activity and typically attempts to utilize the entire field. Although this is not very efficient, the quality of the effort generally is quite good as illustrated by the data for Steps 4 (*DQ* distribution) and 5 (*Zd* and PSV). Seven of his 16 responses are synthesized (only two of those are minus responses), and his scanning effort is more substantial than that of most people.

Case 3 Summary   Overall, there are no significant problems in his information processing, even though he appears to be hyperalert and probably paranoid. He invests considerable effort in processing information and may be inefficient at times in his quest to account for all features of a field, but this inefficiency is a low price to pay when judged against the payoff for him.

Controls

The issue of controls and stress tolerance is important in this case because questions regarding irresistible impulse or loss of control may be raised. The data for this cluster are shown in Table 61.

[margin handwriting: impulse control]

Case 3 Findings   None of the data in this cluster are especially striking. If they were reviewed independent of any other information, one might guess that the subject is a nonpatient. The Step 1 (Adj D Score and CDI) data suggest that his capacity for control and tolerance for stress is probably very much like that of most adults. The Step 2 review of the *EA* suggests that he probably has as much accessibility to resources as most adults. The Step 3 (*EB*) finding supports the notion that the *EA* is apparently valid and the Step 4 (*es*) data appear to confirm the reliability of the Adj D Score. In fact, when the components of the *eb* are examined, there is no evidence of any unusual demand experiences except for a slight elevation in peripheral ideation that is being created by situationally-related stress.

Case 3 Summary   No problems are evidenced in the area of controls and stress tolerance. His capacity for control is like that of most adults. He appears to have about as much resource available for forming decisions and implementing behaviors as is expected for a person of his age. There is no unusual magnitude of internal demand experiences, although situational stress appears to have increased

Table 61.   Control-Related Variables for Case 3

EB = 5 : 3.0	*EA* = 8.0	D = 0	CDI = 2
eb = 6 : 2	*es* = 8 Adj*es* = 6	AdjD = 0	
FM = 3 *m* = 3 *C'* = 2 *T* = 0 *V* = 0 *Y* = 0			

the presence of ideational activity that is not in the direct focus of attention. The latter is easily understood in light of his present circumstances.

Affective Features

Information concerning affect is also very important in this case because of its forensic nature. Data concerning the cluster related to affect are shown in Table 62.

Case 3 Findings   The DEPI is positive, having a value of 5. This indicates that his psychological organization is marked by features that give rise to frequent experiences of depression and/or emotional disruption. This is not uncommon among schizophrenics. As Strauss (1983) pointed out, the frequent presence of post-psychotic depression and severe affective symptoms in schizophrenia suggest that an affective problem or an affective situation may be present in schizophrenia. The finding regarding the presence of or predisposition to depression or affective disruption seems important here because the results of the Step 1 review (*EB*) indicate that he usually prefers to keep his feelings apart from this thinking during decision making. At the same time, as noted earlier, the Step 2 data (*EBPer*) suggest that some flexibility exists in this coping style. Thus, in some circumstances, feelings may become quite influential in his thinking during decision or coping operations.

The Step 3 (right-side *eb*) review is not particularly revealing, although it seems interesting to note that the only experienced emotional demands concern the containment of emotional expression by internalization. This is consistent with the findings from Steps 4 (*FC* : *CF* + *C*) and 6 (*Afr*). It seems clear that he attempts to exert stringent controls over his emotional discharges and, in fact, prefers to avoid emotional stimulation as much as possible. He is probably very uncomfortable when in emotionally arousing situations and may be fearful of losing the tight controls that he has imposed upon his feelings. People such as this tend to be withdrawn and/or socially isolated. The findings from these three steps are important in light of the positive DEPI; that is, there is no evidence of emotional chaos. Thus, the positive DEPI probably reflects more of a cognitive type of depression or at least a predisposition to a cognitive-type depression.

Steps 5 (Pure *C*) and 7 (Color Projection) are not applicable in this case but the Step 8 (*S*) finding is quite dramatic. He harbors a very negative, angry

Table 62.   Affect-Related Variables for Case 3

$EB = 5 : 3.0$	$EBPer = 1.7$	DEPI = 5		BLENDS
$eb = 6 : 2$	$(C' = 2,$ $T = 0,$ $V = 0,$ $Y = 0)$		M.C'F.m	M.FC.FD
$FC{:}CF + C = 4 : 1$	Pure $C = 0$		M.m	
$Afr = 0.33$	CP = 0			
$S = 5$	Col-Shd Bl = 0			

attitude toward the environment. It seems logical to speculate that his fearfulness of or inability to deal with this anger has contributed to the stringent controls that he attempts to place on his emotional displays and his marked avoidance of emotional stimulation. This anger probably has also contributed significantly to the implementation of the violent acts to which he has confessed.

The Step 9 (number of blends) data suggest that, ordinarily, he is not a very complex person. In fact, the review of Steps 10 (*m* and *Y* blends) and 11 (blend complexity) suggests that, even though the current level of complexity is modest, it may even be greater than usual because of situational stress. Steps 12 and 13 are not applicable.

Case 3 Summary   This is a very angry young man who usually prefers to keep his feelings aside during coping or decision making activities. He attempts to exert very stringent controls over his emotional displays and usually prefers to avoid emotionally stimulating situations. Other than his intense anger, there is no evidence of serious emotional disruption. Nonetheless, he seems to be experiencing some form of depression or, at the very least, is predisposed to frequent depressive episodes that are marked mainly by cognitive features. *? Not clear*

Self-Perception

The data concerning self-perception have special importance in this case because of the positive DEPI. The findings from the review of the cluster pertaining to affect did not include evidence of severe emotional disruption. Therefore, it is reasonable to predict that the presence of depressive features, or of a predisposition to depression, has some obvious direct relationship to issues of self-value and self-image. The data concerning the variables in this cluster are shown in Table 63.

Case 3 Findings   There are no reflections in the record but the Step 2 (Egocentricity Index) datum forms a linchpin that helps to draw together some earlier findings. He perceives himself quite negatively when compared with others and probably focuses much more on the external world than on himself. The Step 3 (*FD* and VISTA) data are not very important, except to note that he seems to self-examine about as much as most adults, but this should be viewed in the

Table 63.   **Self-Perception Variables for Case 3**

STRUCTURAL DATA		RESPONSES TO BE READ	
$Fr+rF = 0$ $3r+(2)/R = 0.19$		*MOR* RESPONSES	= 3, 8, 10, 16
$FD = 1$ $V = 0$		MINUS RESPONSES	= 2, 3, 7, 8, 10, 14
$H:(H)+Hd+(Hd) = 1 : 7$		*M* RESPONSES	= 7, 9, 11, 14, 16
$An+Xy = 2$		*FM* RESPONSES	= 1, 2, 6
$MOR = 5$		*m* RESPONSES	= 9, 16

context of his flawed thinking, the negative self-value and the Step 4 (human contents) data. The latter seem to make it clear that his self-concept is based largely on imagination. Thus, when he does self-inspect, he is viewing an image that is probably far removed from reality.

The Step 5 ($An + Xy$) data hint at some unusual body concern that may be related to the finding of the Step 6 (MOR) review. His self-image is marked by many negative features and he tends to perceive himself as damaged or distorted. Whether this was a precursor to his negative self-value or if the reverse is true cannot be ascertained from the data, but the severity of the negative self-perception is illustrated quite well by the Step 7 review of the projected material manifest in the contents of the morbid answers (3. "A torn up body . . . it's torn apart," 8. "some bone . . . a wishbone that has been pulled, it's still connected but it's partly broken . . . nobody will get a wish," 9. "a fist smashing through something," 10. "Somebody was crucified and they cut off his head and legs . . . if you do wrong they'll really get you and cut you up . . . and leave you hanging there," 16. "Somebody is taking revenge, . . . everything is being ripped apart . . . it's all disintegrating . . . it's not very nice to look at"). None of these is modest, and all tend to dramatize the terrible sense of self with which he lives.

Three of the five MOR answers are also minus responses as noted in the Step 8 search for additional projected material. It seems interesting to note that two of the three remaining minus answers have aggressive contents, which probably signify some of the anger and frustration that he feels about himself (7. "a face like an evil looking guy . . . he's a mean person . . . he's really mad at something," 14. "somebody mooning . . . doing it on purpose, like to shock people . . . make fun of them"). The latter answer makes it difficult to avoid speculating about how shocking he would appear to others if he really exposed himself. The remaining minus answer (2. "A face of a frog . . . he's got his mouth open . . . frogs always have big eyes if they are open") contains less direct projected material but could have some relationship to his hypervigilant state.

The perusal through the MOR and minus answers in Steps 7 and 8 has included seven of the 10 responses containing movement. Nonetheless, the remaining three movement answers evaluated in Step 9 contribute added information regarding his rather pathetic and conflicted self-image. The first seems to illustrate a hidden delusion of grandiosity that may exist (1. "maybe it's a queen crow . . . the size lets other crows know that she is majestic"). The second (6. "A gorilla wearing lumberjack boots") is somewhat less revealing except for the boots and the status that they seem to represent to him. The third (11. "Two little girls who have a secret . . . between them, little girls do that you know") is probably the most intriguing. If interpreted in light of the queen crow answer plus the mooning response ("I guess a woman . . ."), a question must be raised concerning the subject's sexual identity confusion. In most cases, such a speculation is very tenuous. However, in this case, he retained undergarments and jewelry of his three victims. Collectively, the responses and the history information raise intriguing questions concerning the etiological motives underlying the acts.

The Step 10 search yields no unusual wording or embellishments in the answers that have not yet been read, but it is interesting to note that all have concealment features (5. "witch's shoes," 12. "a negative of a woman . . . you can't see the features," 13. "A Star Wars mask," 15. "a mask too, probably from New Orleans or Venice when they have those celebrations").

Case 3 Summary   There seems to be little question that this man is tormented by an extremely negative and distasteful self-image. He regards himself very poorly when he compares himself with others and he often examines his self-image, which is based largely on imagination rather than real experience, in a context of disturbed thinking, a pessimistic set, and a possible confusion about his own sexual identification. Although he perceives himself quite negatively and appears to have more body concern than is typical for adults, he also feels that it is important to conceal these features. In addition, he appears to harbor some delusions about power and aggression. Collectively, his self-perception is marked by chaos and disillusionment and it seems logical to assume that many of his behaviors have been designed to maintain some semblance of personal integrity.

Interpersonal Perception and Behavior

In reviewing this final cluster, it seems unrealistic to hope for positive findings, yet the data may shed added light on his complex psychology. The variables for this cluster are shown in Table 64.

Case 3 Findings   The Step 1 (CDI) result is not significant but, as noted earlier, the Step 2 (HVI) finding is very important. The positive HVI not only indicates a chronic pattern of hyperalertness, but also signals an orientation toward the interpersonal world that is scored by mistrust, skepticism, excessive suspiciousness, and a failure to experience needs for closeness in ways that are common among people. In fact, people such as this often become more guarded when gestures of closeness occur because such gestures are unexpected and difficult to comprehend. Usually, these hypervigilant people expend considerable energy in maintaining a defensive psychological posture when dealing with others. They are overly concerned with issues of personal space and become alarmed easily when others are perceived as being intrusive, either physically or emotionally. They tend to keep their interpersonal relationships very casual and superficial and often misread gestures by others. They tend to function best in

Table 64.   Interpersonal Perception Variables for Case 3

STRUCTURAL VARIABLES		RESPONSES TO BE READ
CDI = 2	HVI = Pos	MOVEMENT WITH PAIR = 11
a:p = 3:8	T = 0 Fd = 0	HUMAN CONTENTS = 7, 9, 10, 11, 12, 13, 14, 16
Isolate/R = 0.13		
Total Human Contents = 8		
PER = 4	COP = 0 AG = 4	

safe, reasonably isolated environments over which they feel a sense of control and they usually function at their worst in situations where close contact or exchanges are the rule.

It is not surprising that the Step 3 finding $(a:p)$ reveals a marked tendency toward interpersonal passivity. Avoidance of responsibility is an easy way to avoid emotional involvement and closeness with others. It also provides a convenient source of excuse whenever things do not go well. Steps 4 (Food) and 5 (T) are not applicable, but the datum for Step 6 (total human contents) indicates that he is very interested in people, which is not unusual for a hypervigilant person. The Step 7 result (PER) sheds some light on how he probably interacts with others. He frequently adopts a more rigidly authoritarian approach as a way of avoiding the intrusions and manipulations of others, and to keep them at a distance. The absence of COP responses, as noted in the Step 8 evaluation (COP and AG), is not surprising but the presence of a significant elevation in AG answers is very important. It indicates that he perceives everyday interpersonal relationships as naturally including contentious and belligerent behaviors and has incorporated these features in his own interpersonal activity. Ordinarily, this finding might lead to the postulate that his behaviors have included considerable aggressive behavior that could be documented easily, but in this case, the pronounced commitment to passivity suggests that most of his aggressiveness was probably manifest less directly, as in the instance of the passive-aggressive individual. Nonetheless, the magnitude of this finding seems to ensure that his behavior patterns regularly include aggressive activity. When this set is linked with his long-standing intense anger, couched in the context of his strange and illogical thought processes, and viewed in terms of his fearfulness about emotional arousal, the violence in which he has engaged is not surprising.

The Step 9 (Isolation Index) review is negative, but this is probably a false result. The Step 10 evaluation (movement answers containing a pair) yields only one answer with which to contend. It is the Card VII (11) response of "Two little girls who have a secret." There is no dynamic interaction. They are just "sitting looking at each other," as if deep or meaningful interactions are based on some intellectual sharing that involves no contact. Although the number of human contents is considerable and signals a strong interest in people, the range of human contents, as illustrated in the Step 11 review, tends to reflect his perceptions of others as well as himself (7. "an evil looking guy," 9. "a fist," 10. "somebody crucified," 11. "Two little girls," 12. "A negative of a woman," 13. "A Star Wars mask," 14. 'Somebody mooning," 16. "Somebody is taking revenge"). None is very positive, and most are clearly negative. As implied earlier by the positive HVI, the subject does not look very favorably on others.

Case 3 Summary   Any suggestion that his interpersonal world is impoverished is an understatement and probably misleading. He is very interested in people and apparently devotes considerable time to their study. This is not because of needs to be close or to develop deep and enduring relationships. To the contrary, he perceives people very negatively and regards them as a potential threat to his security. He is easily threatened by the natural everyday emotional friendliness of others and works hard to keep his own feelings on a more intellectual, easily controlled level. Apparently, he has found a passive interpersonal role to be the most safe and productive in terms of his own needs. He also perceives that manifestations of aggressiveness are a routine in the tactics of exchange between people. It is very likely that his own history is marked by many behaviors that, under close inspection, would be regarded as passive-aggressive acts. On a more speculative level, it also seems likely that his perception of aggressiveness has somehow combined with his distorted thinking and his intense anger to promote the violent actions to which he has confessed.

Case 3 Final Description

This young man presents a picture of psychological organization and functioning that closely approximates a paranoid schizophrenic condition. His thinking tends to be strange and disorganized, and frequently is bizarre. He is a very ideationally oriented person who prefers to think things through before forming decisions or initiating behaviors, but, unfortunately, his thinking is often influenced significantly by strong, well-fixed preoccupations and/or delusions. Thus, his judgment is often faulty and concrete, which can produce patterns of decision making and behavior that are quite inappropriate to the situation. Although he makes a strong effort to process information effectively, he does not perceive the world very accurately or conventionally. In some instances his translations of stimuli are not distortions but simply products of his more personal preoccupations. In other instances the translations are marked by a serious perceptual inaccuracy that promotes gross distortions. The result is, at best, a limited grasp of reality.

Ordinarily, he has enough resource available to ensure adequate control over his behavior. His tolerance for stress is like that of most adults and no unusual magnitude of internal demands is pressing on him. Some evidence suggests that current stresses have increased the complexity of his ideation, but not beyond tolerable limits. He is not comfortable with emotion and works hard to keep his feelings very well controlled. He apparently goes to considerable lengths to avoid emotionally arousing situations, including the frequent use of an apparently elaborate fantasy life into which he often takes flight to replace the harshness or stresses of reality. His fearfulness of emotion probably stems from the fact that he harbors considerable anger, which he probably has difficulty acknowledging and controlling.

In part, this anger seems related to his very negative and distasteful self-image, which appears to have evolved more from imagination than real experience, but may include some awareness of his own strangeness. This negative self-image has given rise to a strong sense of pessimism. He does not expect things to go well and probably becomes depressed often because of his plight. He regards himself poorly when compared with others and has adopted an interpersonal approach that is mainly guarded, distant, and passive. He also perceives aggression to be a natural component of interpersonal life, and it is likely that many of his own behaviors include passive-aggressive features. He is defensively preoccupied with people and feels the necessity to be continually alert against the intrusions or manipulations of others. His fearfulness of emotion, when combined with his strange thinking and mistrust of people, often causes him to become easily threatened by others. Most of the time his reaction to these threats is likely to take the form of passive withdrawal; however, the composite of disturbed thinking and perceptual distortion increases the probability for other forms of behavior, including the violent actions to which he has confessed.

Recommendations Based on the Final Description

Most competency laws include two issues: (1) whether the subject is able to comprehend the nature of the charges, and (2) whether the subject is able to participate meaningfully in the preparation and conduct or his or her defense. In this case, it is reasonable to recommend that he be found incompetent with regard to the second issue. It is likely that he can understand the charges, even though he may interpret them in his own idiographic way; however, it is unlikely that he can participate meaningfully in his own defense. His problems in thinking and perceiving are likely to promote frequent distortions of information and events, and his enduring mistrust of others plus his tendency to be very passive are likely to breed activities in relation to his attorney and the court that could be significantly detrimental to his cause.

If he is brought to trial or judgment the etiological basis for his actions can be speculatively explained rather elaborately by drawing inferences from the test findings, and it would not be unreasonable to support a contention of insanity under some statutes. On the other hand, issues such as his adequate controls, ability to formulate and implement behaviors (premeditation), intense anger, and tendencies toward aggressive behaviors, together with his reasonably consistent work history, can all be used as the basis for arguments that can be detrimental to him.

Case 3 Epilogue   A three-judge panel rejected a motion to declare the subject incompetent to stand trial. Subsequently, the defense attorney filed a plea of not guilty by reason of insanity. During the trial the subject did not testify. The state law concerning insanity that was applied in this case reflects a composite of the M'Naghten (laboring under a defective reason from the disease of the mind as to not know the nature and quality of the act he was doing; or, if he did know it, he did not know he was doing what was wrong) and Durham (insanity is considered the product of a mental disease or defect) decisions. He was found guilty on two counts of first degree homicide. The death penalty was recommended in a separate sentencing trial. The last of three appeals caused the verdict to be set aside and a retrial ordered. In the new trial he was found guilty of one count of first degree homicide and a second count of second degree homicide, but the sentencing trial yielded a recommendation of life imprisonment without the possibility of parole.

CASE 4: A SCHIZOTYPAL DISORDER

This 22-year-old female is a voluntary first admission to a private psychiatric facility following the advice of her parents and family physician. The admission was provoked because she recently stole the car of the woman who owns the boarding house in which she lives, with the stated intention of setting out to find people whom she might like. The theft was reported a few hours after it had occurred, and she was apprehended by the state police after having driven approximately 200 miles. She was held in jail overnight and released on bail into the custody of her parents the next morning.

This was her second car theft. At the age of 17, during her third year in high school, she stole her stepfather's car and was missing for five days until apprehended in Florida after taking a position as a waitress in a drive-in restaurant. No charges were pressed, and, after being returned home, she entered psychotherapy with a female therapist. The treatment lasted approximately 13 months (weekly), and she says that it was useful because "it helped me put alot of things into a psychological perspective." She graduated from high school at age 18. Her school record consists mainly of C grades. During her first two years of high school she was on the girl's basketball and field hockey teams and was a member of the library club during all four years. In the fall following her graduation she entered a junior college and continued living at home. Her grades during the year consisted of C's and D's and she decided to drop out and seek work, with the reluctant approval of her parents.

Her natural parents were divorced when she was age eight and she continued living with her mother, who is now age 52. She frequently continued to see her father, who is now age 60. He works in middle management for an industrial firm. She describes him very positively but admits to her disappointment about not seeing him more often, especially during the past two years. Her mother remarried when she was 11. Her stepfather, age 54, works in advertising. It is his second marriage and he has two sons, ages 30 and 28, whom he sees often but with whom the subject has had limited contact. The subject speaks favorably about her stepfather but notes that he is a "weak man who drinks too much." She speaks very unfavorably about her mother, whom she also alleges to be a heavy drinker: "We're on and off. It depends on her mood and how much she drinks. I don't feel close to her most of the time. I feel sorry for her some of the time and I think I hate her most of the time."

After dropping out of college she obtained a job selling cosmetics in a department store and decided to rent her own apartment. She was fired after approximately six months, apparently because of negative interactions with customers. At that time she moved into a shared apartment with two other young women and obtained a job as a dishwasher in a restaurant. She remained in that job for about 10 months, but was fired for absenteeism. Apparently, she was also in arrears for her portion of the rent on the apartment and moved out to live with one of her aunts (her natural father's sister). She did not work for about three months, but then obtained a position as a chambermaid in a motel, leaving her aunt's residence and taking a room in the boarding house in which she now resides. She quit the chambermaid position after six months and affiliated herself with a group of free-lance house painters (two men and three women) who also rent rooms in the boarding house.

Her developmental history, as given by the patient and her mother, is unremarkable. She reports having had several close childhood friendships but admits that these faded early into her high school years. She describes her high school peers as more immature and less interested in life than she. She says that she played basketball and field hockey during her first two high school years because her friends encouraged her, but she discontinued playing because she felt

Case 4: A 22-Year-Old Female

Card	Response	Inquiry
I	1. A bird, yes a bird E: Tak ur time & look more, I'm sur u'll find smthg else S: Can I just use a part? E: If u like	E: (Rpts S's resp) S: Ok, it's all a bird right? The wgs r out here & this is the middle, the body part, just lik a bird
	2. A woman, just the lower part, her legs r togethr	E: (Rpts S's resp) S: Down here (outlines D3) it's formed lik that, lik the lower part of a woman w her legs togethr, u kno lik if u line up in a gym class thy tell u to stand straight up w u'r legs togethr, tht's how she's standing but u can't c her top part m⁹ or F
II	3. I'd say 2 A's getting togethr, lik thyr dancing, yes that's it two birds dancing	E: (Rpts S's resp) S: They really ll 2 chickens that are dancing, thy hav red peaks lik chickens & thyr whirlg around having a good time E: I'm not sur why thy ll chickens, I kno u said thy hav red peaks but help me to c them better S: Oh, I dk, thyr fat I suppose, lik chickens, thy just ll tht
	4. I c love in it too	E: (Rpts S's resp) S: The red down here (D3), anythg red always represents love, thts what is represents to me, it has to b, red couldn't b anythg else
III	5. Two real people trying to come togethr but this red thing in the middl is somethg keeping them apart	E: (Rpts S's resp) S: There's one on each side, c their heads & legs, thyr r lik straining toward each other but thy can't touch because of this red, it represents a thot or a deed E: A thot or a deed? S: It's not really there but its just represented there by the red, I kno red is supp to be love but here its somthg else, mayb a fite, I dk but as long as it's red thy won't get togethr
	V6. If I turn it it's better, the red is just a fly	E: (Rpts S's resp) S: It's got tht shape, these r the wgs & the littl body, just lik a housefly

IV

7. A littl bird, no a big bird but it doesn't hav wgs, don't count ths center thg

E: (Rpts S's resp)
S: Well, it looks big but it must be littl cuz it doesn't hav wgs, it has big feet & a littl head but the wgs haven't grown yet, I don't think birds r born lik tht
E: Born lik tht?
S: Yeah, w.o. wgs, so it must be hurt, it lost its wgs or mayb it never had any, u kno lik deformed
E: U said it looks big but it must be littl?
S: Well at first i figured it was big, it looks big there but then I thot mayb it was littl cuz the wgs aren't there, but I think it really is big & it's hurt or deformed

V

8. Another, no wait, I was going to say bird but I'll say bf

9. Ths way it's lik smbody standg on their head, a gymnast

E: (Rpts S's resp)
S: It's got its wgs spread out, lik it's flying & its got those antennae lik bf's hav
E: (Rpts S's resp)
S: She's got big baggy pants on & her legs are going out in each direction & these r her arms I guess, y kno how thy get in ths position & hold it, it shows good balance, I used to be able to do it lik ths but I don't anymore

VI

10. Well, the first thg is fr the ancients, a weapon but ths down here (D1) isn't part

E: (Rpts S's resp)
S: It has tht structure to it, it has the sharp parts on each side so u can swing it either way & ths is the handle, it's sorta lik a hatchet but its very old, the sharp parts ll stone
E: Stone
S: It's grey colored, lik sk of stone thts sharp

VII

11. Ths bottom ll a blanket, lik a blanket made fr an A

E: (Rpts S's resp)
S: Mayb a bear or a deer blanket, I guess a bear cuz I never heard of a deer blanket but I suppose the Indians had deer blankets
E: I'm not sur wht maks it ll a blanket
S: Well not lik u find in u'r house, it's an A skin blanket, it has those diff textures to it lik diff colors of the hair on it

12. Two kids playing indian

E: (Rpts S's resp)
S: Thy'v got feathers in their hair lik thyr pretending to b indians, thyr jumping up & down on ths rock or platform & thyv painted their faces
E: Painted their faces
S: Thyr diff colors, lik thyv put paint on to pretend is war paint

(continued)

Case 4: (Continued)

Card	Response	Inquiry
	13. This bottom part ll u'r lookg in between s.o.'s thighs	*E:* (Rpts S's resp) *S:* It's lik s.o. is sitting w their thighs spread & u can look right in & c everythg, I kno it sounds vulgar but I'm being honest *E:* I'm not sur I'm seeg it rite *S:* The dark is where the vagina is & where it gets darker is hair & out here is the inside of the thighs, like thyr being held open
VIII	14. A bf, its all diff colors I lik the colors	*E:* (Rpts S's resp) *S:* The wgs out here r pink & white & the center of the wings is blue & up here wld be the head & the back part is pink and orange
	15. If u just take the side thy ll pink wolves	*E:* (Rpts S's resp) *S:* I never heard of pink wolves but tht what thy ll, one on each side, c head & the legs
IX	16. Wow, tht's lik some really loud weird sound, lik the last note of a heavy metal song or smthg	*E:* (Rpts S's resp) *S:* It just re me of tht, it ll its pushing out at the bottom & shootg up at the top & there's ths lin rite in the middl, it's lik the whole thg is gonna burst, if u cld hear it it wld really blow u away *E:* I don't kno if Im seeg it lik u r *S:* It just ll a lot of noise going in all diff directions, up and sideways & out at the bottom
X	17. The top is lik 2 crabs holdg a big club or smthg	*E:* (Rpts S's resp) *S:* C, one on each side w their littl legs & the feelers on their head & thy have littl white eyes & thyr holdg up ths thg, ths club in the center FC
	18. This blue thg ll a crab too	*E:* (Rpts S's resp) *S:* It just ll tht, it has a lotta legs lik crabs do
	19. There r two faces in the pink, lookg at e.o.	*E:* (Rpts S's resp) *S:* Thy ll littl, whadaucallem, elfs, thyr not real people, just elfs, c the nose & the head
	20. This thg cb a bird, a dead one	*E:* (Rpts S's resp) *S:* I dk, it just does, it has the body like a bird & the wgs too, just a bird, I dk what kind *E:* U said a dead one? *S:* Yeah, not moving, lik lying there, lik dead
	21. Ths thg ll a seed, lik fr a tree, I thk a maple	*E:* (Rpts S's resp) *S:* Thy get these seeds in the fall, I see em alot in the fall, thyr shaped lik ths when thy fall off the tree

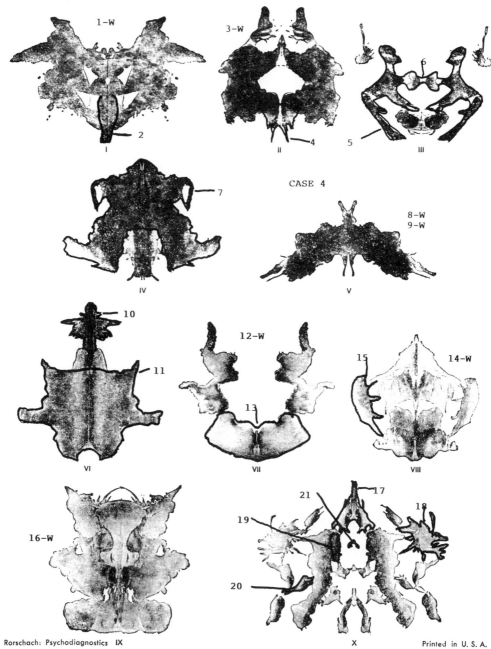

CASE 4

```
CASE 4.    SEQUENCE OF SCORES
================================================================================
CARD  NO  LOC   #      DETERMINANT(S)    (2)   CONTENT(S)   POP  Z  SPECIAL SCORES
================================================================================
  I    1  Wo    1  Fo                           A                1.0
       2  Do    3  Mpo                           Hd                     DR

 II    3  W+    1  Ma.FCu              2          A                4.5   COP,FAB
       4  Dv    3  Ma.C                           Hx                     AB,ALOG

 III   5  D+    1  Ma.Co               2          H,Id        P    4.0   COP,DR,AB
       6  Do    3  F-                             A

 IV    7  Do    7  Fu                             Ad                     MOR,ALOG

  V    8  Wo    1  FMao                           A           P    1.0
       9  W+    1  Mau                            H,Cg             2.5   PER

 VI   10  Do    3  FC'u                           Ay
      11  Do    1  FTo                            Ad          P          DR

 VII  12  W+    1  Ma.FYo              2          H,Id,Ls     P    2.5   COP
      13  Do    4  Ma.FV.FTo                      Hd,Sx

VIII  14  WSo   1  CF.C'Fo                        A                4.5
      15  Do    1  FCo                 2          A           P          INC

 IX   16  Wo    1  Ma-                            Hx               5.5   AB

  X   17  DS+  11  FMa.FC'             2          A,Id             6.0   COP,FAB
      18  Do    1  Fo                             A           P
      19  Dd+  25  Mpo                 2          (Hd)             4.5
      20  Do    7  F-                             A                      MOR
      21  Do    3  Fo                             Bt                     PER
================================================================================
```

it served no useful purpose. She began dating during her third year of high school but was not "really interested" in anyone. During that year, and before she stole her stepfather's car, she became very interested in religion, and although her parents did not attend church, she began going to different churches each Sunday and gradually began attending one more often than the others because "there seemed to be some message that you could get if you went enough."

She claims that her decision to steal her stepfather's car came to her during a church service, during which "something told me to run away and find a new life." She says that she was depressed at the time but cannot account for the cause of the depression. She says that her last high school year and the year in junior college "were wasted because I should have been looking for something else." She denies any drug or alcohol abuse ("I never want to be like my mother") and reports only limited sexual experiences, which include mutual masturbation with both males and females but no experience of intercourse ("I know about it but it must wait"). She says that she had one close friend, a woman her own age, while she worked as a chambermaid but that relationship broke off when the woman

CASE 4.   STRUCTURAL SUMMARY
==

| LOCATION | DETERMINANTS | | CONTENTS | S-CONSTELLATION |

LOCATION FEATURES	BLENDS	SINGLE		S-CONSTELLATION
			H = 3, 0	NO..FV+VF+V+FD>2
Zf = 10	FM.FC	M = 4	(H) = 0, 0	YES..Col-Shd Bl>0
ZSum = 36.0	M.C	FM = 1	Hd = 2, 0	NO..Ego<.31,>.44
ZEst = 31.0	M.C	m = 0	(Hd)= 1, 0	NO..MOR > 3
	M.FY	FC = 1	Hx = 2, 0	YES..Zd > +- 3.5
W = 7	M.FV.FT	CF = 0	A = 9, 0	NO..es > EA
(Wv = 0)	CF.C'F	C = 0	(A) = 0, 0	YES..CF+C > FC
D = 13	FM.FC'	Cn = 0	Ad = 2, 0	YES..X+% < .70
Dd = 1		FC'= 1	(Ad)= 0, 0	NO..S > 3
S = 2		C'F= 0	An = 0, 0	NO..P < 3 or > 8
		C' = 0	Art = 0, 0	NO..Pure H < 2
DQ		FT = 1	Ay = 1, 0	NO..R < 17
.........(FQ-)		TF = 0	Bl = 0, 0	4.....TOTAL
+ = 6 (0)		T = 0	Bt = 1, 0	
o = 14 (5)		FV = 0	Cg = 0, 1	SPECIAL SCORINGS
v/+ = 0 (0)		VF = 0	Cl = 0, 0	Lv1 Lv2
v = 1 (0)		V = 0	Ex = 0, 0	DV = 0x1 0x2
		FY = 0	Fd = 0, 0	INC = 1x2 0x4
		YF = 0	Fi = 0, 0	DR = 3x3 0x6
		Y = 0	Ge = 0, 0	FAB = 2x4 0x7
FORM QUALITY		Fr = 0	Hh = 0, 0	ALOG = 2x5
		rF = 0	Ls = 0, 1	CON = 0x7
FQx FQf MQual SQx		FD = 0	Na = 0, 0	SUM6 = 8
+ = 0 0 0 0		F = 6	Sc = 0, 0	WSUM6 = 29
o = 10 3 4 0			Sx = 0, 1	AB = 3 CP = 0
u = 5 1 2 1			Xy = 0, 0	AG = 0 MOR = 2
- = 5 2 2 1			Id = 0, 3	CFB = 0 PER = 2
none= 1 -- 1 0		(2) = 6		COP = 4 PSV = 0

==
RATIOS, PERCENTAGES, AND DERIVATIONS

R = 21	L = 0.40		FC:CF+C = 2: 3	COP = 4 AG = 0

EB = 9: 5.0	EA = 14.0	EBPer= 1.8
eb = 2: 7	es = 9	D = +1
	Adj es = 9	Adj D = +1

	FC:CF+C = 2: 3	COP = 4 AG = 0
	Pure C = 2	Food = 0
	Afr =0.62	Isolate/R =0.10
	S = 2	H:(H)Hd(Hd)= 3: 3
	Blends:R= 7:21	(HHd):(AAd)= 1: 0
	CP = 0	H+A:Hd+Ad =12: 5

| FM = 2 : | C'= 3   T = 2 |
| m = 0 : | V = 1   Y = 1 |

	P = 6	Zf =10	3r+(2)/R=0.29
a:p = 9: 2	Sum6 = 8	X+% =0.48	Fr+rF = 0
Ma:Mp = 7: 2	Lv2 = 0	F+% =0.50	Zd = +5.0	FD = 0
2AB+Art+Ay= 7	WSum6 = 29	X-% =0.24	W:D:Dd = 7:13: 1	An+Xy = 0
M- = 2	Mnone = 1	S-% =0.20	W:M = 7: 8	MOR = 1
		Xu% =0.24	DQ+ = 6	
			DQv = 1	

| SCZI = 4* | DEPI = 5* | CDI = 1 | S-CON = 5 | HVI = No | OBS = No |

==

became involved with a young man. She reports that her decision to join with the group of house painters occurred because she felt "a great deal of love from them, they enjoy life even though they are poor." She admits being attracted to one of the three women in the group but denies any physical contact.

The assessment is a routine procedure for the fifth or sixth day after admission and typically is designed to focus on a broad description of personality and recommendations for treatment. In this instance, noted peculiarities in her logic and speech have caused some staff to raise a question about the possibility of schizophrenia.

Interpretive Strategy

The record contains 21 answers and should be interpretively useful. The first positive Key variable is the SCZI, which has a value of 4. The search order will be the same as used in Case 3:

IDEATION → MEDIATION → PROCESSING → CONTROLS → AFFECT → SELF-PERCEPTION → INTERPERSONAL PERCEPTION.

Initial Proposition: The subject appears to manifest many features that are common to schizophrenics and uncommon among other psychiatric subjects.

Ideation

The data for the cluster of variables related to ideation are shown in Table 65.

Case 4 Findings The Step 1 (*EB*) and 2 (*EBPer*) results indicate that she is the type of person who prefers to delay, keep feelings aside, and consider alternative possibilities before making a response. However, there is also some flexibility to this coping style and in some instances, she uses an opposite approach; that is, her feelings become more influential in her decisions and tend to prompt trial-and-error behaviors to reach a solution. The Step 3 (left-side *eb*) data show a lower level of peripheral ideation than expected, which suggests that she may not

Table 65. Ideation Variables for Case 4

$EB = 9:5$	$EBPer = 1.8$	M QUALITY	CRITICAL SPECIAL SCORES			
$eb = 2:7$	$(FM = 2 \quad m = 0)$	$+ = 0$	DV	$= 0$	DV2	$= 0$
$a:p = 9:2$	$Ma:Mp = 6:2$	$o = 4$	INC	$= 1$	INC2	$= 0$
$2Ab+(Art+Ay) = 5$		$u = 1$	DR	$= 3$	DR2	$= 0$
MOR $= 2$		$- = 2$	FAB	$= 2$	FAB2	$= 0$
		none $= 1$	ALOG $= 2$		SUM6	$= 9$
RESPONSES TO BE READ FOR QUALITY			CON	$= 0$	WSUM6 $= 29$	
2, 3, 4, 5, 9, 12, 13, 16, 19						

be processing more subtle internal cues as much as most people. The Step 4 ($a:p$) finding is more negative: Her ideational sets, attitudes, and values are apparently well fixed and not very flexible. Thus, it is difficult for her to take a different perspective on things. Step 5 ($M^a:M^p$) is not significant, but the Step 6 (Intellectualization Index) data are important. They suggest that she uses intellectualization routinely as a defense in situations that are perceived as emotionally stressful. Although this tactic tends to neutralize the affective impact of a situation, it increases the vulnerability to disorganization under emotional stress and, when used to excess, it often is transparent to others. Step 7 (MOR) shows a slight, but not significant, elevation.

The most negative data unfold with Step 8 (Sum of six Critical Special Scores). More than one-third of her answers are marked by Critical Special Scores and, at the very least, half seem serious even though no Level 2 scores appear. Thus, it must be concluded that her thinking is disturbed. Instances of discontinuity and/ or flawed conceptualization occur too frequently and tend to impede logic and promote poor judgment. As a result, the possibility of faulty decision making is increased considerably. The Step 9 review of the Critical Special Scores does little to detract from this conclusion.

The INCOM (15. "pink wolves . . . I never heard of pink wolves but . . .") and two of the three DR responses (2. "if you line up in a gym class they tell you to stand straight up with your legs together . . . ," 11. "I never heard of a deer blanket but I suppose . . .") seem more naïve and immature than pathological. The third DR (5. "It's not really there but it's just represented . . . I know red is supposed to be love but here it's something else . . . as long as it's red they won't get together") represents thinking that goes beyond simple naïveté. It is more concrete and disconnected. The two FABCOM's (3. "Animals getting together, like they are dancing," 17. "two crabs holding a big club") also tend to exhibit more immaturity and naïveté than pathology. Both ALOG answers also seem immature, but they are markedly concrete and reflect very poor judgment (4. "red couldn't be anything else," 7. "it looks big but it must be little . . . it looks big but then I thought it was little . . . but I think it really is big"). The latter also illustrates a great deal of vacillation and circumstantiality. Although some of these eight answers seem to exemplify patterns of thinking that are less mature and more juvenile, the composite cannot be taken lightly. Her thinking is strained, concrete, and often disconnected and, although it is not commensurate with the chaos of actively psychotic thinking, it is somewhat similar to that found among schizophrenics at times.

The Step 10 (form quality of M) data seem to confirm that her thinking is peculiar and/or disturbed. There are two $M-$ answers and one formless M response. The latter is especially important because it indicates the likelihood of serious problems in ideational control and may signal the presence of the kinds of ideational disruption that can give rise to hallucinatory experiences. The Step 11 (level of distortions of M) review suggests that both $M-$'s are Level 1 distortions and probably exemplify loose and fluid patterns of thinking.

The Step 12 review of the quality of the M responses reveals more sophistication in her thinking than might have been expected in light of the previous findings. Only one answer, the formless M response (love), seems primitive. Four others (legs together, chickens dancing, kids playing Indian, and faces looking at each other) are somewhat less mature but also very common. The remaining four (people trying to come together, somebody standing on their head, some-one sitting with their thighs spread, and some really loud weird sound) are rea-sonably elaborate and developed in a sophisticated, albeit unusual way. This finding argues strongly against the conclusion that her strained thinking is sim-ply a product of immaturity.

Case 4 Summary   This subject is a very ideational person who relies extensively on her thinking in decision making. Unfortunately, even though her thinking is sophisticated at times, it often is not very clear. Her logic and judgment fre-quently are strained and concrete, and her patterns of thought tend to be recur-rently disconnected and fluid. There is reason to believe that she has problems controlling her ideation as she often vacillates and becomes circumstantial. In fact, there is some likelihood that her thinking is marked by features that give rise to hallucinatory experiences. Thus, many of her decisions are likely to be ineffec-tive because they are generated by flawed, disordered thought.

This problem is exacerbated by two other features. First, she is not very flexible in her ideational sets, attitudes, or values. This increases the probability that faulty decisions or illogical judgments will persist even though external evidence suggests that they are erroneous. Second, she relies heavily on a pseudo-intellectual ap-proach in attempting to contend with stressful situations. This has the effect of neutralizing some of the emotional impact of the situation but is has negative long term effects because the process often is based on disordered thinking that tends to ignore reality. It would be erroneous to suggest that her thinking is markedly pathological, but the extent of the disorganization is considerable and could be commensurate with that found in some instances of schizophrenia.

Cognitive Mediation

The data for the cognitive mediation cluster are shown in Table 66.

Case 4 Findings   The data from Steps 1 (Lambda), 2 (OBS), and 4 ($FQ+$) are not significant. In Step 3, the value of P is in the average range, suggesting that the subject is likely to translate stimuli conventionally when the obvious is present. This is a very important positive finding that can have relevance to treatment

Table 66.   Cognitive Mediation Variables for Case 4

Lambda = 0.40	OBS = Neg		MINUS FEATURES
P = 6	$X+\%$ = .48	III	6. *Do F– A*
$FQx+$ = 0	$F+\%$ = .50	VII	13. *Do Ma.FV.FT– Hd,Sx*
$FQxo$ = 10	$Xu\%$ = .24	VIII	14. *WSo CF.C'F– A 4.5*
FQxu = 5	$X–\%$ = .24	IX	16. *Wo Ma– Hx 5.5 AB*
$FQx–$ = 5	$S–\%$ = .20	X	20. *Do F– 2 A*
FQnone = 1	CONFAB = 0		

planning. The Step 5 $(X + \%)$ datum is also very important because it indicates that, in spite of the positive Step 3 finding, she has a significant tendency to be unconventional in most of her translations, particularly in situations when obvious cues are not present.

The composite of data for Steps 6 $(FQnone)$, 7 $(Xu\%)$, and 8 $(X - \%$ and $S - \%)$ provide some clarification. Many of her unconventional responses are based on idiographic, overly personalized translations. Taken alone, the frequency involved (five answers; $Xu\% = .24$) is only slightly above average. Thus, it could be judged as not very serious and interpreted as representing a strong sense of individuality. However, the magnitude of distortion (five answers; $X - \% = .24$) is far too great and signifies chronic problems in perceptual inaccuracy, even though it is somewhat less than usually found among schizophrenics. When this problem is added to the substantial frequency of overpersonalized translations, the result is an excessive frequency of behaviors that are ineffective and/or inappropriate. Step 9 (sequencing of minus answers) fails to reveal any significant consistency to the pattern of distortions, although four of the five minus answers occur to chromatically colored blots. It may be of special interest to note that none of the eight Critical Special Scores are associated with the minus answers. This is atypical for schizophrenia. Step 10 (homogeneity of minus responses) also does not show any consistency for features or contents of the distortion responses. The Step 11 evaluation for levels of distortion indicates that all are Level 1 minus answers.

Case 4 Summary   The subject tends to make conventional responses when they are obvious but it appears that, when the obvious is not present, problems in cognitive mediation tend to dominate and promote an unacceptably high frequency of behaviors that either ignore conventionality or distort reality. In part, these problems arise from her tendency to translate stimuli in an overly personal way, but they are also based in a more chronic problem of perceptual inaccuracy. The latter may be related, however, to some subtle preoccupation that is not obvious from the data.

The mediational problem is serious and contributes significantly to difficulties in adjustment. On the other hand, the data are not fully congruent with the type of mediational dysfunction that is common among schizophrenics. There are some modest similarities, such as the seeming randomness by which distortions occur, but there are also many features of the data that are quite unlike those found in schizophrenia. For instance, the frequency of mediational distortion is considerably less than would be expected in a schizophrenic, and the fact that there is no obvious merging of distortion and disordered thinking is highly unusual. In that context, the initial proposition concerning the possibility of schizophrenia should be either rejected or deferred.

Information Processing

The data for the variables related to processing are shown in Table 67.

Case 4 Findings   The data for Steps 1 (Lambda) and 2 (OBS and HVI) are not significant but the remaining data in the cluster are somewhat intriguing. The

Table 67.   Information Processing Variables for Case 4

$L = 0.40$	OBS = Neg	HVI = Neg		LOCATION SEQUENCING	
$Zd = +5.0$		$DQ+$ = 6	I W,D	IV D	VII W,D
$Zf = 10$		$DQv/+ = 0$	II W,D	V W,W	VIII WS,D
$W:D:Dd = 7:13:1$		DQv = 1	III D,D	VI D,D	IX W
$W:M = 7:8$		PSV = 0			X D,D,Dd,D,D

Step 3 (Zf, $W:D:Dd$, $W:M$) review suggests a rather conservative or economical processing effort, as if she does not want to become very involved in processing unless the field is easily managed. The Step 4 (DQ) data indicate that she synthesizes about as much as most adults and, interestingly, none of the synthesized responses are minus. This is another finding that is inconsistent with the schizophrenia premise. The Step 5 (Zd) finding reveals that she is an overincorporator. When she does commit herself to processing, she apparently invests extra effort to make sure that no element of the field has been ignored. The Step 6 examination of the sequencing shows that she is reasonably consistent.

Case 4 Summary   There are no obvious information processing problems. She is prone to be conservative or economical in her willingness to deal with new information. Nevertheless, when she commits to process, she tends to invest more energy than is necessary to ensure that she is not negligent. She tends to synthesize details in her processing activity about as much as most adults and, unlike most schizophrenics, does not do this in a manner that leads to mediational distortion. Overall, her processing activities are consistent and not unlike those found among nonpatients.

Controls

Data for the variables in the controls cluster are shown in Table 68.

Case 3 Findings   Step 1 (Adj D Score and CDI) discloses a very important finding. Her capability for control is better than that of most adults, which improves her capacity to deal with stress. This may account for the fact that she has not been in greater disarray in the past. The Step 2 (EA) result indicates that she has considerably more resource than most adults, which is identified and

Table 68.   Control-Related Variables for Case 4

$EB = 9:5.0$	$EA = 14.0$	D = +1	CDI = 1
$eb = 2:7$	$es = 9$ Adj$es = 9$	AdjD = +1	
$FM = 2$ $m = 0$ $C' = 3$ $T = 2$ $V = 0$ $Y = 1$			

organized in ways that make it readily accessible to her. In fact, the magnitude raises a question about whether the Adj D Score might not have been higher in the past. The Step 3 (*EB*) review contains no data from which to challenge the reliability of the *EA,* but the Step 4 (*es*) data indicate that the magnitude of experienced stimulation is somewhat higher than might be expected for the adult. This also raises a question about whether her capacity for control and tolerance for stress might not have been even greater in the past. This postulate also gains some support from the Step 5 evaluation of the *eb* variables that are not related to situational stress. It seems clear that she is experiencing some distress. The values for the variables related to suppression or internalization of affect (*C'*) and needs for closeness (*T*) both are substantially higher than expected. It is remotely possible that these higher values could reflect some situational issues, but there is no obvious evidence to support this hypothesis. Assuming that no situational factors are involved, the distress is apparently chronic and places severe demands on her capacity for control.

Case 4 Summary   Her capacity for control and ability to tolerate stress are somewhat sturdier than those of most adults. In part, this is because she has ready access to considerable resource that can be used to form and implement decisions. At the same time, she appears to be burdened with many aggravating internal emotional demands that have created a chronic state of distress. Thus, although her capacities for control and stress tolerance remain sturdy, the chronicity of the distress may have lowered them to some extent. This might account for some of the ideational confusion that has been noted, and could also contribute in some ways to the problems she has in translating stimuli in overly personal and/or distorted ways.

Affective Features

The data for the variables related to affective features are shown in Table 69.

Case 4 Findings   The DEPI is positive, indicating either the presence of depression or a proclivity to frequent experiences of depression or affective disruption. The data for Steps 1 (*EB*) and 2 (*EBPer*) indicate that the subject usually prefers to keep her emotions at a more peripheral level when involved in decision operations, but also that there is some flexibility to this coping style. Thus, in some

Table 69.   Affect-Related Variables for Case 4

$EB = 9:5.0$	$EBPer = 1.8$	DEPI = 5		BLENDS
$eb = 2:7$	$(C = 3, T = 2, V = 1, Y = 1)$		M.C (2)	M.FV.FT
$FC:CF+C = 2:3$	Pure $C = 2$		M.FY	CF.C'F
$Afr = 0.62$	$CP = 0$		M.FC	FM.FC'
$S = 2$	Col-Shd Bl = 1			

circumstances, she adopts an opposite approach in which her feelings become quite influential in her decisions and may even prompt forms of trial-and-error behavior. This sort of flexibility usually is desirable but in this case that may not be true. The Step 3 (right-side *eb*) data signal the presence of considerable distress, which appears to generate from three sources: elevated C', elevated T, and presence of a Vista response.

The value for C' is elevated indicating that she often internalizes feelings that she would prefer to express outwardly. Excessive suppression or internalization of feelings invariably leads to discomfort that may manifest in the form of chronically aggravating tension, anxiety, apprehension, or sadness. However the discomfort is experienced, it is compounded by the fact that the value for T is also elevated, signifying the experience of atypically strong needs for closeness. In most instances, higher values for T have some obvious situational relationship, but that does not appear to be the case in this instance. If these needs are chronic, they contribute significantly to the distress experience and probably manifest as rather intense loneliness. Chronic discomfort also is suggested by the presence of a *Vista* response, which correlates with an ongoing form of self-inspection in which the focus is on negative features of the self. The resulting experience is often akin to melancholy, and sometimes even becomes a precursor to self-destructive thinking.

The depressive features and the magnitude of distress probably are not more obvious to those around her because she has enough resources to sustain their containment, even though containment is not the most appropriate way to handle the problems. Yet, containment is likely to be a logical tactic for a person who has difficulty controlling emotional displays, and the Step 4 ($FC:CF+C$) data indicate that this is the case for this subject. She has serious modulation problems, often becomes overly intense in her emotional expressions, and at times may convey the impression of emotional impulsiveness. This is very unusual for an ideationally oriented person and suggests that her ideational style of delaying decisions until all alternatives are considered is being short-circuited by other psychological operations. The depressive features and the chronic distress state are the most likely sources.

The Step 5 evaluation of the two Pure C responses offers some very important information from which to speculate about her modulation problems:

4. I see love in it too. (Inquiry) The red down here, anything red always represents love, that's what it represents to me, it has to be, red couldn't be anything else.
5. Two real people trying to come together but this red thing in the middle is something keeping them apart. (Inquiry) There's one on each side, see their heads and legs, they are like straining toward each other but they can't touch because of this red, it represents a thought or a deed . . . It's not really there but it's just represented by the red, I know red is supposed to be love but here it's something else, maybe a fight, I don't know but as long as it's red they won't get together.

The dramatic projections of these answers will be reviewed in the context of other clusters, but the characteristics of the answers highlight the pathos that marks her affect. Both answers have a pseudo-intellectual quality that seems to represent a very naïve and limited effort to modulate. Both also are very concrete, include strained logic, and seem to illustrate some of the disruption that occurs when her thinking and emotions collide or merge. Her feelings become dominant even though she struggles to maintain control ("I know red is supposed to be love but here it is something else").

Many people who have difficulties in modulating emotion become prone to avoid emotional stimulation to escape the internal hassles that often ensue. The Step 6 (*Afr*) finding indicates that this is not true for her. She seems as willing to process emotional stimuli as most adults. Although this tends to fuel her present problems, it can be an asset when viewed in the context of treatment planning. The data for Steps 7 (color projection) and 8 (*S*) are not significant. The Step 9 (number of blends) finding reveals that her level of complexity is somewhat higher than expected for an introversive subject but this may not be unusual in light of her considerable resource and the difficulties that she is experiencing. The Step 10 (*m* and *Y* blends) data do not show any increase in complexity because of situational factors, and the Step 11 (blend complexity) finding is not significant. The more important findings occur in the Step 12 (Color-Shading blends) and 13 (Shading blends) reviews. The Step 12 finding suggests a chronic confusion about feelings and the Step 13 finding indicates the presence of intensely negative, painful, and disruptive feelings. The latter is especially important because these painful experiences often have a pervasive influence on thinking.

Case 4 Summary This young woman has many emotional difficulties that may be contributing significantly to her problems in thinking and mediation that were detected earlier. At the very least she has a marked predisposition toward frequent experiences of depression and/or emotional disruption. It is clear that she is in chronic distress and this probably manifests as some form of depression. Some of the distress is created because of a tendency to internalize feelings excessively, some evolves from a strong sense of loneliness, and some is of a more melancholic variety that is generated by tendencies to become introspectively preoccupied with her own negative features. These elements have accumulated to create a considerable burden for her, which is magnified by the fact that she does not find it easy to modulate her own emotional expressions very effectively.

As noted in earlier findings, she is the type of person who prefers to keep her feelings aside when formulating decisions, but there is some flexibility in that coping style. At times, her feelings merge into her thinking and become quite influential to her decisions. Unfortunately, her feelings are marked largely by aggravation and problems in modulation. They tend to interfere with, instead of facilitate, effective decision operations. As a result, her emotional expressions often are overly intense and she may sometimes even convey the impression to others that she is impulsive.

Her methods of dealing with her feelings are marked by substantial naïveté and concreteness, and these features are very likely exacerbated by experiences of very intense psychological pain with which she is unable to contend. She is more complex than is usually expected for one with an ideational style. The sources of the added complexity are not completely clear, but it seems apparent that some of the complexity is being provoked by a chronic confusion about her feelings. It seems equally plausible to assume that the chronic distress/depression elements are also playing an important role.

Self-Perception

The self-perception cluster of variables takes on special importance in this case. Numerous problems have already been detected, but etiological data seem lacking. Possibly, more information concerning self-image can provide a source from which previous findings will weave together more neatly. The data for the variables related to self-perception are shown in Table 70.

Case 4 Findings Step 1 (reflections) is not significant, but the findings in Step 2 (Egocentricity Index) are quite important. She tends to value herself more negatively than others, and probably tends to focus much more on the external world than on herself. This appears to coincide with the Step 3 (*Vista*) finding, which was detected during the review of the cluster regarding affect. She apparently does engage in considerable introspection in which the focus is on her own negative features. The Step 4 (human content) data suggest that her self-concept is probably based mainly on experience rather than imagination. This is also an important finding because it raises a question that may not be answered from the Rorschach data: Have the negative features that she perceives in herself and her low self-esteem resulted from an awareness of her strangeness, or has the strangeness resulted from her attempts to contend with her negative features?

The Step 5 ($An + Xy$) result is not significant and the Step 6 (MOR) data are somewhat equivocal. The presence of two MOR answers is not always significant. They may be common answers and, as such, be misleading. Conversely, they may signal the presence of negative features in the self-image. The resolution usually comes from the Step 7 evaluation of the specific responses. The first (7. "A little bird, no a big bird but it doesn't have wings . . . (Inquiry) the wings haven't grown yet, I don't think birds are born like that . . . it must be hurt, it lost its wings or maybe never had any, you know like deformed") is fairly dramatic, both by reason of the content and the vacillation that occurs. The second is also gruesome (20. "This thing could be a bird, a dead one. (Inquiry) . . . not moving, like lying there, like dead"). Both of these answers are very unusual and seem to support the postulate that her self-image is marked by some distinctly negative features.

Table 70. Self Perception Variables for Case 4

STRUCTURAL DATA		RESPONSES TO BE READ	
$Fr+rF = 0$	$3r+(2)/R = 0.29$	*MOR* RESPONSES	= 7, 20
$FD = 0$	$V = 1$	MINUS RESPONSES	= 6, 13, 14, 16, 20
$HH)+Hd+(Hd) = 3 : 3$		*M* RESPONSES	= 2, 3, 4, 5, 9, 12, 13, 16, 19
$An+Xy = 0$		*FM* RESPONSES	= 8, 17
$MOR = 2$		*m* RESPONSES	=

The Step 8 review of the minus responses does not reveal as consistent information regarding the self-concept. Four of the five minus answers do have some negative implications:

  6. just a fly. (Inquiry) . . . the wings and the little body, just like a housefly.
13. you are looking in between someone's thighs. (Inquiry) . . . someone is sitting with their thighs spread and you can look right in and see everything, I know it sounds vulgar but I'm being honest . . . like they are being held open.
16. some really loud weird sound, like the last note of a heavy metal song . . . (Inquiry) . . . it's pushing out at the bottom and shooting up at the top . . . like the whole thing is gonna burst . . .
20. a bird, a dead one. (Inquiry) . . . not moving, like lying there, like dead.

The remaining minus appears to be more positive (14. "A butterfly, it's all different colors, I like the colors"). Responses 13 and 16 are probably the most important, or at least the most easy to deal with in terms of projected material. Response 13 is important in three respects: the exposure, the vulgarity, and the fact that the thighs are "being held open." It is tempting to interpret this answer as representing a view of "the real me." Response 16 is more ominous. It is the "last note" and the "whole thing is gonna burst." It seems to reflect some sense of futility.

The Step 9 evaluation of the content of the M answers reveals much variability. Some responses convey a mixture of fearful caution and indecisiveness about herself. (2. "her legs are together . . . stand up straight with your legs together," 5. "real people . . . straining toward each other but they can't touch," 19. "faces looking at each other . . . they look like little . . . elves . . . not real people"). Others convey a more direct and optimistic sense of the self (3. "two animals getting together, like they are dancing," 4. "I see love," 9. "somebody standing on their head . . . it shows good balance," 12. "two kids playing Indian"). Two are more ominous and reflect a vulnerable self-image (13. "you're looking in between someone's thighs . . . you can look right in and see everything, I know it sounds vulgar," 16. "a loud weird sound . . . the last note"). Overall, there seems to be a great deal of confusion about self-image illustrated in these answers. The two animal movement responses are less confusing (8. "I'll say a butterfly . . . it's wings spread out, like it's flying," 17. "two crabs holding a big club or something"), even though one involves an illogical form of cooperation. The Step 10 search through unread responses for unusual wording or embellishments is not significant.

Case 4 Summary The subject's self-image seems to be much more negative than positive and also includes a great deal of confusion. She does not appear to have any definitive sense of herself. Instead, she tends to compare herself to others in very unfavorable ways and reinforces this view by considerable introspection in which she focuses on her own perceived negative features. She seems to feel quite vulnerable and harbors a sense of pessimism about her prospects. It is somewhat surprising to note that much of her self-concept seems to emerge more from experience than from imagination. This suggests that much of the current notion that she has about herself probably developed because of an awareness of her strange, idiographic, often inept ways. There are also some ominous features in her sense of self that appear to provoke a sense of futility. These features probably tend to enhance her proclivities for depression, distress, or other forms of emotional disruption, and it seems important to recommend that the possibilities for self-destructive ideation, even though not evident in the data, be explored very carefully.

Interpersonal Perception and Behavior

The findings from this last cluster may flesh out a broader understanding of her self-perception, as much of it seems to be based on her perceptions of others and their expectations. The data for the cluster are shown in Table 71.

Case 4 Findings   The data for Steps 1 (CDI), 2 (HVI), 3 ($a:p$), 4 (*Food*), and 7 (*PER*) are not significant, but the Step 5 (*T*) data, which have already been reviewed twice, are important. She has strong needs for closeness and probably feels very lonely. The history and test data suggest that this is a chronic condition and, as such, invariably has had an impact on her interpersonal relationships. Needy, lonely people frequently tend to try too hard. In doing so they become vulnerable and transparent and are easily manipulated by others in ways that often have negative endings.

According to her history, she joined with a group of free-lance house painters only a few months prior to the recent car theft because she felt "a great deal of love from them," and she admits to being attracted to one of the women in the group. She also says that the car theft was related to a need to set out and find people that she "might like." Based on her own statements, it seems logical to hypothesize that her continuing search for closeness somehow was rejected once again, and, in the context of her strange thinking and poor judgment, another flight seemed to be the only viable alternative. The Step 6 (total human contents) and Step 8 (COP) data seem to support this contention. She is quite interested in people and perceives interpersonal activity as a very important part of her life. It seems likely that she is viewed by others as likable and outgoing, at least at first glance. It is also likely that her peculiar thinking and problems with emotional control cause people to withdraw gradually from potentially close ties. This only serves to reaffirm her confused and negative sense of self and probably intensifies her perceived need to defend herself.

The Step 9 (Isolation Index) finding is not significant, but the Step 10 evaluation of the five movement responses containing pairs sheds some added light on

Table 71. Interpersonal Perception Variables for Case 4

STRUCTURAL VARIABLES		RESPONSES TO BE READ
CDI = 1	HVI = Neg	MOVEMENT WITH PAIR = 3, 5, 12, 17, 19
$a:p$ = 9:2	T = 2 Fd = 0	HUMAN CONTENTS = 2, 4, 5, 9, 12, 13, 16, 19
Isolate/R = 0.10		
Total Human Contents = 6		
PER = 2 COP = 4 AG = 0		

her interpersonal perceptions. Three involve human figures ("two real people coming together but . . . something is keeping them apart," "two kids playing Indian," "two faces . . . looking at each other . . . not real people"). The only direct interaction occurs when it is a game of pretend; otherwise, people do not or cannot have close interaction. Conversely, when the figures are not human, the interaction is much more direct (two chickens dancing; two crabs holding a big club or something). The inconsistency that marks her perception of people is also reflected in the Step 11 review of human contents (lower part of a woman, real people, somebody standing on their head, kids, in between somebody's thigh's, and elves' faces). The only positive response is the "pretend" answer involving the kids playing Indian. In other words, her conceptions about people are probably no better formulated than her conception of herself.

Case 4 Summary She is quite interested in people and perceives positive interactions as an important part of everyday living. She feels very lonely, and many of her behaviors are formulated in relation to her needs for closeness. Unfortunately, her perceptions of people are inconsistent and often unrealistic, and this often misleads her about how to create and maintain close relationships with others. Thus, although at first glance she may be perceived as likable and outgoing, her strange thinking and problems with emotional modulation gradually cause others to keep her at a distance. Thus, the loneliness and sense of isolation are exacerbated and she becomes prone to flee from one interpersonal situation to another.

Case 4 Final Description

This is a very ideational person who relies extensively on her thinking in decision making. Unfortunately, even though her thinking is sophisticated at times, it often is not very clear. Her logic and judgment are strained and concrete, and her patterns of thought tend to be recurrently disconnected and fluid. There is reason to believe that she has problems controlling her ideation, and there is some likelihood that her thinking is marked by features that give rise to hallucinatory experiences. Thus, many of her decisions are ineffective because they are generated by flawed, disordered thought.

She is not very flexible in her ideational sets, attitudes, or values. This increases the probability that faulty decisions or illogical judgments persist even though external evidence suggests that they are erroneous. She also relies heavily on a pseudo-intellectual approach in attempting to contend with stressful situations. This neutralizes some of the emotional impact of the situation, but it has negative effects because the process often is based on disordered thinking that tends to ignore reality.

She tends to make conventional responses when cues concerning them are obvious, but, when these cues are not present, problems in cognitive mediation tend to dominate and promote an unacceptably high frequency of behaviors that either ignore conventionality or distort reality. In part, these problems arise from her tendency to translate stimuli in an overly personal way, but they are also based in a more chronic problem of perceptual inaccuracy that promotes frequent distortions when inputs are translated. There are no obvious information processing problems. She is prone to be conservative or economical in her willingness to deal with new information but, when she makes commitment to process, she tends to invest more energy than is necessary to ensure that she is not negligent. In general, her processing activities are consistent and not unlike those found among nonpatients.

Her capacity for control and ability to tolerate stress are somewhat sturdier than typical for most adults. This is because she has ready access to considerable resource that can be used to form and implement decisions. However, she is currently burdened with many aggravating emotional demands that have created a chronic state of distress. Thus, although her capacities for control and tolerance of stress remain sturdy, the chronicity of the distress may have lowered them to some extent.

She has many emotional difficulties. She has a marked predisposition toward frequent experiences of depression and/or emotional disruption. She clearly is in chronic distress, which is likely to manifest as some form of depression. Some of the distress is created because of a tendency to internalize feelings excessively, some evolves from a strong sense of loneliness, and some is of a more melancholic variety that is generated by tendencies to become introspectively preoccupied with her own negative features. This problem is made more destructive because she does not modulate her emotional expressions very effectively.

As noted in earlier findings, she is the type of person who prefers to keep her feelings aside when formulating decisions, but there is some flexibility in this coping style. At times, her feelings merge with her thinking and become very influential in her decisions. When this occurs, they tend to interfere with instead of facilitate effective decision operations. As a result, her emotional expressions often are overly intense, and she may at times convey the impression to others that she is impulsive. Her methods of attempting to deal with her emotions frequently are naïve and concrete, and these features are exacerbated by experiences of very intense psychological pain with which she is unable to contend. She is more complex than is usually expected for one with an ideational style. This added complexity is being produced by a chronic confusion about her feelings plus the chronic distress/depression elements noted earlier.

Her self-image seems to be much more negative than positive and includes a great deal of confusion. She lacks a definitive sense of herself and is prone to compare herself with others in very unfavorable ways. She reinforces this view by considerable introspection in which she focuses on her own perceived negative features. She seems to feel quite vulnerable and harbors a sense of pessimism about her prospects. Much of the current notion that she has about herself probably developed because of an awareness of her strange, idiographic, often inept ways. She has a sense of futility about herself that tends to enhance her proclivities for depression, distress, or other forms of emotional disruption. In this context, it seems important to recommend that possibilities for self-destructive ideation, even though not evident in the data, be explored very carefully.

She is quite interested in people and perceives positive interactions as an important part of everyday living. She feels very lonely and many of her behaviors are formulated in relation to her needs for closeness. Unfortunately, her perceptions of people are inconsistent and often unrealistic and this misleads her about how to create and maintain close relationships with others. Thus, although at first glance she may be perceived as likable and outgoing, her strange thinking and problems with emotional expression gradually cause others to keep her at a distance. Thus, she feels very lonely and isolated and moves often from one interpersonal situation to another in search of some sense of belongingness.

Overall, this is a rather pathetic, lonely, depressed person whose strange and sometimes muddled thinking has consigned her to be more of an observer than an active participant in the world. She is not schizophrenic but does have many features that, at best, cause her to be viewed by others as markedly eccentric. She is confused and naïve about emotions and emotional exchanges; perceives herself quite negatively; and, although very interested in people, is lacking in the judgment and skills necessary to create and sustain close relationships.

Recommendations Based on the Final Description

A diagnosis of schizotypal personality disorder with depressive features is appropriate, but the diagnosis is far less important than a useful treatment plan. The subject has many assets on which to draw: (1) she has considerable resource; (2) her ideational coping style is marked by some flexibility; (3) she is prone to make conventional responses when cues concerning them are obvious; (4) as an overincorporator, she invests considerable energy in processing information; (5) she is quite willing to process emotional stimuli; (6) she is lonely and seeks contact with others; and (7) she perceives interpersonal relationships very favorably.

The liabilities for treatment are also numerous, and each can be viewed as a target for change: (1) her judgment is very poor, (2) she is prone to distort or overpersonalize translations of stimuli, (3) her ideational sets and values are not very flexible, (4) she tries to defend herself far too much through intellectualization, (5) she does not seem to know how to manifest feelings effectively and she is quite confused about emotion, (6) her self-image is quite negative and confused, and (7) she does not have very realistic conceptions about people.

Probably the issues of loneliness and her experiences of distress/depression pose the best opening objectives, because focus on them should facilitate the development of a working therapeutic relationship. Possibly the greatest challenge to the therapist or therapeutic community with which she works will be to help prevent her from feeling overly threatened or rejected. Either or both of these feelings can easily provoke another flight reaction.

Case 4 Epilogue This subject remained hospitalized for 38 days during which time she was involved in both individual and group psychotherapy. During the last two weeks of hospitalization she began voluntary work in a public library and she was offered a part time position there following her release from the hospital. Prior to her discharge it was agreed that she would live at home and continue for an indefinite period in outpatient care with her primary therapist who was cautiously optimistic that a reorganization of her social environment could provide a major support element from which further developmental progress might be expected.

SUMMARY

The importance of accurate differentiation of schizophrenia and nonschizophrenia cannot be overemphasized, mainly because of the different treatment considerations. The treatment of the schizophrenic is generally quite different from that of the nonschizophrenic, primarily in that a neuroleptic is prescribed for the former. Numerous studies support that approach (Exner & Murillo, 1977; Hogarty, Goldberg, Schooler, & Ulrich, 1974; Klein, Rosen, & Oaks, 1973; May, 1968; May, Tuma & Dixon, 1976; Murillo & Exner, 1973; Rappaport, Hopkins, Hall, Belleza, & Silverman, 1976). The prescription of a neuroleptic is very infrequent among nonschizophrenics. It usually is contraindicated because of its potent effects on neural transmission and related physiological operations.

The SCZI, taken alone, often highlights the possibility of schizophrenia. As illustrated in Case 4, however, it should never be interpreted casually or independently of other data because the circumstances in which a false positive SCZI can occur vary considerably.

REFERENCES

Andreasen, N. C. (1989). The American concept of schizophrenia. *Schizophrenia Bulletin,* **15,** 519–531.

Beck, S. J. (1965). *Psychological process in the schizophrenic adaptation.* New York: Grune & Stratton.

Exner, J. E. (1986). *The Rorschach: A Comprehensive System. Volume 1: Basic foundations* (2nd ed.). New York: Wiley.

Exner, J. E., and Murillo, L. G. (1977). A long term follow-up of schizophrenic treated with regressive ECT. *Diseases of the Nervous System,* **38,** 162–168.

George, L. and Neufeld, R. W. J. (1985). Cognition and symptomatology in schizophrenia. *Schizophrenia Bulletin,* **11,** 264–285.

Grinker, R., Werble, B., and Drye, R. (1968). *The borderline syndrome.* New York: Basic Books.

Hoch, P. H., and Polatin, P. (1949). Pseudoneurotic forms of schizophrenia. *Psychiatric Quarterly,* **23,** 248–276.

Hogarty, G. E., Goldberg, S. E., Schooler, N. R., and Ulrich, R. F. (1974). The collaborative study group: Drug and sociotherapy in the aftercare of schizophrenic patients. II. Two year relapse rates. *Archives of General Psychiatry,* **31,** 603–608.

Kant, O. (1941). A comparative study of recovered and deteriorated schizophrenic patients. *Journal of Nervous and Mental Disorders,* **93,** 616–624.

Kantor, R. E., Wallner, J. M., and Winder, C. L. (1953). Process and reactive schizophrenia. *Journal of Consulting Psychology,* **17,** 157–162.

Kasanin, J. S. (1944). The disturbance of conceptual thinking in schizophrenia. In J. S. Kasanin (Ed.), *Language and thought in schizophrenia.* Berkeley: University of California Press.

Kendler, K., Gruenberg, A., and Strauss, J. S. (1982). An independent analysis of the Copenhagen sample of the Danish adoption study of schizophrenia: Childhood social withdrawal and adult schizophrenia. *Archives of General Psychiatry,* **39,** 1257–1261.

Kernberg, O. F. (1967). Borderline personality organization. *Journal of the American Psychoanalytic Association,* **15,** 641–685.

Kety, S. S., Rosenthal, D., Wender, P. H., and Schulsinger, F. (1968). The types and prevalence of mental illness in the biological and adoptive families of adoptive schizophrenics. In D. Rosenthal and S. S. Kety (Eds.), *The transmission of schizophrenia.* Oxford: Pergamon Press.

Kety, S. S., Rosenthal, D., Wender, P. H., Schulsinger, F., and Jacobsen, B. (1975). Mental illness in the biological and adoptive individuals who have become schizophrenic: A preliminary report based on psychiatric interviews. In R. R. Fieve, D. Rosenthal, and H. Brill (Eds.), *Genetic research in psychiatry.* Baltimore: Johns Hopkins University Press.

Khouri, P. (1977). Continuum versus dichotomy in theories of schizophrenia. *Schizophrenia Bulletin,* **3,** 262–267.

Klein, D. F., Rosen, B., and Oaks, G. (1973). Premorbid asocial adjustment and response to phenothiazine treatment among schizophrenic patients. *Archives of General Psychiatry,* **29,** 480–484.

Knight, R. P. (1953). Borderline states. *Bulletin of the Menninger Clinic,* **17,** 1–12.

May, P. R. A. (1968). *Treatment of schizophrenia.* New York: Science House.

May, P. R. A., Tuma, A. H., and Dixon, W. J. (1976). Schizophrenia—A follow-up study of results of treatment: I. Design and other problems. *Archives of General Psychiatry,* **33,** 474–478.

Meyer, A. (1948). Fundamental concepts of dementia praecox (1907). In A. Lief (Ed.), *The commonsense psychiatry of Dr. Adolph Meyer.* New York: McGraw-Hill.

Murillo, L. G., and Exner, J. E. (1973). The effects of regressive ECT with process schizophrenics. *American Journal of Psychiatry,* **130,** 269–273.

Phillips, L. (1953). Case history data and prognosis in schizophrenia. *Journal of Nervous and Mental Disorders,* **117,** 515–525.

Piotrowski, Z., and Lewis, N. D. C. (1950). An experimental Rorschach diagnostic aid for some forms of schizophrenia. *American Journal of Psychiatry,* **107,** 360–366.

Polatin, P., and Hoch, P. H. (1947). Diagnostic evaluation of early schizophrenia. *Journal of Nervous and Mental Disorders,* **105,** 221–230.

Rapaport, D., Gill, M., and Schafer, R. (1946). *Psychological diagnostic testing* (Vol. 2). Chicago: Yearbook.

Rappaport, M., Hopkins, H. K., Hall, K., Belleza, T., and Silverman, J. (1976). *Acute schizophrenia and phenothiazine utilization: I. Clinical outcome* (Final Report, NIMH Grant 16445). Bethesda, MD: National Institute of Mental Health.

Strauss, J. H. (1983). What is schizophrenia? *Schizophrenia Bulletin,* **9,** 7–9.

Thiesen, J. W. (1952). A pattern analysis of structural characteristics of the Rorschach test in schizophrenia. *Journal of Consulting Psychology,* **15,** 365–370.

Watkins, J. G., and Stauffacher, J. C. (1952). An index of pathological thinking in the Rorschach. *Journal of Projective Techniques,* **16,** 276–286.

Weiner, I. B. (1966). *Psychodiagnosis in schizophrenia.* New York: Wiley.

Whittman, R. M. (1944). The use of the Rorschach test in schizophrenia. *Psychiatric Quarterly Supplement,* **28,** 26–37.

Wittman, P. (1941). A scale for measuring prognosis in schizophrenic patients. *Elgin State Hospital Papers,* **4,** 20–23.

CHAPTER 12

Issues of Distress and Depression

Most efforts to develop precise diagnoses for instances of affective disruption, especially when the disruption includes negative feelings, have not been very satisfactory. This is especially true when the term *depression,* or any of its several variants, is applied. Wiener (1989) presented an excellent review of the ambiguity, inconsistency, and overgeneralization that is evident among the current applications of the term depression, and harshly criticized the DSM approach to defining features of depression. As Wiener noted, "Depression is used indiscriminantly as a label for a state, trait, sign, syndrome, disease, as a category name and, at the same time, as an explanatory concept" (p. 297).

Much of the problem seems to occur because many view depression as having a homogeneous psychological and/or biological predisposition, and several diversified concepts of depression have been put forth based on this assumption (Abramson, Metalsky, & Alloy, 1989; Beck, 1967; Blatt, Quinlan, Chevron, McDonald, & Zuroff, 1982; Brown & Harris, 1978; Chadoff, 1974; Kendell, 1976; Millon & Kotik, 1985; Seligman, 1975). Some identify the developmental years as the breeding ground from which a predisposition evolves, whereas others focus on faulty attribution, negative self-concept, adverse social interaction, or poor psychobiology. Whichever cause or group of causes are identified, the notion of homogeneity persists. Yet, the criteria for the DSM diagnostic categories tend to stray far from the notion of homogeneity. Instead, they reflect an amalgam of signs and symptoms from which any of a seemingly endless number of combinations yield the same diagnosis. For instance, Wiener (1989) pointed out that, provided a dysphoric mood is present, 286 possible combinations of signs and symptoms can lead to the diagnosis of Dsythymic Disorder.

THE DEPI AND CDI

Obviously, the admixture of features that are used as a basis for identifying and classifying affective problems poses a considerable challenge for any assessment instrument or technique. As noted earlier, the work leading to the revision of the Depression Index (DEPI) included an attempt to make some differentiation based on whether the disruption was mainly cognitive or affective, but that effort was futile. Thus, the revised DEPI includes variables related to both features, but a positive fallout of the effort was the development of the Coping Deficit Index (CDI). When these indices are used separately, or collectively, they correctly identify a very large proportion of people who have serious affective problems. This does not mean, however, that either affords diagnostic precision.

As stressed earlier, with the exception of schizophrenia, Rorschach data do not correlate very directly with specific diagnostic categories or labels. Instead, the data usually only provide descriptive information that is often useful in diagnostic considerations. Thus, although the DEPI and CDI are useful in formulating initial propositions, these propositions are only starting points that become modified and embellished as additional information regarding the subject is uncovered. In that context, it is probably useful to review the initial propositions for each of the indices.

DEPI 5

A DEPI value of 5 is significant, but not necessarily definitive. It indicates that the subject has many features that are common among those diagnosed as being depressed or having an affective disorder, but other diagnoses may be assigned depending on presenting symptoms and history. In effect, the value of 5 probably reflects the presence of a psychological organization that can easily give rise to experiences of depression or fluctuations in mood.

6 - 7

DEPI values of 6 and 7 are more definitive. Subjects having these values almost always are diagnosed as having some significant affective problem. The exceptions to this occur most often among schizophrenics who are depressed but who have schizophrenia as the primary diagnosis.

CDI 4+ 4-5

The CDI is not a second depression index. People with scores of 4 or more on this index are likely to have impoverished or unrewarding social relationships. The data suggest that people who have values of 4 or 5 on the CDI often have difficulty contending with the natural demands of a social world and often are helpless or inept because of their coping limitations or deficiencies. It is reasonable to assume that these coping difficulties give rise to the kinds of affective disruption that sometimes include features that are compatible with the diagnostic criteria for some types of depression. This assumption is supported by the fact that a sizable majority of subjects with affective disorder diagnoses *who are not positive on the DEPI* obtain CDI values of 4 or 5. This is not to suggest that the diagnosis is in error, but rather to point out that people who have coping problems often find themselves in dreadful situations that can easily give rise to depressive features.

coping + dep.

FALSE NEGATIVE AND FALSE POSITIVE ISSUES

False negatives

Whereas false positives are an issue with the SCZI, false negatives are more of a concern for the DEPI. Extrapolating from some of the data presented in Chapter 1, about 25% of patients diagnosed as having a serious affective problem are positive on both the DEPI and CDI, another 50% are positive on the DEPI but not on the CDI, and about 18% are positive on the CDI but not on the DEPI. Taken together, the two indices should identify about 90% of those who are in affective disarray, but, taken alone, each index has shortcomings. The DEPI is not positive for between 20 and 30% of those diagnosed as having a major affective problem. Obviously, a negative DEPI does not exclude the possibility of a serious affective problem. In some instances the problem manifests in other ways that can be detected from Rorschach data, but often that is not the case. In other instances, the problem is more reactive or situational and, as such, does not impact on the variety of features measured by the DEPI variables.

The CDI, taken alone, should never be interpreted as indicating the presence of a serious affective problem. The highest percentage of positive CDI's have been found among people with inadequate personalities (88%), alcohol and substance abuse problems (74%), and adjudicated character disorders (69%). In other words, although a positive CDI does signify a predisposition to distress, and may indicate the presence of marked helplessness, it does not indicate that distress is present.

Cases 5 and 6 illustrate a variety of interpretive challenges that can occur when complaints of distress and/or depression are present.

CASE 5: A MAJOR DEPRESSIVE DISTURBANCE

This 49-year-old male is being evaluated on referral from a psychiatrist whom he has been seeing for the past four weeks. The subject had been referred to the psychiatrist by his family physician who is actively involved in the treatment of the subject's wife for alcoholism. The subject reports that he has become more and more depressed during the past year, and that recently he has had considerable difficulty sleeping and feels very anxious at work.

He attributes some of his difficulties to the problems that he has experienced in supporting his wife through her alcoholism treatment. She apparently has had a drinking problem for approximately five years, but did not seek help for it until she began having blackouts about six months ago. The subject reports that his appetite is good and that, in fact, he has gained about 20 pounds during the past five months. He reports that he has trouble falling asleep and that he also has early morning awakening. Typically, when he wakes, he is sweating and feels very apprehensive. He was treated for a gastric ulcer approximately four years ago, but there has been no recurrence of symptoms associated with it. He denies use of drugs or alcohol.

The subject is the older of two children, having a sister, age 45, who is married and has four children. She lives in a distant state. The subject's father died 10 years ago at the age of 76, from kidney failure. He had been a pharmaceutical salesman until his retirement. The subject's mother died four years ago at age 70. She had been a housewife. The subject gives an unremarkable developmental history and reports that, to the best of his knowledge, there is no psychiatric history in the family. He graduated from high school at age 18 and joined the Navy shortly thereafter. He remained in the Navy for five years, and, after being discharged at age 23, entered college. He graduated from college with honors at age 27, having majored in electrical engineering.

He married the next year after obtaining his first position. His wife was 26 years old at that time. He and his wife had hoped to have children early in their marriage, but she had difficulty conceiving, which ultimately caused them to seek the assistance of a fertility therapist, after which there was successful conception. They now have a daughter, age 7, whom the subject describes as "the light of my life."

The subject reports that his wife began drinking shortly after their daughter was born. By that time, he had changed jobs twice and had accepted the position that he now holds, which involves the management of a systems architecture group for a large satellite communications firm. The subject states that he enjoys his work and generally gets along well with the people who work for him. He complains that he has lost interest in several of his hobbies, including golf, reading about archaeology, photography, and music: "I just don't seem to have much energy lately, and none of those things interest me anymore."

He openly admits to being frustrated by his wife's alcoholism: "There are a lot of times that I get pretty angry because I have to do a lot of things that she ordinarily would do, and I can't complain about them." He also states that he *anger* has been worrying more about his health since his treatment for ulcers and since the death of his mother: "I just become tired more easily, and I'm always wondering if there is something serious wrong." He states that there are times when he feels like crying, but usually holds back the tears.

The referring psychiatrist asks the following questions: (1) Is a diagnosis of major depressive episode warranted, or is this more of a situationally-related phenomenon? (2) Is there any evidence suggesting the presence of a bipolar disorder? (3) Is the depression sufficiently intense to warrant hospitalization for at least a brief period? (4) What recommendations concerning a treatment plan can be made that acknowledge the fact that the patient's wife is currently being treated?

Tactics of Reviewing the Data

In the preceding cases the reviews have been meticulous and sometimes laborious for purposes of demonstration. In Case 1, all potential findings were identified and tested. In Cases 2, 3 and 4, all steps applicable in searching the data for each cluster were identified. The process seems quite arduous on paper, but in reality it does not need to be so ponderous. The practice of reviewing each data source step by step and then integrating findings is a good training tactic for the novice, but it detracts from efficiency. The optimal routine should flow more smoothly, focusing on the task of weaving together the data from various *relevant* sources into a summary of findings.

As proficiency increases, interpreters usually can scan the data for a cluster and easily identify the significant variables. Obviously, the data for some variables, such as the *EB* and *EA,* are always important, and some responses always must be read with the expectation that some homogeneity of contents and/or projected material will augment hypotheses. But in most cases, an intelligent scan accurately differentiates the relevant and irrelevant data sources. In the routine for this case, only the relevant findings are addressed, with the sources identified at the outset.

The Interpretive Strategy

There is no reason to question the interpretive usefulness of the subject's protocol. The first positive Key variable is the DEPI. Therefore, the search strategy is:

AFFECT → CONTROLS → SELF-PERCEPTION → INTERPERSONAL PERCEPTION → PROCESSING → MEDIATION → IDEATION.

Initial Propositions: In this case two initial propositions are warranted. First, the DEPI value of 6 suggests that a major affective problem exists. Second, the

Case 5: A 49-Year-Old Male

Card	Response	Inquiry
I	1. 2 owl eyes, u know, the 2 orbits	E: (Rpts S's resp) S: 2 eyes, orbit section, almost an owl's head formed here, the pupils here and the circle around it
	2. Smbdy with their hands up lik this here	E: (Rpts S's resp) S: Hands here, lik a priest holdg hands up in that sort of gesture, arms, hands, thumb, finger, body, robe here
	3. Looks lik bird wings	E: (Rpts S's resp) S: 2 bird wings, one bird here, head, and another one here A o Pd?
	4. The bottom of a female form	E: (Rpts S's resp) S: Legs, hips, feet, this area just ll the lower half
	5. Darth Vader's helmet	E: (Rpts S's resp) S: This piece, almost bell shaped, this darker shading ll the shield he has to talk thru, the way its shaded
II	6. A cpl of gnomes dancing	E: (Rpts S's resp) S: I've seen them in pictures, red hats, bearded, dark robes, 2 hands, dancg, kickg up one foot, elbow back as they swing around, u can only c part of the arm (motions backward) E: U said the robes are dark? S: It ll fur, the mottled effect E: I'm not sure about the beard S: Here, it's white, a white beard
	7. It ll a bearded cat here	E: (Rpts S's resp) S: This ll a reddish cat, eyes, whiskers, an abstract Japanese cat with a long beard, these tufts of fur, the way it comes down (outlines), ever c an Abyssinian cat?, they have it
	8. The white part ll a spaceship	E: (Rpts S's resp) S: This ll the spaceship going up and the red exhaust is thrusting out this way
	9. I now c 2 bears touching noses	E: (Rpts S's resp) S: Bears, heads, snouts touching, ears, its just the front portion here
III	10. It ll 2 native women	E: (Rpts S's resp) S: Black women, bust, big kettle theyr workg over, the legs, waist, white loin cloth here, the buttocks, face, back, jaw
	11. It ll a bf	E: (Rpts S's resp) S: Right here, the shape of the wings, flyg upward

12. It ll a tiny bird fallg out of a tree, lik Wood-stock

E: (Rpts S's resp)
S: Woodstock, the head, fallg down this way, a pair of them, feathers look ruffled (outlines)

13. It ll, s.t. lik a face, not quite a skull

E: (Rpts S's resp)
S: The eyes, mouth, the nose is this white spot, a muttonchop beard FC'
E: What makes that ll a beard?
S: It looks bushy, fluffy, lik it has depth, c the diff shades of grey there

IV 14. Hmm! ll a cartoon monster I c on t.v., head, big feet, I guess that's it

E: (Rpts S's resp)
S: Big feet, long tail, lik it jumped up in the air, black and furry lik a stuffed doll, he has flipper lik hands, I've been watching too many cartoons w my daughter
E: U said he looks furry?
S: The lines here, indistinct, as if it were covered with fur
E: U said he jumped in the air?
S: Just the way the arms and legs are out

V 15. It ll a bf, antennae

E: (Rpts S's resp)
S: Antenna, tail, wings, a bf just coming out of the cocoon, wings still wet, not completely unfurled
E: Wet?
S: They don't look wet but the wings look folded, not all open, this crease angle where its shaded, looks folded up

16. A cpl of furry bisons lying back to back

E: (Rpts S's resp)
S: Body, head, tail, 2 of them, they look furry bec the ink is smudgy in here and also the edges look irregular

17. It ll a feminine leg here, on either side

E: (Rpts S's resp)
S: Part of one, the calf, toe, part of the thigh, on both sides

VI 18. What could this be? First impression, a bear rug

E: (Rpts S's resp)
S: This whole part ll a bear rug, cut off head part, just ll a furry throw rug, somebody's going to think I have a fixation on bears, but it just struck me as one bec this is shaded and ll fur

19. It ll an otter popping up, splashing out of the water so to speak, that's it, I'm not too imaginative today

E: (Rpts S's resp)
S: Here's the little head, eyes, whiskers, nose, and the water is splashing, seems is splashing, seems to be movg away as if he just popped up

VII 20. It ll 2 girl's faces facing each other, lookg at e.o.

E: (Rpts S's resp)
S: Hairdo, bangs, nose, sort of lik a silhouette, no distinct features, just the black outline

(continued)

307

Card	Response	Inquiry
	21. Some croutons? I dkno, that's all	E: (Rpts S's resp) S: Croutons broken up, soggy in soup E: What makes them look soggy? S: They've lost their square distinct shape, no longer a definite edge (outlines), a bunch of soggy croutons.
VIII	22. Looks colorful lik a story book cover, mice crawl-g up, lizards here, old corset stretched across here, a flower opening up, some critter with hands reachg down, pullg the flower, ll an old fountain pen lik the artist who was drawing this laid it on top of the pict	E: (Rpts S's resp) S: Lik s.t. out of a fairy tale book, pink mice here, the lizards with the combed head, the old corset sort of split here & stretched, thes fragments mak it ll it was torn. Here's the flower, the pink & orange flower & littl hands here lik pulling on the stamen & here's the pen, the tip here, the artist laid in on the picture when he was done
IX	23. Let's c, I don't know, ll a strange creature, eyes, hands	E: (Rpts S's resp) S: Have u seen the "Dark Crystal"?, it's a strange creature, eyes, strange orange hair, a mystical creature, ill defined, almost translucent in here, the lighter part here, lik it's see-thru
	24. It ll part of a crustacean, a cpl of claws	E: (Rpts S's resp) S: It ll claws, lik on a lobster, the shape of a claw
V <V>	25. It ll colored inkblots	E: (Rpts S's resp) S: Colored portions, green, pink, looks pretty, the whole thing
X	26. Hm, ll spiders holdg up s.t. here	E: (Rpts S's resp) S: Here, legs holding a green leaf, here and here, lik holding it up
	27. It ll maybe caterpillars, green caterpillars	E: (Rpts S's resp) S: 2 of them, legs, they look segmented bec of the diff shades of ink, curved here
	28. Rem me of the pelvis, if u will, the bone	E: (Rpts S's resp) S: It ll pelvic bone structure, pubic bone area, spinal column here, the shape of the structure
X	29. Beginning of a flower beginning to open up	E: (Rpts S's resp) S: Here, the first petal unfurling one on each side, the pretty yellow color, the petals here where the shading is darker
	30. It ll 2 little critters, furry cartoon critters, talkg to e.o.	E: (Rpts S's resp) S: The legs, mouth, eyes, antennae, and they look furry, not crisp lines (outlines) and bec of the shading here (rubs)

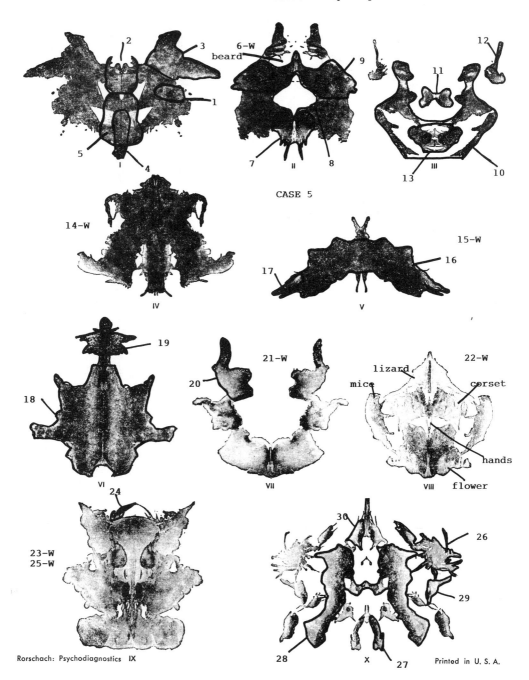

CASE 5

Rorschach: Psychodiagnostics   IX
Printed in U. S. A.

```
CASE 5.   SEQUENCE OF SCORES
===========================================================================
CARD NO   LOC   #      DETERMINANT(S)    (2)   CONTENT(S)   POP   Z    SPECIAL SCORES
===========================================================================
  I    1  Ddo   99  F-            Ad
       2  D+     4  Mp+               H,Cg              4.0
       3  Do     7  Fo         2      A
       4  Do     3  Fo                Hd
       5  Ddo   99  FYu               Sc

 II    6  WS+    1  Ma.FC.FD.FT.FC'+  2  (H),Cg         4.5   PER,COP
       7  Do     3  FC-               Ad                      DV
       8  DS+    5  ma.CFo            Sc,Fi             4.5
       9  Dd+   21  FMpo          2   Ad                3.0

III   10  DS+    1  Ma.FC'+       2   H,Hh,Sx      P    4.5   COP
      11  Do     3  FMao              A
      12  Do     2  FMpo          2   (A)
      13  DSo    7  FV-               Hd                4.5   DR

 IV   14  Wo     1  Ma.FC'.FT+        (H)          P    2.0   PER

  V   15  Wo     1  FMa.FVo           A            P    1.0
      16  D+     4  FMp.FTu       2                     2.5   FAB
      17  Do     1  Fo            2   Hd

 VI   18  Do     1  FTo               Ad           P          MOR
      19  D+     3  FMa.mpu           A,Na              2.5

VII   20  D+     1  Mp.FC'o       2   Hd           P    3.0
      21  W/     1  F-                Fd                2.5   MOR

VIII  22  W+     1  FMp.mp.Mp.CF.FDu  2  Art,A,(Hd),Cg P  4.5  MOR

 IX   23  Wo     1  FV.FCu            (Hd)              5.5   PER
      24  Ddo   25  Fu            2   Ad
      25  Wv     1  C                 Art

  X   26  D+     1  FMp.FCo       2   A,Bt         P    4.0   FAB
      27  Do     4  FC.FYo        2   A
      28  Ddo   99  F+                An
      29  Do    15  mp.FC.FYo     2   Bt
      30  D+     8  Mp.FTo        2   (H)               4.5
===========================================================================
```

CASE 5. STRUCTURAL SUMMARY

```
================================================================================
LOCATION            DETERMINANTS          CONTENTS      S-CONSTELLATION
FEATURES         BLENDS        SINGLE                   YES..FV+VF+V+FD>2
                                         H   = 2, 0     YES..Col-Shd Bl>0
Zf    = 16    M.FC.FD.FT.FC'    M  = 1   (H) = 3, 0     YES..Ego<.31,>.44
ZSum  = 57.0  m.CF             FM  = 3   Hd  = 4, 0     NO..MOR > 3
ZEst  = 52.5  M.FC'            m   = 0   (Hd)= 1, 1     YES..Zd > +- 3.5
              M.FC'.FT         FC  = 1   Hx  = 0, 0     YES..es > EA
W  =  7       FM.FV            CF  = 0   A   = 7, 1     NO..CF+C > FC
 (Wv = 1)     FM.FT            C   = 1   (A) = 1, 0     YES..X+% < .70
D  = 18       FM.m             Cn  = 0   Ad  = 5, 0     YES..S > 3
Dd =  5       M.FC'            FC' = 0   (Ad)= 0, 0     NO..P < 3 or > 8
S  =  4       FM.m.M.CF.FD     C'F = 0   An  = 1, 0     NO..Pure H < 2
              FV.FC            C'  = 0   Art = 2, 0     NO..R < 17
  DQ          FM.FC            FT  = 1   Ay  = 0, 0      7.....TOTAL
.........(FQ-) FC.FY           TF  = 0   Bl  = 0, 0
 +  = 11  ( 0) m.FC.FY         T   = 0   Bt  = 1, 1    SPECIAL SCORINGS
 o  = 17  ( 4) M.FT            FV  = 1   Cg  = 0, 3        Lv1    Lv2
v/+ =  1  ( 1)                 VF  = 0   Cl  = 0, 0    DV  = 1x1   0x2
 v  =  1  ( 0)                 V   = 0   Ex  = 0, 0    INC = 0x2   0x4
                               FY  = 1   Fd  = 1, 0    DR  = 1x3   0x6
                               YF  = 0   Fi  = 0, 1    FAB = 2x4   0x7
                               Y   = 0   Ge  = 0, 0    ALOG = 0x5
      FORM QUALITY             Fr  = 0   Hh  = 0, 1    CON  = 0x7
                               rF  = 0   Ls  = 0, 0      SUM6  = 4
    FQx  FQf  MQual  SQx       FD  = 0   Na  = 0, 1      WSUM6 = 12
 +  = 4   0    4     2         F   = 7   Sc  = 2, 0
 o  = 14  3    2     1                   Sx  = 0, 1    AB = 0    CP  = 0
 u  =  6  1    1     0                   Xy  = 0, 0    AG = 0    MOR = 3
 -  =  5  3    0     1                   Id  = 0, 0    CFB = 0   PER = 3
none=  1  --   0     0         (2) = 14                COP = 2   PSV = 0
================================================================================
            RATIOS, PERCENTAGES, AND DERIVATIONS

R = 30          L =  0.30          FC:CF+C = 6: 3     COP = 2    AG = 0
-----------------------------      Pure C  =    1     Food       = 1
EB = 7: 6.5  EA = 13.5  EBPer= N/A Afr     =0.43      Isolate/R  =0.13
eb =12:15    es = 27      D  =  -5 S       =    4     H:(H)Hd(Hd)= 2: 9
             Adj es = 22  Adj D =  -3     Blends:R=14:30     (HHd):(AAd)= 5: 1
-----------------------------      CP      =    0     H+A:Hd+Ad  =14:11
FM = 8 :  C'= 4   T = 5
m  = 4 :  V = 3   Y = 3
                          P    = 7      Zf  =16        3r+(2)/R=0.47
a:p    = 7:12   Sum6 =  4  X+% =0.60    Zd  = +4.5     Fr+rF   = 0
Ma:Mp  = 3: 4   Lv2  =  0  F+% =0.43    W:D:Dd = 7:18: 5   FD      = 2
2AB+Art+Ay= 2   WSum6 = 12 X-% =0.17      W:M = 7: 7    An+Xy   = 1
M-     = 0      Mnone =  0  S-% =0.20    DQ+  =11        MOR     = 3
                           Xu% =0.20    DQv  = 1
-----------------------------------------------------------------
   SCZI = 1    DEPI = 6*   CDI = 4*    S-CON = 7    HVI = No   OBS =YES
================================================================================
```

CDI value of 4 suggests that the subject's interpersonal relations are impoverished and unrewarding and that he probably has considerable difficulty coping
with the natural demands of everyday living. This second proposition is very
important because it is somewhat contradictory to his history. If it is supported,
it strongly suggests the presence of an ongoing deterioration.

Affective Features

The data for variables concerning affect are shown in Table 72.

Case 5 Findings   All of the data in this cluster, except Step 2 (*EBPer*) and Step 7
(*CP*), are relevant to the interpretation.

The DEPI has been addressed in the initial proposition. The subject appears to
have a major affective disturbance, which, in this case, most likely involves severe
depression. The *EB* indicates that he is inconsistent in the way that he uses emotion in problem solving or decision making. In some instances, he is prone to keep
emotion aside and to rely on a logical weighing of alternatives before reaching a
conclusion. At other times he merges his feelings with his thinking and his decisions become much more intuitively influenced. Neither of these tactics is necessarily ineffective, but his inconsistency in their use often leads to vacillation and
increases the likelihood of errors in problem solving behaviors.

The data for the right side of the *eb* are disconcerting because of the magnitude
of the value. The value signals very intense emotional aggravation, some of which
is caused by an excessive constraint and internalization of feelings, and some of
which is provoked by a great deal of introspection that focuses on his perceived
negative features, but most of which seems to be precipitated by very intense feelings of isolation and emotional loneliness. As a collective, these feelings are overwhelming, going well beyond levels that any human can be expected to tolerate
easily. Surprisingly, these intensely negative experiences have not diminished the
controls that he exerts over his emotional displays. The *FC:CF + C* ratio suggests
that he modulates his displays much more than most people, even though there
may be instances in which he seems forced to give way to his feelings and then

Table 72.   Variables Related to Affective Features for Case 5

			BLENDS	
EB = 7 : 6.5	*EBPer* = NA	DEPI = 6		
eb = 12 : 15	(*C* = 4, *T* = 5, *V* = 3, *Y* = 3)		M.FC.FD.FT.FC′	FM.m.M.CF.FD
FC:CF+C = 6 : 3	Pure *C* = 1		M.FC′.FT	FM.FV
Afr = 0.43	CP = 0		M.FC′ (2)	FM.FT
S = 4	Col-Shd Bl = 4		M.FT	FM.FC
			m.FC.YF	FM.m
			m.CF	FV.FC
			FC.FY	

they become more intense (Pure $C = 1$). But even then, as illustrated by the content of the single Pure C answer (colored inkblots), he attempts to exert some modest control through a very concrete pseudo-intellectual process.

The *Afr* suggests that he tends to avoid emotionally provocative stimuli. This is probably because he feels some sense of fragility in dealing with feelings. Some of the data (*S*) also indicate that he is very negative or angry, but the fact that all of these responses occurred during the first three blots suggests that this negativism was created by being evaluated and not that it represented a chronic trait-like feature.

The data for the blends are possibly most important in understanding the subject's current state. He is a very complicated person. The number of blends is very high. Also, the number of variables within two blends is high; one contains five variables (*M.FC.FD.FT.FC'*), and a second contains four variables (*FM.m.M.CF.FD*). Answers such as these are quite rare. They not only emphasize the complexity that exists but also give some hint about the kind of activities that are contributing to this subject's complexity. The first contains both a color-shading combination and a shading combination, indicating confusion and exquisite pain. The second consists mainly of ideation-related variables, which seem to reflect a great deal of confusion in thinking. Only two of the 14 blends seem to be related to situational stress but, even if they are disregarded, the total remains excessive. The presence of four Color-Shading blends signifies a great deal of confusion about feelings, but more important are the two shading blends. Neither contains obvious situationally-related features, but both include texture features. They hint at the presence of devastating feelings that have some relation to his strong sense of loneliness.

Case 5 Summary   The subject probably is experiencing a serious depression. There is no question that he is in intense emotional distress. Some of this distress is being caused by an excessive internalization of feelings and by a great deal of rumination about his perceived negative features. Much is also generated by very intense feelings of isolation and loneliness. Collectively, these feelings have a very disorganizing influence and have contributed to a substantial increase in psychological complexity. He seems to be experiencing both confusion and pain and some of his thinking is likely to be less clear than may have been the case in the past.

The subject is very inconsistent in decision making activities. Sometimes he pushes his emotions aside and relies on a logical weighing of alternatives before reaching a decision or conclusion; at other times he merges his feelings with his thinking and his decisions become much more intuitively influenced. Although neither tactic is necessarily ineffective, his inconsistency in their use often leads to vacillation and increases the likelihood of errors in problem solving behaviors.

Surprisingly, the subject's intense distress has not diminished his ability to control his emotional displays. In fact, he is somewhat more conservative than most about modulating his displays, although there is a hint that he gives way to his feelings more often than may have been the case in the past. He tends to avoid emotional stimuli, probably because he feels a sense of fragility in dealing with feelings.

Controls and Stress Tolerance

The data for the variables related to the capacity for control and tolerance for stress are shown in Table 73.

no controls
out of con
overload

Case 5 Findings   The Adj D Score of -3 reveals that he is highly vulnerable to loss of control and disorganization under stress. This limited capacity for control is unusual because, as noted by the above average *EA,* he has considerable resource available for use in formulating decisions and implementing behaviors. The problem is caused by the huge magnitude of internally experienced demands, which are reflected in the very high *es* and Adj *es*. They have created a chronic overload state. The experience of the overload is quite severe, and the impact is creating a considerable interference in some of the subject's customary patterns of thinking and/or behavior. The potential for disorganization in complex or highly ambiguous situations is increased substantially.

impulsive

The overload also makes him extremely vulnerable to impulsive behaviors, and he usually will not function very effectively except in environments that are highly structured and routine and over which he has control. This is inconsistent with his history of occupational success and, as such, offers support for one of the initial propositions that was based on the positive CDI, namely, that some ongoing deterioration may be present.

The D Score of -5 indicates that the matter is made worse by the fact that he is also experiencing a significant increase in stimulus demands as a result of some situationally-related stress, which serves to increase his vulnerability to disorganization. The cause of the situationally-related stress is not completely clear. A parsimonious hypothesis suggests that it may relate to some awareness of his deterioration; however, the history suggests that there could be a direct relationship to his wife's alcoholism. The elevation in *T* argues for the presence of a strong sense of emotional loss and the corresponding feelings of loneliness. This issue is important to review again when treatment considerations are formulated.

Case 5 Summary   The subject has very limited capacities for control and is vulnerable to disorganization. In fact, some process of disorganization or deterioration already appears to exist. Actually, he has considerable resource available for use in formulating decisions and implementing behaviors, but the magnitude of internally experienced demands has created a chronic overload state. The overload is severe and interferes with his usual patterns of thinking and/or behavior. It makes him vulnerable to impulsive behaviors and limits his potential for effective functioning to environments that are highly structured and routine. The matter is made worse by the current experience of some situationally-related stress. The

Table 73.   Control Related Variables for Case 5

EB $= 7:6.5$	*EA* $= 13.5$	D $= -5$	CDI $= 4$
eb $= 12:15$	*es* $= 27$ Adj*es* $= 22$	AdjD $= -3$	
FM $= 8$ *m* $= 4$ *C'* $= 4$ *T* $= 5$ *V* $= 3$ *Y* $= 3$			

cause of the stress is not completely clear and may simply relate to an awareness of his disorganization; however, it may relate to difficulties that he is experiencing in attempting to contend with his wife's alcoholism.

Self-Perception

The data for the variables related to self-perception are shown in Table 74.

Case 5 Findings   The data relevant to the interpretation are in Steps 2 (Egocentricity Index), 3 (*FD* and *Vista*), 4 $H:(H)+Hd+(Hd)$, and 6 (MOR), plus the evaluation of minus, MOR, and movement responses in Steps 7, 8, and 9.

The Egocentricity Index is higher than expected, indicating that the subject is very self-focusing or self-centered. This does not necessarily equate with a positive self-image. Instead, it signifies more concern with the self and less attention to the external world than is typical. This is not an unusual finding among those who are seriously depressed. His excessive self-concern is also reflected in the data for *FD* and *Vista*. The combined value is very high, indicating that he is involved with much more introspection than is customary. The very large number of *Vista* answers confirms that much of the self-inspecting focuses excessively on perceived negative features of his self-image. This gives rise to very painful feelings. The disproportionately low number of Pure *H* responses is quite interesting and seemingly inconsistent with the history. It suggests that his self-image tends to be based largely on imaginary rather than real experience. That seems very unusual for a successful businessman and raises a question about whether his affective disruption may be creating some unusual delusions about his self-image. The presence of the three MOR responses indicates that his self-image includes some very negative, unwanted features that tend to promote a pessimistic view of the self that influences many of his decisions.

The contents of the three MOR answers (18. "a bear rug, cut off head part," 21. "Croutons broken up, soggy in soup," 22. "the old corset sort of split here and stretched, these fragments make it look like it was torn") are not nearly as dramatic as anticipated in light of the DEPI value and the intense distress. The second two, broken croutons and split torn corset, hint at a sense of damage and, if considered very speculatively, may raise a question about some loss of potency or virility.

Table 74. Self Perception Variables for Case 5

STRUCTURAL DATA		RESPONSES TO BE READ	
$Fr+rF = 0$	$3r+(2)/R = 0.47$	*MOR* RESPONSES	= 18, 21, 22
$FD = 2$	$V = 3$	MINUS RESPONSES	= 1, 7, 13, 21, 28
$HH)+Hd+(Hd) = 2:9$		*M* RESPONSES	= 2, 6, 10, 14, 20, 22, 30
$An+Xy = 1$		*FM* RESPONSES	= 9, 11, 12, 15, 16, 19, 22, 26
$MOR = 3$		*m* RESPONSES	= 8, 19, 22, 29

The contents of the five minus answers (1. "Two owl eyes . . . the two orbits," 7. "a bearded cat . . . an abstract Japanese cat," 13. "a face, not quite a skull . . . a muttonchop beard," 21. "Croutons broken up, soggy in soup . . . lost their square distinct shape," 28. "the pelvis . . . pubic bone area") are not very revealing, although three (not quite a skull, croutons broken, pubic bone area) also contain subtle cues that might relate to a sense of pending doom regarding the integrity of his self-image and possibly his masculinity.

The contents of the seven *M* responses do not provide a very consistent yield, although all have a distant or concealed quality. The first three (2. "Somebody with their hands up . . . like a priest . . . robe here," 6. "A couple of gnomes dancing . . . dark robes," 10. "two native women . . . big kettle they're working over . . . white loin cloth") include the two Pure *H* contents, but none are simply people. Instead they are more distant (priest, gnomes, natives), and all three have some concealment (robes, loin cloth). The remaining four are more elusive and/or unreal (14. "a cartoon monster . . . like it jumped up in the air," 20. "two girls' faces looking at each other . . . like a silhouette, no distinct features," 22. "some critter with hands reaching down pulling the flower . . . like pulling on the stamen," 30. "furry cartoon critters, talking to each other"). Collectively, they seem to illustrate a person whose self-concept is distant and ill defined. As with other findings, this seems inconsistent with the history and may reflect the sense of disorganization that he is experiencing.

Most of the eight animal movement responses are very passive or tentative (9. "Two bears touching noses," 11. "a butterfly . . . flying upward," 12. "a tiny bird falling out of a tree," 15. "a butterfly just coming out of the cocoon," 16. "A couple of furry bisons lying back to back," 19. "an otter popping up, splashing out of the water . . . moving away," 22. "mice crawling up," 26. "spiders holding up something"). Even the most active (otter popping up) is moving away. The butterfly coming out of the cocoon is the most intriguing, partly because it is a very unusual response and partly because it is very similar to two of the four inanimate movement answers (22. "a flower opening up," 29. "Beginning of a flower, beginning to open up"). Responses such as these are sometimes found among the records of adolescents, and occasionally in the protocols of recovering patients, but they are inconsistent with the presence of a severe depression. Obviously, these three responses have some special importance, but the meaning is far from clear. It was suggested earlier that his self-image seems to be based largely on imagination, and a question was raised about whether the affective disruption was fomenting delusions about his sense of self. If that is true, these answers relate to such operations, but, obviously, numerous other speculations might be generated as well. The two remaining *m* answers (8. "a spaceship . . . the exhaust is thrusting out," 19. "the water is splashing") offer no significant additional information.

Case 5 Summary   It seems clear that he is very preoccupied with himself. This is not unusual for those who are seriously depressed. He engages in much more introspection than do most people, most of which is devoted to perceived negative features of his self-image. This gives rise to very painful feelings. His self-image tends to be based more on imaginary rather than real experience, which seems very unusual in light of the history, and raises a question about whether his affective disruption may be creating some unusual delusions about his self-image. His self-image does include some very negative, unwanted features that tend to promote a pessimistic view of himself, and there is some hint at a sense of damage that may relate to a loss of potency or virility. There are also subtle cues that may signal a sense of threat to the integrity of his self-image. Actually, the data do not portray a consistent or clear picture of the self. Instead, they seem to illustrate a person whose self-concept is distant and ill defined. As with other findings, this seems inconsistent with the history and may reflect the sense of disorganization that he is experiencing.

Interpersonal Perception and Behavior

The data for the variables related to interpersonal perception are shown in Table 75.

Case 5 Findings   The data relevant to the interpretation are in Steps 1 (CDI), 3 ($a:p$), 4 (Fd), 5 (T), 6 (number of human contents), 7 (PER), 8 (COP), 10 (contents of movement answers containing pairs) and 11 (contents of responses containing human figures).

Ordinarily, a positive CDI identifies a person who experiences frequent difficulties when interacting with the environment, and these difficulties usually extend into the interpersonal sphere. As a result, most interpersonal relationships tend to be superficial and less mature than might be expected. Usually, this has been a chronic problem; but if the history for this case is valid, the current state of coping deficit and interpersonal ineptness could reflect the massive pathology that is present. On the other hand, it may be premature to make this judgment as there is little in the history to confirm that he has had many deep and enduring relationships or that his interpersonal skills have been very effective. He works in a highly specialized area and, although he manages the activities of his colleagues, this is not evidence of smooth or mature interpersonal skills. In fact, the $a:p$ data indicate that he usually prefers to take a passive, but not necessarily submissive, role in interpersonal relationships.

People such as this usually like to avoid responsibility for decision making and are less prone to seek new solutions to problems. This ratio is very stable and usually does not change, even under conditions of severe pathology. Thus, the finding

Table 75.   Interpersonal Perception Variables for Case 5

STRUCTURAL VARIABLES	RESPONSES TO BE READ
CDI = 4 HVI = Neg	MOVEMENT WITH PAIR = 6, 9, 10, 12, 16, 17, 20, 22, 26, 29, 30
$a:p$ = 7:12 T = 5 Fd = 1	
Isolate/R = 0.13	HUMAN CONTENTS = 2, 4, 6, 10, 13, 14, 17, 20, 22, 23, 30
Total Human Contents = 11	
PER = 3 COP = 2 AG = 0	

creates a confusion about how best to interpret the history of apparent leadership skills. This confusion is increased by the presence of one *Food* response, which suggests that he is the type of person who has stronger needs to be dependent on others than do most people. Such people tend to rely on others for support and often are more "naïve" in their expectations about interpersonal relationships. The composite of passivity findings, when combined with the suggestion of dependency, raises the issue of whether a marked passive-dependent feature has been an important core component in his personality structure and, as such, may underlie much of the current depression. In other words, if he has been passively dependent, and his wife has played an important role in sustaining this style, her absence of support, because of alcoholism, could undermine the relationship quite easily and leave him without the support to which he is accustomed. As already noted, the significant elevation for *T* indicates that he is in extreme discomfort because of unmet needs for closeness and that experience can be very influential in directing, and possibly even disrupting, many of his daily interpersonal behaviors.

The large number of human contents makes it clear that he is very interested in people, but the relatively higher value for PER suggests that he is quite insecure about his personal integrity and tends to be overly authoritarian when interpersonal situations appear to pose challenges to the self. People such as this are often regarded as rigid or narrow by others and frequently have difficulty in maintaining close relationships, especially with those who are not submissive to them.

The COP value of 2 indicates that he generally perceives positive interactions among people routinely and is willing to participate in them, but this does not necessarily mean that his interpersonal relationships will be positive or mature. The large number of human content responses (11) indicates that he has a definite interest in people; however, a review of the contents of the 11 movement answers containing pairs yields less appealing findings (6. "gnomes dancing," 9. "bears touching noses," 10. "two native women . . . big kettle they are working over," 12. "a tiny bird falling out of a tree . . . a pair of them," 16. "furry bisons lying back to back," 17. "a feminine leg here . . . on both sides," 20. "two girls' faces facing each other," 22. "mice crawling up, lizards here," 26. "spiders holding something up," 29. "a flower beginning to open," 30. "two . . . furry cartoon critters, talking to each other"). The most positive are the two COP responses, gnomes dancing and women working, but the remaining nine tend to be sterile and nondescript. Even the spiders that are holding something up in Response 26 are not proximate and have nothing to do with each other.

A similar sense of sterility is noted in the review of the human contents in the record (priest, bottom of a female form, gnomes, native women, a face, not quite a skull, a cartoon monster, a feminine leg, two girls' faces, some critter with hands, a strange creature, furry cartoon critters). It is, at best, difficult to believe that anyone who perceives humans in this way has a realistic understanding of them or can interact positively with them.

Case 5 Summary   The data create some confusion, not so much because they are inconsistent, but more because they seem to be at odds with what appears to be a very positive history. The findings suggest that he has frequent difficulties when interacting with the environment and these difficulties usually extend into the interpersonal sphere. As a result, most interpersonal relationships tend to be superficial and less mature than might be expected. The data also indicate that he usually prefers to take a passive, but not necessarily submissive, role in interpersonal relationships. People such as this usually like to avoid responsibility for decision making and are less prone to seek new solutions to problems. He seems to have stronger needs to be dependent on others than most people do. People such as this tend to rely on others for support and often are more naïve in their expectations about interpersonal relationships. The composite of findings raises the issue of whether a marked passive-dependent feature has been an important core component in his personality structure and, as such, may underlie much of the current depression. Stated differently, his wife may have played a very important role in sustaining his passive-dependent style. Her alcoholism could undermine the relationship quite easily and leave him without the support to which he is accustomed. As noted earlier, he is in extreme discomfort because of unmet needs for closeness and a sense of loneliness, which can be very influential in directing, and possibly even disrupting, many of his daily interpersonal behaviors.

Some support for the notion that his depression may have evolved because of the absence of a source on which he can be dependent is gleaned from several sources. First, he is quite insecure about his personal integrity and tends to be overly authoritarian when interpersonal situations appear to pose challenges to the self. People such as this are often regarded as rigid or narrow by others and frequently have difficulties in maintaining close relationships, especially with those who are not submissive to them. Second, although he has a strong interest in people, generally anticipates positive interactions among people, and is willing to participate in them, he also tends to perceive those interactions as being superficial and somewhat sterile. This same kind of sterility and lack of animation appears to mark his perceptions of people in general. In that context, it is difficult to believe that he has had a realistic understanding of people or has interacted in more than a superficial way with them.

Information Processing

The data for the variables related to information processing are shown in Table 76.

Case 5 Findings All data for this cluster are relevant to the interpretation.

The relatively low Lambda suggests that he becomes overly involved in stimuli. This could be a function of the severe depression that he is experiencing, but

Table 76. Information Processing Variables for Case 5

$L = 0.30$	OBS = Pos	HVI = Neg	LOCATION SEQUENCING		
$Zd = +4.5$	$DQ+ = 11$	I Dd,D,D,D,Dd	IV W	VII D,W	
$Zf = 16$	$DQ\text{v}/+ = 0$	II WS,D,DS,Dd	V W,D,D	VIII W	
$W{:}D{:}Dd = 7{:}18{:}5$	$DQ\text{v} = 0$	III DS,D,D,DS	VI D,D	IX W,Dd,W	
$W{:}M = 7{:}7$	PSV = 0			X D,D,Dd,D,D	

it is more likely that a low Lambda value would exist even if the depression were not present. This is because the Obsessive Index is positive. A positive OBS is very unusual, especially among those manifesting adjustment difficulties. It signifies the presence of a very marked obsessive style that is pervasive in almost all decisions and behaviors. People with this feature are very meticulous about processing as they are strongly influenced by needs to be correct. They are perfectionistic and often become overly preoccupied with details, sometimes to the point of being inefficient.

The obsessive style is illustrated quite well by the data for several variables. The Zf is very high, reflecting the strong effort to organize, and the $W:D:Dd$ and $W:M$ ratios portray the conservative, overattention to details and the orientation to be economical in setting goals. The excessive attention to details increases the likelihood that some of his processing may not be very effective. Actually, the quality of his processing tends to be complex and sophisticated as illustrated by the DQ distribution and the Zd score. He synthesizes much of what he processes and his overincorporative style causes him to invest considerable energy in scanning activities. The inefficiency of his obsessive style is probably best represented in the location sequencing and the distribution of the responses. Both are very inconsistent. Although five of his W's are first responses, two others are last responses. Similarly, his Dd answers are scattered. One is the first response to the test, two others are last responses, and the remaining two are middle responses. He gives five answers to the first and last cards, four answers to Cards II and III, but only one response to Cards IV and VIII. The lack of consistency in overall pattern strongly suggests that much of his processing activity will fall short of the perfectionistic objectives that he appears to set for himself and this can have a significant effect on his mediational activity.

Case 5 Summary   He has a markedly obsessive personality style that causes him to become overly involved in stimuli. This style is pervasive in almost all of his decisions and behaviors. He tries to be very meticulous about processing and is strongly influenced by needs to be correct. He is perfectionistic and often becomes overly preoccupied with details. He makes a strong effort to organize and, at times, the quality of his processing tends to be reasonably sophisticated. He synthesizes much of what he processes and his overincorporative style causes him to invest considerable energy in scanning activities. However, he is very inconsistent and it is likely that much of his processing activity will fall short of the perfectionistic objectives that he appears to set for himself.

Cognitive Mediation

The data for variables related to mediation are shown in Table 77.

Case 5 Findings   All variables in the cluster, except the Step 1 (Lambda) data, are relevant to the interpretation.

As with the data concerning processing, the most important variable is the positive Obsessive Index. People with an obsessive style usually are very cautious about translating stimuli because they want to be correct or conventional. When an obsessive style is functioning effectively, the data regarding mediation typically include (1) an average or above average number of Popular answers,

Table 77. Cognitive Mediation Variables for Case 5

Lambda = 0.30	OBS = Pos	MINUS FEATURES		
P = 7	*X+%* = .60	I	1. *Ddo F– Ad*
FQx+ = 4	*F+%* = .43	II	7. *Do FC– Ad DV*
FQxo = 14	*Xu%* = .20	III	13. *DSo FV– Hd 4.5 DR*
FQxu = 6	*X–%* = .17	VII	21. *Wv/+ F– Fd 2.5 MOR*
FQx– = 5	*S–%* = .20	X	28. *Ddo F– An*
FQnone = 1	CONFAB = 0		

(2) an $X+\%$ that is either well into the average range or is above average, (3) some *FQ+* answers, (4) the absence of *FQnone* responses, and (5) *Xu%* that is no greater than average and an $X-\%$ that is quite low. The data for this case are not like that. There are seven Popular responses, indicating that, in obvious situations, expected or acceptable responses are likely to occur, and there are four *FQ+* answers, confirming the tendency to be precise. Nonetheless, the $X+\%$ is lower than expected, there is one *FQnone* response, and the values for the *Xu%* and $X-\%$ are both higher than expected. The latter suggest that he may display a higher than usual frequency of behaviors that disregard social demands or expectations and that concern is warranted about the elevated incidence of perceptual inaccuracy and/or mediational distortion. In other words, the obsessive style is not functioning very adequately.

A review of the sequencing of the minus responses is not very revealing. Minus answers occur in five of the 10 cards. One is a first answer, two are last answers, and two are middle responses. The Step 10 search for homogeneity among the minus answers also is somewhat disappointing, although it may offer a clue about the distortion process. If a prediction were to be made about the kind of homogeneity to be expected among minus answers in this case, the presence of the intense distress could be used as a basis from which to hypothesize that all would include some evidence of the distress. That is not the case. Only Response 13 contains such evidence. In fact, three of the five minus answers are Pure *F* responses. This might indicate that distortions become more likely when he attempts to extract himself from becoming overwhelmed by the complexity of a stimulus field but this is a very speculative postulate. All minus answers appear to be Level 1 distortions, although Responses 7 and 13 ("a bearded cat . . . eyes, whiskers . . . a long beard"; "a face, not quite a skull . . . eyes, mouth . . . a muttonchop beard") both represent relatively severe distortions.

Case 5 Summary   The subject's obsessive style is not functioning very effectively in spite of his orientation to make correct or conventional responses. In obvious situations, expected or acceptable responses are likely to occur, and he does strive to be precise. Nevertheless, he is more prone to overpersonalize or distort inputs than should be the case and this leads to a higher than usual frequency of behaviors that disregard social demands or expectations. The mediational distortions may be related to his attempts to avoid becoming overwhelmed by the complexity of a stimulus field, but this is a very speculative postulate. On a more positive note, the extent of distortion and overpersonalization is considerably less than might be expected in light of the earlier findings concerning emotional disarray, and this could bode well for treatment.

Ideation

Data for the variables related to ideational activity are shown in Table 78.

Case 5 Findings   All data for this cluster, except that for Steps 2 (*EBPer*), 4 (*a : p*), 6 (Intellectualization Index), and 11 (*M*– responses), appear to be relevant to the interpretation.

The *EB* indicates that his ideational activity tends to be less consistent. He sometimes delays and ponders alternative responses, but other times searches for external feedback through trial-and-error tactics. People such as this are inconsistent in their judgments and often find it more difficult to reach a firm decision. Their lack of consistency in thinking makes them more vulnerable to errors in decision making. The left-side *eb* data add to the problem. He is experiencing a higher than expected level of ideational activity that is outside the focus of attention. This kind of peripheral ideation, which is promoted by needs states, can serve as a positive stimulus, but it can also become quite distracting once it exceeds natural levels. His level of peripheral ideational activity appears to be chronically high, and is being increased by situationally-related stress. As a result, it serves to exacerbate the long-standing pattern of limited concentration, and interruptions in the flow of deliberate thinking are likely to be even more frequent.

The $M^a : M^p$ ratio suggests that he has a stylistic tendency to use fantasy as a defensive substitute for reality in stress situations much more than do most people. This form of denial provides some temporary relief by replacing an unpleasant situation with one that is easily managed; however, it also breeds a dependency on others because of the implicit assumption that external forces will bring resolution to the situation if it can be avoided long enough. The presence of the three MOR answers indicates that his thinking is often influenced by

Table 78.   Ideation Variables for Case 5

		M QUALITY	CRITICAL SPECIAL SCORES			
EB = 7 : 6.5	*EBPer* = NA					
eb = 12 : 15	(*FM* = 8 *m* = 4)	+ = 4	DV	= 1	DV2	= 0
a:p = 7 : 12	*Ma:Mp* = 3 : 4	o = 2	INC	= 0	INC2	= 0
2*Ab*+(*Art*+*Ay*) = 2		u = 1	DR	= 1	DR2	= 0
MOR = 3		– = 0	FAB	= 2	FAB2	= 0
RESPONSES TO BE READ FOR QUALITY			ALOG	= 0	SUM6	= 4
2, 6, 10, 14, 20, 22, 30			CON	= 0	WSUM6	= 12

a pessimistic set that causes him to view the world with a sense of doubt and/or discouragement.

The presence of four Critical Special Scores indicates that his ideation is marked by more slippage than should be the case. It does not necessarily reflect pathological thinking but does suggest that some of his ideation is unsophisticated and sometimes marked by flawed conceptualizations and/or judgment. This seems to be confirmed by the qualitative evaluation of the Critical Special Scores (abstract Japanese cat; not quite a skull; bisons lying back to back; spiders holding up something). None is serious, and some barely meet criteria. The Step 10 review of the form quality for the M responses reveals that four have a *plus* form, whereas the other three are *ordinary* or *unusual*. This suggests that his obsessive style is very influential in his thinking and orients him toward being very precise.

In spite of this, the quality of most of the M answers generally is not very sophisticated (2. "Somebody with their hands up . . . like a priest . . . robe here," 6. "A couple of gnomes dancing . . . dark robes," 10. "two native women . . . big kettle they're working over . . . white loin cloth," 14. "a cartoon monster . . . like it jumped up in the air," 20. "two girls' faces looking at each other . . . like a silhouette, no distinct features," 22. "some critter with hands reaching down pulling the flower . . . like pulling on the stamen," 30. "furry cartoon critters, talking to each other"). Only Response 6 (gnomes) is very elaborately developed, even though some of the others are very detailed. In other words, the quality of his thinking probably tends to fall far short of his own expectations. The history implies that he is a very bright, creative person. If that is or has been true, it is not confirmed here and suggests that his present condition may have a much more negative impact on the quality of his thinking than is readily apparent.

Case 5 Summary   His ideational activity related to decision making tends to be inconsistent. He vacillates between thoughtful delay and searching for external feedback through trial-and-error tactics. As a result, his judgments are also inconsistent, and he often finds it difficult to reach a firm decision. This problem is increased by the fact that he is experiencing considerable ideational activity that is outside the focus of attention. Although peripheral ideation usually serves as a positive stimulus, it becomes distracting once it exceeds natural levels. In this case, the activity that is chronically high is being increased by situationally-related stress. As a result, it exacerbates his already limited concentration and results in even more frequent interruptions in the flow of deliberate thinking.

He tends to use fantasy as a defensive substitute for reality much more than do most people. Although this form of denial provides some temporary relief, it also breeds a dependency on others. His thinking is often influenced by a pessimistic set that causes him to view the world with a sense of doubt and/or discouragement. His ideation also is marked by more slippage than should be the case. It is not pathological, but does contribute to faulty conceptualizations and/or judgment. His obsessive style is very influential in his thinking and orients him toward being very precise. In spite of this, the quality of his thinking is not very sophisticated. The history implies that he is a very bright and creative person. If that is or has been true, it is not confirmed here and suggests that his present condition may have a much more negative impact on the quality of his thinking than is readily apparent.

Case 5 Final Description

This 49-year-old male appears to be experiencing a serious depressive episode that seems to be superimposed on a very obsessive but passive-dependent personality structure. He is in intense emotional distress, caused by an excessive internalization of feelings, rumination about his perceived negative features, and very intense feelings of isolation and loneliness. These feelings have a very disorganizing influence and it is likely that some of his thinking is less clear than might otherwise be the case. He is very inconsistent in decision making activities, which increases the likelihood of errors in problem solving behaviors.

Even though intensely distressed he continues to maintain tight control over his emotional displays but this control may be quite fragile. He tries to avoid emotionally provocative stimuli, probably because he feels some sense of fearfulness about dealing with feelings; however, his overall capacity for control is very limited, and he is vulnerable to disorganization. In fact, some process of disorganization or deterioration already appears to exist. Actually, he has considerable resource available but he is currently in a chronic overload state that is severe and creating a considerable interference in some of the customary patterns of thinking and/or behavior. It makes him vulnerable to impulsive behaviors and limits his potential for effective functioning to environments that are highly structured and routine. The matter is made worse by the experience of some situationally-related stress. The cause of the situational stress is not completely clear and may simply relate to an awareness of his disorganization.

He is very preoccupied with himself, engaging in considerable introspection, most of which is devoted to perceived negative features of his self-image. His self-image tends to be based more on imaginary than on real experience, which seems very unusual in light of the history and raises a question about whether his affective disruption may be creating some unusual delusions about himself. He has a rather pessimistic view of himself, and there is some hint of a sense of damage that may relate to a loss of potency or virility. The findings seem to portray a person whose self-concept is distant and ill defined. As with other findings, this seems inconsistent with the history and may reflect the sense of disorganization that he is experiencing.

Many of the findings are at odds with the history. For example, it seems clear that he has frequent difficulties when interacting with the environment and these difficulties usually extend into the interpersonal sphere. As a result, most of his interpersonal relationships tend to be superficial and less mature. The findings also indicate that he prefers a passive, but not necessarily submissive, role in interpersonal relationships. People such as this usually like to avoid responsibility for decision making and are less prone to seek new solutions to problems. He also seems to be more dependent on others. People such as this often are more naïve in their expectations about interpersonal relationships. These findings suggest that a marked passive-dependent feature has been an important core component in his personality structure, and may underlie the current depression.

In this context, it seems reasonable to speculate that his wife has played a very important role in sustaining his passive-dependent style. Her alcoholism has undermined the relationship and he has lost the support to which he is accustomed. One result is the extreme discomfort that he experiences because of unmet needs for closeness and a sense of loneliness. This speculation seems supported in several ways. He is quite insecure about his personal integrity and tends to be overly authoritarian when interpersonal situations appear to pose challenges to the self. Although he is strongly interested in people and generally anticipates positive interactions among them, he tends to perceive those interactions as being superficial and somewhat sterile. This same kind of sterility and lack of animation appears to mark his perceptions of people in general. In that context, it is difficult to believe that he has had a realistic understanding of people or has interacted in more than a superficial way with them.

He has a markedly obsessive personality style that causes him to become overly involved in stimuli. This style is pervasive in almost all of his decisions and behaviors. He tries to be very meticulous about processing and is strongly influenced by needs to be correct. He is perfectionistic and often becomes overly preoccupied with details. He makes a strong effort to organize and the quality of his processing is reasonably sophisticated at times. He synthesizes much of what he processes and invests considerable energy into scanning activities. He is very inconsistent, however, and much of his processing activity is likely to fall short of the perfectionistic objectives that he appears to set for himself. Some of the findings make it clear that his obsessive style is not functioning very effectively in spite of his orientation to make correct or conventional responses. In obvious situations, expected or acceptable responses are likely to occur, and he strives to be precise. Nevertheless, he is more prone to overpersonalize or distort inputs than should be the case and this leads to a higher than usual frequency of behaviors that disregard social demands or expectations. His distortions possibly are related to his attempts to avoid becoming overwhelmed by the complexity of a stimulus field, but this is a very speculative postulate. On a more positive note, the extent of distortion and overpersonalization is considerably less than might be expected in light of the earlier findings concerning emotional disarray, and this could bode well for treatment.

His inconsistency in decision making is complicated further by the presence of considerable ideational activity that is outside the focus of attention. This kind of peripheral ideation usually serves as a positive stimulus but, in this case, it becomes distracting once it exceeds natural levels. Currently, this chronically high level of peripheral ideation is increased by situationally-related stress. As a result, limited concentration and interruptions in the flow of deliberate thinking will be even more frequent.

He tends to use fantasy as a defensive substitute for reality much more than do most people. Although this provides some temporary relief, it also breeds a dependency on others. His thinking is often influenced by pessimism, causing him to view the world with a sense of doubt and/or discouragement. His ideation also is marked by more slippage than should be the case. It is not pathological, but does contribute to faulty conceptualizations and/or judgment. His obsessive style is very influential in his thinking and orients him toward being very precise. In spite of this, the quality of his thinking is not very sophisticated. The history implies that he is a very bright, creative person. If that is or has been true, it is not confirmed here. His present condition may have had a much more negative impact on the quality of his thinking than is readily apparent.

Recommendations Based on the Final Description

Many problems are evidenced in this case, not the least of which is the intense discomfort that he currently experiences and that seems to be causing considerable disorganization. A reduction of the distress will probably occur as the result of concern, tenderizing, and support. Each of these therapeutic gestures will feed into his needs for closeness and his passive-dependent style. But these tactics are short term and can falter quickly if any added stresses are experienced. His relationship with his wife seems to be a very key factor in his psychological demise and will be equally important to his revival. Thus, although individual psychotherapy that focuses on his negative self-image is important, some therapeutic venture that involves both him and his wife may be the sustaining action. It also seems likely that he may be "out of place" in his current occupational assignment. This should be carefully evaluated and, if some change is warranted, it should be strongly recommended to his employers. Finally, this does not seem to be the kind of case in which pharmacotherapy will be beneficial over a long period. Free and Oei (1989) and McLean and Hakistan (1990) found that cognitive-behavioral models of treatment tend to fare better than pharmacotherapy over long periods. This is probably the type of case in which the former will promote greater gains than the latter.

whew! ethics of this. He didn't address my ques 2 + 3

Case 5 Epilogue   The subject was hospitalized for 114 days. During the first two weeks of hospitalization his depression intensified and he was unresponsive to pharmacological intervention. A course of unilateral ECT was initiated in the fourth week and he received 12 treatments during a 26 day period. The response seemed very favorable and he began participating in individual and group therapy shortly thereafter. During the last four weeks of hospitalization he and his wife were seen together seven times by a couples therapist. He returned to work three weeks after being discharged and continued in individual psychotherapy for approximately 15 months. According to the therapist reports, the subject's relationship with his wife improved considerably as she also continued in individual treatment. The therapist noted that, although the subject improved considerably and his job performance seemed more than adequate, deeply embedded obsessive features continued to pose obstacles throughout the course of treatment.

CASE 6: A DYSTHYMIC DISORDER

This 33-year-old female was referred for evaluation by a psychiatrist whom she contacted recently for treatment on the advice of a physician in the company at which she is employed. This is the third time that she has entered psychotherapy. Currently, she complains of being depressed, and says that recently she has considered cutting her wrists. She complains of difficulties concentrating and reports frequently feeling very lethargic concerning her work and her future.

   She is currently employed as a technical representative in customer relations for a large manufacturing firm. She has been with the firm for nearly eight years, having begun as a service representative. She has been promoted twice but each promotion has required her to move to a different state. She has been in her current position for slightly more than two years. She is the second of two children, having a brother, age 39, who is married and has two children. He works in the forestry service. Her parents are both age 64 and have recently retired from their respective jobs. The father, a civil engineer, had been employed by the same city government for nearly 40 years. The mother had been employed in a secretarial position in a school system for more than 30 years. The subject states that she was not very close to either parent, partly because they both worked, but also because she felt they treated her more harshly than they did her older brother. She usually sees them once a year during a brief visit home, but otherwise has only brief telephone contact with them. She has not seen her brother for seven years.

She gives a developmental history that is essentially unremarkable. She progressed satisfactorily in elementary and high school, and graduated from high school at the age of 18 in the upper 25% of her class. She entered a large university shortly thereafter, being supported partly on a state scholarship and partly by funds supplied by her parents. She majored in economics and received a B.A. degree at age 22. Her cumulative grade point average was 2.6. During the first two years after graduation she worked as an office manager for an automobile rental agency. She left that position at age 24 for what she thought would be a better position in an advertising agency. She states that she had difficulty adjusting to the demands of the position and found herself in frequent conflict with coworkers. She quit after one year, accepting the position with the firm in which she is now employed. She states that she used to enjoy her work, but that, since her last promotion and transfer, her interest has declined: "I lose my temper alot when I shouldn't, it's a very demanding job and I get frustrated alot."

Her first experience in psychotherapy occurred following an abortion at age 22, shortly after graduating. She admits that, at that time, she was quite active sexually and was not certain who may have impregnated her: "It would not have made any difference if I had known, I still would have gone ahead with it." That course of treatment lasted approximately nine months and the major focus appears to have been on "all of the bad feelings and sadness that I had about that stupid episode." She feels that course of treatment also helped her to plan more realistically for her occupational future. The second course of psychotherapy began when she was 26 and lasted approximately one year. It was prompted by considerable depression that she experienced following the suicide of a male coworker with whom she was quite friendly and whom she had dated several times. During that course of treatment she was prescribed Elavil™, Ludiomil™, and Mellaril™ for approximately three months each. She says that the treatment aided in contending with the trauma of her friend's death and also "it helped me even some things out in my mind."

She reports a varied social history. She began dating during high school and had her first experience of intercourse at age 16. She reports having dated very frequently during college: "nobody really steady, just a lot of different guys." She reports that after college she did have two relationships that lasted more than four months, and she was tempted to live with one of the men believing that marriage might occur, but decided against that commitment: "Things just didn't work out. We couldn't find the kind of common interests that I really wanted and we began to argue alot, just about little things but they piled up. Finally, I knew that I could never really live with him and he knew he couldn't live with me and we split."

Case 6: A 33-Year-Old Female

Card	Response	Inquiry
I.	1. It ll a cut up bf *E:* I thk if u tak ur time u'll find sthg else too	*E:* (Rpts S's resp) *S:* Its got the shape of a bf but it ll its cut up along the edges, thy r ragged & the white parts ll holes in it, c the wgs r here & the body (points)
	2. If u don't count the stuff on the side it it ll a wm standg in a negligee	*E:* (Rpts S's resp) *S:* Here's the figure in the cntr, (D4) c the littl feet & her hands r up lik ths (demos) u don't c her head very clear *E:* U said she's in a negligee? *S:* Well, it's transparent, u can c thru it, the waist & the full skirt
II	*S:* I'm having troubl w ths, it doesn't ll athg to me *E:* Tak u'r time, everybdy finds s.t. 3. I guess it cb 2 bears, lik thy got into some paint or smthg, thats the only way I can fig wht the red is	*E:* (Rpts S's resp) *S:* Just all of it ll tht, lik thyr standg there w red paint all over them, it's on their heads & on their feet too, I don't kno if thy got into it or smbody thru it on them, anyhow thyv got it all ovr them
	4. The center ll a spaceship	*E:* (Rpts S's resp) *S:* It just has tht form lik the shuttle
III	5. Now ths ll an interesting needlepoint design tht someone has been doing, it has a bf in the cntr, its blk on white w a red bf design ↑ *thms'shances how*	*E:* (Rpts S's resp) *S:* Here's the bf, in the middle, c the wgs & littl body & the rest is just a design thts not finished yet *E:* I'm not sur I'm seeing it lik u r, help me *S:* When u do needlepoint it's intricate, the designs hav to b precise lik tht, just the bf in the middl is finished, this black will b smthg else but its too early to tell what, I've done a few, thy tak a lot of patience and it takes a long time
	6. Thes ll sk of prehistoric A's	*E:* (Rpts S's resp) *S:* Thes thgs, 2 of them, the long necks & the pointed bony kind of structures, I don't thk I've ever seen athg lik tht, thts why I thot mayb thyr lik prehistoric A's of some sort, thyr almost human lik, (laughs) mayb the missing link or smthg
IV	7. Sk of an A w big feet & a tail & a small head	*E:* (Rpts S's resp) *S:* Here's the big feet & the tail & up here is the littl head & mayb thes r arms, just sk of big A, at least his feet r big

V

8. This ll an ugly moth flyg around

E: (Rpts S's resp)
S: I don't lik moths much, it just ll one, the wgs & the body part & the antennae

9. No wait, its mor lik a bat, an ugly bat

E: (Rpts S's resp)
S: Its more a bat than a moth cuz the wgs r big, big black wgs, lik the wgspread of a bat & its got thes antennae thgs up here *do bats have antinae*
E: You said its ugly?
S: All bats r ugly

VI

10. Ths part of it ll the head of cat, the whiskers

E: (Rpts S's resp)
S: Ths part rite here (D3), thes just stick out lik cat's whiskers, thts wht I thot of when I saw them, just a cat's head w the big whiskers

11. I guess it cld ll a bear rug, lik wld b near a fireplace in a cabin

E: (Rpts S's resp)
S: The W thg, it looks really furry, the head & the legs, lik a bear rug
E: U said it looks really furry?
S: It just has texture to it esp in here, (points to mid) it looks tht way very very furry, it's all rough around the edges too lik a furry rug wld b

VII

12. (Laughs) 2 little Indians boys jumpg up & dwn

E: (Rpts S's resp)
S: Ok, here's the feather, the face, & nose, forehead, I guess thes r their littl hands thy ll thyr jumping up & dwn on ths thing, mayb its a rock or smthg

VIII

13. Oh, pretty, 2 mt lions on the sides

E: (Rpts S's resp)
S: Ths ll 2 A's, mt lions, here is the face, the legs & the tail, c one on each side

14. It cb an exotic plant

E: (Rpts S's resp)
S: Very pretty, it has pink and blues leaves, mayb lik some special orchid or something fr the jungle, here is the stalk & ths dwn here (D2) is the pot

IX

15. Some coral or sthg, lik u'd c if u were lookg underneath the ocean

jump CF
not FC

E: (Rpts S's resp)
S: Well its got lots of colors lik u'd c in the ocean, part of it looks deepr & part looks closer lik if u were underwater & lookg down
E: U'll have to help me a littl more
S: The pink & orange r closer, lik coral, thyr brighter in some parts, lik higher & the white ll it is deeper lik sand, white sand but w a blue overlay, lik the water & the green is lik vegetation or sthg

(continued)

Case 6: (Continued)

Card	Response	Inquiry
X	16. I guess the blue cld b spiders, fuzzy one's lik tarantulas	E: (Rpts S's resp) S: Thes blu thgs, all the legs, thy look fuzzy lik tarantulas E: Fuzzy? S: Yeah, thy way the ink is makes them look not precise, more fuzzy, lik hairy, mostly in the cntr part, c here (points) there r diff shades there, it gives a fuzzy appearance
	17. Thes thgs here ll flowers sort of opening up, & thes dwn here ll green worms, it all ll a garden setting w littl bugs & worms & flowers	E: (Rpts S's resp) S: These 3 parts, c the brwn & yellow, thyr colord lik flowr buds, the yellow ll thyr opening lik thy r attached to ths brown, the stem & down here r the worms lik thyr crawling around, thyr green ones lik in the garden, & the rest is lik diff kinds of bugs or foliage, just diff kinds, tht's it

330

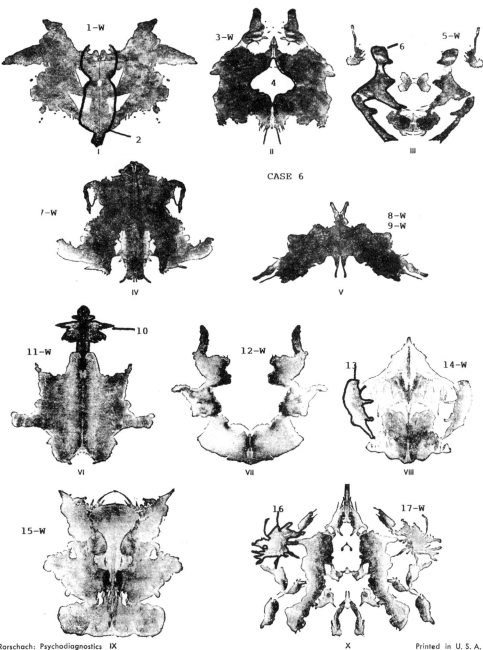

CASE 6

```
CASE 6.  SEQUENCE OF SCORES
```

CARD	NO	LOC	#	DETERMINANT(S)	(2)	CONTENT(S)	POP	Z	SPECIAL SCORES
I	1	WSo	1	Fo		A	P	3.5	MOR
	2	D+	4	Mp.FVo		H,Cg		4.0	
II	3	W+	1	CF.FMpo	2	A,Art		4.5	
	4	DSo	5	Fo		Sc			
III	5	WS+	1	FC'.FCu		Art,A		5.5	PER
	6	Do	9	Fu	2	A,Ay			
IV	7	Wo	1	Fo		A		2.0	
V	8	Wo	1	FMao		A		1.0	
	9	Wo	1	FC'o		A	P	1.0	INC
VI	10	Do	3	Fu		Ad			
	11	Wo	1	FTo		Ad	P	2.5	
VII	12	W+	1	Mao	2	H,Cg,Ls	P	2.5	
VIII	13	Do	1	Fo	2	A	P		
	14	W+	1	CFo		Bt,Hh		4.5	
IX	15	WS/	1	CF.VF.C'Fo		Na		5.5	
X	16	Do	1	FTo	2	A	P		
	17	W+	1	mp.FMa.FCo	2	Bt,A		5.5	

She reports that she began dating considerably less after her last transfer and attributes this to several factors: "It seemed to become more difficult to meet people, and then you always have to worry about herpes or AIDS." She points out that, until her last transfer, she usually dated once or twice a week and reports continuing satisfying sexual relationships. Since her last transfer, her dating frequency has dropped significantly: "I go out every now and then, but not very much." She admits experimenting with different drugs during college but says that she has only smoked marijuana from time to time since then. She reports that she liked to drink beer and wine in college, but after graduating her use of alcohol became less frequent and typically limited to social occasions. She also reports that she has had considerable variation in her weight. Approximately 18 months ago she went on "an eating binge" and gained 35 pounds in one month. Shortly thereafter, she began a stringent diet and ultimately lost 40 pounds. Currently, she is slightly overweight but does not feel that this is any source of concern.

She is not able to identify any major cause for her current depression. She states that she worries about some of her financial investments that have not turned out well. She feels that there must be something wrong with her because she has no close friends. She is beginning to believe that she is probably in the wrong occupation and that she might be more successful in some other work, but does not know what type of work that might be. She has considered making a résumé to give to an employment agency but feels that would be futile unless she had a specific type of position in mind.

The referring psychiatrist asks for a personality description and recommendations concerning a treatment plan. He also raises a question about whether pharmacological intervention seems contraindicated.

CASE 6.   STRUCTURAL SUMMARY
==

LOCATION	DETERMINANTS		CONTENTS	S-CONSTELLATION
FEATURES	BLENDS	SINGLE		NO..FV+VF+V+FD>2

LOCATION FEATURES	DETERMINANTS BLENDS	SINGLE	CONTENTS	S-CONSTELLATION
			H = 2, 0	YES..Col-Shd Bl>0
Zf = 12	M.FV	M = 1	(H) = 0, 0	NO..Ego<.31,>.44
ZSum = 42.0	CF.FM	FM = 1	Hd = 0, 0	NO..MOR > 3
ZEst = 38.0	FC'.FC	m = 0	(Hd)= 0, 0	YES..Zd > +- 3.5
	CF.VF.C'F	FC = 0	Hx = 0, 0	YES..es > EA
W = 11	m.FM.FC	CF = 1	A = 8, 2	YES..CF+C > FC
(Wv = 0)		C = 0	(A) = 0, 0	NO..X+% < .70
D = 6		Cn = 0	Ad = 2, 0	YES..S > 3
Dd = 0		FC'= 1	(Ad)= 0, 0	NO..P < 3 or > 8
S = 4		C'F= 0	An = 0, 0	NO..Pure H < 2
		C' = 0	Art = 1, 1	NO..R < 17
DQ		FT = 2	Ay = 0, 1	5.....TOTAL
........(FQ-)		TF = 0	Bl = 0, 0	
+ = 6 (0)		T = 0	Bt = 2, 0	SPECIAL SCORINGS
o = 10 (0)		FV = 0	Cg = 0, 2	Lv1 Lv2
v/+ = 1 (0)		VF = 0	Cl = 0, 0	DV = 0x1 0x2
v = 0 (0)		V = 0	Ex = 0, 0	INC = 1x2 0x4
		FY = 0	Fd = 0, 0	DR = 0x3 0x6
		YF = 0	Fi = 0, 0	FAB = 0x4 0x7
		Y = 0	Ge = 0, 0	ALOG = 0x5
FORM QUALITY		Fr = 0	Hh = 0, 1	CON = 0x7
		rF = 0	Ls = 0, 1	SUM6 = 1
FQx FQf MQual SQx		FD = 0	Na = 1, 0	WSUM6 = 2
+ = 0 0 0 0		F = 6	Sc = 1, 0	
o = 14 4 2 3			Sx = 0, 0	AB = 0 CP = 0
u = 3 2 0 1			Xy = 0, 0	AG = 0 MOR = 1
- = 0 0 0 0			Id = 0, 0	CFB = 0 PER = 1
none= 0 -- 0 0		(2) = 6		COP = 0 PSV = 0

==
RATIOS, PERCENTAGES, AND DERIVATIONS

R = 17   L = 0.55   FC:CF+C = 2: 3   COP = 0   AG = 0
-------------------------------------- Pure C =   0   Food   = 0
EB = 2: 4.0 EA =   6.0   EBPer= 2.0   Afr   =0.42   Isolate/R =0.29
eb = 4: 7   es = 11   D = -1   S   =   4   H:(H)Hd(Hd)= 2: 0
             Adj es = 11 Adj D = -1   Blends:R =5:17   (HHd):(AAd)= 0: 0
-------------------------------------- CP   =   0   H+A:Hd+Ad =12: 2
FM = 3 : C'= 3   T = 2
m = 1 : V = 2   Y = 0
                             P   = 6   Zf =12   3r+(2)/R=0.35
a:p   = 3: 3   Sum6 = 1   X+% =0.82   Zd = +4.0   Fr+rF = 0
Ma:Mp = 1: 1   Lv2   = 0   F+% =0.67   W:D:Dd =11: 6: 0   FD   = 0
2AB+Art+Ay= 3 WSum6 = 2   X-% =0.00   W:M =11: 2   An+Xy = 0
M-   = 0   Mnone = 0   S-% =0.00   DQ+ = 6   MOR   = 1
                            Xu% =0.18   DQv = 0

  SCZI = 0   DEPI = 5*   CDI = 4*   S-CON = 5   HVI = No   OBS = No
==

Interpretive Strategy

The record contains 17 answers and there is no reason to question its interpretive usefulness. The first positive Key variable is the CDI. Thus, the search order for the clusters will be:

CONTROLS → AFFECT → SELF-PERCEPTION → INTERPERSONAL PERCEPTION → PROCESSING → MEDIATION → IDEATION.

Initial Proposition   The CDI value of 4 suggests that her personality organization is less mature than might be expected. Her interpersonal relationships are probably impoverished and unrewarding and she tends to have difficulty coping with the demands of everyday living.

Controls and Stress Tolerance

The data for the variables related to capacity for control and stress tolerance are shown in Table 79.

Case 6 Findings   All data in the cluster are relevant to the interpretation.

The subject's Adj D Score of −1 signals the presence of a chronic overload state, which reduces her capacity for control and creates a marked proclivity for impulsiveness. Some of her decisions are not well thought out or implemented, and she is quite susceptible to disorganization under stress. People such as this usually function most effectively in familiar environments in which demands and expectations are predictable. The *EA* indicates that she has fewer resources available than most adults, and the data for the *EB* provide no cause to question the reliability of the *EA*. Thus, it does seem likely that her personality is somewhat less mature than might be expected. The value of *es* is slightly higher than expected, with the elevation being created mainly by right-side variables, which signifies the presence of considerable internal stimulus demand, much of which takes the form of negative emotional experience.

If some of the negative emotional demands were eliminated the potential for impulsiveness would be reduced but the potential for problems in control probably would continue. For instance, if the *Vista* features were eliminated and the tendency to internalize feelings were to diminish, the value for *es* could be lowered to about eight, thereby creating an Adj D Score of zero. The level of accessible resource would not be improved, however, so any added internal demands would again exceed her tolerance limits and the Adj D Score would be −1 again.

Table 79.   Control-Related Variables for Case 6

$EB = 2 : 4.0$	$EA = 6.0$	$D = -1$	$CDI = 4$
$eb = 4 : 7$	$es = 11$ $Adjes = 11$	$AdjD = -1$	
$FM = 3$ $m = 1$ $C' = 3$ $T = 2$ $V = 2$ $Y = 0$			

In other words, the lack of accessible resource, or psychological immaturity, creates a chronic vulnerability to disorganization.

Case 6 Summary   The subject is in a chronic state of stimulus overload which reduces her capacity for control and creates a potential for impulsiveness. Some of her decisions will not be well thought out or implemented, and she becomes easily disorganized under stress. The overload occurs in part because she has fewer resources available than most adults and it is provoked in part by considerable stimulus demand, much of which takes the form of aggravating emotion. But even if she were relieved of some of that aggravation she would remain vulnerable to disorganization because of her limited resources. In other words, she is considerably less mature than might be expected, especially for a college graduate. People such as this often have difficulty functioning effectively unless they are in familiar environments in which demands and expectations are predictable.

Affective Features

Data for the variables related to affect are shown in Table 80.

Case 6 Findings   All data, except those for Steps 5 (Pure *C*), 7 (Color Projection), and 10 (stress-related blends), are relevant to the interpretation.

The DEPI value of 5 indicates that her personality organization is very similar to those who have frequent and reasonably intense experiences of depression and is consistent with her presenting complaint. The right-side *eb* data confirm the presence of considerable distress or discomfort. These aggravating feelings appear to be generated by three sources: a marked tendency to hold in and internalize feelings, excessive self-inspecting behavior that focuses on negative features that she perceives in herself, and a chronic state of loneliness or emotional deprivation.

The *EB* reveals that her basic coping style involves a tendency to merge feelings with thinking during problem solving or decision making. People such as this are prone to use and be influenced by emotion, and usually prefer to test out postulates through trial-and-error behaviors. The *EBPer* suggests that there is some flexibility to the style and that instances will occur in which feelings are put aside in favor of a more clearly ideational approach. The *FC* : *CF* + *C* ratio indicates that, as with many people who have coping styles such as this, she is somewhat less stringent about modulating her emotional displays. People with this style often are more willing than others to display feelings and are less concerned about carefully

Table 80.   Affect-Related Variables for Case 6

			BLENDS	
EB = 2 : 4.0	*EBPer* = 2.0	DEPI = 5		
eb = 4 : 7	(*C* = 3, *T* = 2, *V* = 2, *Y* = 0)		M.FV	FM.FC'
FC:CF+C = 2 : 3	Pure *C* = 0		CF.VF.C'F	FC'.FC
Afr = 0.42	CP = 0		CF.FM	m.FM.FC
S = 4	Col-Shd Bl = 2			

modulating those displays. This is not a negative finding but can become a liability because of problems with control. The *Afr* shows a marked tendency to avoid emotionally loaded stimuli. Apparently, she is quite uncomfortable around emotion, which is very unusual for one with her coping style. This may relate to some awareness of her limited controls.

A very significant finding is the high value for *S*. She has a very negative, angry attitude toward the environment. This is a trait-like feature that is bound to have some impact on her psychological functioning. This does not necessarily mean that the anger will be manifest overtly, but it will have some impact on decision making and coping activities. People like this often have difficulty sustaining deep and/or meaningful relationships with others as they tend to be less tolerant of the routine compromises usually required in social intercourse. Although the number of blends is not excessive, their characteristics add important information. Two of the five are triple determinant blends, suggesting more complexity than might be expected in light of the low *EA*. In addition, two of the five are Color-Shading blends, signaling that she finds emotions confusing and may frequently experience both positive and negative feelings about the same stimulus situation. People such as this often experience feelings more intensely than others and sometimes have more difficulty in bringing closure to emotional situations. The Color-Shading blend reveals the presence of intensely negative and painful emotion. This kind of intense irritation often dominates the translation of affective experiences and can become pervasive in influencing thinking.

Case 6 Summary   Her personality organization is very similar to that of people who have frequent and reasonably intense experiences of depression, and evidence confirms the presence of considerable distress or discomfort. Her dysphoric feelings are being caused by a marked tendency to hold in and internalize feelings, excessive self-inspecting behavior that focuses on negative features that she perceives in herself, and a chronic state of loneliness or emotional deprivation.

She is prone to merge feelings with thinking during problem solving or decision making and usually prefers to test postulates through trial-and-error behaviors. There is some flexibility to the style and instances occur in which feelings are put aside in favor of a more clearly ideational approach. She is somewhat less stringent about modulating her emotional displays, which is not a negative finding but can become a liability because of her problems with control. She tries to avoid emotionally provoking situations, probably because she has some awareness of her limited controls.

She harbors a chronic negative, angry attitude toward the environment. The anger may not be manifest overtly, but it has some impact on decision making and coping activities, and on her relationships with others. She is more complex than might be expected in light of her immaturity. Some complexity seems to be related to the fact that she finds emotions confusing and is more ambivalent than is common. Presently, she is experiencing intensely negative and painful emotion, which can often dominate her translation of emotional experiences and can become very pervasive in her thinking.

Self-Perception

The data for the variables that are related to self-perception are shown in Table 81.

Table 81. Self Perception Variables for Case 6

STRUCTURAL DATA		RESPONSES TO BE READ	
$Fr+rF = 0$ $3r+(2)/R = 0.35$		*MOR* RESPONSES	= 1
$FD = 0$ $V = 2$		MINUS RESPONSES	= NA
$HH)+Hd+(Hd) = 2 : 0$		*M* RESPONSES	= 2, 12
$An+Xy = 0$		*FM* RESPONSES	= 3, 8, 17
MOR = 1		*m* RESPONSES	= 17

Case 6 Findings   All data, except Steps 1 $(Fr + rf)$, 5 $(An + Xy)$, 6 (frequency of MOR), and 8 (minus responses), are relevant to the interpretation.

The Egocentricity Index suggests that she does not regard herself any more or less favorably than others. Conversely, the presence of the two *Vista* answers indicates that she engages in considerable introspection that focuses on her negative features. These findings may seem contradictory but, if taken literally, they are not. The *Vista* responses suggest that she perceives herself negatively, and the Egocentricity Index suggests that she regards herself as favorably as others; thus, she probably perceives others as also having negative features. If this is true, it tends to bode poorly for her interpersonal relationships.

Both of her human responses are Pure *H,* implying that her self-concept is based more on experience than imagination. The single MOR answer is the first response ("a cut up butterfly"), which is negative and carries the implication that the damage was done by someone else (cut up).

The contents of the movement answers do not contain much directly projected material (2. "a woman standing in a negligee . . . her hands are up like this," 3. "two bears . . . like they are standing there with red paint all over them . . . I don't know if they got into it or if somebody threw it on them," 8. "an ugly moth flying around," 12. "Two little Indian boys jumping up and down," 17. "flowers sort of opening up . . . worms like they are crawling around"). The first of the two *M* answers suggests a sense of vulnerability, and the first of the three *FM* responses seems to raise a question: "Is this my fault?" The content for Response 8, ugly, is clearly negative, but the content for Response 17, opening up, tends to be more positive. Overall, the contents are not remarkably enlightening regarding her self-image. It appears to be more negative than positive and she seems to feel quite vulnerable. It is also possible that she is somewhat preoccupied with the origins of her negative sense of self, but this is quite speculative.

Case 6 Summary   The subject does not regard herself any more or less favorably than others, yet she engages in much self-examining behavior that focuses on her perceived negative features. It seems possible that she also perceives others as having negative features which, if true, does not portend well for her interpersonal relationships. Her self-concept seems to have some experiential basis and there is a hint that she may attribute her negative status to the actions of others. The trauma of her abortion may have some importance in this respect. She seems to harbor a sense of vulnerability that probably has a relationship to her perceived negative features. Although her self-image is more negative than positive, there may be a glimmer of some optimism concerning a better status for the future. ✓

Interpersonal Perception and Behavior

The data for this cluster are especially important because of the positive CDI and the finding from the self-perception cluster that she may perceive others as negatively as she perceives herself. The data for the variables concerning interpersonal perception are shown in Table 82.

Case 6 Findings   The data for Steps 1 (CDI), 5 (T), 6 (number of human contents), 7 (COP and AG), 8 (Isolation Index), 9 (evaluation of movement answers containing a pair), and 10 (human content responses) are relevant to the interpretation.

The positive CDI has already prompted a postulate that her interpersonal relationships probably are impoverished and unrewarding. That notion seems clearly supported by some of the other data. The elevation in T signals a strong sense of emotional deprivation and loneliness. If the history is accurate, this appears to be a chronic problem that is very serious, not so much because of the loneliness, but because of the limited probability that it can be resolved easily. The record contains only two human contents and no COP or AG answers, which suggests that she has little interest in people and probably does not anticipate much interaction, either positive or negative, among people as a routine event. People such as this tend to feel less comfortable in group situations and are often regarded by others as more distant or aloof. The positive Isolation Index adds to the already bleak picture. She is less involved in social interaction than are most people. There are only three movement answers containing a pair (3. "two bears . . . standing there with red paint all over them," 12. "Two little Indian boys jumping up and down," 17. "flowers sort of opening up . . . worms like they're crawling around"). Only one (Indian boys) is animated, but there is no clear interaction. This is also one of only two human contents. The other ("a woman standing in a negligee . . . you don't see her head very clear . . . it's transparent") suggests a passive and insecure kind of isolation.

Case 6 Summary   She lives in a very impoverished and unrewarding interpersonal world. She has a strong sense of emotional deprivation and loneliness, which is very serious because she seems unable to deal directly with it. Her own

Table 82.   Interpersonal Perception Variables for Case 6

STRUCTURAL VARIABLES		RESPONSES TO BE READ
CDI = 4 HVI = Neg		MOVEMENT WITH PAIR = 3, 12, 17
$a{:}p$ = 3:3 T = 2 Fd = 0		HUMAN CONTENTS = 2, 12
Isolate/R = 0.29		
Total Human Contents = 2		
PER = 1 COP = 0 AG = 0		

interpersonal skills probably are not very well developed and, as a result, she has become less and less interested in people and seems to anticipate little more than superficial interaction with them. She is probably uncomfortable and/or confused in group situations and is likely to be regarded by others as cool and aloof. She seems to be less involved in social interaction than most people and probably has little understanding about how to create and sustain meaningful relationships. In effect, she seems to be a socially inept person who interacts with her world only on a superficial level and, as a result, suffers the torment of her own isolation.

Information Processing

Data for the variables related to processing activity are shown in Table 83.

Table 83.   Information Processing Variables for Case 6

$L = 0.55$	OBS = Neg	HVI = Neg	LOCATION SEQUENCING			
$Zd = +4.0$	$DQ+$ = 6		I W,D	IV W	VII W	
$Zf = 12$	$DQv/+$ = 1		II W,D	V W,W	VIII WS,D	
$W{:}D{:}Dd = 11{:}6{:}0$	DQv = 0		III W,D	VI D,W	IX W	
$W{:}M = 11{:}2$	PSV = 0				X D,W	

Case 6 Findings   All data, except Steps 1 (Lambda) and 2 (OBS and HVI), are relevant to the interpretation.

The composite data for Zf, $W{:}D{:}Dd$, and $W{:}M$ indicate that she is highly motivated and makes a considerable effort in processing information. In fact, the $W{:}M$ ratio suggests that her aspirations may sometimes exceed her capacities and this can lead to faulty processing. Actually, the data for the DQ distribution suggest that, generally, the quality of processing is similar to that of most other people. The Zd signals the presence of an overincorporative style, and indicates that she invests considerably more effort and energy in scanning activities. Although somewhat less efficient because of the added effort involved, the style is often an asset, because the cautious, thorough approach to scanning usually ensures that all stimulus cues are included in the input.

Case 6 Summary   The subject makes a strong effort to process new information and generally does so adequately. At times her aspirations may exceed some of her capacities, which can breed faulty processing, but the likelihood of this occurring is reduced considerably by the fact that she invests considerable effort and energy in scanning activity.

Cognitive Mediation

Data for the variables related to mediation are shown in Table 84.

Case 6 Findings   The data for Steps 3 (P), 5 ($X+\%$), 7 ($Xu\%$), and 8 ($X-\%$) are relevant to the interpretation.

Table 84.   Cognitive Mediation Variables for Case 6

$Lambda = 0.55$	OBS $=$ Negative	MINUS FEATURES
$P \quad = 6$	$X+\% = .82$	NOT APPLICABLE
$FQx+ = 0$	$F+\% = .67$	
$FQxo = 14$	$Xu\% = .18$	
$FQxu = 3$	$X-\% = 0$	
$FQx- = 0$	$S-\% = 0$	
$FQnone = 0$	CONFAB $= 0$	

The number of Popular responses is average, indicating that she translates stimuli conventionally when cues concerning expected or acceptable responses are obvious. The finding for the $X+\%$ is more important. It is well into the average range and signifies that, generally, she is oriented toward making conventional translations or responses. The $Xu\%$ is also average, indicating that idiosyncratic features occur in her mediational activity about as often as for most people. There are no minus responses in the record, which is a very favorable finding and can be quite important to treatment considerations.

Case 6 Summary   Overall, the subject's mediational activity is very similar to that of many nonpatients. She is oriented toward conventionality most of the time and incorporates her own idiographic features into her translations and behaviors no more than do most adults.

Ideation

The data for the variables related to ideation are shown in Table 85.

Case 6 Findings   Data from Steps 1 (*EB*), 2 (*EBPer*), 8 (number of Critical Special Scores), 9 (quality of Critical Special Scores), 10 (*M* form quality), and 12 (quality of human movement responses) are most relevant to the interpretation.

As noted earlier, the *EB* indicates that she often merges her feelings with her thinking, and they become influential in most of her decision making. Nonetheless, there is some flexibility to this coping style and she sometimes keeps her feelings at a more peripheral level while evaluating the potential merits of various responses. This can be a very useful coping style, especially if there are no significant problems in thinking or in emotional control. She does have some control problems, however, which can reduce the overall effectiveness of the style. Nonetheless, the record contains only one Critical Special Score, an INCOM, but examination reveals that it is a very minor slip (antennae) that is common among many people. The two *M* answers have *ordinary* form quality and, although not very sophisticated, reflect clear and reasonably logical thought.

Table 85. Ideation Variables for Case 6

$EB = 2 : 4.0$	$EBPer = 2.0$	M QUALITY		CRITICAL SPECIAL SCORES			
$eb = 4 : 7$	$(FM = 3 \; m = 1)$	$+ = 0$		DV	$= 0$	DV2	$= 0$
$a{:}p = 3 : 3$	$Ma{:}Mp = 1 : 1$	$o = 2$		INC	$= 1$	INC2	$= 0$
$2Ab+(Art+Ay) = 3$		$u = 0$		DR	$= 0$	DR2	$= 0$
MOR $= 1$		$- = 0$		FAB	$= 0$	FAB2	$= 0$
RESPONSES TO BE READ FOR QUALITY				ALOG	$= 0$	SUM6	$= 1$
2, 12				CON	$= 0$	WSUM6	$= 2$

Case 6 Summary   The subject's thinking appears to be clear and reasonably consistent. Her feelings often become quite influential in her thinking and, because many of her feelings currently are negative, this can create a gloomier attitude than might be desired. Nevertheless, no evidence suggests that those feelings are leading to peculiarities in her thinking, and her judgment seems reasonably logical.

Case 6 Final Description

This 33-year-old female is in a chronic state of stimulus overload that reduces her capacity for control and creates a potential for impulsiveness. Some of her decisions are not well thought out or implemented, and she can become easily disorganized under stress. The overload occurs because she has fewer resources available than most adults and cannot contend with the level of internal stimulation that she experiences, much of which takes the form of irritating emotion. But, even if she were relieved of some of that aggravation she would remain vulnerable to disorganization because of her limited resources. This is because she is less mature than might be expected. People such as this often have difficulty functioning effectively unless they are in familiar environments in which demands and expectations are predictable.

She is prone to frequent and reasonably intense experiences of depression and evidence confirms the presence of considerable distress or discomfort. Her dysphoric feelings are being caused by a marked tendency to hold in feelings, excessive self-inspecting behavior that focuses on negative features that she perceives in herself, and a chronic state of emotional deprivation that probably translates as loneliness.

She is the kind of person who is prone to merge feelings with thinking during problem solving or decision making and usually prefers to test postulates through trial-and-error behaviors. There is some flexibility to the style and she sometimes puts aside feelings in favor of a more clearly ideational approach. She is not as concerned as others about modulating her emotional displays. This is not a negative finding, but it can become a liability because of her problems with control. She tries to avoid emotionally provoking situations, probably because she has some awareness of her limited controls.

She harbors a chronic angry attitude toward the world. The anger may not be manifest overtly, but it has some impact on decision making and coping activities, and on her relationships with others. She finds emotions confusing and experiences considerable ambivalence. Currently, she feels a great deal of negative and painful emotion that tends to be very pervasive in her thinking.

She does not regard herself any more or less favorably than others, yet she engages in much rumination about her own negative features. It is possible that she attributes her negative status to the actions of others. The trauma of her abortion may have some importance in this respect. She seems to feel vulnerable because of her negative features, but also appears to harbor some optimism concerning a better future.

One of the most important findings concerns her interpersonal world, which seems very impoverished and unrewarding. This makes her long-standing sense of emotional deprivation and loneliness more serious because she is unable to deal directly with it. Her interpersonal skills probably are not very well developed and as a result, she has become less and less interested in people and seems to anticipate little more than superficial interaction with them. She is probably uncomfortable and/or confused in group situations and is likely to be regarded by others as cool and aloof. In effect, she seems to be a socially inept person who interacts with her world only on a superficial level and, as a result, suffers the torment of her own isolation.

Her cognitive operations are her greatest asset. She makes a strong effort to process new information and generally does so adequately. At times, her aspirations may exceed some of her capacities, which can breed faulty processing, but the likelihood of this occurring is reduced considerably by the fact that she invests considerable effort and energy into scanning activity. Most of her translations of inputs are very similar to those of nonpatients. She is oriented toward being conventional but, like most adults, incorporates her own ideographic features into her translations and behaviors from time to time. Her thinking seems to be clear and reasonably consistent. As noted earlier, her feelings usually are quite influential in her thinking and, because many of her feelings currently are negative, this can create a gloomier attitude than might be desired. Nevertheless, no evidence suggests that those feelings are leading to peculiarities in her thinking, and her judgment seems reasonably logical.

Recommendations Based on the Final Description

A diagnosis of dysthymic disorder is not inappropriate, but the underlying condition is much more important. Her personality is marked by considerable inadequacy and immaturity, and many might consider an Axis II diagnosis of borderline personality disorder as appropriate. Whatever the diagnosis, treatment should not focus simply on her mood problems. Intervention should follow a developmental model that, at the outset, converges on three interrelated issues: (1) the formation of more effective social skills and the implementation of those skills in ways that will reduce her loneliness without causing her to be manipulated by others, (2) the identification and/or development of more resources in ways that will make them readily accessible to her, and (3) the emergence of a more definitive and realistic self-image.

She has numerous assets for treatment. Her loneliness and current misery should facilitate the necessary therapeutic working relationship. Her cognitive operations are commendable. She processes quite well and has an overincorporative style. She translates in very conventional ways and is oriented toward acceptable responses, and her thinking, even though influenced by her misery, is reasonably clear. Finally, she has an established coping style that can be quite useful, especially because it orients her toward a trial-and-error testing of her decisions. A group process could be quite advantageous as a supplement to individual treatment once some initial progress has been experienced.

Case 6 Epilogue This subject entered individual treatment with a male therapist whom she saw twice a week. During the first two months of the treatment issues such as her continued rumination concerning suicide, her occupational discontent, and her detachment from her family consumed much time. However, beginning in the third month she began to explore various avenues for expanding her social contacts and in the fourth month joined in a women's group, led by a female therapist. She continued in treatment for approximately 15 months during which time her social activities increased considerably. She began dating regularly although with no one person, and became active in a bowling league sponsored by the firm for which she continued to work. Her reported sense of well being improved substantially.

REFERENCES

Abramson, L. Y., Metalsky, G. I., and Alloy, L. B. (1989). Hopelessness Depression: A theory based sub-type of depression. *Psychological Review, 96,* 358–372.

Beck, A. T. (1967). *Depression: Clinical, experimental and theoretical aspects.* New York: Harper & Row.

Blatt, S. J., Quinlan, D. M., Chevron, E. S., McDonald, C., and Zuroff, D. (1982). Dependency and self criticism: Psychological dimensions of depression. *Journal of Consulting and Clinical Psychology, 50,* 113–124.

Brown, G. W., and Harris, T. (1978). *Social origins of depression.* New York: Free Press.

Chadoff, P. (1974). The depressive personality: A critical review. In R. J. Friedman and M. M. Katz (Eds.), *The psychology of depression.* Washington, DC: Winston.

Free, M. L., and Oei, T. P. S. (1989). Biological and psychological processes in the treatment and maintenance of depression. *Clinical Psychology Review, 9,* 653–668.

Kendell, R. E. (1976). The classification of depression: A review of contemporary confusion. *British Journal of Psychiatry, 129,* 15–28.

McLean, P. D., and Hakistan, A. R. (1990). Relative endurance of unipolar depression treatment effects: A longitudinal follow-up. *Journal of Consulting and Clinical Psychology, 58,* 482–488.

Millon, T., and Kotik, D. (1985). The relationship of depression to disorders of the personality. In E. E. Beckham and W. R. Leber (Eds.), *Handbook of depression: Treatment, assessment and research.* Homewood, IL: Dorsey Press.

Seligman, M. E. P. (1975). *Helplessness: On depression, development and death.* San Francisco: Freeman.

Wiener, M. (1989). Psychopathology reconsidered: Depressions interpreted as psychosocial transactions. *Clinical Psychology Review, 9,* 295–321.

CHAPTER 13

Severe Reactive Conditions

Circumstances that promote negative feelings and psychological chaos are extremely varied, and the magnitude of the disruption also varies enormously from one person to another, even though there is a shared etiology for the experience. Stresses or traumas that prompt mild irritation for one person can become extremely distressing or even psychosis provoking for another. Similarly, the time frame for the recovery from distress, depression, or disorganization differs considerably among people. Whereas some are quite resilient, others tend to become trapped in their own agony, and, as a result, their behaviors and overall adjustment become affected very significantly. The differences among people are created by many elements, both internal and external, and altogether are not well understood.

Sometimes the reactions to stress manifest in ways that resemble more chronic conditions. The similarity frequently raises questions about appropriate treatment. Thus, the issue of differentiating chronic from reactive conditions can be quite important. As noted in Case 1, the difference between the D Score and the Adj D Score often provides important information concerning the presence of situationally-related stress; but in other instances that difference does not exist or, if it does exist, it might plausibly be attributed to the trauma associated with the ongoing disorganization. The following cases fall into this category. In both, a severe disruption followed a clearly terrorizing event and manifested in ways that raised questions about some latent predisposition to a serious disturbance that simply had been triggered by the event.

CASE 7: REACTIVE PSYCHOSIS

This 23-year-old female was tested 12 days after an involuntary admission to a public psychiatric facility. Initially, she had been admitted to a general medical facility by her parents' family physician following a two-day episode of chaotic behavior during which she seemed very disoriented and probably hallucinatory. She was transferred to the psychiatric unit the next day. On admission, she identified herself correctly, but was disoriented for time and place. Shortly thereafter, she became very withdrawn and nontalkative. On the fifth day after admission (the sixth day of hospitalization), she began to carry on limited conversations with staff and ate willingly, and the sedative that had been prescribed for her was discontinued. Shortly thereafter, she became cooperative with hospital staff and participated willingly in interviews. On the seventh day following admission, she signed herself to a voluntary status, but only after clear assurance that she could leave the hospital of her own accord at any time.

She had been living with her father and mother, both age 48, for the past three months following her release from a general medical hospital. That admission resulted from an automobile accident in which her husband of two years was seriously injured and remains comatose. He has been declared brain dead, and is being sustained on life support systems. The accident occurred following the wedding reception of a close friend for whom the husband served as best man. According to witnesses and the subject, both she and her husband consumed large quantities of wine and also used cocaine. When they prepared to leave the reception, an argument ensued about who would drive. A friend offered to drive them home or to call a taxi, but the husband refused and the couple left together in their own car.

The subject states that her husband did not seem to be driving badly, but, approximately three miles from the wedding reception, he crossed the center line of the road and had a head-on collision with a delivery van. The driver of the delivery van was killed. The subject was wearing a seatbelt and, although the car was badly demolished, she suffered only fractures of the left arm and ankle and minor abrasions. Her parents have cared for her since the accident. Both fractures have healed satisfactorily, and casts have been removed. She returned to work three weeks ago and has visited her husband's bedside daily during the past month. According to her parents, her grief has been intense and obvious.

Her father, a highway maintenance supervisor, expresses disbelief at her breakdown. He states that she has "held up" very well through this trying situation and finds her current state difficult to understand. Her mother, a housewife, attributes her daughter's condition to some sort of head injury suffered during the accident. Neurological and neuropsychological evaluations conducted two days prior to the personality assessment yielded no positive findings. A review of medical records concerning her hospitalization following the accident tends to support these findings.

The subject, the older of two children, has a sister, age 19, who is a freshman at a state university. According to the subject and her parents, the family was always "close," and both parents describe the subject as a lively, independent person. Her mother describes a normal developmental history. The subject began menstruation late in her 12th year and reports no problems related to it. Her academic grades in both elementary and high school were above average. She was a cheerleader in high school, was a member of the school choir, and was active in a social services club involved in soliciting funds for meals for the elderly. After high school, she decided against entering a university and completed a one-year secretarial course in a local business college. Her grades there were A's and B's. On completing that course, she obtained a position as a receptionist-secretary in a law firm and, after one year, was selected to be a personal secretary for two attorneys. She continues to hold that position.

She and her husband were classmates in high school, although they dated only occasionally. According to the subject, she dated "many" fellows during her four years of high school and admits to her first sexual experience at age 16. She reports that it was disappointing because "he was awfully gross, and I guess I wasn't ready." During the next two years, she had sexual relationships with at least four other men and reports experiencing her first orgasm during her senior year in a relationship with her husband-to-be. They began dating regularly

Case 7: A 23-Year-Old Female

Card	Response	Inquiry
I	1. I dk, mayb two birds r flyg off with a carcass of ss, I dk, prob a cow or horse	E: (Rpts S's resp) S: It ll lik a bird on each side & thyr pickg up ths dead thg in the cntr, it ll a carcus of som A, lik a cow or a horse, I guess a cow E: I'm not sur I'm seeg it rite, help me S: There's a bird on each side, c the wgs r out lik birds get when thy pick on smthg or thyr ready to fly w it lik these, ths is their body E: And the carcus? S: It's smthg dead, I thot of a cow bec of the horns on top & it's pretty fat too lik a cow
	2. It cb a face too, it must b a wolf	E: (Rpts S's resp) S: Well, it has the big ears & the eyes (S) and mouth is curled up lik it's growling, wolves r always growling E: U said it must be a wolf? S: Yeah, lik I said wolves r always growling, thts why I said a wolf
II	3. Some A's r fiting & thyr both hurt, pretty bad	E: (Rpts S's resp) S: Thy cb bears I guess, thyr big enuff to b, but thyv got blood all over, on their feet & on their heads, I don't thk either one will live, it's gory E: I'm not sur wht makes them ll bears? S: I guess thy just ll bears, u cld c them better but all ths red, ths bld covers their faces
III	4. Ths one's gory too, it ll a cpl skeletons, lik thyr dancing around some pot, lik thy killed smthg	E: (Rpts S's resp) S: There's one on each side, lik thyr dancing around this pot tht thy cooking som poor A tht thy killed, c all the blood around them E: Wht maks them ll skeletons? S: Thyr all thin, bony lookg, lik skeletons E: And the blood? S: All ths red, it's blood & ths is the pot
IV	5. Thts ugly, sk of monster, mayb a gorilla, yes thts it	E: (Rpts S's resp) S: It's big, huge, lik I'm layg under it lookg up,' it has big feet & its, . . . I dk, all fur w a littl head, mayb its sittg on smthg E: U said all fur? S: It's all dark lik fur, lik gorilla's hav E: U said it's sittg on smthg? S: Lik a stool I guess, no a stump of a tree, yeah a tree stump

6. I suppose it cb one of thos Darth Vader masks too

E: (Rpts S's resp)
S: It has those thgs tht come dwn around the ears, lik flaps & ths straight piece over the mouth and it's black . . . my husband really liked those movies (cries) . . . cld we stop
E: Take u'r time we're in no hurry (the subject stood for about a minute and then)
S: Ok, I'm ok

V 7. A moth, trying to keep away from the flame

E: (Rpts S's resp)
S: U can't really c the flame, jst the moth flyg upward
E: I'm not sur what makes it ll a moth
S: It's dreary lookg, grey, its got it's wgs stretched out lik it was flyg upward lik thy do when thyr too near a light or flame

8. It cb 2 people too, thyv fallen asleep, leaning on each othr

E: (Rpts S's resp)
S: Thy just hav their legs sprawled out in frnt of them & their head r kind of bent ovr lik thyr sleeping, propped up against each other, c the leg here & these r the heads

VI 9. Tht's strange, it's lik a crucifix, a medal like u wear

E: (Rpts S's resp)
S: Just the top, it ll a crucifix, its elaborate showing Christ's body & it has a sunburst design, u can c the darker outline of the body, lik a human, lik the Turin cross, all dark lik tht, imprinted on the cross

v10. Ths way it ll a cat tht got run over by a car or truck

E: (Rpts S's resp)
S: It's all flattened out, like it was run over by a car or smthg, u can still c the head & the whiskers & I guess these wld b the legs all flattened & the rest is just a furry mess
E: Furry mess?
S: It just looks lik fur, all the lines & dots lik the fur of a cat

VII v11. Ugh, it sorta ll bones

E: (Rpts S's resp)
S: Just smthg lik bones, thy seem connected but I can't tell very much about them, maybe it's lik one piece of the rib cage of a big A, lik if u go to a museum and lik at a dinosar's bone ths is lik tht, sorta lik one huge piece

12. It's better ths way, it ll 2 littl girls going up & dwn on a teeter-totter

E: (Rpts S's resp)
S: It's happy times, thyr playg togethr on the teeter, a see-saw, I used to lov to do tht w my friends when I was littl, u just didn't hav any cares, just had fun
E: I'm not sur I'm seeg it rite, can u help?
S: There's one here (D2) & here, c the nose & their hair is flyg up & dwn here is the teeter

(continued)

347

Case 7: (Continued)

Card	Response	Inquiry
VIII	13. Somethgs been all tore apart, its just insides, lik a carcus	E: (Rpts S's resp) S: It looks horrible, just remains of some poor A, there's ribs & lungs & I guess wht's left of the stomach, part is decayed E: Decayed? S: All the blue, thgs get blue when thy decay, the rest is still bloody but the center is all decayed E: The rest is all bloody? S: Oh God, I dk, it just is, it's colored lik blood, alright!
	v14. It's better ths way, but I dk wht it is, a top, yes, a kid's top	E: (Rpts S's resp) S: Well ths pointed part is wht it spins on, it's round & it's diff colors, it's lik I got my nephew, he's only 3
IX	15. I don't lik ths one, it re me of a woman's insides	E: (Rpts S's resp) S: It's lik the lower parts, the center is the uterus & there's a tube in there, inside of it, & the pink is down around the vagina and the rear, I dk wht the green is, part of the stomach I guess & the orange is nothing, maybe heartburn E: I'm not sur I followed all of tht, the uterus is the center & there's a tube in there and the pink? S: It's pink, lik the vagina is pink & the rear is pink, it's all pink there E: And U said the orange is heartburn? S: I dk, I just said heartburn bec its orange, lik fire, tht's wht hearburn is, all fire in your stomach
X	16. I c 2 littl yellow birds	E: (Rpts S's resp) S: One on each side, thyr just sitting there lik on ths limb here, ths brown part E: Wht maks them ll birds? S: Thy hav tht form, thyr yellow, lik yellow birds
	17. These mite be spiders, blue spiders	E: (Rpts S's resp) S: Thy do, thy hav a lotta legs lik spiders, one on each side, I've always hated spiders but I guess u shouldn't hate anythg cuz it will come home to haunt u. I'm not gonna hate spiders anymore, at least I'll try to lik blue ones
	18. Ths ll a sad rabbit, he's crying, green tears	E: (Rpts S's resp) S: His head, it's rite here (D5), but he's cryg, all this green (D4) is his tears, he's really sad
	v19. Ths way is better, it's a lot of flowers, all diff colors, just scattered	E: (Rpts S's resp) S: Just a lot of flowers, all diff colors but some r wilting, thyr fading, c the pink one's hav diff shades of pink, & dwn here thes r grey already. It's lik smbody just thru them away

348

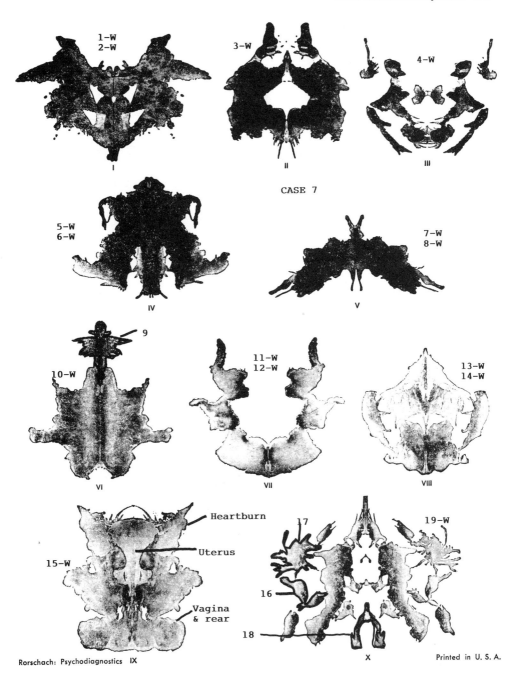

CASE 7

Rorschach: Psychodiagnostics IX

Printed in U. S. A.

CASE 7. SEQUENCE OF SCORES

```
=====================================================================
CARD NO  LOC  #   DETERMINANT(S)    (2)  CONTENT(S)    POP  Z  SPECIAL SCORES
=====================================================================
  I   1  W+   1 FMa-             2   A,Ad              4.0  FAB2,MOR,COP
      2  WSo  1 FMao                 Ad                3.5  AG,ALOG

 II   3  W+   1 FMa.CFo          2   A,Bl              4.5  AG,MOR

III   4  W+   1 Ma.Cu            2   (H),Bl,Hh     P   5.5  COP,MOR,FAB2

 IV   5  W+   1 FD.FT.FMpo           A,Bt          P   4.0
      6  Wo   1 FC'u                 (Hd)              2.0  PER

  V   7  Wo   1 FMa.FC'o             A                 1.0  ALOG
      8  W+   1 Mpo              2   H                 2.5  COP

 VI   9  Do   3 FYo                  Art,(H)                DV
     10  W+   1 FTo                  Ad            P   2.5  MOR

VII  11  Wo   1 Fu                   An,Ay             2.5
     12  W+   1 Ma.mpo           2   H,Sc          P   2.5  COP,PER

VIII 13  Wo   1 CF-                  An,Bl             4.5  MOR
     14  Wo   1 FCu                  Sc                4.5  PER

 IX  15  Wo   1 FD.CF.Mp-            An,Hx,Sx          5.5  DR,MOR

  X  16  D+  15 FC.FMpo          2   A,Bt              4.0
     17  Do   1 FCo              2   A             P        INC,DR
     18  D+  10 Mp.FC-               Ad,Hx,Id          4.0  FAB2,MOR
     19  Wv   1 CF.YF.C'Fo           Bt                     MOR
=====================================================================
```

CASE 7. STRUCTURAL SUMMARY

```
==================================================================================
    LOCATION              DETERMINANTS                    CONTENTS        S-CONSTELLATION
    FEATURES           BLENDS         SINGLE                              NO..FV+VF+V+FD>2
                                                  H    = 2, 0            YES..Col-Shd Bl>0
    Zf    = 16      FM.CF          M   = 1        (H)  = 1, 1            NO..Ego<.31,>.44
    ZSum  = 57.0    M.C            FM  = 2        Hd   = 0, 0            YES..MOR > 3
    ZEst  = 52.5    FD.FT.FM       m   = 0        (Hd) = 1, 0            NO..Zd > +- 3.5
                    FM.FC'         FC  = 2        Hx   = 0, 2            YES..es > EA
    W     = 15      M.m            CF  = 1        A    = 6, 0            YES..CF+C > FC
     (Wv = 1)       FD.CF.M        C   = 0        (A)  = 0, 0            YES..X+% < .70
    D     = 4       FC.FM          Cn  = 0        Ad   = 3, 1            NO..S > 3
    Dd    = 0       CF.YF.C'F      FC' = 1        (Ad) = 0, 0            NO..P < 3 or > 8
    S     = 1                      C'F = 0        An   = 3, 0            NO..Pure H < 2
                                   C'  = 0        Art  = 1, 0            NO..R < 17
      DQ                           FT  = 1        Ay   = 0, 1            5.....TOTAL
   .........(FQ-)                  TF  = 0        Bl   = 0, 3
    +  =  9  ( 2)                  T   = 0        Bt   = 1, 2            SPECIAL SCORINGS
    o  =  9  ( 2)                  FV  = 0        Cg   = 0, 0              Lv1    Lv2
    v/+ = 0  ( 0)                  VF  = 0        Cl   = 0, 0      DV  =  1x1    0x2
    v  =  1  ( 0)                  V   = 0        Ex   = 0, 0      INC =  1x2    0x4
                                   FY  = 1        Fd   = 0, 0      DR  =  2x3    0x6
                                   YF  = 0        Fi   = 0, 0      FAB =  0x4    3x7
                                   Y   = 0        Ge   = 0, 0      ALOG=  2x5
      FORM QUALITY                 Fr  = 0        Hh   = 0, 1      CON =  0x7
                                   rF  = 0        Ls   = 0, 0       SUM6  = 9
       FQx  FQf  MQual  SQx        FD  = 0        Na   = 0, 0       WSUM6 = 40
    +  = 0    0    0     0         F   = 1        Sc   = 1, 1
    o  = 11   0    2     1                        Sx   = 0, 1      AB = 0     CP  = 0
    u  = 4    1    1     0                        Xy   = 0, 0      AG = 2     MOR = 8
    -  = 4    0    2     0                        Id   = 0, 1      CFB= 0     PER = 3
  none= 0    --    0     0         (2) = 7                         COP= 4     PSV = 0
==================================================================================
                    RATIOS, PERCENTAGES, AND DERIVATIONS

    R = 19          L =  0.06          FC:CF+C = 4: 5     COP = 4     AG = 2
   ----------------------------------  Pure C  =    1     Food        = 0
    EB = 5: 7.5  EA = 12.5  EBPer= 1.5 Afr     =0.58      Isolate/R  =0.16
    eb = 7: 7    es = 14      D  = 0   S       =   1      H:(H)Hd(Hd)= 2: 3
                Adj es = 13  Adj D = 0 Blends:R= 9:19     (HHd):(AAd)= 3: 0
   ----------------------------------  CP      =  0       H+A:Hd+Ad  =10: 6
    FM = 6 :  C'= 3   T = 2
    m  = 1 :  V = 0   Y = 2              P   = 4        Zf  =16       3r+(2)/R=0.37
                                         X+% =0.58      Zd  = +4.5    Fr+rF   = 0
    a:p   = 6: 6   Sum6  = 9   F+% =0.00      W:D:Dd =15: 4: 0  FD      = 2
    Ma:Mp = 2: 3   Lv2   = 3   X-% =0.21           W:M =15: 5    An+Xy   = 3
    2AB+Art+Ay= 2  WSum6 = 40  X-% =0.21           DQ+ =10       MOR     = 8
    M-    = 2      Mnone = 0   S-% =0.00      DQv = 1
                               Xu% =0.21
   ---------------------------------------------------------------------------
     SCZI = 5*    DEPI = 3    CDI = 1    S-CON = 5    HVI = No    OBS = No
==================================================================================
```

following high school and considered the possibility of living together, but she declined, assuming that her parents would object too strenuously. They became engaged a few months before she completed her business school course and married shortly after she took her job with the law firm. Her husband also had decided against college and accepted a position in a firm manufacturing canned food products. He had done well in that position and had been promoted twice, ultimately becoming an assistant foreman, overseeing an assembly line.

The subject is puzzled by her psychotic-like behavior. She denies any abuse of alcohol or drugs, although she admits that she and her husband have used cocaine on several occasions, including the wedding reception. She hints at agreement with her mother's postulate that she may have experienced some hidden head injury. She expects to be discharged shortly, but also admits that she is unwilling to sign herself out until she feels assured that this will not happen again.

The assessment is part of a routine procedure. Several staff members have been impressed by the lack of clarity in her thinking and her tendency to become detached during interviews or conversations. Thus, the issue of early schizophrenia has been raised in the referral.

The Interpretive Strategy

There is no reason to question the interpretive usefulness of the protocol as it contains 19 responses. The first positive Key variable is the SCZI. Thus, the search strategy will be:

IDEATION → MEDIATION → PROCESSING → CONTROLS → AFFECT → SELF-PERCEPTION → INTERPERSONAL PERCEPTION.

Initial Proposition   The SCZI value is 5, which signals a strong probability of the presence of schizophrenia or a schizophreniform disorder.

Ideation

Data for the cluster of variables related to ideation are shown in Table 86.

Table 86.   Ideation Variables for Case 7

$EB = 5:7.5$	$EBPer = 1.5$	*M* QUALITY	CRITICAL SPECIAL SCORES			
$eb = 7:7$	$(FM = 6\ m = 1)$	$+ = 0$	DV $= 1$		DV2 $= 0$	
$a:p = 6:6$	$Ma:Mp = 2:3$	$o = 2$	INC $= 1$		INC2 $= 0$	
$2Ab+(Art+Ay) = 2$		$u = 1$	DR $= 2$		DR2 $= 0$	
MOR $= 8$		$- = 2$	FAB $= 0$		FAB2 $= 3$	
RESPONSES TO BE READ FOR QUALITY			ALOG $= 2$		SUM6 $= 9$	
4, 8, 12, 15, 18			CON $= 0$		WSUM6 $= 40$	

Case 7 Findings   The important findings from this cluster are found in the review of Steps 1 (*EB*), 2 (*EBPer*), 3 (left-side *eb*), 5 ($M^a:M^p$), 7 (MOR), 8 (sum of Critical Special Scores), 9 (evaluation of Critical Special Scores), 10 (*M*– frequency), 11 (characteristics of *M*– responses), and 12 (quality of *M* answers).

The subject's *EB* and *EBPer* indicate that she usually is prone to merge her feelings into her thinking when making decisions. In most situations, she prefers a trial-and-error approach and relies extensively on feedback from her actions. However, there is some flexibility to this style and, at times, she pushes emotion to a more peripheral level and relies more on an internal evaluation of various alternatives before forming behaviors. Regardless of which approach she uses, some problems are likely to occur for two reasons. First, the left-side *eb* value suggests that her ideational world is marked by more peripheral, potentially distracting thought than is common for most people. Part of this may be related to situational stress, but most is provoked by her own experience of unmet needs. Second, the $M^a:M^p$ data reveal that she tends to slip into fantasy more often than should be the case. This permits her to avoid the harshness of reality, but she also fails to deal with reality and, as a result, some of her decision making could be very faulty. Another, much more serious problem in her current thinking is evidenced by the presence of eight MOR responses. She is very pessimistic. She anticipates negative outcomes as the result of her actions and may often misread stimuli because of this set.

The most serious problem is indicated by the presence of nine Critical Special Scores, having a weighted sum of 40. Her thinking is strange and disordered. The fact that three of the responses are FAB2 answers suggests that, at times, she makes very irrational and bizarre associations. A review of the content of these responses confirms this (1. "birds are flying off with the carcass of . . . a cow or horse," 4. "skeletons . . . dancing around a pot," 18. "a sad rabbit . . . crying, green tears"). The two ALOG answers suggest that her judgment often becomes more concrete than should be the case, although neither is a serious or bizarre ALOG response (2. "wolves are always growling, that's why I said a wolf," 7. "flying upward like they do when they are too near a light or flame"). The contents of the two *M*– answers hint that some of her peculiar thinking may be related to considerable emotional pain, (heartburn, a sad rabbit crying green tears). In spite of the bizarreness that marks her thinking, the quality of *M* answers does not afford any evidence to suggest that her ideation is primitive or juvenile. In fact, sometimes it is reasonably sophisticated (4. skeletons dancing around a pot, 8. people fallen asleep leaning on each other, 12. little girls going up and down on a teeter-totter, 15. heartburn, 18. a sad rabbit). Nonetheless, the disordered thinking is very pervasive and not unlike that found among more serious psychiatric disturbances, including schizophrenia.

Case 7 Summary   This is the type of person who usually is prone to merge her feelings into her thinking when in a decision making situation. In most situations, she prefers a trial-and-error approach and relies extensively on feedback from her actions. However, there is some flexibility to this style and, at times, she pushes emotion to a more peripheral level and relies more on an internal evaluation of various alternatives before forming behaviors. Regardless of which approach she uses, some problems are likely to occur. Her ideational world is marked by more peripheral, potentially distracting thought than is common for most people. Most of this is provoked by her own experience of unmet needs. She also tends to slip into fantasy more often than should be the case. This permits her to avoid the harshness of reality but, in doing so, she fails to deal with reality and, as a result, some of her decision making could be very faulty.

A much more serious problem is that her thinking is marked by considerable pessimism. She anticipates negative outcomes as the result of her actions and may often misread stimuli because of this set. The most serious problem is that her thinking is strange and disordered. At times, she makes very irrational and bizarre associations. Her judgment also is sometimes much more concrete than should be the case. On a more positive note, no evidence suggests that her thinking is primitive in spite of the bizarreness that is evident. In fact, sometimes her ideation is reasonably sophisticated. Nonetheless, the disordered thinking is very pervasive and disabling.

Cognitive Mediation

The data for the variables in this cluster are shown in Table 87.

Case 7 Findings   The relevant findings are derived from Steps 3 (P), 5 ($X + \%$), 7 ($Xu\%$), 8 ($X - \%$), 9 (sequence of minus responses), 10 (homogeneity of minus responses), and 11 (levels of distortion).

The lower than average number of Popular responses suggests that she is less prone than others to make conventional responses, even when cues concerning the obvious are readily apparent. In fact, the low $X + \%$ indicates that her tendency to make less conventional translations of stimuli is rather pervasive, regardless of whether obvious cues are present. The values for the $Xu\%$ and $X - \%$ reveal that her unconventional translations reflect a composite of overpersonalizations and distortions. Neither is of sufficient frequency to warrant major concern, but collectively they indicate that many of her behaviors are likely to be more idiosyncratic and/or inappropriate than is typical for the well-adjusted adult.

On a more positive note, the relatively low frequency of minus answers (4) tends to rule out the probability of schizophrenia or a schizophreniform disturbance. Support for this premise is also noted in two additional sources. First,

Table 87.   Cognitive Mediation Variables for Case 7

Lambda = 0.06	OBS = Negative		MINUS FEATURES
P = 4	$X+\% = .58$	I	1. *W+ FMa– 2 A,Ad 4.0 FAB2, MOR, COP*
$FQx+ = 0$	$F+\% = 0$	VIII	13. *Wo CF– An,Bl 4.5 MOR*
$FQxo = 11$	$Xu\% = .21$	IX	15. *Wo FD.CF.Mp– An,Hx,Sx 5.5 DR, MOR*
FQxu = 4	$X–\% = .21$	X	18. *D+ Mp.FC– Ad,Hx,Id 4.0 FAB2, MOR*
$FQx– = 4$	$S–\% = 0$		
$FQnone = 0$	CONFAB = 0		

the sequence of the four minus answers shows that the first, Response 1, is followed by a series of 11 answers across seven cards in which no distortions occur. In fact, eight of the 11 have *ordinary* form quality. Such a sequence is highly unusual in a schizophrenic record. Second, all four minus answers contain morbid content. This is also highly unusual for a schizophrenic record, and leads to the speculation that her tendency to distort probably is stimulated more by affective disruption than by some chronic problem in perceptual accuracy. A similar speculation was generated from reviewing the contents of her *M*– answers during the search through data concerning ideation. Although all of her minus answers are somewhat dramatic by reason of their content, none are Level 2 distortions of the field. In fact, it is intriguing to note that, in at least three of the four answers, the response becomes minus because of something that is added to an otherwise *ordinary* answer. In Response 1, the major features are two birds; the carcass creates the minus. In Response 13, the minus occurs only because specific organs or parts were identified. In Response 18, the major element is the head of a rabbit; the addition of tears causes the minus to be assigned. This pattern seems to highlight her preoccupation and the devastating effects that it is having.

Case 7 Summary She is not as oriented as others to make conventional responses, even when cues concerning the obvious are readily apparent. Actually, this tendency is pervasive, regardless of whether obvious cues are present. It reflects a composite of overpersonalizations and mediational distortions. Although neither occurs so frequently as to warrant major concern, together they form a strong likelihood that many of her behaviors are more idiosyncratic and/ or inappropriate than is typical for the well-adjusted adult. On the other hand, the overall picture concerning mediation tends to be quite different from that found commonly among schizophrenics or in most conditions that fall within the schizophrenia spectrum. In fact, her tendency to distort seems to be stimulated more by affective disruption than by some chronic problem in perceptual accuracy.

Information Processing

The data for the variables related to processing are shown in Table 88.

Case 7 Findings The relevant data are found in Steps 1 (Lambda), 3 (*Zf*, $W:D:Dd$, $W:M$), 4 (*DQ*), 5 (*Zd*), and 6 (Location Sequencing).

Table 88. Information Processing Variables for Case 7

$L = 0.06$	OBS = Neg	HVI = Neg		LOCATION SEQUENCING		
$Zd = +4.5$		$DQ+ = 9$	I W,W	IV W,W	VII W,W
$Zf = 16$		DQv/+ $= 0$	II W	V W,W	VIII W,W
$W{:}D{:}Dd = 15{:}4{:}0$		DQv $= 1$	III W	VI D,W	IX W
$W{:}M = 15{:}5$		PSV $= 0$			X D,D,D,W

The very low Lambda value suggests that she becomes overly immersed in stimulus complexity. It represents a failure to economize that may result from an overincorporative style, but sometimes it is produced because of a disorganization in thinking or a preoccupation with emotion. If the latter is true it becomes a liability because overinvolvement creates many more demands which, in turn, can provoke even more complexity in emotion. This failure to economize is also reflected in her processing effort. The very high Zf, the disproportionate relationship of W to D, and the unusual $3:1$ relationship noted in $W:M$ all signify an effort that is commendable but very unrealistic. People such as this tend to be almost obsessive in their strivings and invariably encounter frustration when they fail to achieve some of their objectives. As the experiences of frustration accumulate, they breed distress and often have the potential for damaging self-esteem.

Actually, the $DQ+$ value suggests that the quality of her processing effort is very good, and the Zd score seems to confirm an overincorporative style. The nature of her processing approach is best illustrated by the location sequence, which shows that in the first 15 answers, only one common detail segment of a blot was used. The remaining 14 answers involve the entire blot. Only in the most broken blot does she falter, giving three common detail answers and then "signing out" with a final whole response that is not well organized.

Case 7 Summary   She seems to become overly involved in her efforts to process stimuli. In doing so, she fails to economize as much as most people. In this case the overinvolvement is probably stylistic; that is, she invests considerably more energy than most people to ensure that all aspects of a field are processed. This style can be very useful, but it can become very detrimental if problems in adjustment exist. People like this set very high goals and invariably encounter frustration when they fail to achieve some of their objectives. As frustrations accumulate distress occurs and can have a negative impact on self-esteem. Actually, the quality of her processing is very good, but evidence points to a fatigue effect which considerably reduces the quality of her processing.

Controls

The data for the variables related to controls and stress tolerance are shown in Table 89.

Case 7 Findings   All data in this cluster are relevant, except those for the D Score and the CDI.

Table 89.   Control-Related Variables for Case 7

$EB = 5:7.5$	$EA = 12.5$	$D = 0$	$CDI = 1$
$eb = 7:7$	$es = 14$ Adj$es = 13$	Adj$D = 0$	
$FM = 6$ $m = 1$ $C' = 3$ $T = 2$ $V = 0$ $Y = 2$			

The Adj D Score indicates that her capacity for control and tolerance for stress are very similar to those of most people, even though the *es* value indicates that she is experiencing many more internally irritating demands than is typical for most people. As noted by the higher than average *EA* value, she has access to considerable resource. The *EB* data provide no source from which to question that conclusion. The very high value for the Adj *es* (13) signals the presence of an unusually intense and apparently chronic experience of irritating internal demands.

The values on both sides of the *eb* provide some insight into the source of these demands. The *FM* value is higher than expected, suggesting that many unmet needs are causing an increase in peripheral ideational activity. The values for *C'* and *T* are also elevated substantially, indicating excessive internalization of feelings and strong unmet needs for closeness. In this case, both may be related to the tragic circumstances concerning her husband. Collectively, the needs states and the emotional aggravation have probably increased her experienced demands considerably and pose a serious challenge to her resources. In fact, should the situationally-related demands continue to intensify, her capacities for control could falter badly.

These findings raise a question about whether her capacity for control might not have been greater in the past. For instance, if only two *FM*'s, one *C'*, and one *T* were subtracted from the Adj *es* on the premise that they may reflect a more accurate picture of preaccident demands, the value for the Adj *es* would be reduced to 9, and the Adj D Score would be +1. However, the flaw in this position is an assumption that the value for *EA* would remain constant, which might not be the case. For instance, it is logical to question whether at least one *M* response (sad rabbit) would have occurred in her preaccident state, and whether either of the blood responses (Cards II and III) would have been given in the same form. If not, the *EA* would be correspondingly lowered and the Adj D Score would still be zero. Thus, it is probably best to conclude that her current controls are adequate even though she is experiencing much more internal demand irritation than is common.

Case 7 Summary   Her capacity for control and tolerance for stress are similar to those of most people. Fortunately, she has considerable resource available and it appears to be sustaining these capacities even though she is experiencing more internal irritation than is common.

Affective Features

Data for the variables related to affective features are shown in Table 90.

Case 7 Findings   The relevant data are found in Steps 1 (*EB*), 2 (*EBPer*), 3 (right-side *eb*), 4 (*FC* : *CF* + *C*), 5 (Pure *C*), 6 (*Afr*), 9 (blends), 11 (blend complexity), 12 (Color-Shading blends), and 13 (Shading blends).

As noted earlier, the subject's *EB* and *EBPer* indicate that she is the type of person who typically merges her feelings with her thinking during decision making. She is trial-and-error oriented, preferring to test decisions. There is some flexibility to this coping style and, in some circumstances, she may take an

Table 90.   Affect-Related Variables for Case 7

				BLENDS		
$EB = 5:7.5$	$EBPer = 1.5$	$DEPI = 3$				
$eb = 7:7$	$(C = 3, T = 2, V = 0, Y = 2)$		M.C	FM.CF	CF.YF.C'F
$FC:CF+C = 4:5$		Pure $C = 1$	M.m	FC.FM	
$Afr = 0.58$		$CP = 0$ M.FC	FM.FC'		
$S = 1$		Col-Shd Bl $= 1$	FD.CF.M	FD.FT.FM	

(handwritten margin notes: "color shading", "shading blends")

opposite approach in which emotions are set aside and possible decisions or behaviors are carefully reviewed before any action occurs. The right-side *eb* data indicate that, currently, she experiences considerable internal emotional aggravation that is provoked mainly from two sources. One is the result of excessively internalized feelings that she might prefer to discharge, and the second is a strong need for closeness that has probably been made more intense because of her recent tragedy.

The *FC:CF + C* ratio suggests that she is less stringent than most adults about controlling the discharge of her emotions. This is not necessarily a negative finding because she has no obvious problems in control but, in many instances, the expression of her feelings may be somewhat more obvious and intense than expected of the average adult. Her single Pure *C* answer (Response 4) of blood has a more primitive quality, yet it is tempered to some extent because of the greater emphasis on two formed objects (skeleton and pot) in the response.

The *Afr* suggests that her interest in processing emotional stimuli seems no different from that of most adults. The presence of nine blend responses suggests that she is a very complex person and there is little reason to suspect that this complexity has been increased inordinately by her present circumstance. The presence of a Color-Shading blend (*CF.YF.C'F*) indicates a sense of confusion about her feelings. This may be situationally-related, but could also be a more chronic feature. This same response includes a Shading blend, signaling the presence of very intense pain that probably is situationally related.

(handwritten margin note: "but only 1 blend of pure shading")

Case 7 Summary
As already noted, she is the type of individual who relies extensively on her feelings during decision making. She prefers a trial-and-error orientation through which she can test out decisions. There is some flexibility to this coping style and, in some circumstances, she may take an opposite approach in which emotions are set aside and possible decisions or behaviors are carefully reviewed before any action occurs. Currently, she is experiencing considerable emotional irritation that results from the internalization of feelings plus a strong need for closeness or experience of loneliness that has probably resulted because of her recent tragedy.

Generally, she is prone to be less cautious about her emotional displays than most adults and, at times, she may become overly intense in some of her emotional behaviors. This is not necessarily a negative finding because she has no obvious problems in control but, in some instances, the expression of her feelings will be more obvious than expected of the average adult. She seems as interested as most adults in processing emotional stimuli. She is a very complex person who seems to have some confusion about her feelings. This may be situation related, but it could also be a more chronic feature. There is no question that she is currently experiencing intense pain that is probably situationally related.

Self-Perception

The data concerning variables related to self-perception are shown in Table 91.

Case 7 Findings   All data in this cluster except Step 1 $(Fr + rF)$ are relevant to the interpretation.

The Egocentricity Index suggests that she is no more or less concerned with herself than are most people and that her self-value tends to be similar to that found among most adults. The *FD* answers suggest that she engages in self-examination somewhat routinely, but not excessively. The number of Pure *H* contents is lower than expected and less than half of the total human contents. Thus, her self-image probably includes more features based on imagination than experience, as contrasted with most adults, although it may be important to note that one of her *(H)* responses (skeletons) might have been Pure *H* if her ideational confusion did not exist. The elevated value for $An + Xy$ suggests some unusual body concern. This could be related to her recent physical injury but it is equally plausible that it reflects a preoccupation with her husband's status.

The most devastating finding concerns the extraordinarily large number of MOR responses. MOR is a relatively stable variable over time but values greater than 5 or 6 are extremely rare. In this case, the high value probably represents negative feelings about herself, as well as a strong sense of damage, but both are likely to have a more situational than chronic base. Certainly, the contents of the MOR responses are commensurate with that postulate (1. "a carcass, it's something dead," 3. "they're both hurt pretty bad . . . I don't think either one will live, it's gory," 4. "some poor animal that they killed, see all the blood around them," 10. "a cat that got run over . . . just a furry mess," 13. "all tore apart . . . like a carcass . . . part is decayed," 15. "maybe heartburn . . . all fire in your stomach," 18. "a sad rabbit, he's crying green tears . . . he's really sad," 19. "flowers . . . just scattered . . . but some are wilting, they're fading").

Table 91. Self Perception Variables for Case 7

STRUCTURAL DATA		RESPONSES TO BE READ	
$Fr+rF = 0$	$3r+(2)/R = 0.37$	*MOR* RESPONSES	$= 1, 3, 4, 10, 13, 15, 18, 19$
$FD = 2$	$V = 0$	MINUS RESPONSES	$= 1, 13, 15, 18$
$HH)+Hd+(Hd) = 2:3$		*M* RESPONSES	$= 4, 8, 12, 15, 18$
$An+Xy = 3$		*FM* RESPONSES	$= 1, 2, 3, 5, 7, 16$
$MOR = 8$		*m* RESPONSES	$= 12$

All but two are marked by death or decay and the remaining two (heartburn and sadness) are both Human Experience (*Hx*) responses. The collective yield of projections in these responses portrays a tormented and miserable sense of the self that seems directly related to her husband's condition. He is brain dead and decaying, and she is torn apart by the experience. In fact, although there are no direct supporting data, it seems very likely that part of her torment and negative view of herself evolve from a series of "if" questions that people invariably ask when a tragedy occurs (if we had taken a taxi, if we had let a friend drive us, if I had been driving, etc.).

The review of the minus responses adds little because all four are also MOR responses. This seems to highlight her preoccupation and the devastating effect that it is having. The review of the movement responses offers a somewhat different view of her self-image. Three of the five *M* answers contain positive features (skeletons dancing around some pot; people, fallen asleep, leaning on each other; little girls going up and down on a teeter-totter). Similarly, three of the six *FM* answers are not really negative (a gorilla sitting on a stump, a moth trying to keep away from the flame, little yellow birds sitting on a limb). Instead, they hint at a sense of fragility or passivity. The *m* response (hair flying up) is associated with the positive *M* response. This is not to suggest that her self-image is really positive, or that it is not damaged, but the composite does hint at remnants of a more favorable view of the self.

Case 7 Summary   A firm and reliable picture of the self-image of this woman is difficult to generate because so much of it appears to have been sharply impacted by her ongoing tragedy. Historically, it seems that she has been no more or less concerned with herself than most people and that her self-value has been similar to that of most adults. She seems prone to engage in self-examination somewhat routinely, but not excessively. It is possible that her self-image includes more features based on imagination than experience, but this may be a misleading conclusion. She has substantial body concern, but this could be related to her recent physical injury or a preoccupation with her husband's current status.

The most devastating finding concerns very negative feelings about herself as well as a strong sense of damage. Both are likely to have a more situational than chronic basis. A tormented and miserable sense of the self is portrayed. It seems very doubtful that this has been a chronic feature. Rather, it seems to depict her current state of preoccupation and the devastating effects that it is having. Some of the findings do hint at a much more favorable self-image in the past, but they are difficult to sort out from the intensely negative sense of the self that appears to exist now.

Interpersonal Perception and Behavior

The data related to variables in the cluster are shown in Table 92.

Case 7 Findings   The relevant data from this cluster are found in Steps 5 (*T*), 6 (total human contents), 7 (PER), 8 (COP and AG), 10 (movement answers containing pairs), and 11 (human content).

Table 92.   Interpersonal Perception Variables for Case 7

STRUCTURAL VARIABLES			RESPONSES TO BE READ
CDI = 1	HVI = Neg		MOVEMENT WITH PAIR = 1, 3, 4, 8, 12, 16
$a{:}p = 7 : 7$	$T = 2$	$Fd = 0$	HUMAN CONTENTS = 4, 6, 8, 9, 12
Isolate/R = 0.16			
Total Human Contents = 5			
PER = 3	COP = 4	AG = 2	

The elevation in T is a dominant feature in this cluster. She is a very needy, lonely person who is struggling with the consequences of her loss. As with several features in the record, this appears to be a situationally-related phenomenon but nonetheless, it has an impact on her current interpersonal behaviors. The presence of five human contents suggests that she is interested in people. The slight elevation in PER responses suggests that she tends to be more defensively authoritarian with others, but it is not clear whether this is a chronic trait or more of a situationally developed tactic that helps her contend with her bad feelings about herself. Whichever may be the case, it is not a serious flaw when considered in light of the data for COP and AG. She probably is regarded by others as likable and gregarious. She seems to anticipate that most of her exchanges will be positive and strives to create and maintain harmonious relationships.

The review of human contents presents a somewhat more equivocal view of people. The two Pure H answers (people leaning on each other, little girls playing together) seem positive, and one of the parenthesized contents (skeletons dancing) also has some positive features. The remaining two (one of those Darth Vader masks, a crucifix . . . it's elaborate) are less positive, but not negative. Thus, it seems likely that her overall view of others is marked by a positive but not naïve set.

Case 7 Summary   At the moment, her own struggles with her sense of loneliness and loss undoubtedly has an impact on her interpersonal perceptions and behaviors. She has a tendency to be more defensively authoritarian with others, but it is not clear whether this is a chronic trait or more of a situationally developed tactic that helps her contend with her bad feelings about herself. Whichever may be the case, it is not a serious liability because generally she is likely to be regarded by others as likable and gregarious. She generally is positive, but not naïve about people. She seems to anticipate that most of her exchanges will be positive and, in that context, strives to create and maintain harmonious relationships.

Case 7 Final Description

This subject is the type of person who usually is prone to merge her feelings into her thinking when in a decision making situation. She prefers a trial-and-error approach and relies extensively on feedback from her actions. However, there is some flexibility to this style and, at times, she pushes emotion to a more peripheral level and relies more on an internal evaluation of various alternatives before forming behaviors. Regardless of which approach she uses, some problems are likely to occur. Her thinking is strange and disordered. At times, she makes very irrational and bizarre associations. Her judgment also is sometimes much more concrete than should be the case.

Her ideation also is marked by more peripheral, potentially distracting thought than is common for most people. Most of this is provoked by her own experience of strong, unmet needs. She tends to slip into fantasy more often than should be the case. Although this permits her to avoid the harshness of reality, her failure to deal with reality contributes to faulty decision making. Another serious problem is that her thinking is marked by considerable pessimism. She anticipates negative outcomes as the result of her actions and may often misread stimuli because of this set.

She is not as oriented as others to make conventional responses. This results from a tendency to overpersonalize or distort inputs. Although neither occurs so frequently as to warrant major concern, the composite forms a strong likelihood that many of her behaviors are likely to be more idiosyncratic and/or inappropriate than is typical for the well-adjusted adult. Her tendency to distort appears to be prompted more by affective disruption than by some chronic problem in perceptual accuracy. She is the type of person who becomes very involved in her efforts to process information. She invests considerably more energy than most people to ensure that all aspects of a field are processed. This processing style can be very useful, but, if problems in adjustment exist, it can become very detrimental. People like this often set very high goals and invariably encounter frustration when they fail to achieve some of those goals. As frustrations accumulate, they breed distress and can have a negative impact on self-esteem.

Her capacity for control and tolerance for stress are very similar to that of most people. She has considerable resource available, and it appears to be sustaining these capacities even though she is experiencing much more internal aggravation than is common. This is being produced by an excessive internalization of feelings plus a strong need for closeness or experience of loneliness that has probably resulted because of her recent tragedy. Generally, she is less cautious about her emotional displays than most adults and, at times, she may become overly intense in some of her emotional behaviors. This is not necessarily a negative finding because she has no obvious problems in control. She seems as interested in processing emotional stimuli as most adults, but she is a very complex person who seems to have some confusion about her feelings. This may be situationally related, but it could also be a more chronic feature. There is no question that she is currently experiencing intense pain, which is probably situationally related.

A firm and reliable picture of the self-image of this woman is difficult to generate because so much of it appears to have been sharply impacted by the ongoing tragedy that she is experiencing. A tormented and miserable sense of the self is portrayed. It seems very doubtful that this has been a chronic feature. Instead, it seems to depict her current state of her preoccupation and the devastating effects that it is having. Historically, it seems that she has been no more or less concerned with herself than most people and her self-value has been similar to that of most adults. She seems prone to engage in self-examination somewhat routinely, but not excessively. She has substantial body concern, but this could be related to her recent physical injury or a preoccupation with her husband's status. The most devastating finding concerns very negative feelings about herself as well as a strong sense of damage. Both are likely to have a more situational than chronic basis. Some of the findings do hint at a much more favorable self-image in the past but they are difficult to sort out from the intensely negative sense of the self that appears to exist now.

At the moment, her own struggles with her sense of loneliness and loss has a considerable impact on her interpersonal perceptions and behaviors. She has a tendency to be more defensively authoritarian with others, but it is not clear whether this is a chronic trait or more of a situationally developed tactic that helps her contend with her bad feelings about herself. Whichever may be the case, it is not a serious liability because generally she will be regarded by others as likable and gregarious. Her view of others usually is positive but not naïve and she strives to create and maintain harmonious relationships.

Recommendations Based on the Final Description

Although much of her thinking appears to be disturbed, there is no firm support for the notion of a schizophreniform disturbance. When considered in light of the history, the picture is much more like that of a brief reactive psychosis that has not subsided fully. It is obvious that she is in considerable distress and this is having a very negative impact on her thinking and many of her behaviors. She needs considerable assistance to deal more directly with her grief and provide direction for some of the decisions that she must make in reconstructing her life. This should include individual supportive psychotherapy and the utilization of whatever additional support sources may be available. The possibility of some group interaction is worth considering but should be implemented only after the individual therapy contact has been firmly established. Continued hospitalization may be warranted for a very brief period while the support structure is organized but should not be prolonged more than necessary as it risks exacerbating her very pessimistic state.

Case 7 Epilogue The subject remained hospitalized for an additional 10 days following the psychological evaluation. During that time, which included daily individual therapy, her improvement was marked. After discharge she continued in individual treatment twice weekly for three months and once weekly for an additional three months. She returned to work two weeks after being discharged. A second round of psychological tests were administered at the end of six months at the request of her therapist. The second Rorschach showed remarkable improvement and was essentially free of any indices of pathology. An elevation T persisted and some of the data evidenced a sense of cautiousness about social relationships, but otherwise the data are very similar to a well adjusted nonpatient. Following the retest, she and the therapist agreed to continue with weekly visits for a period of at least three months.

CASE 8: REACTIVE DEPRESSION

This 22-year-old male was referred for evaluation by a psychiatrist who has been seeing him twice weekly for six weeks. The treatment began approximately four months after the subject had been involved in an automobile accident in which his two roommates were killed. According to the subject, the three companions were returning to their apartment from the university that they attended, following a basketball game. They were driving in a small two-seater sports car, with one roommate driving, the subject in the passenger seat, and the other roommate squatting in the storage space behind the two seats. Apparently, they had stopped for some pizza and beer en route, and each had consumed one or two glasses of beer with the meal. After leaving the restaurant, they drove onto a divided highway and were proceeding at an estimated speed of 50 miles per hour. Shortly thereafter, a large tractor trailer passed them and was lengthening the distance between them when it suddenly jackknifed, swerving from side to side until the cab struck a guard rail, throwing the trailer horizontally across both lanes of the roadway. The friend who was driving attempted to stop but the car skidded and ran underneath the trailer and became wedged there, shearing off the windshield and convertible top. Both the driver and the subject ducked just before the impact, but the roommate squatting in the back of the car was unable to do so and was killed instantly. The driver and the subject were wedged underneath the dashboard of the vehicle for approximately 90 minutes before being extricated by an emergency crew. The driver suffered a crushed chest and fractured skull. He expired without regaining consciousness after four days. The subject suffered a broken jaw, a broken collarbone, and a shattered elbow. He remained in the hospital for three weeks and wore a shoulder and arm cast for two months after being discharged.

At the time of the accident the subject was nearing the end of the first semester of his senior year at the university. He was a prelaw and political science major and an honor student. His cumulative grade point average was 3.54. He had taken the LSAT six weeks before the accident and obtained scores that ranked him nationally in the top 10%. He had completed two interviews regarding law school admission and was scheduled for four others. The timing of the accident precluded him from taking his regularly scheduled final exams, but his professors arranged for makeup exams following his release from the hospital. He completed the five exams within two weeks of being discharged, scored very well on all of them, and his grades for the semester included three A's and two B's.

He had preregistered for five courses for the second semester and began attending as scheduled, and completed two of the law school interviews for which he had been scheduled. During the fourth week of the semester his class attendance fell sharply and he failed to complete assigned papers in two courses. The department chairman, who was also his adviser, became concerned and called him in for an interview. During that interview, and a subsequent interview with a psychologist at the university health center, the subject complained about difficulties in concentration, insomnia, and nightmares about the accident. At that time, he was referred to the psychiatrist who rendered a preliminary diagnosis of posttraumatic stress disorder. The psychiatrist prescribed an antidepressant and arranged for the biweekly treatment sessions, which have been mainly supportive, with special focus on feelings concerning the accident and the loss of his friends.

The psychiatrist has become increasingly concerned because all of the symptoms have intensified. On mutual agreement with the department chairman, the subject has withdrawn from three courses, one of which is prerequisite for law school admission, but his attendance in the remaining two courses has been

Case 8: A 22-Year-Old Male

Card	Response		Inquiry
I	1. It ll a man w a cape on, lik dracula, standg there w his arms out, lik w his cape ovr his arms	E:	(Rpts S's resp)
		S:	Well dracula always wears black, & ths is lik his big cape extended out & his body & littl funny legs & his head. It ll he's got sk of hat on w horns on it or sthg
	E: I thk if u tak ur time u'll c sthg else too		
II	2. Well, let me c . . . I guess u cld thk of it as a bf, but it wld be dead	E:	(Rpts S's resp)
		S:	Well bf's r usually pretty colorful. Ths 1 isn't, it's all black lik. I wld thk of decay when I c tht, the wgs & the body r still there but it's discolored, prob lik it was dead
	3. Thts not too great, it ll smthg pretty gory, sorta lik a wound or sthg tht got all torn up	E:	(Rpts S's resp)
		S:	Well I thot of the red as being bld & the dark part as being lik burnt flesh flesh or skin or sthg. Anyhow, I thot of a wound bec of the hole in the middl, lik mayb a bullet wound
		E:	U said the dark prt ll burnt flesh or skin?
		S:	Well if it was burnt it wld be black lik ths & u can c some bld spots on it too
III	4. U kno, if I look at it diff it cb 2 people, mayb at a costume party, mayb toasting e.o.	E:	(Rpts S's resp)
		S:	Well its lik thy are hunched ovr toward e.o., & each has a big cloak on & thyr wearing red hats & thy seem to b holdg sthg, poss glasses, lik champagne glasses, lik thyr touchg them as if thy were toastg e.o.
	5. Ths ll 2 people, 2 men who r pickg sthg up	E:	(Rpts S's resp)
		S:	Well 1 here & 1 here, thyr thin guys, here's the head & the legs & the arm & & ths is what thy r pickg up
IV	6. Ths ll some giant out of sc fict who's sittg on a stump	E:	(Rpts S's resp)
		S:	Just some big giant, all covrd w fur, black fur, c his big legs stretched out in frt of him & he's sorta leang backwrd cuz his head looks so small
		E:	U said he has blk fur?
		S:	Yeah, its all black but its diff colors of black lik fur looks, lik a fur coat looks unless its a really expensive one, then the colors better match
V	7. Tht cb a bat, his wgs r out lik he's flyg, lik swooping	E:	(Rpts S's resp)
		S:	I thk thy extend their wgs more when thy swoop dwn, I thk I heard tht in biol class, it gives them enuff surface to zoom back up when thy want to. C the big wgspan & the narrow body & little legs & I guess bigger legs in frt altho I always heard thy had only 2 legs

(continued)

365

Case 8: (Continued)

Card	Response	Inquiry
VI	8. Tht rem me of tht cartoon, the Roadrunner where the fox or wolf whatevr he is just got run ovr	E: (Rpts S's resp) S: It just ll tht, all flattened out w tire marks up & down his back, c his nose is stretched out in front & the whiskers & the legs out to each side E: U mentioned tire marks up & down his back? S: Well some of the marking just ll his fur but there r other discolorations in there tht cld be tire marks
VII	9. Ths ll 2 littl guys riding on a teeter, thyr made up lik littl Indian kids	E: (Rpts S's resp) S: Well here's the feathers in their hair, & down here is the teeter lik on a playgrnd. Thyr kinda squattg on it, just goin up & down, I guess ths thg back here (Dd21) is is lik a brace or sthg so thy won't fall backwards
	10. If u use the white part in the middl as water the whole thg cb an island	E: (Rpts S's resp) S: Well just an island w the white prt being lik a harbor & the rest is lik the island, lik u'd c it from a plane E: From a plane? S: Well lookg down fr above, quite a ways up cuz u can c the whole thg
VIII	11. Tht ll a cpl of rats eatg on the remains of some dead A	E: (Rpts S's resp) S: Well thy r on each side & it ll thy r tryg to pull ths top part apart. U can c some of the bones here (DS3) & ths red looks all bloody lik torn flesh or some organ & I guess ths blue prt is some skin or sthg. U really can't tell what kind of A it was E: U said the red part looks bloody? S: Well more fleshy colored, lik blood but flesh too
	12. Just the top ll a jellyfish	E: (Rpts S's resp) S: I dk, it just re me of a jellyfish w the legs out here & the body, just a jellyfish or Man O War I thk thy call them smtimes
IX	13. Well the 2 at the top cb a cpl of clowns, lik thry leang back lik laughing or sthg	E: (Rpts S's resp) S: Well u kno lik in a circus, thyr dressed all in orange w big fat stomachs & peaked peaked hats. Thy ll thyr leang backwrd lik thy just did sthg & thyr leang back havg a good laugh
	14. This cntr ll an hourglass w the sand running in it	E: (Rpts S's resp) S: Well it kinda has the shape of an hourglass & it looks transparent & here in the cntr, ths darker part (D5) ll it cb the sand falling, lik time is running out cuz there's not much sand in the top

366

X

15. Well tht top part rem me of the helmet & face piece that Darth Vader wore

E: (Rpts S's resp)

S: Its not as black as it shld b, his was real shiny black, ths is a duller black, but it has the general shape to it w the white parts for the eye slots, u hav to stretch ur imag a littl to thk of it lik tht

16. If u just take the upper prt of the pink & ths blue, its lik a cpl guys talking to eo, not real, but lik in a cartoon

E: (Rpts S's resp)

S: Well the blue is lik what thyr sayg to eo, lik u c in a cartoon, there's no words there but it repres smthg thyr sayg to eo. Thy hav peaked hats on, lik elves or smthg, c the nose & chin & the indentation for the eye & the forehead, its just sort of an abstract representation of 2 guys talkg, u can't c their whole body, just their heads & the upper prt of their body

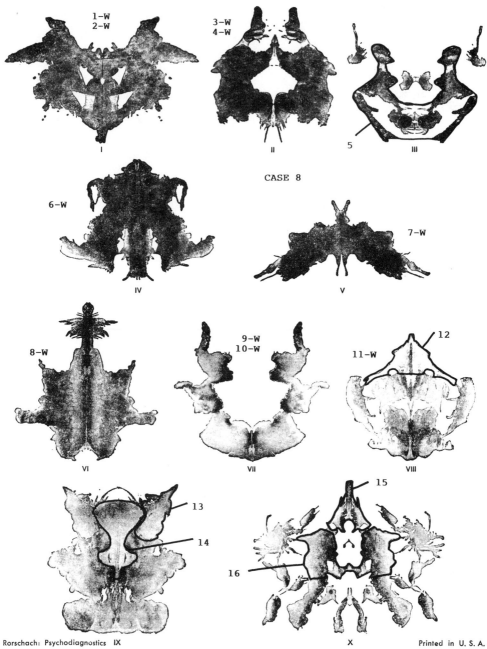

CASE 8

CASE 8. SEQUENCE OF SCORES

CARD	NO	LOC	#	DETERMINANT(S)	(2)	CONTENT(S)	POP	Z	SPECIAL SCORES
I	1	W+	1	Mp.FC'+		(H),Cg		4.0	
	2	Wo	1	FC'o		A	P	1.0	MOR
II	3	WS/	1	CF.C'Fu		Bl,Hd		4.5	MOR
	4	W+	1	Ma.FCo	2	H,Cg,Hh		4.5	COP
III	5	D+	1	Mao	2	H,Id	P	3.0	COP
IV	6	W+	1	Mp.FC'.FT.FDo		(H),Bt	P	4.0	
V	7	Wo	1	FMao		A	P	1.0	PER
VI	8	Wo	1	FT.YFo		(A)	P	2.5	MOR
VII	9	W+	1	Mpo	2	H,Id	P	2.5	COP
	10	WS+	1	FDo		Na		4.0	
VIII	11	W+	1	FMa.CFu	2	A,Ad,An	P	4.5	MOR
	12	Do	4	F-		A			INC
IX	13	D+	3	Mp.FCo	2	(H),Cg	P	4.5	COP
	14	D+	8	mp.FVo		Sc,Na		2.5	
X	15	DSo	11	FC'o		(Hd),Sc		6.0	
	16	Dd+	99	Mpu	2	(Hd),Cg,Art		4.0	AB

CASE 8. STRUCTURAL SUMMARY

```
================================================================================
LOCATION              DETERMINANTS            CONTENTS      S-CONSTELLATION
FEATURES         BLENDS          SINGLE                     YES..FV+VF+V+FD>2
                                            H   = 3, 0      YES..Col-Shd Bl>0
Zf   = 15      M.FC'           M  = 3       (H) = 3, 0      NO...Ego<.31,>.44
ZSum = 52.5    CF.C'F          FM = 1       Hd  = 0, 1      YES..MOR > 3
ZEst = 49.0    M.FC            m  = 0       (Hd)= 2, 0      NO...Zd > +- 3.5
               M.FC'.FT.FD     FC = 0       Hx  = 0, 0      YES..es > EA
W    = 10      FT.YF           CF = 0       A   = 4, 0      NO...CF+C > FC
(Wv  = 0)      FM.CF           C  = 0       (A) = 1, 0      NO...X+% < .70
D    = 5       M.FC            Cn = 0       Ad  = 0, 1      NO...S > 3
Dd   = 1       m.FV            FC'= 2       (Ad)= 0, 0      NO...P < 3 or > 8
S    = 3                       C'F= 0       An  = 1, 0      NO...Pure H < 2
                               C' = 0       Art = 0, 1      YES..R < 17
   DQ                          FT = 0       Ay  = 0, 0        5.....TOTAL
........(FQ-)                  TF = 0       Bl  = 1, 0
 +  = 10  ( 0)                 T  = 0       Bt  = 0, 1      SPECIAL SCORINGS
 o  =  5  ( 1)                 FV = 0       Cg  = 0, 4           Lv1    Lv2
v/+ =  1  ( 0)                 VF = 0       Cl  = 0, 0      DV  = 0x1    0x2
 v  =  0  ( 0)                 V  = 0       Ex  = 0, 0      INC = 1x2    0x4
                               FY = 0       Fd  = 0, 0      DR  = 0x3    0x6
                               YF = 0       Fi  = 0, 0      FAB = 0x4    0x7
                               Y  = 0       Ge  = 0, 0      ALOG= 0x5
   FORM QUALITY                Fr = 0       Hh  = 1, 0      CON = 0x7
                               rF = 0       Ls  = 0, 0         SUM6  = 1
    FQx  FQf  MQual  SQx       FD = 1       Na  = 1, 1         WSUM6 =  2
 +  = 1   0    1     0         F  = 1       Sc  = 1, 1
 o  = 12  0    5     2                      Sx  = 0, 0      AB  = 1    CP  = 0
 u  = 3   0    1     1                      Xy  = 0, 0      AG  = 0    MOR = 4
 -  = 1   1    0     0                      Id  = 0, 1      CFB = 0    PER = 1
none= 0   --   0     0         (2) = 6                      COP = 4    PSV = 0
================================================================================
            RATIOS, PERCENTAGES, AND DERIVATIONS

R = 16        L = 0.07         FC:CF+C = 2: 2    COP = 4      AG = 0
-----------------------------  Pure C  =    0    Food        = 0
EB = 7: 3.0  EA = 10.0  EBPer= 2.3  Afr =0.60    Isolate/R  =0.31
eb = 3: 9    es = 12     D = 0      S   =  3      H:(H)Hd(Hd)= 3: 6
          Adj es = 12  Adj D = 0    Blends:R= 8:16  (HHd):(AAd)= 5: 1
-----------------------------  CP    = 0        H+A:Hd+Ad  =11: 3
FM = 2 : C'= 5   T = 2
m  = 1 : V = 1   Y = 1
                       P    = 8    Zf   =15       3r+(2)/R=0.38
a:p   = 4: 6  Sum6  = 1  X+% =0.75  Zd  = +3.5    Fr+rF   = 0
Ma:Mp = 2: 5  Lv2   = 0  F+% =0.00  W:D:Dd =10: 5: 1  FD   = 2
2AB+Art+Ay= 3 WSum6 = 2  X-% =0.06  W:M =10: 7    An+Xy   = 1
M-    = 0     Mnone = 0  S-% =0.00  DQ+ =10       MOR     = 4
                         Xu% =0.19  DQv = 0
-------------------------------------------------------------------
  SCZI = 0    DEPI = 5*   CDI = 2    S-CON = 5    HVI = No   OBS = No
================================================================================
```

erratic and his work substandard. He complains about flashbacks concerning the accident and reports bouts of anxiety if riding in a car or on a bus. He says that he has lost interest in school and in law school and is considering withdrawing altogether. The psychiatrist is considering brief hospitalization and raises a question about whether the accident has provoked a major depressive disorder that will require long term treatment.

The subject is the older of two children, having a younger brother, age 19, who is a freshman at another university. His father, age 49, owns and operates a small grocery store. His mother, age 46, also works in the store. He gives an unremarkable developmental history. He was an honor student in high school and has attended college on a partial scholarship that pays three-quarters of his tuition. He has been on the high school and university baseball teams, is reportedly well liked by his peers, and has been regarded as an outstanding student by faculty. He began dating in high school and had his first sexual experience at age 17. Prior to the accident, he dated frequently but not with the same person. He has stated that he does not want to marry before finishing law school, but also points out that that is not a "firm" decision. He is interested in politics and has considered that area as something to be explored in the future.

The referral specifically asks whether this is a Post-Traumatic Stress Disorder and/or whether there is evidence of a Major Depressive Disorder. Recommendations concerning treatment are also requested, with special consideration of his academic status, that is, whether he should be encouraged or discouraged about withdrawing from school. Complete neurological and neuropsychological examinations have been conducted, both yielding negative findings.

Interpretive Strategy

The protocol contains only 16 answers but there is no reason to question its interpretive usefulness. The first positive Key variable is the introversive *EB*. Thus, the order for the clusters is:

IDEATION → PROCESSING → MEDIATION → CONTROLS → AFFECT → SELF-PERCEPTION → INTERPERSONAL PERCEPTION.

Initial Propositions   Two initial propositions can be formulated at the outset. The first is from the positive Key variable and is that he prefers to delay formulating decisions or initiating behaviors until all apparent alternative possibilities have been considered. People such as this tend to rely heavily on internal evaluation in forming judgments. The second is derived from the positive DEPI. It has a value of 5 and, as such, is not a Key variable; however, it does imply that the current personality organization is very similar to that of people who have frequent and reasonably intense experiences of depression.

Ideation

Data for the variables related to ideation are shown in Table 93.

Case 8 Findings   All data, except Steps 3 (left-side *eb*), 4 (*a : p*), 6 (Intellectualization Index), and 11 (*M*– level of distortion), are relevant to the interpretation.

Table 93. Ideation Variables for Case 8

EB = 7 : 3	EBPer = 2.3	M QUALITY	CRITICAL SPECIAL SCORES			
eb = 3 : 9	(FM = 2 m = 1)	+ = 0	DV	= 0	DV2	= 0
a:p = 4 : 6	Ma:Mp = 2 : 5	o = 6	INC	= 1	INC2	= 0
2Ab+(Art+Ay) = 3		u = 1	DR	= 0	DR2	= 0
MOR = ~~0~~ 4		– = 0	FAB	= 0	FAB2	= 0
RESPONSES TO BE READ FOR QUALITY			ALOG	= 0	SUM6	= 1
1, 4, 5, 6, 9, 13, 16			CON	= 0	WSUM6	= 2

The basic finding from the *EB* has already been stated in an initial proposition. He is an ideationally oriented person who usually likes to think things through before coming to a decision. The *EBPer* suggests that there is flexibility to the style, and instances occur in which feelings contribute significantly to decisions. The data for the $M^a : M^p$ are quite important. They signal the presence of a routine tactic that involves flights into fantasy to avoid dealing with unpleasant situations. People such as this have a "Snow White Syndrome," characterized mainly by the avoidance of responsibility and decision making. They use fantasy with an abusive excess to deny reality and the results often are counterproductive to many of their own needs. This mode of coping involves the creation of a self-imposed helplessness because it requires a dependency on others. The pervasiveness of this fantasy abuse is particularly detrimental for the introversive subject because the basic ideational coping orientation becomes subservient to the avoidant orientation in situations that seem overly complex or potentially stressful.

The presence of four MOR responses is also an ominous sign. It indicates that much of his thinking includes a significant pessimistic set that affects how he views the world. He anticipates negative outcomes regardless of his own effort and this gloomy attitude often reduces motivation considerably. Actually, his thinking appears to be clear and free of slippage. Only one INCOM occurred ("a jellyfish with the legs out here") and is a minor finding. The quality of the *M* answers is quite sophisticated (1. "a man with a cape on . . . standing there with his arms out"; 4. "two people, maybe at a costume party, maybe toasting each other"; 5. "two men who are picking something up"; 6. "some giant out of science fiction who is sitting on a stump"; 9. "two little guys riding a teeter, they are made up like little Indian kids"; 12. "a couple of clowns . . . leaning back like they are laughing"; 16. "a couple of guys talking to each other . . . the blue is like what they are saying to each other, like you see in a cartoon"). This sophistication is not surprising in light of his excellent academic performance and can be a valuable aid to treatment.

Case 8 Summary   The subject is an ideational person who usually likes to delay and think things through before coming to a decision. There is flexibility in his coping style and sometimes he merges his feelings more directly into his thinking so that some decisions have a more intuitive influence. His thinking usually is clear and relatively free of slippage, and the quality of his ideation is quite sophisticated. Unfortunately, his thinking is also marked by two very negative features. First, he is very abusive of his fantasy life. In other words, he flees into fantasy to avoid dealing with unpleasant situations. In doing so he abrogates responsibility and decision making and denies reality too often. This tends to create a self-imposed helplessness. The pervasiveness of his fantasy abuse is particularly detrimental for him because his basic ideational coping style becomes subservient to the avoidant orientation. Second, much of his thinking seems to be very pessimistic. Apparently, he anticipates negative outcomes regardless of his efforts, and this gloomy attitude tends to reduce his motivation considerably. In light of the history, it seems reasonable to hypothesize that the abuse of fantasy and the extreme pessimism have resulted from an inability or unwillingness to confront his recent trauma and the variety of negative elements that it has brought into his life.

Information Processing

The data for variables related to processing activities are shown in Table 94.

Case 8 Findings   All data except Step 2 (OBS and HVI) are relevant to the interpretation.

The low Lambda value indicates that he becomes more involved with stimuli than is common for most people. This may be a consequence of his overincorporative style which is reflected in the Zd score but the value is so low that it may also reflect some unusual preoccupation with emotional stimuli. Whatever the cause, the high Zf and the $W:D:Dd$ ratio make it clear that he is highly motivated in processing new information, especially when the information relates to problem solving or decision making. The $W:M$ ratio suggests that his efforts usually are well within his capabilities, and the DQ distribution indicates that the quality of processing is complex and sophisticated. This finding is common among more intelligent or better educated subjects. As noted earlier, he does have an overincorporative style that causes him to invest considerable effort and energy in scanning activities. This style is often an asset because the cautious, thorough approach to scanning usually ensures that all stimulus cues are included in the input. The evaluation of the Location Sequencing reveals that he is quite consistent in his processing approach, and also that he seems reasonably cautious at times. On three of the more broken or complex blots (III, IX, and X), he avoided the W and settled for detail answers, synthesizing four of the five given in the process.

Table 94.   Information Processing Variables for Case 8

$L = 0.07$	OBS = Neg	HVI = Neg		LOCATION SEQUENCING		
$Zd = +3.5$	$DQ+$ $= 10$		I W,W	IV W	VII W,WS	
$Zf = 15$	DQv/+ $= 1$		II WS,W	V W	VIII W,D	
$W:D:Dd = 10:5:1$	DQv $= 0$		III D	VI W	IX D,D	
$W:M = 10:7$	PSV $= 0$				X DS,Dd	

Case 8 Summary The subject becomes engrossed with stimuli more than do most people. In part, this is a product of an overincorporative style that causes him to invest considerable effort and energy in scanning activities. It promotes a cautious, thorough approach to scanning that usually ensures that all stimulus cues are included in the input. However, the excessive involvement may also reflect some unusual preoccupation with emotional stimuli. Regardless of the cause, he is highly motivated in processing new information. Although he works hard at processing, his efforts usually are well within his capabilities, and the quality of processing is consistent, complex, and sophisticated.

Cognitive Mediation

The data for variables related to mediational activity are shown in Table 95.

Table 95. Cognitive Mediation Variables for Case 8

Lambda = 0.07	OBS = Negative	MINUS FEATURES	
P = 8	$X+\% = .75$	VIII	12. *Do F− A INC*
$FQx+ = 1$	$F+\% = 0$		
$FQxo$ = 11	$Xu\% = .19$		
FQxu = 3	$X-\% = .06$		
$FQx- = 1$	$S-\% = 0$		
$FQnone = 0$	CONFAB = 0		

Case 8 Finding All of the data except those for Steps 1 (Lambda), 2 (OBS), 6 (*FQnone*), and 10 (homogeneity of minus) are relevant to the interpretation.

The number of Popular responses plus the value for the $X+\%$ indicate that conventional or expected translations of stimuli are likely to occur about as frequently as is the case for most people. The single $FQ+$ response indicates that, at times, he is likely to be detailed in forming a translation, which is consistent with his apparent above average intellectual level. At the same time, he expresses his idiosyncratic features in some of his translations, but no more than do most people. His single minus answer is not a serious distortion. These findings seem to be advantageous for treatment.

Case 8 Summary His mediational activities are not different from those expected of an intelligent nonpatient. He is prone to translate stimuli in conventional and expected ways but with no sacrifice of his individuality.

Controls and Stress Tolerance

The data variables related to capacity for control and tolerance for stress are shown in Table 96.

Case 8 Findings All data in the cluster are relevant to the interpretation.

The Adj D Score of zero and the value for the *EA* indicate that he usually has enough resource accessible to participate meaningfully in the formulation and

Table 96.   Control-Related Variables for Case 8

$EB = 7 : 3.0$	$EA = 10.0$	$D = 0$	$CDI = 2$
$eb = 3 : 9$	$es = 12$ Adj$es = 12$	AdjD = 0	
$FM = 2$ $m = 1$ $C' = 5$ $T = 2$ $V = 1$ $Y = 1$			

direction of responses. His tolerance for stress is like that of most people and controls are unlikely to falter unless the stress is unexpected and intense or prolonged. The data for the *EB* offer no reason to challenge that assumption. The values for *eb, es,* and Adj *es* also tend to support this postulate, but they also raise some concern. The *es* and Adj *es* both have values higher than the *EA,* which suggests that the capacity for control may be a bit more tenuous than meets the eye. Obviously, the higher right-side *eb* value is creating this problem. Under other circumstances there would be no cause for concern.

Case 8 Summary   Ordinarily, he has enough resource accessible to exert adequate control over the formation and direction of responses. His tolerance for stress is like that of most people and controls are unlikely to falter unless the stress is unexpected and intense or prolonged. Nonetheless, there is some cause for concern. Current levels of internal stimulation are higher than expected; thus, his capacity for control and tolerance of stress may be more tenuous than is usual, even though they continue to be within normal limits.

Affective Features

Data for the variables related to affect are shown in Table 97.

Case 8 Findings   All data in the cluster, except Steps 5 (Pure *C*), 7 (CP), and 10 (*m* and *Y* blends), are relevant to the interpretation.

The fact that the DEPI is positive has already been noted in an initial proposition. It is consistent with his report of being depressed. As noted earlier, the *EB* indicates that emotions typically do not play an important role in his decision making activities but, as noted by the *EBPer,* they become influential in some situations and can prompt more intuitive kinds of ideational activity. This kind of flexibility usually is desirable; however, the right-side *eb* shows that he is currently experiencing considerable distress or discomfort, which is consistent with

Table 97.   Affect-Related Variables for Case 8

$EB = 7 : 3.0$	$EBPer = 2.3$	$DEPI = 5$	*shad* BLENDS	
$eb = 3 : 9$	$(C = 5, T = 2, V = 1, Y = 1)$		M.FC'.FT.FD	CF.C'F — *color shady*
$FC:CF+C = 2 : 2$	Pure $C = 0$		M.FC (2)	FT.FY — *shady*
$Afr = 0.60$	CP = 0		M.FC'	m.FV
$S = 3$	Col-Shd Bl = 1		FM.CF	

the positive DEPI. This can create a more negative influence on decision operations than should be the case. A review of the variables in the right-side *eb* reveals several negative findings. The elevated value for C' indicates a substantial containment and internalization of feelings, which invariably lead to discomfort that may manifest as anxiety, sadness, tension, or apprehension. In addition, the presence of one *Vista* answer signifies irritating feelings that are being generated by negative self-inspecting behavior. Taken alone, this is often a precursor to depression. A third source of the aggravation is a strong sense of loneliness or emotional deprivation. In this instance, it is probably related to the traumatic loss of his two friends.

The $FC:CF+C$ suggests that he is somewhat less stringent about modulating emotional displays than most ideationally oriented subjects. This is not a negative finding for an adult, but it does not bode well if problems with controls develop. The *Afr* suggests that he appears to be as willing to process emotional stimuli as most adults. This is a favorable finding because people who are depressed or seriously disturbed often find it more convenient to withdraw from emotionally provoking situations.

The value for S indicates that he seems to be more negativistic or hostile toward the environment than most people. This may reflect a preexisting sense of individualism that could be very healthy, or it may represent a growing sense of hostility that ultimately can become very detrimental to him. The number of blends indicates that his psychological functioning is more complex than should be the case, particularly for one with an ideational style. This level of complexity is almost always the result of emotional experiences and can contribute easily to dysfunction. The Color-Shading blends suggest that part of the complexity is created because he finds emotions confusing and may frequently experience both positive and negative feelings about the same stimulus situation. This may be a more chronic trait and, if so, suggests that he often experiences feelings more intensely than others and sometimes has more difficulty in bringing closure to emotional situations. The Shading blend signals that the presence of intensely negative, probably painful emotion is also contributing to the complexity. This appears to be situational in origin and it tends to dominate his interpretation of affective experiences and usually becomes pervasive in influencing thinking.

Case 8 Summary There is no reason to challenge his report about being quite depressed. Usually, his emotions do not play an important role in his decision making activities, but they become influential in some situations and can prompt more intuitive kinds of ideational activity. He seems to be experiencing one of those situations and, unfortunately, his emotions are dominated by distress or discomfort, which create a more negative influence on decision operations than should be the case. He is involved with a substantial containment and internalization of feelings, which invariably lead to discomfort; he is involved with considerable negative self-inspecting behavior; and he is experiencing a strong sense of loneliness or emotional deprivation. The latter is probably related to the traumatic loss of his two friends.

Currently, he seems less concerned about modulating emotional displays than most ideationally oriented subjects. This is not a negative finding, but it does not portend well if problems with controls develop. He appears to be as willing to process emotional stimuli as most adults. This is a favorable finding, because people who are depressed or seriously disturbed often find it more convenient to withdraw from emotionally provoking situations. On the other hand, he also seems to be more negativistic or hostile toward the environment than most people. This could reflect a preexisting sense of individualism that might be healthy, but it more likely represents a growing sense of hostility that ultimately can become very detrimental to him. His psychological functioning is more complex than should be the case, particularly for one with an ideational style, and this level of complexity is almost always the result of emotional experiences and can contribute easily to dysfunction. Part of the complexity is created because he finds emotions confusing and may frequently experience both positive and negative feelings about the same stimulus situation. This may be a more chronic trait and, if so, suggests that he often experiences feelings more intensely than others and sometimes has more difficulty in bringing closure to emotional situations. Another element that contributes to the complexity is intensely negative, probably painful emotions. This appears to be situational in origin and it tends to dominate his interpretation of affective experiences and usually becomes pervasive in influencing thinking.

Self-Perception

The data for variables related to self-perception are shown in Table 98.

Case 8 Findings All data except Steps 1 ($Fr + rf$) and 5 ($An + Xy$) are relevant to the interpretation.

A very positive finding is the value for the Egocentricity Index, which is in the average range. It suggests that his self-esteem is average. In other words, he does not appear to be focusing more or less on himself than do most people, and tends to regard himself as positively as he regards others. This is quite important in light of the depressive features. A lowered self-value is often a precursor in cases of dysthymia or chronic depression. The values for *FD* and *Vista* reaffirm the fact that he engages in considerably more introspection than is common, and that much of this focuses on perceived negative features. The relationship of Pure *H* answers to other human contents is somewhat surprising in light of the subject's history and raises a question about whether his self-image has always been more imaginary than real, or whether his current fantasy abuse and pessimism are creating some distortion in self-concept.

There is no question that his self-image currently is marked by many negative features. This is evidenced by the presence of four MOR answers, which constitute

Table 98. Self Perception Variables for Case 8

STRUCTURAL DATA		RESPONSES TO BE READ	
$Fr + rF = 0$	$3r + (2)/R = 0.38$	*MOR* RESPONSES	= 2, 3, 8, 11
$FD = 2$	$V = 1$	MINUS RESPONSES	= 12
$HH) + Hd + (Hd) = 3:6$		*M* RESPONSES	= 1, 4, 5, 6, 9, 13, 16
$An + Xy = 1$		*FM* RESPONSES	= 7, 11
$MOR = 4$		*m* RESPONSES	= 14

one-fourth of his responses, and by the rather grim features in those answers (2. "you could think of it as a butterfly, but it would be dead . . . it's discolored," 3. "like a wound or something that got all torn up," 8. "where the fox or wolf, whatever he is just got run over . . . there are other discolorations in there that could be tire marks," 11. "rats eating on the remains of some dead animal"). The single minus response (a jellyfish) raises a question about the integrity or firmness of his self-concept. Although jellyfish can be dangerous, they seem somewhat helpless and transparent.

The overall content of the *M* responses is much more positive, although four have an unreal quality (1. "a man with a cape on, like Dracula . . . standing there with his arms out," 6. "some giant out of science fiction who is sitting on a stump . . . his head looks so small," 13. "a couple of clowns . . . leaning back like they are laughing . . . like they just did something and they are leaning back having a good laugh," 16. "a couple of guys talking to each other, not real, but like in a cartoon . . . the blue is like what they are saying to each other, like you see in a cartoon, there's no words there but it represents something"). The remaining three are very positive (4. "two people maybe at a costume party, maybe toasting each other," 5. "two men who are picking something up," 9. "two little guys riding a teeter, they are made up like little Indian kids . . . like on a playground . . . I guess this thing back here is like a brace . . . so they won't fall backwards"). It is always dangerous to overemphasize content, but most of these answers contain hints of fragility and/or a need to conceal (big cape, big cloak, thin guys, small head, a brace so they won't fall backwards, there's no words). When considered in light of the unreal characters noted earlier, this might suggest that a serious flaw is developing in his sense of self.

The first of the two *FM* answers (7. "a bat . . . like swooping . . . it gives them enough surface to zoom back up when they want to") might be interpreted positively, but that requires considerable speculation. The second (11. "rats eating on the remains of some dead animal . . . all bloody like torn flesh or some organ") may be more direct and is not difficult to translate as reflecting a sense of guilt about having survived. The single inanimate movement answer is quite dramatic (14. "an hourglass with the sand running in it . . . like time is running out"). It has an almost hopeless quality, but may also signal some awareness that if he does not "zoom back up" soon, he may run out of time. The remaining two answers (an island, a helmet) do not contain dramatic wording or unusual embellishments.

Case 8 Summary   The subject's self-esteem appears to be similar to that of most people, but he engages in considerably more self-examining than is common, and much of it focuses on negative features. His self-image seems to reflect a composite of older, positive features plus many more recently developed negative features that have evolved from fantasy abuse and pessimism. They are creating some distortion in self-concept and there is no question that the negative features currently are having a significant impact and challenging his integrity. It seems likely that his sense of self is confused and is marked by an almost hopeless quality. He is probably aware of this and of a sense of guilt that he apparently harbors concerning his survival, but he seems unable to contend with these elements effectively.

Interpersonal Perception and Behavior

Data for the variables related to interpersonal perception are shown in Table 99.

Case 8 Findings All data, except Steps 1 (CDI), 2 (HVI), 4 (*Food*), and 7 (PER), are relevant to the interpretation.

The $a : p$ ratio suggests that he usually prefers to take a passive, but not necessarily submissive, role in interpersonal relationships. People such as this usually prefer to avoid responsibility for decision making and are less prone to seek new solutions to problems. As noted earlier, the higher values for T indicate a strong sense of loneliness or emotional loss that can be quite influential in interpersonal relationships. People who are passive and lonely often become quite vulnerable to the manipulations of others. In light of the history, it seems reasonable to postulate that both of these features are more reactive than chronic. Nonetheless, both are now present, which does not forecast a rewarding interpersonal world.

The number of human contents indicates that he has strong interest in people and the significant number of COP responses suggests that he is likely to be regarded by others as likable and outgoing. People such as this often view interpersonal activity as a very important part of their daily routines and are usually identified by those around them as among the more gregarious in group interactions. Nonetheless, the Isolation Index is positive, revealing that he is probably less involved in social interaction than most people. It seems certain that this finding is a direct product of his current state. The six movement responses containing pairs generally are positive, even though one is also morbid (two people at a costume party, maybe toasting each other; two men picking something up; two little guys riding on a teeter; two rats eating on remains; a couple of clowns leaning back laughing or something; a couple of guys talking to each other). Five of the six are also included among the nine human contents. The remaining four are negative (Dracula, a wound or something that got all torn up, giant out of science fiction, the helmet and facepiece that Darth Vader wore). Thus, it seems that his perception of others is very mixed and probably reflects some of the confusion that he is currently experiencing.

Case 8 Summary As with the findings concerning the subject's self-perception, these data convey two very different pictures. One illustrates a person with a strong interest in people and indicates that he is likely to be regarded by others as

Table 99. **Interpersonal Perception Variables for Case 8**

STRUCTURAL VARIABLES			RESPONSES TO BE READ
CDI = 2	HVI = Neg		MOVEMENT WITH PAIR = 4, 5, 9, 11, 13, 16
$a:p$ = 4:6	T = 2	Fd = 0	HUMAN CONTENTS = 1, 3, 4, 5, 6, 9, 13, 15, 16
Total Human Contents = 9			
Isolate/R = 0.31			
PER = 1	COP = 4	AG = 0	

likable and outgoing. It suggests that he regards interpersonal activity as very important to his daily routine and is likely to be identified by those around him as among the more gregarious in group interactions. The second is much more negative and suggests that he usually prefers to take a passive role in his relationships with others. He feels very lonely and is less involved in social interaction than most people. His perception of others is very inconsistent and confused.

It seems likely that the first finding reflects his preaccident view and activity, whereas the second illustrates the rather foreboding consequences that now mark his social perceptions. Obviously, they do not forecast a good future.

Case 8 Final Description

This is an ideational person who usually likes to delay and think things through before coming to a decision. There is flexibility in his coping style; sometimes he merges his feelings more directly into his thinking and some decisions have a more intuitive influence. His thinking usually is clear and relatively free of slippage, and the quality of his ideation is quite sophisticated. Currently, his thinking is also marked by two very negative features. First, he is very abusive of fantasy, using it often as an escape from unpleasantness. This is particularly detrimental for him because his basic ideational coping style becomes subservient to the avoidant orientation. Second, much of his thinking is very pessimistic. He anticipates negative outcomes regardless of his efforts, and this tends to reduce his motivation considerably. In light of the history, it seems reasonable to hypothesize that his abuse of fantasy and extreme pessimism have resulted from an inability or unwillingness to confront his recent trauma and the variety of negative elements that it has brought into his life.

He usually has enough resource available to exert adequate control over the formation and direction of responses, and his tolerance typically does not falter unless the stress is unexpected and intense or prolonged. However, there is some cause for concern because his current level of internal stimulation is higher than it should be. Thus, his capacity for control and tolerance of stress may be more tenuous than usual. He becomes engrossed with stimuli more than do most people. This seems to be the product of a scanning style that causes him to invest considerable effort and energy in processing activities. It promotes a cautious, thorough approach and ensures that all stimulus cues are included in the input. He is highly motivated in processing new information. Although he works hard at processing, his efforts usually are well within his capabilities and the quality of processing is consistent, complex, and sophisticated. His mediational activities are not different from what might be expected of an intelligent nonpatient. He is prone to translate stimuli in conventional and expected ways, but with no sacrifice of his own individuality.

There is no reason to challenge his report about being quite depressed. His emotions are clearly marked by considerable distress or discomfort, which have a much more negative influence on his thinking and decision making than should be the case. He has internalized much negative feeling and this breeds discomfort. The discomfort is increased by his tendency to ruminate about his negative features, and exacerbated even more by a strong sense of loneliness or emotional deprivation. The latter is probably related to the traumatic loss of his two friends. Currently, he seems less concerned about modulating emotional displays than may previously have been the case. This is not a negative finding, but it does not bode well if problems with controls develop. He appears to be as willing to process emotional stimuli as most adults. This is a favorable finding because people who are depressed usually withdraw from emotionally provoking situations. However, he seems to be more negativistic or hostile toward the environment than most people. This may represent some preexisting sense of individualism, but it more likely reflects a growing sense of hostility that ultimately can become very detrimental to him. His psychological functioning is more complex than should be the case. Part of this is generated by relatively strong feelings of ambivalence that cause difficulty in bringing closure to emotional situations. Another element that contributes to the complexity is intensely negative, probably painful emotion. This appears to be situational in origin, and it tends to dominate his interpretation of affective experiences and usually becomes pervasive in influencing thinking.

His self-esteem appears to be similar to that of most people, but, as noted earlier, he engages in considerably more self-examining than is common, and much of it focuses on negative features. His current self-image seems to reflect a composite of older features that are positive, plus many more recently developed negative features that have evolved from fantasy abuse and pessimism. They are creating some distortion in self-concept, and there is no question that the negative features currently are having a significant impact and challenging his integrity. It seems likely that his sense of self is confused and is marked by an almost hopeless quality. He is probably aware of this and of a sense of guilt that he apparently harbors concerning his survival.

As with the findings concerning self-perception, his interpersonal perception is marked by two very different pictures. One illustrates a person with a strong interest in people and indicates that he is likely to be regarded by others as likable and outgoing. It suggests that he regards interpersonal activity as a very important part of his daily routine and is likely to be identified by those around him as among the more gregarious in group interactions. The second is much more negative and suggests that he usually prefers to take a passive role in his relationships with others. He feels very lonely and is less involved in social interaction than most people. His perception of others is very inconsistent and confused. It seems likely that the first finding reflects his preaccident view and activity, whereas the second illustrates the rather foreboding consequences that now mark his social perceptions.

Recommendations Based on the Final Description

His current condition, even though severe, does not really approximate a chronic depression. His thinking is clear, he translates stimuli realistically and conventionally, and he continues to have a strong motivation to process new information accurately. He is tormented because he has been suppressing a great deal of very negative emotion that relates to his experienced loss of his friends and probably some guilt regarding his own survival. He has been grieving internally and, in doing so, has placed an enormous burden on himself that now tends to cloud his thinking about himself and his relationship to the world.

The 12 therapy sessions in which he has participated have probably been very supportive, but he has tended to cover over feelings rather than ventilate them. In addition, the prescription of antidepressant medication may have created an unwanted form of agitation that serves only to increase complexity rather than reduce it. Hospitalization at this time has a high risk of exacerbating his passivity and promoting more fantasy abuse. It seems more appropriate to recommend an outpatient form of crisis intervention that would include daily contacts and the possible entry into a group in which the focus is on recent loss. Obviously, he needs to explore his feelings and contend with them more directly. He should be counseled against withdrawing from school and his adviser should be solicited to provide whatever assistance might be available to ensure his continuation. Some social support structure would be ideal if one can be generated. In light of his many assets, the overall prognosis should be very favorable. A reevaluation should occur within the next four to six weeks.

Case 8 Epilogue   After the assessment, the therapy routine was altered to a crisis intervention model in which the subject was seen daily and antidepressant medication discontinued. His university department advisor arranged for special tutoring to assist in completing the two courses for which he remained enrolled. The therapist reported reasonably favorable progress once the issue of guilt feelings began to be addressed. Approximately four weeks after the evaluation, a financial settlement was made regarding a psychic injury claim that had been filed on behalf of the subject. According to the therapist, progress increased remarkably once the issue of litigation was resolved, and the therapy schedule was reduced to once per week. The subject completed final examinations and received grades of "A" for both of his university courses. He proceeded to register for four summer courses and remained in weekly treatment. Ultimately, he completed all four courses (3 "A's" and 1 "B"), terminated treatment, and entered a law school in the fall.

CHAPTER 14

Personality Deficits

During the past two decades there has been a substantial shift in attention among professionals toward greater concern with issues of personality deficiencies or disorders. Much of this shift in attention can probably be attributed to Kernberg's (1967) provocative work concerning borderline personality organization and Kohut's (1971) intricate work regarding narcissism. Whereas focus had been on the borderline personality, a renewed interest in various personality deficits has occurred and numerous expositions have focused on this issue (Frances, 1980, 1982; Koenigsberg, Kaplan, Gilmore, & Cooper, 1985; Millon, 1981; Morey, 1988; Widiger & Frances, 1985).

This attention has been further stimulated by the fact that a substantial number of patients presenting depressive symptoms also show evidence of a deficient or disordered personality (Farmer & Nelson-Gray, 1990). This fact is not surprising because depression is a much more socially acceptable complaint, whereas few people are prone to seek intervention because of some undefined but irritating personality deficiencies. In most instances, people who have personality deficits present symptoms that are predisposed by the deficit, but that often are not readily attributable to the presence of a deficit. For instance, Cases 1 and 2 both presented anxiety and somatic symptoms that had origins in their respective personality structures. In Case 1, a rather immature, histrionic picture unfolded. In Case 2, the findings reflected a more withdrawn, schizoid personality structure. In Case 4 the picture was more complex as the underlying schizoid features gave rise to faulty thinking as the struggle to maintain contact with the world intensified. A basic obsessive personality constituted an important foundation in Case 5, whereas a more naïve and immature borderline structure seemed to predispose the chronic depressive complaints in Case 6. Cases 9 and 10 have been selected to illustrate some other forms of personality organization in which significant deficits exist.

CASE 9: A NARCISSISTIC DISORDER

This 23-year-old male was evaluated in conjunction with entry into a substance abuse program. He had been using cocaine daily for at least two years and recently had an episode of disorientation that was very frightening to him and the woman with whom he lives. The episode lasted for several hours. According to his girlfriend, he was alternately violent and suicidal, striking her several times and threatening her with a knife, and sitting on a window ledge for about 45 minutes threatening to jump. She called his brother, who was able to subdue him and took him to an emergency room. He was admitted overnight and sedated, and the next morning he signed himself out and returned home. His girlfriend was already packing to move out before his return. He pleaded with her to stay and she agreed, provided he seek help. She has agreed to enter treatment with him.

The subject is the younger of two sons, having a brother, age 25, who is a certified public accountant. His father, age 48, is also a certified public accountant and owns his own small firm. His mother, age 48, is a college graduate and has taught elementary school for the past five years. She did not finish her degree until the subject had graduated from high school, although she had completed two years of college before her oldest son was born. There is no reported psychiatric history in the immediate family. The subject graduated from college at age 21, having majored in business administration. His cumulative grade point average was 2.9. Since graduation he has been employed as an industrial salesman for a chemical firm that manufactures solvents. His work history is reported to be good and he has received three salary increases during his 27 months of employment, plus a bonus during the past year. He says that he enjoys his work and expects to become an assistant sales manager in the near future. He has asked for and received a one-month unpaid leave of absence.

He reports an unremarkable developmental history and has been free of serious injuries or illnesses. He states that he was close to both parents and especially close to his brother, with whom he shared a bedroom until age nine. He and his brother both played Little League baseball and both were in the Boy Scouts until he was 15. He had become a First Class Scout by that time. He claims to have had many high school and college friends, and was in a fraternity in college. He reports that his first sexual experience occurred when he was age 15. He denies any homosexual experiences. Apparently, he dated one girl regularly during his sophomore year in college but she broke up with him before the end of that year. He met his current girlfriend about 18 months ago at a party given by a mutual friend. They dated regularly for about eight months and, when the lease on her apartment expired, they decided to live together in his apartment. He states that they have discussed marriage but he is reluctant until he feels more secure in his work. He admits that their sexual relationship is "not always good," but attributes this to his cocaine addiction. She has reported that he has frequently been impotent and sometimes has ejaculated prematurely. She also notes that he frequently asks her to dress in unusual ways to stimulate him.

He says that he became casually involved with cocaine during his senior year in college, although he admits that he had been using marijuana since high school and experimented with other drugs during his college years. He reports that he found it helpful to him in dealing with the pressures of his job and ultimately began using it daily. He claims that he usually would not use it during the day except during the past month, but did use it each evening at home. He says that he also drinks one or two glasses of wine daily.

He is 5 feet 11 inches, 175 pounds, athletic looking, attractive, and neatly dressed. During the initial interview he often asked that questions be repeated, but he seemed open and cooperative when responding. He was especially cautious in describing his feelings for his girlfriend: "She's just great, I don't know how she's put up with me. She really deserves better. I hope everything works out for her, I owe her a lot."

The treatment program that he is entering requires a minimum of 14 days of inpatient routine, followed by a minimum of six weeks of twice-per-week

Case 9: A 23-Year-Old Male

Card	Response	Inquiry
I	1. A bf, sbody told me tht thy all ll bf's	*E:* (Rpts S's resp)
	E: Tak ur tim & look som more, I thk u'll find sthg else too	*S:* Well its got the wgs, thyr out lik it is in flight & the body in the cntr & the littl antennae, jus a bf
	v2. Ths way it ll a pagoda	*E:* (Rpts S's resp)
		S: U kno lik thy hav thos thgs going up & weird designs & the crown is at the top, it comes to a point & it has thes opengs in it (S) not windows but opengs tht r part of the design, I'v seen em in magazines
II	3. Two people at a party or sthg, it ll thyr shaking hands	*E:* (Rpts S's resp)
		S: Mayb a costume party cuz u can't mak out a lot of features. It ll thyv got their hands togethr lik thyr shaking hands, it ll thyr wearing cloaks or big coats & thyr bending forward, lik greeting e.o.
		E: U said thyr at a party or sthg
		S: Well thyr wearing red hats & those big cloaks so I figure a party
	4. The red down here ll a crab, lik a horseshoe crab but I don't thk thy have 2 tails	*E:* (Rpts S's resp)
		S: Well it has tht shape except for the 2 tails & the variations in the coloring gives it the impression of a hard shell
		E: A hard shell?
		S: It has kind of a shiny appearance lik it was hard
III	5. Ths ll a wm lookg in the mirror kinda checking herself out	*E:* (Rpts S's resp)
		S: Ths stuff down here (D7) doesn't count, just this part (D9), she's bendg forward a littl lik she's just checkg herself out, c the big nose & her arm, her leg & her breast
IV	6. I'd say a tree at night	*E:* (Rpts S's resp)
		S: Ths is the trunk & the big arching top, lik a big maple or oak, we hav alot on our street tht hav ths shape
		E: U said at nite?
		S: Well its all black, lik a silhouette
V	7. A bird, no wait I'll say a bf	*E:* (Rpts S's resp)
		S: It really looks more lik a bf w the wgs extended lik thy do when the air lifts them & the antennae r here

(continued)

385

Case 9: (Continued)

Card	Response	Inquiry
	v8. When I look ths way it looks mor lik a bird	E: (Rpts S's resp) S: Well the othr way the wgs were rite for a bf but ths way thy come forward, lik a bird thts flapping its wgs & ths (D9) is lik the beak is open, it re me of a swallow, I'v seen pict's lik ths of them
VI <9.	Ths re me of an iceberg thts floating in the water & its reflected down here	E: (Rpts S's resp) S: Well it has an irreg shape & ths line is lik the water & down here its the same, it has a cold look to it thts why I thot of an iceberg E: I'm not sur what there is tht gives it a cold look S: Its all diff shades of grey & blk lik a big huge chunk of ice, lik it wld really b cold if u sat on it
VII 10.	Ths ll a weird statue of 2 people w their heads turned backward lookg at e.o.	E: (Rpts S's resp) S: Ths cb their arms & noses & faces & ths is ss of hair style if thyr wm or mayb a feather if thry supp to b kids, I guess thy cb either
v11.	Ths way it re me of one of thos arch thgs lik u grow flowers on, usually roses or smthg, we had one in our backyrd tht my mother was always trimming	E: (Rpts S's resp) S: Well it has the gen shape of an arch & these thgs cb the flowers stickg out on sides & ths white cntr is where u can walk thry, its lik a trellis tht u can walk thur, we used to run thru it playg tag & my mothr wld hav a fit cuz we'd grab it & she was always worried we'd pull it down
VIII 12.	Well, the first thg I thot of was a big birthday cake	E: (Rpts S's resp) S: It has all different colors of icing on it & it has 2 little candles on top E: I'm not sur I'm seeg it lik u r S: Well it has three layers, c here (D4), here (D5) & here (D2) & each is a diff color & then there's pink designs out here & white frosting too, sort of lik in between the layers, its very pretty & up here it ll 2 littl candles (Dd24)
13.	It cb a crown too, lik one u c in Nat'l Geo-graphic tht some oriental prince mite wear at special occasions	E: (Rpts S's resp) S: Well it has all the diff colors & the designs on the sides ll 2 A's & it has the peak, it all looks glittery lik it had a look of glass or jewels in it E: Glass or jewels? S: Well each section, it has 3 sections, has various shades of the coloring, it gives it a glittery look, Iv seen some lik ths in Nat'l Geographic

IX
14. Up here it ll a cpl of wizards or witches mak-ing sthg in ths cauldron

E: (Rpts S's resp)
S: Well thyv got pointed hats & orange robes & it ll thy hav got their arms out ovr ths cauldron, c ths round cntr thg, its all white lik it contains magic fog or smoke, lik u can c in it & its all hazy lik u c in the movies
E: U can c thru it?
S: Not thru it, in it, lik its transparent, c the white looks hazy, lik smthg is bubblg in it & thyv got their arms ovr it lik thyr makg smthg

v15. Ths way ths part ll a corkscrew

E: (Rpts S's resp)
S: C ths part (D5) is what goes into the bottl & here (D6) is the handle, just lik a corkscrew lik to open wine

X
16. The 1st thg I thk of here is a firewrks display, lik on the 4th of July

E: (Rpts S's resp)
S: It just ll its bursting outward, all of the colors are going outward in a symmetrical fashion, lik to represent celebration, just a lot of colors exploding outward at the same time lik u c if u watch fireworks

17. Ths part up here re me of the Eiffel Tower

E: (Rpts S's resp)
S: It just has that shape to it, I've been to Paris & it looks very much lik ths

18. These thgs cb fancy blue earrings

E: (Rpts S's resp)
S: Yes, lik made out of some pretty blue sapphires, its a blue jewel, thry irregular in shape & thy hav a shimmery effect to them
E: Shimmery effect?
S: The diff variations of blue mak them ll thyr moving slightly, sort of the way jewels sparkle as lite hits thm differntly

19. Ths othr blue cb a wm's bra

E: (Rpts S's resp)
S: Sort of a fancy one, blu, it just ll tht, I'd guess about a 36C

20. U kno w the symmetrical effect & all the colors it ll a mobile, lik abstract art w all the pieces hangg in a symmetrical pattern

E: (Rpts Ss resp)
S: If u'v evr been to a museum where thy specialize in abstracts thy always hav mobiles, ths one is very colorful, mor lik a child mite do, most of the ones I'v seen by artists r made of metal but ths one is just loaded w colors & up here is where it wld hang from & evthg goes out fr these lrge pink thgs alth u can't c all of the connections, lik ths green dwn here ll its suspended by itself, evthg is interconnected

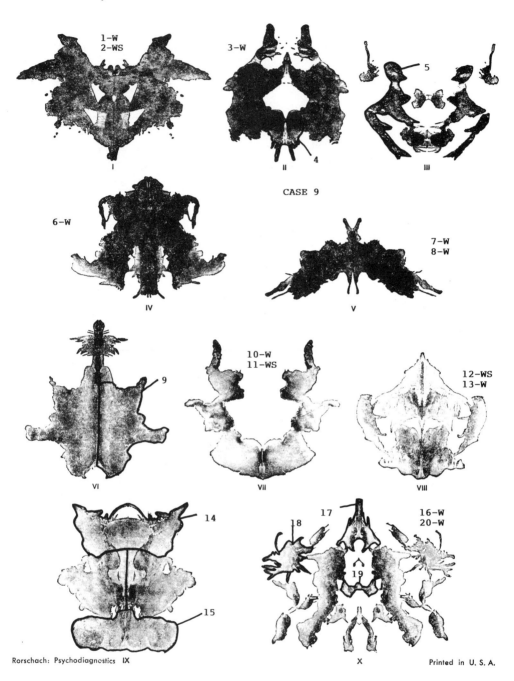

CASE 9

Printed in U. S. A.

CASE 9   SEQUENCE OF SCORES

CARD	NO	LOC	#	DETERMINANT(S)	(2)	CONTENT(S)	POP	Z	SPECIAL SCORES
I	1	Wo	1	FMao		A	P	1.0	
	2	WSo	1	Fu		Ay		3.5	PER
II	3	W+	1	Ma.FCo	2	H,Cg		4.5	COP
	4	Do	3	FTo		A			
III	5	D+	9	Mp.Fro		H	P	4.0	
IV	6	Wo	1	FC'o		Bt		2.0	PER
V	7	Wo	1	FMpo		A	P	1.0	
	8	Wo	1	FMao		A		1.0	PER
VI	9	D/	4	mp.rF.TFo		Na		2.5	
VII	10	W+	1	Mpo	2	Art,(H)	P	2.5	
	11	WS+	1	Fu		Id,Bt		4.0	PER
VIII	12	WS+	1	CF.C'F-		Fd,Id		4.5	
	13	Wo	1	CF.YFu	2	Art,(A)		4.5	PER
IX	14	DS+	3	Ma.FC.FVo	2	(H),Cl		2.5	AB,COP
	15	Do	9	Fu		Hh			
X	16	Wv	1	ma.CFu		Ex			
	17	Do	11	Fo		Ay			PER
	18	Do	1	CF.YF.mpu	2	Art			
	19	Do	6	FCu		Cg,Sx			
	20	Wo	1	CF.mpu		Art		5.5	

CASE 9 STRUCTURAL SUMMARY

```
===============================================================================
LOCATION              DETERMINANTS            CONTENTS      S-CONSTELLATION
FEATURES         BLENDS        SINGLE                       NO..FV+VF+V+FD>2
                                         H   = 2, 0         YES..Col-Shd Bl>0
Zf   = 14    M.FC          M   = 1       (H) = 1, 1         YES..Ego<.31,>.44
ZSum = 43.0  M.Fr          FM  = 3       Hd  = 0, 0         NO..MOR > 3
ZEst = 45.5  m.rF.TF       m   = 0       (Hd)= 0, 0         NO..Zd > +- 3.5
             CF.C'F        FC  = 1       Hx  = 0, 0         YES..es > EA
W   = 12     CF.YF         CF  = 0       A   = 4, 0         YES..CF+C > FC
 (Wv = 1)    M.FC.FV       C   = 0       (A) = 0, 1         YES..X+% < .70
D   = 8      m.CF          Cn  = 0       Ad  = 0, 0         YES..S > 3
Dd  = 0      CF.YF.m       FC' = 1       (Ad)= 0, 0         NO..P < 3 or > 8
S   = 4      CF.m          C'F = 0       An  = 0, 0         NO..Pure H < 2
                           C'  = 0       Art = 4, 0         NO..R < 17
  DQ                       FT  = 1       Ay  = 2, 0          6.....TOTAL
.........(FQ-)             TF  = 0       Bl  = 0, 0
 +  =  6  ( 1)             T   = 0       Bt  = 1, 1         SPECIAL SCORINGS
 o  = 12  ( 0)             FV  = 0       Cg  = 1, 1            Lv1     Lv2
v/+ =  1  ( 0)             VF  = 0       Cl  = 0, 1       DV   = 0x1    0x2
 v  =  1  ( 0)             V   = 0       Ex  = 1, 0       INC  = 0x2    0x4
                           FY  = 0       Fd  = 1, 0       DR   = 0x3    0x6
                           YF  = 0       Fi  = 0, 0       FAB  = 0x4    0x7
                           Y   = 0       Ge  = 0, 0       ALOG = 0x5
    FORM QUALITY           Fr  = 0       Hh  = 1, 0       CON  = 0x7
                           rF  = 0       Ls  = 0, 0          SUM6  = 0
    FQx  FQf  MQual  SQx   FD  = 0       Na  = 1, 0         WSUM6  = 0
 +  = 0   0    0     0     F   = 4       Sc  = 0, 0
 o  = 11  1    4     1                   Sx  = 0, 1       AB  = 1    CP  = 0
 u  = 8   3    0     2                   Xy  = 0, 0       AG  = 0    MOR = 0
 -  = 1   0    0     1                   Id  = 1, 1       CFB = 0    PER = 6
none= 0   --   0     0     (2) = 5                        COP = 2    PSV = 0
===============================================================================
                RATIOS, PERCENTAGES, AND DERIVATIONS

R = 20          L = 0.25           FC:CF+C = 3: 5     COP = 2    AG = 0
------------------------------     Pure C  =    0     Food       =  1
EB = 4: 6.5  EA = 10.5  EBPer= 1.6 Afr    =0.82       Isolate/R  =0.30
eb = 7: 7    es = 14      D  = -1  S      = 4         H:(H)Hd(Hd)= 2: 2
         Adj es = 10   Adj D =  0  Blends:R= 9:20     (HHd):(AAd)= 2: 1
------------------------------     CP     = 0         H+A:Hd+Ad  = 9: 0
FM = 3  :  C'= 2   T = 2
m  = 4  :  V = 1   Y = 2
                       P     = 4      Zf    =14        3r+(2)/R=0.55
a:p   = 5: 6  Sum6  = 0  X+% =0.55    Zd    = -2.5     Fr+rF     = 2
Ma:Mp = 2: 2  Lv2   = 0  F+% =0.25    W:D:Dd=12: 8: 0  FD        = 0
2AB+Art+Ay= 8 WSum6 = 0  X-% =0.05    W:M   =12: 4     An+Xy     = 0
M-    = 0     Mnone = 0  S-% =1.00    DQ+   = 6        MOR       = 0
                         Xu% =0.40    DQv   = 1
------------------------------------------------------------------------
  SCZI = 0    DEPI = 4    CDI = 1    S-CON = 6    HVI = No    OBS = No
===============================================================================
```

outpatient treatment that consists of one individual session and one group session. If his girlfriend enters treatment, she will not go through the inpatient routine, but instead will begin an eight-week outpatient routine of individual and group sessions.

Drug screening prior to the evaluation was positive but not toxic. Neuropsychology screening was essentially negative. The assessment issues are as follows: (1) Is there any serious psychiatric disturbance? (2) How well will he respond to a highly structured inpatient program? (3) What is the prognosis for his staying in treatment? (4) Are there any specific recommendations for focus in individual treatment?

Interpretive Strategy

The record contains 20 answers, therefore it appears to be interpretively useful. The first positive Key variable is that the D Score is less than the Adj D Score. This identifies the search strategy for only the first two groups of data, the cluster regarding controls and the array of data concerning situational stress. The second positive Key variable is that $Fr + rF$ is greater than zero. This finding adds two more clusters to the search routine: self-perception and interpersonal perception. A third positive Key variable, EB is extratensive, fleshes out the remainder of the interpretive procedure. Thus, the entire routine is:

CONTROLS → SITUATIONAL STRESS → SELF-PERCEPTION → INTERPERSONAL PERCEPTION → AFFECT → PROCESSING → MEDIATION → IDEATION.

Initial Proposition: In this instance, as many as three initial propositions could be generated (one concerning situational stress, one concerning the reflection finding, and the third regarding the extratensive EB), but this is probably not a good idea because too many assumptions become involved that could prove to be misleading or erroneous in light of early findings. Accordingly, it is best to formulate only one initial proposition based on the first Key variable, that is, that the subject is experiencing a significant increase in stimulus demands as a result of situationally-related stress. Thus, some decisions and/or behaviors may not be as well organized as is usually the case, and the subject is more vulnerable to impulsiveness in thinking, affect, and/or behavioral disorganization in complex or highly ambiguous situations.

Controls and Stress Tolerance

Data for the variables related to capacities for control and tolerance for stress are shown in Table 100.

Table 100.   Control-Related Variables for Case 9

$EB = 4:6.5$	$EA = 10.5$	$D\ \ = -1$	$CDI = 1$
$eb\ = 7:7$	$es = 14$ Adj$es = 10$	AdjD $= 0$	
$FM = 3$ $m = 4$ $C' = 2$ $T = 2$ $V = 1$ $Y = 2$			

Case 9 Findings All data in the cluster are relevant to the interpretation.

The subject's Adj D Score is zero and CDI is negative, which suggests that he typically has enough resource accessible to participate meaningfully in the formulation and direction of responses. His tolerance for stress is like that of most people; that is, controls usually falter only if the stress is unexpected and intense or prolonged. The *EA* value is well into the average range, and the *EB* contains no zero values. The *es* has a value of 10, which is also in the average range, and the *eb* shows values on both sides. Therefore, there seems to be no reason to challenge the reliability of the Adj D Score.

Case 9 Summary Ordinarily, his capacities for control and tolerance for stress are like that of most people. He has enough resource accessible to formulate and implement responses and his stress tolerance is likely to be exceeded only under unusual conditions.

Situation-Related Stress

Data for the array of variables related to situational stress are shown in Table 101.

Case 9 Findings All data in the array are relevant to the interpretation.

The difference between the two D Scores has already been noted in the initial proposition that he is currently in stimulus overload because of situationally-related stress. The fact that the D Score is −1 suggests that he is not necessarily disorganized, but it does indicate that some of his decisions or behaviors may not be well thought out, and he is vulnerable to impulsiveness in thinking or emotions. The elevated value for *T* indicates that some of this vulnerability is generated by a sense of emotional deprivation, loss, or loneliness, but the history does not make it clear that this is a recent event. Thus, this feature may be more chronic than situational. The increased values for *m* and *Y* suggest that the effects of the stress are more diffuse than specific, although there is a more notable increase in peripheral ideation that probably affects attention and concentration. The fact that three of his nine blends are constituted by *m* or *Y* determinants makes it very probable that the current stress is creating substantially more complexity than is common. Two of the three are Color-Shading blends, suggesting that one result of the current condition is an increase in confusion about feelings.

Table 101. Array of Stress Related Variables for Case 9

				BLENDS		
D = −1	ADJ D = 0			M.FC.FV	m.CF	CF.YF
m = 3,	*Y* = 2,	*T* = 2		M.Fr	CF.YF.m	
Pure *C* = 0		Blends	= 9	M.FC	CF.m	
M− = 0		*M*Q none = 0		m.rF.TF	CF.C'F	

Case 9 Summary   He is currently in stimulus overload because of situationally-related stress. This does not mean that he is disorganized, but it does indicate that some of his actions may not be well thought out. The effects of the stress have also created a vulnerability to impulsiveness in thinking or emotions. The effects of the stress appear to be more diffuse than specific, although there is a more notable increase in peripheral ideation that probably affects attention and concentration. The stress has also increased his complexity and confusion about his feelings.

Self-Perception

The data for variables related to self-perception are shown in Table 102.

Case 9 Findings   All data except those for Steps 5 ($An + Xy$), 6 (MOR), and 7 (MOR contents) are relevant to the interpretation.

The presence of the reflection answers indicates that a core element in his personality is a narcissistic-like tendency to overvalue his personal worth. This is natural among children but it usually disappears during early adolescence. When it persists it tends to be a dominant psychological influence that, although not necessarily pathological, has a substantial influence on perceptions of the world, as well as on decisions and behaviors. A by-product is the development of a marked style oriented toward the reaffirmation and protection of the exaggerated self-value. This style contributes significantly to the development of motives for status, and the formation of an elaborate defense system that typically involves an excessive reliance on rationalization, externalization, and denial. People such as this often find it difficult to establish and maintain deep, meaningful interpersonal relationships, and, in instances in which the environment is unrewarding, asocial or antisocial sets can evolve easily. The value for the Egocentricity Index confirms the fact that he is very self-focusing or self-centered.

Interestingly, he is involved in introspection that focuses on his perceived negative features. As a result, painful feelings that are difficult to contend with often occur. This is an unusual finding for one with narcissistic features and might be an asset to psychotherapy as it could represent some ongoing struggle with the issue of high self-value versus perceived negative features of the self. The number of Pure H responses is somewhat low and difficult to interpret; however, it may indicate that his self-concept is based less on imagination than

Table 102.   Self Perception Variables for Case 9

STRUCTURAL DATA		RESPONSES TO BE READ
$Fr+rF = 2$	$3r+(2)/R = 0.55$	MOR RESPONSES = NA
$FD = 0$	$V = 1$	MINUS RESPONSES = 12
$HH)+Hd+(Hd) = 2 : 2$		M RESPONSES = 3, 5, 10, 14
$An+Xy = 0$		FM RESPONSES = 1, 7, 8
$MOR = 0$		m RESPONSES = 9, 16, 18, 20

might be suspected. The single minus response is quite interesting (12. "a big birthday cake . . . all different colors of icing . . . and it has two little candles on top"). It is a rather juvenile response and, of course, has a self-glorifying content.

Three of the four *M* answers also seem more juvenile than adult when considered in the context of self-image (5. "a woman looking in the mirror kinda checking herself out," 10. "a weird statue of two people with their heads turned backward looking at each other," 14. "a couple of wizards or witches making something in this cauldron"). On the other hand, the fourth is much more sophisticated and adult-like (3. "Two people at a party or something, it looks like they are shaking hands"). The three *FM* answers do not contain any easily detectable projected material (1. "A butterfly . . . it's got the wings, they are out like it is in flight," 7. "A butterfly . . . with the wings extended like they do when the air lifts them," 8. "like a bird that's flapping its wings . . . like the beak is open").

The *m* answers are more intriguing (9. "an iceberg . . . floating in the water . . . it has a cold look to it," 16. "a fireworks display, like on the Fourth of July . . . like to represent celebration," 18. "fancy blue earrings . . . it's a blue jewel . . . they have a shimmery effect to them," 20. "a mobile, like abstract art . . . more like a child might do . . . just loaded with colors . . . this green thing down here looks like it's suspended by itself"). Three of the four are elaborately exhibitionistic, whereas the fourth seems to convey something guarded, concealed, impenetrable, and threatening. In searching through the eight remaining answers for unusual wording or embellishments, it is difficult to avoid being impressed by the contents. Five are also exhibitionistic (2. "a pagoda," 11. "one of those arch things like you grow flowers on," 13. "a crown . . . that some oriental prince might wear at special occasions," 17. "the Eiffel Tower," 19. "a woman's bra"). The remaining three have much the same impenetrable feature as the iceberg (4. "a horseshoe crab," 6. "a tree at night . . . the trunk and the big arching top," 15. "a corkscrew . . . like to open wine").

The characteristics of the two *T* answers are quite unusual and raise a question about his sense of deprivation. The first (horseshoe crab) is described as, "a shiny appearance like it was hard." The second (iceberg) is described as, "like it would really be cold if you sat on it." Empirical data regarding these highly unusual forms of *T* are lacking because the frequencies are so low. People who give answers such as these are likely to regard and experience tactile exchange very differently from those who give the soft or furry descriptions that characterize most *T* answers.

Case 9 Summary   The subject's personality is clearly marked by a narcissistic tendency to overvalue his own worth. This feature exerts a dominating influence on his perceptions of the world as well as on decisions and behaviors. Its presence requires that it be reaffirmed and protected, and an elaborate system of defense typically evolves that relies mainly on rationalization and denial. It also tends to promote substantial motives for status. People such as this often find it difficult to establish and maintain deep relationships and often use their interpersonal skills to manipulate others to their own ends. If the environment is unrewarding, asocial or antisocial sets evolve easily.

It is interesting to note that he often engages in self-inspecting behaviors that focus on his negative features, and this results in aggravating feelings. This is an unusual finding and may signal some ongoing struggle with the issue of high self-value versus perceived negative features of the self. His self-concept appears to include many juvenile and exhibitionistic features that tend to sustain his exquisite self-centeredness. At the same time, he tries to conceal any flaws and ensure his own aloofness and impenetrability.

Interpersonal Perception

The data for the variables related to interpersonal perception are shown in Table 103.

Case 9 Findings   All of the data, except those for Steps 1 (CDI), 2 (HVI), and 3 ($a:p$), are relevant to the interpretation.

The Food response suggests that he has stronger needs to be dependent on others than is usual. People such as this tend to rely on others for support and often are more naïve in their expectations about interpersonal relationships. The two T responses indicate that he is experiencing a sense of loneliness or emotional deprivation that can be very influential in his interpersonal relationships. As discussed previously, the characteristics of the two T answers (crab and iceberg) are quite unusual and raise a question about his sense of loneliness or deprivation. It is possible that his needs for closeness manifest in rather unusual ways. His girlfriend's report that he often asks her to dress in unusual ways to arouse him may relate to this finding.

The four human contents indicate that he appears to have as much interest in others as do most people. However, the six PER responses indicate that he is quite insecure about his personal integrity and tends to be overly authoritarian when interpersonal situations appear to pose challenges to the self. People such as this are often seen as rigid or narrow by others and they frequently have difficulties in maintaining close relationships, especially with those who are not submissive to them. The two COP answers suggest that he perceives positive interactions among people to be a routine, and he is willing to participate in them, but this does not necessarily mean that his relationships will be positive or mature. In fact, the positive Isolation Index suggests that he tends to be less involved in social interaction than most people. This does not necessarily mean that he avoids social relationships, but it does suggest that they will be less broad or diversified than expected.

Table 103.   Interpersonal Perception Variables for Case 9

STRUCTURAL VARIABLES			RESPONSES TO BE READ
CDI = 1	HVI = Neg		MOVEMENT WITH PAIR = 3, 10, 14, 18
$a:p$ = 5:6	T = 2	Fd = 1	HUMAN CONTENTS = 3, 5, 10, 14
Total Human Contents = 4			
Isolate/R = 0.30			
PER = 6	COP = 2	AG = 0	

One of the four movement answers containing a pair seems to reflect a very positive view of interpersonal contact (two people at a party shaking hands) but the answer is also marked by guardedness or concealment (both are wearing cloaks or big coats). The remaining three answers are more negative (a weird statue of two people with their heads turned backward looking at each other; a couple of wizards or witches making something in a cauldron; fancy blue earrings that have a shimmery effect). At best, his perception of interaction is unusual. Similarly, the four human contents do not seem to illustrate a very mature perception of others (two people shaking hands, a woman looking in a mirror, a statute of two people with their heads turned backward, and two wizards or witches).

Case 9 Summary   He appears to need to be dependent on others and may be more naïve in his expectations about relationships than should be the case. He is lonely or feels deprived, but his sense of neediness may not equate directly with that experienced by others. Instead, it may manifest in more atypical ways. The report of his girlfriend that he often asked her to dress in unusual ways to arouse him may have some relation to this finding. He appears to be interested in people, but he is insecure about his personal integrity and tends to be overly authoritarian when interpersonal situations appear to pose challenges to him. He is probably regarded by others as being rigid or narrow, and he is likely to have difficulties in maintaining close relationships, especially with those who are not submissive to him. He seems to anticipate that most interpersonal relationships will be positive, and he is willing to participate in them. Nevertheless, it seems likely that he is less involved in social interaction than most people. This does not necessarily mean that he avoids social relationships, but it does suggest that they will be fewer in number and have less depth than might be expected. A sense of guardedness or concealment appears to mark much of his interpersonal contact, and it is doubtful that his perceptions of others are very realistic.

Affective Features

Data for the variables related to affect are shown in Table 104.

Case 9 Findings   All data, except Steps 5 (Pure C), 7 (Color Projection), and 13 (shading blends), are relevant to the interpretation.

The EB indicates that his basic coping style is one in which he tends to merge feelings with thinking during problem solving or decision making. People such as

Table 104.   Affect-Related Variables for Case 9

				BLENDS	
$EB = 4 : 6.5$	$EBPer = 1.6$	$DEPI = 4$			
$eb = 7 : 7$	$(C = 2, T = 2, V = 1, Y = 2)$		M.FC.FV	m.CF	CF.YF
$FC:CF+C = 3 : 5$	Pure $C = 0$		M.FC	CF.YF.m	
$Afr = 0.82$	CP = 0		M.Fr	CF.m	
$S = 4$	Col-Shd Bl = 4		m.rF.TF	CF.C'F	

this are prone to use and be influenced by emotion, and usually prefer to test postulates through trial-and-error behavior. They also are more willing to display feelings openly and often are less concerned about carefully modulating those displays. The *EBPer* suggests that there is some flexibility to this style and that, at times, he puts feelings aside in favor of a more clearly ideational approach.

The right-side *eb* value is substantial, indicating that he is experiencing considerable negative emotional stimulation. Some of this is situationally-related (*Y*), but some also is being generated by his sense of loneliness or deprivation (*T*), and some derives from his previously mentioned negative introspection (*V*). He does not modulate his emotional displays as much as most adults do, and at times these displays are overly intense, even to the casual observer. He is as willing to process emotional stimuli as most adults, which is not a problem except that, when processing emotion occurs, some exchange often is required. If the exchange is overly intense, it can be counterproductive. One of the most important findings is the elevated value for *S*, which signifies that he has a very negative, angry attitude toward the environment. This is a trait-like feature that has some impact on his functioning. The anger may not manifest overtly, but it has some impact on decision making and coping activities. People like this often have difficulty sustaining deep and/or meaningful relationships with others as they tend to be less tolerant of the routine compromises usually required in social intercourse.

The number of blends reveals that his functioning is more complex than ordinarily expected. This complexity in functioning increases the possibility that emotion can have a detrimental influence on his behavioral consistency. As noted earlier, most of this complexity results from situationally-related stress. The presence of four Color-Shading blends indicates that he often finds emotions confusing and may frequently experience both positive and negative feelings about the same stimulus situation. Although this ambivalence has been increased by situational stress, it is likely that it existed at a lower level prior to the current state.

Case 9 Summary   The subject usually merges feelings with his thinking during problem solving or decision making. People such as this are prone to use and be influenced by emotion, and usually prefer to test postulates through trial-and-error behavior. There is some flexibility to this style, and he sometimes puts aside feelings in favor of a more clearly ideational approach. This coping style can be very effective, especially if there are no problems in control and if emotions do not become overly intense. In this case, both of these problems exist. He has potential problems in control because of his current overload state but, even without the situational stress, he is less stringent about modulating emotional discharges than most adults. In other words, his emotions may often become overly intense, and, as such, may become excessively influential in his thinking and decision operations.

He is experiencing considerable negative emotion, some of which is situationally-related, but some is more chronic, provoked by his sense of loneliness or deprivation and his previously mentioned negative introspection. His failure to modulate his emotional displays as much as most adults may sometimes call attention to his intense feelings, even to the casual observer. A very important finding is the presence of a seriously negative, angry attitude toward the environment that invariably affects his functioning. The anger may not manifest overtly, but it is likely to have some impact on decision making and coping activities. People like this often have difficulty sustaining deep relationships with others as they tend to be less tolerant of the routine compromises usually required in social intercourse.

His current functioning is more complex than is ordinary for him. Most of the added complexity results from the situationally-related stress that he is experiencing. The stress has also exacerbated a marked confusion that he has about emotion. This tendency to become ambivalent in emotional situations existed prior to his current state, but the overload has increased the frequency by which it occurs.

Information Processing

Data for the variables related to processing are shown in Table 105.

Case 9 Findings   All data are relevant to interpretation except Step 2 (OBS and HVI).

The lower than expected value for Lambda suggests that he becomes overly involved in stimulus complexity. This is probably related to the current stress situation and coincides with the earlier finding that his functioning has increased in complexity. The values for Zf, $W:D:Dd$, and $W:M$ indicate that he makes a considerable effort in processing, especially when the information involved relates to problem solving or decision making. The DQ distribution suggests that the quality of processing is similar to that of most adults and the Zd score indicates that the same is true for scanning efficiency. The location sequencing is reasonably consistent, although it is interesting to note that he gives two W responses to five of the 10 blots. This probably reflects his strong motivation to process new information.

Case 9 Summary   Overall, his processing activities are marked by considerable effort and the quality of the input seems to be similar to that found among most nonpatient adults.

Cognitive Mediation

Data for the variables related to mediational activity are shown in Table 106.

Case 9 Findings   The data for Steps 3 (Populars), 5 ($X+\%$), 7 ($Xu\%$), 8 ($X-\%$), and 11 (minus distortion level) are relevant to the interpretation.

Table 105.   Information Processing Variables for Case 9

$L = 0.25$	OBS = Neg	HVI = Neg		LOCATION SEQUENCING		
$Zd = -2.5$	$DQ+$ = 6		I W,WS	IV W	VII WS,W
$Zf = 14$	$DQv/+$ = 1		II W,D	V W,W	VIII WS,W
$W:D:Dd = 12:8:0$	DQv = 1		III D	VI D	IX DS,D
$W:M = 12:4$	PSV = 0				X W,D,D,D,W

Table 106.   Cognitive Mediation Variables for Case 9

		MINUS FEATURES
Lambda = 0.25	OBS = Neg	
P = 4	*X+%* = .55	VIII 12. *WS+ CF.C′F− Fd,Id 4.5*
FQx+ = 0	*F+%* = .25	
FQxo = 11	*Xu%* = .40	
FQxu = 8	*X−%* = .05	
FQx− = 1	*S−%* = 1.00	
FQnone = 0	CONFAB = 0	

The relatively low value *P* suggests that he is not likely to translate stimuli in conventional ways, even in situations that are simple and/or precisely defined in ways that make the conventional translation obvious. This lack of conventionality is also reflected in the lower than expected *X + %* and the much higher than expected value for the *Xu%*. He does not distort stimulus inputs, as evidenced by the modest *X − %*, which involves only one minus answer that is a Level 1 distortion. Instead, he has a marked tendency to overpersonalize or individualize translations much more than most people. As a result, he is likely to display a higher than usual frequency of behaviors that disregard social demands or expectations. A high frequency of atypical behaviors frequently sets the stage for confrontation with the environment.

Case 9 Summary   He tends to perceive the world through his own special set of psychological lenses. He translates events much less conventionally and much more in accord with his own needs or sets. Thus, many of his behaviors ignore social expectations or demands, and these less conventional behaviors are likely to occur with sufficient frequency to make confrontations with the environment inevitable.

Ideation

Data for the variables related to ideation are shown in Table 107.

Table 107.   Ideation Variables for Case 9

		M QUALITY	CRITICAL SPECIAL SCORES			
EB = 4 : 6.5	*EBPer* = 1.6					
eb = 7 : 7	(*FM* = 3 *m* = 4)	+ = 0	DV = 0		DV2 = 0	
a:p = 5 : 6	*Ma:Mp* = 2 : 2	o = 4	INC = 0		INC2 = 0	
2*Ab*+(*Art*+*Ay*) = 8		u = 0	DR = 0		DR2 = 0	
		− = 0	FAB = 0		FAB2 = 0	
MOR = 0			ALOG = 0		SUM6 = 0	
RESPONSES TO BE READ FOR QUALITY			CON = 0		WSUM6 = 0	
3, 5, 10, 14						

Case 9 Findings   The data for Steps 1 (*EB*), 2 (*EBPer*), 3 (left-side *eb*), 6 (Intellectualization Index), 10 (*M* form quality), and 12 (quality of *M* responses) are relevant to the interpretation.

As noted earlier, the *EB* and *EBPer* reveal that his ideational activity associated with problem solving usually includes some merging of feelings and, as such, is marked by intuitive features. People such as this tend to be more accepting of logic systems that are not precise or are marked by greater ambiguity. This coping style has some flexibility and sometimes he puts aside feelings in favor of a more clearly ideational approach. The left-side *eb* value indicates that his ideation currently is marked by a higher than expected level of ideational activity that is outside the focus of attention. Although this kind of peripheral ideation can serve as a positive stimulus, it can also become quite distracting once it exceeds natural levels. The increase in peripheral ideation is being generated by situationally-related stress, and while it lasts, a pattern of more limited concentration and interruptions in the flow of deliberate thinking will be present.

The data for the Intellectualization Index are quite important. They reveal that he uses intellectualization as a major defensive tactic in situations that are perceived as stressful. This is a pseudo-intellectual process that conceals and/or denies the presence of emotion and, as a result, reduces the likelihood that feelings will be dealt with directly and/or realistically. People such as this are more vulnerable to disorganization during intense emotional experiences, because the tactic becomes less effective as the magnitude of affective stimuli increases.

An evaluation of his human movement responses suggests that there is no reason for concern about the quality of his thinking (3. "Two people at a party or something, it looks like they are shaking hands . . . maybe a costume party . . . they are bending forward, like greeting each other"; 5. "a woman looking in the mirror kinda checking herself out . . . she's bending forward a little"; 10. "a weird statue of two people with their heads turned backward looking at each other . . . arms and noses and this is some sort of hair style"; 14. "a couple of wizards or witches making something in this cauldron . . . they've got pointed hats and orange robes and it looks like they have got their arms out over this cauldron . . . like it contains magic fog or smoke"). Even though they have some juvenile features, all are elaborate and well developed and two of the four (3 and 14) are reasonably sophisticated.

Case 9 Summary   He usually prefers a more intuitive approach to problem solving in which his feelings play an important role. This coping style has some flexibility, and sometimes he puts aside feelings in favor of a more clearly ideational approach. Currently, his thinking includes more peripheral ideation than is expected. This appears to be related to situational stress. Usually, this serves as a stimulus but, when excessive, it tends to interfere with attention and concentration. His thinking usually is clear and, although some of his ideation includes more juvenile features that probably relate to his extreme self-centeredness, it is often elaborate, well developed, and reasonably sophisticated.

A major finding concerning his ideational activity is that he uses intellectualization as a major defensive tactic in situations that are perceived as stressful. This process tends to conceal and/or deny the presence of emotion and, as a result, reduces the likelihood that feelings will be dealt with directly and/or realistically.

People such as this are more vulnerable to disorganization during intense emotional experiences because the tactic becomes less effective as the magnitude of affective stimuli increases.

Case 9 Final Description

This 23-year-old male currently is in stimulus overload because of situationally-related stress. He is not disorganized, but some of his actions may not be well thought out and a vulnerability to impulsiveness in thinking or emotions exists. The stress has made him more confused about his feelings and he is likely to experience more distracting thoughts than is usually the case. Ordinarily, his capacities for control and tolerance for stress are like that of most people. He has enough resource accessible to formulate and implement responses and his stress tolerance is likely to be exceeded only under unusual conditions.

Although the current stress is probably related to his recent disorganization, the antecedents of the disorganization appear to abide in a personality organization that is less mature or sophisticated than he prefers to accept or reveal. It is clearly marked by a narcissistic tendency to overglorify his own worth. This has a dominant influence on his perceptions of the world as well as on his thinking, and has created a strong motivation for status. People such as this usually find it difficult to establish deep relationships with others, and often use their interpersonal skills to manipulate others to their own ends. If the environment is unrewarding, asocial or antisocial sets evolve easily. It is important to note that he often engages in self-inspecting behaviors that focus on his negative features, and this results in aggravating feelings. This is an unusual finding and may signal some ongoing struggle with the issue of high self-value versus perceived negative features of the self.

His self-image includes many juvenile and exhibitionistic features that tend to sustain his extreme self-centeredness. At the same time, he tries to conceal any flaws and ensure his own aloofness and impenetrability. He has developed an elaborate system of defense to protect his overvalued self-image. It involves rationalization, denial that is used to avoid responsibility, a marked abuse of intellectualization to neutralize affect, plus a form of authoritarianism that he invokes to ward off challenges to his integrity. He appears to seek dependency on others but, because his perceptions and expectations of others are not very realistic, most of his relationships with others are more superficial. Currently, he feels emotionally deprived, but this sense of deprivation is probably related more to his loss of self-value than to any deep experience of loneliness. Generally, he is the type of person who probably is regarded by others as being rigid or narrow, and who has difficulties in maintaining close relationships, especially with those who are not submissive to him.

Emotions play a significant role in his thinking and most of his decisions have an intuitive influence. This coping style can be very effective, especially if there are no problems in control and if emotions do not become overly intense. In his case, both problems exist. He has potential problems in control because of his current overload state, but even without the situational stress, his emotions often are likely to become overly intense and, as such, to have excessive influence in his thinking and decision operations. He is experiencing considerable negative emotion, some of which is situationally related, but some is more chronic, provoked by his sense of deprivation and his previously mentioned negative introspection. He also harbors a very negative, angry attitude toward the environment that invariably affects his functioning. The anger may not manifest overtly, but it has some impact on decision making and coping activities and adds to his tendency to be intolerant of those around him. The current stress has also exacerbated a marked confusion that he has about emotion. This tendency to become ambivalent in emotional situations existed prior to his current state, but the overload has increased the frequency by which it occurs.

Overall, his cognitive activities are intact but they pose some additional problems. His processing activities are marked by considerable effort and the quality of the input seems to be similar to that found among most nonpatient adults. The problems occur because of his mediational activities. He tends to perceive the world through his own special set of psychological lenses and translates events much less conventionally and more in accord with his own needs or sets. Thus, many of his behaviors ignore social expectations or demands, and these less conventional behaviors are likely to occur with a sufficient frequency to make confrontations with the environment inevitable. His thinking usually is clear and, although some of his ideation includes more juvenile features that probably relate to his extreme self-centeredness, it is often elaborate, well developed, and reasonably sophisticated.

Recommendations Based on the Final Description

Although the primary diagnosis in the case will, no doubt, focus on the substance abuse issue, the more major problem is his enduring narcissistic personality. It is interesting to note that he has received a one-month leave of absence to involve himself in treatment, and probably with the naïve and somewhat grandiose expectation that such a treatment effort will bring satisfactory resolution to his problems. Brief treatment can work wonders at times, but not when the basic personality structure is so warped and immature.

The referral asks whether the subject has any serious psychiatric disturbance. Technically, the answer is no, but there is a serious personality disturbance. The referral also asks for a prediction about how well he may respond to a highly structured two-week inpatient program and for a prognosis concerning the likelihood that he will stay in treatment. He will probably respond well to the structure for a brief period and, in light of his elaborate defenses, he will probably exhibit considerable intellectualization during its early phases and couple this with his authoritarian dogmatism as he becomes more accustomed to the routines. At that point he is likely to begin competing directly with his therapists. The overall prognosis for staying in treatment should probably be considered in two segments, one related to relief from current stresses and the second related to enduring change. It is likely that he will persist in treatment until some immediate relief is experienced. His sense of deprivation and his need to be dependent, plus his current increase in emotional distress, should assure this. Once relief is experienced, however, the prognosis becomes relatively poor. Prospects of change will be very threatening. At best, it will be difficult to create a long term working relationship with him. On the other hand, if such a relationship can be created, there are several beginning assets with which to work. He processes well. His thinking is clear and can be sophisticated. He is interested in people and has substantial needs for status. In addition, he is already involved in some negative introspection, which may signal a glimmer of hope that he would like to change. Keeping him motivated for treatment will require a skillful therapist who is able to handle two very important but very delicate issues: control and self-integrity. In other words, if he perceives himself as losing control over his behavior or as relinquishing his overglorified sense of self, he will probably bolt the situation.

Case 9 Epilogue   The subject was accepted into the relatively brief substance abuse program. He was judged to be very cooperative during the 14 inpatient days, and described by at least two staff members as being outgoing, likeable, and helpful with other patients. It was noted that he organized at least three inter-ward basketball games during his second week of hospitalization. Following his discharge he returned to work, and participated in all six individual therapy sessions, but only the first four of the six group therapy sessions that were a formal part of the program. His therapist, a male, reports that much of the time during the individual sessions focused on complaints by the subject about the hospital routine and about the extreme pressures that are experienced when working as a salesman. The therapist felt that it was difficult to create a working relationship with the subject and, apparently, was not surprised when the subject opted not to continue treatment after the sixth session. According to his girlfriend, the subject began using cocaine occasionally about one month after the termination.

CASE 10: AN INADEQUATE PASSIVE-DEPENDENT

This 25-year-old female is the girlfriend of the subject described in Case 9. As noted in that history, she expressed a willingness to enter treatment with him, and was evaluated in conjunction with her application for outpatient treatment in the substance abuse program. She admits to the frequent use of cocaine with her boyfriend. She says that she wants to enter treatment (1) to help with his rehabilitation, and (2) because she feels unable to "say no" when drugs are offered to her. She does not want to go through the inpatient program for fear of losing her job. If accepted into the outpatient program, she will be seen twice per week, once individually and once in a group for a minimum of eight weeks.

   She is the only child of a couple who divorced when she was nine. She lived with her mother, now age 47, and an aunt, now 51, until she was age 22. Her mother works as an assistant manager in a bookstore and her aunt is a secretary. She has had no contact with her father, age 50, for the past six years except occasional letters or cards. He remarried and moved to a distant state shortly after her high school graduation. Prior to that time he visited five to eight times per year, usually on special occasions such as Christmas or her birthday. He apparently was treated for alcoholism when she was in junior high school and, to the best of her knowledge, he has not used alcohol since that time. He works for an oil company in a blue collar position. She is vague about the reasons for her parents' divorce but suspects that his alcoholism plus the fact that he was unfaithful were the main causes.

   She reports that a series of upper respiratory infections caused her to be bedridden quite often when she was between the ages of three and six and that she entered school a year late. She had problems with skin rashes while in sixth, seventh,

Case 10: A 25-Year-Old Female

Card	Response	Inquiry
I.	1. It ll a person in a costume, lik a ballerina, mayb lik fr Swan Lake or sthg	E: (Rpts S's resp) S: Well u can c her outline here (D4) & ths wld b wings, lik a costume, it's lik she's standg w the wgs out, lik mayb in a pose, u can c her outlin thru the costume
		E: Thru the costume? S: Well c here (D3) is the outline of her legs lik her costume was transparent, lik u can c thru it
	E: Look som mor, I thk u'll find smthg else too	
	2. Ths mite be a bell, just ths part	E: (Rpts S's resp) S: Well, it has the outline of a bell & ths wld be the clapper, lik a church bell or the Liberty bell
II	3. Ths part up here ll 2 chickens sort of looking at e.o.	E: (Rpts S's resp) S: Well thy hav the outline of chickens & thyr facing e.o., thts why I thot thyd lookg at e.o.
	4. Ths part ll a partly decayed tooth	E: (Rpts S's resp) S: Well u c some pretty strange lookg teeth if u work for a dentist & ths re me of one tht we had to reconstruct last wk, it had decayed more on the outside & it was all black lik ths one
		E: I'm not quite sur I'm seeg it lik u r S: Rite here & c the littl cone shaped edges, lik decay
III	5. Ths ll 2 wm talking to e.o.	E: (Rpts S's resp) S: Well thy ll wm to me, c their heads & breasts & legs & thyr standg ovr some pot or sthg & tallkg to e.o.
IV	6. Ths part up here ll a fan lik an oriental fan	E: (Rpts S's resp) S: Well u can c the folds in it, c the lines, lik it is opened up, at least partially but mayb not all the way, thy usually mak them out of paper, at least the ones tht don't cost much are made out of paper
		E: I'm not sur about the folds S: C these dark lines mak it ll folds lik when u begin to open one up
	7. Ths dark cntr part in here ll an x-ray of the spine	E: (Rpts S's resp) S: Well, it just has tht shape to it, when I looked it just re me of tht, its dark lik an Xray of a spine
V	8. Tht re me of a bat	E: (Rpts S's resp) S: Its lik when thy hav their wgs way out lik when thy fly real fast, I guess when thyr swooping & ths is his hands out here in front & the little feet

404

9. Ths part out here ll a leg but u can't c a foot, lik its been cut off

   E: (Rpts S's resp)
   S: Well it really has the shape of a leg to it but u can't c a foot, its lik it was severed & it stops at the ankle

   E: What kind of leg?
   S: A person's leg, I dk of any A legs lik tht

VI 10. I dkno about all ths (D1) but up here it ll a fly

   E: (Rpts S's resp)
   S: Well it just does, it has wgs & the body, just lik a fly

VII 11. Ths ll 2 littl rabbits sittg on a ledge

   E: (Rpts S's resp)
   S: Well thy hav their ears & the littl tails & the round face lik a rabbit face & thyr sittg on ths thg, it ll a piece of rock lik a rocky ledge or smthg lik tht

12. Down here it ll 2 people standg next to e.o., lik thy hav formal clothg on

   E: (Rpts S's resp)
   S: U can just barely make them out, its lik thyr both dressed in dark clothg & thyr standg there, lik at a ceremony, mayb its a couple gettg married or smthg but she ought to b in white if thy r

   E: I'm not sur I'm seeg it lik u, help me
   S: Look, rite here, standg next to e.o., its lik a man on the left & a wm & ths cb a big train from her gown but it shld b white, mayb it looks dark cuz thyr in the shadows

VIII 13. Tht looks lik sbody's insides

   E: (Rpts S's resp)
   S: Well ths cb the rib cage (DS3) & the stomach (D2) & the lungs & smthg else up here (D4) mayb a neckbone

   E: I'm not sur why it ll that
   S: I don't either, its ugly, it just ll smbody was opened up & u c all the parts

IX 14. If u just tak the pink it cb a cpl of A's

   E: (Rpts S's resp)
   S: Sort lik dogs or cats, c the legs & the head & the body, I thk mor lik a dog

15. A clown's face lik u'd c on a circus poster

   E: (Rpts S's resp)
   S: Well its painted all diff colors, c his ears r orange & his cheeks r green & his his neck is pink, & he's got orange hair arranged to stick up lik clown's do, its lik a poster more than real, lik thy show to advertise the circus

X 16. Well up here it ll 2 littl bugs tryg to lift up this stick

   E: (Rpts S's resp)
   S: Well thy ll littl ants or sthg c the antennae & the legs & thyr tryg to lift ths pole or stick or smthg up or at least thry pushg on it. Thyr prob ants cuz thyr grey colored lik ants

(continued)

Case 10: (Continued)

Card	Response	Inquiry
17. Ths ll the face of a rabbit		E: (Rpts S's resp)
		S: Well it just does, c the ear & the eyes, just lik a rabbits face
18. Ths part ll one of those spaceships lik Luke Skywalker flew in **Star Wars**, its lik coming toward u		E: (Rpts S's resp)
		S: It has the big pods on each side & the littl cabin in the middle, it ll it's traveling in space
		E: Traveling in space?
		S: Yes if u thk of the white as being space, ths ll its coming toward u, way off in the distance, its so littl it wb far off
19. Ths part ll 2 cherubs or smthg lik tht drinking smthg out of a straw, thy hav littl pointy caps on		E: (Rpts S's resp)
		S: Well thy hav littl pudgy noses & the forehead & ths blue is lik a straw & thy each r sharing whatvr is in the container, ths othr blue part
		E: U said thyr cherubs or sthg?
		S: Well thry pink, I guess cherubs cb pink & thy hav littl pointy caps on, lik nitecaps, mayb its fr a cartoon or smthg, u can't c the rest of their bodies

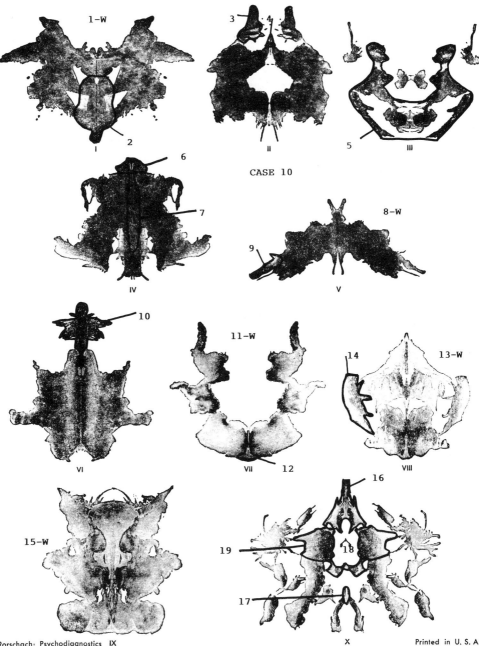

CASE 10

CASE 10. SEQUENCE OF SCORES

CARD NO	LOC	#	DETERMINANT(S)	(2)	CONTENT(S)	POP	Z	SPECIAL SCORES
I	1 W+	1	Mp.FVo		H,Cg		4.0	
	2 Ddo	24	Fo		Id			
II	3 D+	2	FMpu	2	A		5.5	
	4 Do	4	FC'-		Hd			PER,MOR
III	5 D+	1	Mpo	2	H,Hh	P	3.0	
IV	6 Do	3	FV.mpu		Id			DR
	7 Ddo	33	FYo		Xy			
V	8 Wo	1	FMao		A	P	1.0	INC
	9 Do	1	Fo		Hd			MOR
VI	10 Do	3	Fu		A			
VII	11 W+	1	FMpo	2	A,Ls		2.5	
	12 Dd+	28	Mp.FYu		H,Cg		1.0	AB,COP
VIII	13 Wo	1	F-		An		4.5	MOR
	14 Do	1	Fo		A	P		
IX	15 Wo	1	CFu		Art,(Hd)		5.5	
X	16 D+	11	FMa.FC'o	2	A,Bt		4.0	COP
	17 Do	5	Fo		Ad			
	18 DdS+	29	ma.FDu		Sc		6.0	
	19 Dd+	99	Mp.FCo	2	(Hd),Fd		4.0	DV,COP

```
CASE 10. STRUCTURAL SUMMARY
===============================================================================
LOCATION              DETERMINANTS              CONTENTS      S-CONSTELLATION
FEATURES          BLENDS          SINGLE                      YES..FV+VF+V+FD>2
                                           H   = 3, 0         NO..Col-Shd Bl>0
Zf    = 11        M.FV          M   = 1     (H) = 0, 0        YES..Ego<.31,>.44
ZSum  = 41.0      FV.m          FM  = 3     Hd  = 2, 0        NO..MOR > 3
ZEst  = 34.5      M.FY          m   = 0     (Hd)= 1, 1        YES..Zd > +- 3.5
                  FM.FC'        FC  = 0     Hx  = 0, 0        YES..es > EA
W     = 5         m.FD          CF  = 1     A   = 6, 0        NO..CF+C > FC
 (Wv  = 0)        M.FC          C   = 0     (A) = 0, 0        YES..X+% < .70
D     = 9                       Cn  = 0     Ad  = 1, 0        NO..S > 3
Dd    = 5                       FC' = 1     (Ad)= 0, 0        NO..P < 3 or > 8
S     = 1                       C'F = 0     An  = 1, 0        NO..Pure H < 2
                                C'  = 0     Art = 1, 0        NO..R < 17
   DQ                           FT  = 0     Ay  = 0, 0         5.....TOTAL
........(FQ-)                    TF  = 0     Bl  = 0, 0
  +  =  8   ( 0)                 T   = 0     Bt  = 0, 1        SPECIAL SCORINGS
  o  = 11   ( 2)                 FV  = 0     Cg  = 0, 2             Lv1    Lv2
  v/+ =  0   ( 0)               VF  = 0     Cl  = 0, 0        DV  = 1x1    0x2
  v  =  0   ( 0)                 V   = 0     Ex  = 0, 0        INC = 1x2    0x4
                                FY  = 0     Fd  = 1, 1        DR  = 1x3    0x6
                                YF  = 0     Fi  = 0, 0        FAB = 0x4    0x7
                                Y   = 0     Ge  = 0, 0        ALOG= 0x5
   FORM QUALITY                 Fr  = 0     Hh  = 0, 1        CON = 0x7
                                rF  = 0     Ls  = 0, 1          SUM6  = 3
     FQx  FQf  MQual  SQx        FD  = 0     Na  = 0, 0          WSUM6 = 6
  +  =  0    0    0    0         F   = 6     Sc  = 1, 0
  o  = 11    4    3    0                     Sx  = 0, 0        AB  = 1   CP  = 0
  u  =  6    1    1    1                     Xy  = 1, 0        AG  = 0   MOR = 3
  -  =  2    1    0    0                     Id  = 2, 0        CFB = 0   PER = 1
none=  0   --     0    0       (2) = 5                         COP = 3   PSV = 0
===============================================================================
                 RATIOS, PERCENTAGES, AND DERIVATIONS

R = 19          L = 0.46              FC:CF+C = 1: 1      COP = 3     AG = 0
---------------------------------     Pure C  =   0       Food    = 1
EB = 4: 1.5   EA =  5.5   EBPer= 2.7  Afr     =0.58       Isolate/R  =0.11
eb = 6: 6     es = 12     D  = -2     S       = 1         H:(H)Hd(Hd)= 3: 4
           Adj es = 10   Adj D = -1   Blends:R= 6:19      (HHd):(AAd)= 2: 0
---------------------------------     CP      = 0         H+A:Hd+Ad  = 9: 5
FM = 4 :  C'= 2   T = 0
m  = 2 :  V = 2   Y = 2
                          P    = 3        Zf  =11         3r+(2)/R=0.26
a:p    = 3: 7   Sum6  = 3   X+% =0.58     Zd  = +6.5      Fr+rF   = 0
Ma:Mp  = 0: 4   Lv2   = 0   F+% =0.67     W:D:Dd = 5: 9: 5  FD    = 1
2AB+Art+Ay= 3   WSum6 = 6   X-% =0.11     W:M = 5: 4      An+Xy   = 2
M-     = 0      Mnone = 0   S-% =0.00     DQ+ = 8         MOR     = 3
                            Xu% =0.32     DQv = 0
-------------------------------------------------------------------------------
  SCZI = 1     DEPI = 3    CDI = 4*    S-CON = 5     HVI = No    OBS = No
===============================================================================
```

and eighth grades. These apparently were caused by allergies, so she was exempt from gym classes. The rash problem cleared by the time she entered high school although she continued with allergy shots until age 16. She graduated from high school at age 19. Her grades had been mostly C's and B's. She worked one year in the bookstore where her mother is employed and then began training to become a dental technician. She completed that course, was certified at age 22, and obtained a dental assistant position in a group practice. She continues in that job, which she says she likes and anticipates staying on indefinitely.

She says that because she was frail, she often did not join in the games of other children during elementary school and, because of her allergy problems, she did not have many friends in junior high or in her first two years of high school. She began menstruation at age 13 and had serious cramping problems for the next two years. She went to her first school dance at age 16. Not long after, at another dance a boy kissed and fondled her. She had her first experience of intercourse with that boy about 4 months later, which she says was not very pleasant for her. She abstained from further sex until she was in dental training. After completing her training, she began sharing an apartment with two other girls (a secretary, age 27, and an airline agent, age 25).

Since that time she has "slept with eight or 10 guys" but did not experience orgasm until she met her current boyfriend at a party about 18 months ago. They began living together when the lease on her shared apartment expired about nine months ago. She says, "I love him and he loves me. If we didn't do all the coke we'd get along a lot better, but when we get high things just don't go right and he loses his temper a lot when that happens." She says that sex with him is "really good except when he has trouble and then he makes me do a lot of weird things." Apparently he buys exotic underwear for her and asks her to dance in it and has also bought her a vibrator. If she is reluctant he loses his temper, although he has not been assaultive to her until his recent episode of disorientation. She is clearly concerned about his treatment and implies that she is quite apprehensive about their future relationship.

She is 5 feet 5 inches, weighs 126 pounds, and has long brown hair. Although her overt appearance is not striking, she is reasonably attractive, is very cooperative, and smiles a great deal while talking about herself. Drug screening was negative although some trace activity was noted. Neuropsychological screening was negative. The assessment issues are as follows: (1) Is there any evidence of a serious psychiatric disturbance? (2) What are her motivation for treatment and prognosis for staying with the program? (3) What are the specific treatment objectives? (4) Should couples therapy be considered?

Interpretive Strategy

There is no reason to question the interpretive usefulness of the record as it contains 19 answers. The first positive Key variable is the difference in the D scores, which requires that the interpretive routine begin with the cluster regarding controls and stress tolerance, followed by a study of the array of variables concerning situational stress. The second positive Key variable is the CDI, which means that the entire search routine is:

CONTROLS → SITUATIONAL STRESS → AFFECT → SELF-PERCEPTION → INTERPERSONAL PERCEPTION → PROCESSING → MEDIATION → IDEATION.

Initial Proposition: Because the D Score is less than the Adj D Score, it can be assumed that the subject is currently experiencing a significant increase in stimulus demands as a result of situationally-related stress. Thus, some decisions and/or behaviors may not be as well organized as is usually the case, and the subject is more vulnerable to impulsiveness in thinking, affect, and/or behavioral disorganization in complex or highly ambiguous situations.

Controls and Stress Tolerance

Data for the variables related to capacities for control and tolerance for stress are shown in Table 108.

Table 108.   Control Related Variables for Case 10

$EB = 4 : 1.5$	$EA = 5.5$	$D = -2$	$CDI = 4$
$eb = 6 : 6$	$es = 12$ Adj$es = 10$	AdjD $= -1$	
$FM = 4$ $m = 2$ $C' = 2$ $T = 0$ $V = 2$ $Y = 2$			

Case 10 Findings   All data in this cluster are relevant to the interpretation.

The Adj D Score of −1 and the positive CDI indicate that her personality organization is somewhat less mature than might be expected. This tends to breed problems in coping with the requirements of everyday living and lowers her capacity to deal with stress. Her controls are fragile and, because she is in a chronic overload state, some of her decisions will not be well thought out or implemented. This chronic overload creates a proclivity for impulsiveness and a susceptibility to disorganization under stress. People such as this usually function most effectively in familiar environments in which demands and expectations are predictable. The low EA and the finding that neither side of the EB contains a zero value supports the notion that the Adj D Score is reliable. She has fewer resources available than most people. The value for the Adj es is substantial but not higher than average. The values for the eb indicate that it is elevated slightly because of aggravating emotions, but even if some of that aggravation did not exist, the Adj D Score would not change. In other words, she has at least as much internal stimulus demand as most adults and, when considered in light of her limited resource, the susceptibility to problems in control is not surprising. The problem becomes even more profound because the positive CDI suggests that her immaturity makes her vulnerable to difficulties in the interpersonal sphere.

Case 10 Summary   Her overall personality is less mature than expected. This creates problems in dealing with the requirements of everyday living and reduces her capacity to deal with stress. Her controls are fragile and, because she is in a state of chronic stimulus overload, some of her decisions are not well formulated or implemented. This chronic overload creates a proclivity for impulsiveness and a susceptibility to disorganization under stress. People such as this usually function most effectively in familiar environments in which demands and expectations are predictable. She has fewer resources available than most people, but the demands that she experiences are no less than most people experience. Thus, it is not surprising that this uneven mixture leads to a susceptibility for problems in control. The problem becomes even more profound because her immaturity makes her vulnerable to difficulties in the interpersonal sphere.

Situationally-Related Stress

Data for the variables in the array related to situational stress are shown in Table 109.

Case 10 Findings   All data except Step 5 (Color-Shading blends) are relevant to the interpretation.

Table 109. Stress-Related Variables for Case 10

			BLENDS	
$D = -2$	ADJ D = -1		M.FV	FM.FC′
$m = 2$,	$Y = 2$,	$T = 0$	M.FC	m.FD
Pure $C = 0$		Blends = 6	M.FY	FV.m
$M- = 0$		MQ none = 0		

The 1-point difference between the D Scores and the Adj D Score indicates that she is experiencing a significant increase in stimulus demands as a result of situationally-related stress. The fact that the D Score has a value of −2 suggests that she is quite disorganized. Her potential for impulsiveness in thinking, affect, and/or behavior is considerable. People such as this usually have difficulty functioning in most environments, no matter how structured. They are easily distracted and often lose continuity in their thinking. The values for m and Y indicate that the impact of the stress is diffuse and has significant effects on both thinking and emotions. A review of the number of blends created exclusively by either of those variables suggests that she is considerably more complex now than has been the case previously.

Case 10 Summary   She is currently experiencing the impact of some situational stress that has caused her to be quite disorganized. Her potential for impulsiveness in thinking, affect, and/or behavior is increased considerably. People in this state usually have considerable difficulty functioning effectively in most environments, no matter how structured. They are easily distracted and often lose continuity in their thinking. The impact of the stress tends to be diffuse and has significant effects on both thinking and emotions, and has increased her complexity to a level well beyond her previous experience.

Affective Features

Data for the variables related to affective features are shown in Table 110.

Table 110. Affect-Related Variables for Case 10

			BLENDS	
$EB = 4 : 1.5$	$EBPer = 2.7$	DEPI = 3		
$eb = 6 : 6$	$(C = 2, T = 0, V = 2, Y = 2)$		M.FV	FM.FC′
$FC:CF+C = 1 : 1$	Pure $C = 0$		M.FC	m.FD
$Afr = 0.58$	CP = 0		M.FY	FV.m
$S = 1$	Col-Shd Bl = 0			

Case 10 Findings   All data, except the DEPI, and Steps 5 (Pure *C*), 7 (Color Projection), 11 (blend complexity), 12 (Color-Shading blends), and 13 (Shading blends), are relevant to the interpretation.

The *EB* indicates that she prefers to keep emotions away from her thinking, especially during problem solving or decision making activities. This is a very pervasive style, and it is reasonable to assume that emotions usually play only a very limited role in her decision making activity. The right-side *eb* data indicate that she is experiencing more discomforting negative emotions than should be the case. Most of this is provoked by a frequent tendency to self-examine and focus on her negative features or shortcomings. This kind of introspection tends to breed sadness and unhappiness, and it is likely that she experiences both feelings. The $FC:CF+C$ ratio suggests that she does not display her feelings very freely but, when she does, they are usually modulated as well as those of most adults. She appears to be willing to process emotional stimuli, but generally tries to keep herself reasonably free of emotional complexity. Unfortunately, her current level of complexity has been increased by the situationally-related stress and probably tends to create more confusion for her than is normal.

Case 10 Summary   She prefers to keep emotions away from her thinking, especially during problem solving, and emotions typically play a very limited role in decision making activity. She is experiencing more discomforting emotions than should be the case, mainly because of a frequent tendency to self-examine and focus on her own shortcomings. This behavior often causes sadness and unhappiness and it is likely that she experiences both feelings. She does not care to display her feelings very freely and tries to keep them well controlled. She seems interested in being around emotion but tries to keep herself reasonably free of emotional complexity. Unfortunately, her level of complexity has been increased by the situational stress and tends to create more confusion for her than usual.

Self-Perception

Data for the variables related to self-perception are shown in Table 111.

Case 10 Findings   All data except those for Step 1 $(Fr + rF)$ are relevant to the interpretation.

Table 111.   Self Perception Variables for Case 10

STRUCTURAL DATA		RESPONSES TO BE READ	
$Fr+rF = 0$ 3r+(2)/R = 0.26		*MOR* RESPONSES	= 4, 9, 13
$FD = 1$ $V = 2$		MINUS RESPONSES	= 4, 13
$H:(H)+Hd+(Hd) = 3:4$		*M* RESPONSES	= 1, 5, 12, 19
$An+Xy = 2$		*FM* RESPONSES	= 3, 8, 11, 16
$MOR = 3$		*m* RESPONSES	= 6, 18

The low Egocentricity Index indicates that she is the type of person who regards herself less favorably when compared with others. The composite of one *FD* and two *Vista* answers reveals that she engages in much more self-examining behavior than is customary. This probably relates to her lower self-esteem and much of the focus is on the perceived negative features of her self-image. The proportion of human contents that are Pure *H* responses is lower than expected, suggesting that her self-image contains many features that are based mainly on imaginary rather than on real experience. People such as this are often less mature and frequently have very distorted notions of themselves and others.

The slight elevation in *An + Xy* answers hints at some unusual body concern but the source is not obvious. The presence of the three MOR contents indicates that her self-image includes some very negative, unwanted features. All three include rather dramatic forms of projected material (4. "a partly decayed tooth . . . you see some pretty strange looking teeth if you work for a dentist . . . we had to reconstruct last week, it has decayed more on the outside and it was all black like this," 9. "a leg but you can't see the foot, like it's been cut off . . . it's like it was severed and it stops at the ankle," 13. "somebody's insides . . . somebody was opened up and you can see all the parts"). All represent a sense of damage and two of the three (4 and 13), her only minus answers, may reflect some aspects of the current vulnerability and deterioration that she is experiencing.

All four of the *M* responses are passive; however, the contents are more positive, even though two are marked by fantasy characteristics (1. "a ballerina, maybe from "Swan Lake" or something . . . standing with the wings out, maybe in a pose, you can see her outline through the costume," 5. "two women talking to each other . . . standing over some pot," 12. "two people standing next to each other . . . like at a ceremony, maybe it's a couple getting married . . . but she ought to be in white if they are," 19. "two cherubs . . . drinking something out of a straw . . . sharing whatever is in the container"). In Response 1, the issue of vulnerability is raised again, and Response 12 is especially interesting because of the somewhat confused or morose comment, "she ought to be in white if they are."

The four *FM* responses also are more tentative than is common, but none are negative and one (16) is quite positive (3. "two chickens sort of looking at each other," 8. "a bat . . . like when they have their wings way out when they fly real fast," 11. "two little rabbits sitting on a ledge," 16. "two little bugs trying to lift up this stick"). The two *m* answers are intriguing because both have dimensional features (6. "an oriental fan . . . it is opened up, at least partially . . . the ones that don't cost much are made out of paper," 18. "one of those spaceships like Luke Skywalker flew in *Star Wars* . . . it's coming toward you, way off in the distance"). Both convey a sense of things yet to come and may reflect some optimism that she harbors about herself. The remaining six answers (a bell, an X-ray, a fly, two animals, a clown's face on a circus poster, and the face of a rabbit) do not contain any unusual wording or embellishments. Nonetheless, Response 15 (clown's face) is quite interesting because of the possible implication concerning a facade: "it's painted all different colors . . . it's like a poster more than real, like they show to advertise the circus."

Case 10 Summary   Her view of herself seems to reflect a mixture of naïvely positive features that are linked together with a sense of vulnerability or apprehension and a view of being damaged. It is clear that she regards herself less favorably when compared with others, and that she engages in much self-examining, most of which focuses on the perceived negative features of her self-image.

Her self-image includes many features that are based mainly on imaginary rather than on real experience and probably reflects her immaturity. She may have some unusual body concern but the source is not obvious. It could relate to her sense of damage and the current vulnerability and deterioration that she is experiencing. On the other hand, it may relate to some body experience that has occurred because of her substance abuse. She seems to have a positive but naïve optimism about herself, but she also gives a distinct impression of harboring some awareness that the optimism is not well founded in reality.

Interpersonal Perception

Data for the variables related to interpersonal perception are shown in table 112.

Case 10 Findings   All data, except Steps 2 (HVI), 7 (PER), and 9 (Isolation Index), are relevant to the interpretation.

The positive CDI signals that she is prone to experience frequent difficulties when interacting with the environment. Usually, these difficulties extend into the interpersonal sphere; thus, most of her interpersonal relationships tend to be more superficial and less mature than might be desired. The disproportionately high number of passive movement answers shown in the $a : p$ ratio signifies that she usually prefers to take a passive role in interpersonal relationships. People such as this usually prefer to avoid responsibility for decision making and are less prone to seek new solutions to problems. The presence of a *Food* content indicates that she makes many more dependency gestures in her behaviors than is typical. This preference to be dependent on others, when combined with the finding concerning her marked passivity, leads to the conclusions that a passive-dependent coping style is present.

The finding concerning her passive-dependency is especially interesting when considered in light of the absence of any *texture* response. This absence suggests that she does not experience needs for emotional closeness in ways similar to

Table 112.   Interpersonal Perception Variables for Case 10

STRUCTURAL VARIABLES			RESPONSES TO BE READ
CDI = 4	HVI = Neg		MOVEMENT WITH PAIR = 5, 19
$a:p$ = 3:7	T = 0	Fd = 1	HUMAN CONTENTS = 1, 4, 5, 9, 12, 15, 19
Total Human Contents = 7			
Isolate/R = 0.11			
PER = 1	COP = 3	AG = 0	

most people. This does not mean that the needs are not present, but rather that she probably is less comfortable in close relationships, especially those involving tactile exchange. People such as this usually prefer to maintain some distance or safety in their relationships and sometimes become excessively concerned with issues of personal space. Her passive-dependent style seems to create a conflict situation for her. In other words, she wants to take from others while remaining distant from them.

The presence of seven human content responses signals that she is reasonably interested in people, and the fact that three of these responses include cooperative movement indicates that she probably is regarded by others as likable and outgoing. In fact, she tends to view interpersonal activity as a very important part of her daily routine, and it is likely that she is identified by those around her as gregarious. At first glance, this may seem contradictory to other findings concerning her immaturity, her chronic vulnerability to impulsiveness, and her passive-dependent style, but it is not necessarily. She has selected an occupation that is structured, involves controlled interpersonal exchange, and permits her to be dependent on the direction provided by others; under these circumstances, features that might otherwise be liabilities can become assets.

The kind of interpersonal activity that probably marks her behavior seems to be illustrated by the five movement answers that include pairs (chickens sort of looking at each other, women talking to each other, rabbits sitting on a ledge, bugs trying to lift up a stick, cherubs drinking something out of a straw . . . sharing whatever is in the container). All but one (bugs) are passive but none are negative and, in fact, two (women talking, cherubs sharing) are positive. Generally, her perceptions of people seem to be more positive than negative. The positive is illustrated in the answers about a ballerina, two women talking, two people at a ceremony, a clown's face, and two cherubs sharing. The negative impressions are more personal (a partly decayed tooth, a leg with a severed foot).

Case 10 Summary Her immaturity and limited resources make her susceptible to difficulties when interacting with the environment and these difficulties often extend into the interpersonal sphere. In this case the interpersonal difficulties are not so readily apparent, probably because she prefers to take a passive-dependent role in relationships. This permits her to avoid responsibility for decision making and reduces the likelihood of any open conflict with others. Apparently, she does not experience needs for emotional closeness in ways similar to most people and, as a result, probably makes few demands for closeness with others. This does not mean that the needs for closeness are not present, but that they are probably fulfilled more easily through dependency than through tactile exchange. This permits her to take from others while remaining at a safe distance from them.

She is reasonably interested in people, and her perceptions of people appear to be more positive than negative. She probably is regarded by others as likable, outgoing, and gregarious. She seems to feel most secure in situations that are structured, involve controlled interpersonal exchange, and permit her to be dependent on the direction provided by others. Under those circumstances, features that might otherwise be liabilities can become assets.

Information Processing

Data for the variables related to processing activity are shown in Table 113.

Table 113. Information Processing Variables for Case 10

$L = 0.46$	OBS = Neg	HVI = Neg		LOCATION SEQUENCING	
$Zd = +6.5$		$DQ+ = 8$	I W,Dd	IV D,Dd	VII W,Dd
$Zf = 11$		$DQv/+ = 0$	II D,D	V W,D	VIII W,D
$W{:}D{:}Dd = 5{:}9{:}5$		$DQv = 0$	III D	VI D	IX W
$W{:}M = 4{:}5$		PSV = 0			X D,D,Dd,Dd

Case 10 Findings All data except Steps 1 (Lambda) and 2 (OBS and HVI) are relevant to the interpretation.

Although the value for Zf is in the expected range, the data for the $W:D:Dd$ and $W:M$ ratios indicate that she prefers to deal with less complex, more easily managed stimulus fields. This finding is not unusual in light of her passive style and probably represents an inclination to feel uncomfortable about her decision making capabilities. This tendency could lead to less effective processing; however, the DQ distribution shows that the quality of her processing is similar to that of most people.

The good quality yielded in her processing is at least partly attributable to her overincorporative style, as evidenced by the Zd score. Obviously, she invests considerable effort and energy into scanning activities and, although overincorporation can be less efficient because of the added effort involved, it is often an asset because the cautious, thorough approach to scanning usually ensures that all stimulus cues are included in the input. The Location sequencing is quite consistent and reflects some of the overincorporative activity. She begins each blot with either a W or a D response, but in four of the blots she moves to the more conservative but more precise Dd answer.

Case 10 Summary Generally, she prefers to deal with less complex, more easily managed stimulus fields. This is in keeping with her passive style and probably represents an inclination to feel uncomfortable about her decision making capabilities. Nonetheless, the quality of her processing is similar to that of most people, partly because of her overincorporative style that causes her to invest considerable effort and energy in scanning activity. Thus, although she is more conservative in her processing effort, the process is reasonably consistent and sophisticated.

Cognitive Mediation

Data for the variables relating to mediational activity are shown in Table 114.

Table 114. Cognitive Mediation Variables for Case 10

Lambda = 0.46	OBS = Negative		MINUS FEATURES
P = 3	X+% = .58	II	4. *Do FC' – Hd PER,MOR*
FQx+ = 0	F+% = .67	VIII	13. *Wo F– An 4.5 MOR*
FQxo = 11	Xu% = .32		
FQxu = 6	X–% = .11		
FQx– = 2	S–% = 0		
FQnone = 0	CONFAB = 0		

Case 10 Findings All data, except Steps 1 (Lambda), 2 (OBS), 4 (*FOx+*), and 6 (*FOnone*), are relevant to the interpretation.

The low number of Popular responses suggests another potential problem. She rarely translates stimuli conventionally, even when the cues are obvious. The lower than average $X+\%$ also calls attention to the fact that she gives a higher than usual frequency of atypical translations. The composite of the low number of Populars and the low $X+\%$ suggests that many of her behaviors may disregard social demands or expectations. Her lack of conventionality seems best explained by the finding for the $Xu\%$. She has a marked tendency to overpersonalize in translating stimuli, that is, to interpret situations in the context of her own needs, sets, and attitudes. The $X-\%$ reveals that she does not distort more than most people, but instead gives way to her own individuality more than expected. People who do this excessively, as she does, have a much greater potential for confrontations with the environment.

The sequencing of the minus answers is not especially revealing, although it may be important to note that both occur to colored blots and may have been prompted by the emotionally loaded stimuli. They are somewhat homogeneous (decayed tooth, somebody's insides), although the content codings differ. Both are MOR responses that reflect exposed features. Thus, it may be that the tendency to distort is related to her own sense of damage. Neither is a Level 2 form of distortion.

Case 10 Summary She does not translate stimuli very conventionally, even when cues are obvious. This suggests that many of her behaviors may disregard social demands or expectations. This does not mean that she is perceptually inaccurate, for that is not the case. Her perceptual inaccuracies or distortions of inputs occur no more often than for most people and, when they do occur, it is usually because she is preoccupied with her own sense of damage. She tends to yield to her own individuality more than most people. Thus, many of her behaviors probably are formed in the context of her own needs, sets, and attitudes. People who do this excessively, as she does, have a much greater potential for confrontations with the environment. If no other problems exist, they are often accepted as simply being eccentric or overly individualistic; in her case, however, such confrontations may tend to be unfavorable because of her immaturity and low tolerance for stress.

Ideation

Data for the variables related to ideation are shown in Table 115.

Case 10 Findings   All data except Steps 6 (Intellectualization Index) and 11 ($M-$ distortion levels) are relevant to the interpretation.

The *EB* and *EBPer* indicate that she prefers to delay formulating decisions or initiating behaviors until all apparent possibilities have been considered. She relies heavily on internal evaluation in forming judgments, and her feelings usually play only a very limited role in decision making activity. The data for the left-side *eb* show that her level of peripheral ideation is being increased by situationally-related stress even though it continues to fall within expected limits. The difference between the values in the $a:p$ ratio suggests that her ideational sets and values are reasonably well fixed and would be somewhat difficult to alter.

Possibly the most negative finding concerns the $M^a:M^p$ ratio, which signals that the subject routinely takes flight into fantasy as a tactic for dealing with unpleasant situations. This "Snow White Syndrome" is characterized mainly by the avoidance of responsibility and decision making through an abusive use of fantasy to deny reality. The presence of this style is not surprising, as it coincides with the subject's self-imposed helplessness that requires a dependency on others. In other words, it is very consistent with her passive-dependent style. Unfortunately, it also makes her quite vulnerable to the manipulations of others. In her case, the pervasiveness of this coping style is especially detrimental because her basic ideational coping style becomes subservient to her avoidant-dependent orientation.

The MOR responses indicate another source that can limit the effectiveness of her ideational style. They illustrate features that can create a very pessimistic attitude in her thinking, so that some of her decision making is marked by doubts and the anticipation that her actions have little to do with the outcome of a situation. She has three Critical Special Scores but all are of a very mild variety, and an evaluation of their quality seems to reflect more immaturity than serious slippage ("they usually make them out of paper, at least the ones that don't cost much are made out of paper"; "this is [the bat's] hands; they have

Table 115.   Ideation Variables for Case 10

$EB = 4:1.5$	$EBPer = 2.7$	*M* QUALITY	CRITICAL SPECIAL SCORES			
$eb = 6:6$	$(FM = 4\ m = 2)$	$+ = 0$	DV	$= 1$	DV2	$= 0$
$a{:}p = 3:7$	$Ma{:}Mp = 0:4$	$o = 3$	INC	$= 1$	INC2	$= 0$
$2Ab+(Art+Ay) = 3$		$u = 1$	DR	$= 1$	DR2	$= 0$
MOR $= 3$		$- = 0$	FAB	$= 0$	FAB2	$= 0$
RESPONSES TO BE READ FOR QUALITY			ALOG	$= 0$	SUM6	$= 3$
1, 5, 12, 19			CON	$= 0$	WSUM6	$= 6$

little pointy caps"). The quality of her human movement answers tends to be quite adequate, even though some seem to reflect more of the juvenile fantasy than characterizes much of her thinking (1. "a ballerina, . . . standing with the wings out, maybe in a pose"; 5. "two women talking to each other . . . standing over some pot . . ."; 12. "two people standing next to each other . . . like at a ceremony, maybe . . . getting married . . . but she ought to be in white"; 19. "two cherubs . . . drinking something out of a straw . . . sharing whatever is in the container").

Case 10 Summary   She is the type of person who likes to delay formulating decisions or initiating behaviors until she has considered all apparent possibilities. As such, she relies heavily on internal evaluations in forming judgments, and her feelings usually play only a very limited role in decision making activity. Her ideational sets, attitudes, and values are reasonably well fixed and would be somewhat difficult to alter.

Unfortunately, she does not use her ideational style very well. Much of her deliberate thinking is committed to developing an elaborate fantasy world into which she takes flight as a routine tactic for dealing with unpleasant situations. This permits her to avoid responsibility and decision making. The presence of this defensive style is not surprising as it is consistent with her passive-dependent style. Unfortunately, it makes her quite vulnerable to the manipulations of others. Her thinking is also marked by a pessimistic attitude that tends to create doubts and the anticipation that her actions have little to do with the outcome of a situation. The quality of her ideation is clear but less mature than might be desirable, as it often includes much of the naïve juvenile fantasy that she has developed so extensively.

Case 10 Final Description

This 25-year-old female is considerably less mature than expected. She has fewer resources available than most people but she experiences as many demands on those resources as do most adults. This uneven relationship between resource and demand creates problems in her everyday living and reduces her capacity to deal with stress. Her controls are fragile because she is in a state of chronic stimulus overload. Thus, some of her decisions are not well formulated or implemented. This overload creates a proclivity for impulsiveness and a susceptibility to disorganization under stress. People such as this usually have difficulty functioning effectively except in familiar environments in which demands and expectations are predictable.

She is currently experiencing some situational stress that has caused her to be quite disorganized and her potential for impulsiveness in thinking, affect, and/ or behavior is increased considerably. People in this state usually have significant difficulty functioning effectively in most environments. They are easily distracted and often lose continuity in their thinking. Usually, she likes to keep her emotions well controlled and away from her thinking, especially during problem solving. This is more difficult for her now because she is experiencing more distress. Most of this is provoked by a frequent tendency to self-examine and focus on her shortcomings, but some is also generated by the current stress.

This often gives rise to sadness and unhappiness and it is likely that she experiences both feelings. She does not care to display her feelings very freely, although she seems interested in being around emotion.

Her view of herself seems to reflect a mixture of naïvely positive features that are linked together with a sense of vulnerability or apprehension and a view of being damaged. Clearly, she regards herself less favorably when compared with others, and she focuses a great deal on her perceived negative features. Her self-image includes many features that are based mainly on imaginary rather than real experience, and this is probably reflected in her immaturity. She may have some unusual body concern but the source is not obvious. It could relate to her sense of damage and the current vulnerability or it may relate to some body experience that has occurred because of her substance abuse. She seems to have a positive but naïve optimism about herself but she also gives a distinct impression of harboring some awareness that the optimism is not well founded in reality.

Her immaturity and limited resources make her susceptible to interpersonal difficulties. In this case those difficulties are not readily apparent, probably because she prefers to take a passive-dependent role in interpersonal relationships. This role permits her to avoid responsibility for decision making and reduces the likelihood of any open conflict with others. She probably makes few demands for closeness with others. This does not mean that needs for closeness are not present, but that they are probably fulfilled more easily through dependency than through tactile exchange. This permits her to take from others while usually remaining at a safe distance from them. She is reasonably interested in people, and her perceptions of people appear to be more positive than negative. She probably is regarded by others as likable, outgoing, and gregarious. She seems to feel most secure in situations that are structured, involve controlled interpersonal exchange, and permit her to be dependent on the direction provided by others. Under those circumstances, features that might otherwise be liabilities can become assets.

Generally, she prefers to deal with less complex, more easily managed stimulus fields, which is in keeping with her passive style and probably represents an inclination to feel uncomfortable about her decision making capabilities. Nonetheless, the quality of her processing is similar to that of most people, partly because of an overincorporative style that causes her to invest considerable effort and energy in scanning activity. Thus, although she is more conservative than most in her processing effort, the process itself is reasonably consistent and sophisticated. Although she processes information adequately, she does not translate stimuli very conventionally, even when the conventional is obvious. This suggests that many of her behaviors disregard social demands or expectations, but it does not mean that she is perceptually inaccurate, for that is not the case. Perceptual inaccuracies or distortions of inputs occur no more often than for most people. However, she does tend to yield to her own individuality more than most people. Thus, many of her behaviors probably are formed in the context of her own needs, sets, and attitudes. People who do this excessively, as she does, have a much greater potential for confrontations with the environment.

Her thinking is reasonably clear although it is marked by considerable juvenile-like fantasy. As noted earlier, she likes to delay forming decisions or behaviors until she has had time to consider all apparent alternatives. Thus, she relies heavily on internal evaluations in forming judgments. Her ideational sets, attitudes, and values are reasonably well fixed and would be somewhat difficult to alter. Unfortunately, she does not use her ideational style very well. Instead, much of her deliberate thinking is committed to the development of an elaborate fantasy world into which she takes flight as a routine tactic for dealing with unpleasant situations. This permits her to avoid responsibility and decision making, which is consistent with her passive-dependent style. A negative by-product is the fact that she is quite vulnerable to the manipulations of others. Her thinking is marked by a pessimistic set that causes her to anticipate that her actions will have little to do with the outcome of a situation.

Recommendations Based on the Final Description

It is unclear whether an Axis I diagnosis concerning substance abuse will be afforded, but there is no question that the subject's passive-dependent features should be given some emphasis if a diagnostic label is required. The referral asks if a major psychiatric disturbance is present. The answer is no, but there is a major personality deficit. The referral also asks for estimates regarding her motivation for treatment and prognosis for staying in treatment. Unfortunately, she is probably too naïve to be well motivated for treatment. She may believe that she has a substance abuse problem but it is doubtful that she would recognize it as being very important except that her significant other appears to need treatment. Thus, her prognosis for staying in treatment depends largely on his reactions. Apparently, he is her main source of emotional income. He probably not only permits her to be passively dependent on him, but encourages that behavior. Thus, she becomes a victim of a relationship that she needs.

The referral also asks for recommendations concerning treatment objectives, and there are many but few if any that can be achieved in a brief treatment orientation. Obviously, her immaturity and chronic overload state are prime treatment targets, as are her extreme passiveness and extensive fantasy abuse. She does not know who she is or what she is and will remain vulnerable to the manipulations of others until those issues are resolved. She does not understand conventional behaviors or, if she does, cannot perceive herself in those roles. A reasonable treatment plan must have a developmental focus and is certain to require considerable time and effort. A women's group could be highly beneficial but would probably generate progress only if she has more resource identified with which to ward off some of the everyday stresses of living that threaten to overwhelm her. The referral asks whether couples therapy might be appropriate. This raises an ethical question. Surely, she wants to continue in her pathological relationship with the fellow described in Case 9 who appears to be manipulating her at will. To interfere with the relationship violates her own wishes, yet to encourage the continuation and/or strengthening of the relationship will doom her to a continuation of her fragile passive-dependent role in life. If her best interests are to be given proper weight, any consideration of couples therapy would be abandoned.

She does have assets. She processes information quite well. There is no evidence of mediational distortion. Her thinking is reasonably clear. She tends to regard others positively and probably is perceived by others as a likable person. The key to therapeutic success with her lies in the development of a working relationship with someone with whom she feels comfortable and can identify.

Obviously, this means a female therapist who can employ the skills necessary to maintain motivation for change and interfere when necessary with pathologically dependent relationships that she may create.

Case 10 Epilogue   This subject was accepted into the substance abuse program with the proviso that she participate in at least eight weekly individual and group psychotherapy sessions. She did so, and at the end of the eighth week asked to continue in individual treatment. Her therapist, a female, notes that much of the time in the first sessions focused on her relationship with her boyfriend, but that the main topic gradually shifted to concerns about her social fears and feelings of insecurity as time progressed. Apparently, the group interactions also played a significant role in provoking her to look more closely at herself, so that when she requested continuation, she was able to identify outcome that seemed realistic in the opinion of the therapist. During the twelfth week of treatment she decided to move out of her boyfriends apartment after he became angry when she refused to use cocaine. She moved to her parents home where she remained for three weeks, after which she moved into an apartment shared by a female medical technician. She was seen twice each week during that interval. The therapist reports that, after seven months of treatment, the subject is progressing slowly but favorably. She has two dating relationships, has remained drug free, has developed a close relationship with her roommate, and is actively involved in expanding her social network and experience. She is currently considering taking some evening courses at a local university.

REFERENCES

Farmer, R., and Nelson-Gray, R. O. (1990). Personality disorders and depression: Hypothetical relations, empirical findings, and methodological considerations. *Clinical Psychology Review, 10,* 453–476.

Frances, A. (1980). The DSM-III personality disorders section: A commentary. *American Journal of Psychiatry,* **137,** 1050–1054.

Frances, A. (1982). Categorical and dimensional systems of personality diagnosis: A comparison. *Comprehensive Psychiatry,* **23,** 516–527.

Kernberg, O. (1967). Borderline personality organization. *Journal of the American Psychoanalytic Association,* **15,** 641–685.

Koenigsberg, H. W., Kaplan, R. D., Gilmore, M. M., and Cooper, A. M. (1985). The relationship between syndrome and personality disorder in DSM-III: Experience with 2,462 patients. *American Journal of Psychiatry,* **142,** 207–212.

Kohut, H. (1971). *The analysis of the self.* New York: International Universities Press.

Millon, T. (1981). *Disorders of personality: DSM-III: Axis II.* New York: Wiley.

Morey, L. C. (1988). Personality disorders in DSM-III and DSM-IIIR: Convergence, coverage, and internal consistency. *American Journal of Psychiatry,* **145,** 573–577.

Widiger, T. A., and Frances, A. (1985). The DSM-III personality disorders: Perspectives from psychology. *Archives of General Psychiatry,* **42,** 615–623.

PART V

Other Issues

CHAPTER 15

Simulation and Malingering

INTRODUCTION

It has often been proposed that one value of the Rorschach is its immunity to faking or simulation, but the validity of that axiom seems questionable. Certainly, the interpretation of Rorschach data is sometimes more knotty when the test is used for other than routine types of consultation that involve formulating diagnoses, recommending treatment plans or objectives, or evaluating treatment effects. This added challenge occurs most frequently when the circumstances under which the test is administered provoke unusual situational sets to convey false impressions of the self. In some instances, motivational sets can have an impact on some of a subject's decision operations and/or response patterns. Some subjects hope to appear more healthy or well adjusted than they are in reality, whereas other subjects seek to feign serious maladjustment. In either instance, the transient set may create unusual censoring of responses or promote the selection of responses that otherwise would have been discarded. This is not to suggest that the sets are unreal. On the contrary, although transient, they are quite real. As such, they can have an impact on some aspects of performance, just as the presence of situational stress increases the likelihood that certain features will occur more frequently than they would otherwise.

The product of these situational sets varies considerably depending on the set's strength, the subject's objectives, and whatever information (true or false) the subject may have concerning the test or the condition to be simulated. Undoubtedly, very direct sets can produce some alterations in a record. For example, Hutt, Gibby, Milton, and Pottharst (1950) demonstrated that increases in the frequencies for location types, movement, color, and form occur when subjects are specifically instructed to give those kinds of responses. Gibby (1951) reported that subjects increase the number of *W* or *A* responses if instructed to look for those types of answers. Even more subtle sets that capitalize on the issue of social desirability, such as those employed to study projection (Exner, 1989), tend to have an impact on the frequency with which some types of movement or contents are given.

Although none of these studies addressed the issues of simulation or malingering, the findings have some parallels to circumstances in which a subject is motivated to simulate or malinger. For instance, if a subject believes that it is to his or her advantage to appear seriously disturbed, as in issues of incompetency, insanity, or psychic injury, that set may produce answers that are dramatic or elaborated in a bizarre manner. On the other hand, a subject already adjudicated as insane or incompetent who is seeking probation or release may be very guarded, offering a relatively low number of responses, or being unwilling to elaborate adequately concerning responses during the inquiry. Subjects seeking promotion or special employment placement, or parents embroiled in a custody dispute usually try to do their best, and, in doing so, often seek more direction or reassurance or become more defensive by personalizing answers.

Any sets that are present, whether long term or situational, will manifest in the test data and should be readily apparent if the strength of the set is strong enough to influence the response process. Sometimes, the manifestations are obvious in the structural data. In other instances, the composite of structural and content material is sufficient to key the appropriate interpretive discrimination. However, in many instances, a merging of history information with the data of the test is necessary to identify the presence of discrepant and/or discordant data.

The challenge to the interpreter is to determine if the product of the set is an integral part of the subject's psychological organization, or if it reflects an element that is transient or even incompatible with the basic personality structure or psychological functioning of the subject. In most cases, none of these sets cloud the data of the test so much that all the information concerning the basic personality organization is completely distorted, but the presence of any of these situation-specific sets does add complexity to the interpretive process. Thus, any Rorschach interpreter should be alert to the possibility of some unusual situation-specific set, especially those clinicians seeking to use the Rorschach in employment or forensic consultations.

The presence of any of three conditions seems particularly important: (1) the perceived advantage to malinger serious pathology, (2) the perceived advantage to simulate good adjustment, and (3) the perceived advantage to conceal and be overly guarded.

SIMULATION OF GOOD ADJUSTMENT

Data concerning attempts to simulate or approximate a state that is regarded as positive or desirable are very sparse. Fosberg (1938, 1941) was the first to test the "fakability" hypothesis by using a counterbalanced retest design with instructions to give good and bad impressions. He found that the basic structural features of the test data were not altered and that many variables he studied showed retest reliabilities exceeding .80. Carp and Shavzin (1950) also used a counterbalanced retest design with 20 subjects instructed to give good and bad impressions. They found differences between the groups, but the direction in which the data were altered could not be predicted based on the instructional set. Phares, Stewart, and Foster (1960) used standard instructions with one group of subjects but informed a second group that there were specific right and wrong answers. They did not find significant differences between the groups and concluded that the effects of the instructional set were negligible.

Exner and Sherman (1977) retested 10 schizophrenics on the same day that the first test had been administered. Prior to the second test, each subject was informed that the results of the first test had been reviewed and that the staff agreed that the subject could probably improve his or her performance. Although most of the second records differed from the first for location selection, content, and length, all 10 were judged as schizophrenic by each of three judges naïve to the purpose of the study or the fact that the subjects had been tested previously. Seamons, Howell, Carlisle, and Roe (1981) used 48 subjects with varying degrees of pathology in a counterbalanced retest design. Subjects were asked to respond as if they were normal and well adjusted in one testing and as if they were seriously mentally ill in the second. They found that when instructed to approximate normality, subjects gave significantly more P responses and significantly fewer answers containing *es*-related variables, inappropriate combinations, and dramatic contents.

It seems likely that subjects involved in custody disputes would be prone to attempt simulation of very good adjustment. In that context, the protocols of 25 pairs of nonpatient men and women who were tested in conjunction with custody litigation were reviewed and compared with equal size random samples drawn from the nonpatient normative population. Essentially, the distribution of scores for the combined group of 50 subjects differed very little from that of the normative population, although some differences were found when the groups were compared by sex. For instance, the 25 male subjects averaged nearly 25 responses, which is slightly higher than normative data for males. Conversely, the 25 female subjects averaged only 19 responses, which is slightly lower than the normative data for females. The males had an average EA of 10.5 (median = 9), which is slightly higher than the normative sample, and none of the males gave Pure C responses. The males also averaged 15.4 Z responses, significantly more than the control sample or the female group. None of the 50 subjects was positive on the CDI and only two, one male and one female, were positive on the DEPI. One subject, a male, was also positive on the OBS. Some frequency data for the sample are shown in Table 116.

Obviously, the absence of baseline records, taken prior to litigation, makes it impossible to use these data for more than a basis for speculation. Nonetheless, the findings suggest that if attempts at simulation were common, the results were often less than favorable. As noted in Table 116, 10% of the group have Adj D Scores of less than zero, 12% have $CF + C$ values that are considerably greater than the FC value, 40% have an $X + \%$ that is less than 70%, 16% have $X - \%$'s of more than 15%, 12% are underincorporators, 20% have more passive than active M responses, 18% gave at least one $M-$ response, 22% have more than four Critical Special Scores, 18% are *T-less,* 18% gave at least one reflection answer, and 46% have Egocentricity Indices that fall outside of the average range.

All 50 records contained at least one characteristic that usually would be judged as a liability when compared with an optimal standard, and 41 of the 50 included at least three such characteristics. The presence of some liabilities in the protocols of nonpatients is common but, if someone were successful at simulating exceptional adjustment, it seems doubtful that any liabilities would appear.

Possibly the most intriguing findings in both male and female groups concern the Intellectualization Index, the PER special score, and the number of Popular responses. More than half the subjects in both groups have an interpretively significant Intellectualization Index, and 52% of the total group gave more than two PER answers. These substantial frequencies seem to reflect efforts to appear more mature or sophisticated when confronted with test demands. The frequencies are so much greater than the normative data that it seems reasonable to assume that the elevations were produced by the situational motive. Similarly, 36%

Table 116.   Some Frequency Data for 25 Nonpatient Male-Female Pairs Involved in Custody Litigation

VARIABLE	FEMALE		MALE		TOTAL	
	N	%	N	%	N	%
Ambitent	6	24%	8	32%	14	28%
D Score >0	3	12%	6	24%	9	18%
D Score <0	4	16%	4	16%	8	16%
Adjusted D Score >0	3	12%	6	24%	9	18%
Adjusted D Score <0	2	8%	3	12%	5	10%
$FC>(CF+C)+2$	2	8%	5	20%	4	8%
$FC>(CF+C)+1$	9	36%	8	32%	17	34%
$CF+C>FC+1$	8	32%	6	24%	14	28%
$CF+C>FC+2$	3	12%	3	12%	6	12%
$X+\%>.89$	2	8%	4	16%	6	12%
$X+\%<.70$	11	44%	9	36%	20	40%
$Xu\%>.20$	12	48%	10	40%	22	44%
$X-\%>.15$	5	20%	3	12%	8	16%
Popular <4	3	12%	2	8%	5	10%
Popular >7	8	32%	10	40%	18	36%
$Lambda>0.99$	1	4%	2	8%	3	6%
$Zd>+3.0$	5	20%	8	32%	13	26%
$Zd<-3.0$	4	16%	2	8%	6	12%
$Mp>Ma$	6	24%	4	16%	10	20%
$M->0$	5	20%	4	16%	9	18%
Sum 6 Spec Scores >4	5	20%	6	24%	11	22%
Intellectual Index >3	16	64%	14	56%	30	60%
Intellectual Index >5	12	48%	7	28%	19	38%
COP >1	15	60%	12	48%	27	54%
COP >2	10	40%	9	36%	19	38%
AG >1	6	24%	7	28%	13	26%
AG >2	3	12%	5	20%	8	16%
PER >2	15	60%	11	44%	26	52%
$T=0$	5	20%	4	16%	9	18%
$T>1$	6	24%	3	12%	9	18%
$Pure\ H<2$	7	28%	7	28%	14	28%
$Pure\ H>2$	9	36%	7	28%	16	32%
All human content >6	8	32%	9	36%	17	34%
Egocentricity Index $<.33$	5	20%	4	16%	9	18%
Egocentricity Index $>.44$	8	32%	6	24%	14	28%
$Fr+Rf>0$	5	20%	4	16%	9	18%

of the group gave more than seven Popular answers, which is quite different from the normative sample. These findings coincide with those of Seamons et al. (1981) and support the notion that people attempting to do well are prone to respond more to obvious cues and give more conventional answers.

Overall, research concerning simulation is spotty and incomplete. The composite of data suggest that it is probably quite difficult to simulate good psychological health unless some elements of good health already exist and, even then, any existing liabilities of substance are likely to be conveyed in the data.

MALINGERING

Empirical findings regarding efforts to malinger or approximate serious disturbance are more extensive than those dealing with the simulation of good adjustment, but the literature is more sparse than should be the case, and some findings
must be regarded with equivocation. Malingering, as such, is a rather broad category. The issue or question that must be addressed is not simply whether an effort
at malingering may have occurred, but what kind of pathology might a subject
have attempted to approximate.

As noted earlier, Fosberg (1938, 1941) was the first to test the potential for
malingering by using a counterbalanced retest design. He concluded that the
test data were not easily alterable and that, regardless of instructions, the basic
features of personality continue to be displayed by the structural features of the
test. Carp and Shavzin (1950), who also used a counterbalanced retest design
with instructions to give good and bad impressions, concluded that subjects can
produce a different personality picture under different sets. Easton and Feigenbaum (1967) used a similar design but with a control group that was tested twice
under standard instructions. They detected a decrease in *R, D, H, A, Ad*, and *P*
as a result of instructions to malinger.

Malingering Psychosis or Schizophrenia

Most published studies concerning malingering have focused on schizophrenia or
schizophrenic-like conditions, and most of these works are limited by the fact that
each involved the use of nonpatient subjects who were requested to simulate the
protocols of markedly pathological subjects. Probably the best design of this variety was created by Albert (1978; Albert, Fox, & Kahn, 1980). In this study, 24
subjects, six nonpatients, six paranoid schizophrenics, and 12 nonpatients were
asked to approximate a schizophrenic condition in their Rorschachs. Six of the 12
nonpatients were asked to simulate schizophrenia with no additional information
(uninformed malingerers), and the remaining six were provided with information
concerning paranoid schizophrenia by an audio recording (informed malingerers).

Unfortunately, this excellent design was confounded by several errors in implementation. Albert administered the tests and he may have been influenced in his
inquiry questioning by his own hypotheses-related biases. This error was made
more complex by the fact that the records were not scored before being passed
along to judges for their evaluation. These problems were compounded by the fact
that he obtained no information from the 46 judges concerning their experience
with the test or the approach they used in their evaluations. His results revealed
that 48% of the judgments rendered concerning the schizophrenic records indicated the presence of a psychotic condition, as were 46% of the judgments of the
protocols given by the uninformed malingerer group; however, 72% of the judgments regarding the records of informed malingerers identified those protocols
as having been taken from schizophrenic subjects. Moreover, 24% of the judgments regarding protocols used as controls, that is, records taken from nonpatients under standard conditions, were also identified as representing psychotic
or schizophrenic records. In light of the array of judgments, Albert concluded that

expert clinical judgments about the Rorschach are apparently very susceptible to faking a serious disturbance. Taken at face value, these findings are quite disconcerting; however, they are open to question when reviewed in light of the several major errors that occurred in implementing the design.

The findings of the Seamons et al. (1981) study tend to contradict Albert's results. They found that, when subjects were asked to appear seriously mentally ill, a decrease in Popular responses occurred, as well as an increase in Blood responses, answers containing variables related to *es,* inappropriate combination answers, and dramatic responses. One expert judge was used and was able to differentiate with 80% accuracy protocols collected according to instructions either to appear normal or to appear mentally ill. The judge was also 92% correct in differentiating nonschizophrenic subjects and 75% accurate in identifying schizophrenic subjects.

Mittman (1983) attempted to correct for the methodological errors that occurred in Albert's study. She used 12 naïve examiners to collect 30 protocols. Eighteen of the 30 were taken from nonpatient adults recruited to participate in a standardization study. All were workers in a manufacturing plant. Following Albert's model, six were administered the test with no other instruction. The other 12 were asked to try to simulate a schizophrenic protocol; six were provided with no additional information, and the other six were asked to listen to the Albert audio recording concerning paranoid schizophrenia before taking the test. The remaining 12 records were collected from six inpatient schizophrenics and six inpatient depressives, all of whom were first-admission patients who were administered the test as part of the admission routine. The 30 records were scored and Structural Summaries calculated, although the Schizophrenia Index and Depression Index were not included, as the research concerning their development had not been completed at the time.

Each of 110 volunteer judges received a randomly selected packet of four of the protocols as well as a questionnaire to be completed for each concerning psychological characteristics, including a listing of 12 possible diagnostic categories that included normal and malingered classifications. Ninety judges responded, yielding a range of between 81 and 99 judgments per record. Eighty-nine judgments were rendered concerning the six schizophrenic protocols, but only 51 (57%) correctly identified the presence of that condition. Twelve (13%) of the remaining 38 judgments concerning the schizophrenic records identified serious pathology (endogenous depression, manic depression, borderline personality with psychotic features), but the remaining 26 (29%) were obviously deceived in some way and assigned less serious diagnosis from the listing of 12 provided in the questionnaire. No records were identified as normal, but one judgment of malingering was assigned.

Judgments concerning the records of the six depressive protocols were no more consistent. Thirty-eight of the 81 judgments (47%) concerning this group of six records correctly identified the presence of a major affective disturbance. Twelve (15%) judgments assigned the schizophrenia category. Thirty (37%) of the remaining 31 judgments identified the records as those from personality disorder subjects, and one assigned the malingering category. None of the records was identified as normal.

Five (5%) of 91 judgments rendered concerning the six records of uninformed malingerers identified the presence of schizophrenia. Interestingly, four of the five were assigned to the same record. Twenty-three (25%) of the remaining 86 judgments incorrectly identified the presence of a major affective disturbance, and an additional 44 (48%) judgments assigned one of five personality disorder categories. Eighteen (20%) judgments used the normal classification, and only one (1%) identified a record as being malingered.

Sixteen (18%) of 90 judgments rendered concerning the six records of informed malingerers identified the presence of schizophrenia. Thirteen of the 16 schizophrenia decisions were assigned to two of the six records. Fifteen (16%) other judgments concerning this group of six records identified the presence of a major affective problem and, interestingly, 10 of the 15 were assigned to the same two records that had been identified as schizophrenic 13 times. Fifty-four (59%) of the additional judgments concerning this group of records used one of the five personality disorders categories, whereas only four (4%) used the normal classification and one (1%) identified a record as being malingered.

None of the six nonpatient control records was identified as being schizophrenic, but 12 (12%) of the 99 judgments rendered used a major affective disorders classification. Twenty-three (23%) of the remaining 87 judgments used a category of reactive depression, and 43 (43%) others used the five personality disorders categories. Only 19 (19%) of the judgments identified the records as normal, and two (2%) assigned the malingering classification.

There seem to be two important findings from the study. First, three of the 12 subjects asked to malinger schizophrenia, two from the informed group and one from the uninformed group, were able to do so with considerable success. Actually, 17 of 35 judgments concerning those three protocols identified them as being schizophrenic, whereas 14 of the remaining 18 judgments identified them as being major affective disturbances. These findings tend to support Albert's (1978) conclusions that the Rorschach is susceptible to malingering, especially if subjects have some awareness of the type of condition they are trying to approximate. Second, it seems clear that the 90 judges who rendered a total of 450 judgments concerning the 30 protocols were set or disposed to find pathology or psychological liabilities. Approximately 45% of the judgments used one of the five personality disorders categories. When major pathology was present, the majority of judgments were in that direction (about 70% of the decisions made for the six schizophrenic records and about 60% of those made concerning the depressive protocols) but, when major pathology was not obvious, as in the two malingered groups and the nonpatient group, slightly more than 50% of all judgments used the personality disorders classifications.

As noted earlier, neither the SCZI nor the DEPI were part of the *Comprehensive System* when the 30 records were collected for Mittman's (1983) study. Mittman and Exner (1989) recoded the records, taking into account the variety of newer special scores that had been developed after 1982 and differentiating Critical Special Scores into the Level 1 and Level 2 classifications. The purpose was to determine if the original or revised SCZI and/or the revised DEPI might have influenced some of the judgments that were made had they been available at the time the judgments were rendered, or if they might shed some light concerning the judgments that were made concerning the three malingered records. Calculations for the two SCZI's, the revised DEPI, and the CDI are shown by subject and group in Table 117, together with the diagnosis afforded each record by the majority of judgments.

An examination of the data in Table 117 provides some clues concerning the majority of judgments made for almost all of the cases. The record of the one uninformed malingerer identified by the majority of judgments as being schizophrenic contained enough serious signs to obtain a value of 5 on the original SCZI, but that value dropped to 3 on the revised SCZI. Similarly, the two informed malingerers identified by the majority of judgments as being

Table 117.   Scores for Several Indicies Plus Consensus Diagnosis for 30 Records Used in the 1983 Mittman Study

GROUP	ID	AGE	SEX	R	ORGINAL SCZI	REVISED SCZI	DEPI	CDI	CONSENSUS DIAGNOSIS
SCHIZOPHRENIA									
	15	37	M	35	4	5	4	2	SCHIZOPHRENIA
	12	22	F	25	2	4	6	4	AFFECT DISORDER
	2	28	M	32	5	6	2	1	SCHIZOPHRENIA
	17	58	F	28	5	4	6	2	SCHIZOPHRENIA
	27	32	M	12	5	4	6	1	SCHIZOPHRENIA
	24	50	F	18	3	1	4	4	BORDERLINE
AFFECTIVE DISORDER									
	19	52	M	16	1	0	5	3	AFFECT DISORDER
	6	37	F	12	3	4	3	4	BORDERLINE
	5	31	M	14	5	3	7	3	AFFECT DISORDER
	9	26	F	16	1	1	4	5	BORDERLINE
	30	48	1	31	3	3	5	1	AFFECT DISORDER
	20	26	2	24	4	3	5	1	AFFECT DISORDER
UNINFORMED MALINGERER									
	16	38	F	14	0	0	3	2	NORMAL
	14	39	F	15	1	0	5	4	AFFECT DISORDER
	3	32	M	16	1	1	3	4	INADEQUATE
	28	54	F	12	0	0	5	4	INADEQUATE
	1	26	M	27	5	3	4	1	SCHIZOPHRENIA
	29	30	F	22	0	0	4	3	REACTIVE DEPRESS
INFORMED MALINGERER									
	10	36	F	17	0	0	4	2	HYSTEROID
	8	35	M	16	5	6	5	4	SCHIZOPHRENIA
	7	58	M	24	3	2	3	1	BORDERLINE
	4	22	M	19	4	3	5	1	SCHIZOPHRENIA
	25	51	M	21	0	1	1	2	BORDERLINE
	26	48	F	20	1	1	3	2	HYSTEROID
NONPATIENT									
	18	59	F	20	0	0	5	3	REACTIVE DEPRESS
	11	22	F	10	1	1	4	4	INADEQUATE
	23	30	F	12	1	0	1	2	NORMAL
	13	19	F	14	1	1	2	5	INADEQUATE
	21	56	M	19	4	1	4	0	SCHIZOID
	22	52	F	20	1	1	3	3	NORMAL

schizophrenic also gave records in which the original SCZI was positive, and one of the two (ID #8) had a value of 6 on the revised SCZI. All subjects identified by the majority of subjects as having affective disorders had positive values on the DEPI. The four subjects whom the majority of judgments identify as inadequate all had positive CDI values, as did three of the five subjects identified by the majority as being borderline.

The partial reanalysis of Mittman's data yielded nothing that would alter the conclusion that, under some circumstances, nonpatient subjects may be able to approximate serious disturbance if set to do so. It is also possible that the likelihood of success in malingering is increased because most clinicians seem set to give greater weight to features that may relate to pathology or psychological liabilities.

The notion that information concerning schizophrenia and/or the Rorschach will enhance the possibility of successfully malingering schizophrenia, although logical, is somewhat debatable. That premise seems subject to challenge in light of findings from five small sample studies that used designs in which graduate students, nearing the completion of courses in assessment with emphasis on Rorschach training, were instructed to write a schizophrenic protocol within a given time limit. The first study (Exner & Wylie, 1975) involved 12 students who were allowed two hours to complete the task. Only one of the 12 records submitted by that group was appraised unanimously by five judges as being a schizophrenic protocol, although three other records were appraised by two judges as schizophrenic. In 1984, the 12 records were recalculated for the original SCZI and the one judged unanimously as schizophrenic was found to have an SCZI of 5. The remaining 11 records had SCZI's of 2 or 3.

In the other four studies (Exner & Levantrosser, 1982; Exner & Sternklar, 1980; Exner, Viglione, & Hillman, 1983; Exner & Wasley, 1984), a time limit of one hour was imposed for the same task for groups of 13 to 16 students. Six of the resulting 57 records had values of 5 on the original SCZI, nine had values of 4, and the remaining 42 had values of 2 or 3. When recalculated for the revised SCZI, two records had values of 6, four had values of 5, and four had values of 4. In other words, 15 of the 57 (26%) were positive on the original SCZI, and 10 (18%) of those 15 remained positive on the revised SCZI. If the postulate that information about the Rorschach or about schizophrenia enhances the capacity to malinger schizophrenia is true, it would seem likely that more than 10 of 57 students, trained extensively in both subjects, could easily create a schizophrenic protocol when requested to do so spontaneously.

Moreover, a closer inspection of the 10 protocols that have positive revised SCZI's reveals that the data for the variables in the SCZI were so extreme in four cases that it is unlikely that anyone trained in Rorschach would be deceived by them. Two had $X+$%'s of zero, one had an $X+$% of 15%, and the fourth an $X+$% of 18%. One record had an $X-$% of 100%, and the other three had $X-$%'s of between 75 and 83%. One record, consisting of 20 responses, contained 23 of the six Critical Special Scores, with a weighted sum of 114, whereas the remaining three contained between 15 and 18 Critical Special Scores, with weighted sums ranging from 69 to 80. All four records contained at least five $M-$ answers. In other words, although all four records clearly contained the features of the schizophrenic, all were so bizarre that they reflected the kind of extreme psychotic disorganization that would preclude the subject from being amenable to testing. These findings are commensurate with those reported by Overton (1984), who randomly assigned 30 undergraduate psychology students to three groups. Subjects were administered the Rorschach by examiners blind to the conditions. A control group received standard instructions, a noninformed group received malingered instructions, and an informed group was given instructions on how to malinger in the role of a schizophrenic. The results indicated that the noninformed fakers appeared to be closer to psychotic than the informed fakers who produced protocols too pronounced to be believed and whose behavioral presentation was inconsistent with the presence of psychosis.

Obviously, the issue of malingering schizophrenic like Rorschach's is far from resolution. Unfortunately, with the exception of Seamons et al.'s (1981) investigation, the studies reported thus far have used nonpatient subjects tested under conditions that are quite dissimilar to those under which a true malingerer might attempt to approximate serious disturbance.

Malingering Depression

Investigations concerning efforts to malinger or approximate depression are far fewer than those concerning schizophrenia. The data are sparse and somewhat equivocal but tend to suggest that malingered depression may be less easily detected than malingered schizophrenia.

Meisner (1984) used five trained examiners, blind to the experimental condition of the study, to administer the Rorschach to 58 nondepressed university students. Immediately prior to taking the Rorschach, half of the subjects were trained in the clinical symptoms of depression and asked to fake depression. The remaining 29 were administered the test under standard instructions. Meisner found that, when subjects attempted to fake depression, their protocols showed a reduction in R and an increase in blood content and MOR Special Scores. No determinants were significantly affected by attempts to fake depression; thus, Meisner concluded that the susceptibility of the Rorschach indices of depression to faking is markedly limited.

Exner (1987) used a modified Albert design to study this issue. Twenty-four nonpatient adults recruited from an electronics manufacturing firm were randomized into three groups of eight subjects each. Eight naïve examiners administered the Rorschachs, each testing three subjects. One group was informed that they were participating in a standardization project, a second was instructed to take the test as if they were feeling very severely depressed, and the third was given the same instruction as the second but, before taking the test, each listened to a 15-minute audio recording that provided a detailed description of the symptoms and characteristics of seriously depressed adults. The protocols of eight first-admission major depressive disturbance inpatients were randomly selected from the protocol pool of the Rorschach Research Foundation to be used as a comparison group.

Data from the 32 records were analyzed by group for seven structural variables using a series of chi-squares, the results of which are shown in Table 118. The data show that three of the 16 subjects asked to malinger depression were able to render protocols with a positive DEPI. A close inspection of the three

Table 118.   **Frequency Data for Seven Variables for Four Groups, Each Containing Eight Subjects**

VARIABLE	NONPT	UNIFORMED MALINGER	INFORMED MALINGER	DEPRESSED
DEPI > 4	0	1	2	7**
CDI > 3	1	3	2	4
RT eb > LFT eb	1**	6	7	6
MOR > 2	1**	7	6	7
$3r+(2)/R$ < .33	1	2	3	6*
Afr < .35	0	0	1	6**
Isolate > .24	1	0	1	6**

* = significantly different from two groups, $p < .02$
** = significantly different from all other groups, $p < .01$

records reveals that, although some of the MOR answers were quite grotesque, they were not markedly unlike those found in the protocols of the depressed patients and, overall, the records themselves offer no distinct clues that depression might be malingered. Only the addition of the history (all three are gainfully employed and socially active) would raise a question about malingering, as the records themselves are not commensurate with those of socially active or occupationally productive people.

It is also of considerable interest to note that even though none of the remaining 13 malingering subjects failed to achieve a positive DEPI, 10 of the 13 produced records in which the right-side eb value is greater than the left-side value, and 10 also produced more than two MOR responses. The former seems especially important because it signals distress. In this instance, all 10 higher right-side values were created by an elevation in C' responses. This suggests that MOR and C' may have less stability than has been reported previously, or that they are more subject to variation under sets to approximate distress or depression. Obviously, this possibility has important implications for the forensic setting in which psychic injury is the focus of attention.

Ros (1990) also used a modified Albert design to study the malingering of depression on both the Rorschach and the Minnesota Multiphasic Personality Inventory. Her study involved 40 subjects in five cells with eight subjects each. Twenty-four subjects were nonpatients randomized into three groups. One group was administered both tests using standard instructions, a second group was asked to take the tests as if they were seriously depressed and the third group was asked to listen to an audio cassette concerning depression, which included a statement by a seriously depressed subject, and then take the tests with the intent of approximating the records of the seriously depressed patient. The remaining 16 Rorschachs and MMPI's were collected from depressed patients, six of whom were outpatients and six were inpatients.

Ros found that six of the 16 malingering subjects gave protocols in which the DEPI value was 5 or higher. It is not necessarily surprising to learn that four of the six were from the informed malingering group. She also found that the two malingering groups gave as many MOR, *C'*, and *Vista* responses as did her two patient comparison groups. Two of the most important findings in this study concerned the MMPI and CDI data. Almost all of the informed malingerers produced *invalid* MMPI's that had extremely high T-scores on the *F*, 2, 7, and 8 scales. Conversely, four of the uninformed malingerers produced valid MMPI's that do approximate the profile of a seriously depressed subject. None of the malingerers produced a positive CDI although most of the patient records included a positive CDI.

The number of studies concerning the malingering of depression are too few to draw firm conclusions. Nonetheless, the data suggest a distinct possibility that depression and/or features of distress can be approximated deliberately by some people. Although the findings are based on very small samples of nonpatient subjects asked to approximate depression, they are difficult to cast aside. On the contrary, they represent the sort of findings that argue for caution against concluding that the subject is distressed and/or depressed, especially in instances in which it is clearly to the advantage of the subject to appear distressed and/or depressed.

ADJUDICATED MALINGERING

From 1974 to 1989, the Rorschach Research Foundation accumulated the protocols of 31 adjudicated malingerers, that is, subjects who have admitted efforts to convey the presence of serious psychological problems. Twenty-one of these subjects were involved in criminal proceedings and attempted to malinger a form of disturbance that could be used as a basis for being declared incompetent to stand trial, or not guilty of an offense by reason of insanity. The remaining 10 were involved in cases of psychic injury and hoped to produce records that would lead others to agree to the presence of a disabling affective problem. The samples have been subjected to statistical analysis, but each group is notably heterogeneous for structural features.

In two of the 21 criminal cases, values of 6 were achieved on the revised SCZI, but both records were so bizarre that they were unbelievable and both were highly inconsistent with the cooperativeness of the subject during the testing. One of the 10 civil cases had a DEPI of 7 and a CDI of 5, but was given by a subject who, only two days before the record was taken, was at a racetrack celebrating with friends.

Although each group of records lacks homogeneity for structural features, some common features among most of the records should create a sense of skepticism in the skilled Rorschacher. First, all contain an inordinate number of lengthy responses, that is, the basic answer, excluding the inquiry. Most answers given by the typical subject, whether a schizophrenic, nonschizophrenic, or nonpatient, are between 10 and 16 words. The mean for a random sample of 200 nonpatient adults is 13.2, whereas the mean for 200 schizophrenic, *nonpsychotic* subjects is 11.1. More than 40% of the answers given by adjudicated malingerers have between 25 and 40 words, and another 5% exceed 40 words. A word of caution should be inserted here: Subjects from the upper-upper socioeconomic group (SES1) and those of superior intelligence (I.Q. > 125) also tend to give a larger number of lengthy verbalizations in the basic response. Thus, length of response, by itself, is not necessarily a good discriminator. However, the longer answers given by the malingering group tend to be marked by much more bizarreness than is found in the records of either the SES1 or the superior intelligence subjects. Those attempting to malinger often mix a marked bizarreness in words with a good or even excellent use of form. In other words, the form quality for the majority of answers is much different from that found among truly disturbed subjects. Even when the form quality is minus, the distortion seems to have been developed only by a struggle. A response to Card III may serve as a good example: "This looks like two evil people dancing around a pot that has their evil spirits in it ready to be released. They want to destroy the world because it is so evil and they are bending there saying their chants . . . [long pause]. They must be succeeding because the red intestines of some of their previous victims are falling all around them [D2 and D3]." The definition of D2 and/or D3 as intestines makes the entire response a minus; prior to the pause, however, the response includes only adequate form use and, in fact, even after the minus components are introduced, the response remains a Popular.

The records of adjudicated malingerers usually contain a larger number of Critical Special Scores than is common, but the $X + \%$ is at least 65% in 22 of the 31 cases. The larger frequency of Special Scores is generated by efforts at bizarreness, and also by many comments and phrases that are legitimately scored as DR because they seem out of place: "This looks too scary for me, I can't look at it"; or "I wouldn't dare tell you what I see cause you'll think I'm crazy"; or "I hope that no one else will ever know I said this"; or "It's too vulgar, please don't make me tell you"; or "I've been hoping all my life that I'd never see one like this." It is important to note that the efforts to malinger in these 31 cases are not readily obvious to the casual observer and even press the wisdom of the experienced clinician. A class of 13 second-year graduate students in clinical psychology decided that seven of the 10 civil cases were truly pathologically depressed.

Overall, if anything is to be gleaned from these 31 cases, it is the fact that the record "doesn't sound right" in light of other information, mainly history data, available concerning the subject. Two of these cases, one criminal and one civil, are described below. They are in no way unique with regard to the sample and, in fact, represent more conservative efforts at malingering than noted in the total group.

Case 11: A Rapist

This 20-year-old male was administered the Rorschach as part of an evaluation requested by the office of a district attorney. The request was made after the subject's attorney had filed a plea of "not guilty by reason of temporary insanity" in a sexual assault case.

The subject was apprehended by a university security officer while raping a 19-year-old sophomore in her dormitory room. According to the victim, he had knocked on her door and, when she opened it, "he pushed a gun in my face and pushed me backward into the room." According to the allegation, he then instructed her to disrobe. During the next several minutes, he talked to her explaining that he knew that she had been waiting for him. He then proceeded to ask her many questions about herself, her parents, her dating behaviors, her prior sexual experiences, and her vocational interests. Ultimately, he used his belt to tie her hands together behind her and forced her to lie on the bed, at which time he commenced the actual rape. According to the victim, approximately 15 minutes elapsed before the act began.

Apparently someone in another dormitory room saw the subject in the building and notified the university security and they began checking through the building in a systematic manner. Shortly after the physical act began, a security guard knocked on the door, causing the subject to discontinue the act and he began to untie the victim at about the same time the security guard opened the unlocked door. When apprehended, the subject claimed that he had been invited into the room by the victim and that she had also asked him to bind her hands with his belt.

The subject was incarcerated overnight and accompanied by an attorney arranged for by his parents to an arraignment hearing the next morning. At that time, the subject acted confused and claimed to have no recollection of the event. He was released on bail after his attorney filed the temporary insanity plea. Prior to this evaluation, he had been examined by a psychologist and a psychiatrist acting on behalf of the defense.

The subject is the older of two siblings, having a brother age 17 who currently is in his third year of high school. His father, age 50, is the manager of a clothing store. His mother, age 45, works full time in that store. There is no reported psychiatric history in the immediate family. The birth and developmental history provided by the mother is unremarkable, and the subject has no significant medical history. He graduated from high school at age 17 and was ranked in the top 20% of his class. During his last two years in high school he was on the varsity track team as a distance runner. He applied and was admitted to several universities, and ultimately selected a large state university with the intention of completing a premedical curriculum.

At the time of his arrest, he was in the second semester of his junior year, carrying a 3.26 grade point average. Although he had been interested in a premedical major, he decided to change his major to psychology during his second year. He has lived in a single room in a men's dormitory. Reports from various professors, including his adviser, tend to be favorable, although none seemed to know him very well. Interviews with other students suggest that he does not have many close relationships, but does participate in a variety of group activities in the dormitory and in some intramural sports. The victim claims that she does not know the subject and does not remember ever seeing him in school. According to records, they have never taken the same class together.

According to the subject, he has no recollection for the event. He states that he drinks beer occasionally and has smoked marijuana, but denies the use of any other substance. He says that he has had several girlfriends while at the university, but that none of his relationships have lasted very long, "I guess because I spend so much time on my studies." He says that his first heterosexual experience was at age 15 during high school and that he has never experienced any sexual problems. He argues strenuously that if he was in the room of the victim, it would have "been because she wanted me and probably asked me to be there, but I can't remember that." He admits owning a revolver, and says that he

Case 11: A 20-Year-Old Male

Card	Response	Inquiry
I	1. A bat	E: (Rpts S's resp) S: I thk I said that bec I saw the proj's comg out of ths area (points) & the 2 whole sides comg out lik wgs, but I thk I only saw it as rite here (points to D1 projections) E: Outline it for me S: Right here (outlines W)
	2. It ll some kind of satanic demon w his hands raised & around him r, I dk, hell bats. A preacher preaching fire & brimstone. Som kind of being w his hands raised & ths shaded area around it & the gaps in between	E: (Rpts S's resp) S: Here's the figure right here (points) E: Hell bats? S: Hell bats? Is that wht I said? E: Yes S: Hell, yeah, just ths, nothin concrete about him, yet there's smthg omnipresent perhaps E: I'm not sur I c it lik u do S: Well just the idea of ths preacher in a cloaked puritannical garb & the whole idea of puritannical preaching lik Whitehead conjurs up visions of hell, thy were common in the 1600's, the entity brings on the idea of the surroundings bringing on the idea of the entity. He's praising the power of the Lord and his Evangelical manner is scaring his audience with pict's of hell, and the gaps—there's nothing concrete about him & yet smthg's there
II	3. U kno wht it c.b., when my girlfriend used to be menustrating s.t. there'd b bld on the sheet, & the shading & the spaces here caus my girfrd's black & ths cld b her vagina w bld comg out S: Do u want me to keep look? Is thr a a proce-dur u want me to follow cuz if u want I cld keep lookg at it E: It's up to u	E: (Rpts S's resp) S: The red areas wb bld & I did say she was black & here r black areas here, & the red against the black wb the bld against her E: Where is the vagina? S: The space in the middl is the vaginal area, c the slit & the open area (outlines)
II	4. This ll a spaceship being propelld into dark-ness & on the othr side there's light	E: (Rpts S's resp) S: Ths wld b the lite area in the middl w a satellite kind of form & the red underneath is the fiery propulsion & the dark is the space *(continued)*

441

Case 11: (Continued)

Card	Response	Inquiry
	I guess tht's about it, I've really got a good imagination	E: The dark? S: Around the spaceshp is darkness, I guess I wld interpret the darkness as a space, lik a spaceshp does, go into space E: U said on the other side there's lite? S: On top, kind of passg thru the space & then back out into ths light area (points)
III	5. 2 blk people, um, um, sk of tribal ritualistic dance. Thy seem to b playg a drum & the red around mite be the energy comg out of it	E: (Rpts S's resp) S: One, two (points), at first I saw a dance but then I saw the instrument (points) E: U mentioned the red around it? S: To beat on a drum there wld be vibrations & red is a vibrating kind of color tht represents that
IV	6. Bigfoot, yeah tht's wht it ll, it ll st u c in a monstr movie, tht's my interpretation of it	E: (Rpts S's resp) S: Exactly, a monstr movie, comic book char, some kind of swamp monster E: I'm not sur I c it as u do S: 2 feet a larg body, & there's the head, thse wb the arms yet there's no hands, no real hands anyway, thyr strangely shaped, & ths mite b a tail, it ll thos Big Foot commercials on TV, c how TV influences this?
V	7. Um, a bf or a bat, there's wgs & antennae E: Which did u say it is? S: Um, the shape c.b. that of a bf or a bat, but the shp is more lik a bf but the color is more lik a bat, a black bf-mixed marriage perhaps	E: (Rpts S's resp) S: Yeah, its the W thg, c (outlines), its lik a cross betw a bf & a bat, a weird marriage but interesting
	8. The 2 sides seem to be merging togethr & yet tryg to repel e.o. at the same time (long pause) Its interesting	E: (Rpts S's resp) S: There seems to b s.k. of fusion here in the middl & yet it spreads here at the bttm & at the top E: Spreads? S: C the way it spreads (motions w fingers). Then I said its interesting—I thk I said tht in ref to how interestg it is tht u can tell me to c s.t. & kno inevitably u'll mak judgements about ths & I find that interesting

VI

9. Good question! I don't really c it as being athg concrete, um, the only thg I mite c is some stratification, there's a small bit at the top, it comes out a bit & a big mass at the bttm, the Aristoi of society is at the top & the bttm is the lower classes, I'm trying to c st here—if so were to show ths to me I wldn't c anythg, its just an inkblot

E: (Rpts S's resp)

S: I took a Sociology cours, thy showd the stratification in the shape of a triangle, ths isn't a triangle but it does hav a small Aristoi, rich at the top & the more u go down, the more, the largr the mass of people wb, hav the large mass of thos of us who aren't rich at the bottm & here's that small area at the top

VII

10. With the dark area around the white area in the middl there seems to b some penetration going on, intercourse perhaps

E: (Rpts S's resp)

S: The round area is perhaps the head of the penis & the drk area around it is the vaginal area, penetration has been achieved, its in—I'm talkg about the white area in the middl & the drk area around it

VIII

11. To look at it another way, an old wm in a rockg chair & a mirror image of herself on the othr side

Going back to what I originally said, the white area seem to b forcing itself into the blk area, lik intercourse

E: (Rpts S's resp)

S: An old wm sittg here in a rockg chair, & the mirror image here (points), the only thg inconsistent wb the prorusion on top of the head & I dkno wht it is, mayb a hair style

E: U said an old wm?

S: The head is thin, emaciated, ths prt wb lik her dress & its the position she's in, & the hook prt comg up, & the rockg chair below, the bttm swgs up lik an arc

12. Its a pleasant chg from all the dark blots to come to s.t. w a littl color in it, its like one of those prehistoric paintgs on a cave wall

E: (Rpts S's resp)

S: I went to a movie a few months ago, "The Other Side of Midnight"—the color scheme & pattern ll the prehistoric paintings he showd her in the cave, all yellows & oranges & greens and blues

13. The 2 pink figs on the outside seem to ll beavers, thy seem to b tryg to reach the top but thy can't cause theyr part of the bttm of it

E: (Rpts S's resp)

S: Right here (points), thy seem to b connectd here, but thyr tryg to climb up, thyl never attain the heights thyr tryg for, thyv been held back, thyr prt of ths, thy can't reach the top bec thyr simply not long enuff

(continued)

Case 11: (Continued)

Card	Response	Inquiry
	14. And ths space in the middl kind of ll vertebrae	E: (Rpts S's resp) S: Ths part rite here (points) wb the spine & here r the bones coming out
	15. And the grey area on top ll a gargoyle	E: (Rpts S's resp) S: Kind of a reptilian fig. & a gargoyle is concrete, st u'd c on the side of a bldg & its grey basically, now ur going to want to kno why its a reptilian fig rite? Well, thes seem to b legs, the head, & ths line wld mak it look bowed dwn, the head isn't visible, its bec of the shape
IX	16. To look at ths, ths litd area on top w a brightly colrd dome, it appears to b arnd it, I dk, it seems lik a height u'd want to attain, lik heaven perhaps, it seems to opn in the middl & get bright, kinda lik what u'd c in a movie where thyd play movie music, u kno, da, da, u kno, I'm seeing st in the cards bec I'm askd to c st in thes cards, getting back to wht I said bef abt heaven, uv got the pink on the bttm, grn & orange on top, & red signfyg hell, the green is purgatory & orange, blue & white heaven, it seems to open up	E: (Rpts S's resp) S: Yes, ths is the heights, the heaven ths area, the way its open, light & serene E: U said it's open, lite & serene? S: It's open bec of the shape, & the orange is arnd it & I'm talkg about the opening betwn tht orange & the serene feeling comes fr the lite blue & green in the middle here, it's hard to describe ur own craziness to someone else
X	17. Hallucinations. It ll s.t. an alcoholic mite c on the wall, nothg cohesive & yet thrs littl thgs thr littl crawlg thgs. It ll littl beings or creaturs who seem to b both sides of ths r the same yet seem to b opposit, opposing one anothr, thy seem hav the same outcome in mind whil opposng one anothr, the small or-ange in the middle mit b wht thyr tryg to obtain, its serene & tranquil—outside is all turmoil	E: (Rpts S's resp) S: Littl thgs (points to several), littl creatures thts wht thy ll, lookg at eo by themselves, not collectively, thy come in pairs, each side has a pair on the othr side, I said little creaturs w a battl going on, thes 2 on top bring it to mind more thn anythg else, & the orange lik thg its just hanging there in space, protected by ths area around it & it seems lik evthg is tryg to get it, the turmoil, thyr all diff colors, the arrangement of the colors seems tumultuous

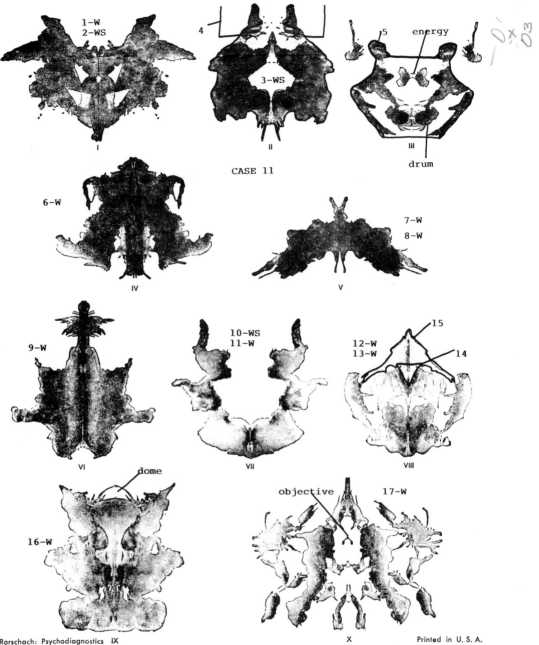

CASE 11

Rorschach: Psychodiagnostics IX
Printed in U. S. A.

CASE 11. SEQUENCE OF SCORES

```
===================================================================================
CARD NO  LOC   #    DETERMINANT(S)   (2)   CONTENT(S)  POP  Z    SPECIAL SCORES
===================================================================================
  I    1 Wo    1 Fo                        A            P  1.0
       2 WS+   1 Ma.YF-             2  (H),(A)             4.0  DR2,AB

  II   3 WS+   1 Mp.CF.C'Fu               Sx,Bl             4.5  PER
       4 DdS+ 99 ma.YF.CFo               Sc,Fi,Na          4.5

 III   5 D+    1 FC'.Ma.ma.Cu      2  H,Id          P  4.0  COP,AB,ALOG

  IV   6 Wo    1 Fo                        (H)          P  2.0

   V   7 Wo    1 FC'o                     A            P  1.0  DR2
       8 W/    1 Mau               2  Hx                2.5  AG,DR,AB

  VI   9 Wv    1 F-                        Art               DR,PER,AB

 VII  10 WS+   1 Ma-                      Sx                4.0
      11 W+    1 Mp.Fro                   H,Hh         P  2.5  MOR

VIII  12 Wv    1 CFo                      Art,Ay            PER
      13 W+    1 FMao             2  A            P  4.5  FAB
      14 Do    3 Fo                       An
      15 Do    4 FC'.FDu                  (A),Art

  IX  16 WS+   1 CFu                      Hx                5.5  DR,PER,AB

   X  17 WS/   1 Ma.FC.mpo        2  Hx,(A)            6.0  AG,AB
===================================================================================
```

CASE 11. STRUCTURAL SUMMARY
===

LOCATION FEATURES	DETERMINANTS BLENDS	SINGLE	CONTENTS	S-CONSTELLATION

```
LOCATION                DETERMINANTS              CONTENTS        S-CONSTELLATION
FEATURES            BLENDS      SINGLE                          NO..FV+VF+V+FD>2
                                            H   = 2, 0          YES..Col-Shd Bl>0
Zf    = 13      M.YF            M   = 2     (H) = 2, 0          YES..Ego<.31,>.44
ZSum  = 46.0    M.CF.C'F        FM  = 1     Hd  = 0, 0          NO...MOR > 3
ZEst  = 41.5    m.YF.CF         m   = 0     (Hd)= 0, 0          YES..Zd > +- 3.5
                FC'.M.m.C       FC  = 0     Hx  = 3, 0          NO...es > EA
W    = 13       M.Fr            CF  = 2     A   = 3, 0          YES..CF+C > FC
 (Wv = 2)       FC'.FD          C   = 0     (A) = 1, 2          YES..X+% < .70
D    = 3        M.FC.m          Cn  = 0     Ad  = 0, 0          YES..S > 3
Dd   = 1                        FC' = 1     (Ad)= 0, 0          NO...P < 3 or > 8
S    = 6                        C'F = 0     An  = 1, 0          NO...Pure H < 2
                                C'  = 0     Art = 2, 1          NO...R < 17
   DQ                           FT  = 0     Ay  = 0, 1          6.....TOTAL
.........(FQ-)                  TF  = 0     Bl  = 0, 1
  +   = 8  ( 2)                 T   = 0     Bt  = 0, 0          SPECIAL SCORINGS
  o   = 5  ( 0)                 FV  = 0     Cg  = 0, 0            Lv1      Lv2
  v/+ = 2  ( 0)                 VF  = 0     Cl  = 0, 0      DV  = 0x1      0x2
  v   = 2  ( 1)                 V   = 0     Ex  = 0, 0      INC = 0x2      0x4
                                FY  = 0     Fd  = 0, 0      DR  = 3x3      2x6
                                YF  = 0     Fi  = 0, 1      FAB = 1x4      0x7
                                Y   = 0     Ge  = 0, 0      ALOG= 1x5
    FORM QUALITY                Fr  = 0     Hh  = 0, 1      CON = 0x7
                                rF  = 0     Ls  = 0, 0        SUM6  = 7
        FQx  FQf  MQual  SQx    FD  = 0     Na  = 0, 1        WSUM6 = 30
  +   =  0    0    0     0      F   = 4     Sc  = 1, 0
  o   =  9    3    2     2                  Sx  = 2, 0      AB  = 6    CP  = 0
  u   =  5    0    3     2                  Xy  = 0, 0      AG  = 2    MOR = 1
  -   =  3    1    2     2                  Id  = 0, 1      CFB = 0    PER = 4
none  =  0    --   0     0      (2) = 5                     COP = 1    PSV = 0
```
===
                        RATIOS, PERCENTAGES, AND DERIVATIONS

```
R = 17         L = 0.31           FC:CF+C = 1: 5      COP = 1    AG = 2
----------------------------------  Pure C  = 1       Food     = 0
EB = 7: 6.0   EA = 13.0   EBPer= N/A  Afr   =0.55      Isolate/R =0.12
eb = 4: 6     es = 10      D = +1   S       = 6        H:(H)Hd(Hd)= 2: 2
             Adj es = 7  Adj D = +2  Blends:R= 7:17    (HHd):(AAd) = 2: 3
----------------------------------  CP      = 0        H+A:Hd+Ad  =10: 0
FM = 1 :  C'= 4   T = 0
m  = 3 :  V = 0   Y = 2
                              P    = 6      Zf   =13     3r+(2)/R=0.47
a:p   = 8: 3   Sum6  = 7    X+%  =0.53     Zd   = +4.5   Fr+rF   = 1
Ma:Mp = 5: 2   Lv2   = 2    F+%  =0.75   W:D:Dd=13: 3: 1 FD      = 1
2AB+Art+Ay=16  WSum6 = 30   X-%  =0.18     W:M  =13: 7   An+Xy   = 1
M-    = 2      Mnone = 0    S-%  =0.67     DQ+  = 8      MOR     = 1
                            Xu%  =0.29     DQv  = 2
-------------------------------------------------------------------------------
   SCZI = 2    DEPI = 4    CDI = 0    S-CON = 6    HVI =YES    OBS = No
```
===

originally purchased it because he wanted to learn how to shoot a gun and decided to keep it for his own self-protection.

Case 11 Overview The subject did a good job of presenting convincing evidence for a thought disturbance. The 17-response record contains seven Critical Special Scores, including two Level 2 responses, and there are two *M−* answers. When the Special Scores are read, however, a sense of intellectualizing becomes emphasized much more than distorted or circumstantial thinking. Similarly, the two *M−* responses, although legitimately scored minus, seem to reflect answers in which the minus form quality is forced. Whether this critique is valid is almost irrelevant to the issues of dissociation or temporary insanity, as no data suggest that a pattern of chronically disturbed thinking underlies either condition.

The data concerning processing and mediation are even less convincing. The processing data show a hypervigilant style and a considerable effort to input data carefully. The mediation data are clearly inconsistent with serious pathology, although the high *S− %* suggests that distortions occur as the result of negativism or anger. The data for the cluster regarding controls probably offer the most compelling argument against dissociation. The D Score is lower than the Adj D Score, but both are in the *plus* range, suggesting little likelihood for loss of control. The notion of dissociation also tends to be negated by the data concerning self-perception. He has a marked narcissistic-like quality that promotes externalization of cause and protection of self-integrity.

The data regarding affect, especially the high value for *S* and the deviant *FC : CF + C* ratio can probably be used to help understand his actions, as might some of the limited significant data regarding interpersonal perception. Similarly, some data from the array regarding situational stress can be used to understand his current psychological state. But anyone would be hard-pressed to use the test data to support either the dissociative or temporary insanity defense. At best, they might be used to provide mitigating information concerning his personality disorder; that is, the composite of his hypervigilant style and narcissistic features are likely to have combined in ways that led to his assaultive, antisocial activity.

Case 11 Epilogue A jury rejected the defense of "not guilty by reason of temporary insanity," and found him guilty of breaking and entering, assault with intent to do bodily harm, and rape. He was sentenced to 12 to 25 years. In an interview conducted approximately one year after his incarceration, he freely admitted attempting to malingering a "crazy state" when taking the Rorschach and noted that he felt quite upset when a psychologist testified that much of the data in the record reflected an attempt at malingering. At the time of the interview the subject continued to study psychology through an accredited correspondence course arranged by the Department of Corrections, and looked forward to seeking an advanced degree in psychology after his release from prison.

Case 12: A Psychic Injury Complaint

This 42-year-old male was evaluated in conjunction with a claim of work-related psychic injury. He had been employed for approximately four months as an X-ray technician in a medical support unit in a large industrial complex. According to the claim, the subject slipped on some wet tile while taking some X-rays of the leg of an injured worker. In falling, he injured his back, which he states became more and more painful as the day wore on. He was subsequently prescribed pain medication and did not attempt to return to work for three days. On the fourth day, he returned to work but complained that the pain continued to intensify and stated that he was unable to walk without the assistance of a cane.

During the next two weeks, he was examined by several physicians, including two neurologists, all of whom reported negative findings. By that time, he was reporting intense depression, insomnia, inability to sleep, and a continuing increase in lower back pain. He was placed on leave and ultimately filed a lawsuit for disability, which included a request for a large sum of money because of the psychic injury leading to his chronic depression. The firm's insurance company has offered a modest settlement, but he has also been examined by three other physicians and one psychiatrist who agree that his disability is severe. Thus, this evaluation is related to a pending trial.

The subject was born in a foreign country and immigrated to the United States at age 20. During his first two years in the United States he attended a technical training institute specializing in medicine support training and obtained a certificate as an X-ray technician. According to the subject, he has worked in four different medical settings, each for approximately five years. He cites an interest in relocating as the main reason he left each position. He states that he has never been married, but reports that he has had close relationships with many women. He states that he spends much of his free time attending various university classes to "enrich my education."

He says that he is fearful of leaving his apartment; he finds himself too anxious to drive his automobile and must rely on public transportation; and, although medication has reduced the intensity of his pain, it often becomes very intense and causes him to remain immobile. He states that he has become more and more depressed by his handicap and has given some consideration to the possibility of suicide. He states that he has seen a therapist a few times, but does not find this to be of practical assistance at this time.

Case 12 Overview In this case, the subject was not very successful in conveying a picture of a very helpless and/or depressed person. There is some situational stress, but the magnitude of the overload is very modest. The higher left-side *eb* signals distress, but this could easily be the result of the situational element rather than a more chronic state. The most striking finding is the very high number of Critical Special Scores, almost all of which are DR responses. If the subject were in a hypomanic state, these responses would probably reflect considerable circumstantiality in thinking that is causing difficulty in closure. When they are reviewed, however, it becomes obvious that most are simply transparently dramatic efforts to convey a sense of helplessness.

One might be tempted to argue that the majority of the DR answers are manifestations of an active psychotic process, such as might be noted in cases of toxicity. A few of the answers have that quality but, if an active psychotic process were present, the probability of also having an $X-\%$ of zero is astronomical, even though the record contains only 15 answers.

Case 12: A 42-Year-Old Male

Card	Response		Inquiry
I		I don't like the black it makes me feel more depressed, it makes me nerv	
	1.	It's a terribl blk Bf, u don't c thm very often, its very very ugly, it makes me nervous, the way its flyg around here	E: (Rpts S's resp)
		E: Tak ur time, I thk u'll find sthg else too	S: It has wgs, big wgs (yawns), its terribl, all black, its makg me depressd again, lik I'll lose my mind lookg at it, it even shows the littl feelers up here on the body
		S: I can't look anymore, its too frightening, it maks me feel crazy	
II	2.	I don't lik ths either, there's another bf down here, lik gettg ready to land on this black part ths so ugly, why would a bf land on ths beautiful land on ths ugly part, mayb bf's r blind	E: (Rpts S's resp)
			S: Dwn here's the bf, pretty, c a pretty red red one, I lik pretty red red one's but it's gonna land on ths black dirt, its ugly dirt, it scares me about wht will happen to the bf
			E: I'm not sur how u c it abov the dirt
			S: It just is & the dirt is down below, if its flyg the dirt must b below
	3.	Thes r bloodstains, ugly, do I hav to look at it. I don't lik it	E: (Rpts S's resp)
			S: Oo! thy'r awful, I don't lik them
			E: What is there thy makes thm ll bldstns?
			S: Just the red, oo its awful
III	4.	Ha, that's terrible, its a very funny picture, I don't thk I can tell u about them, its too awful	E: (Rpts S's resp)
		E: Tak ur tim	S: I just can't say, its too awful
		S: It's really awful, it's shamful	E: Take ur time, u said 2 men, wht thyr doing, its vulgar
		E: What is?	S: Thyr peeing, two men peeing on ths rock
		S: It's terrible, 2 men thry doing, its vulgar	E: Show me
			S: I told u it was awful, vulgar, it maks me sick to look at them, here & here (points) (outlines I can't look anymore
	5.	Only the cntr is a clear picture its a bf, that same red one, he got away	E: (Rpts S's resp)
			S: I'm happy for him, c he's flyg again, rite there, don't look at the othr part tho
IV	6.	Oh, I don't lik ths one, its terribl, lik my nitemares, Oh God, its tht monstr chasing me, big black w thos huge feet tryg to crush me, I can't look or I'll go crazy again	E: (Rpts S's resp)
			S: Do I hav to look, its so scary, oh I can't its just big & scary lik my nitemares only I'm not asleep I just c it all the time, tryg to crush me, I can't look at it (hides head in arms)
V	7.	Oh God, wht is it, all the pic's r so scary, just a black ugly bird flyg there, so depressing it makg me sick to c it, take it away	E: (Rpts S's resp)
			S: Not again, I can't look again at tht bat, its too terrible and scary, its an ugly creature

VI

Oh God, I can't look, I dk what it is, its so ugly

E: Tak u'r time, we're in no hurry, we hav all day

8. Its s.t. tht crawls, lik an ant, it cld get on u & bite u, the big ones r so scary, one bit me once, thy can fly

E: (Rpts S's resp)
S: Its so ugly I can't look
E: Show me the ant
S: Oh no, up here, c the ant lik w wgs lik he'll fly up & bite, I can't look its too awful (sobs)

VII

9. Ha, ha, a funny cloud

E: (Rpts S's resp)
S: Its dark lik clouds but its funny too cuz it goes around in a half circle, lik prt is missing
E: Half circle?
S: There's no top to it

10. Oh its magic too, lik 2 genies rising fr a magic lamp so to cast a spell on the world

E: (Rpts S's resp)
S: Thy ll smok, greyish lik the clouds but thy hav faces & body parts & here is the magic lamp, its spooky but I lik it cuz I understand magic

VIII

11. Aha, better, I lik colors, mayb its a tree up here, a magic tree

E: (Rpts S's resp)
S: It has a magic point on the top, lik to mak thgs happen when u dkno thy will, & a littl trunk, magic trees always hav a littl trunk

12. An A jumping, I don't kno why mayb he's scared lik me, & he is seeing himself down here in the water

E: (Rpts S's resp)
S: Its really strange but bettr than the others, its a scared A, scared out of his wits, he's jumpg across all of ths & seeg himself do it down here in the water
E: Water?
S: The blue is water, anybody knows tht

IX

13. Oh God, I dk, I can't take much more, its lik a plant tht can eat u up, its terrible, don't mak me look at it or I'll b crazy more

E: (Rpts S's resp)
S: Oh no, its got those big branches up here tht grab u, I've seen thm, thy eat peopl in the parks, c the green leaves thyr deceiving but the orang leaves can reach out & grab u
E: I'm not sur I c it lik u do
S: Well u'r not crazy mayb but thyr real, I kno, I don't want to look

X

14. I lik ths color, there's a map there, lik islands

E: (Rpts S's resp)
S: Its a map of two big islands, I can't rem the name but I used to kno

15. Oh God there's 2 creatures too thyr terrible, thy scare me

E: (Rpts S's resp)
S: Lik big blue lobsters that can eat u up thy hav thm some places & thy can get u w all the big legs & claws, thyr terrible, I can't look its too scary, it maks me depressed

451

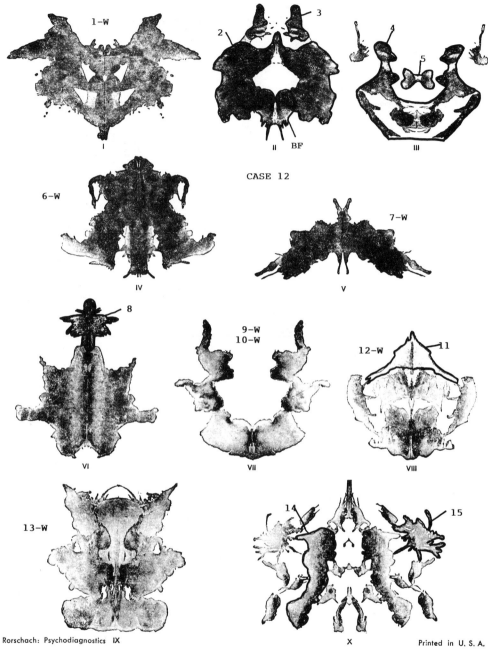

CASE 12

```
CASE 12. SEQUENCE OF SCORES
=======================================================================
CARD NO  LOC  #    DETERMINANT(S)      (2)  CONTENT(S)  POP  Z    SPECIAL SCORES
=======================================================================
   I   1 Wo   1 FC'.FMao                    A           P   1.0  DR

  II   2 D+   3 FMa.C'F.FC.FDo              A,Ls            3.0  DR
       3 Dv   2 C                      2    Bl

 III   4 D+   1 Mao                    2    H,Ls            3.0  DR
       5 Do   3 FC.FMao                     A                    PSV

  IV   6 Wo   1 Ma.FC'o                     (H)         P   2.0  DR,PER

   V   7 Wo   1 FC'.FMao                    A           P   1.0

  VI   8 Do   3 Fu                          A                    PER

 VII   9 Wv   1 YFo                         Cl
      10 W+   1 Mp.YFo                 2    (H),Hh      P   2.5  DR

VIII  11 Do   4 Fu                          Bt                   ALOG
      12 W+   1 FMa.Fr.CFo                  A,Na        P   4.5  DR

  IX  13 Wo   1 FCo                         Bt              5.5  DR2

   X  14 Dv   9 Fu                     2    Ge
      15 Do   1 FCu                    2    A                    INC,DR
=======================================================================
```

CASE 12. STRUCTURAL SUMMARY

```
===============================================================================
LOCATION                  DETERMINANTS          CONTENTS        S-CONSTELLATION
FEATURES            BLENDS          SINGLE                      NO..FV+VF+V+FD>2
                                              H   = 1, 0        YES..Col-Shd Bl>0
Zf   = 8        FC'.FM          M   = 1       (H) = 2, 0        YES..Ego<.31,>.44
ZSum = 22.5     FM.C'F.FC.FD    FM  = 0       Hd  = 0, 0        NO...MOR > 3
ZEst = 24.0     FC.FM           m   = 0       (Hd)= 0, 0        NO...Zd > +- 3.5
                M.FC'           FC  = 2       Hx  = 0, 0        YES..es > EA
W    = 7        FC'.FM          CF  = 0       A   = 7, 0        NO...CF+C > FC
  (Wv = 1)      M.YF            C   = 1       (A) = 0, 0        YES..X+% < .70
D    = 8        FM.Fr.CF        Cn  = 0       Ad  = 0, 0        NO...S > 3
Dd   = 0                        FC' = 0       (Ad)= 0, 0        NO...P < 3 or > 8
S    = 0                        C'F = 0       An  = 0, 0        YES..Pure H < 2
                                C'  = 0       Art = 0, 0        YES..R < 17
     DQ                         FT  = 0       Ay  = 0, 0         6.....TOTAL
........(FQ-)                   TF  = 0       Bl  = 1, 0
  +  = 4 ( 0)                   T   = 0       Bt  = 2, 0        SPECIAL SCORINGS
  o  = 8 ( 0)                   FV  = 0       Cg  = 0, 0           Lv1    Lv2
 v/+ = 0 ( 0)                   VF  = 0       Cl  = 1, 0        DV  =  0x1    0x2
  v  = 3 ( 0)                   V   = 0       Ex  = 0, 0        INC =  1x2    0x4
                                FY  = 0       Fd  = 0, 0        DR  =  7x3    1x6
                                YF  = 1       Fi  = 0, 0        FAB =  0x4    0x7
                                Y   = 0       Ge  = 1, 0        ALOG=  1x5
     FORM QUALITY               Fr  = 0       Hh  = 0, 1        CON =  0x7
                                rF  = 0       Ls  = 0, 2         SUM6  =10
     FQx  FQf  MQual  SQx       FD  = 0       Na  = 0, 1        WSUM6 = 34
  +  = 0    0    0    0         F   = 3       Sc  = 0, 0
  o  = 10   0    3    0                       Sx  = 0, 0        AB  = 0    CP  = 0
  u  = 4    3    0    0                       Xy  = 0, 0        AG  = 0    MOR = 0
  -  = 0    0    0    0                       Id  = 0, 0        CFB = 0    PER = 2
none = 1   --    0    0         (2) = 5                         COP = 0    PSV = 1
===============================================================================
                  RATIOS, PERCENTAGES, AND DERIVATIONS

R = 15        L =  0.25             FC:CF+C = 4: 2    COP = 0      AG = 0
------------------------------------ Pure C  =   1    Food        = 0
EB = 3: 4.5  EA =  7.5  EBPer= N/A   Afr     =0.50    Isolate/R =0.60
eb = 5: 6    es = 11       D  = -1   S       = 0      H:(H)Hd(Hd)= 1: 2
             Adj es = 10  Adj D = 0  Blends:R=7:15    (HHd):(AAd)= 2: 0
------------------------------------ CP      = 0      H+A:Hd+Ad =10: 0
FM = 5 :  C'= 4   T = 0
m  = 0 :  V = 0   Y = 2
                            P   = 5      Zf   = 8      3r+(2)/R=0.53
a:p   = 7: 1  Sum6  = 10   X+% =0.67    Zd   = -1.5   Fr+rF   = 1
Ma:Mp = 2: 1  Lv2   =  1   F+% =0.00    W:D:Dd = 7: 8: 0  FD  = 1
2AB+Art+Ay= 0 WSum6 = 34   X-% =0.00    W:M  = 7: 3   An+Xy   = 0
M-    = 0     Mnone = 0    S-% =0.00    DQ+  = 4      MOR     = 0
                          Xu% =0.27    DQv  = 3
-------------------------------------------------------------------------------
 SCZI = 1    DEPI = 3   CDI = 3   S-CON = 6   HVI = No   OBS = No
===============================================================================
```

It is difficult to determine which features of the record truly represent the psychological makeup of this subject because many of the answers are contaminated with the dramatic efforts. It seems likely that some of the data concerning self-perception, mediation, processing, and affect are reliable, especially the tendency to overvalue personal worth, the ability to modulate affect displays, the conservative processing effort, and the awareness of conventionality. These all involve highly stable variables. The data concerning interpersonal perception could be more misleading as the Isolation Index is extraordinarily high.

If the data are taken at face value, one could argue that he is disturbed, but not in the way he attempts to convey. He seems to be immature and possibly prone to give way to his feelings at times. He is extremely self-centered and probably interacts with the world in only the most superficial ways.

Case 12 Epilogue   Other data collected in the subject's evaluation tend to coincide with the notion of malingering. His performance on the Wechsler Adult Intelligence Scale yielded a Verbal I.Q. of 61 and a Performance I.Q. of 54. On neuropsychological screening, he obtained 99 errors on the Categories Test and 14 errors on Trails A. Insurance investigators found that his employment history on his job application was false, but were able to establish that he had completed training as an X-ray technician. Subsequently, they discovered that he had feigned disability as the result of a similar accident in a hospital setting and was compensated with a sizable disability pension. This led the company to file charges of attempted fraud, which were dropped later when the subject withdrew his disability claim.

REFERENCES

Albert, S. (1978). *The susceptibility of the Rorschach to faking psychosis by normal individuals.* Unpublished doctoral dissertation, Arizona State University, Tempe.

Albert, S., Fox, H., and Kahn, M. (1980). Faking psychosis on the Rorschach. *Journal of Personality Assessment,* **44,** 115–119.

Carp, A. L., and Shavzin, A. R. (1950). The susceptibility to falsification of the Rorschach psychodiagnostic technique. *Journal of Consulting Psychology,* **14,** 230–233.

Easton, K., and Feigenbaum, K. (1967). An examination of an experimental set to fake the Rorschach test. *Perceptual and Motor Skills,* **24,** 871–874.

Exner, J. E. (1987). A pilot study on efforts by nonpatients to malinger characteristics of depression. *Alumni Newsletter.* Asheville, NC: Rorschach Workshops.

Exner, J. E. (1989). Searching for projection in the Rorschach. *Journal of Personality Assessment,* **53,** 520–536.

Exner, J. E., and Levantrosser, C. (1982). *Collection and analysis of protocols simulating schizophrenia by 15 graduate students* (Workshops Study No. 294, unpublished). Rorschach Workshops, Bayville, NY.

Exner, J. E., and Sherman, J. (1977). *Rorschach performance of schizophrenics asked to improve their protocols* (Workshops Study No. 243). Rorschach Workshops, Bayville, NY.

Exner, J. E., and Sternklar, S. (1980). *Analysis of 13 protocols created by psychology graduate students attempting to simulate schizophrenia* (Workshops Study No. 249, unpublished). Rorschach Workshops, Bayville, NY.

Exner, J. E., Viglione, D., and Hillman, L. (1983). *Collection and analysis of protocols simulating schizophrenia by 14 psychology graduate students* (Workshops Study No. 297, unpublished). Rorschach Workshops, Bayville, NY.

Exner, J. E., and Wasley, J. (1984). *Collection and analysis of protocols simulating schizophrenia by 16 graduate students* (Workshops Study No. 304, unpublished). Rorschach Workshops, Bayville, NY.

Exner, J. E., and Wylie, J. (1975). *Attempts at simulation of schizophrenia-like protocols by psychology graduate students* (Workshops Study No. 211, unpublished). Rorschach Workshops, Bayville, NY.

Fossberg, I. A. (1938). Rorschach reactions under varied instructions. *Rorschach Research Exchange,* **3,** 12–30.

Fosberg, I. A. (1941). An experimental study of the reliability of the Rorschach psychodiagnostic technique. *Rorschach Research Exchange,* **5,** 72–84.

Gibby, R. G. (1951). The stability of certain Rorschach variables under conditions of experimentally induced sets: The intellectual variables. *Journal of Projective Techniques,* **15,** 3–25.

Hutt, M., Gibby, R. G., Milton, E. O., and Pottharst, K. (1950). The effect of varied experimental "sets" upon Rorschach test performance. *Journal of Projective Techniques,* **14,** 181–187.

Meisner, J. S. (1984). Susceptibility of Rorschach depression correlates to malingering. *Dissertation Abstracts International,* **45,** 3951B.

Mittman, B. L. (1983). Judges' ability to diagnose schizophrenia on the Rorschach: The effect of malingering. *Dissertation Abstracts International,* **44,** 1248B.

Mittman, B. L., and Exner, J. E. (1989). *Rescoring and reanalysis of the 1983 Mittman data* (Workshops Study No. 303, unpublished). Rorschach Workshops, Asheville, NC.

Phares, E. J., Stewart, L. M., and Foster, J. M. (1960). Instruction variation and Rorschach performance. *Journal of Projective Techniques,* **24,** 28–31.

Ros Plana, M. (1990). *An investigation concerning the malingering of features of depression on the Rorschach and MMPI.* Unpublished doctoral dissertation, University of Barcelona.

Seamons, D. T., Howell, R. J., Carlisle, A. L., and Roe, A. V. (1981). Rorschach simulation of mental illness and normality by psychotic and non-psychotic legal offenders. *Journal of Personality Assessment,* **45,** 130–135.

CHAPTER 16

Research and the Rorschach

Most of this volume has been devoted to issues of interpretation, and most of what has been written has evolved from information derived from research. That is the way of psychology. Assuming that the Rorschach test will continue to be explored and developed, research will be at the core of that effort. Rorschach research is not easy because of the many complexities that often are involved in collecting or analyzing data. Twenty years have elapsed since the idea for the *Comprehensive System* first took shape. During that period, many of the investigations concerning it have been marked by errors in design, implementation, and analysis. An entire book would probably be necessary to itemize them in detail. Possibly, however, some wisdoms have accumulated that can be passed along as suggestions to others interested in exploring the world of the inkblot. In that context, it seems appropriate to devote the last few pages of this work to some issues relevant to researching the test.

The issues included here are not new or different from those stressed in academic courses on measurement or design, but they often are not considered with regard to Rorschach research. Texts concerning experimental methods are plentiful with illustrations of published works but few include examples of credible or even incredible Rorschach research. Similarly, contemporary textbooks on measurement and statistics seem to neatly sidestep confrontations with the knotty issues that sometimes plague Rorschach data analyses. To some, the test is an aberration that does not fit well into the grand designs of psychology. To others, it is overly complex and difficult to understand and probably not worth the time to study thoroughly in order to contribute to research endeavors concerning it. The paucity of contemporary interest in Rorschach research methodology should be cause for concern because future research could easily repeat some of the disasters of the past if some guidelines are not firmly in place.

CRITICAL USE OF THE LITERATURE

Those thoroughly familiar with the abundant Rorschach literature are well aware that a multitude of studies have been published that are marked by inappropriate methodology, faulty analyses, and/or conclusions that overgeneralize or distort findings. The majority of these studies were published early in Rorschach history, when a lack of sophistication in research design and methodology was common, and tactics of data analysis were laborious, simplistic, and often misunderstood. It is likely that the rapid outpouring of such studies during the 1940s and 1950s increased the shrill of criticism leveled against the test and its efficacy, and diverted the attention of many interested in Rorschach research to areas of less controversy and more easily managed subject matter. This is not to suggest that the criticisms were unwarranted. On the contrary, they were appropriate and necessary broadsides that, at the very least, caused the seemingly runaway "inkblot train" to be slowed and evaluated more thoroughly.

Nevertheless, the abstracts of all published works remain in place, and contemporary publications often are marked with citations of older works that fall far short of optimal standards for methodology and/or analysis, simply because the conclusions drawn from the recent works tend to agree with hypotheses or conclusions previously formulated or a method previously used. For instance, in the preceding chapter on simulation and malingering, no mention is made of an investigation by Feldman and Graley (1954), although most studies concerning malingering published since 1954 probably have mentioned it. Most authors who have mentioned it simply listed it among those studies that seem to support the notion that the Rorschach is susceptible to some degree of faking. Others have gone further and noted that Feldman and Graley found significant differences on 14 of 35 variables in comparing the results of standard instructions with the results of instructions to simulate the record of an institutionalized patient. Some authors have expanded the description to note that the simulators gave more *m, CF + C, An,* and *Sx* responses, and fewer Populars than those people given standard instructions.

In reality, Feldman and Graley created a very interesting design and approached the data analysis very cautiously, and overall it was a much more sophisticated study than much Rorschach research of that time. However, because they used a *group* administration with two groups, one of which was tested twice and one tested once, the results are not subject to extrapolation to situations in which the test is administered individually and in a standardized manner. One could argue that the inclusion of a more expanded description of Feldman and Graley's work in an investigation concerning malingering enhances an understanding about prior efforts to study the issue, but it would also be necessary to point out that their findings are irrelevant. Actually, the design itself remains intriguing as a possible tactic to study malingering efforts when the test is administered individually and by different examiners.

EXAMINER BIAS AND MULTIPLE EXAMINERS

A problem that is often neglected in designing Rorschach research concerns the potential bias effect that may result when a single examiner is used. The magnitude of the problem increases considerably when the research design focuses on the collection of data to test specific hypotheses. The side-by-side seating arrangements recommended for use in the *Comprehensive System* were not selected casually. In fact, when several methods of testing—face-to-face, side-by-side, or the examiner sitting behind the subject—were examined, some findings suggested that the latter might be preferable if the objective of minimizing inadvertent nonverbal influences was given priority. The side-by-side seating was selected because it reduced the apparent discomfort of subjects when they could not see an examiner and because it made the mechanical procedures of recording and inquiring much easier. Therefore, some trade-off occurred. Clearly, side-by-side seating considerably reduced the possibilities of inadvertent examiner influence when compared with face-to-face testing. Nonetheless, the potential for nonverbal influence remains, and the potential for inadvertent verbal reinforcement prior to the test and during the inquiry remains a major hazard. In other words, the possibility of experimenter bias continues to exist. Thus, in most instances, the principal investigator for a research project should not collect any of the records. Instead, the data collection should be left to others who are naïve to the nature of the project.

The importance of multiple examiners who, preferably, are naïve to the nature of the study cannot be underestimated. Ideally, any one examiner should not test more than 10 to 20% of the subjects in an investigation and, if more than one group is involved, subjects should be randomly assigned to examiners so that each examiner tests some subjects from each group. For example, if three groups of 15 subjects each are included in a design, it would be appropriate to use five naïve examiners, with each testing nine subjects and no more than four from any one group. Obviously, the number of qualified, available examiners is limited at times, and some compromise with the optimal is necessary. When no hypothesis testing is involved, the compromise can be more liberal; however, if hypothesis testing is involved, the compromise should be weighed very carefully in the context of the potential importance of controlling for examiner bias when drawing conclusions from whatever findings have evolved.

ISSUES OF INTERSCORER AGREEMENT

The examiner who administers the test should always score it but it is always important to challenge the integrity of the scoring or coding for records used in research. This does not mean that the examiner and a second person who has also scored the record should sit down, discuss their differences, and reach some consensus; that procedure, which has nothing to do with interscorer reliability, is a naïve tactic that assumes scoring criteria cannot be applied uniformly. Hopefully, scoring criteria are applied uniformly by anyone qualified to administer the test. Certainly, differences in scoring across examiners are inevitable. Some are legitimate differences of opinion created because the verbiage in a response is not sufficiently precise to indicate whether a criterion is met. Others are simply errors, usually of neglect. Nevertheless, the number of differences should be small across any group of qualified examiners.

Some researchers have evaluated levels of agreement by calculating a form of interscorer reliability. Typically, this involves applying the Spearman-Brown formula to the total scores for each variable (number of M's, T's, etc.) to derive correlation coefficients. This is probably not the best approach to use with Rorschach data. Instead, a simpler calculation of a *percentage* of interscorer agreement seems more definitive and understandable. Ordinarily, it is not necessary to have all responses for every protocol scored a second time to evaluate interscorer agreement. Usually, a randomly selected 25 to 35% of the records or responses should suffice if several examiners are used, but that proportion should be larger if the number of examiners is small.

Interscorer agreement can be calculated in either of two ways. The most practical approach is to calculate the percentage of concurrence by segments of the scoring or coding. Usually, this means that each score is broken into eight segments and a cumulative tally of agreements and disagreements is recorded for all responses that are considered. The eight segments are (1) location score (includes the location and developmental quality codes), (2) determinant(s) (whether a single determinant or a blend), (3) form quality, (4) pairs, (5) contents (can be taken as a single segment or subdivided into main and secondary contents), (6) Popular, (7) Z score, and (8) Special Scores (can be taken as a single segment or subdivided in Critical and noncritical). When this procedure is used, the expected percentage of agreement may vary to some extent by segments. Typically, the percentages of agreement for location, pairs, Z score, and Popular should approach 100%. The percentages of agreement for form quality and content may be somewhat lower, but well over 85%. The percentages of agreement for determinants and Special Scores are likely to be lowest, but should not fall below 80%.

Several variations of this procedure can be used. For example, when one scorer codes *FC* and a second codes *CF,* the difference usually is tallied as a disagreement; however, if the study has nothing to do with the weighted sum of color or with the $FC:CF+C$ ratio, an investigator might tally an agreement because the presence of color was noted.

A second, much more stringent approach to evaluating scorer concurrence should be applied to research designs in which the integrity of the total score is critical to the research objective. Generally, this occurs only when sequencing effects are important. In this method, randomly selected responses from numerous protocols, usually approximating no fewer than 20% of the total responses involved, are coded by several scorers. The results are then tallied, using a straightforward "yes" or "no" procedure. In this instance, the "yes" category is used when the entire score (location, determinants, form quality, pairs, contents, Popular, Z score, and Special Scores) is identical with that of other scorers, and the "no" category is used when the entire score is not identical. Experience demonstrates that this very demanding criterion for calculating the percentage of agreement yields, in the best of circumstances, agreement levels between 70 and 75%. The flaw with this tactic concerns those judgments that are recorded in the "no" category. One scorer might record a coding for a response that differs almost completely from that of a second scorer, whereas another person might agree with the second scorer except for one secondary content category. Nonetheless, both would be considered disagreements and recorded in the "no" category.

NORMATIVE DATA AND RESEARCH

Occasionally, researchers use published norms as a control sample against which comparisons for small groups are made. This tactic is naïve at best, and invariably leads to faulty and misleading conclusions. Almost any group that is homogeneous for some features should differ from the published normative data. If they do not, they are not homogeneous.

The normative samples for both adults and children represent a conglomeration of subjects from eight socioeconomic levels and three geographic distributions. They have been deliberately stratified, to the extent possible, to approximate distributions of the 1970 or 1980 U.S. Census figures. The only element common to all subjects is the absence of psychiatric history. The subjects are not necessarily normal; they are simply not patients. As such, they represent a vast array of individual differences, with dimensions ranging from introversive to extratensive, well controlled to poorly controlled, gregarious to isolated, strange to sturdy, and so on.

The normative data are important because they provide some references and, in many instances, highlight deviations. The only time the data might be useful as a "control" group would be if they are used to generate comparisons with another large heterogeneous sample of nonpatient subjects such as from another culture or country. Attempts to use the normative data or extrapolations from them as a control group for small sample research are no more logical than comparing the data collected for 40 bulimics with the data for 700 psychiatric subjects that include inpatients, outpatients, depressives, schizophrenics, substance abusers, and a host of other diagnostic entities. The results of such a comparison would be meaningless.

The designs for any research in which Rorschach variables serve as dependent measures should not differ from those typically accepted for any psychological experiment. At least one control sample, drawn from a similar population, is necessary and, in some designs, a single control group may not be sufficient. This is particularly true when the research focuses on specific types of pathology. For instance, if one were attempting to study some characteristics of hospitalized ulcer patients, it would be important to control for hospitalization effects. Thus, at least one control group of hospitalized non-ulcer patients would be required. It would also be important to control for specific somatic features. Thus, other control groups, such as chronic headache patients and dermatology patients, could be important to determine if features discovered in the ulcer group are unique to that group.

In some instances, it may be useful to call attention to normative data, especially when a group deviates markedly for some features. For example, a review of two tables in Chapter 2 reveals that only 1% of the 700 subjects in the nonpatient sample have $X-$ % greater than 20%, compared with 90% of the 320 subjects in the reference sample of schizophrenics. The data are obvious and no statistical manipulations would enhance the meaning.

STATISTICAL APPLICATIONS

A resurgence of interest in research related to the Rorschach appears to have occurred during the past decade and has spewed forth a large number of dissertations and publications that seem to span a wide range of sophistication. Obviously, all are well intended but many are scored by problems. Some have problems in design, but more often the tactics of analyses tend to stretch the credibility of the findings or conclusions. In many cases very robust statistical routines are inappropriately applied to samples that are far too small from which to draw credible conclusions. In other instances scores are inappropriately scaled, smoothed, or weighted, or ratios are inappropriately reduced so that robust parametric methods can be applied in testing hypotheses.

Even the best pieces of research can be marred by inappropriate statistical applications. During the past three or four decades, psychology has profited enormously from the development of many very sophisticated statistical methods. Whereas the simple analysis of variance was once considered the pinnacle of statistical accomplishment, it is now often viewed as a pedestrian tactic that has only limited usefulness in many situations. A phenomenal increase in the frequency by which discriminant function analyses, multivariate techniques, multiple regression models, and factor analysis are applied has paralleled the development of computer technology, and has opened many doors that permit the analyses of data samples in ways that few would have considered possible less than a half century ago.

Nonetheless, some new ways are not always the best ways, and it seems that, in the struggle to teach the new ways, some old ways have been neglected. Most students learn quite a bit about statistics, but few seem to learn much about measurement and/or individual differences. Rorschach data first must be considered in the context of measurement, and many research revelations that have evolved concerning the test have not involved the more powerful or robust statistical applications but, instead, have relied extensively on applications of some older methods. This has been necessary because many Rorschach variables fall into classifications that do not coincide with the requirements for the more robust analyses. Many variables are nonparametric. They do not have normal distributions or broad ranges. Thus, it is frequently necessary to revert to some of the older nonparametric statistical tactics, even though less robust, to ascertain whether data are truly meaningful or whether differences between groups actually exist. Other Rorschach variables are parametric but sometimes fall on distributions that are so sharply skewed that parametric forms of analyses may be inappropriate.

Decisions concerning which statistical procedures should be applied to a data set should not be made because an investigator happens to prefer one method over another, or because one method may yield the sought-after confidence levels whereas another may not. They should be selected in light of the issue(s) at hand: the hypotheses to be tested, the data to be used, the characteristics of the variables to be analyzed, and the demands or prerequisites of the procedures being considered. The final selection of a procedure or procedures must afford major weight to the objective of presenting findings in the most accurate way, not simply in a way that might support a hypothesis or theoretical position.

VALUE OF DESCRIPTIVE STATISTICS

Some of the most valuable information concerning any data set is provided in the descriptive statistics. If thorough, they convey the unconcealed picture of the data and often provide information about distributions that may not be clear otherwise. This is especially true when more than the mean and standard deviation is included. As noted earlier, many Rorschach variables do not have neat Gausian-like distributions; for those variables, the data for means and standard deviations have only limited value and, in some cases, can be quite misleading. Often, the median, range, and frequency data for a variable aid considerably in generating a better picture of a distribution, particularly when the distribution is markedly skewed. If the data for skewness and kurtosis are added, the picture is usually expanded, and sometimes the use of the mode can flesh it out even further, but it is important to note that some variables may have more than one mode.

SIGNIFICANCE TESTING

In many studies, the publication of descriptive statistics is more than sufficient to make a point or provide information and the ritual of testing for significance becomes unnecessary. When significance testing seems important, the data should be addressed in a way that provides the clearest and most accurate picture of the data.

Ideally, anyone interested in Rorschach research needs to be familiar with a classic article by Lee J. Cronbach that was published in 1949. It should be required reading for anyone interested in learning about the Rorschach. It is a rich, constructive, and very important piece that had considerable influence in improving the caliber of Rorschach research. Even though it was written four decades ago, it remains an important source of advice to those pondering which statistic might be best suited to the data. In it, Cronbach reviewed the variety of statistical methods that had been used with Rorschach data and, citing numerous published studies, neatly differentiated those methods that were appropriate and those that were inappropriate in light of the data used or the conclusions drawn.

One theme stressed repeatedly by Cronbach concerns the advantages of using counting (frequency) procedures rather than additive (means) procedures for many kinds of Rorschach investigations. This recommendation continues to have much value for contemporary Rorschach research. Median tests and chi-squares and Fisher's Exact Z have formed a sturdy foundation for many investigations that have been completed in developing the *Comprehensive System.* In fact, it has been almost a matter of routine to ask whether data can be compiled in ways to which any of the three methods can be applied. This is not to suggest that tests for differences in proportions or the number of specific types of responses or response features should be ignored. In many Rorschach studies, however, the question is not simply whether differences between groups exist, but whether there is an interpretive difference between groups. The two issues are quite different.

For example, the *Affective Ratio,* which usually is a normally distributed variable, tends to be somewhat lower during or following the experience of stress. It is not unusual to find retest values for *Afr* that are between .10 and .15 less than baseline values if situational stress is occurring or has occurred recently. Thus, if a t test is calculated comparing the baseline mean for a group with the retest or stress mean for the same group, the result is usually significant, at least to a level in which $p < .05$, or, if for some reason a retest correlation is calculated, the result is usually a value for r that is much lower than those for retest studies in which the only independent variable is time. But if the data are sorted in terms of interpretive ranges, such as .15 to .25, .26 to .35, .36 to .45, .46 to .80, and so on, and analyzed using a chi-square, the results usually are not significant because most of the second test values often remain in the same interpretive range as the first test values. Similarly, if the data sorted by range are subjected to a categorical correlation, the resulting r is usually very similar to those found in routine temporal consistency studies.

Some investigators prefer to use correlational techniques to demonstrate relationships between some Rorschach variables and other measures or criteria. Often this tactic is justified, but some cautions should be noted. First, if the distribution for any of the variables is markedly skewed, the result will probably convey a distorted picture concerning the relationship(s). Second, there has been a notable tendency among some investigators to correlate everything with everything, usually in a multiple regression or discriminant function analysis. The wonders of computer technology and sophisticated statistical packages makes this quite easy to accomplish and often surprisingly important findings can result. But these techniques can be abused. For instance, it is very inappropriate to include both parametric and nonparametric variables in the same matrix. The skewness problems of the latter can cause a distortion in weights to occur so that some variables appear to have substantially more or less predictive capability than is truly the case.

A third problem that is more common than should be the case is the failure to recognize some of the inevitable consequences of multiple significance testing. This is a particular problem when multiple correlations are involved. A certain proportion can be expected to reach the magical .05 or .01 levels of significance by chance. Many investigators seem to believe that the chance proportion is simply 5%, but that is not true unless *all* variables in the matrix are completely independent. Numerous formulas can be used to derive estimates concerning the number of chance significant findings, and most include the entry of interdependency information. But even after the number of chance estimates have been determined, the astute investigator will ruminate about which levels of significance are acceptable. Probability values of less than .05 are often not convincing, especially if culled from numerous significance tests and, at times, p values of less than .01 are cause for suspicion if the data have been subjected to many correlational manipulations.

Historically, much psychological research has been based on the premise that $p < .05$ offers some proof and that $p < .01$ is conclusive. Although those positions can be argued from probability theory, the actual numbers required to obtain these differences when using correlations are quite modest. For instance, a correlation of .18 is statistically significant at the .01 level if two groups of 100 subjects each have been compared. A correlation with that probability level may be meaningful, but that may not always be the case. Such a correlation accounts for approximately only 3% of the total variance and, if multiple correlations have been calculated, the likelihood of obtaining a correlation of .18 for two groups of 100 subjects increases substantially with the number of correlations completed. In other words, the finding may be spurious but, even if it is not spurious, the finding may not be very meaningful because an additional 97% of variance remains unaccounted.

PARTIALING OR CONTROLLING FOR R

As recent interest in Rorschach research has increased, an old issue regarding tactics of analysis is sometimes resurrected. It concerns R and the oft debated issue about whether differences in R require that other scores be normalized in relation to R. Most who advocate normalization or partialing for R cite

Cronbach's (1949) article as the basis for their argument. Slightly more than two of the article's 36 pages were devoted to problems of partialing out differences in R, and that segment was summarized in a five-line paragraph at the end of the article as one of 10 numbered paragraphs suggesting guides for future practice. However, that segment of the article has often been used as a basis from which to conclude that Rorschach data are not readily subject to methods of statistical analysis because of an unequal R (Holtzman, Thorpe, Swartz, & Herron, 1961; Murstein, 1965) or that, if Rorschach data are to be subjected to statistical analysis, differences in R must be controlled "to the maximal extent possible" (Perry & Kinder, 1990).

Actually, Cronbach reached neither of these conclusions. He simply pointed out that some studies had been published in which the R's for the groups varied so significantly that conclusions based on the comparison of other variables, such as $D, Dd, M\%,$ and $P\%,$ were not appropriate. Obviously, Cronbach was correct in drawing attention to the problem of R. In one study he cited, differences for the mean R were 41 responses, and he undoubtedly was also concerned with a finding reported by Guilford (1947) in which R varies significantly from examiner to examiner. He also allowed, as was common for the time, that any number of answers constituted a usable Rorschach, citing a sample of 289 protocols with which he had done some work. In that sample, 74 cases had values for R ranging from five to 19 responses, and a second group of 82 cases had R values ranging from 40 to 109 answers. Cronbach made several suggestions about how to address the problem of differences in R, one of which would be to divide a sample into groups, "within which R is nearly uniform (e.g., R 20–29)," and make significance tests for each grouping.

A second study commonly cited regarding problems with varying R's is that of Fisk and Baughman (1953), which, in effect, followed Cronbach's suggestion of dividing samples into groups in which R is nearly uniform. They used 633 records taken from the Chicago Veterans Administration Mental Hygiene Clinic (outpatients) plus 157 protocols of employees in a mail order house (normals) that had been analyzed earlier (Beck, Rabin, Thiesen, Molish, & Thetford, 1950). The resulting pool of 790 records were then subdivided into nine groups based on the number of responses given. Group 1 contained records in which the R ranged from zero to nine answers, Group 2 included R from 10 to 14, Group 3 included R from 15 to 19, and so on, so that Group 7 included R from 35 to 39, Group 8 included R from 40 to 49, and Group 9 included R from 50 to 175. They then calculated median frequencies by group and by subject type (patients or normals).

Fisk and Baughman also reported contingency coefficients comparing R, by outpatient versus normal, for 29 scoring categories of which at least 16 ($Dd, C, CF, FC, FM, m, YF, FY, FV, H, Hd, A, Ad, An, Ge,$ and Sex) are nonparametric. Most resulting correlations were positively significant, but Fisk and Baughman pointed out that the coefficients are actually spurious because they are "part–whole" correlations; that is, the total number of responses includes the frequency in each scoring category (which is not necessarily true if any blends were involved). They also presented graphs showing the relationships between R and eight of the 29 variables for each of the nine groupings that had been created based on R. In every graph, sharp increases or decreases are noted but, in almost every instance, the distinct increase or decrease occurred in the extreme groups, that is, the three involving 19 or fewer answers or the three involving 35 or more answers.

There can be no question that Fisk and Baughman's (1953) data are thoroughly analyzed and quite intriguing. Their work represents another important milestone in Rorschach history that served to temper the casual approaches to data analysis that had been so common. On the basis of their data, it would be difficult to argue with their conclusion that it is important to account for R when analyzing data, but, as with Cronbach, the authors allowed for much greater variation in the number of responses than is currently the practice.

For example, the adult nonpatient normative or standardization samples for the *Comprehensive System,* consisting of 700 subjects, has a mean R of 22.67 ($SD = 4.23$), as contrasted with means of 22.7 ($SD = 8.52$) for depressives and 23.44 ($SD = 8.66$) for schizophrenics. Obviously, a difference in variance exists when the nonpatients are contrasted with either patient sample, but is the variance so deviant among the three groups that some control for R is necessary? Cronbach addressed that question by suggesting the use of a test of significance. In other words, if R for one group is significantly different from R for another, some sort of control for R may be necessary.

Another approach that can be applied is much easier to calculate now than only two or three decades ago. It involves the calculation and review of the data in a matrix of correlations to try to ascertain the extent to which R seems to influence the data. In most instances, the results probably lead to the conclusion that controlling for R is not necessary for most or all variables to be included in an analysis. This is because the relationship between R and most variables in most samples is not nearly as direct as was often thought to be the case. Table 119 shows the correlations between R and 14 parametric variables for four groups. The groups were randomly selected from much larger samples and the size of each group was designed to be large enough to represent the sample and to avoid the pitfalls that can occur in such a matrix when a small sample is involved, yet small enough that the resulting correlations might seem so negligible as to be uniformly unimportant.

The data in Table 119 do not provide any absolute answers about when to control or partial for R, but they do offer some hints about when partialing may or may not be important. Obviously, R correlates with some variables at statistically significant levels for some groups but, if the correlations are examined carefully, it is noted that only those related to D account for more than 10% of the variance. In fact, if the D location variable is excluded from consideration for the moment, only two other correlations (Zf for nonpatient males and blends for schizophrenics) are significant at .001. The conservative investigator might review these data and opt to control or partial for all variables because some correlate at statistically significant levels. A less conservative investigator might opt to omit from the analyses those variables that correlate with R at significant levels. At the Rorschach Research Foundation, the decision would probably be to drop the location D scores from consideration and use the other data in planned analyses, mainly on the assumption that the findings will replicate in other samples. If no replication were planned, then the analyses might proceed both ways, that is, partialing for R in one set of analyses and not partialing for R in the second. If partialing were unnecessary, the data should replicate in each set of analyses.

Table 119.   Correlations Between *R* and 14 Other Rorschach Variables for Four Groups of Randomly Selected Subjects

VARIABLE	NONPATIENT MALES N = 70a	NONPATIENT FEMALES N = 125b	INPATIENT SCHIZOPHRENIC N = 100c	INPATIENT DEPRESSIVE N = 125b
RANGE OF *R*	14–30	15–34	14–31	14–28
CORRELATIONS OF *R* WITH				
W	.3098*	.3106*	.0139	−.1637
D	.6171**	.5252**	.4245**	.8721**
M	.0377	.1314	.1207	.1490
FM + m	.2199	.2299*	.2573*	.2807*
Pair	.2356	.0771	.2073	.2765*
Popular	.2597	−.0172	.1184	.1155
Zf	.3800**	.3135*	.2794*	.1279
Blends	.3168*	.2522*	.3338**	.1331
Color resp	.2593	.1537	.2474	.2888*
EA	.3259*	.2174	.2173	.2168
es	.2699	.2070	.2794	.2505
Afr	.1816	.0951	.0910	.1049
3r + (2)/R	−.0930	−.1139	.1357	−.0659
Lambda	.0536	.0800	−.0904	−.0316
X + %	−.1932	−.2057	−.1397	−.2081
Xu%	.3009	.2413*	.2072	.1265
X-%	.0113	−.0052	.2082	.2501

* = significant, $p < .01$; ** = significant, $p < .001$
a = *r* of .302 is significant at .01, *r* of .379 is significant at .001
b = *r* of .228 is significant at .01, *r* of .314 is significant at .001
c = *r* of .254 is significant at .01, *r* of .321 is significant at .001

If it is decided that some control for *R* is important, the next issue to be addressed is what kind of control might best contend with the issue. Some researchers have attempted to use a percentage or proportion score. These are far too simple and lead to major distortions. Others have used logarithmic transformations or scaled score transformations. These are misleading because they become trapped in assumptions of equal distance between values. A partialing technique can be appropriate for parametric variables but it is likely to present a distorted picture if applied to nonparametric variables. If a factorial analysis is to be employed, partialing usually creates spurious correlations and should be avoided. *R* can be regressed out for parametric variables and this is the most appropriate tactic to use if factor analysis is to be used. If data are to be subjected to factor analysis, the nonparametric variables should be excluded because they often have spuriously high correlations with some parametric variables and can distort clustering effects.

If, for some reason, it seems important to control for *R* in studies that include nonparametric variables, some kind of ranking method can be used, but the potential for a distorted output is considerable. Most nonparametric Rorschach variables have very few data points, usually not more than three or four for nearly 99% of a subject group. Thus, the effect of attempting to partial or smooth the distribution into ranks, other than those to be used in a nonparametric analysis, is to create a distorted curve that in turn can affect other variables in the analysis rather dramatically.

SUMMARY

The few pages that make up this brief chapter on research can hardly provide much instruction concerning Rorschach research. They are offered to draw attention to some of the issues and problems that face the Rorschach researcher, in part with the hope that some reminders of the problems of the past will help those of the future to avoid making the same mistakes.

REFERENCES

Beck, S. J., Rabin, A. I., Thiesen, W. G., Molish, H. B., and Thetford, W. N. (1950). The normal personality as projected in the Rorschach test. *Journal of Psychology,* **30,** 241–298.

Cronback, L. J. (1949). Statistical methods applied to Rorschach scores: A review. *Psychological Bulletin,* **46,** 393–429.

Feldman, M. J., and Graley, J. (1954). The effects of an experimental set to simulate abnormality on group Rorschach performance. *Journal of Projective Techniques,* **18,** 326–334.

Fisk, D. W., and Baughman, E. E. (1953). Relationships between Rorschach scoring categories and the total number of responses. *Journal of Abnormal and Social Psychology,* **48,** 25–32.

Guilford, J. P. (Ed.). (1947). *Printed classification tests* (AAF Aviation Psychology Program Research Reports, No. 3). Washington, DC: U.S. Government Printing Office.

Holtzman, W. H., Thorpe, J. S., Swartz, J. D., and Herron, E. W. (1961). *Inkblot perception and personality.* Austin, TX: University of Texas Press.

Murstein, B. I. (1965). Factor analysis of the Rorschach test. In B. I. Murstein (Ed.), *Handbook of projective techniques.* New York: Basic Books.

Perry, G. G., and Kinder, B. N. (1990). The susceptibility of the Rorschach to malingering: A critical review. *Journal of Personality Assessment,* **54,** 47–57.

Author Index

Subject Index